The Prehistory of the Netherlands

Volume 1

The Prehistory of the Netherlands

Volume 1

Edited by

L.P. Louwe Kooijmans
P.W. van den Broeke
H. Fokkens
A.L. van Gijn

AMSTERDAM UNIVERSITY PRESS

The publication of this book was made possible by grants from:
- the Netherlands Organisation for Scientific Research (NWO)
- Archol BV, Leiden
- The Prince Bernhard Cultural Foundation (PBCF)

Cover illustration: Flint arrowhead from the Middle Bronze Age burial at Wassenaar, c. 1700 BC, see feature L, p. 459 (photo J. Pauptit, Faculty of Archaeology, Leiden University).

Cover design: Studio Jan de Boer BNO, Amsterdam
Lay-out: Perfect Service, Schoonhoven

ISBN 90 5356 160 9 (both volumes)
ISBN 90 5356 806 9 (volume 1)
ISBN 90 5356 807 7 (volume 2)
NUR 682

Contents Volume 1

Contents Volume 2

Conclusion

Note on the dates used in this book

Dates before 50,000 are based on various physical dating techniques, other than radiocarbon, and expressed as 'years ago'.

Dates in the period 50,000-10,000 years ago are based on uncalibrated radiocarbon dates and expressed as 'years ago' or 'years BP' (= Before Present).

Dates in the last 10,000 years are based on calibrated radiocarbon dates and expressed as 'years BC'. Only these dates can be equated with calender or solar years.

See chapter 1, section 'periods and dates' for the principles of radiocarbon dating.

Preface

More than ten years ago, in 1991 to be precise, the plan was born to combine our knowledge of Dutch prehistory in a single volume, to be written by specialists. The reason behind this plan was the explosive increase in archaeological research, in particular settlement excavations, in the Netherlands in the decades after World War II. The reports of those excavations were published in numerous different periodicals, making it difficult for archaeologists, even professional ones, to gain an overall view of the know-how outside their own fields of specialisation. This know-how, it was felt, should also be better accessible to the public at large. So it was decided to present a comprehensive survey of Dutch prehistory, one that would open up the primary sources.

What is true for our Dutch-speaking regions holds in an even greater degree for countries outside the Netherlands. Although ever more findings are in the Netherlands nowadays reported in English, many publications are nevertheless in Dutch, and have appeared in periodicals that are not widely distributed outside our country. Even reports of major excavations are still often written in Dutch, and for most foreigners that is a handicap. What is more, the available information is highly fragmented. The last – as well as only – English survey of Dutch prehistory, written by professor Siegfried De Laet from Ghent in 1958 (!), is to be found in the 'The Low Countries' volume of the well-known Ancient Peoples and Places series. Quite a lot has been published since then, but the shelves reserved for the Netherlands in most archaeological libraries outside our country are fairly unimpressive.

This would not matter all that much if our research related solely to issues of regional importance, but that is not the case. In our opinion, the high research density and large-scale character of many of our projects make the Netherlands one of the hotspots for present-day knowledge of European prehistory. Our two main foci of interest are wetland archaeology and settlements. The first is largely attributable to the fact that in former days 50% of the Netherlands consisted of wetlands, and the second is partly associated with large-scale threats to ancient living areas in the building explosion that occurred in our country after World War II. The Dutch knowledge should be widely accessible to enable archaeologists to integrate it in their view of prehistoric Europe.

Our plan for a comprehensive survey of Dutch archaeology was therefore expanded to include the simultaneous publication of an English edition. This actually proved to be rather a lot on the editors' plate. The project involved a good deal more effort, while the editors' daily tasks left them progressively less time to spend on it. Furthermore, as work progressed the book became thicker and thicker, as we found there was so much to be told. But our efforts were to pay off in the end, in the form of a new comprehensive survey that is also a work of reference for anyone requiring prehistoric data from the Netherlands.

This book owes its publication in the first place to the *Prins Bernhard Cultuurfonds* (Prince Bernhard Cultural Fund), which commissioned the work. The editors are most grateful to this fund for its patience and firm belief that the project would eventually be successfully completed. The same holds for the confidence of Amsterdam University Press. We would also like to thank Medy Oberendorff for the final editing of the visual material, Susan Mellor for her conscientious translation of the Dutch texts, and the many authors for their meticulously written contributions.

On behalf of the editorial team,
Leendert P. Louwe Kooijmans

Introductory

1   A prehistory of our time

Peter van den Broeke,
Harry Fokkens and Annelou van Gijn

A NEW SURVEY

The last detailed survey of Dutch prehistory, *De voorgeschiedenis der Lage Landen* ('Prehistory of the Low Countries') by De Laet and Glasbergen, was written more than forty years ago (fig. 1.1). Since its publication, in 1959, our knowledge of the past has increased tremendously. Many sites have been excavated, excavation methods have changed and dating and analytical techniques have been drastically modified. Moreover, under the influence of changed theoretical insights, entirely novel sources of information have been tapped and new explanation models have been formulated.

Over the years, these developments have created a need for a new survey of Dutch prehistory. The large number of publications, some in poorly accessible journals, has made it very difficult for Dutch archaeologists, but certainly also for the interested public and colleagues in other countries, to see the wood for the trees. It is for the benefit of the latter group that this English translation of *Nederland in de prehistorie* has been published.

fig. 1.1

Two previous surveys that covered the prehistory of the Netherlands.

This book is essentially a handbook. In that respect it clearly differs from *Pre- en protohistorie van de Lage Landen* ('Pre- and protohistory of the Low Countries'), the textbook published by the Open University, which, besides presenting a survey of the pre- and protohistory of the Low Countries, also pays much attention to the theoretical and methodological backgrounds of the science of archaeology.[1] The latter work moreover covers not only prehistory, but also the Roman period and the Middle Ages and hence – from sheer necessity – pays fairly little detailed attention to material remains. And that is precisely one of the main aims of the present book, and also one of the reasons why the book is restricted to prehistory. The other reason is that we already have an excellent comprehensive study focusing on the Netherlands in the Roman period, namely *De Romeinen in Nederland* ('The Romans in the Netherlands') by W.A. van Es.[2]

In this book the Netherlands is the main area of attention. But as our present-day borders have no meaning with respect to our view of the past, surrounding areas will also be considered in the discussions presented on the following pages, in particular in the chapters on the earliest occupation periods.

As our aim was to let as many researchers as possible present their views on their own, specific areas of research, we have divided the subject matter into periods and themes tied in with Dutch research traditions. A consequence of this approach is that the early prehistoric periods are discussed in chronological order, whereas the Bronze Age and the Iron Age are covered in chapters focusing on different themes. The biologists involved in this project have summarised the results of their research into subsistence activities in two chapters. We have tried to divide the span of many thousands of years covered in this book into relatively long periods, to avoid the risk of providing too much detail for the broader pattern to be discernable. Topics of particular interest are discussed in separate features of a few pages inserted between the main chapters.

The great advantage of involving a large number of authors in such a project is that the information is presented at first hand, by researchers who have moreover carefully selected their data from the great mass of information available on their particular subject. A disadvantage, however, is the unavoidable variation in emphasis and style. The editors' primary task was therefore to coordinate the individual contributions and integrate them into a sufficiently unified whole. Their second task was to write introductory and concluding chapters for the four parts of the book covering the different prehistoric periods. The concluding editorial chapters can be read as brief surveys, summarising the basic information presented on the preceding pages.

In the present, introductory, chapter we intend to discuss various methodological and theoretical developments that have taken place over the past decades,[3] highlight several factors that affect our understanding of the past, and explain the chronological framework used in this book.

NEW RESEARCH METHODS AND NEW SOURCES

One of the most important methodological developments in archaeology of the past decades has been the introduction of digging machines in excavation work (fig. 1.2). This innovation led to a shift in emphasis from research into funerary monuments and burial practices – which were until the late 1950s our main sources of information on the past – to settlement research. Together with the introduction, in the 1970s, of new survey methods, whose use was greatly boosted by the work of the RAAP Foundation[4] in the Netherlands, this resulted in a wealth of data of an entirely novel kind.

Within a relatively short time, large-scale settlement research came to be one of the trademarks of Dutch archaeology. The evidence obtained in such research in the Low Countries, combined with that from Scandinavia and northern Germany, where similar developments have taken place, formed an important basis for subsistence and settlement models for Northwest Europe. The great abundance of new evidence, in particular botanical macroremains, tiny bones and fragments of flint, is in part the consequence of the introduction of flotation techniques and

fig. 1.2
Excavations carried out in 1959 by the State
Service for Archaeological Investigations
in the Netherlands (ROB) at a Neolithic
settlement site near Elsloo. This was only
a few years after the first attempts had
been made to use digging machines in
archaeological research. They made it
possible to conduct fieldwork on a larger
scale.

the systematic use of sieves since the 1970s (fig. 1.3). As an aid to understanding prehistoric agriculture, pollen research (palynology) has been pushed into the background by research into macroremains, but pollen research is still often our only available instrument for reconstructing past vegetations. This is true especially where late prehistory is concerned, because for the Palaeolithic the analysis of the bones of small rodents has proven particularly important. Information derived from the bones of rodents has played a part in reconstructing Palaeolithic

fig. 1.3
Use of a sieving installation and a water
nozzle for recovering small finds such as
bone splinters and fish remains.

man's natural environment, but the rodents' skeletal morphology has also helped us to date deposits and very early sites. This research, too, would be inconceivable without the use of sieves.

Another important development has been the introduction of new measuring equipment, including instruments coupled to computers. The positions and measurements of finds and features are nowadays often determined by teams us-

fig. 1.4
Where thousands of finds have to be three-dimensionally recorded an infrared-theodolite is an indispensable instrument. Here such an instrument is being used at a prospective excavation in the province of North Brabant.

ing an infrared theodolite coupled to a computer (fig. 1.4), which stores the measurements and can even print them in drawings. More and more use is being made of computers in analysing field data, too. In the 1960s and '70s the data were analysed essentially with the aid of statistical techniques, but the 1980s and '90s saw the introduction of new analytical systems, in particular Geographical Information Systems (GIS).

Archaeometry and related research have also become very popular, for example in studies on the provenance of stone and flint.[5] Such studies are important for our understanding of exchange systems, and hence also the social organisation of prehistoric communities. Archaeometry is also used in the analysis of food residues in cooking pots, which can provide information on prehistoric diet. In an entirely different manner, the analysis of microwear polishes, in particular on flint but also on bone implements, likewise sheds light on prehistoric man's economic basis and subsistence activities.

THEORETICAL INNOVATIONS

No one who now reads *De voorgeschiedenis der Lage Landen* can fail to notice the great influence of the most important archaeologist of the first half of the twentieth century: Gordon Childe. It is he who first defined the archaeological term 'culture', which has remained one of the most important concepts in archaeological theory to this day. An archaeological culture differs markedly from what anthropologists understand by the term 'culture'. Childe defined it as a constantly recurring assemblage of elements, such as certain types of settlements, burials and pottery. He was moreover of the opinion that 'culture' thus defined could be equated with 'people'.

The latter view has however been superseded. The distributions of certain types of finds are no longer seen to correspond to the distributions of peoples. The 'culture' concept is however still used to distinguish assemblages in chronological and spatial terms, in particular on the basis of flint and pottery – especially decorated pottery. A constantly recurring question is whether the distribution of a particular type of artefact may indeed be seen to reflect a certain cultural identity, or whether it is associated with certain widespread economic practices, or should perhaps be seen as reflecting ideological or social aspects of a community. The answer to this question differs per category of artefacts, per region and per period, and this issue will therefore crop up in several places throughout this book.

Childe not only defined the term 'culture', he also advanced models for interpreting changes observable in time and space. In his opinion, innovations had spread from the ancient Near East to the west via diffusion. The spread of and changes in elements of material culture were to be interpreted in terms of the migration of cultures or peoples. De Laet and Glasbergen formulated this view as follows:

> 'An infiltration of new population elements will usually have involved a relatively small number of people. The host that set out on a "pan-European" migration will have dissolved en route into many groups of varying sizes that settled at favourable locations. The settlements and burials that have been found scattered across our region are the remains of only hundreds, or more likely only dozens of people. Such small numbers would have been decimated or exterminated by an epidemic or a natural disaster, while newcomers who represented a ruling class among a native population were frequently totally absorbed by the subject population within a few generations and rapidly lost their distinct culture.'[6]

This dynamic view of culture led to a new approach, whose primary aim was to determine the earliest developments and the area of origin of a culture, after which attempts were made to trace its local developments. Childe moreover tried to use archaeological evidence as a source of information on social aspects of the cultures he studied. The latter approach however found little support among Dutch archaeologists and no social aspects are therefore to be found in *De voorgeschiedenis der Lage Landen*. To quote Glasbergen once again, this time from his preface to the Dutch translation of Childe's 'The prehistory of European society':

> 'In elaborating his themes in the works which he wrote for a wide public, Childe has supplemented his scientifically founded interpretations based on technological evolution and subsistence evidence with his interpretation of the unsound evidence relating to social conditions, religion and spiritual life. What the resultant picture has gained in terms of detail and literary qualities it has however lost in terms of scientific cogency.'[7]

Now, more than forty years later, the interpretation of material culture in sociocultural terms is one of the most important aspects of archaeology, alongside the study of the relations between prehistoric man and his natural environment. The 1960s saw the introduction of anthropological models and concepts in archaeology, first of all in the United States. The consequence of this was that ethnographic data gradually became the main sources of inspiration for the interpretation of archaeological evidence. But the available ethnographic information often proved deficient for archaeologists and these conditions ultimately led to the birth of a new science: ethnoarchaeology, whose aim is the systematic study of material aspects of human behaviour in present-day societies.

These developments inspired entirely novel views on the interpretation of changes in the archaeological record. In Childe's opinion all changes were ultimately attributable to only two processes: migration and diffusion. Under the influence of scholars like Lewis Binford and David Clarke those same processes became the focus of intensive research. Over the years, the diffusionist and migrationist model has gradually been superseded by models of cultural continuity, in which changes in material culture are regarded as the consequences of social and ideological processes. This approach is consequently known as processual archaeology.

Processual archaeology pays great attention to the relations between man and his natural environment (fig. 1.5). Culture is regarded as an adaptive system that responds to the natural surroundings of a human group, with the surrounding human communities constituting a major influential factor. In processual models of explanation the interaction between different communities consequently receives far more attention than it ever did in the past. In that respect anthropology, in which thoughts on exchange play an important part, is a source of inspiration for new archaeological research. The aforementioned developments have influenced all branches of archaeology, in studies ranging from the Palaeolithic to the Middle Ages and from Europe to Australia.

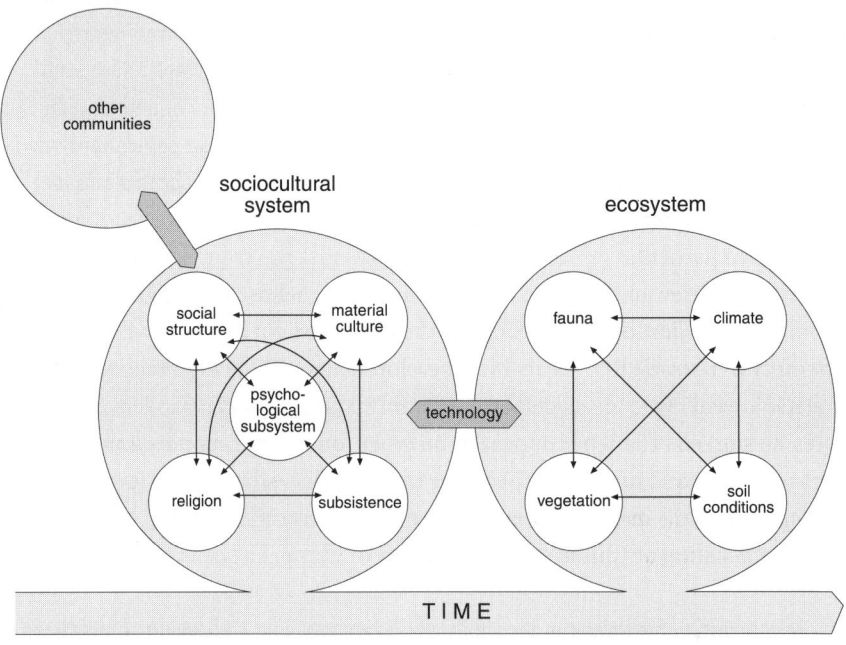

fig. 1.5

Model of the socio-cultural system of a human community showing internal subsystems and relations with the natural environment and other communities, as presented by David Clarke, one of the founders of the New Archaeology.

The past decades have seen the emergence of yet new approaches, especially in England. Some of these new approaches continue along the lines of processual archaeology, but most are reactions against that way of thinking. In the 1980s these approaches were collectively referred to as contextual archaeology. Nowadays they are known as post-processual, interpretive or post-modern archaeology. Hodder, Shanks, Tilley, Thomas and other authors of these new trends emphasise that material objects may have different meanings in different cultures, regions and contexts. They point out that it is impossible to speak of objectively observable facts, because the meanings that we attribute to our data are coloured by our Western perceptions and our scientific and social backgrounds.[8] Like most ideologies, the processual and contextual trends attracted and still continue to attract ardent and more moderate supporters.

In the Netherlands, all these developments were closely followed, but the different trends never really gave rise to a controversy and the most extreme views received little support. The development of theoretical and methodological aspects of archaeology has never been a prime objective in the Netherlands. Instead, the emphasis has been on gathering and interpreting information in field research. Over the years, the questions raised by the results of surveys and material research have inspired a selective and creative use of models and theories. Pragmatism has prevailed over dogmatism. Generally speaking, the Dutch approach to the past can be placed in between between modest positivism and moderate relativism. The authors of this book all agree that any statement they make on the past will inevitably be influenced by their assumptions and their preconceptions. Nevertheless, their approach to the past is rather positivistic. And that is understandable: the raw archaeological data – the features and artefacts – have a tangible relation with the past. They tempt us into believing that the past is to some extent knowable. But we must bear in mind that our evidence is limited, and may moreover be distorted by various factors. The latter topic is also an important aspect of present-day Dutch archaeological research.

DISTORTED IMAGES

The pictures that we are able to present of the past are biased as a result of the excavation methods we use and our theoretical frameworks. But there are more factors that affect our understanding of the past. For example, some regions appear to have been far more densely occupied than others. Such an impression may correctly reflect the actual situation, but it may also be the consequence of comparatively more intensive research, as for example in the case of the high density of finds discovered on the Dutch island of Texel.[9] In other cases it is a scholarly preference for a particular period or class of objects that has led to a distorted image. For example, the Stone Age is well represented at the many sites that have been discovered by amateur archaeologists. That is because many amateur archaeologists tend(ed) to search primarily for flint artefacts; pot sherds attract less interest and moreover disintegrate relatively quickly at the surface.

Our understanding of early communities is also greatly influenced by aspects of prehistoric behaviour. For example, our knowledge of large numbers of showpieces of the material culture of Neolithic and later communities we owe to those communities' custom of deliberately depositing unused valuable objects in swampy depressions, valleys and watercourses. The large flint axes, heavy bronze swords, strings of beads and the like are found in their primary contexts, i.e. the contexts in which they were last in use, although in this case that use was probably of a special – ceremonial – nature. Finds recovered from such primary contexts offer us the best possible starting points for studying prehistoric human behaviour and the underlying ideas, unlike most domestic remains, which were usually thrown away or removed from a site as refuse and consequently ended up in secondary contexts.

Concepts like 'primary refuse', 'secondary refuse' and 'de facto refuse' feature prominently in the systematic work that the American archaeologist Schiffer has been carrying out in the field of so-called archaeological formation processes since the 1970s.[10] Schiffer makes a distinction between cultural and natural processes (fig. 1.6). The most important cultural processes are the discarding and abandoning of artefacts. The human practices and customs associated with those processes greatly determine what aspects of the socio-cultural system ('system context') are represented in the archaeological record. They are hence site-formation processes.[11]

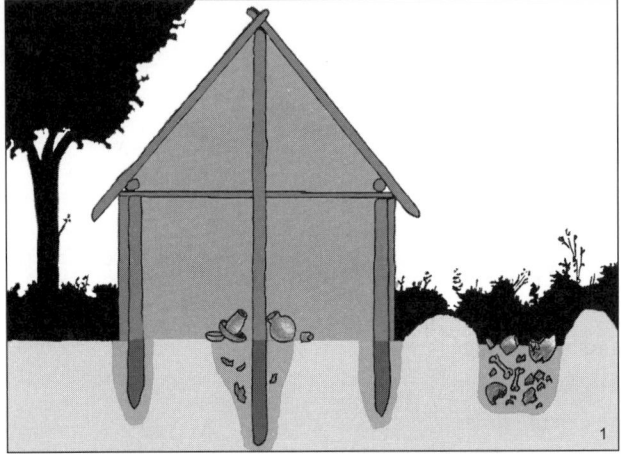

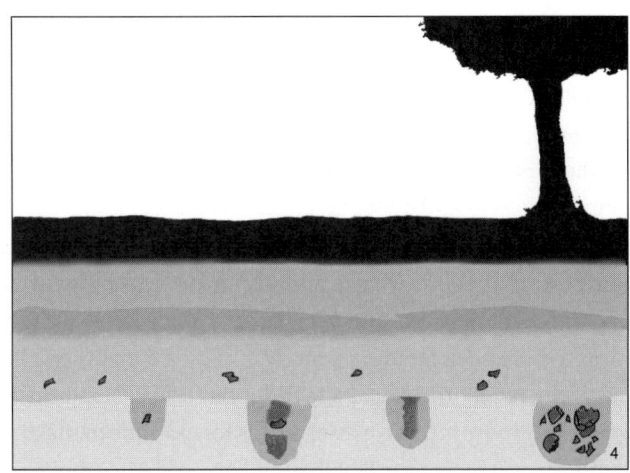

fig. 1.6

Examples of post-depositional processes
that have taken place since the period of
prehistoric occupation.

1 A settlement in the sandy part of the Netherlands.

2 After the settlement has been abandoned
   the building gradually becomes dilapi-
   dated; the top parts of the posts begin to
   rot; the vegetation starts to invade the area
   and root growth will displace structural
   remains.

3 The layer containing the occupation
   remains is disturbed by ploughing and the
   remains are displaced and fragmented;
   only those buried deeper beneath the
   surface will survive in part; all bones have
   meanwhile decayed.

4 Manuring with dung mixed with sods in the
   Middle Ages resulted in the formation of
   a *Plaggen* soil, as a result of which the site
   has not been disturbed further by the usual
   agricultural activities.

The processes to which remains are subjected before they are ultimately excavated
are classed as site-*deforming* or *post-depositional* processes. Many of the latter are
natural processes. The most important, besides burial by sediments, soil frost,
the burrowing of animals and the effects of roots (bioturbation), are deterioration
owing to chemical processes and bacterial action. But nature is not the only source
of distortion; man, too, has affected what survives in the archaeological record. All
the communities that succeeded those being studied, from prehistoric times to the
present and even the future, may have disturbed or may still disturb the evidence.
The search for flint at abandoned camps is an example of disturbance by human
activities in the distant past. Deep-ploughing, house construction, the digging of
gravel pits and trenches for pipelines are contemporary, more devastating examples of damage. Of particular influence, finally, are the archaeologists themselves.
It is their research methods and their interests that largely determine where and
what remains from the past are discovered.

Schiffer's ideas have won a wide acceptance in the Netherlands, as well, where
they have played a predominant part in the interpretation of archaeological evidence, especially in regional studies.[12] That is the main reason why each of the
following parts of this book is preceded by an introductory review of the representativeness of the evidence available for the period discussed in the part in
question. A conspicuous aspect of the representativeness of the Dutch evidence
is the great variation observable within this small country. For example, we know
virtually nothing about the Palaeolithic and Mesolithic of the coastal region. This
is entirely attributable to the melting of the northern ice cap in the final phase of
the last glaciation, which started about 18,000 years ago. The Palaeolithic and Mesolithic sites in the low-lying parts of the North Sea Basin that were submerged

by the melted ice were subsequently covered by thick layers of sediments and are now practically inaccessible for archaeological research. Our understanding of these periods is based on finds recovered from higher grounds and is hence biased: in certain seasons the Upper Palaeolithic hunter-gatherers will have left the higher parts to exploit the resources of the lowlands, where their way of life will have differed. Only in rare circumstances, for example when a beach is raised with sand from the North Sea or when finds are recovered by trawl nets, do we catch a glimpse of earlier human existence on what is now the bottom of the North Sea.

The reverse of the above situation holds for the later periods. The evidence from the coastal region from the Neolithic and later periods is richer and more varied than that from the interior, comprising as it does many wooden objects, uncarbonised seeds, bones and other organic remains. These finds in fact all come from watery environments, including stream and river valleys and the raised bogs of Drenthe, which have now all been dug away. Organic remains that end up beneath groundwater level – and remain there – or that become buried beneath clay or manure relatively quickly remain virtually unaffected by bacterial action owing to the lack of oxygen in the surrounding environment. Skeletal remains, however, survive only in soils with an acidity favouring their preservation. In raised bogs bones may disappear, whereas skin may survive, preserved by a natural tanning process.

THE IMPORTANCE OF THE WETLANDS FOR OUR IMAGE OF THE PAST

The most diverse archaeological record to be found in the Netherlands is that of the wetlands (fig. 1.7). Finds from the waterlogged soils of these regions show that the Stone Age was also a Bone Age. One of the best represented categories of bone objects is that of Mesolithic points (see feature B). The rare spades, plough shares, cart wheels, vessels and wool combs of organic material offer us a more varied picture of Bronze Age and Iron Age farming practices than the more numerous – for more durable – querns, earthenware spindle whorls and loom weights.

Apart from the fact that they have yielded a wider diversity of remains of material culture than any other region in the Netherlands, the wetlands are also the only environments in this country where answers to various specific research questions

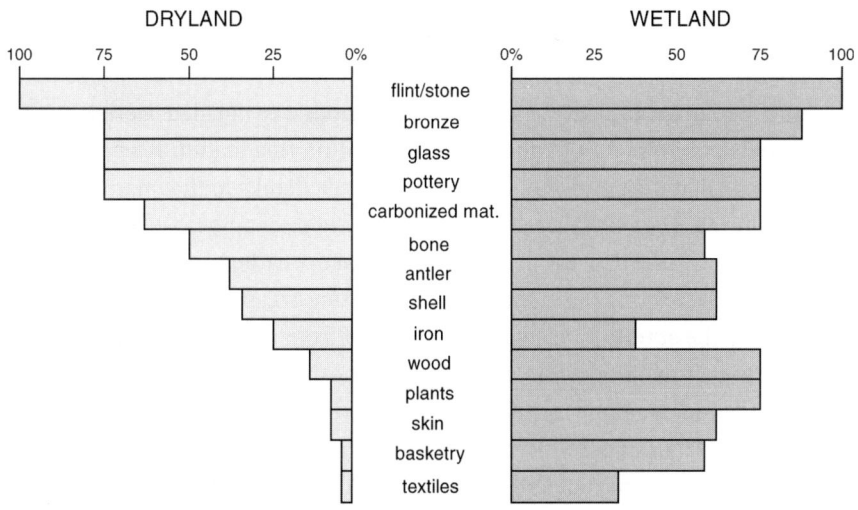

fig. 1.7

Estimates of different materials surviving after centuries of burial in dry and wet soils in Europe. At the many dry sites in the aerated Dutch sandy soils with their low calcium contents the proportion of organic remains will be much lower than indicated here.

25

fig. 1.8
In peat with a certain acidity even hair may be preserved, as can be inferred from this pair of plaits that was found near Odoorn. The plaits were cut off and deposited here between 800 and 400 BC, presumably as votive gifts.

can be found.[13] From research on the higher grounds we already knew that sedentary life in late prehistoric times was of a dynamic nature ('unsettled settlement'), but exactly how dynamic could be estimated only there where remains of timber structures had survived. Those remains showed that the farms in the peat regions were inhabited for no more than a few dozen years (see feature O). The inhabitants of the farms on more solid ground will not have stayed put for much longer.

Bones and plant remains preserved at camps and in farmyards provide excellent information on exploitation patterns and farming strategies. It is no coincidence that the first quantitative models of prehistoric farming developed in the Netherlands are based on data obtained in the wetlands of Westfrisia.[14] The comparatively large proportion of remains of young rhinoceros at the Middle Palaeolithic camps in the Meuse valley near Maastricht even raise the fundamental question whether the earliest occupants of this region were hunters or perhaps scavengers. Wetland sites also offer us a much clearer picture of prehistoric man himself, for example in places where the remains of a fully dressed Bronze Age man come to light (see features Q and S) or where the remains of the last meal and dental plaque are found to have resisted the ravages of time for 4500 years.[15]

These relatively large differences in surviving material remains show that the factor preservation constitutes an important filter between what was once present at a site and what still remains today. It therefore goes without saying that throughout this book we will repeatedly have to 'dress' prehistoric man on the basis of incidental finds (fig. 1.8).

PERIODS AND DATES

Early divisions and chronologies

The system devised by the Danish museum curator C.J. Thomsen in the first half of the 19th century is still used to divide prehistory today. On the basis of the most characteristic types of materials employed in particular periods he distinguished a Stone Age, a Bronze Age and an Iron Age. This Three Age System proved applicable to the whole of Europe. As our knowledge of the past increased, the system was refined, while the phases that were distinguished within this general system differed from one country to another or from one cultural area to another. Only the division of the Stone Age into an Old Stone Age or Palaeolithic and a New Stone Age or Neolithic was commonly adopted at a relatively early stage; later a Middle Stone Age (Mesolithic) was distinguished too.

In the Netherlands, a first official division (from the Neolithic until the end of the Iron Age) was accepted in 1965. The criteria for distinguishing the beginning of a new period and the cultural phenomena characterising the distinguished periods were then also formulated.[16] The different periods were not dated, even though reasonable consensus had by then been reached on this matter. Many absolute dates were at that time available in the Netherlands thanks to the important part that the University of Groningen had played in the development of radiocarbon dating, a method based on the decay of the radioactive carbon isotope ^{14}C.[17] Scientists had discovered that the moment of death of any organism that had absorbed carbon from the atmosphere could be calculated from a given decay rate, on the assumption that the proportion of ^{14}C in the atmosphere had remained constant throughout time. A simple formula was all that was needed. Subtraction of 1950 years from the laboratory result expressed in ^{14}C years BP (= Before Present), with an unavoidable margin (standard deviation), yielded a date expressed in 'years be-

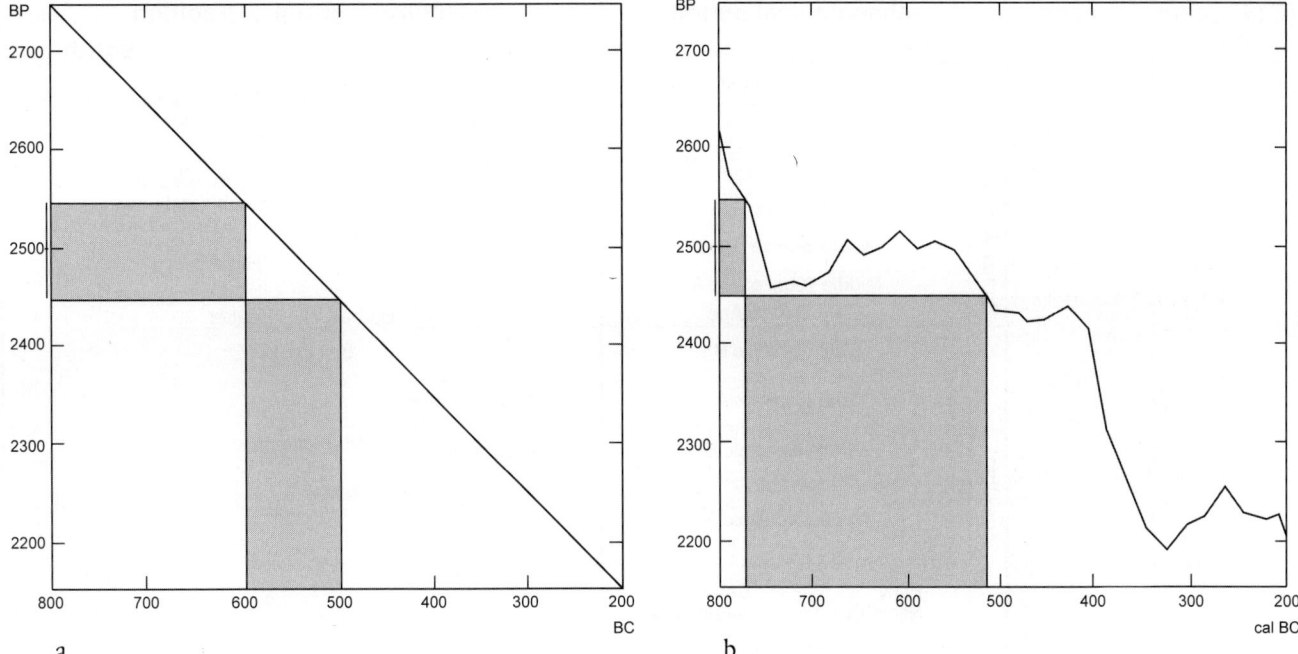

fore/after Christ' (fig. 1.9a). A ^{14}C date of 2050 ± 40 BP hence resulted in a date around 100 BC. This method implied a tremendous advance on the dating methods available up to 1950,[18] in spite of the margins that had to be included, which ranged from a few dozen years for late prehistoric dates to many hundreds of years in the earliest part of the range covered by this dating method, around 50,000 years ago.[19] In 1977 a slightly modified chronology was developed for the Netherlands, with dates based on the results of ^{14}C research.[20]

From radiocarbon years to calendar years

The chronological framework used in this book (fig. 1.10) reflects the continuous developments in the field of absolute dating methods.[14]C measurements of Egyptian mummy coffins of a known age had at an early stage already shown that ^{14}C years cannot be equated with calendar years. The ^{14}C dates consequently had to be corrected. Trees were found to provide the solution to this problem. In cross-section, tree-trunks show patterns of annual growth rings of varying thicknesses. These varying thicknesses are the consequence of variations in environmental conditions, in particular fluctuations in climatological conditions. Recent and fossilised trees with partly overlapping annual ring patterns yielded master sequences of annual growth rings spanning many millennia, first of all in the United States and later also in Europe. Measurements of the ^{14}C contents of these tree rings of known ages showed that the assumption that the concentration of this isotope in the atmosphere had remained constant was not correct. The concentration was found to have fluctuated considerably in certain periods. Moreover, the dates of samples from before 2500 BP were found to be consistently too young.

The results of these measurements of annual rings were plotted in calibration curves expressing the relation between the ^{14}C dates and tree-ring or calendar years (fig. 1.9b). Nowadays, the laboratory results in years BP are converted into years cal BC and cal AD, but always with a margin.[21] The present composite curves go back to 9439 BC, but the parts before 7875 BC are still poorly founded.[22] That is why the dates in the time scale shown in figure 1.10 are given in two columns:

fig. 1.9
Past and present approaches to ^{14}C dating. It was originally assumed that ^{14}C values were linearly related to dates in solar years (left). A ^{14}C date of, say, 2500 ± 50 years BP (Before Present) was assumed to correspond to 600-500 BC. But when the proportion of ^{14}C in the atmosphere was found to fluctuate, the straight line was replaced by a calibration curve (right). The aforementioned ^{14}C date now corresponds to a range of solar years comprising almost three centuries.

(C14) years ago	years BC	archaeological period		culture / group / tradition		
		north	**south**	**north**	**south**	
	12	Roman period		Frisian	other native-Roman and Iron Age groups	
2000		Late Iron Age				
2250	250	Middle Iron Age				
2450	500	Early Iron Age		Zeijen		
2600	800				Niederrheinische Grabhügel	
2900	1100	Late Bronze Age		Sleen		
		Middle Bronze Age B				
3300	1500	Middle Bronze Age A		Elp	Hilversum	
3450	1800	Early Bronze Age		Barbed Wire Beaker		
3650	2000					
		Late Neolithic B		Bell Beaker		
3950	2500	Late Neolithic A		Single Grave		
4300	2900	Middle Neolithic B		Funnel Beaker	Vlaardingen	Stein
4700	3400	Middle Neolithic A			Hazendonk-3	
				Swifterbant	Michelsberg	
5300	4200	Early Neolithic	Early Neolithic B		?	Rössen
6000	4900		Early Neolithic A			Linear Pottery
6400	5300	Late Mesolithic		Late Mesolithic tradition		
7600	6450	Middle Mesolithic		Northwest Group	Rhine Basin Group	
8200	7100					
		Early Mesolithic		Earlly Mesolithic tradition		
9600	(8800)					
10.000				Ahrensburgian		
11.000		Late Palaeolithic		Tjonger / Federmesser		
12.000		Upper Palaeolithic B		Hamburgian	Creswellian	Magdalenian
13.000				uninhabited		
18.000		Upper Palaeolithic A				
35.000						
300.000		Middle Palaeolithic		Mousterian		
		Lower Palaeolithic				

fig. 1.10

Schematic chronology of Dutch prehistory.

calibrated dates until in the Early Mesolithic and uncalibrated dates from the Early Mesolithic to the Middle Palaeolithic.[23]

It goes without saying that this use of two different dating standards also holds for the text of this book. The dates in calendar years given in the time scale and in the following chapters are not always the actual 'translations' of the conventional ^{14}C dates; many are interpreted dates. The reason for this is that the margins in the calibrated dates in some periods have been found to be much greater than the margins of the original laboratory results. This is attributable to wiggles in those particular parts of the calibration curve. Particularly notorious are dates between c. 2500 and 2400 BP, which span about four centuries (c. 800-400 BC), and dates between c. 4250 and 4050 BP (c. 2900-2600 BC). The latter range comprises dates of both the Funnel Beaker culture and the Single Grave culture. It was only when we found that the relative order of two ^{14}C dates in such time ranges has no meaning that we were able to abandon the view that these two cultures had existed side by side for three centuries.[24] The most likely conclusion is that the Single Grave culture succeeded the Funnel Beaker culture without interruption, although the exact date of the transition between the two is still unknown.

Recent developments have even tightened our grip on the time factor. In the first place, the amount of carbon needed for ^{14}C analysis has been reduced from a few grammes to a few microgrammes.[25] This allows us, for example, to date pottery on the basis of adhering food residues. Secondly, in areas with favourable conditions, especially the wetlands, we are able to take advantage of the most accurate absolute dating method: dendrochronology (*dendron* is Greek for tree). The same annual growth rings that form the basis for the calibration of ^{14}C dates have been found to be of even more direct benefit. There where a substantial piece of wood, such as a beam from a house, has survived with its bark, the date at which the tree in question was felled can be calculated in principle to within a year, sometimes even to within the season. In spite of the hiatuses that still remain in the Dutch tree-ring chronology and the highly regional annual ring patterns, coupling of the Dutch curves to reference curves obtained in Germany in particular has led to surprisingly favourable results. With two interruptions of several centuries, the Dutch tree-ring chronology now goes back to the year 2258 BC.[26]

In the past few decades new radiometric methods have become available for sites with ages that fall outside even the wide span covered by the ^{14}C method, i.e. sites from more than c. 50,000 years ago.[27] For example, the oldest archaeological remains recovered in the Netherlands, at the Middle Palaeolithic camps of Maastricht-Belvédère, have been dated largely by means of thermoluminescence. The results, which were found to lie around 250,000 years BP, we owe to the fact that the contemporary hominids knew how to make fire. They therefore produced the heated material that is required for this dating method, in this case flint flakes.

The Dutch periodisation

The increased 'chronological resolution' in the expanding body of archaeological information has enabled further refinements and modifications in the commonly accepted periodisation developed by Lanting and Mook in 1977, which has resulted in the scheme presented in figure 1.10. Nowadays, the main aim of any periodisation is to provide a coarse-meshed framework in which cultural phenomena can be placed. The lines that have been drawn between the different periods distinguished in the scheme hence apply to the Netherlands as a whole, in spite of the fact that the actual times at which the elements defining the periods made their appearance differed from region to region.[28] We have made only one exception, for the beginning of the Neolithic. After farming communities had settled in the loess zone, hunter-gatherers continued to adhere to their Mesolithic way of life in regions outside that zone for many centuries. The final phase of the Late Mesolithic of the northern (and western) Netherlands consequently coincides chronologically with the Early Neolithic A of the southern part of the Netherlands.

A major problem that had to be solved in establishing a chronology that applies to the Netherlands as a whole is the fact that the cultural sequence of the northern part of the country is linked to that of Northern Europe, whereas the sequence of the southern part is linked to that of Central and Western Europe. The periods distinguished in the frameworks of those two areas, especially those within the Neolithic, differ considerably. In the Dutch periodisation the differences have been reconciled where possible.

Besides the archaeological periodisation there is also a geological division, comprising periods whose names differ from those of the archaeological periods. A final point that should be added here is that the text of the following chapters may differ in terms of periodisation and chronology from that in the original sources employed. This is the consequence of changed views on dates and on the limits of periods and the cultural contents attributed to the periods.[29]

It goes without saying that future finds and changed insights will show that the contributions in this book are also products of their time. Only the finds and observations on which they are founded will retain their value, as A.E. van Giffen, the founding father of modern Dutch archaeology, already pointed out in 1913, in his doctoral thesis, which contains the eternally valid motto: *Die Tatsachen bleiben, Die Interpretation schwankt.*[30]

NOTES

1 Bloemers/Van Dorp 1991.

2 Van Es 1981.

3 For a more detailed survey see Slofstra 1994.

4 RAAP stands for *Regionaal Archeologisch Archiverings Project* (Regional Archaeological Filing Project), an organisation that carries out archaeological surveys and assessments.

5 For a provisional survey see Kars 1988, 1990.

6 De Laet/Glasbergen 1959, XI-XII.

7 Childe 1959.

8 For surveys see *e.g.* Hodder 1986; Hodder *et al.* 1995 (in which in particular Shanks/Hodder 1995); Trigger 1989.

9 Woltering 1979, 1994.

10 A more specific term is 'site formation processes'. See in particular Schiffer 1972, 1976, 1987.

11 For a discussion of the concept 'site' see Butzer 1982 and Fokkens 1991a, 54. A 'site' is often understood to be a place where human activities took place in the past. In practice, the term 'site' is often taken to be synonymous with 'settlement', which, strictly speaking,

is not correct, for some activities took place outside settlements. Neither is it correct to define a site as a place where evidence for human activities may be found, in other words, a findspot. A findspot need not necessarily coincide with a site, for example if remains from a site are recovered from sand or soil used to raise terrain elsewhere (as in the case of the Mesolithic bone points recovered from the Maasvlakte).

12 *Cf.* Bos 1985, 126 ff; Bult 1983, 81 ff; Fokkens 1991a, 53 ff.

13 For a survey see *e.g.* Coles 1991, table 6.

14 Brandt/IJzereef 1980; IJzereef 1981.

15 Pasveer/Uytterschaut 1992.

16 See *De periodisering van de Nederlandse prehistorie* (The periodisation of Dutch prehistory), *Berichten van de Rijksdienst voor het Oudheidkundig Bodemonderzoek* 15-16 (1965-'66), 7-12.

17 Waterbolk 1959a, 1970a.

18 For a survey of those early dating methods see *e.g.* Eggers 1959.

19 The laboratory gives these margins as figures that correspond to a single standard deviation, *i.e.* a 68% probability range. If the result

is, say, 3650 ± 40 BP, there is a 68% probability that the actual date lies between 3690 and 3610 BP. For a probability of 95% the margin has to be doubled, *i.e.* to 80 years.

20 Lanting/Mook 1977.

21 See especially *Radiocarbon* vol. 28, number 2B (1986), and vol. 35, number 1 (1993). For accurate results a computer program is required, for example the program developed by the *Centrum voor Isotopen Onderzoek* (Centre for Isotope Research) of the University of Groningen, which is commonly used in the Netherlands (*cf.* Van der Plicht 1993; Van der Plicht/Mook 1987). See Mook/Waterbolk 1985 for a concise summary of the many facets of this dating method.

22 Kromer/Becker 1993. The date of 8800 BC for the beginning of the Dutch Mesolithic is hence based on an estimate.

23 The periodisation and the indicated dates were for the greater part established jointly by P.W. van den Broeke, J. Deeben, E. Drenth, J.N. Lanting and L.P. Louwe Kooijmans. With a few minor differences this periodisation was recorded in the Archaeological Basic Records of the Dutch archaeological expertise centre ARCHIS in Amersfoort.

24 See *e.g.* Louwe Kooijmans 1976b, fig. 2. Large time margins that are attributable to wiggles in the calibration curve can to some extent be reduced via 'wiggle-matching' (*cf.* Van der Plicht 1993, 236), but only if *series* of radiocarbon dates are available.

25 Lanting/Van der Plicht 1993-'94.

26 Jansma 1995. In the past it was thought that only oak could be used for dating purposes, but it has recently been found that other types of wood, such as ash and various types of coniferous wood, are also suitable for deriving dendrochronological dates.

27 See *e.g.* Aitken 1990.

28 Some elements are represented in part of the Netherlands only; in one case (Early Mesolithic) we were forced to take the *absence* of certain phenomena as the criterion for the beginning of the period.

The criteria for the periodisation as a whole are:

Middle Palaeolithic:	first use of Levallois technique
Upper Palaeolithic A:	beginning of Aurignacian (Central Europe)
Upper Palaeolithic B:	beginning of Magdalenian (Central Europe)
Late Palaeolithic:	beginning of Tjonger/Federmesser culture
Early Mesolithic:	end of Ahrensburgian culture
Middle Mesolithic:	first surface retouch on flint tools
Late Mesolithic:	first wide trapezium-shaped flint artefacts
Early Neolithic A:	beginning of *Linearbandkeramik*
Early Neolithic B:	beginning of Rössen culture
Middle Neolithic A	beginning of Michelsberg culture
Middle Neolithic B:	beginning of Funnel Beaker culture
Late Neolithic A:	beginning of Single Grave culture
Late Neolithic B:	beginning of Bell Beaker culture
Early Bronze Age:	beginning of Barbed Wire Beaker culture
Middle Bronze Age A:	first ring ditches around Bronze Age barrows
Middle Bronze Age B:	first post circles around Bronze Age barrows
Late Bronze Age:	first urnfields
Early Iron Age:	beginning of Gündlingen phase (Central Europe)
Middle Iron Age:	first Marnian pottery
Late Iron Age:	beginning of La Tène C (Central Europe)

29 After this chapter was written unexpected progress was made in the field of age determination, when it was found that burned bone can also be dated with the aid of the ¹⁴C method (Aerts-Bijma *et al.* 1999). This means that cremated remains will play a role in the revised Dutch ¹⁴C chronologies (published: Lanting/Van der Plicht 1995-'96, 1997-'98, 1999-2000, 2001-'02).

30 'The facts remain, their interpretation varies' (Van Giffen 1913, 1).

2 The discovery of prehistory in the Netherlands

Ayolt Brongers

The professional study of history and archaeology can be said to have started around the beginning of the nineteenth century.[1] In the seventeenth and eighteenth centuries there had hardly been what we would today consider a scientific approach to the past in the Low Countries or anywhere else in Western Europe. Finds were collected, but very few excavations were carried out and hardly anything was actually recorded. The antiquarians of those days were ministers – such as the well-known Johan Picardt (1600-1670) – and schoolmasters, who interlaced their descriptions of monuments visible aboveground with myths about giants (fig. 2.1) and 'will-o'-the-wisps'. Around 1800 things began to change. The research that started to be carried out from then onwards, which included excavations, reflects a new approach to the past. The discovery of finds was no longer left to chance. Archaeologists started to take the place of antiquarians. In the Netherlands the name associated with this transition is that of C.J.C. Reuvens.

THE 19TH CENTURY

C.J.C. Reuvens

Caspar Jacob Christiaan Reuvens (1793-1835, fig. 2.2) was the first Dutch professional archaeologist.[2] In 1818 he was appointed professor of archaeology at Leiden

fig. 2.1
In the 17th century people couldn't imagine that the megalithic monuments were built by the region's original occupants. In the absence of a more conceivable alternative they assumed that the monuments were the works of giants or *Huinen*, which explains the name *hunebed*. This plate by Johan Picardt from 1660 shows the little people watching.

fig. 2.2

Caspar Jacob Christiaan Reuvens as painted
by Louis Moritz. Collection of the Leiden
University Museum.

University. King William I commissioned him to create a museum of antiquities at
Leiden. A collection of classical sculptures assembled by Gerard van Papenbroek
(1673-1743), which had been in the possession of Leiden University since 1744,
was to be the core of the museum's collection. To this Reuvens added a fairly large
collection of Egyptian objects and architectural remains, which were all the rage in
those days. He also collected finds from the Netherlands, though. The collection
of Leiden's *Theatrum Anatomicum*, which focused on the various aspects of death,
included, besides mummies, pottery from Roman cemeteries near Nijmegen. And
the geological department of the Museum of Natural History contained stone axes
that had been found in the Netherlands. Reuvens also negotiated the transfer of
Dutch archaeological finds from a number of Royal collections to his museum.

His inaugural lecture was a eulogy on predecessors whose main interest had
been classical archaeology, but it also contained the question, 'What do we in the
Netherlands know about the Huns, the builders of the tumuli?'[3] This question,
which shows that Reuvens dated all the Dutch barrows to the first millennium of
our era, reflects the short chronological perspective of those days.

1818 was a very special year for Dutch archaeology. As already mentioned above,
in the western Netherlands it saw the foundation of a National Museum of Antiquities and the introduction of the study of archaeology at Leiden University. In the
northern part of the country a bog trackway was excavated that year. No finds were
recovered, but that did not matter to the hydraulic engineer, J.W. Karsten (1775-
1825), who was purely interested in the structure and the course of the trackway.[4]
It was also in 1818 that the first list of ancient monuments, the *Schultesrapport*, was
drawn up for Drenthe. This province had already had a kind of Ancient Monuments Act since 1734. These legal provisions had been made to prevent the demolition of *hunebedden* in connection with the demand for stone for dike construction.
In 1818 the Royal Commissioner, P. Hofstede (1755-1839), asked all the mayors,
the *Schultes*, to submit lists of all ancient remains or monuments in their districts.
This, among other matters, gave rise to the archaeological-cartographical work
carried out by B.W. Cranssen (1779-1860).[5]

In 1813, after the end of the French rule, the present Kingdom of the Netherlands was established. King William I was full of plans which he hoped to realize
unhindered by any long-standing democracy. One of these plans was the foundation of the aforementioned museum. Others concerned the construction of for-
tresses and the digging of canals to improve the infrastructure for transport. Many
discoveries were made during these earth-moving activities. When news of these
discoveries reached Reuvens he would try to acquire the finds for his museum. He
eventually came to an agreement with the various ministries that all finds were
from then on to be reported and handed over to him. All these finds were recorded
in alphabetical order of their findspots. Reuvens travelled all over the country to
inspect these sites. He supplemented his records with information from older literature[6] and in this way he created what was essentially the basis of the same inventory of sites and finds which is still being used today.

In 1826 the Dutch government purchased the estate Arentsburg near The Hague
for the sole purpose of enabling Reuvens to investigate the site, which had in the
past yielded many Roman finds (fig. 2.3). Here Reuvens carried out the first 'modern' excavation ever. Horizontal and vertical sections were drawn and drawings
were made that were to give a three-dimensional impression of the excavation[7]
as is nowadays done by means of photographs. It was at this site that Reuvens
learned the ins and outs of an archaeological excavation, including all the technical, financial and staffing problems it may involve.

Around 1830 there came an end to all these fine initiatives that had been so important from a cultural point of view. The king ran up against difficulties with the population of the southern part of his kingdom. In the end, these problems led to the division of the kingdom into the Netherlands in the north and Belgium in the south. One of the consequences of this was that there was very little money left for cultural matters of the kind described above now that an army in the field had to be financed. The Arentsburg estate had to be sold and although the new owner allowed the investigations to continue for a short while, Reuvens decided to start

work on the publication of the discoveries made at the site. However, the desire familiar to most archaeologists – the desire to work in the field – soon got the better of him. And so, in the Easter holiday of 1833, when he did not have to give lectures, he planned a trip to Drenthe, the province of the ancient monuments that had already aroused his interest when he first visited them in 1819.[8] He prepared his trip well and made useful contacts with people who gave him all the help he needed. In Drenthe he carried out true archaeological fieldwork. He was most interested in the remains of what are now known as Celtic fields: low balks enclosing more or less square plots of land. These remains of Iron Age field systems encountered in the sandy areas of the Netherlands had been referred to as the remains of Roman army camps in the Dutch literature since the eighteenth century.[9] Reuvens, who in connection with his research at Arentsburg had undertaken to locate in the field the places mentioned on the Dutch part of the *Tabula Peutingeriana*, decided to investigate these 'Roman structures'. He soon discovered that the banks had nothing to do with either Romans or armies.[10] Unaffected by this discovery, however, he continued to record the structures. He believed that they dated from heathen times and that they were in some way connected with the bog trackway that had been discovered at Valthe in 1817.[11]

Reuvens' journal reflects his great interest in what we now call prehistory. He himself went in search of an answer to the question he had asked in his inaugural speech. In the Easter holiday of 1834 he investigated barrows near Remmerden,

fig. 2.3

Excavation of the Roman provincial town Forum Hadriani, capital of the *Cananefates*, on the Arentsburg country estate near Voorburg (1827-1833). It is assumed that the illustration shows Reuvens (centre) with his assistant Van der Chijs and the draughtsman Gordon (right). Visible in the background are the unearthed foundations and the estate's garden gate.

Maartensdijk, and Loosdrecht and in September of that year he excavated a barrow known as *Witte Wijvenbult* (will-o'-the wisps mound) at Gorssel near Zutphen.

In July 1835 Reuvens went to London to attend the auctioning of Salt's collection of Egyptian antiquities. On the journey back a brain haemorrhage put an end to the pioneering work of the man with whom prehistoric research in the Netherlands had made a very promising start.

C. Leemans, L.J.F. Janssen and W. Pleyte

C. Leemans (1809-1893) succeeded Reuvens as director of the Museum of Antiquities. Although he did some research on Roman remains in the Netherlands, he was first and foremost an Egyptologist and spent most of his time on work in this field and on his tasks as director of the museum. However, this did not stop him from working on the inventory of sites and finds together with L.J.F. Janssen (1806-1869), one of the staff members of the museum. The result of their efforts was published in 1845 in the form of an inventory of the recovered finds and recorded monuments, alphabetically arranged according to their findspots, accompanied by a map of the investigated area.[12]

Janssen also studied Roman remains but he showed a clear interest in what we now call prehistory, too. He continued work on the inventory practically all by himself. In Leiden he made contacts with students who later became clergymen or landowners all over the country.[13] They kept him informed of any discoveries made in their neighbourhoods, which he recorded in a special filing system.[14]

Janssen's chronological perspective was also very 'short': he dated a *hunebed* to the period of Roman occupation on the basis of a single fragment of tufa found in the vicinity of the grave. On the other hand, he was of the opinion that *hunebedden* could not be associated with the Celts because they did not contain any iron objects.

Much digging work was done around the middle of the nineteenth century, too: canals were dug, peat was cut and fortifications were built. At the same time there was a great need for humus and animal bones to help improve soil conditions for agricultural purposes. The former led to the recovery of finds from *terpen*,[15] the latter to the location of the early medieval town of Dorestad.[16] These discoveries put an end to the hegemony of the museologically so attractive Roman remains.

The second half of the nineteenth century also saw the foundation of a number of local museums, such as those of Nijmegen, Assen, Leeuwarden, Barneveld, Heerlen, and Amersfoort; several of these were founded primarily to house archaeological finds.[17]

In 1846 De Haan Hettema (1796-1873), who was later a staff member of the museum of Leeuwarden, published the translation of a Danish book on the excavation and conservation of antiquities.[18] In this way the Three Age System for dating finds to a Stone Age, a Bronze Age, and an Iron Age used by C.J. Thomsen (1788-1865) in the museum of Copenhagen was introduced into the Netherlands.[19]

The work of W. Pleyte (1836-1903) in the State Museum of Antiquities brings us to the end of the 19th century. In addition to a written and illustrated inventory of sites and finds, he designed a map showing the distribution of archaeological finds discovered in the Netherlands in relation to a geological background.[20] His work on Dutch archaeology at the Museum of Leiden was continued by J.H. Holwerda (1873-1951).

fig. 2.4
Jan Hendrik Holwerda as a young man,
drawn by his wife Nicolette Jentink, the
daughter of the director of the National
Museum of Natural History. Collection of the
National Museum of Antiquities in Leiden.

THE FIRST HALF OF THE 20TH CENTURY

J.H. Holwerda

Jan Hendrik Holwerda (fig. 2.4) was originally a classicist. During his practical training he participated in the excavation of the remains of a *limes* fort supervised by Carl Schuchhardt (1859-1943) at Haltern in 1905. There he learned to interpret certain discolourations of the soil as postholes. Back in the Netherlands he applied this newly acquired knowledge to groups of barrows in the Veluwe region. His observations and his – unfortunately – insufficient knowledge of the mechanical properties of soil led to his 'corbelled tomb grave hypothesis'. Influenced by his classical training he concluded that some (if not all) of the Dutch barrows were imitations in wood and sand of the *tholoi* known from the Mediterranean area. In addition to Roman remains at Arentsburg and Nijmegen and the early medieval remains of Dorestad, Holwerda investigated Iron Age settlements in the Betuwe and urnfields in the south of the Netherlands. He published quickly; on four occasions he summarised his latest theories, one of which was that the Netherlands never had a Bronze Age.[21] He also too quickly established connections between archaeological finds and classical literary traditions. In 1910 he was appointed lecturer of prehistoric and Roman archaeology at Leiden University. The ties between the university and the museum, which had been broken since Reuvens' death, were thus restored. In his capacity of director of the Museum of Leiden, he took great pains to acquaint the public at large with the results of his archaeological

research, for example through school books and through an educational service
at the museum.

A.E. van Giffen

One of the most-influential Dutch archaeologists of the twentieth century is Albert Egges van Giffen (1884-1973, fig. 2.5). From 1912 until 1917 Van Giffen was an
assistant at the Leiden Museum. During the continuation of Reuvens' excavations
at Arentsburg supervised by Holwerda, he became acquainted with the German
excavation method involving the study of traces of posts and postholes. He employed this method himself in the excavations that he was to conduct in the north
of the Netherlands from 1917 onwards.

He started with the investigation of a *terp* (1916)[22], a number of barrows, and
Celtic fields.[23] They were the first of a long series of excavations. The commercial
excavation of *terpen* in the coastal region of Groningen and Friesland and the reclamation of the heath-lands on the sandy soils in Drenthe stimulated much archaeological research. Van Giffen improved the methods of excavation and recording.
For example, he developed the quadrant method and introduced the use of graph
paper on site. He also delegated much of the actual excavation work to field techni-
cians. Unlike Holwerda, who arrived at incorrect conclusions by extrapolating the
information obtained in excavation trenches to a whole site, Van Giffen conducted
relatively large-scale excavations. In 1930 he became a lecturer at the University
of Groningen. It was around that time that he started to publish his books on the
Dutch *hunebedden*[24] and on Dutch barrow research.[25] The results of this excavation
of the *terp* of Ezinge in the early 1930s remained largely unpublished. However,
colleagues who often visited the excavation were very impressed by his work and it
was this dig that gained him the reputation of an exemplary excavator.

Van Giffen was not a theoretician. In his opinion theories had to be based on a
large number of chronologically arranged observations made in a limited area, as

he pointed out in a speech he gave in 1947.[26] For his own limited area of research he chose the province of Drenthe,[27] in particular the area around the Noordsche Veld, where he had conducted research from 1917 onwards. Many archaeologists followed his example and his *Festschrift*, written by his pupils, friends and scientific relations, hence contains a good survey of archaeological research in the Netherlands up to the end of World War II.[28]

Early amateur archaeologists

In the 1920s and 1930s the almost professional activities of a few amateur archaeologists led to two important publications. The first was the book published by P.C.J.A. Boeles (1873-1961) in 1927, which contained a systematic chronological survey of all the archaeological discoveries made in Friesland.[29] By the time that Van Giffen started his *terpen* research in 1916 Boeles had already been studying finds from *terpen* for almost twenty years.[30]

The second publication was that written by H.J. Beckers (1862-1950) and G.A.J. Beckers (1908-1978), father and son, who recorded the discoveries made in South Limburg. Their work, which was published in 1940, discussed finds with dates up to the early Middle Ages; they paid much attention to *Bandkeramik* finds.[31]

A number of original contributions came from related geographical disciplines. C.A.J. von Frijtag Drabbe (1889-1975), for example, the director of the Ordnance Survey and one of the first to have made use of aerial photographs for topographical purposes, pointed out the significance of aerial photography for archaeology to Van Giffen.[32] And in 1936 the soil scientist W.A.J. Oosting (1898-1942) discovered a systematic connection between pedological conditions and the occurrence of archaeological finds.[33]

THE SECOND HALF OF THE 20TH CENTURY

World War II

Preparations for the – entirely legitimate – centralisation of archaeological research in the Netherlands proposed by the Dutch government had already started before World War II. Just after the German invasion, in May 1940, they resulted in the foundation of the *Rijksbureau voor Oudheidkundig Bodemonderzoek* (State Bureau for Archaeological Investigations) at Leiden.[34] Owing to war-time circumstances, however, persons with 'Blut und Boden' sympathies got control of the bureau. Their efforts in the field of archaeology involved carrying out research, drawing up an inventory to serve as the basis of a list of archaeological monuments, taking action in response to reports of archaeological finds and seeing to it that an injunction was issued against excavations by unauthorised persons. However, they also organised exhibitions, wrote articles for journals and books and assisted in making films which were all aimed at indoctrinating the Dutch people with Nazi ideologies.[35]

In the north of the Netherlands, Van Giffen continued his work more or less unaffected by the war. Oosting's ideas led to a gradual increase in field surveys in and around Wageningen. P.J.R. Modderman (1919), for example, conducted surveys in the clay region of the great rivers[36] in 1942 and 1943 and in the Noordoostpolder[37] later on. For him and his colleagues this was an excellent way of going into hiding to avoid being deported to join the labour forces in Germany.

Around this time another survey of Dutch prehistory was published.[38] The author, A.W. Byvanck (1884-1970), a classical archaeologist, was in a way an outsider. For many years he had edited a bibliography on Dutch archaeological publications in one of the art history journals. He had read the works of Van Giffen, Holwerda and several others. He too had his doubts about Holwerda's corbelled tomb grave hypothesis and agreed with those who pointed out the mechanical instability of such a structure. He claimed that the Aryans came from southern Russia – a comment that apparently escaped German censure.

After World War II

After the war the study of archaeology developed rapidly. 1947 saw the foundation of the Rijksdienst voor het Oudheidkundig Bodemonderzoek (ROB; the State Service for Archaeological Investigations), in a way the successor of the Rijksbureau, which was discontinued in 1945. Shortly after its foundation the Rijksdienst moved to Amersfoort. In addition, departments of archaeology were introduced at some Universities: the Instituut voor Prae- en Protohistorie in Amsterdam (1951) and the Instituut voor Prehistorie in Leiden (1963). W. Glasbergen (1923-1979)[39], H.T. Waterbolk (1924), and P.J.R. Modderman (1919) contributed much to archaeological research in their capacities of university professors.

The general public started to become interested in archaeology and in 1951 an association of amateur archaeologists was founded in Haarlem at the initiative of H.J. Calkoen (1894-1979). At first, the members of the association concentrated on the coastal region of the western Netherlands, which is why it was called Archeologische Werkgemeenschap voor Westelijk Nederland (Archaeological Study Group of the Western Netherlands). This association deserves the credit for having for the first time systematically demonstrated the archaeological potential of this region. When amateur archaeologists from areas further inland later joined the association, its name was changed to Archeologische Werkgemeenschap voor Nederland (Archaeological Study Group of the Netherlands). The association publishes the archaeological journal Westerheem. Since 1951 the ROB has been encouraging contacts between amateur and professional archaeologists by organising annual correspondents days at Amersfoort.

Dutch archaeological research since World War II has been characterised by the large-scale use of a number of new methods and techniques, including pollen analysis[40], archaeozoological and geological research, the use of machines for excavation (fig. 1.2)[41] and the ^{14}C method.[42] One of the most important consequences of the use of the ^{14}C method was the lengthening of the prehistoric chronology. After the large-scale excavations carried out between 1950 and 1958 the Bandkeramik culture, which had always been dated to around 2500 BC, was dated to around 4000 BC. The results obtained with these new methods were used for the first time in 1959, in the well-known survey De voorgeschiedenis der Lage Landen by De Laet and Glasbergen (fig. 1.1).[43]

The use of scientific methods in archaeology started already in the 1950s. Waterbolk and Van Zeist were the first to employ methods used in botanical research. The next discipline from which archaeologists were to borrow analytical methods was zoology.[44] Other scientific (archaeometric) methods were to follow, such as the chemical and thermal analysis of ceramics and the petrographic study of stone tools.[45] With this new scientific approach the need arose for a new survey of the prehistory of the Netherlands based on the results obtained with these methods.[46] Impressive syntheses of the results of archaeological research carried out in collaboration with geologists and soil scientists are to be found in the works of J.F. van Regteren Altena (1930)[47] and L.P. Louwe Kooijmans (1940)[48], who were in fact upholding a tradition of contacts between these two disciplines already established in 1910 in connection with research on the rise in sea level.[49]

Another important new method was that of regional surface survey. In 1966 W.A. van Es (1934), then director of the ROB at Amersfoort, pointed out the importance of field archaeology, to which Haarnagel and, indirectly, Van Giffen had already drawn attention.[50] In the Netherlands field archaeology came to focus on Westfrisia, the island of Texel, the Kromme Rijn region to the southeast of Utrecht, and the area known as Kempen. The results of the field surveys of course constituted a valuable source of information for archaeologists, but, incorporated in the inventory of sites and finds, they were also of great importance to institutions responsible for the protection and conservation of ancient monuments. In addition, they encouraged work on the Archaeological Map of the Netherlands and led to closer contacts between professional and amateur archaeologists.

The introduction of the Dutch Ancient Monuments Act in 1961 was very important for Dutch archaeology. It provided the legal means necessary for protecting important archaeological sites from destruction. Lists of monuments and sites requiring such protection had to be drawn up and these lists were incentive to the development of a national inventory of sites and finds, which was computerized in the early 1970s. This has resulted in one of the most modern and extensive archaeological databanks in the world. ARCHIS, as this databank is called, is managed and updated jointly by the ROB and the Dutch archaeological institutions.[51]

1962 saw a breakthrough in the field of the description and interpretation of finds and the formulation of models. In that year H.T. Waterbolk published the results of an entirely new, dynamic, interpretative study of a large area[52], which showed that there was a connection between the occupation of the Pleistocene sandy soils and that of the Holocene clays with their *terpen* surrounding it. Waterbolk's example of integrated regional research has been followed by many Dutch archaeologists. The early part of the 1960s was hence a very productive period, as is also testified by the many contributions to the first volumes of *Helinium*, the only Dutch journal besides *Westerheem* that is not published by an archaeological institution.

With the great increase in building activities and all of the archaeological research involved, archaeology is more and more frequently being brought to the attention of the general public. And the public is clearly interested, as is evident from the fact that the first edition of *Verleden Land* (Land of the Past), which was chosen as one of the 'books of the month' in 1981, was sold out fairly quickly and was followed by a second edition.[53] The awareness of the importance of the cooperation and interest of the public is slowly inducing archaeologists to emerge from their ivory towers. A spin-off of this popularization process, which is now sometimes referred to as 'archaeo-education', is the archaeological theme park ARCHEON which was built near Alphen aan den Rijn in 1993.

In the 1960s attitudes towards archaeology started to change in the United States and Britain. The pioneers of this new approach, which became known as the New Archaeology, were Lewis Binford and David Clarke. In tune with the spirit of the times it was felt that archaeology should be a useful science; its aim should be to find laws that would explain human behaviour. This led to the formulation of rigorous research strategies and the use of computers in testing hypotheses. According to Binford the only possible way of arriving at meaningful statements about communities of the past was by comparing archaeological evidence with anthropological data. The New Archaeologists also stressed the importance of reconstructing the former landscape and studying man's role in this landscape, something which in their opinion was hardly being done in America at that time.

In the Netherlands this new approach met with little response at first, mainly because it was – quite rightly – believed that much of the criticism that the New Archaeologists levelled at their predecessors did not apply in the Netherlands. A few young archaeologists, however, did appreciate certain innovative aspects of the New Archaeology, in particular its British version. In the 1970s they launched a number of large research projects of this new style. The first of these were R.R. Newell's Bergumermeer project[54] and the Swifterbant project supervised by H.T. Waterbolk and J.D. van der Waals[55], which were both carried out under the auspices of the BAI. These early projects were still largely based on American prototypes. The British influence was more apparent in the Assendelver polder project of the IPP[56] and the Kempen project launched jointly by the IPP and the AIVU.[57] Characteristic of these projects are the clearly defined objectives, research strategies aimed at realizing these objectives, the use of computers for data processing and the integration of archaeological data and theories drawn from anthropology and, in the past few years, sociology and philosophy.

Partly because of its belief in the feasibility of arriving at provable statements on the past, many archaeologists now consider the New Archaeology outdated. Under the influence of new trends in sociology and philosophy the whole idea of objective knowledge is being called into question; a more critical, and more relativistic (post-modern), approach is now gradually taking the place of the New Archaeology.

NOTES

1 Several researchers have discussed aspects of the history of prehistoric research in the Netherlands. To mention a few: A.E. van Giffen (1884-1973) in his book on the Dutch *hunebedden* (megalithic tombs); H. Brunsting (1902-1997) and his publication on the history of barrow research (1947); W. Glasbergen (1923-1979) on barrows with rings of posts and the related pottery from the Bronze Age (1954) and J.A. Bakker (1935) on the TRB culture and *hunebedden* (1973). For a detailed survey of publications on the early history of the study of archaeology in the Netherlands, see Brongers 1976.

2 Brongers 2002.

3 Reuvens 1819, 12.

4 Karsten 1819.

5 Brongers 1973; Brongers 1972-'73.

6 For example from Picardt 1660; Van Lier 1760 and Westendorp 1815.

7 Brongers 1974.

8 Brongers 1973.

9 For a full survey of the history of Celtic field research in the Netherlands, see Brongers 1976, chapter II.

10 Brongers 1973a, 7.

11 Brongers 1973a, 8. 'From heathen times' means: from the period before the missionary activities of Willibrord and Boniface in this area, i.e. before c. 700.

12 Reuvens *et al.* 1845.

13 Brongers 1980, 33.

14 Kramer-Clobus 1978.

15 Arjaans 1990.

16 Van Es/Verwers 1973.

17 Brongers 1980.

18 De Haan Hettema 1846; this is a translation of *Om Nordiske Oldsager og deres Opbevaring*, Copenhagen, 1831.

19 Jensen 1987.

20 Pleyte 1877-1903.

21 The last two surveys are Holwerda 1925 and 1935.

22 Wierhuizen, municipality of Appingedam.

23 Noordsche Veld near Zeijen, municipality of Vries, in 1917.

24 Van Giffen 1925-'27.

25 Van Giffen 1930.

26 Van Giffen 1947.

27 Van Giffen 1943.

28 Van Gelder *et al.* 1947.

29 Boeles 1927.

30 Knol 1991.

31 Beckers/Beckers 1940.

32 Van Giffen 1939; this work contains an aerial photograph of a Celtic field interpreted by Von Frijtag Drabbe.

33 Oosting 1936.

34 Van Es 1972.

35 Van Heemskerck Düker/Felix; the book was published in connection with a travelling exhibition in April 1943. Staff members of the bureau also published articles in the monthly journal *Hamer*, associated with the SS department for Nazi science *Ahnenerbe*.

36 Edelman *et al.* 1950.

37 Modderman 1945.

38 Byvanck 1941.

39 Glasbergen 1954.

40 Waterbolk 1954, Van Zeist 1955.

41 In 1957 P.J.R. Modderman, who was then still with the *Rijksdienst voor het Oudheidkundig Bodemonderzoek* at Amersfoort, for the first time used a dragline during his excavations of *Bandkeramik* remains at Elsloo.

42 Barendsen 1955. This work discusses the technical aspects of the theories of H. de Vries (1916-1959); it is this work that made the results of the pioneering work of W.F. Libby (1908-1980) usable in practice and on a large scale. As a result of this the Netherlands now has a close network of ^{14}C dates (Lanting/Mook 1977).

43 De Laet/Glasbergen 1959.

44 Clason 1967; Van Wijngaarden-Bakker 1970.

45 Slager *et al.* 1978, Arps 1978. For early systematic petrographic work, see Addink-Samplonius 1968.

46 Brongers/Woltering 1978.

47 Jelgersma *et al.* 1970.

48 Louwe Kooijmans 1974.

49 Van Giffen 1910.

50 Bos 1985.

51 This project, which is led by R.W. Brandt, was launched in 1988 with a subsidy granted by the Dutch Ministry of Welfare, Health and Cultural Affairs.

52 Waterbolk 1962.

53 Bloemers *et al.* 1981.

54 Newell 1980.

55 Waterbolk/Van der Waals 1972.

56 Brandt *et al.* 1987.

57 Slofstra *et al.* 1982.

3 Shaped by water, ice and wind: the genesis of the Netherlands

Kier van Gijssel and Bert van der Valk

THE QUATERNARY

Cold and warm periods

Viewed on the geological timescale, the formation of the Netherlands was a short process. It spanned predominantly the youngest geological period, the Quaternary, which began about 2.5 million years ago. For a large part of this period the Netherlands was a sedimentation zone at the boundary of land and water (the North Sea). The Quaternary sequence comprises sands and clays with a thickness of several hundred metres. They form part of the sedimentary fill of the subsiding

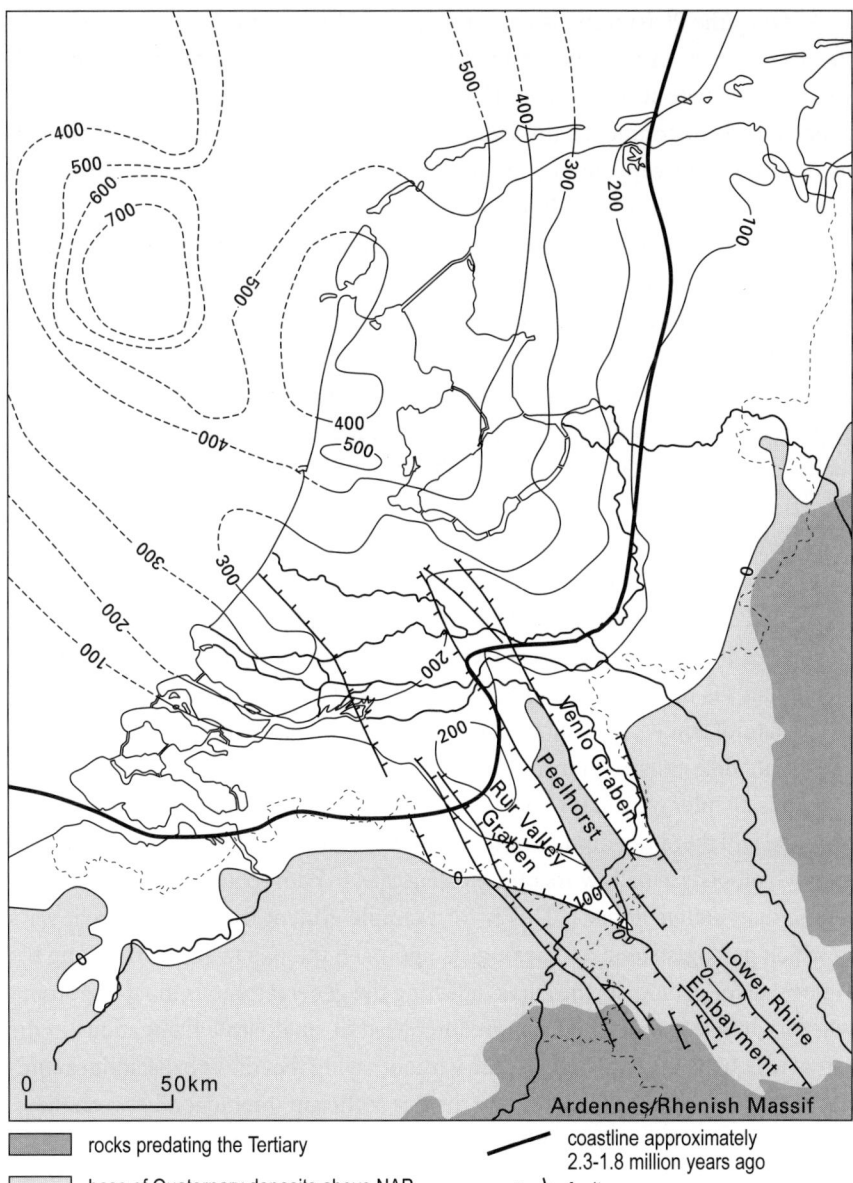

0   50km

rocks predating the Tertiary

base of Quaternary deposits above NAP

coastline approximately 2.3-1.8 million years ago

fault

fig. 3.1

Depth of the base of the Quaternary deposits in the Netherlands, insofar as they lie below the present sea level (depths given in metres below NAP). Also indicated are the most important faults that were active in the Quaternary.

basin of the southern North Sea (fig. 3.1). A large part of the Quaternary geological history of the Netherlands was determined by the deposition of river sediments transported from the hinterland and – at more or less the same rate as the subsidence in the subbasins – sea level fluctuations. Outcrops of older deposits are to be found only in the areas along the German and Belgian borders.

The Quaternary is subdivided, on the basis of major climatic changes, into *glacial stages* or ice ages, in which vast ice sheets spread over large parts of the continents, and *interglacial stages*, characterised by climatic conditions comparable with those of today. Cold and warm phases within a glacial stage are called *stadials* and *interstadials*. Indications of these fluctuations in climate are to be found in the various Quaternary deposits, in their fossil contents and in many landforms.

Two epochs are distinguished within the Quaternary: the Pleistocene and the Holocene. Their lengths differ tremendously. The Pleistocene comprises the period from about 2.5 million years ago until the end of the last glaciation on the northern hemisphere, about 10,000 years ago. Prehistoric man started to play a role in geological history only in the last part of the Pleistocene. After the Pleistocene comes the Holocene. This geological epoch, characterised by the temperate climate in which we live today, has not yet come to an end. The two epochs will be discussed separately below.

As far as the Pleistocene is concerned, we will focus on the reconstruction of the development of the climate and the natural environment of the Netherlands and its immediate surroundings. The changes that took place in this epoch in the depositional environments, the sedimentation and erosion patterns, the development of the landscape and of the natural environments of plants, animals and humans were largely caused by climatic fluctuations.[1]

The major factor that has determined the natural evolution of the Netherlands in the temperate-warm Holocene is the rise in sea level, which has had a particularly powerful influence on the development of the Dutch lowlands, *i.e.* the coastal plain, including the drainage areas of the major rivers. The present landscape of those areas is largely the result of geological (sedimentary) processes. In the higher parts of the country, *i.e.* the Pleistocene sandy areas lying above NAP (*Normaal Amsterdams Peil*, the Dutch Ordnance Datum), erosion and soil-formation have been the prevailing formative processes in the Holocene.

Around 5000 BC human influence on the natural development of the Netherlands increased. Prehistoric man started to create clearances in the forests for pasturing and crop cultivation, but it was only some 1000 years ago that man himself became an influential geological factor. The present cultivated landscape of the Netherlands is the visible proof of this, a result of man's large-scale interference in the natural landscape from the Middle Ages onwards (deforestation, drainage, extraction, dike construction and land reclamations)[2].

In this chapter we can give only a brief outline of the country's geological history, and will therefore discuss only those details that are of interest to archaeologists. Geologists usually work on a greater scale, in both spatial and chronological terms, than archaeologists. This is for example evident from the different ways in which geologists and archaeologists approach the rise in sea level during the Holocene: for geologists the curve reflecting the general trend is most important, whereas archaeologists are far more interested in small-scale fluctuations in the rate at which the sea level rose. It goes without saying that the two disciplines complement one another well, providing there is sufficient interaction between them. In the Netherlands, this has indeed been the case for many years.[3]

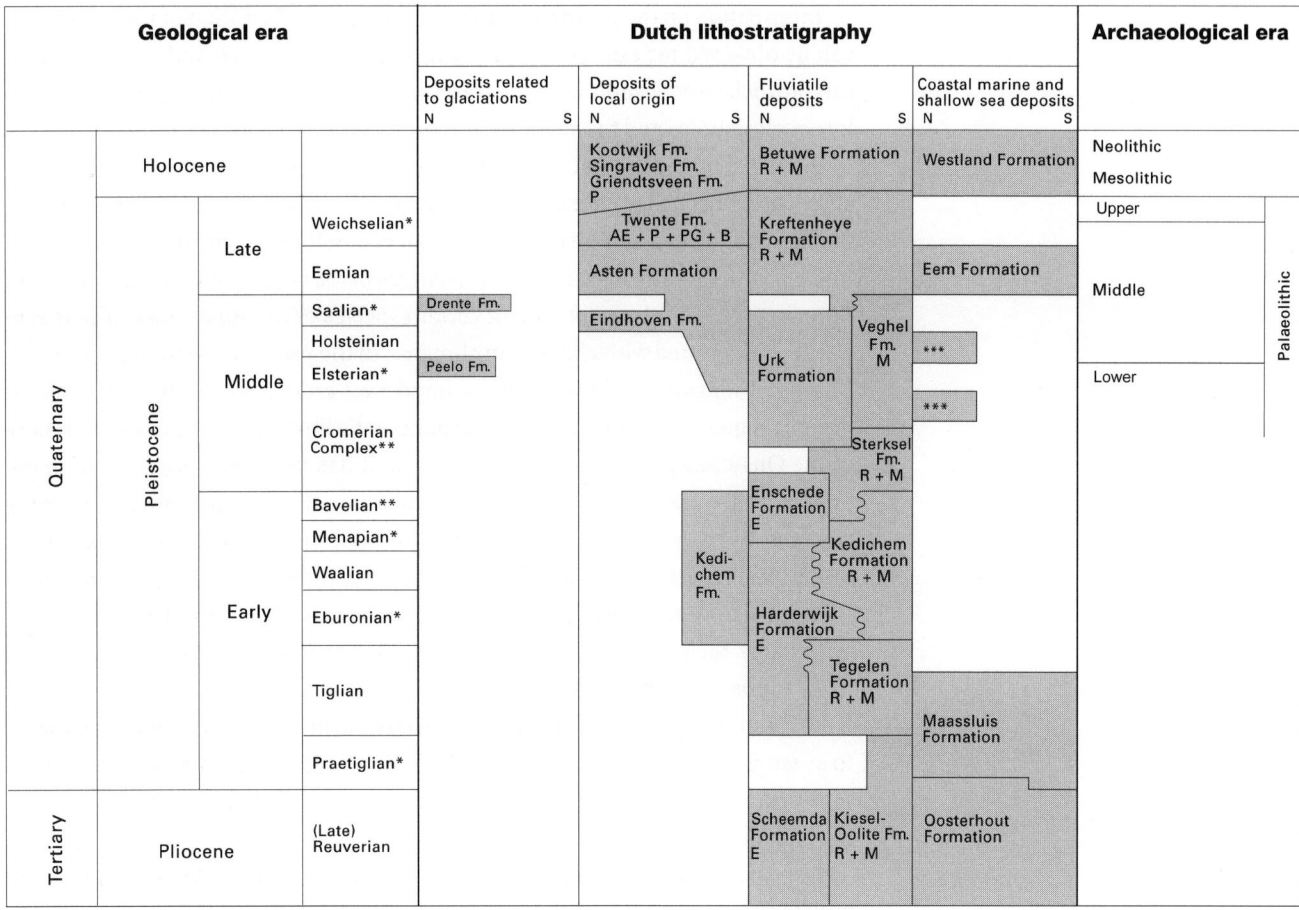

Explanation:

AE = aeolian deposits
PG = periglacial deposits
B = stream deposits
P = peat
R = Rhine deposits
M = Meuse deposits
E = deposits easterly rivers

* cold phase
** complex unit consisting of warm and cold phases
*** still undetermined, for the time being assumed to form part of the Urk Formation

fig. 3.2

Survey of the Quaternary stratigraphy of the Netherlands: more than twenty formations arranged according to age, nature of the sedimentation context and rough geographical position. To the diagram an outline of the prehistory of the Netherlands is added. The nomenclature of the Dutch stratigraphic units has recently been revised; the units have now been defined on the basis of lithostratigraphic instead of chronostratigraphic characteristics (Westerhoff et al. 2003). It was, however, decided to use the former nomenclature in this chapter. Cf. note 36.

Dating methods and stratigraphic units

The chief concern of geological research is to study the composition and characteristics of deposits (= lithology) for the purpose of gaining an understanding of how and under what conditions they were laid down. To this end, comparable deposits are classified layer by layer and arranged in a stratigraphic order, both spatially and in terms of the time of their formation.

Lithostratigraphy orders the deposits on the basis of their composition, the way in which they were formed, the provenance of the sediments and the positions of the deposits in relation to other deposits. The fundamental unit is the formation. One of the basic principles of lithostratigraphy is that of every two successive strata, the top deposit is always younger than the bottom deposit. The formations on which the classification of the Quaternary deposits in the Netherlands is based (fig. 3.2) comprise: (glacial) sediments and landforms formed by the ice sheets, deposits formed by the sea (marine) and the rivers (fluvial) and deposits of local origin (aeolian or wind-blown deposits, peat and stream deposits).

Information on the geological stratification and composition of the subsurface can be obtained for example from borings, seismic research and – often temporary, artificial – exposures in sand, gravel and clay pits or in building pits. Research into rock samples and fossils yields important additional information.

Biostratigraphy is the study of the fossil contents of the deposits, which are classified into units called *biozones*. By identifying the different species represented by the fossils and determining their numbers it is possible to reconstruct the environment in which a deposit was formed. Changes in the composition of the fauna and flora, in particular the extinction of certain species or the appearance of new species, are associated with changes in climate.[4] In the past, palaeontology, the study of animal remains, yielded the most important criteria for a Quaternary stratigraphic sequence on land. Partly on account of the limited evolutionary differences in the Quaternary macrofauna, much research has lately been carried out in the field of pollen analysis, or palynology. Pollen provides clearer records of climatic changes. By analysing pollen samples it is possible to reconstruct the composition of the local vegetation at the time when a particular deposit was laid down. Pollen is found mainly in clay and peat deposits formed in relatively warm environments. Palynology, then, is of particular importance for obtaining information on the climatic ratios of interglacials and interstadials. Similar information can be obtained from fossil soils (palaeosols). Under relatively warm conditions, changes referred to as *soil-forming processes* take place at the surface, often under the influence of the vegetation or organisms living in the soil. Examples of such processes are leaching and illuviation of humus and minerals.

Deposits from cold phases are recognisable mainly by their lithological and structural characteristics; till, for instance, is a glacial deposit. Frost wedges (fig. 3.7) and collapsed pingos (fig. 3.8) are examples of structural features characteristic of permanently frozen ground (permafrost) in areas adjacent to ice sheets, which are also known as periglacial areas.

Litho- and biostratigraphic units yield only relative ages. The branch of stratigraphy that is concerned with *absolute* ages, whose aim, therefore, is to determine when the successive members of a formation were laid down, is called *chronostratigraphy*. The Dutch stratigraphic sequence has been dated to about 50,000 years ago with the aid of ^{14}C dates. K/Ar measurements and palaeomagnetic observations have yielded absolute dates in the older parts (fig. 3.3). K/Ar research involves determining the age of various volcanic rocks by measuring their potassium/argon ratios. Palaeomagnetic research focuses on the determination of the direction of the earth's magnetic field (polarity) at the time of the volcanic eruptions. It has proved possible to date the global variations in the polarity of the earth's magnetic field over the past few million years by comparing a large number of such measurements. As fine-grained sediments, such as clay, can also be used for palaeomagnetic research, many of the Quaternary deposits in the Netherlands have been dated with the aid of this relative timescale. The last change in polarity in the Pleistocene occurred about 780,000 years ago (the Brunhes/Matuyama reversal). This leaves us with a major chronological hiatus for the last part of the Pleistocene. Recently developed dating methods such as thermoluminescence (TL) and uranium/thorium determinations present considerable limitations and are not always reliable. They can yield dates up to about 300,000 years BP.

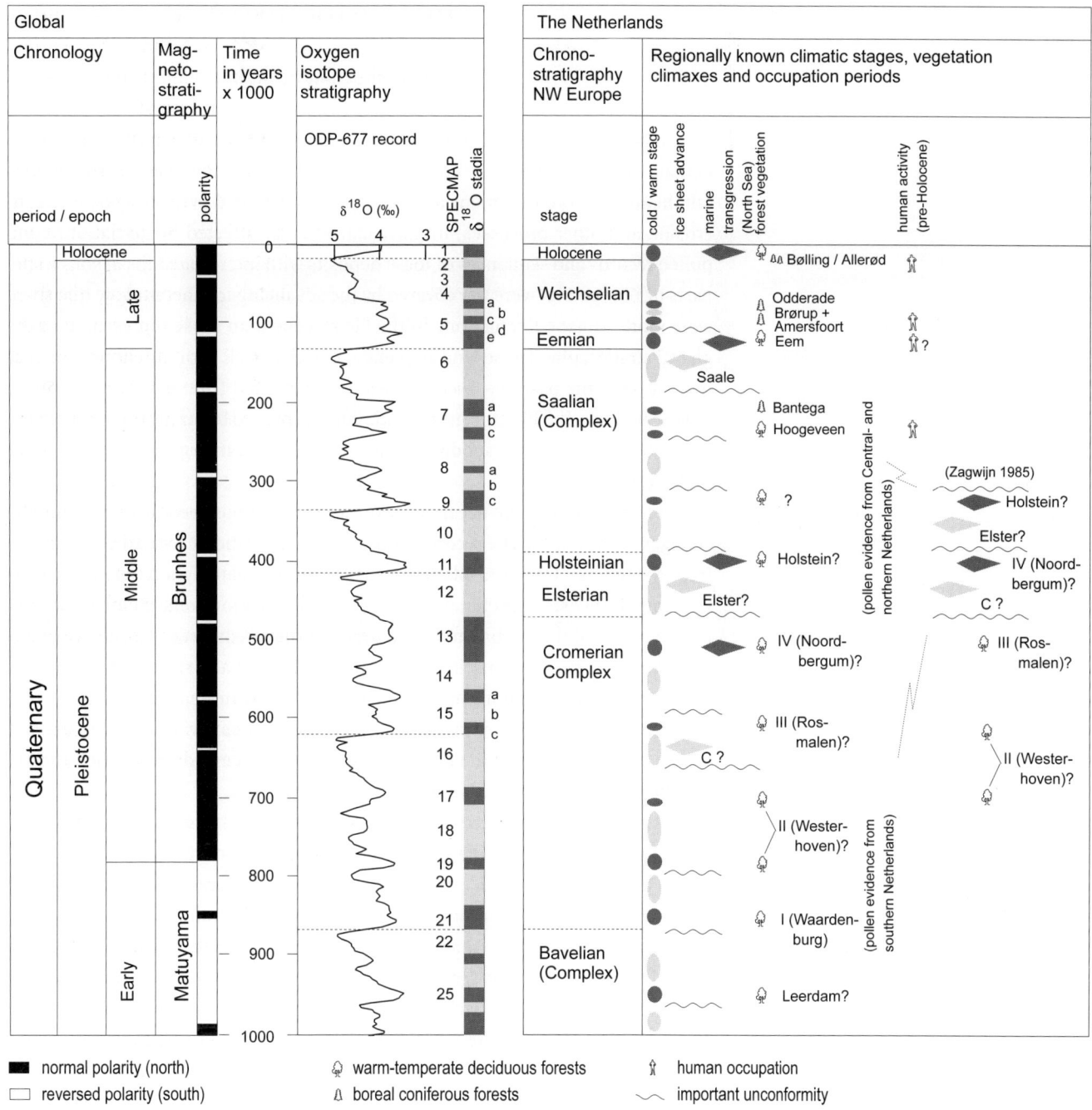

fig. 3.3

Comparison of the global palaeomagnetic time scale and the oxygen isotopes curve of
core ODP-677 from the Pacific (after Shackleton *et al.* 1990) with the climate curve and
chronostratigraphic classification of the last one million years of the Dutch Quaternary. The
odd numbered peaks of the isotope stratigraphy represent warm phases, during which the ice
caps were relatively small. The number of warm phases that can be inferred from deposits in
the Dutch subsoil is substantially smaller, in particular due to unconformities ('hiatuses') in
the sequence of sediments. Some of these phases are moreover difficult to date. Opinions vary
about the Holsteinian and the Elsterian in particular.

Chronology of the climatic changes

The many sequences of stratified deposits on land from which information on climate can be inferred were not formed in continuous processes and hence contain hiatuses. Moreover, many deposits have disappeared over the ages, owing to erosion and other processes, in particular in areas affected by glaciation. Long pollen records and sequences of loess deposits with intercalated fossil soils in the parts of Europe that were not covered by the advancing ice sheets show that there were more climatic fluctuations in the Pleistocene than those represented in the glacial stratigraphy. Those land sequences correlate well with the climatic history that has over the past two decades been reconstructed from dated sediments in the ocean floor. The Pleistocene climatic curve proves to be far more complex than suggested by the simple subdivision into glacials and interglacials presented in figure 3.2.

Cores drilled from the ocean floor present continuous records of the climatic changes in the ocean. The recorded variations in the ratio of two oxygen isotopes (represented as $^{18}O/^{16}O$) in plankton fossils are particularly suitable for reconstructing the Pleistocene climate. These $^{18}O/^{16}O$ fluctuations reflect global changes in the volume of the continental ice sheets. Ice sheets consist of frozen precipitation, which, deriving primarily from evaporated ocean and sea water, contains a comparatively high proportion of light ^{16}O isotopes. Some deposits in the deep sea cores show sharp decreases in the ^{18}O content of the ocean water. These are called terminations and represent the melting of vast ice sheets, during which the ^{16}O isotopes locked up in the ice returned to the ocean water.

In the oxygen isotope record (fig. 3.3) the *interglacial/glacial cycle*, the period between two successive terminations, is used as a climatostratigraphic unit. The cycles in the last part of the Pleistocene have an average duration of 100,000 years. Each cycle starts with an interglacial, with a maximum duration of 20,000 years, followed by a glacial. More than twenty Pleistocene interglacial/glacial cycles have been identified in the deep-sea cores.

A number of standard isotope curves have been set up on the basis of the evidence obtained from the many cores from the northern hemisphere. These curves have been calibrated with the aid of palaeomagnetic dates and through comparison with the astronomical Milankovich curve, which is based on calculations of the intensity of solar radiation on the earth.[5] This has resulted in a number of consistent absolute chronologies for the Pleistocene. The most frequently used chronology is the so-called SPECMAP timescale[6] for the increases and decreases in the global ice volume over the past 700,000 years. The cold and warm climatic phases distinguished in the isotope curve have been assigned even and odd numbers, respectively. As can be inferred from the saw-tooth shape of the curve, various short-term climatic changes occurred within the individual isotope stages.

The dated climatic curves based on evidence from deep-sea cores help us to interpret the Pleistocene sediment sequences on land and to place them in a sound chronological framework.

In figure 3.3 the composite climatic curve for the Quaternary in the Netherlands is shown alongside the isotope curve inferred from deep-sea core ODP-677. The Dutch curve shows the estimated mean temperatures of the warmest month as inferred from pollen data. So far, fifteen periods of temperate, interglacial climatic conditions have been inferred from the Dutch evidence, but owing to the incomplete Pleistocene terrestrial sequence and the lack of absolute dates, only the correlation with the last interglacial/glacial cycle (Eemian-Weichselian) is well-founded and commonly accepted.

The most drastic climatic changes occurred in the periods of glacial advances. In the North European Plain, of which the Netherlands forms part, they are best characterised as protracted periods of cold, generally dry climatic conditions. The main features of the physical environment were the regular occurrence of permanently frozen ground, which was susceptible to erosion, treeless tundra or steppe vegetations, little soil formation, mostly braided river systems and low sea levels. Large parts of the southern North Sea Basin emerged from the sea, the shoreline sometimes retreating beyond Dogger Bank. These general conditions were interrupted by phases of extremely cold conditions (resulting in the formation of so-called 'polar deserts'), with considerable wind activity, in which the ice sheets advanced beyond Scandinavia and Scotland. On at least two occasions the Scandinavian ice sheets extended into the Netherlands. It was during those phases of glacial advance and the subsequent melting of the ice sheets (= deglaciation) that the greatest changes in sedimentation and erosion patterns took place.

The cold periods in the Pleistocene were interspersed with warmer interludes, the aforementioned interglacials and interstadials. Interstadials are short episodes of warmer conditions within a glaciation, with durations of a few thousand years at the most. Interglacials are much longer periods of temperate, humid climatic conditions comparable with those of today. The Pleistocene interglacials were characterised by dense forest vegetations, little erosion, extensive soil formation, mostly meandering river systems and relatively high sea levels in the North Sea Basin. On several occasions the sea expanded inland beyond the present Dutch coastline. The Netherlands constituted a near-shore, densely forested plain in which large meandering rivers, such as the Rhine and the Meuse, discharged their waters into the sea.

A broad spectrum of vegetation cover can be inferred from the pollen diagrams, ranging from thermophile deciduous forests during phases of temperate climatic conditions to mixed forests in cooler phases, and exclusively coniferous forests and open grass steppe and tundra vegetations in the cold climates typical of the interstadials.[7] The vegetational zones moved alternately northwards and southwards, in accordance with the climatic fluctuations (fig. 3.4). Another factor that has had a major influence on climate, besides temperature, is the amount of precipitation, which in Europe is dependent on the west-east oriented maritime influence of the Atlantic Gulf Stream.[8] On the basis of these considerations two types of temperate climatic phases are distinguished in the pollen records of Western Europe.[9] The occurrence of silver fir (*Abies*) is indicative of an oceanic influence associated with high sea levels and the deposition of marine sediments in the present coastal areas along the North Sea. Pollen spectra containing *Abies* date from the Cromerian IV, the Holsteinian and the Eemian interglacials. In the second type of temperate climatic phases the vegetation underwent little or no oceanic influence. In these phases the climate was apparently less humid. However, the mean summer temperatures may well have been the same as those of the present interglacial. These

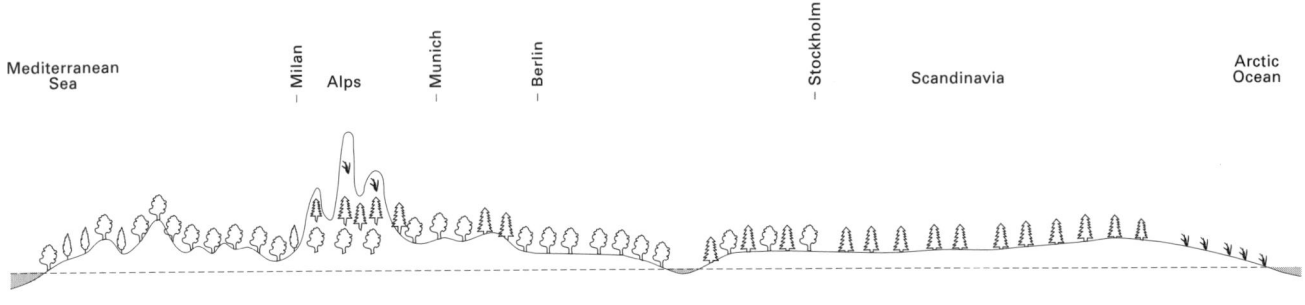

A Interglacial stage (Holocene)

Mediterranean Sea | Milan | Alps | Munich | Berlin | Stockholm | Scandinavia | Arctic Ocean

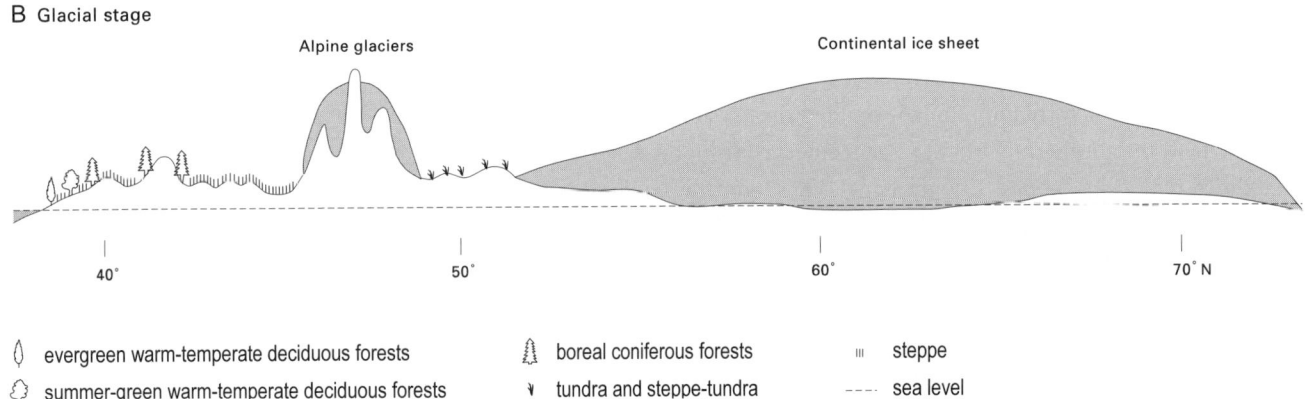

B Glacial stage

Alpine glaciers   Continental ice sheet

40°   50°   60°   70° N

◊ evergreen warm-temperate deciduous forests   ♈ boreal coniferous forests   ⦀ steppe

♤ summer-green warm-temperate deciduous forests   ⥥ tundra and steppe-tundra   ---- sea level

fig. 3.4
Schematic representation of vegetation zones and landscape during the warmest and coldest phases of the Pleistocene in Europe. Section A shows the present distribution of the natural vegetation. We see an almost completely forested continent. During a glacial maximum, as shown in section B, forests were to be found only in parts of the Mediterranean. Open vegetations (tundra or steppe grassland) prevailed to the north of the Alps and to the south of the continental ice sheet on permanently frozen soil.

more continental climatic conditions were probably the consequence of the sea retreating from the North Sea Basin (resulting in a lower sea level) and a change towards a drier and sunnier (anticyclonic) climate.

An additional source of information on the Pleistocene climatic ratios on the European continent are the remains of mammals that have been found in many deposits. For example, the occurrence of remains of grazing animals may point to the presence of a steppe vegetation during a warmer phase. The animal species represented in glacial and periglacial deposits, such as mammoth and reindeer, but also smaller mammals, such as mouse and lemming, differ considerably from those found in interglacial deposits. The latter usually represent forest faunas closely resembling those of our time, except that they also include animal species that are extinct or live further south today.[10]

Geological history

Palaeogeographical reconstructions
Another important aim of geological research, besides studying the sequence and character of stratified deposits and reconstructing changes in climatic conditions, is to construct and interpret palaeogeographical maps. A palaeogeographical map shows an interpretation of the distribution of certain deposits and landforms in a certain period in the past. In spite of their large-scale character, such maps are often used as bases for the presentation of archaeological evidence. Together with the (chrono)stratigraphic chart (fig. 3.3) and the climatic curve (fig. 3.6), the palaeogeographical maps shown in figure 3.5 and plate 1 constitute bases of reference for the following discussion of the three main parts of the Pleistocene:
– the Lower Pleistocene, which spans the period from 2.5 million until about 800,000 years ago;

- the Middle Pleistocene, which lasted until the end of the last, Saalian, glaciation in the Netherlands, approximately 130,000 years ago;
- the Upper Pleistocene, which comprises the last (Eemian-Weichselian) interglacial/glacial cycle.

The Lower Pleistocene (Praetiglian until the end of the Bavelian)
The deposits that were laid down in the earliest part of the Pleistocene form an important part of the Quaternary sediments in the Netherlands. At the beginning of the Pleistocene, large areas of the Netherlands still lay submerged beneath the sea. Marine deposits were laid down in those areas. The sediments that were deposited in the sedimentary basin were supplied by two major river systems: from the southeast by the Rhine, of which the Meuse was a relatively unimportant tributary, and from the northeast by a river system that no longer exists today, known as the 'Baltic River system'. As the degree of erosion increased under the influence of the first cold conditions in the Praetiglian (owing to the sparser vegetation), these river systems built large deltas into the sea.

During warmer phases in the subsequent Tiglian, the coastline moved inland and marine sands and clayey fluvial deposits were laid down. This renewed marine influence in the southern part of the North Sea Basin lasted until the end of the Tiglian, about 1.8 million years ago. After that, the deltas of the two river systems expanded rapidly within a relatively short time, pushing the coastline far beyond its present position.

The vast delta complex of the Rhine and the eastern rivers remained in existence throughout the Eburonian, the Waalian and the Menapian. The eastern rivers influenced an area extending to what are now the provinces of Utrecht and North Holland. The Rhine no longer flowed through the Roer/Rur rift valley and the Venlo graben, having shifted its course to its present basin. Eroded rocks of Scandinavian provenance in fluvial sediments dating from the Menapian[11] are the earliest indications that the ice sheets had advanced to within the vicinity of the Netherlands.

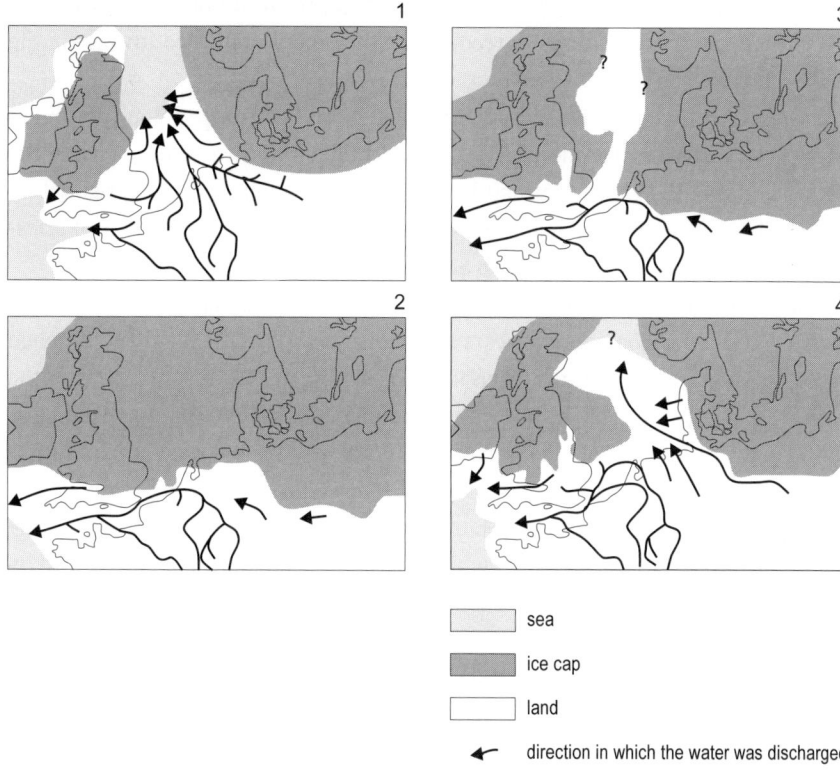

fig. 3.5
The most important expansions of the continental ice sheet and the palaeogeography of Northwest Europe during the Pleistocene.

1 The situation during a glaciation in the Early Pleistocene.
2 The situation during the Elsterian.
3 The maximum expansion of the ice during the Saalian. Exactly how the ice sheet in Great Britain and the North Sea area expanded is not known.
4 The situation in the Weichselian, the last glacial. It is not entirely certain whether the ice caps of Scandinavia and Great Britain touched one another.

sea

ice cap

land

← direction in which the water was discharged

From the Bavelian onwards, about 900,000 years ago, the rhythm of the climatic fluctuations gradually changed. The glacials and interglacials started to alternate in a regular cycle, each glacial and interglacial together spanning 100,000 years. This cyclic pattern remained unchanged throughout the Middle and Upper Pleistocene.

The Middle Pleistocene (Cromerian Complex to the end of the Saalian)
In the Middle Pleistocene, which began about 800,000 years ago, various changes took place in the development of the Netherlands and the surrounding areas. During the cold stages the ice sheets repeatedly expanded far beyond Scandinavia. On at least two occasions part of the Netherlands was also covered with ice. Glacial erosion put an end to the supply of sediments by the eastern rivers (the 'Baltic River system'); from this time onwards the Rhine and the Meuse determined the formation of the river delta in the Netherlands.

In addition to these geological changes, there were also changes in ecological conditions. The European pollen diagrams from the warm stages of the Middle Pleistocene reveal the gradual disappearance from the forest vegetations of exotic (Tertiary) plant species, such as the wing nut (*Pterocarya*) and the Chinese rubber tree (*Eucommia*). The composition of the fauna also changed. For example, zebras, which in the Tiglian had been present in the Netherlands, disappeared. They became extinct in the cold phases or they emigrated, never to return.

The Cromerian (fig. 3.5:1) is a complex unit, in which four interglacials have been distinguished on the basis of palynological evidence.[12] Relatively little is known about the intermediate cold phases. In the last interglacial (IV) the Netherlands once again underwent marine influence, for the first time since the Waalian. By this time the Rhine, which had definitively adopted its present course, to the east of the graben area was transporting volcanic ash ejected during eruptions in the German Eifel.

During the Elsterian the Scandinavian ice sheets reached the Netherlands and the southern part of the North Sea Basin (fig. 3.5:2). It is fairly certain that the ice did not advance as far south as in the later Saalian, but owing to the almost complete lack of till and ice-pushed ridges dating from the Elsterian glaciation it is virtually impossible for us to reconstruct the exact limit of ice advance in the Netherlands.

The Holsteinian, which succeeded the Elsterian,[13] comprised one prominent interglacial with a high sea level. The sea penetrated into the northern part of the Netherlands via the valleys formed in the Elsterian, which had not yet silted up entirely. The Rhine emptied itself into the sea in what is now the province of Friesland. The southern part of the North Sea Basin was dry in this period.

The penultimate glacial in the Pleistocene sequence is the Saalian. In the last part of this glacial (200,000-130,000 years ago: isotope stage 6) the ice sheets reached their maximum extent in the Netherlands, stretching to the present course of the Rhine (fig. 3.5:3). The ice-pushed ridges and till plateaus that were formed in this period in the central and northeast parts of the country, respectively, still dominate the relief and the landscape in those regions today. The ridges were formed in different phases of glacial advance. Material accumulated in terminal basins at the end of the tongues of the ice sheet, which was at least 200 m thick, was pushed up frontally and laterally. The ridges pushed up by the ice in the northern and eastern parts of the Netherlands were later covered by the advancing ice sheets, but those in the central part of the country (now the ridges of the Utrechtse Heuvelrug and the Veluwe) mark the maximum extent of the Saalian ice sheets.[14] The till was deposited beneath the ice.

fig. 3.6 (p. 55)
Geological chronology, vegetation and climate characteristics of the Netherlands in the Late Pleistocene. The (relative) time units and some (absolute) ^{14}C dates have been plotted along the vertical axis.

Geological period			C14-years	Inferred mean temperature in July	Pollen zone	Vegetation
HOLOCENE		Pre-Boreal			H I	birch and pine forests
WEICHSELIAN	Late Weichselian (Late Glacial)	Late Dryas St.	10.000		LW III	park landscape (subarctic)
		Allerød Interst.	11.000		LW II	birch forests changing into pine-birch forests
		Early Dryas St.	11.800		LW Ic	open park landscape (subarctic)
		Bølling Interst.	12.000		LW Ib	birch increasing park landscape and birch forests
			13.000		LW Ia	Artemisia increasing
	Middle Weichselian (Pleniglacial)				PW	tundra
						polar desert
						tundra
		Denekamp Interstadial	29.000		PWd	scrub tundra (dwarf birch)
			32.000		PW	tundra
		Hengelo Interstadial	37.000		PWh	scrub and steppe tundra (dwarf birch)
			39.000			polar desert
		Moershoofd Interstadial	43.000		PW	tundra
			50.000			polar desert
	Early Weichselian (Early Glacial)	Odderade Interst.			EW VI	pine and birch forests with oak hazel and others
					EW V	subarctic open landscape
		Brørup Interst.			EW IV	forests with pine, spruce, omorica spruce, birch, alder and others
					EW III	subarctic open landscape, birch, pine
		Amersfoort Interstadial			EW II	open landscape with willow
					EW Ib	pine and birch forests with oak, alder, spruce and others
					EW Ia	subarctic park landscape with heather (dominating), pine, birch
EEMIAN					E6b	pine and birch forests with spruce and others
					E6a	spruce and pine forests with fir, alder, hornbeam, oak and others
					E5	hornbeam forests with alder, oak, hazel, spruce, fir and others
					E4b	oak, hazel and yew forests with elm, ash, hornbeam and spruce
					E4a	hazel and oak forests, no yew, no hornbeam
					E3	oak, elm, ash and alder forests with some hazel, pine decreasing
					E2	pine forests with oak, elm, ash and alder
					E1	birch and pine forests
SAALIAN		Late Saalian			LS	open subarctic landscape

Inferred mean temperature in July scale: 0°C   5°   10°   15°   20°

beyond the limit of radiocarbon dating

The Rhine and the Meuse flowed as wide braided rivers against the ice and were deflected to a westerly course. In the southern part of the Netherlands periglacial conditions prevailed, characterised by permafrost and little or no vegetation. The wind had free play, which resulted in aeolian deposits of fine sand and loess.[15]

How the climate developed during the first part of the Saalian, before the advance of the ice, is not quite clear. Periglacial sands that were laid down in the Netherlands in this period have been found to contain two layers of organic matter indicative of warmer phases with a forest vegetation; they are known as the Hoogeveen and Bantega intervals. The Hoogeveen pollen spectrum in particular shows interglacial characteristics. The climatic and environmental conditions of this temperate phase can be fairly accurately reconstructed on the basis of floral and faunal evidence from other parts of Europe.[16] The absence of maritime plant species points to a period of warm, fairly continental climatic conditions, in which large parts of the North Sea Basin were dry land.

The Upper Pleistocene (Eemian until the end of the Weichselian)

The changes that took place in the climatic and environmental conditions in the last Pleistocene interglacial/glacial cycle are the best known and best documented. The chronology of this period is also comparatively well known. Figure 3.6 presents the chronostratigraphic scale, the vegetational characteristics and the climatic conditions, with estimated temperatures.

The cycle starts with the Eemian interglacial,[17] which lasted from about 126,000 until 116,000 years ago and corresponds to isotope substage 5e. That this phase lasted for 10,000 years could be inferred from varves in northern Germany.

The melting of the Saalian ice sheets caused the sea level to rise, and part of the Netherlands was submerged. This marine transgression largely followed the proglacial lakes and valleys left behind by the retreating ice sheets (plate 1.3). Those lakes and valleys were filled up with predominantly clay- and shell-bearing sands (Eem Formation). During the Eemian the sea level was at most a few metres higher than it is now. Today, the marine Eemian deposits in the Netherlands lie at depths of 8 m and more below NAP. These depths provide an indication of the overall subsidence of the southern part of the North Sea Basin over the past 100,000 years or so.[18]

The Rhine's principal drainage stream flowed through what is now the valley of the river IJssel. The course of the Meuse was very much the same as it is today.

The vegetational sequence of the Eemian bears a close resemblance to that of the Holocene (compare fig. 3.6 with 3.11). During the Eemian climatic optimum, which lasted for only a few thousand years, the forest vegetation consisted entirely of deciduous trees.[19] The mean summer temperature (about 19 °C) was slightly higher than it is today.[20] After this climatic optimum, the deciduous trees once again gave way to conifers, which in turn gave way to an open park tundra dominated by heather. That marked the beginning of the last glacial stage, the Weichselian.

During the Weichselian the Netherlands was not covered by ice (fig. 3.5:4). Periglacial conditions prevailed, with recurrent permafrost. But these cold conditions did not persist throughout the entire period. The first part of the Weichselian saw a number of warm interludes, of which the Brørup and Odderade interstadials, with their boreal forest vegetations, are the most important (fig. 3.6).[21]

In the Middle Weichselian the climatic fluctuations were less pronounced than in the Lower Weichselian. The entire Middle Weichselian is characterised by low temperatures, tundra vegetations and polar deserts. Frost wedges and structural modifications caused by cryoturbation in this period are observable in the sediments (fig. 3.7).[22] The many round lakes on the Drenthe Plateau are the relics of frost hummocks or *pingos* dating from this period (fig. 3.8). Pollen analysis has revealed three intervals of warmer conditions in the Middle Weichselian: the Denekamp, Hengelo and Moershoofd intervals, which have been dated with the aid of the ^{14}C method. Owing to the absence of forest vegetations these intervals cannot be classed as interstadials proper.

The bare landscape was highly susceptible to erosion. Colluvial deposits were transported in the active layer above the permanently frozen ground (solifluction). In the absence of a vegetation cover, soil began to drift on a large scale. Most of the deposits that were laid down in this period are hence aeolian deposits (Older

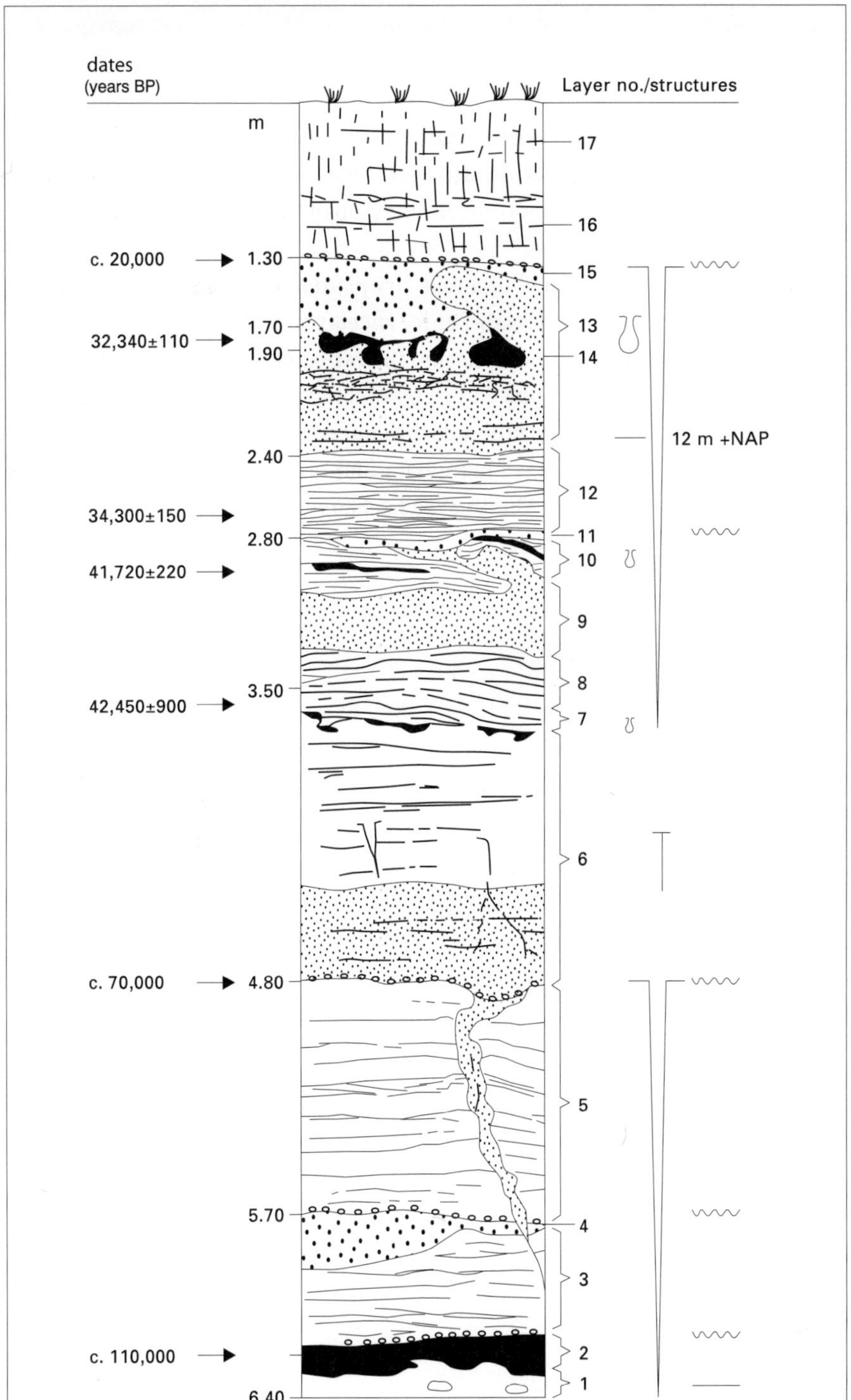

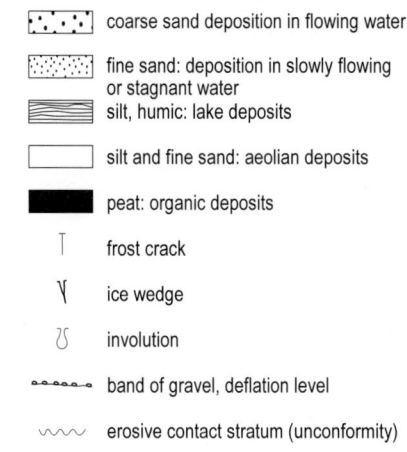

	coarse sand deposition in flowing water
	fine sand: deposition in slowly flowing or stagnant water
	silt, humic: lake deposits
	silt and fine sand: aeolian deposits
	peat: organic deposits
⊤	frost crack
Ⅴ	ice wedge
Ⅴ	involution
∘∘∘∘∘	band of gravel, deflation level
∿∿	erosive contact stratum (unconformity)

fig. 3.7
The climatic history of the last glacial has been documented in a sequence of deposits and periglacial structures on many locations in the subsoil of the uplands of the Netherlands, as in the section of the motorway near Borne (Ov.) depicted here. The deposits belong to the Formation of Twente (nos. 3-16). They date from the last glacial (Weichselian) and are lying on a peat deposit from the preceding Eemian (2). The ages given are ^{14}C dates and estimates in years BP.

fig. 3.8
The Esmeer (Drenthe), a collapsed pingo. During the last glacial an ice-cored mound of earth known as a 'pingo' formed at the site of what is now a round pond. When the ice core thawed, the mound's centre collapsed, resulting in a depression in the landscape surrounded by a low bank. This depression was filled with water.

Coversand I/II and in particular loess in southern Limburg). The greater part of this sand came from the valleys of the major rivers and from sand drifts elsewhere. Such locally formed sediments are also to be found in large parts of the southern North Sea Basin. The distribution and orientation of the sand ridges show that the prevailing winds were westerly.

Northwest Europe consisted of a vast, dry plain to the south of the Scandinavian and British ice caps (fig. 3.5:4). The ice sheets reached their maximum extent, stretching into northern Germany, during the extremely cold last part of the Middle Weichselian, between 25,000 and 18,000 years ago. The Netherlands then lay in the permafrost zone. The Rhine was a braided river, which at first flowed via the valley of the IJssel and the ice-marginal valley of the Vecht in Overijssel to the Straits of Dover, but from the Middle Weichselian onwards it followed its present course again, as did the Meuse (plate 1.4).

fig. 3.9
Section through a sequence of coversands and peat seams, which in the course of the Late Glacial filled a depression near Usselo (Twente). The peat layers date from the Bølling and Allerød periods. Extensive forest fires occurred in the pine-forests during the transition from Allerød to the Late Dryas, reflected by charcoal particles in the soil horizon, the so-called Usselo Layer, visible in the photo as a thin line, linked to the Allerød peat. See also fig. 7.1.

The last 3000 years of the Pleistocene constitute the transition to the Holocene. In this relatively short period, which is known as the Upper Weichselian or Late Glacial in the Netherlands, the climate ameliorated intermittently. There were two warmer phases in which birch and coniferous forests developed: the Bølling and Allerød interstadials. During the colder phases with sparse vegetation (the Older and Younger Dryas stadials) coversand was again deposited on a large scale (Younger Coversand I and II). In many places a thin leached horizon or a layer of soil containing charcoal dating from the Allerød has been observed between the latter two Coversand deposits, in addition to peat horizons dating from that same period (fig. 3.7 and fig. 7.1). This is known as the Usselo Horizon.

The improvement of the climate caused the major rivers to adopt meandering courses. As the sea level was still low, the rivers cut deep channels into their drainage basins. These channels gradually silted up again, but they also granted the encroaching sea access to the hinterland. This marks the beginning of the Holocene history of the Dutch coastal region.

A vegetation developed on the drift sand deposited along the river channels and in the Holocene this sand was covered with peat and clay. Small parts of the tops of some of the former river dunes (donken) still project above the surface today.

Possibilities for human occupation in the Pleistocene

Prehistoric man was very much dependent on ecological factors and had to adjust to the regional changes and the migrations of floral and faunal communities. The biogeographical and palaeogeographical reconstructions based on the deposits laid down in the different climatic periods hence also shed light on prehistoric man's living conditions. Man first appeared in Northwest Europe in the Middle Pleistocene. The oldest occupation remains discovered at several sites (e.g. Boxgrove, England; Miesenheim, Germany) were embedded in the uppermost interglacial deposits of the Cromerian Complex. The bones of 'Boxgrove man' have recently been assigned an age of 500,000 years.[23]

The Middle Palaeolithic artefacts that have been found in the Netherlands, in the Belvédère gravel pit near Maastricht, in fine-grained fluvial deposits laid down by the Meuse,[24] are correlated with the Saalian. Burned flint found in these deposits has yielded thermoluminescence dates of approximately 250,000 ± 20,000 years BP.[25] They permit correlation with the temperate stage 7 of the isotope sequence. That this flint dates from before the expansion of the Saalian ice sheets is confirmed by geological and palaeontological evidence.[26] Comparable Middle Palaeolithic artefacts have been found at Rhenen, in deposits pushed up by the Saalian ice.

In the higher parts of the country, artefacts that may also date from the Middle Palaeolithic have been found in surface deposits laid down in the Eemian, when the Netherlands was a densely forested coastal region. No reliable dates are available for these finds though. Site J at Maastricht-Belvédère yielded evidence for human occupation during a warm phase in the Early Weichselian. No occupation remains whatsoever are known from the cold Middle Weichselian. It was only about 13,000 years ago, around the end of the Ice Age, that the Netherlands – and Northwest Europe in general – was recolonised.

General

The Holocene is the most recent epoch in the earth's history. It began some 10,000 (^{14}C) years ago, i.e. around 9000 BC. This epoch may be regarded as a single inter-glacial, in which minor climatological changes have taken place. Those climato-logical fluctuations will be briefly outlined below.[27] The Holocene has also seen major geological and environmental changes, especially in the Dutch lowlands (the coastal and rivers areas), which suffered the effects of the rapid rise in sea level (fig. 3.10). Around 7000 BC the first consequences began to manifest them-selves in the area approximately coinciding with the present coastline. Until 4400 BC the coastline as a whole rapidly moved inland; after that time the developments varied from one region to another. In the higher parts of the Netherlands, gener-ally speaking those lying above the present Mean Sea Level, soil formation and erosion became dominant factors.

Geological/Archaeological periodization

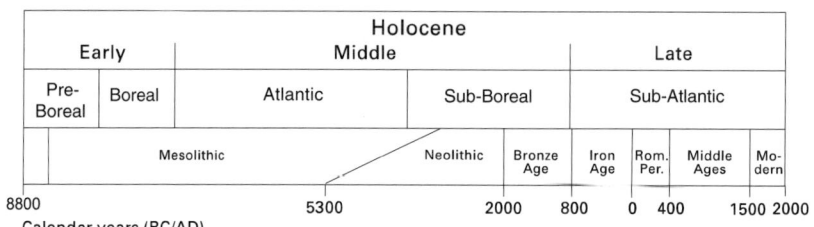

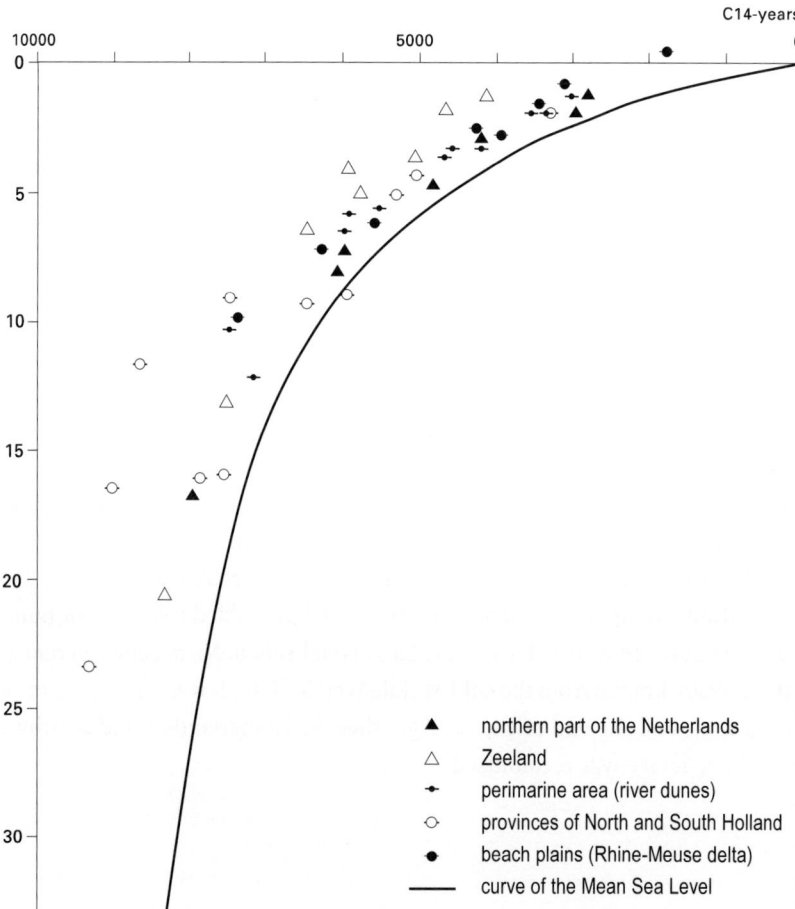

fig. 3.10

Curve of the rise in sea level in the Netherlands and the adjacent part of the North Sea during the Holocene. The older part of the curve lies far below the sample points indicated in this diagram. The results of the analyses of samples from Zeeland are invariably higher than those from other areas. This is probably due to the fact that the coastal area of Zeeland underwent less tectonic subsidence than the rest of the Dutch coastal area.

Age (yrs.) C14	real	Geological time		Pollen zone	Pollen characteristics	
				Vb2	beech over 5%	many cultivated plants (rye, later also cornflower and buckwheat)
1250	750 AD	Late Holocene	Sub-Atlantic	Vb1		hornbeam >1%
1950	0			Va		hornbeam <1%
2900	1100 BC			IVb		
3700	2100		Sub-Boreal		beech<1% elm less than 5%; first agricultural influence	
		Middle Holocene		IVa		
5000	3800					
			Atlantic	III	alder and oak dominant; pine decreasing; elm over 5%	
8000	7000					
		Early Holocene	Boreal	II	pine dominant; oak, elm, hazel	
9000	8000					
			Pre-Boreal	I	birch and pine dominant	
10,000						
		Pleistocene	Late-Weichselian	LW III	herbs; open park landscape	

fig. 3.11

The Holocene in the Netherlands: chronology and vegetation characteristics derived from pollen analyses and climate data. The beginning of the Sub-Atlantic is sometimes dated to 800 BC or later.

Climatological changes and palaeogeography

The Early Holocene (the Pre-Boreal and Boreal: 9000-7000 BC)

The increase in the mean annual temperature at the end of the last glaciation caused the polar ice caps and glaciers all over the world to melt, which resulted in a rapid rise in the sea level. In the oceans, the $^{18}O/^{16}O$ isotope ratios changed drastically. The polar front above the Atlantic Ocean moved northwards, reaching Scotland around 8000 BC. The North Sea hence became exposed to the influence of the Gulf Stream, which resulted in permanently higher seawater temperatures and more precipitation. Around this time the level of the North Sea was more than 25 m lower than it is today, as a result of which this area consisted of two separate parts. The Rhine, the Meuse and the Scheldt discharged their waters towards the southwest, via an intertidal zone in the southern part of the North Sea Basin.[28] Between 8000 and 7000 BC the greater part of the southern North Sea Basin was submerged, including the land bridge between East Anglia and Texel. The waters of the North Sea consequently joined with those of the Channel, which resulted in the permanent isolation of the British Isles (fig. B1).[29] The temperatures on the vast continent rose to values comparable with those of today. The vegetation changed in accordance with this rapid climatic improvement (fig. 3.11). Whereas only plant species adjusted to low temperatures had grown in the Netherlands at the end of the Weichselian, a few hundred years later, thermophile species were already growing all over the country (fig. 3.12). A vegetation of heliophilous shrubs, in particular hazel and Scotch pine, dominated the young Early Holocene soils.

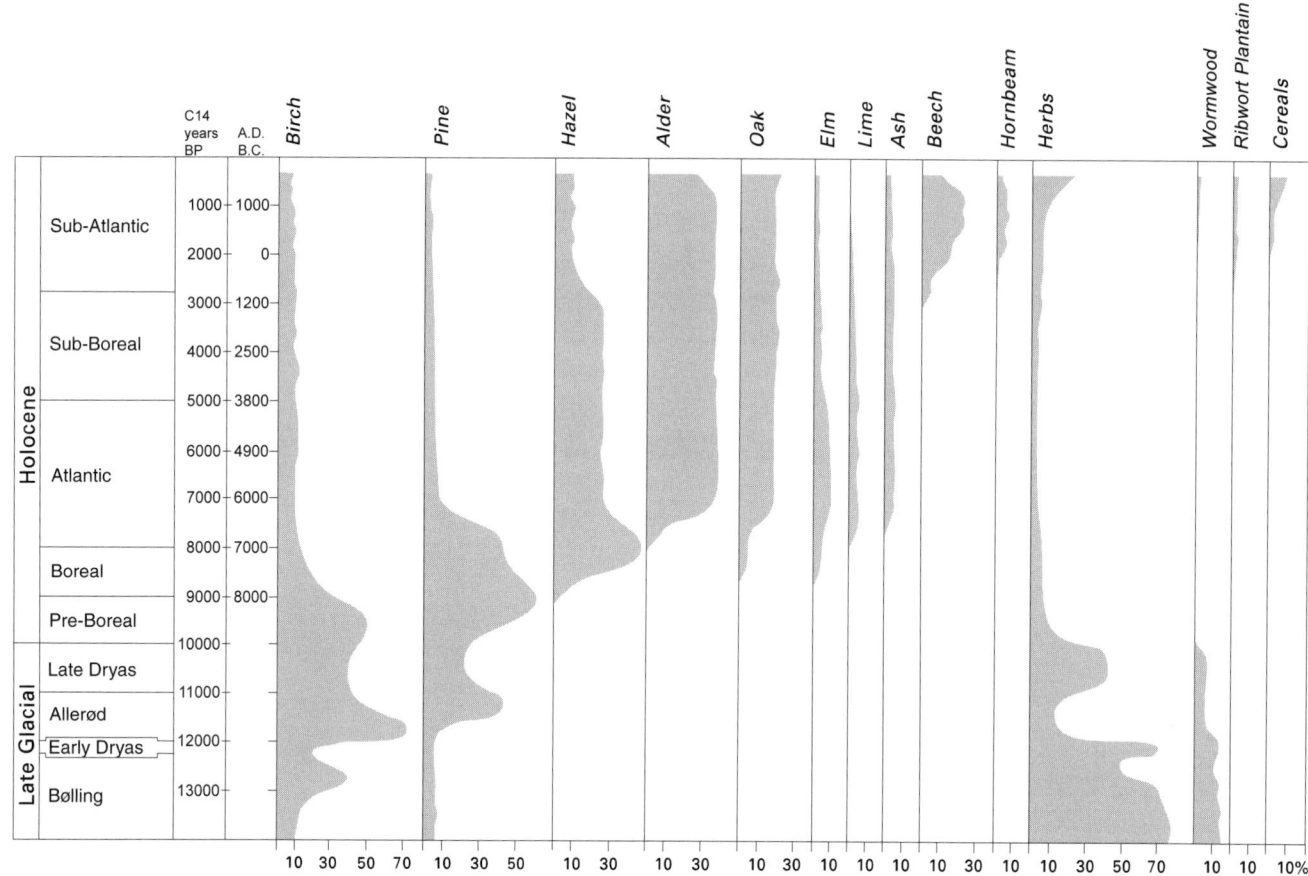

fig. 3.12

Generalised pollen diagram of the Late Weichselian and the Holocene in the Netherlands.

The Middle Holocene (the Atlantic and Sub-Boreal: 7000-1100 BC)

It is generally assumed that a climatic optimum prevailed for several millennia in the Atlantic. Exactly how much warmer this climatic optimum was we do not know, but it is believed that the mean July temperature was about 1-2 °C higher than it is today. This is based largely on evidence from countries surrounding the Netherlands, in particular on fossil remains of temperature-sensitive plant and animal species. The best known example is the occurrence of the European pond tortoise (*Emys orbicularis*).[30]

In spite of the higher temperatures, the climate of the early part of this period is believed to have been drier than that of today, with 10-15% less rainfall. This was probably attributable to a higher degree of continentality owing to the lower sea level.

At the end of the Atlantic, when the level of the North Sea was above −15 m NAP and there was more precipitation, the proportion of hygrophytes in the vegetations rapidly increased. Northwest Europe was beginning to be dominated by the present-day, more Atlantic climatic conditions and the Netherlands became exposed to marine influence. Pools of brackish water and freshwater swamps formed in the low-lying parts behind the coastal barriers, where seepage and stagnation of the groundwater initiated the growth of peat (fen peat). In many places in the higher parts, cores of this peat that became dependent on rainfall for their growth rose above the groundwater level, evolving into what are known as raised bogs. Prehistoric man must have been acutely aware of these rapid changes in palaeogeographic ratios.

As we approach the present it becomes increasingly difficult to infer the changes in climatic conditions from the primary sources. With the introduction of crop cultivation and pasturing (around 5300 BC in the loess region) human interference in the regional vegetation increased tremendously. As a result, the climatologically interpretable evidence from this stage onwards is often overshadowed by the more sharply visible signs of man's impact on the vegetation. The more intensive use of the land also meant that more sediments were washed away than in the past;[31] the transport of sediments was probably retarded less owing to the sparser vegetation and this, among other factors, led to soil erosion.

The Late Holocene (the Sub-Atlantic: 1100 BC-present)

From regions outside the Netherlands we have evidence testifying to a climatic deterioration in the Sub-Atlantic. This is attributed to a somewhat greater degree of oceanity: a change in depression paths led to more clouds and higher precipitation rates. The aforementioned evidence consists of a decrease in the altitude of the tree line of Scotch fir in upland regions and the occurrence of so-called *Grenzhorizonte*[32] in raised bogs. From vegetational evidence Zagwijn has recently inferred a 1 °C decrease in the mean temperature in the warmest month in the Netherlands; the mean temperature of the coldest month does not seem to have changed.[33] This deterioration around 800 BC or a little later was succeeded by several minor climatic fluctuations, namely the medieval climatic optimum between about 700 and 1300 AD and the so-called Little Ice Age (14th-18th century).

The geological development of the higher parts of the Netherlands

The geological map of the Netherlands[34] teaches us a good deal about the conditions that determined the possibilities for human occupation in the higher parts of the Netherlands. The greater part of this area consists of sandy Pleistocene deposits. The flat, sometimes undulating landscape is traversed by coversand ridges and river plains, with the Saalian ice-pushed ridges and till plateaus completing the picture in the central and northern parts of the country. In the early part of the Holocene, transportation of sand by the wind, denudation and fluvial erosion were the prevailing geological processes in this relatively flat area, which extended far beyond the present coastline. The intensity of these processes rapidly decreased with the expansion of the vegetation and the rise in sea level. Under the influence of the constantly rising sea level and the related rise in the groundwater level, the comparatively high parts of the Netherlands gradually decreased in size in the course of the Holocene. In the transitional zone conditions became wetter, causing the peat to expand from the plains behind the coastal barriers and the flood plains of the major rivers across the adjacent, gently undulating, coversand landscape. As a result, prehistoric sites that originally lay in the higher parts of the Netherlands came to be buried beneath younger deposits.[35] Examples of such sites are the megalith grave (*hunebed*) of Heveskesklooster near Delfzijl and the Bronze Age settlements of Ittersumerbroek in the valley of the IJssel near Zwolle.

In the higher parts of the Netherlands sediments were deposited largely on a local scale in the Holocene. The different geological formations[36] that are to be found at or near the surface comprise:
- the fluvial deposits of small rivers and streams and also peat formed in the stream valleys, which are collectively known as the Singraven Formation;
- biogenic and sedentary deposits, which are jointly referred to as the Griendtsveen Formation. This formation also includes the raised bogs. Raised bogs had started to develop here and there in the Early Holocene already;[37] many more formed later on in the Holocene. The greater part of the peat has been systematically exploited over the past centuries;

– coversand deposits of the Kootwijk Formation, most of which are of post-Roman age. There are however a few coversand deposits that were formed in prehistory, in particular in Drenthe and also in Limburg (in the vicinity of Budel-Weert).

At surfaces where these formations do not occur, soil formation and/or erosion dominated, the latter increasingly also owing to human interference. Leached soils, varying in nature in accordance with the composition of the original soil, formed in contexts above the local groundwater level, as a result of decalcification (in the case of calcareous soils) and eluviation of iron and humus. Sometimes the leached substances were precipitated again in soil horizons further down or elsewhere in the vicinity.

Settlement concentrated in areas at the transition from comparatively high parts of the landscape (in particular coversand ridges) to lower-lying parts (the stream

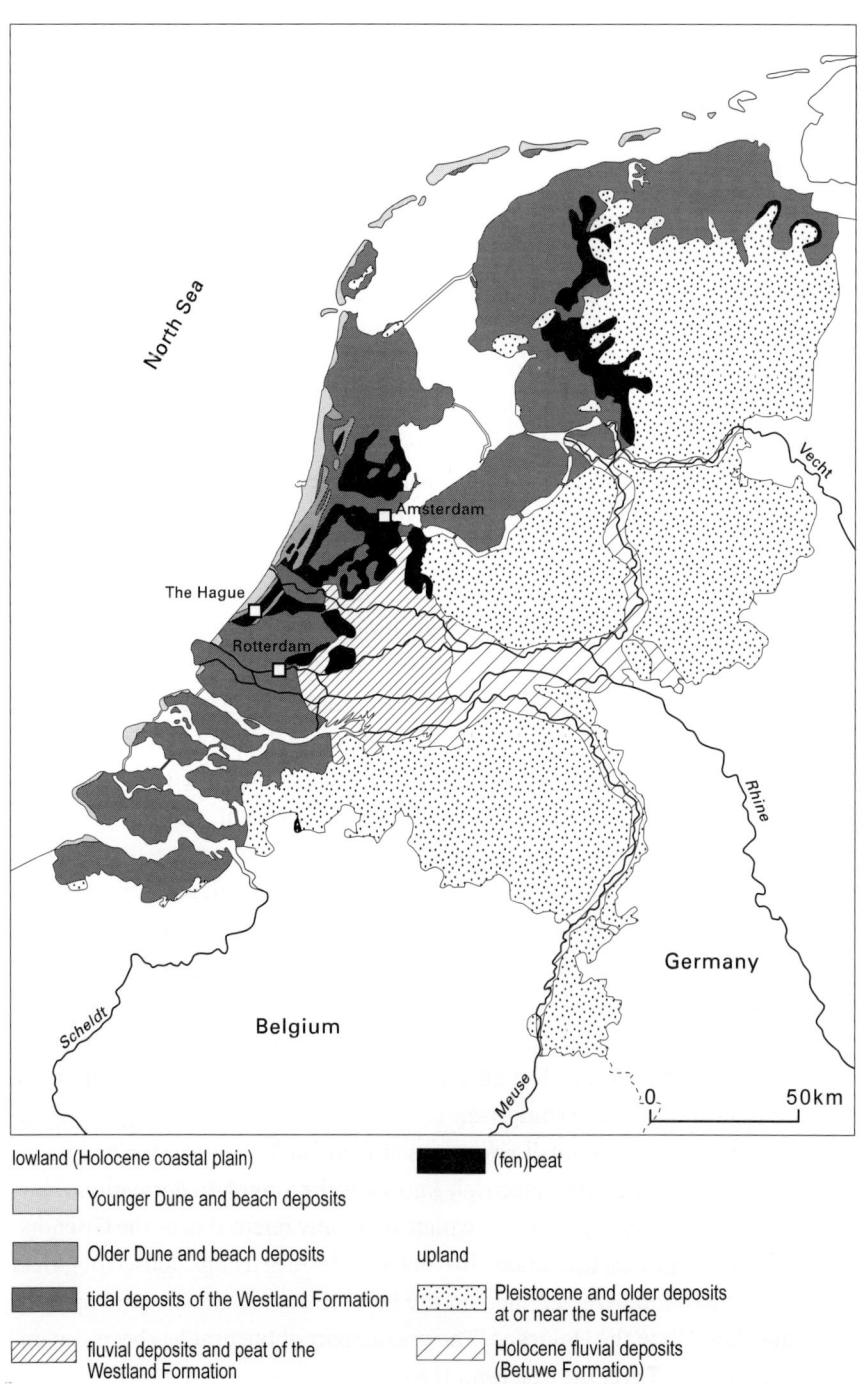

fig. 3.13

Distribution of outcrops of Quaternary deposits. Wind blown sands, brook valley floors and peat bogs (for the greater part now reclaimed) are not mapped.

lowland (Holocene coastal plain)

Younger Dune and beach deposits

Older Dune and beach deposits

tidal deposits of the Westland Formation

fluvial deposits and peat of the Westland Formation

(fen)peat

upland

Pleistocene and older deposits at or near the surface

Holocene fluvial deposits (Betuwe Formation)

and river valleys), i.e. areas with considerable gradients. After the beginning of the Bronze Age sand began to drift on an increasing scale, as a result of – we assume – degradation of the soil owing to overcropping and high grazing pressure on the impoverished vegetation. The production of charcoal may also have been an influential factor from the Iron Age onwards. In the loess zone degradation of the soil, leaching and the subsequent formation of colluvial deposits started only in the Roman period.

The geological development of the lower part of the Netherlands (fig. 3.13)

The deposits in the coastal and rivers areas

The Dutch coastal zone is generally agreed to be one of the best geologically investigated areas worldwide. A wide range of largely chronostratigraphically defined units has been distinguished in the Holocene sediments, which are about 20 m thick along the present coastline. All the deposits of the coastal zone belong to the Westland Formation (figs. 3.14 and 3.15). This formation comprises:

– coastal deposits: the Older and Younger Beach deposits and the wind-blown Older and Younger Dune deposits;
– marine, estuarine and lagoonal deposits: the Calais and Dunkirk deposits;
– so-called perimarine (freshwater intertidal) deposits: the Gorkum and Tiel deposits;
– peat and other biogenic sediments: what is known as *Hollandveen* ('Holland Peat').

In addition, there are also various local underwater deposits in the so-called Almere lagoon.[38]

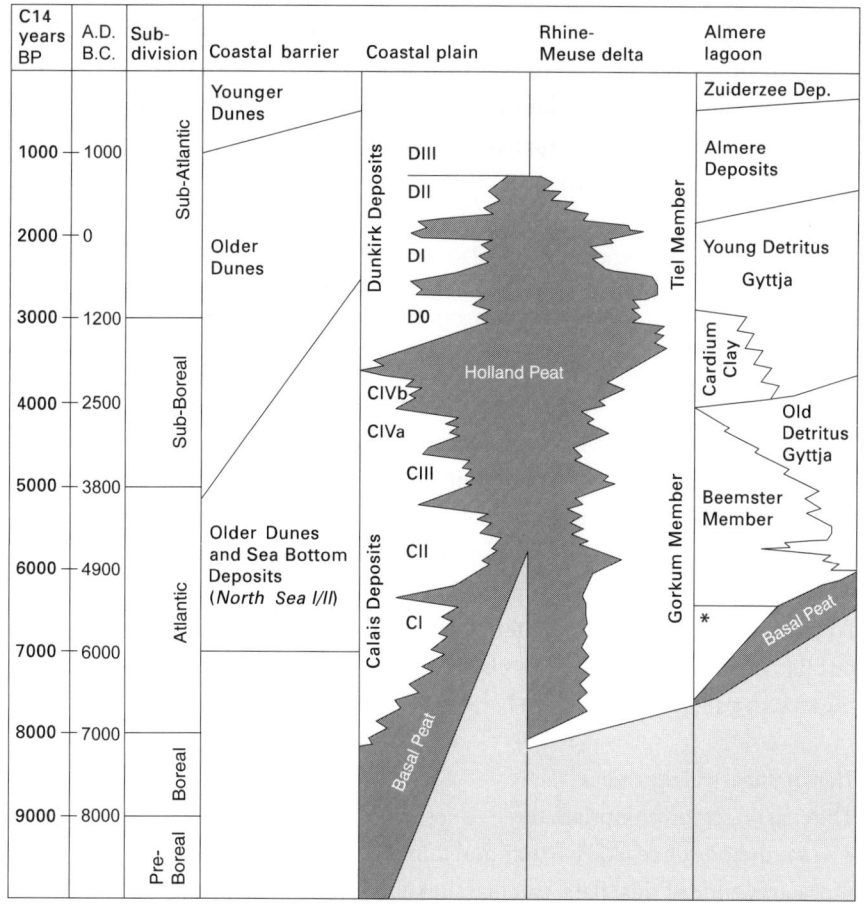

fig. 3.14
Schematic representation of the sediments of the Westland Formation arranged according to the conditions under which they were formed. The Westland Formation comprises all the deposits in the coastal area, including the aeolian deposits (dune sands) and the organic sedentates (peat, gyttja).

* Velsen Clay

West   East

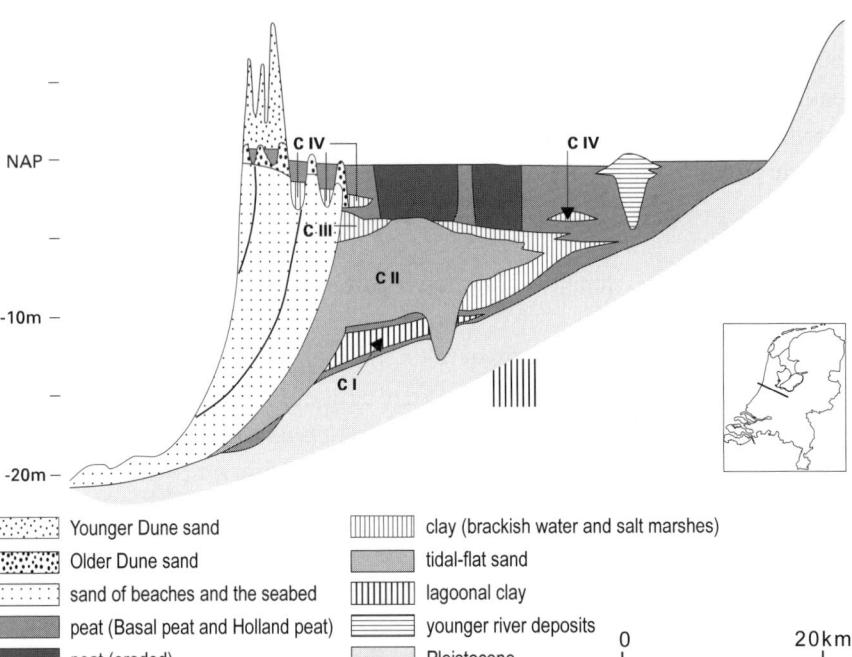

fig. 3.15
Schematic west-east section through the
coastal plain near Haarlem. The expansion
of the coastal barriers led to a steeper coast.
C I-IV: Calais deposits.

Younger Dune sand		clay (brackish water and salt marshes)
Older Dune sand		tidal-flat sand
sand of beaches and the seabed		lagoonal clay
peat (Basal peat and Holland peat)		younger river deposits
peat (eroded)		Pleistocene

0   20km

Layers of Holland Peat are to be found between both the marine deposits and the perimarine deposits; in both cases this peat separates older and younger deposits. The Calais and Dunkirk deposits have been distinguished on chronostratigraphic grounds (they were formed before and after 2500 BC, respectively). They are separated predominantly by layers of reed peat (Holland Peat). The Calais deposits generally consist of layers of (fine) sand and clay of a marine nature. The layer of peat at the base of this marine sediment is often referred to as *Basisveen* ('Basal Peat'). To our knowledge, very little, if any, salt marsh formation took place in these areas. Expansive Dunkirk deposits are to be found only in the southwest and northern parts of the Netherlands. Like the Calais deposits, they are marine horizons; a major difference is that large salt marshes formed in the areas of the Dunkirk deposits, also around the tidal inlets along the western coast. This is undoubtedly attributable to the greatly decreased rate at which the sea level rose.

Both of the aforementioned marine members have chronological equivalents in the perimarine zone between the purely marine and the purely fluvial zones. Those equivalents are the Gorkum and Tiel deposits, respectively. In many places the latter deposits, consisting predominantly of clay and sand, show high concentrations of plant and tree roots, which indicate that they were laid down in fresh water.

The fluvial deposits further upstream the major rivers all belong to the Betuwe Formation, which consists of alternating layers of sand and clay with the odd intercalated peat horizon. Sand or clayey sand occurs predominantly in and along the stream gullies, clay chiefly in backswamps (fig. 3.16).

Transgressions and regressions
The coastal region comprises three zones, from west to east:
– a sandy zone of coastal barriers and dunes;
– a clayey zone of tidal flats, salt marshes and brackish lagoons;
– a zone with peat growth.

It was initially proposed that these three zones gradually moved inland in the Holocene, under the influence of the rise in sea level.[39] Viewed on a large scale, the Holocene sediments indeed wedge out in an easterly direction. However, various recently discovered data are inconsistent with this postulated inland movement of sedimentary zones. They are, first of all, the distribution of the sediments in the coastal region, secondly, the westward movement of the coastline of North and South Holland and part of that of Zeeland (which began around 4400 BC and continued until 300 BC at least) while the sea level continued to rise and, thirdly, the extents of the peat horizons intercalated between the sediments.

Until recently, marine sediments were associated exclusively with an encroaching sea (transgression) and peat horizons with a retreating sea (regression). In the early 1960s the marine, perimarine and fluvial deposits in the Dutch coastal plain were dated by means of radiocarbon research. Most of the samples used for the ^{14}C analyses were derived from the bases of peat horizons between the clastic members (sand and clay deposits). However, as more radiocarbon dates became available (many of which were based not only on peat, but also on for example shells from the sandy and clayey sediments), it became clear that it is not so easy to date stratigraphic sequences as was originally thought in the early days of radiocarbon dating. Clastic sediments were increasingly often found to be non-synchronous.

fig. 3.16

Schematic section through the Rhine/Meuse delta between Voorne and Arnhem. The younger marine sediments (Calais and Dunkirk deposits) extended less far inland. This was largely attributable to the slower rate at which, in the second half of the Holocene, the sea level rose in this particular area through which the major rivers flowed to the sea. Also clearly visible is that the Holland peat has meanwhile filled up the area between the younger marine and perimarine deposits in the absence of sand and clay in this area.

D 0-III   Dunkirk deposits
C I-IV   Calais deposits
T   Tiel deposits
G   Gorkum deposits

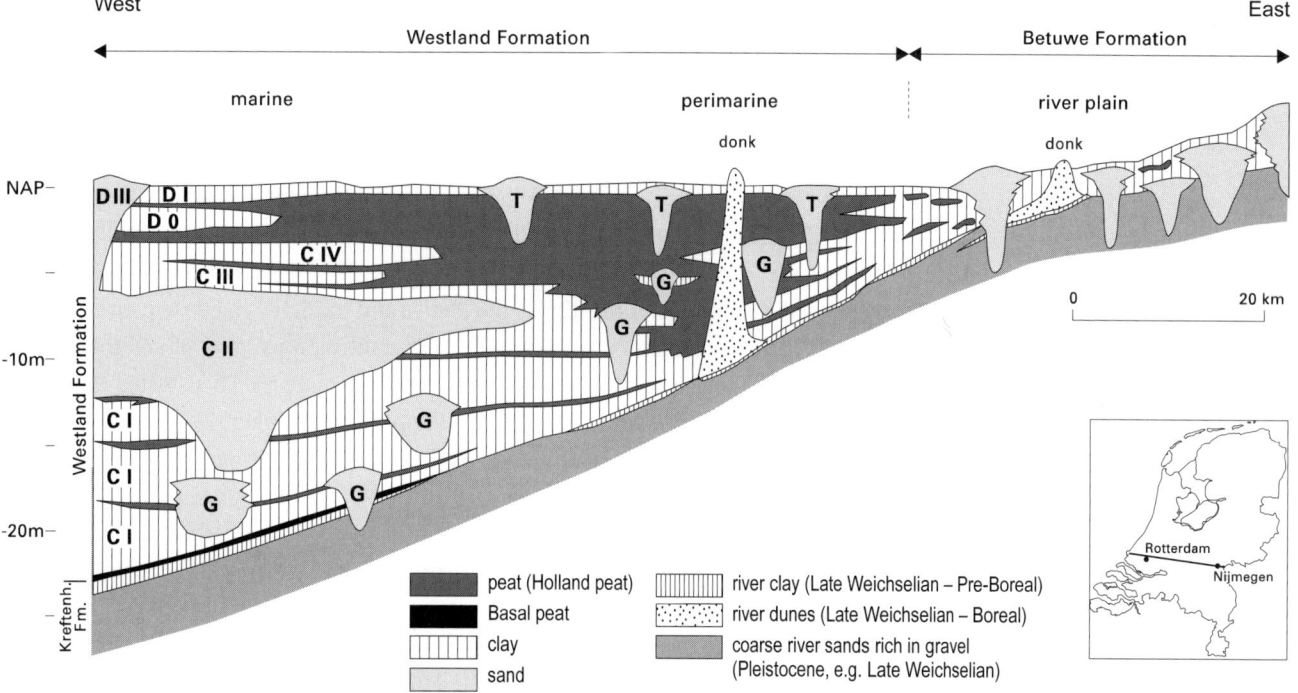

This is for example the case with the various phases of the Calais and Gorkum deposits.[40]

In the 1980s this led to new views on the evolution of the coastal zone. These views have recently been more explicitly publicised.[41] The simple transgression/regression model is no longer commonly accepted, but it is still useful as a point of departure for further research.[42] It has been found that other factors besides the rate of the rise in sea level (high at first and then lower later on) have played important parts in the development of the Dutch coastal region and more attention is hence being paid to the effects of subsidence, the transport and deposition of sand and clay and the growth of peat.

The Atlantic (7000-3900 BC)

The Atlantic is characterised by a very rapid rise in sea level until about 4400 BC.[43] The coastline of the western Netherlands consisted of a narrow coastal barrier. By analogy with the oldest preserved coastal barriers it is believed that the coastal barriers of this period were low and narrow and practically devoid of dunes. The coastline was interrupted by two major inlets: the mouth of the Rhine valley (including the Meuse valley) in the central part of the country and that of the Vecht in the north. As a result of the rise in the rivers' base level of erosion, the mouths of these rivers evolved into tidal basins or estuaries. As the sea level rose, the tidal basins rapidly expanded inland. The relief was eroded in the process (plate 2). In this period the southern inlet of the Rhine-Meuse estuary underwent considerable freshwater influence from the great mass of water of the Rhine.[44] As the amount of sediments that the river transported to the basins was insufficient to compensate for the rise in the level of the water in the basins, the coastline moved eastwards. The comparatively low rate of sedimentation in the tidal basins prevented the formation of linked sand bars intersected by tidal channels of the kind that are to be found in the Dutch *wadden* area (the tidal flats area in the north of the country) today.

In the plain behind the coastal barriers the rising groundwater levels led to the formation of swamps between the tidal basins. This zone of (fen) peat growth (*Basisveen*) also moved inland, across the Pleistocene hinterland.

The Sub-Boreal and early Sub-Atlantic (3900 BC until the beginning of the Christian era)

From approximately 4400 BC onwards, the rate at which the sea level rose fell to about 30 cm or less per century. The tidal basins consequently became filled up with clastic material (sand and clay) that continued to be supplied to them.[45] The coastal system as a whole moved no, or only very little, further inland in this period, which, unlike the preceding period, saw important regional developments.

Between 3900 and 1300 BC the tidal basins of South and North Holland were filled up, successively from the south to the north. The tidal inlets, with the exception of the mouths of the Rhine, the Meuse and the Scheldt, consequently sanded up. The coast became a straight line. The continuing supply of sediments ultimately led to the progradation of the coastline (plate 3). This started on a local scale between 5000 and 3900 BC, at the northern periphery of the Rhine/Meuse plain.[46] Further north, near Alkmaar, the coast began to prograde only around 2900 BC, after the tidal basin in that area had filled up (plate 4). This process, which lasted probably until the early Middle Ages, led to the fusion of a series of coastal barriers and beach plains into a body of sand with a width of 8-10 km, with dunes with maximum heights of 10 m on the coastal barriers (plate 5). The coastlines from the earliest centuries AD have disappeared owing to later erosion. It is assumed that the coast can never have lain much more than 1-1.5 km to the west

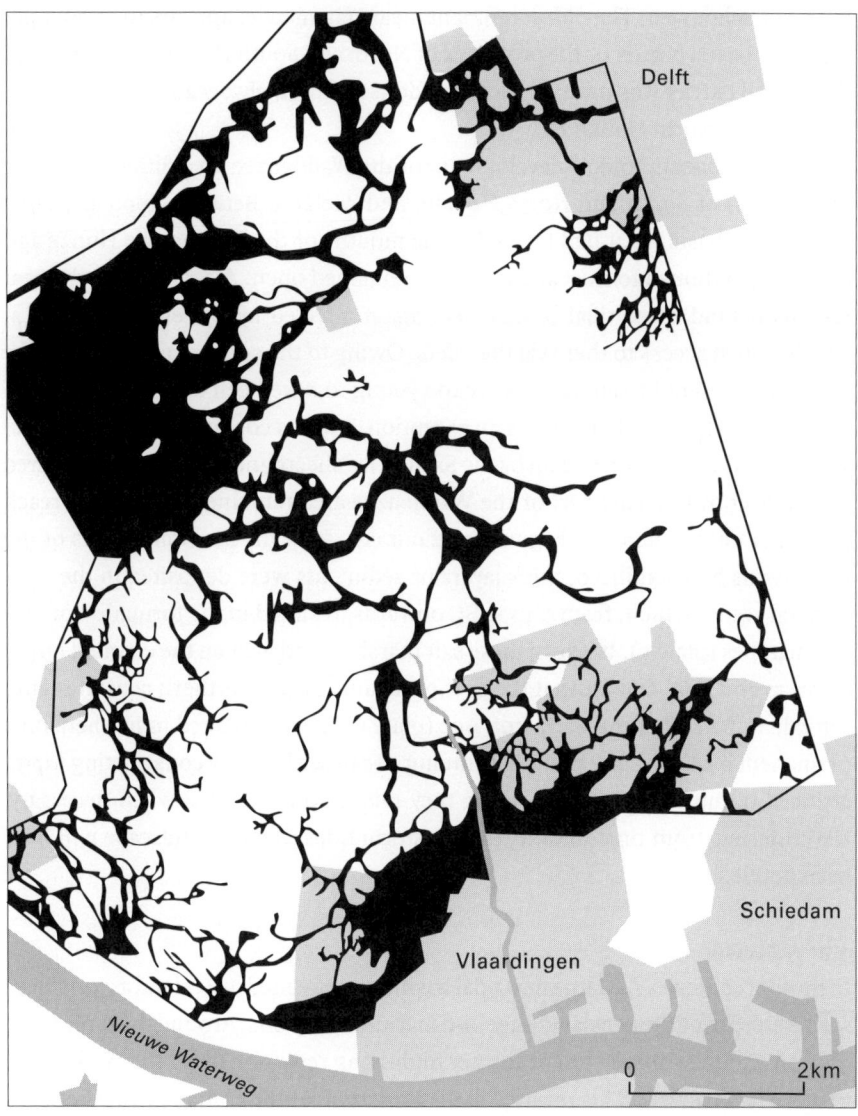

Delft

Schiedam

Vlaardingen

Nieuwe Waterweg

0   2km

fig. 3.17
Example of stream systems (belonging to
the Dunkirk O and I deposits) that have
been filled with sediments in the Delfland
region. The more sandy stream fills stand
out in the present Dutch landscape because
they have become visible as low ridges due
to compaction of the backswamp deposits
(relief inversion). The differences in height
will have been much less pronounced shortly
after deposition.

of the present coastline.[47] The water in the former tidal basins behind what was at
first still a very narrow barrier became fresh and the basins evolved into swamps,
in which plant remains accumulated as peat (Holland Peat), alternating with lakes,
some of which were quite large.[48] The peat regions were however vulnerable to
environmental change. The sea had easy access to them through the openings in
the coastline. The marine incursions often resulted in drainage, subsidence and
flooding of the peat. When the subsided areas had after some centuries filled up
with sand and silt, the tidal channels sanded up and those areas again evolved into
freshwater swamps with peat growth (fig. 3.17). As the sea level continued to rise,
this process repeated itself over and over again, resulting in sequences of clastic
sediments alternating with layers of peat (figs. 3.16).[49] By the time that the tidal
inlet at Bergen/Alkmaar had sanded up, around 1600 BC, an uninterrupted coast
had been formed, which, in spite of the continuing rise in sea level, was no longer
subject to major inroads of the sea. The lowmoor bogs behind the coast consequently soon evolved into raised bogs lying above groundwater level (plate 6).

Until 3300 BC the coast of Zeeland had many inlets, through which marine
sediments were washed into the basin behind the coast. After that date the coast in
this area was more or less closed, except for the small mouth of the Scheldt. Here
too, peat bogs rapidly expanded behind the coastline, as further north. In the province of Zeeland remnants of the former coastal barrier are to be found only on the

island of Schouwen. The oldest remnant, near Haamstede, appears to be younger than the coastal barrier of the provinces of North and South Holland.[50] In Zeeland, the coastal barrier was probably not as wide as it ultimately became further north, in South and North Holland.

The palaeogeographical development of the Waddenzee area differs from that of the coast of South and North Holland and Zeeland. Between 3900 and 2500 BC the tidal basins that had formed in the mouths of the Boorne, the Hunze and the Eems continued to exist and the inlets remained open. After 2500 BC the peat regions behind these tidal basins were again affected by the encroaching sea, which gained access to them via the inlets. Owing to the continuous retreat of the coast, the present Frisian Islands are too young to have been occupied in prehistoric times. The island of Texel is an exception, with its core of Pleistocene fluvial sediments that were pushed up by the Saalian ice sheets and subsequently covered with a layer of till. This part of the Waddenzee area remained beyond the reach of the sea until around the beginning of our era. After the landward limits of the tidal basins had stabilised, thick layers of sediments were deposited in their peripheral zones, which, from c. 1900 BC onwards, resulted in the formation of true salt marshes (plate 5). It was in these salt marshes, and also on the elevated levees of rivers and tidal creeks, that the first occupants of the northern coastal region settled, at the end of the Early Iron Age (plate 6). They managed to live here on a permanent basis, in spite of the continuing rise in sea level, by constructing terpen, artificial occupation mounds, which they raised and extended when necessary. Nevertheless, from time to time, during storm tides, the flat landscape will have been flooded.

After prehistory
In the first centuries AD large new tidal basins were formed in Zeeland as a result of severe erosion of the peat landscape and marine incursions. Around the same time, erosion and the submersion of former high-lying regions caused the Waddenzee to move further west. This resulted in the formation of the Marsdiep inlet between North Holland and the island of Texel and links with the Flevo lakes, which ultimately, in the Middle Ages, led to the birth of the (former) Zuiderzee. The coast of South and North Holland underwent fairly few changes after the beginning of the Christian era, except for the formation of the Younger Dunes (plate 7).

The present Dutch coastline, with the uninterrupted coast of South and North Holland and the interrupted coasts of the Waddenzee region and Zeeland, is largely the result of the developments outlined above.

Possibilities for occupation in the Dutch coastal region in prehistory

We may assume that until c. 5000 BC people will have ventured into the coastal region only temporarily, and for specific purposes, such as hunting and fishing and procuring various resources. It was only after 5000 BC, when the coastal system gradually became less dynamic as a result of the drop in the rate at which the sea level rose, that the conditions for settlement began to improve.

The coastal barrier zone
The low Older Dunes, built from drift sand blown onto the coastal barriers of the western Netherlands, were suitable for occupation from 4400 BC onwards.[51] Until recently there appeared to be a hiatus of more than 500 years between the assumed period of formation of the coastal barriers and their prehistoric colonisation. But

it has recently been found that this was attributable to a poor understanding of the ages of the individual coastal barriers and insufficient information on their colonisation. The preliminary analysis of evidence obtained in a recent excavation near Rijswijk has shown that the first occupants settled on the very low coastal barriers (lower than 1.5 m above the former average line of high tides) shortly after they had formed. Another recent discovery is a settlement of the Vlaardingen group on the Haarlem coastal barrier, which had formed only shortly before the colonists' arrival. These discoveries have greatly reduced the gap between the formation of the coastal barriers and their colonisation.

In the west, large parts of the Older Dunes were later covered with Younger Dune deposits. Here the conditions for the preservation of archaeological remains are consequently better than average (fig. 3.18 and plate 7).[52]

The estuaries

The colonisation of the tidal flats is closely connected with the availability of drinking water. In these regions, small reservoirs of fresh water became available fairly soon after the sea's retreat (after a dozen to several dozens of years). In North Holland the tidal flat deposits were occupied shortly after they had emerged from the sea, around 2600 BC.[53] No prehistoric finds have yet come to light in the parts of the Dutch tidal flat region around Zoetermeer and Hoofddorp, which became fit for occupation at the end of the Atlantic.

After transgression phases, the newly formed soils were colonised as soon as conditions permitted it, or the former occupation areas – if still fit for settlement – were reoccupied. The ever-changing environment of the dynamically developing coast meant that the possibilities of occupation kept shifting from one place to another (or periodically recurring in the same places). All over the coastal region we find evidence showing how time and time again prehistoric man managed to find ways of exploiting the resources of this instable, yet very attractive environment.

The coastal peat areas

During the intermittent development of the peat (Holland Peat), the nutrients content of the groundwater in the coastal plains periodically decreased. The peat growth caused the supply of nutrient-rich river water to stagnate.[54] In large parts

fig. 3.18
Schematic section though the Velserbroek area. The section clearly reveals the alternation of aeolian (dune formation) and estuarine (tidal deposition and salt marsh formation) processes on the one hand and peat growth and occupation/cultivation in periods without deposition on the other. Detailed evidence shows that man expediently exploited the land's natural fertilisation with clay, which was rich in organic matter. The clay was deposited during the annual flooding of the land by the former river Oer-IJ.

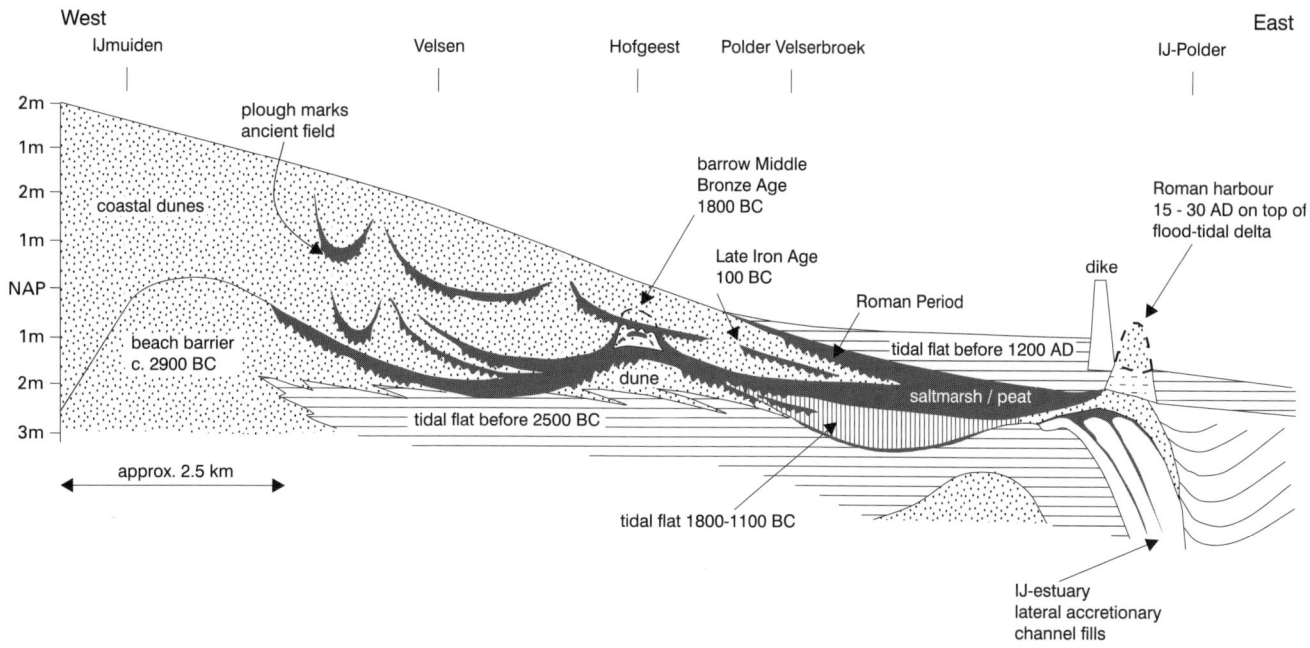

of the western Netherlands this led to changes in the plant communities and to a switch from eutrophic/mesotrophic peat growth (in carrs and reed and sedge swamps) to the development of raised bogs (formed by bog mosses, especially *Sphagnum*). In areas which lay beyond the reach of the sea and the rivers and were moreover entirely dependent on rainfall for their water supplies the environment acidified. The raised bog plant communities benefited most from this development. As the sea level continued to rise, these conditions persisted for a relatively long time. Only the peripheries of the raised bogs were colonised, that is, subject to the relatively exceptional condition that they had been drained by tidal channels. In the Iron Age, for instance, the newly drained peat around all the estuaries was colonised.

The river district
Characteristic of the landscape of the rivers area in the central part of the Netherlands are the tops of former river dunes projecting from the surrounding peat and clay sediments, the so-called donken (fig. 3.16 and feature D).[55] From a geological viewpoint, these river dunes, being of pre-Holocene date, are small, more or less isolated, remnants of the former elevated parts of the Netherlands rather than features of the coastal plain. Almost all of these river dunes were occupied from an early stage onwards.[56] This is connected with the nature of the surroundings, viewed in the context of the contemporary subsistence patterns: those surroundings were freshwater areas abounding in wild animals and fish. For many centuries the river dunes constituted safe occupation areas, especially when the surrounding areas were drowned and the area fit for occupation decreased considerably.[57] In late prehistoric times, when agriculture started to be practised on a larger scale, their importance as occupation areas declined.

From examples quoted in this and other chapters we may infer that prehistoric man appreciated the environmental and ecological diversity of the Dutch lowlands. Salt marshes unprotected by dikes, estuaries near tidal inlets, drained peat and other areas that would in our eyes appear only marginally suitable for occupation were evidently by no means such to prehistoric man, who, rapidly adjusting to the constantly changing conditions, resourcefully exploited the rich resources they offered him.

NOTES

1 Besides by the Quaternary climatic fluctuations, long-term environmental and palaeogeographic changes were also affected by the consequences of tectonic movements in the earth's crust. Active fault systems and the weight of overlying sediments or ice sheets caused land to rise and subside periodically. It is a well-known fact that the mainland of Scandinavia was depressed in the periods that it was covered by the ice sheets and subsequently rose several hundreds of metres after deglaciation (*isostasy*). It is not clear what consequences this had in Northwest Europe.

2 For the last two activities see in particular Van de Ven 1993.

3 Earlier articles discussing the genesis of the Netherlands are to be found in *e.g.* Vos 1983, Van Es *et al.* 1988 and Bloemers/Van Dorp 1991.

4 Much information on (regional) changes in climatic conditions can be inferred from biostratigraphic evidence. Such evidence indirectly reflects the climatic development and constitutes the basis for climatostratigraphy – the classification of deposits and fossils according to climatic criteria. Sensitive temperature indicators on land are, for example, insects (Coope 1977). The most important indicators of climate are however plankton fossils from the ocean floor. Oxygen isotope analysis of the calcareous skeletons of these organisms has led to a new (global) climatic curve for the Quaternary.

5 The results of other independent research methods, such as the determination of the CO_2 contents of deep-sea cores and ice cores and radiometric dating of calcite deposits in caves and crevasses, have largely confirmed and further refined the dates of the oxygen isotope curve, but the phasing and intensities of some periods still remain uncertain.

6   Imbrie *et al.* 1984.

7   In Europe it is not always possible to distinguish between interglacials and interstadials on the basis of palynological evidence, owing to the geographical situation of the sampling sites and the fact that their positions in the Pleistocene stratigraphy are often unknown. The durations of several of the warmer phases in question are also poorly known.

8   The development of the climate on the northwestern European continent was in all probability partly governed by the polar front, which in the Pleistocene lay above the Atlantic Ocean. It is nowadays assumed that the position of the polar front is determined by the Atlantic Gulf Stream. Cold periods are consequently seen as the consequences of temporary changes in the ocean currents, which put an end to the flow of comparatively warm ocean water to high latitudes.

9   Zagwijn 1992.

10 Roebroeks 1990a; Van Kolfschoten 1990.

11 The so-called Hattem beds in the Enschede Formation; Zandstra 1971.

12 Zagwijn 1975. The oxygen isotope stratigraphy and the results of recent research in the Meuse valley in southern Limburg suggest that there were more interglacials in the Cromerian Complex. Six separate terraces distinguished in the Meuse valley can all be correlated with interglacials in this chronological unit (Veltkamp/Van den Berg 1993; Van den Berg 1996). Each of these terraces was formed by the Meuse cutting into the land during the transition from a cold to a warm stage; they were preserved by the slow uplift of the area.

13 The chronostratigraphic positions of the Holsteinian interglacial and the preceding Elsterian glaciation in the Netherlands are still matters of dispute. Of great importance for the dating of these two periods are the volcanic eruptions that took place in the Eifel some 400,000 years ago. A concentration of minerals (dominated by augite) ejected during these eruptions and transported by the Rhine has been found in a horizon in the Urk Formation in the northern part of the Netherlands. Overlying these minerals were Elsterian glacial sediments (including pot clay) belonging to the Peelo Formation. From this stratigraphic evidence we may infer that the advance of the Elsterian ice sheets occurred after the deposition of this augite zone in the Urk Formation. Dates obtained for the volcanic activity coincide with the end of the extremely cold stage 12 and the first part of stage 11 in the oxygen isotope record. The Elsterian glaciation may hence be chronologically just equivalent to stage 12, but in the Netherlands it is generally correlated with the next cold stage in the oxygen isotope record (No. 10), approximately 350,000 years ago (Zagwijn 1985). Radiometric determinations of shells from Holsteinian deposits have yielded an age of at least 300,000 years, which could correspond to oxygen isotope stages 9 and 11.

14 Van den Berg/Beets 1987.

15 Extensive loess deposits are characteristic of the parts of Europe to the south of the limits of glacial advance. The sequences of alternating loess sediments and palaeosols constitute important stratigraphic evidence for climatic reconstructions in those areas.

16 Sites that have yielded comparable pollen spectra in the part of Europe that was covered by the advancing ice are Wacken, Pritzwalk and Schöningen, all of which lie in Germany. This period is usually correlated with stage 7 in the oxygen isotope record. There is also evidence suggesting that there was another phase with a vegetation typical of a temperate climate between the Holstein and Hoogeveen interglacials. This phase, which differed from the latter two interglacials, has been called the Reinsdorf interglacial (Urban 1995). The stratigraphic position of this interglacial (isotope stage 9?) is, however, still a matter of debate; it has not yet been soundly identified in geological sections.

17 The interglacial's name was derived from the marine clay beds in the basin of the river Eem, which were described by Harting in 1874 already. The deposits were first defined as a type locality by Zagwijn (1961).

18 Zagwijn 1983.

19 Whereas the development of raised bogs was a common phenomenon in the Holocene, only few raised bogs formed in the Eemian, presumably because the greater differences in relief ensured better drainage.

20 This summer temperature maximum was reached before the highest sea level. One of the causes of this is the ice sheets' relatively slow response to the improvement of the climate.

21 Zagwijn (1961) distinguishes an additional interstadial before the Brørup interstadial: the Amersfoort interstadial. Nowadays this phase is usually regarded as the first part of the Brørup interstadial.

22 *I.e.* disturbances in stratifications attributable to the transport of material in the active layer. Thawing and freezing of the active layer oversaturated with water resulted in the formation of characteristic drop- or festoon-like features (involutions).

23 Roberts *et al.* 1994.

24 Van Kolfschoten/Roebroeks 1985.

25 Roebroeks *et al.* 1993.

26 Meijer 1985.

27 Very little primary climatic evidence unambiguously pointing to changes in temperature is available in the Netherlands for the entire Holocene. There are only few varves with records of climatic changes over a long period. In most of the collapsed pingos in the northern part of the Netherlands and the Peel region in the south the desired information is to be found in fragmentary form only. For more complete records we have to turn to the fills of the volcanic lakes (crater lakes) in the German Eifel and the French Massif Central. A recent survey has been presented by Zagwijn (1994).

28 Eisma *et al.* 1981.

29 Jelgersma 1979; Gerritsen/Berentsen 1998; Van der Molen/Van Dijck 2000; see also Beets/Van der Spek 2000. The submersion of the entire southern part of the North Sea basin between *c.* 6900 and 6400 BC led to a reorientation in the isotherms (from NW-SE to roughly N-S) and continental conditions were forced back to the area that is now Germany (Zagwijn 1994).

30 Terrapin remains have been found in England, Belgium, the Neth-

erlands and Denmark. To be able to reproduce, this animal species requires a summer temperature that is a few degrees higher than that prevailing today (this is connected with the amount of insolation at nesting places).

31 Mannion 1991.

32 Casparie 1972.

33 Zagwijn 1994.

34 Zagwijn/Van Staalduinen 1975.

35 See in particular Fokkens 1991a.

36 The nomenclature of the Dutch stratigraphic units has recently been revised; the units have now been defined on the basis of lithostratigraphic instead of chronostratigraphic characteristics. The publication concerned (Westerhoff et al. 2003) is however not yet internationally accessible (Ebbing et al. 2003) and it was therefore decided to use the former nomenclature in this chapter.

37 Zagwijn 1986; for peat formation see also Casparie 1972.

38 Zagwijn 1986.

39 Jelgersma/Ente 1977. New views on developments in the (Holocene) stratigraphy have led to a much less rigid sequence of trans- and regression phases. Most of the literature predating 1980 is however still based on the former sequence.

40 For different views on the stratigraphy of the Dutch lowlands, see for instance Berendsen (1984) and Van Loon (1981).

41 They are mentioned in e.g. De Mulder/Bosch 1982; Vos 1983; Westerhoff et al. 1987; Westerhoff/Cleveringa 1990, and more particularly in Beets et al. 1992, 1994; Van der Spek 1994; Vos/Van Heeringen 1997; Beets/Van der Spek 2000.

42 For more information on the nomenclature of stratigraphic units see Zagwijn/Van Staalduinen 1975; more specifically the nomenclature of units in the Dutch rivers area: Törnqvist et al. 1994. For a more recent view see Westerhoff et al. 2003.

43 Bennema 1954; Jelgersma 1961 and 1979; Louwe Kooijmans 1974; Van de Plassche 1982.

44 The coastal region of the southwest part of the Netherlands is often described as a delta coast. Strictly speaking this is true up to a very small point only, because geological research has shown that only 5% to 10% of the sand of which the coast is composed can have been deposited by the Rhine (Beets et al. 1992); the subsoil does moreover not show the typical sequence of delta deposits that gradually become coarser towards the surface.

45 Beets et al. 1994; Beets/Van der Spek 2000.

46 The oldest dated coastal barriers, near Rijswijk, date from c. 4400 BC. For recent publications on this area see Cleveringa 2000 and Koot/Van der Have 2001.

47 Pool 1992.

48 De Mulder/Bosch 1982; Westerhoff et al. 1987; Van der Spek 1994.

49 Beets et al. 1994.

50 Van der Valk et al. (1997) have dated the youngest part of the Schouwen coastal barrier to around 1000 BC. The Neolithic settlement on the Brabers may lie not on a coastal barrier, but on a levee (pers. com. A. van der Spek, 2002). This could mean that the entire Schouwen coastal barrier dates from a fairly late phase in the period of formation of the western coastal barrier.

51 Roep et al. 1991.

52 Magendans 1987.

53 Brandt 1988a; Roep/Van Regteren Altena 1988.

54 Pons 1992.

55 Central Netherlands: Berendsen/Stouthamer 2001, 66; Vink 1954; Van der Woude 1981; Flevoland: Gotjé 1993; Van der Waals/Waterbolk 1976.

56 M. Verbruggen, pers. com.; Verbruggen 1992a.

57 Louwe Kooijmans 1985; 1993a; Van der Woude 1981.

Part I

Hunters and gatherers

The Palaeolithic and Mesolithic together span a relatively long period of 2.5 million years, in which the only means of subsistence were hunting, fishing and gathering. As the great majority of the Palaeolithic and Mesolithic artefacts known to us are made of stone, this period is referred to as the 'Stone Age'.

In the Palaeolithic, or Old Stone Age, the earliest hominids gradually evolved into modern humans, first of all exclusively in East Africa and from 1 million years ago also elsewhere, but only in the past 500,000 years in Europe, too. Towards the end of the Palaeolithic, 'fully modern man' or Homo sapiens sapiens, developed an efficient tool kit that enabled him to survive the severe last ice age as a specialist hunter of the large herds of migrating ungulates. His rich spiritual world he expressed in various art forms, the best known being the cave art of the Dordogne and the Pyrenees. The archaeological differences between the Upper Palaeolithic and the preceding period are so great as to have triggered an intensive discussion as to how much the behaviour of the earlier hominids, such as Neanderthal man, resembled that of those later, modern, humans.

At the end of the last ice age, around 10,000 years ago, the hunters switched to an entirely new hunting strategy comprising the broad-range exploitation of the wide diversity of resources that were to be found in the forests and lakes that characterised the landscape of those days. This period of hunters in a temperate climate we call the Mesolithic, or Middle Stone Age. The key archaeological characteristics of this period are small, geometric flint artefacts, or microliths, with which the wooden and bone hunting implements were equipped. In many regions man developed a sophisticated system with strategically positioned sites and seasonal use of different resources. An important innovation was the intensive exploitation of water using canoes, fish weirs and fishing nets.

4 Palaeolithic and Mesolithic: introduction

Wil Roebroeks and Annelou van Gijn

INTRODUCTION

After shaking off the 'Great Chain of Being' – a chain in which the beings created by God all had a fixed and unchanging place – Western mankind has since the 19th century constantly been preoccupied by the question as to what distinguishes us from our evolutionary ancestors and relatives: 'What is a human being?'[1] This question has been answered in anatomical terms (shape of the skull, brain size, upright gait, *etc.*), in terms of cultural criteria (use of tools, 'art', language) and also with a genetic definition (obtained via DNA research). The different perspectives vary considerably and are difficult to combine, because it has been found that for example anatomical characteristics cannot always be correlated with particular types of material culture.

The answers that have been given to the question 'What is a human being?' differ substantially from a historical viewpoint, too. Some anthropologists around the transition to the 20th century maintained that many hunter-gatherers were to be regarded as human beings who were (culturally and anatomically) 'not modern': Tasmanians, Aborigines, Bushmen and Inuit were seen as contemporary 'primitives', as 'savages' who had remained behind on some lower rung of the evolutionary ladder (fig. 4.1). Nowadays such synchronous distinctions are no longer made and the origins of modern man, *Homo sapiens sapiens*, have been pushed back tens of thousands of years. According to one scenario for the origins of modern humans, *Homo sapiens sapiens* individuals originated in Africa more than 200,000 years ago and then gradually spread from there to other parts of the world, where they ultimately replaced the earlier, 'more primitive', occupants. Another theory claims that groups of hominids (*Homo erectus*) spread across the world from Africa at least a million years ago and then gradually evolved into our own species in the different parts of the world.[2]

fig. 4.1
A hundred years after James Cook's draughtsman had depicted occupants of Tierra del Fuego in front of their huts, people from this archipelago who had been taken prisoner were exhibited as 'cannibals', as here at the 1889 World Fair in Paris. This group was later to be exhibited in England and Belgium, too. These people were regarded as direct representatives of 'primitive man' who had roamed Europe in the distant past. They were thought to belong to some subhuman species, and were treated accordingly.

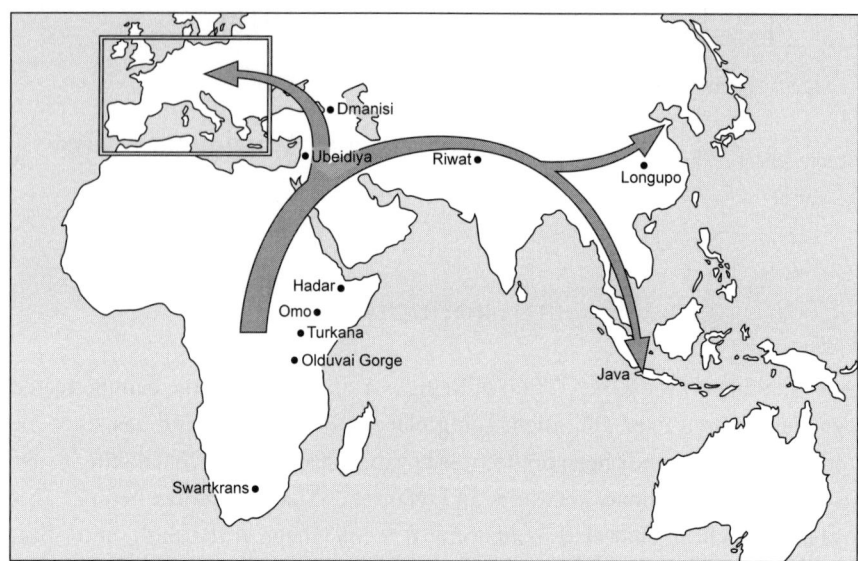

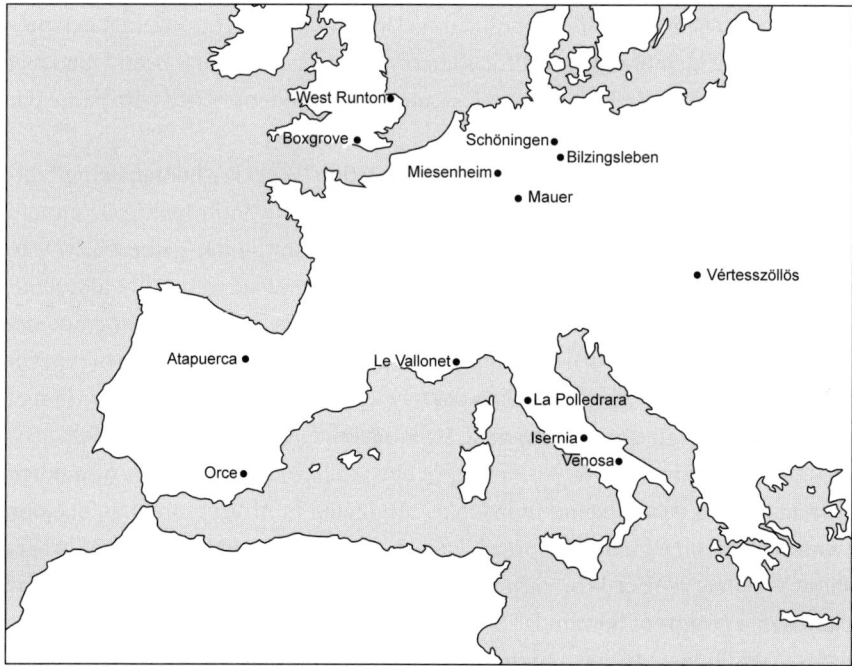

fig. 4.2

It is generally assumed that the first hominids originated in East Africa, on the basis of the many fossil human remains found in that region from the period of 4 to 1 million years ago. From there, these hominids gradually spread all over the world. The map shows some of the key sites in the discussion of the earliest occupation of Eurasia. Evidence found at some of these sites yielded ages suggestive of a very early hominid presence, from 1.8 MA (Java, Longupo) or even earlier (Riwat), though these claims are contested, as are those for a comparable early presence in Europe, *e.g.* at Orce (Spain).

Whether one opts for the first or the second scenario, there is one thing that remains the same and that is that Africa is to be seen as the cradle of humankind (fig. 4.2). Almost all the locations that have yielded human fossils and implements of more than 1.5 million years old lie in Africa. The earliest hominid[3] is *Australopithecus*, with the respectable age of 4 million years. Of the various forms of this hominid, *Australopithecus afarensis* has become very famous thanks to the discovery of 'Lucy', a large part of the skeleton of an approximately 1.10-m-tall adult female who lived in East Africa more than 3 million years ago. Sometime between 2 and 2.5 million years ago the first representatives of the genus *Homo* appeared: *Homo habilis*. The earliest archaeological sites – small concentrations of stone tools and the waste formed in tool manufacture and bones – date from this same period. It is to this tool manufacture that *Homo habilis* thanks his name of 'handy man'. The oldest fossils of *Homo erectus* are some 1.6 million years old, which is also the possible age of the earliest hominids venturing out of Africa, for example into what is now Georgia. They do not seem to have made their appearance in Europe until some time later: that actually makes Europe a peripheral area, in terms of both its earliest occupation and its situation relative to the African area of origin. For historical reasons Europe is however a very important archaeological area, for thanks to its long tradition of geological and archaeological research, the history of occupation of this rich part of the Old World is better known than that of any other area. Consequently, extensive research can be carried out in Europe into the differences in the archaeological remains left behind by 'modern humans' and their ancestors, the Neanderthals and earlier hominids. The key question in this research, however, is again how to define 'modern humanity'. Different perspectives (anatomical, cultural or genetic) yield different answers to this question.

HISTORY OF THE RESEARCH

Our present chronological framework is rooted in nineteenth-century attempts to classify the overwhelming quantity of archaeological remains that came to light in the second half of that century. Many of those remains were found during building and digging projects launched in the wake of the industrial revolution. The chronological sequences that were set up in those days can also be seen in the light of the contemporary economic and social changes: archaeology and geology demonstrated that change was actually something that took place in all eras, something 'natural' that led to progress. This evolutionary perspective, in which 'old' stood for 'primitive' and 'young' for 'complex', more 'developed', had a profound influence on archaeological frameworks; our current chronological sequences are in fact still based on this same perspective.

In the early 19th century Thomsen divided prehistory into three ages: a Stone, Bronze and Iron Age. The many new finds that were discovered in the course of that century led to refinements in this Three Age System. In 1865 a *période de la pierre taillée* or period of chipped stone tools (the Palaeolithic or Old Stone Age) and a *période de la pierre polie* or period of polished stone tools (the Neolithic or New Stone Age) were distinguished. It was assumed that these two periods were separated by a hiatus (in occupation). However, around the end of the 19th century researchers discovered more and more occupation layers between the horizons containing typical Palaeolithic and Neolithic finds. It was only in the 1920s that the term *Mesolithic* came to be commonly used for this transitional phase.[4] The adherents of the aforementioned theory of evolution found it difficult to accept the Mesolithic as a transitional phase, for the material culture of this phase was found to be very poor compared with that of the reindeer hunters of the last phase of the Palaeolithic with its mobiliary art and its well-known rock paintings. For many years the Mesolithic was regarded as a period of degeneration, a view that was not particularly conducive to research into this period.[5]

Dutch research has played virtually no role in these chronological debates; it has in fact played virtually no role in prehistoric archaeology at all. Nevertheless, one of the researchers of the early years of prehistoric archaeology was a Dutchman (be it of Austrian birth), namely the physician Schmerling (1791-1836). In 1833-34 he published the results of his research in caves in the surroundings of Liège, which in his opinion demonstrated that people had lived in those caves in times when extinct animals like mammoths, woolly rhinoceros and cave-bears had roamed those areas.[6] Schmerling's views met with a good deal of scepticism, like those of a later pioneer, Boucher de Perthes (1788-1868), who studied fossils of extinct mammals found in association with stone tools in the gravel pits in the valley of the Somme in northern France. Boucher de Perthes' findings were not to

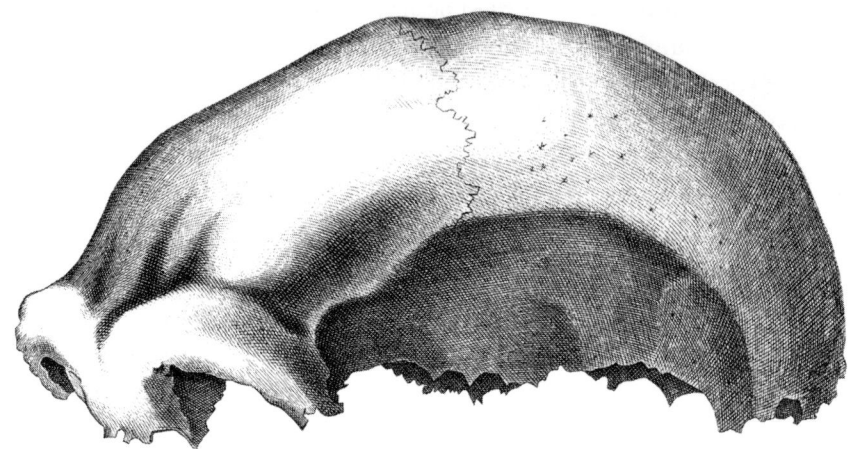

receive scientific recognition until 1859, the year in which Darwin's 'On the Origin of Species' was published.

Another important 19th-century researcher was the Dutchman Eugène Dubois, whose investigations on Java led to the discovery of *Pithecanthropus* (now *Homo erectus*). Dubois, from the village of Eysden near Maastricht, was greatly influenced by the important discoveries that had been made in the vicinity of his home region, such as the Neanderthal skeletons found in the Neanderthal near Düsseldorf (1856, fig. 4.3) and in the cave of Spy in Belgium (1886). One of the excavators of the Spy remains, the archaeologist De Puydt from Liège, described a number of 'Mousterian' tools that had been found in the vicinity of the Neolithic flint-mining site between Rijckholt and Sint-Geertruid, where Dubois had also collected stone tools.[7] This site yielded a large number of Middle Palaeolithic artefacts, which attracted the attention of mostly Belgian archaeologists at first, especially archaeologists from Liège. Among the latter was professor Hamal-Nandrin, who conducted excavations at Rijckholt until the 1950s.[8]

In the Netherlands, research into the Old Stone Age and the Mesolithic was for many years carried out essentially by amateur archaeologists. It was only around 1920 that Upper Palaeolithic and Mesolithic assemblages were identified as such in the Netherlands, in both the northern and southern parts of the country; Middle Palaeolithic artefacts remained scarce. The first hand axe in the northern half of the Netherlands came to light in 1939, near the village of Wijnjeterp in Friesland (plate 8A).[9] The 1950s and 1960s saw an increase in excavations of Palaeolithic and Mesolithic sites, in both the north and the south of the country. Much of the impetus behind this activity came from the fruitful cooperation in excavations and

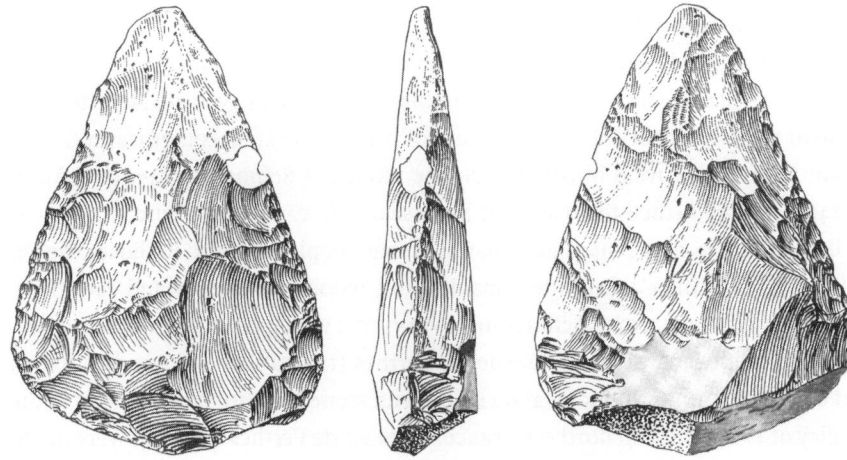

fig. 4.4
Hand axe that was found near Anderen on the boulder clay plateau of Drenthe. The artefact shows an intense orange patination, similar to the hand axe from Wijnjeterp (plate 8A) and is – especially at the top – severely weathered. Scale 1:2.

publications between the archaeologist Bohmers from Groningen and the friar Aq. Wouters, who performed research in the south of the country. Their main concern was establishing typological and chronological sequences.

That was also the primary objective of the excavation of the alleged Middle Palaeolithic site Hoogersmilde, which was discovered by the amateur archaeologist Vermaning in 1965 and was excavated by archaeologists of Groningen University. Ten years and several site publications[10] later, archaeologists of that same university reported that the artefacts were forgeries. The main giveaway was the artefacts' lack of wear: the absence of evidence of natural changes on the surface of stones that must have lain close to the surface for tens of thousands of years made it highly unlikely that the finds were genuine. Another argument was that many of Vermaning's finds showed characteristics (such as rounded edges) that are not observable on natural flints from that region. The commotion caused by Vermaning's finds drew the attention of amateur archaeologists to the older phases of the Stone Age. This found expression in for example research into the deposits that had been pushed up by the advancing Saalian ice sheets in the central part of the Netherlands (fig. 4.5). These deposits were found to contain artefacts from before the Saalian glaciation, which consequently had to be at least 150,000 years old. Palaeolithic finds came to light at many locations in other parts of the country, too, for example in the valley of the Meuse in Limburg.

fig. 4.5
River deposits pushed-up by the ice during the Saalian glacial in the Kwintelooijen quarry near Veenendaal. In the 1970s many flint artefacts were found in this and other quarries in the ice-pushed ridges in the central part of the Netherlands. They show that the Netherlands was occupied already before the advance of the Saalian glaciers, 150,000 years ago.

During the 1970s, the former aim in Palaeolithic and Mesolithic research of establishing typological and chronological sequences gradually gave way to a different approach. One of the main new research topics concerned aspects of early settlement systems, both on site level, as in the thorough excavation of a large Mesolithic site near the Bergumermeer,[11] and on a much larger scale, as in the model developed for the hunting territories of Late Glacial hunter-gatherers.[12] In view of the absence of organic remains, the emphasis in this research was on the interpretation of flint scatters; site typologies were set up for the Mesolithic sites on the basis of the composition, shape and size of those flint scatters.[13]

The 1980s saw a major revival of interest in the Palaeolithic and Mesolithic. One of the projects launched in this period involved the gathering of all the available data on Lower and Middle Palaeolithic occupation remains in the southern part of the Netherlands; that led to the discovery of a series of Middle Palaeolithic sites in the Belvédère gravel pit near Maastricht.[14] The first Magdalenian sites were discovered and excavated in the loess region of southern Limburg and an inventory was made of all the Upper Palaeolithic and Mesolithic sites in the coversand areas of the Kempen region[15] and the three northern provinces.[16] Much of the research in those years was conducted on a regional level and focused on the reconstruction of subsistence patterns, seasonal occupation cycles and site locations.[17] Typological and chronological questions remained important, but the emphasis had clearly shifted to the behaviour of Pleistocene and early Holocene hunter-gatherers.

The employed research methods have also changed over the years. Among the latest dating methods are thermoluminescence and electron spin resonance[18] but more important information can be obtained from for example refitting experiments and microwear analysis[19] and from new methods for the spatial analysis of Stone Age sites.[20] In some cases the combined use of several of these methods and techniques can lead to a clear understanding of the dynamics of prehistoric sites, even those that consist of nothing more than flint scatters.[21]

CLIMATE AND ENVIRONMENT

The Quaternary saw major climatic fluctuations and great changes in the environment. In the coldest phases of the glacials large volumes of water from the oceans were absorbed into the expanding continental glaciers, causing the sea level to fall several dozens of metres worldwide. One of the consequences of this was that the North Sea basin between the Netherlands and Great Britain dried out. During the interglacials the land/sea ratio was largely the same as it is today (see chapter 3).

Most of our information on climatic and environmental conditions during the various Palaeolithic and Mesolithic occupation phases in the Netherlands comes from non-archaeological sites, because organic remains have been preserved at only very few archaeological sites. One of those is Maastricht-Belvédère, where excavations have yielded a wealth of interglacial faunal remains with an approximate age of 250,000 years.[22] Here early humans had camped in a marshy river valley with a dense vegetation surrounded by thickly forested higher grounds. The sites lay along former meanders of the Meuse that were slowly drying out. The mammalian fauna (25 species) and the molluscs (over 70 species) show that the area was visited during the climatic optimum of an interglacial. The mammals included straight-tusked elephant, steppe rhinoceros, giant deer, bear, red deer and roe deer. Remains of the pond tortoise (Emys orbicularis) indicate that the mean summer temperature must have been slightly higher than it is today. Northern Europe was at this time probably covered with dense deciduous forests. The river valleys, however, will have contained large clearances, created by for example grazing herbivores. The Pleistocene vegetation differed somewhat from one interglacial to another. It has been pointed out that Europe was covered with a fairly uniform deciduous forest vegetation during interglacials when the sea level was high, whereas the vegetation must have been more open in interglacials with a relatively low sea level.[23]

There is much discussion about the ecological tolerances of pre-*sapiens sapiens*-groups. Whereas some researchers claim that before the arrival of modern humans in northern Europe full-interglacial environments saw no human occupation as pre-moderns were only able to adapt to intermediate conditions – neither

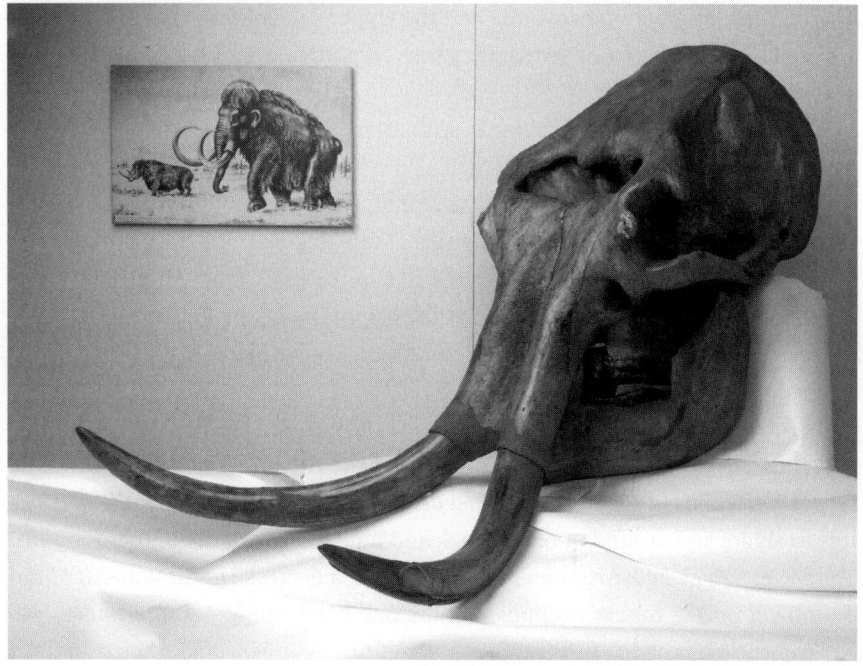

fig. 4.6
Skull of a young mammoth dredged up in
the river district. During the last glacial the
landscape in this part of the world consisted
of a steppe-like environment, inhabited only
in the summertime by cold-resistant animals
such as mammoths.

too cold nor too warm (and densely forested) –, others state that the 'archaics'
were capable of survival in a wide range of environments and that only the oldest
glacial phases led to local occupation gaps. But then, a hiatus of more than 15,000
years is also observable in the Upper Palaeolithic occupation remains, around the
glacial maximum of the Weichselian.[24] The cold loess steppes were already being
exploited during the penultimate glacial, the Saalian, and probably much earlier,
too.[25] This is not surprising, though, as it has been demonstrated that these regions had a wealth of faunal resources.[26] There is little sense in attempting to use
present-day arctic tundras to model the vegetation at the time of the Pleistocene
occupation of these regions, because both fauna and vegetation were then both
far more productive. One of the great differences between the arctic tundras and
the former 'mammoth steppe' is that the latter had no polar nights or polar days;
in the summertime, with the sun high in the sky, it must indeed have been quite
warm. The term 'mammoth steppe' is used to indicate an association of vegetation and fauna for which there are no modern parallels. The vegetation included
both tundra species and a wide range of grasses and herbs: food for the large herbivores, which, as appears from their fossils, lived here in large numbers (fig. 4.6).
In the interstadials the treeless mammoth steppe with its large game population
alternated with a vegetation largely dominated by trees, in particular birch and
pine. It is in those environments that we are to envisage the Late Glacial occupants
of the Netherlands: open types of vegetation with herds of migratory animals like
reindeer during the stadials, and denser forest vegetations with mainly sedentary
game like elk and roe deer during the warmer phases, such as the Bølling and the
Allerød. Each period will however have been characterised by a considerable degree of spatial diversity, with substantial differences between for example the vegetations of river valleys and those of higher grounds.

The transition from the Late Glacial to the present interglacial, the Holocene,
took place in very much the same way as previous glacial/interglacial transitions.
The first Holocene climatic phase, the Pre-Boreal (9000-8000 BC), was characterised by the expansion of birch forests; coniferous forests were dominant in the
southern part of the Netherlands from the start. The steppe-tundra vegetation
disappeared entirely. The substantial rise in sea level caused the amount of area
available for occupation to decrease considerably in the course of the Pre-Boreal.

The reindeer migrated northwards and the Upper Palaeolithic fauna was gradually replaced by a fauna of sedentary game, in particular red deer, roe deer, elk, aurochs and wild boar.

The Boreal (8000-7000 BC) began with an increase in hazel; that species will have dominated the forests, which then also started to include pine and, later on, oak and elm. The forests became denser and more impenetrable. The evidence suggests that the temperature slowly rose a few degrees, reaching a maximum in the Atlantic. As a consequence of the rise in sea level, from 60 metres below Amsterdam Ordnance Datum (NAP) at the beginning of the Pre-Boreal to 8 metres below NAP in the Middle Atlantic, the North Sea basin gradually became submerged.

The marked increase in the pollen of elm and oak and the appearance of lime and alder are taken to mark the beginning of the Atlantic (7000-3800 BC). The vegetation will have varied from mixed deciduous forests in stream and river valleys to alder carrs around pools and oak and lime forests on the higher grounds. The formation of dense canopies will have led to a decrease in the amount of undergrowth on the higher grounds. On the one hand, these Atlantic forests will consequently have been more accessible, but on the other hand, they contained a narrower range of animal and plant resources, making them less attractive for game and human occupation. In the Atlantic, peat started to grow in the Netherlands on a large scale for the first time, especially in Drenthe and eastern Brabant and along the coast.

CULTURAL TRADITIONS

The Old Stone Age has been divided into three phases, the Lower, Middle and Upper Palaeolithic, on the basis of developments in the manufacture of stone tools, which are often the only remains that have survived from this distant past.

Middle Palaeolithic flint industries differ from the industries of the preceding Lower Palaeolithic in that they were produced according to a more complex knapping technique, known as the Levallois technique. This technique enabled the prehistoric flint knappers to make much more efficient use of their raw materials than had previously been the case. The introduction of a blade technology (see feature A) has been taken to mark the transition from the Middle to the Upper Palaeolithic.

Within this general framework a number of 'cultures' or 'traditions' have been distinguished on the basis of typological features of the stone tools. The majority of the cultural sequences were set up in the 19th century, when attempts were made to classify archaeological remains according to a system resembling that used by geologists, with type fossils and type sites. The Lower Palaeolithic 'hand axe tradition' was consequently named the 'Acheulean', after the finds in the gravel quarries at St. Acheul near Amiens in northern France. The Neanderthal period was named the Mousterian, after the site Le Moustier in the Dordogne. Within these rough divisions finer subdivisions have been established. Nowadays, however, these specific cultural classifications are being used increasingly less for the Lower and Middle Palaeolithic because, rather than to provide information, these labels in fact tend to mask variation.

This is less true where the Upper Palaeolithic is concerned. The terms originally introduced for the cultures and traditions of that era are still frequently used today, although the boundaries between the different groups are often vague. The Netherlands has yielded almost exclusively finds from the last phase of the Upper Palaeolithic, the Late Glacial (13,000 to 10,000 BP).[27] Within the short period of time spanned by this phase no fewer than five traditions have been distinguished on the basis of characteristic tool types. The oldest are the (Late) Magdalenian and Hamburgian traditions, which are in the Netherlands dated roughly between 13,000 and 12,000 BP. The Dutch Magdalenian sites lie along the northern periphery of the distribution area of this tradition, which covers large parts of Western and Central Europe. The Hamburgian tradition is a phenomenon of the North European Plain, covering an area from southern England to Poland. It is often assumed to have originated in the Middle Magdalenian.[28] Late Magdalenian finds have been found only in the southernmost part of the Netherlands. This phase is characterised by an advanced blade technology, which was used to produce small backed blades, scrapers on blades and burins. Remains of the Hamburgian tradition have been found in the northern part of the Netherlands. Conspicuous tools among this culture's lithic remains are shouldered points, tanged points and so-called 'Zinken', asymmetrically pointed boring tools.

The latest Upper Palaeolithic traditions, the Creswellian, Tjongerian and Ahrensburgian traditions, are dated between 12,000 and 10,000 BP. The Tjongerian tradition forms part of a large-scale Western European phenomenon, namely that of the *Federmesser* groups, which is characterised by a decrease in the importance of burins and an increase in the proportion of short scrapers, *Federmesser* and points with arched backs (known as Tjongerian points). In the Netherlands this tradition was in the past dated to the Allerød interstadial, but its time span is in fact greater than originally assumed, extending into the Younger Dryas at least and possibly even into the Pre-Boreal.[29]

Little is known about the chronology of the Creswellian culture, but it is believed that it is to be dated to the first half of the Allerød (see chapter 6). Characteristic of this culture are points with one or two obliquely blunted ends, known as Creswellian and Cheddarian points, respectively. As with the Hamburgian tradition, it is not certain where the roots of this culture lie: some archaeologists associate it with the Hamburgian tradition while others prefer to class it with the *Federmesser* group.[30] According to Arts, the Creswellian assemblages that have been identified in the southern part of the Netherlands can in fact not be distinguished from the *Federmesser* remains found in that region.

The youngest tradition is that of the Ahrensburgian group, so called after the site of Ahrensburg-Stellmoor in northern Germany, a reindeer hunters' camp dating from the Younger Dryas. A small tanged type of point is the type fossil of this Upper Palaeolithic tradition, which differs from the other groups in terms of the morphology of the blades, too.[31]

The beginning of the Holocene, around 10,000 BP, is traditionally taken as the base line for the beginning of the Mesolithic. Until recently, there appeared to be a chronological hiatus between the Upper Palaeolithic and the Mesolithic, but that gap is now gradually being filled with ^{14}C dates.[32] Current views place the emphasis on the continuity observable between these two periods, both in a typological and technological respect and in the types of locations selected for occupation. The problem is that it is virtually impossible to define the limits of the Mesolithic on typological and technological grounds. From a typological viewpoint matters are complicated by the fact that microliths, the type fossils of the Mesolithic *par excellence*, were already being produced in the Upper Palaeolithic. Moreover, various Upper Palaeolithic point types are also encountered at Pre-Boreal sites. The theory that the Mesolithic is characterised by a highly specific form of adaptation to the changed environmental conditions (from a steppe-tundra to a forest vegetation) and the related changes in the composition of the fauna (from a fauna dominated by herds of migratory animals like reindeer to one consisting of species with reduced mobility such as red deer, auroch and elk) is no longer tenable. It has been found that similar changes had taken place previously already, for example in the Allerød, without bringing about fundamental changes in the material culture.

It is also difficult to define the end of the Mesolithic in the Netherlands. The criterion used for the beginning of the Neolithic is the appearance of the first agricultural communities. However, they appeared in the southern part of the Netherlands much earlier than in the central and northern parts. It is moreover very difficult to say whether the western and northern parts of the country were around that time occupied by 'Mesolithic' hunter-gatherers or by communities with a more mixed subsistence economy, certainly given the shortage of data available for those parts. Apart from that, some traits that are traditionally considered typically Neolithic are observable in the Mesolithic already, such as the domestication of certain animal species and pottery production. Dogs, for example, were domesticated in the Pre-Boreal, and the Danish Late Mesolithic Ertebølle culture includes pottery. No indisputable cases of associations between Mesolithic flint types and pottery have however been found in the Low Countries (see chapters 8 and 9). The most common, if not entirely satisfactory, definition currently used for the Mesolithic is hence 'the period of the Holocene hunter-gatherers'.[33]

The Early Mesolithic is characterised by a great homogeneity over large parts of Europe. Characteristic of the lithic industries of this period are a versatile blade technology, a fairly limited range of microlith types (most with unretouched bases) and the occurrence of Upper Palaeolithic point types. The transition from the Early

fig. 4.7

North-south cross-section of the Netherlands from the Ardennes (left) to the Drenthe Plateau (right) showing the projections of the locations of the most important Palaeolithic sites and their relation to the geology.

site	Sclayn	Belvédère	Bakel	Rhenen	Mander	Wijnjeterp
region	Namur (B)	South Limburg	Noord-Brabant	Utrecht	Overijssel	Friesland
geo-morphology	plateau edge, cave	middle terrace	Horst	hills	ice-pushed hills	boulderclay plateau
Pleistocene stratigraphy	-	2. between loess dep. 1. below loess	below cover sand	ice-pushed	-	below cover sand?
geological context	cave fill	2. erosion surface 1. top Meuse levee	on top of Meuse deposits	in river deposits	surface	top glacial till
age BP	40 - 130.000	2. 80.000 1. 250.000	> 35.000	> 150.000	< 120.000	< 120.000

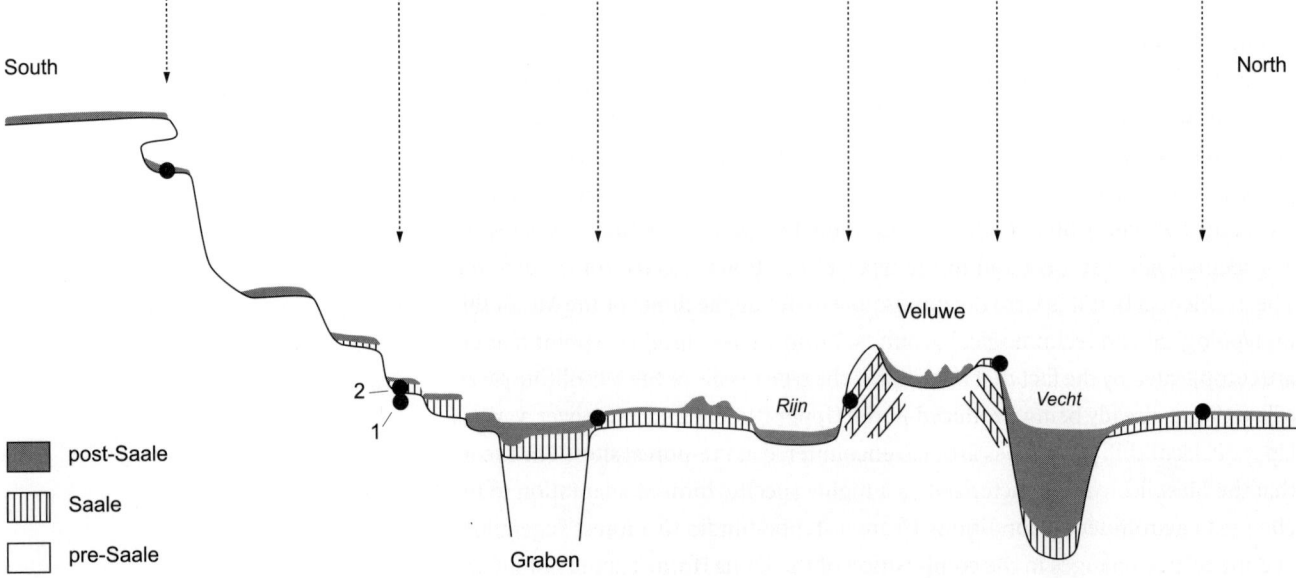

South   North

Veluwe

2

1

Rijn

Vecht

post-Saale

Saale

pre-Saale

Graben

86

to the Middle Mesolithic was very gradual.[34] The appearance of a wider range of microlith types, in particular types made on blade segments, triangles and points with surface retouch has been taken to mark the beginning of the Middle Mesolithic (7100 BC). In the course of the Boreal the degree of regional variation increased. The Late Mesolithic (from 6450 BC) saw the appearance of wide trapezium-shaped microliths across the whole of Europe. This type may definitely be regarded as a type fossil. Other characteristics of this period are an advanced blade technology and the appearance of needle-shaped points. Some archaeologists also distinguish a De Leien-Wartena Group in the Late Mesolithic.[35] That group's sites are very large and often lie on the shores of lakes or along rivers. The best-known site is that of Bergumermeer.[36] But whether these sites are large aggregation sites or palimpsests representing the location's frequent reuse is still a matter of debate.

The first farmers arrived in the loess regions in the south of the Netherlands, the Rhineland and parts of Belgium around 5300 BC (the *Linearbandkeramik* farmers). Most researchers assume that the Netherlands was occupied by groups with a hunter-gatherer way of life, often referred to as 'Late Mesolithic tradition', until the appearance of the Michelsberg culture. The remains of these groups consist largely of small sites, situated on the sandy soils. The nature of the relationship between the hunter-gatherers and the earliest farmers is still poorly understood.[37]

THE REPRESENTATIVITY OF THE EVIDENCE

In the Netherlands, the number of places where Palaeolithic and Mesolithic occupation remains can be found is limited because large parts of the former landscapes are inaccessible for archaeological research. This is to some extent ascribable to the fact that a large area of the Netherlands has undergone subsidence. In

fig. 4.8
Thanks to calm sedimentation in a marine bay near Boxgrove in England, flint and bone scatters dating from some 500,000 years ago have survived in excellent condition. The figure shows an impression of such a scatter at site Q1B, which, besides many other finds, contained hundreds of hand axes and some human remains.

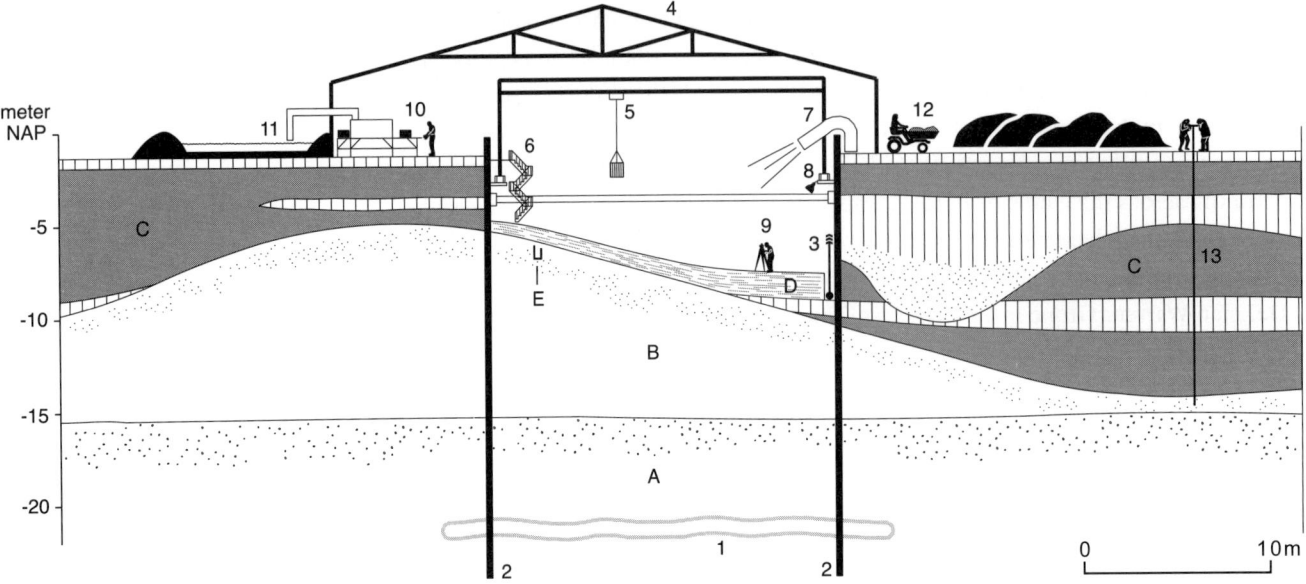

meter NAP

-5

-10

-15

-20

0   10m

fig. 4.9
Schematic cross-section of the excavation
pit of Hardinxveld-Giessendam Polderweg
(1997-'98, feature D) showing the innovative
techniques that make it possible to conduct
excavations at such great depths beneath
the surface. New legislation based on the
regulations of the Malta Convention allows
for financing of such excavation work. Cf.
plate 11 and fig. 10.4.

Explanation:

1   injected impermeable layer
2   steel sheet-piling
3   electric pump
4   tent
5   portal crane
6   staircase
7   hot air blower

8   floodlight
9   total station
10   wet sieving machine
11   water storage basin
12   caterpillar dumper
13   hand drilling

A   Late Glacial river deposits
B   Early Holocene river dune
C   peat and fluvial deposits
D   slope wash deposits
E   burial

the western part of the country and in the area of the major rivers in particular, many finds from the Old and Middle Stone Age lie too far beneath the present surface to be recovered (fig. 4.7). This is because the so-called Central Graben, a zone of long, parallel, geological faults between which the land subsides, extends beneath the Netherlands and part of the North Sea. Land has been subsiding between these faults for more than two million years. Over this period the rate of sedimentation has kept pace with the rate of subsidence and consequently deposits with a total thickness of 600 metres, here and there even 1000 metres, have been formed at an average rate of three to five centimetres per century. This means that in the subsidence areas the land surface of 200,000 years ago now lies buried beneath 60-100 metres of deposits, making it virtually inaccessible for archaeological research. The fluctuations in the sea level have also caused large parts of former settlement systems to disappear. This is for example true of the North Sea floor, which frequently emerged from the sea and must contain both Palaeolithic and Early Mesolithic sites.

Besides this 'geographical' distortion, the evidence, especially that from the older phases, also shows a climatological bias. As sedimentation was usually a much calmer process in interglacials than in colder phases, a large proportion of the well-preserved sites in Northwest Europe date from warmer phases (fig. 4.8). This is all the more remarkable because in total, those phases cover only a relatively small part of the overall Pleistocene time span: about ten to twenty percent. The fine-grained fluvial and lacustrine deposits from these phases are accessible in some gravel pits and other outcrops outside the subsidence areas. Good examples of sites found in fine-grained deposits are the well-preserved sites of Maastricht-Belvédère and the Mesolithic site of Bedburg-Königshoven (German

Rhineland).[38] The recently excavated Late Mesolithic sites of Hardinxveld are good examples in the Netherlands (fig. 4.9, see also feature D).

Such well-preserved sites are however exceptions in the Netherlands, where organic remains are only rarely found. Among the few organic remains that have come to light in the Netherlands are the well-known figurine resembling a male figure from Willemstad, the canoe from Pesse and the finely carved bone points from the Meuse plain. Most sites were not incorporated in deposits favouring their preservation (but at the same time reducing the chance of their recovery) and at such sites flint scatters are all that remain from the prehistoric occupants' activities (fig. 4.10). There is also a category of sites in areas where no sedimentation has taken place, where the occupation remains of successive short periods of use of specific 'magnetic locations' accumulated into substantial assemblages. In such cases the *number* of artefacts in itself may tell us nothing about a site's former function. This distorting effect has sometimes even been strengthened by the drifting of the sandy soil on which many of such sites lie.

A final distorting factor is the difference in the intensity of research carried out in certain areas; this has affected our picture of early settlement patterns in particular. We are, for example, well-informed about the Mesolithic occupation of the Belgian/Dutch Kempen region, thanks to the work by Vermeersch, Bohmers and Wouters, whereas we have much less information on other regions.

CURRENT RESEARCH PROBLEMS

The main current research problems concern issues that are not specifically 'Dutch', but are of importance with respect to the archaeology of hunter-gatherers in general. This is partly due to the fact that the archaeology of mobile hunter-gatherers can only be studied properly from a regional perspective; the

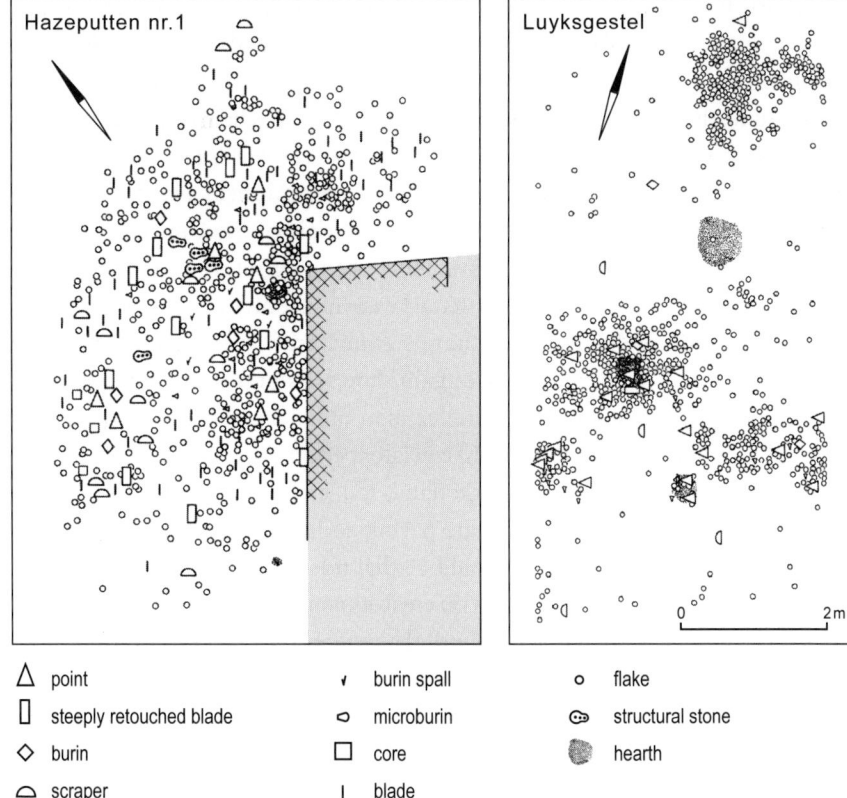

△	point	⌇	burin spall	○	flake
▯	steeply retouched blade	↪	microburin	□	core
◇	burin	□	core	⊕	structural stone
⌒	scraper	∣	blade	▨	hearth

fig. 4.10

Typical plans of Mesolithic flint scatters. The typological composition of the assemblages and the dimensions of scatters of this kind are used to interpret the sites in functional terms. The Luyksgestel site is assumed to represent the remains of a series of short-lived hunting camps, while that of Sint-Oedenrode-Hazeputten is thought to be a hut site forming part of a base camp that was used for a greater length of time.

fig. 4.11
One of the two red deer skullcaps with antlers that were found in the fill of a small lake next to the Pre-Boreal Mesolithic dwelling site of Bedburg-Königshoven (Rhineland). The skullcap was perforated, indicating that it was used as a mask, either for stalking deer or in ritual performances.

studied region may vary from a so-called microregion[39] to the whole of Northwest Europe.[40]

This is one of the main reasons why most researchers nowadays adopt what has been described as a 'landscape approach'.[41] In this form of research the aim is no longer merely to arrive at detailed analyses of individual sites, but to integrate the results of the investigations of individual sites in a regional approach based on, among other things, studies of raw materials and technology. It is thanks to such studies that we now know that already at an early stage of the Middle Palaeolithic there were 'raw material links' between the southernmost part of the Netherlands and a region more than 100 kilometres further southeast: excavations in the eastern part of the Eifel have shown that tools made of flint from the Meuse region were discarded in that area during the penultimate and last glaciations. Such raw material links continued to exist in the Magdalenian. One of the questions we are now interested in concerns the processes behind these raw material transfers: are we to assume that a system of 'barter' or 'exchange' existed between neighbouring groups as early as 150,000 years ago or were the tools taken along in the course of the usual group movements and are we hence to regard them as records of prehistoric mobility patterns?[42] The exotic raw materials of the Upper Palaeolithic and Mesolithic also reflect group movements and/or social contacts. The size of the area across which these exotic materials were transported varied over the ages and, consequently, so did the size of the operational environment of the groups of hunter-gatherers. This probably once again shows that it is irrelevant to look for univocal developments, and that complex, non-unilinear, changes took place in earlier phases of prehistory too, just like in later periods.

One of the reasons why, in the Netherlands too, archaeologists concerned with early hunter-gatherer communities are paying so much attention to the reconstruction of former environments could be that it is believed that the way of life of those groups was more dependent on environmental conditions than on social factors, i.e. human relationships. Indeed, the models that are used to study those communities are based on the assumption that humans adapted to their environment in an 'optimum' manner, presupposing a 'Homo economicus' whose actions were hardly determined by other relationships than this economic 'human nature' one.

However, Dutch and Belgian researchers studying the later phases of the Palae-olithic and the Mesolithic consider social factors as well (fig. 4.11). Issues of current interest are the definition of ethnic units[43] and the degree of 'complexity' of late hunter-gatherer communities.[44] Of importance with respect to the latter topic is that many regard the hunter-gatherers of the Holocene as the people who created 'the breeding ground for the introduction of a farming economy'. The transition from the way of life of a hunter-gatherer to that of a sedentary food producer is a research topic for which many models have been set up.[45] The metaphor of the 'breeding ground' clearly illustrates the unfortunate teleological perspective that is implicitly employed in many of these models.

NOTES

1 See for example Corbey 1989 and Corbey/Theunissen 1995.

2 See Mellars/Stringer (1989) and Stringer/Gamble (1993) for a survey of the different theories in this field.

3 The family of *Hominidae* includes both the present human species and its extinct relatives. To be classed as hominids those relatives must have shown more affinities to modern man than to anthropoids.

4 Price 1987.

5 For many years views on the Mesolithic were largely influenced by Childe's interpretation of this period as a phase of cultural decline (1942). This picture changed with the publication of the lectures presented at the 'Man the Hunter' symposium (Lee/DeVore 1968), at which Sahlins introduced his concept of the 'affluent hunter-gatherer'. Basing himself on anthropological evidence, he argued that hunter-gatherers did not lead such a hard, marginal existence as had always been assumed, but were on the contrary capable of securing sufficient resources within a short space of time and consequently enjoyed a relatively large amount of spare time. Nowadays, anthropologists are however gradually coming to the conclusion that the picture of the hunter-gatherers presented in the 1960s is too idealistic and that their existence was indeed considerably hampered in various respects.

6 Schmerling 1833-'34.

7 For a historical survey of the Palaeolithic research at Rijckholt/Sint-Geertruid, see Roebroeks 1980.

8 See *e.g.* Hamal-Nandrin/Servais 1923.

9 Bohmers 1951.

10 See for example Van der Waals/Waterbolk 1973.

11 Newell 1980.

12 Arts/Deeben 1981.

13 Newell 1973; Price 1975.

14 Roebroeks 1989.

15 See for example Vermeersch 1990 and Gendel *et al.* 1985.

16 See for example Groenendijk 1993.

17 Grahame Clark (1936 and 1975) has had a great influence on the kinds of questions that are asked in Mesolithic research. His analysis of Star Carr (Clark 1954) in particular was most influential.

18 For a survey of these techniques see Aitken 1990. In the Nether-lands, much use was made of these dating methods in the research at Belvédère (see Roebroeks 1988).

19 Van Gijn 1989, 1990.

20 Stapert 1990, 1992a.

21 One of the first examples of the systematic combined use of such techniques concerns the research at Meer (Belgium) (Cahen *et al.* 1979).

22 Van Kolfschoten/Roebroeks 1985.

23 Zagwijn 1992.

24 See Gamble 1986 and 1987 versus Roebroeks *et al.* 1992.

25 See Roebroeks *et al.* 1992.

26 Guthrie 1990. In publications on the Late Magdalenian sites Gönnersdorf and Andernach in the Neuwied Basin near Koblenz (Germany), Bosinski (1992) and others have repeatedly drawn attention to the high productivity of the Late Glacial loess steppe and the wide diversity of its fauna.

27 For the scarce finds from earlier phases of the Upper Palaeolithic, see chapter 6.

28 See for example Bosinski 1987, 129-130.

29 See for example Arts 1988, 299; Deeben 1988.

30 For a discussion of the different viewpoints see for example Stapert 1985b.

31 Arts 1988, 296. Arts has pointed out that the various Upper Palaeolithic groups can be distinguished on the basis of technological criteria besides on the basis of 'type fossils'.

32 Vermeersch 1989; Arts 1988, 1989.

33 Price 1987.

34 Vermeersch used this gradual transition as an argument for dividing the Mesolithic into only two phases, an Early and a Late Mesolithic (Vermeersch 1984).

35 Newell 1973.

36 Newell 1980; Odell 1977, 1980.

37 See Weelde-Paardsdrank in the Kempen region in Belgium (Huyge/Vermeersch 1982), the presence of Early Neolithic points in Late Mesolithic contexts (Van der Graaf 1988) and the research carried out by Verhart/Wansleeben (1990).

38 Street 1991.

39 *Cf.* Verhart/Wansleeben 1990.

40 *Cf.* Gamble 1986; Newell *et al.* 1990.

41 Villa 1991.

42 Roebroeks *et al.* 1988.

43 Gendel 1984; Newell *et al.* 1990; Verhart 1990.

44 See *e.g.* Price/Brown 1985.

45 See *e.g.* Rowley-Conwy 1984; Thomas 1988, 1991; Zvelebil 1986b. In the Netherlands this topic is being studied in the Meuse Valley Project (Verhart/Wansleeben 1990) in particular.

5 Neanderthals and their predecessors Lower and Middle Palaeolithic

Wil Roebroeks

THE NETHERLANDS AS A FIND AREA

Through the ages, the national frontiers of the Netherlands have undergone many changes, but the same can be said of the country's natural frontiers when viewed on the geological time scale: the proportions of land and sea and the course of the coastline varied considerably from one geological period to another. In the coldest phases of the Pleistocene, for example, such large volumes of water were locked up in the vast ice caps that the sea level was repeatedly many dozens of metres lower than it is today. Large parts of the North Sea Basin were then dry and Great Britain formed part of the Continent. The tremendous quantities of bones of mammoths, reindeer, horses and other large mammals that fishermen on the North Sea have recovered in their trawl nets are reminders of this 'North Sea land' that was actually submerged by the sea only during the interglacials, which together spanned not more than 10% of the overall Pleistocene period. Besides the submersion of the North Sea Basin there are several other geological factors (see chapter 3) that greatly reduce our chances of recovering finds from the early phases of the Palaeolithic in large parts of the Netherlands. However, there where old land surfaces were not covered with younger sediments or where overlying deposits have disappeared owing to later erosion, we are able to collect Lower and Middle Palaeolithic finds at the surface.

To obtain a somewhat coherent picture of the earliest occupation of the Netherlands we must also consider the evidence from surrounding areas. We must bear in mind that this chapter discusses the archaeological record of highly mobile groups – small groups of hunter-gatherers with 'no fixed abodes' – whose archaeological visibility in the form of artefacts and features is very poor; apart from being few in number, those artefacts and features have moreover suffered the ravages of time for many tens of thousands of years. We indeed have concrete evidence demonstrating that these groups covered large distances, from for example the chalk hills of southern Limburg to the Neuwied Basin near Koblenz. The evidence for the earliest occupation of what is now the Netherlands will therefore be presented within the context of the history of occupation of Northwest Europe and throughout this discussion reference will be made to sites in England, northern France, Belgium and the adjacent parts of Germany, too.

THE EARLIEST OCCUPATION

Artefacts and pseudo-artefacts

How to determine when a particular region was first occupied has always been a subject of heated discussions. In archaeology, these discussions usually revolve around two issues. The first concerns the nature of finds: does a particular piece of chipped stone show unambiguous signs of human activity? The second relates to the finds' exact age. More than a century ago, the existence of Tertiary man was a source of a furious controversy among European Palaeolithic archaeologists. Eoliths, 'stones from the dawn' of humankind, proved that the history of humankind extended very far back, argued the *eolithophiles*. Their adversaries, the *eolithophobes*, maintained that the stones in question were not related to human activities, but owed their distinctive shape to natural processes. The fierce debate engendered extensive surveys and experiments intended to demonstrate how objects resembling artefacts may have been formed naturally. The results are described in well-known handbooks from the beginning of the twentieth century, such as Obermaier's *Der Mensch der Vorzeit* (1911), Sollas' *Ancient hunters and their modern representatives* (1911) and Boule's *Les Hommes Fossiles* (1921). One of the conclusions of these discussions was that it is indeed possible for natural processes to transform pieces of flint and other stones so as to make them resemble artefacts. In the early twentieth century the British antiquarian Warren maintained that, in view of these resemblances in shape between natural stones and artefacts, the onus of proof should always lie with those who wished to interpret such ancient stones as the products of human workmanship.[1] The stones in question should moreover not constitute a relatively small sample of 'artefacts' from an extensive lithic complex lacking clear evidence for knapping by humans. It was essential that the lithic material be studied and interpreted in its geological and spatial contexts *in its entirety*. There are indeed often quite acceptable explanations in terms of natural processes for seemingly unusually shaped stones. Because of this problem and the continuing quest for ever older tools, the question of 'pseudo-artefacts' has never really disappeared from the archaeological agenda.[2] Another issue that is still a matter of debate today is the exact age of occupation remains; the new dates recently obtained for the earliest occupation of Java have caused quite a stir in the palaeo-anthropological world[3] and the dates of the earliest occupation of the New World and Australia are also topics of never-ending discussions.[4]

period	interglacial context	intermediary context	'cold steppe' context
Late Pleistocene / Upper Palaeolithic			Gönnersdorf
			Andernach
			Mainz-Linsenberg
			Sprendlingen
			Maisières
			Lommersum
Late Pleistocene / Late Middle Palaeolithic	Neumark-Nord	Seclin	Becksteinschmiede
	Grabschutz	Wallertheim	Balve
	Rabutz	Tönchesberg	Kartstein
	Gröbern	Königsaue	Salzgitter-Lebenstedt
	Lehringen		Ariendorf 3
	Veltheim		
	Taubach, Weimar, Burgtonna		
Late Middle Pleistocene	Stuttgart-Bad Cannstatt	Biache-Saint-Vaast	Achenheim 'Sol 74'
	Ehringsdorf		La Cotte de St. Brelade
	Maastricht-Belvédère		Schweinskopf / Wannen
			Ariendorf 2
Early Middle Pleistocene	Bilzingsleben	Cagny-l'Epinette	Ariendorf 1
	Clacton-on-Sea	Hoxne	Mesvin IV
	Barnham	Schöningen	
	Miesenheim I		
	Boxgrove		

fig. 5.1

Schematic survey of well-documented Palaeolithic sites in northern Europe (north of 49° N) and their climatological context.

94

The first hominids in Europe

Until recently, most experts considered about one million years a good estimate of the age of the earliest evidence for occupation in Europe,[5] although some even suggested two million years.[6] According to a new 'short chronology', Europe was not colonised by hominids until a relatively late stage, not much more than about 500,000 years ago. Since the introduction of this short chronology, the European evidence has played an important part in the discussion about the earliest occupation of the regions outside Africa, the cradle of humankind.[7] The adherents of the short chronology are of the opinion that the finds from sites like Kärlich A and B in Germany, Le Vallonet in France and Prezletice and Stránská skála in the Czech republic, which were previously believed to date from before 500,000 years BP, do not constitute sound proof of early occupation because they do not include convincing artefacts. Other sites, such as Isernia in Italy, which have yielded what are assumed to be unmistakable artefacts, are in their opinion actually younger than often claimed. An argument supporting the short chronology, which is not in any way connected with the discussion concerning the natural or artificial nature of lithic assemblages, is that not one human fossil with an age of over 500,000 years has been found anywhere in Europe,[8] whereas fossil human remains have frequently been found in Middle Pleistocene deposits younger than 500,000 years (fig. 5.1).

This scenario leads to an entirely different view on the colonisation of Europe than the various longer chronologies. According to the models based on the latter chronologies, the colonisation of Europe was essentially a *gradual* process, in which the newcomers had sufficient time to adapt to their new surroundings. The short chronology is based on the assumption that hominids lived in the immediate surroundings of Europe for a fairly long time – as testified by the finds from Dmanisi (Georgia) and 'Ubeidiya (Israel) – before finally penetrating into Europe itself around 500,000 years ago, after which they spread across it at a fairly *high rate*. In this model the earliest occupation of northern Europe, documented at sites like Boxgrove (southern England) and Miesenheim I (near Koblenz), is more or less 'contemporary' with that of southern Europe, that is, within the limits of the chronological resolution of our dating methods. But if this model is correct, the question is *why* those hominids should have waited several hundred thousand years at Europe's gates before passing through them around half a million years ago.[9]

With their biostratigraphically founded ages of around 500,000 years, Boxgrove and Miesenheim I are among the oldest sites known in Europe. Boxgrove is actually a former coastal plain at the foot of a limestone cliff with a length of several dozen kilometres, where various scatters of bones and stones have been remarkably well preserved. Throughout an interglacial, about half a million years ago, and for the early part of the subsequent colder phase, groups of hominids regularly visited a lagoon at the foot of the cliff, where they found flint for manufacturing tools, but also an abundance of game. The remains of these groups, excellently preserved by the fine sand and loam that were later deposited on top of them, inform us that these groups collected blocks of flint at the foot of the limestone cliff, which they transported to a nearby location, where they transformed them into tools, often carefully finished hand axes. Those tools they used to butcher animals like rhinoceros and horse. In spite of the excellent preservation conditions, no features of huts or hearths were found at Boxgrove. The remains appear to represent a series of many brief, episodic visits to the former coastal plain. This impression is entirely in keeping with the pattern known from other sites from these early periods, for example those along the former courses of the Somme in northern France, on the shores of lakes in the vicinity of present-day Hoxne in England and

near the travertine deposits of Bilzingsleben in former East Germany. Those sites are actually small 'windows' through which we catch glimpses of former landscapes, including their flora and fauna, and – occasionally – the activities of the first people to have wandered across them.

At the end of 1993 a tibia of a very robust individual with an estimated length of 1.80 m was found at Boxgrove (fig. 5.2). This British fossil is one of the scarce remains of the earliest occupants of Europe, which also include the lower jaw that was found at Mauer (near Heidelberg in Germany) in 1907 and the richer assemblage from Atapuerca TD6 (Spain).[10] These hominids differ from both *Homo erectus*, of which no unambiguous remains have been found in Europe, and the later occupants, the Neanderthals. According to some specialists these earliest Europeans showed so many distinctive features as to deserve a separate name: *Homo heidelbergensis*.[11]

The well-preserved mammal remains from the fill of the La Belle Roche cave, near Sprimont in the Belgian Ardennes,[12] probably date from the same period as the Boxgrove and Mauer remains. Bear (*Ursus deningeri*), panther (*Panthera gombaszoegensis*) and lion (*Panthera leo fossilis*) are among the animals represented in the faunal sample of this highly important palaeontological site, which was excavated in a campaign that lasted for many years. The fills of the karst fissures of this 'cave' also yielded several dozen stones, some severely eroded, which the excavators interpreted as artefacts, in other words, as evidence for human occupation. Other archaeologists however class the stones as pseudo-artefacts.[13]

It has been suggested that another ancient find, a primitive 'core' from the high terrace gravels of the Meuse near Halembaye (Haccourt, Belgian province of Liège), may likewise be a pseudo-artefact.[14] So all in all, no incontestable evidence for human occupation in the Lower Palaeolithic has so far been found in the Benelux, but finds recovered in the surrounding countries make it likely that remains from 500,000 years ago will some day come to light here, too.

THE MIDDLE PALAEOLITHIC

The oldest unmistakable artefacts recovered in the Netherlands date from about 250,000 years ago,[15] *i.e.* from the beginning of the Middle Palaeolithic (fig. 5.3). This period is characterised by the frequent use of the Levallois technique for manufacturing stone tools (see feature A). Hand axes were still used, but tools made on (Levallois) flakes, in particular scrapers, points and denticulate tools, became far more common than in the Lower Palaeolithic.

The Levallois technique made its appearance in large parts of Europe between c. 300,000 and 250,000 years ago, and this appearance marks the beginning of the Middle Palaeolithic. The youngest Middle Palaeolithic assemblages date from approximately 35,000 years BP, although even younger finds are known from Spain. In the Low Countries, both early Middle Palaeolithic artefacts have been found and artefacts dating from the late Middle Palaeolithic, the period of the 'classic' Neanderthal, which spanned the first half of the last, Weichselian, glaciation.

The Neanderthals

Fossil human remains from the early Middle Palaeolithic are still rare in Europe. Nevertheless, the number and quality of the available remains allow us to conclude that by the beginning of the Middle Palaeolithic hominids had evolved into

fig. 5.2
One of the oldest human remains ever found in northern Europe is this tibia, which came to light during excavations at Boxgrove (southern England) and has been dated to around 500,000 years ago. A recent study of this find showed that it belonged to an individual who died when he was around 50 years old and had a relatively robust, stocky physique, adapted to cold conditions. The remains of the earliest Europeans north of the Alps and Pyrenees already show evidence of adaptation to the colder conditions that prevailed in those areas, marking the beginning of a process that ultimately resulted in the 'classic Neanderthal man'.

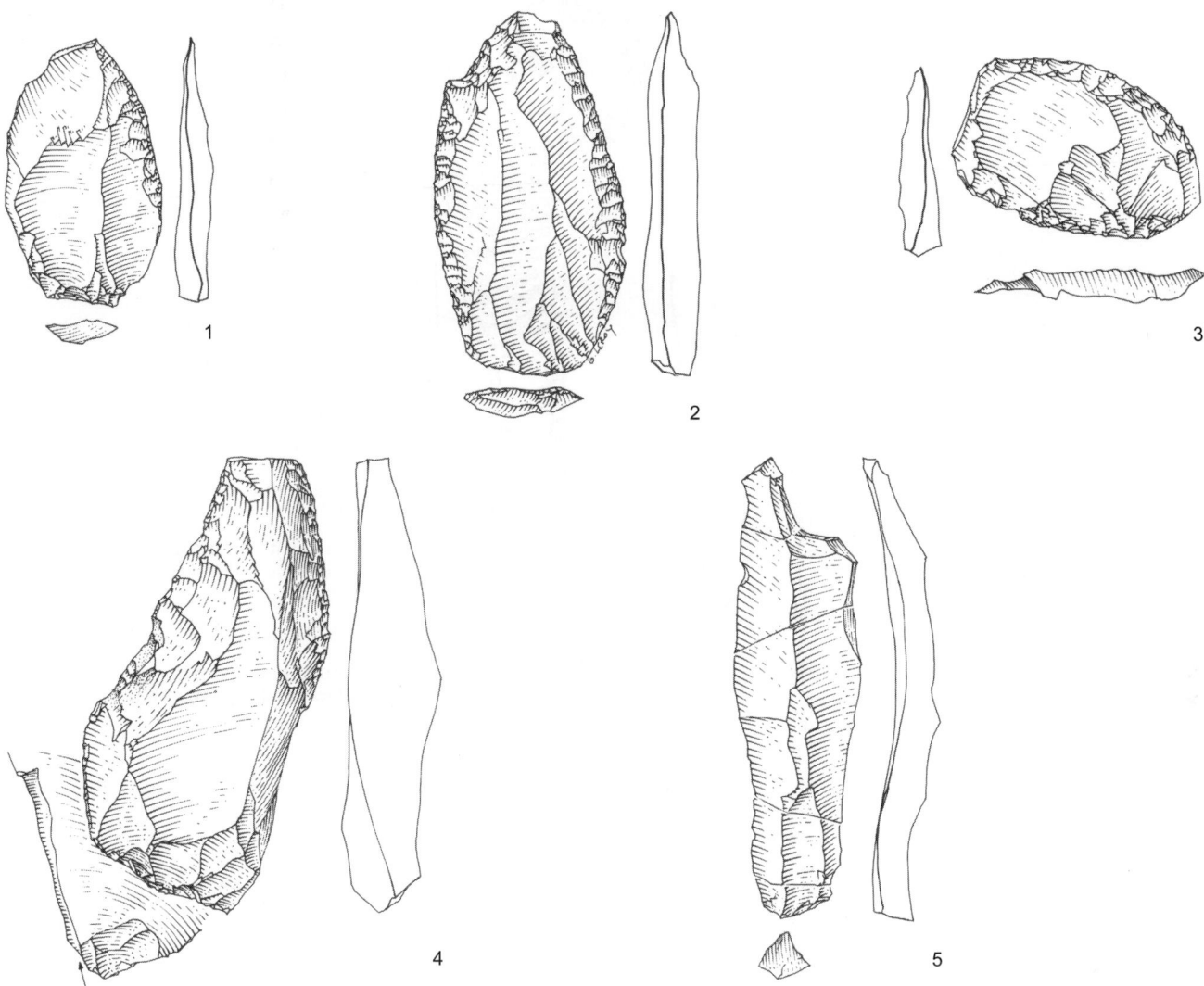

the direct ancestors of the well-known Neanderthals. Important fossil remains of these early Neanderthaloids are known from more or less contemporary sites like Biache-Saint-Vaast (northern France), Swanscombe (at the mouth of the Thames) and Ehringsdorf and Steinheim (Germany). The hominids of the Maastricht-Belvédère site in the Netherlands, who are known to us only through their artefacts, probably also belonged to this group.

The Neanderthals 'proper', or 'classic' Neanderthals, lived in the second half of the Middle Palaeolithic, between 120,000 and 35,000 years ago; they were a distinctively European phenomenon (fig. 5.4). The Neanderthals are generally classed as a subspecies of *Homo sapiens*: *Homo sapiens neanderthalensis*, although some specialists regard them as a separate species, *Homo neanderthalensis*.

The species/subspecies problem broached above involves far more than the classification of fossils alone, namely also the question as to whether the Neanderthals represent an evolutionary dead-end, having been replaced by modern humans some 35,000 years ago, or whether, on the contrary, they are largely ancestral to anatomically modern humans. Those in favour of the latter view see Neanderthals as a simpler version of modern humans, whereas their opponents postulate major differences between the two populations, also in terms of their behaviour. They emphasise for example the lack of clear indications of the use of symbols before the appearance of modern humans and the lack of evidence for the long-distance contacts that are so typical of the behaviour of many present-day hunter-gatherers and also that of their Upper Palaeolithic predecessors.

fig. 5.3

Typical Middle Palaeolithic artefacts found at site N, Maastricht-Belvédère. Scale 1:2

1 single convex side scraper

2 double convex side scraper

3 single convex side scraper

4 double concave/convex scraper

5 blade consisting of refitted fragments

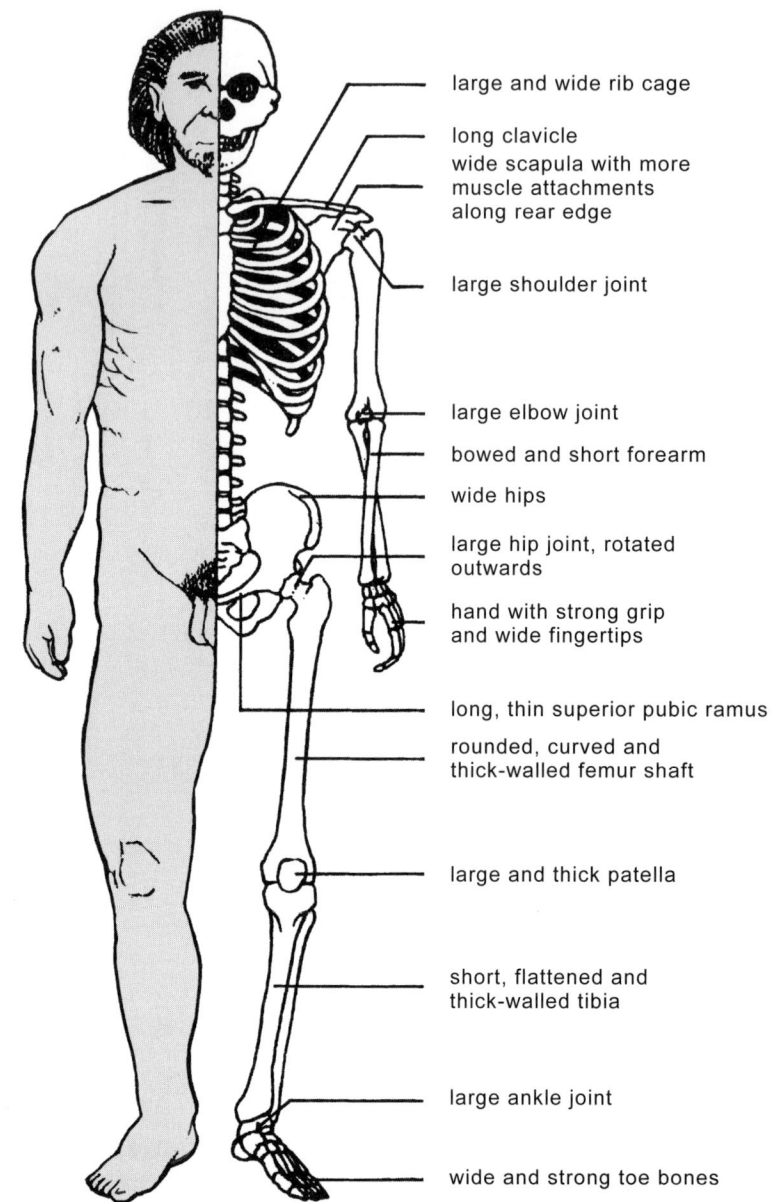

large and wide rib cage

long clavicle
wide scapula with more
muscle attachments
along rear edge

large shoulder joint

large elbow joint

bowed and short forearm

wide hips

large hip joint, rotated
outwards

hand with strong grip
and wide fingertips

long, thin superior pubic ramus

rounded, curved and
thick-walled femur shaft

large and thick patella

short, flattened and
thick-walled tibia

large ankle joint

wide and strong toe bones

fig. 5.4
Anatomical features of a Neanderthal
skeleton. Neanderthal man was far more
robust and stocky than *Homo sapiens sapiens*,
'modern' man.

Sites

A survey

Since the nineteenth century, amateur archaeologists have been finding Middle
Palaeolithic artefacts in ploughed fields in many parts of the Netherlands, in particular in the south, for example on 'De Hej' near Sint-Geertruid (plate 8C),[16] but
also in the east and the north. The absence of overlying deposits makes it difficult
to place such surface finds in a geological-chronological framework: most Middle
Palaeolithic artefact types remained in use for long periods of time throughout the
entire Middle Palaeolithic, which lasted for 250,000 years. Exceptions are the perfectly triangular hand axes from the beginning of the last glaciation and the leaf
points from the end of the Middle Palaeolithic. Having been exposed for such long
periods, sometimes tens of thousands of years, many of those surface finds, like
the hand axes from Wijnjeterp and Anderen, are severely patinated and show frost
cracks (fig. 4.4 and plate 8A).[17] Such finds testify to the presence of Middle Palaeolithic people in these areas, but they tell us next to nothing about when those
people lived here and under what climatological and ecological conditions or what
they did at the different locations. For answers to such questions we must turn to

the evidence from the well-preserved sites that have been found embedded in flu-viatile and loess deposits and from the cave sites discovered in the *Mittelgebirge* to the south and east of the Netherlands.

Cave sites in the Belgian/German Mittelgebirge

The Belgian cave sites have yielded very few finds dating from before the last interglacial, between 125,000 and 115,000 years ago. The vast majority of the finds date from the first half of the last glaciation, the period of Neanderthal man 'proper'.

Unfortunately, most of the cave sites in the Ardennes were excavated many dec-ades ago, as a result of which we now have only little information on the contexts of the many finds. This makes it very difficult to make statements on how and why the caves were occupied: when were they used and were the sites 'settlements' proper or simply transit camps where people spent the night while moving from one area to another? Such questions can regrettably no longer be answered on the basis of the old excavation data.

Good examples of cave sites that were excavated a long time ago are the series of sites from the second part of the Middle Palaeolithic near Huccorgne, a few kilometres northwest of Huy in Belgium. The majority of those sites were all dis-covered and investigated in the nineteenth century. They comprise several open-air sites and ten cave and rock-shelter sites situated closely together in the steep slopes of a narrow, deep valley through which the river Mehaigne passes before flowing into the Meuse, and in the slopes of the valley of the river's tributary the Roua. The best-known of these sites are the Grotte de l'Hermitage and the Grotte du Docteur. Among the finds from the former are fine, regular Levallois flakes and a fair number of hand axes, many of which are heart-shaped. The site's faunal assemblage included remains of hyena (*Hyena spelaea*), bovids (*Bos primigenius*), horse (*Equus caballus*), rhinoceros, cave bear, giant deer and mammoth. The ab-sence of reindeer could imply that this site was occupied fairly early in the last glaciation.[18]

Present-day research a short distance to the east of Namur has shown how informative well-excavated cave sites can be. The fill of the cave Scladina near Sclayn[19] was found to contain several Middle Palaeolithic assemblages. The oldest finds date from shortly before the last warm phase, the Eemian interglacial, which means they are more than 125,000 years old. The youngest assemblage is about 40,000 years old and hence dates from the middle of the Weichselian glacial and the end of the Middle Palaeolithic. The cave's fill, then, constitutes a record of at least 80,000 years of human activity. The composition of the assemblages and the provenance of the chipped stone show that the cave was used predominantly – but not exclusively – as a shelter for brief periods of time during movements between the Hainaut, the Belgian province of Brabant and the Ardennes. According to the excavators, the faunal sample comprised predominantly remains of hunted ani-mals, in particular chamois, deer, reindeer and ibex.

Two caves that are known all over the world for the more or less complete Ne-anderthal skeletons that were found in them lie fairly close to the Dutch border: in the Neanderthal near Düsseldorf and at Spy near Namur (fig. 5.5). It was in the Feldhofer Grotte in the Neanderthal that the holotype of the 'classic' Neanderthal was found in 1856. These remains excited a heated debate about their meaning: did they represent a primitive ancestor, an 'antediluvian man', as some claimed, or had they belonged to a relatively recent 'degenerate' individual? When more such finds began to crop up in ancient deposits it soon became clear that the remains indeed derived from early hominids, in particular when, in 1886, excavators from

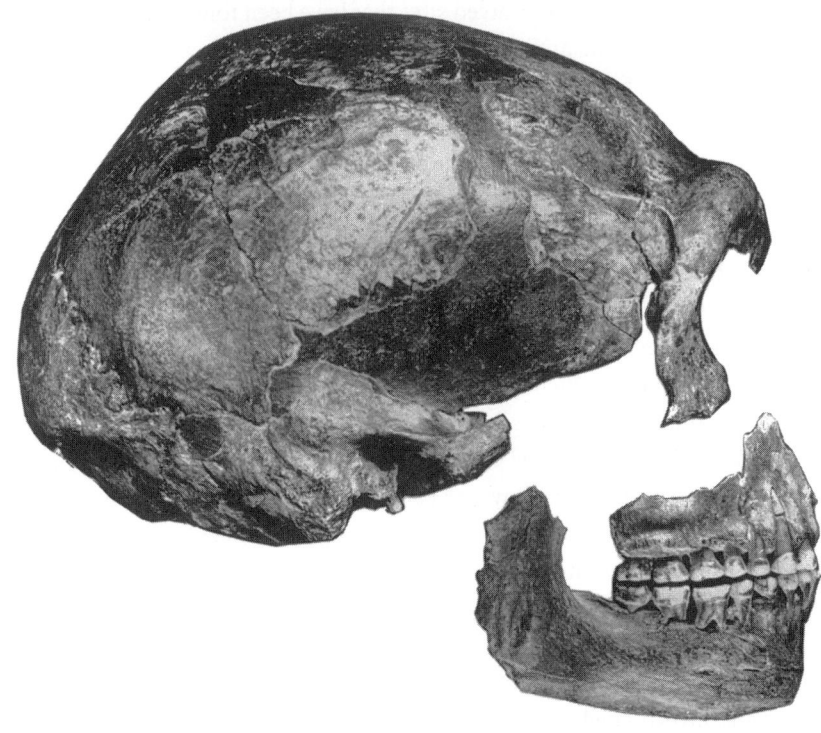

fig. 5.5
Neanderthal skull from the cave of Spy near Namur, where remains of two Neanderthal individuals were found in 1886. These finds played an important part in the ultimate classification of Neanderthal man as an early hominid.

Liège discovered two almost complete Neanderthal skeletons in a cave near Spy in Belgium.

Camp sites buried beneath loess

To the north of the *Mittelgebirge*, Middle Palaeolithic occupation remains are in many places buried beneath thick layers of fluviatile deposits or loess and sand laid down by the wind in the coldest phases of the glaciations. It was indeed in such a geological context that the oldest sites known in the Netherlands were discovered: Maastricht-Belvédère and the sites in the central part of the country, such as those at Rhenen. They were all embedded in deposits, predominantly fluviatile deposits of the Meuse and the Meuse/Rhine, respectively. The sites near Maastricht have been soundly dated to about 250,000 years BP. Those in the central part of the country may be of the same age; we know for sure that they date from before the arrival of the Saalian glaciers here, about 150,000 years ago.[20]

The finds from Liège-St. Walburge also date from before the advance of the Saalian ice sheets. This rich Middle Palaeolithic site was discovered in a gravel quarry in 1911 by the French archaeologist Victor Commont. Further research by other excavators, among whom were De Puydt and Hamal Nandrin from Liège, yielded some 8000 Middle Palaeolithic flint artefacts buried beneath a thick layer of loess. Thanks to Commont's detailed description of the soil sections we now know that this loess dates from the last and penultimate glaciations. That makes the finds – many simple flint flakes, but also beautiful Levallois flakes, scrapers and hand axes – at least 150,000 years old. Unfortunately the way in which the finds were recovered precludes any statements about the former significance of this location. Another sad fact is that no faunal remains had been preserved in the decalcified loess. The latter also holds for the Middle Palaeolithic sites that were excavated in a loess quarry near Rheindahlen in the adjacent German Rhineland, where a series of assemblages of flint artefacts spanning the entire Middle Palaeolithic have survived the ravages of time.[21]

'Absolute' dates (Ka)	Lithostrat. units	Stratigraphical position of sites and isolated finds (*)	'Soils'	Chronostratigraphy
TL 17.2 ± 3.5 TL 17.5 ± 3.4	VII		Holocene Luvisol	WEICHSELIAN
TL 13.3 ± 3.0	VI-E		'Nagelbeek horizont'	
	VI-D	*		
	VI-B/C			
	VI-A	Ⓙ Ⓔ	'Warneton'	
TL > 75	V-B	*	'Rocourt' Luvisol	SAALIAN
	V-A	*	Luvisol	
TL 270 ± 22 ESR 220 ± 40	IV-C-III	* Ⓐ Ⓓ Ⓕ Ⓗ Ⓚ		
	IV-C-II			
	IV-C-I	* Ⓑ Ⓒ Ⓖ		
	IV-B			
	IV-A III-B	*		
	III-A	*		

fig. 5.6

Stratification of the Belvédère quarry near Maastricht.

Top: idealised sequence of the various geological units indicating the stratigraphic positions
of the various findspots. Overlying the Meuse gravels of Unit III are the fine sands and clays
representing the most important find horizon (Unit IV). Above lie deposits laid down during
the penultimate glacial (Unit V) and the last glacial (Units VI and VII). The uppermost unit (VII)
consists of loess, which was deposited between around 20,000 and 16,000 years ago.

Bottom: section showing the stratification; the light band is the calcareous tufa of Unit IV.

Maastricht-Belvédère

The loess and gravel quarry Belvédère near Maastricht was subjected to thorough geological and archaeological research in the 1980s (fig. 5.6 and plate 8E).[22] Between 1981 and 1990 twelve 'sites' were investigated in an area of about 6 hectares. The most important archaeological and palaeontological assemblage was embedded in fine-grained deposits laid down by the river Meuse and was covered by a thick layer of loess-like sediments dating from the penultimate and last glaciations.

About 250,000 years ago, the area where the quarry lies today was a densely vegetated backswamp of the sluggishly meandering Meuse. This landscape, transected by many former river courses that were then slowly silting up, was surrounded by deciduous forests and tracts of more open land in the higher parts. The remains of twenty mammal species and more than seventy mollusc species were identified in the excavations. The mammal remains tell us what animals roamed across this landscape. They included straight-tusked elephant (*Elephas antiquus*), steppe rhinoceros (*Dicerorhinus hemitoechus*), giant deer (*Cervus giganteus*), bear and bison. The archaeological remains show that humans, too, populated this landscape.

Thanks to the detailed geological research that has been carried out in the quarry, and the use of various relative and absolute dating methods, we are well informed about the age of the most important occupation phase (fig. 5.6a). The fluviatile deposits in which the archaeological remains were embedded form part of a sequence of river terraces. After laying down loam and fine sands, the Meuse cut deep into its deposits on at least two occasions. The archaeological remains were moreover covered with layers of loess in two separate cold periods. This stratigraphic evidence yielded a first rough indication of the date of the occupation period. A more accurate date was provided by the rich faunal remains contained in the deposits: the remains of small rodents (mice and water vole), for example, were found to derive from more primitive individuals than those found in the ice-pushed ridges in the central part of the Netherlands. And as the Belvédère fauna dates from an interglacial, the archaeological remains could consequently be dated to a warm phase before the advance of the Saalian ice sheets. The absolute date of this interglacial has been determined with the aid of, amongst other evidence, thermoluminescence dates obtained for burned flints recovered in the excavations. These flints yielded a TL age of 250 ± 22 Kyr for the important oldest assemblage.[23] This assemblage – which will be discussed in greater detail below – hence dates from an interglacial around 250,000 years ago.

The quarry contained several more assemblages. Of a slightly older date are a few artefacts recovered from the underlying gravels, which were laid down in the preceding cold phase. The several thousands of artefacts that came to light in an excavation at the base of the loess dating from the last glaciation (site J) are 'only' 80,000 years old. After the most important assemblage had been covered with sediments, the river cut many metres into its bed; site J was hence originally situated not in the river plain, but on its high edge.

The remains of human activity in the former river valley consist of concentrations of debitage, stone tools, bones, charcoal and, at one site, haematite (red ochre). The latter may have been imported from the Ardennes via the Meuse valley. Most of the assemblages are the remains of very brief visits. Highly spectacular is the way in which the assemblages have been preserved for a quarter of a million years: lying in the floodplain of the Meuse they were covered with a thin layer of sediments every time the river flooded its banks and so they very soon became 'sealed'.

What makes these sites in the Belvédère quarry, so perfectly preserved by Palaeolithic standards, so unusual is their short time span combined with their practically undisturbed spatial patterns. Excellently preserved by geological processes, they provide snapshots of the lives of hunter-gatherers in a distant past. One of the finest sites in Northwest Europe that have provided similar snapshots is Boxgrove, which we have already come across above.

On closer inspection, the excavated Belvédère flint scatters proved to differ considerably from one another. Some consisted of the debris formed in the knapping of a single flint nodule, whereas others comprised several spatially distinct scatters, each from a different lump of flint. A few included several tools and/or burned flint and bone besides debitage. None however included the features of spatial structures such as hearths or huts. Nevertheless, certain spatial aspects of human behaviour could be reconstructed at some of the sites. At site K, for exam-

fig. 5.7

The sites in the Belvédère quarry were covered by sediments so shortly after the period of occupation that even the finest debitage was found in exactly the same place where it was discarded 250,000 years ago. Visible at site C were the areas where flint nodules, picked up in the surrounding hills, were knapped on the bank of the river. Some of the flakes were used at the site itself. The lines connect flakes that could be refitted.

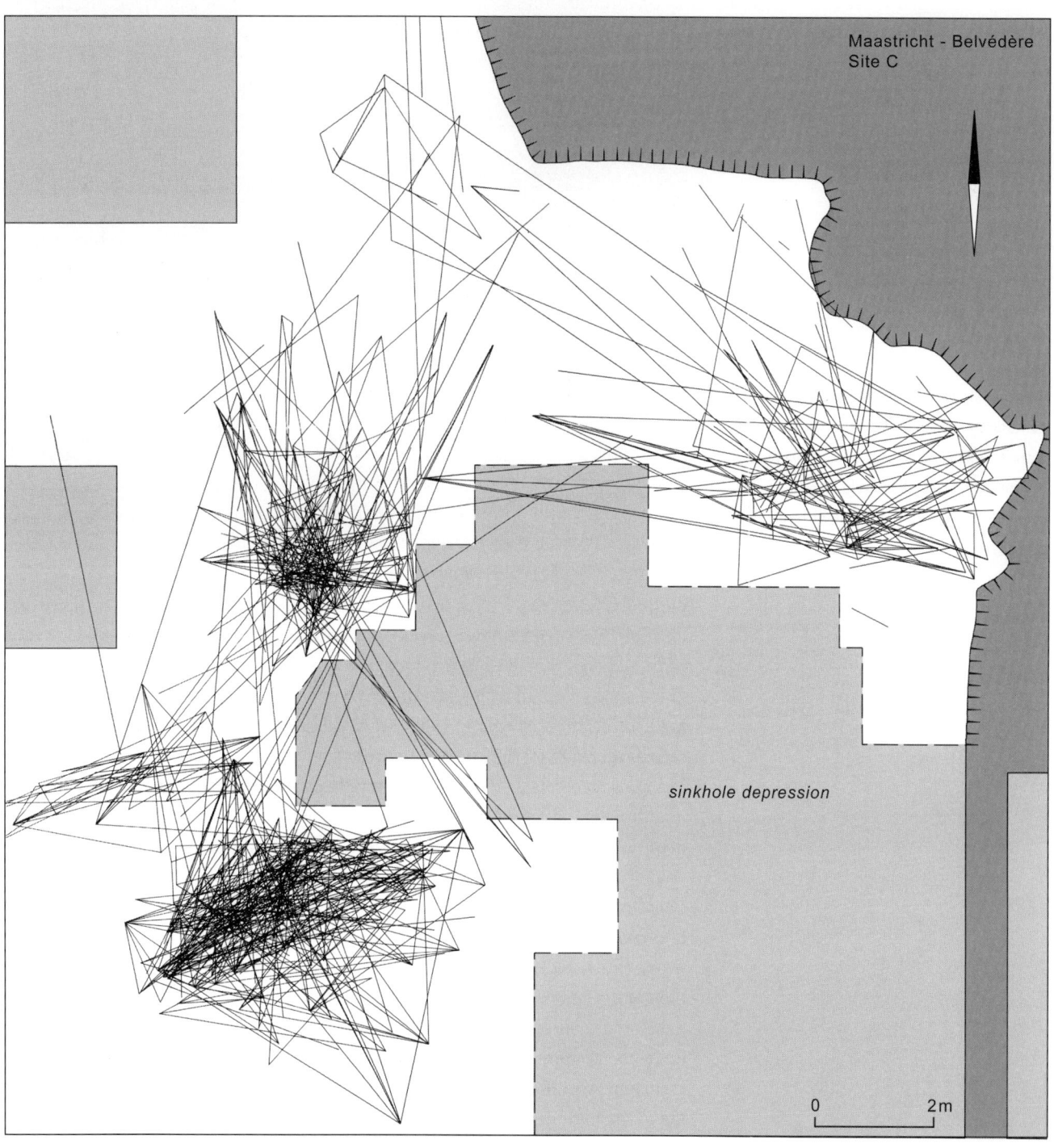

Maastricht - Belvédère
Site C

sinkhole depression

0   2m

fig. 5.8
Refitting shows how people in former days manufactured their tools. Here the researcher Dimitri DeLoecker shows a set of 162 pieces of flint from site C that could be refitted. The core was not found; it was evidently taken elsewhere.

ple, it was found that a large number of flint nodules had been taken to a particular location, where the flint was divided into coarse blocks – cores – after which each of these cores was used to produce flakes at different locations. The many tools that were discovered at this site did however not derive from these cores; they were made of a different type of flint and could not be refitted to any of the nodules reconstructed from the large quantities of debitage. These tools must hence have been produced elsewhere and may have been left behind before or after the flint nodules were knapped. Artefacts that are found in association with one another need not necessarily have been produced or used at the same time.

Close study of the flint from site C showed that each block of flint had left a distinct 'impression' in the excavated area (fig. 5.7). For example, all that remained of one of the nodules were cortical flakes; the resultant core had been taken elsewhere (fig. 5.8). In a different case only the core and a few large flakes remained; the greater part of the original block of flint had been used to produce smaller flakes and tools elsewhere. Such sites actually record only certain phases in a flint nodule's 'knapping history'. The knappers carried carefully prepared cores with them wherever they went and struck fresh flakes from them as need dictated. Owing to the high degree of mobility, the different production phases are often spatially separated, as a result of which we are usually able to reconstruct only parts of a nodule's 'biography'.

The fine-grained fluviatile deposits of Belvédère moreover almost everywhere contained artefacts representing a kind of 'background noise'[24] in the form of very sparse scatters of about one tool per several dozen square metres. This background noise was dominated by tools like knives and scrapers, but also included a few small series of flakes that could be fitted together. They indicate that a core was used very briefly to produce flakes at that particular location. Such finds are perhaps to be seen as representing primarily the *use* of tools, while the richer sites with their large quantities of debitage represent essentially the *production* of tools. A good example of the use of tools produced elsewhere is provided by the 'background noise' site G, the only investigated Belvédère site whose faunal remains could with some degree of certainty be interpreted as the remains of butchering (see below).

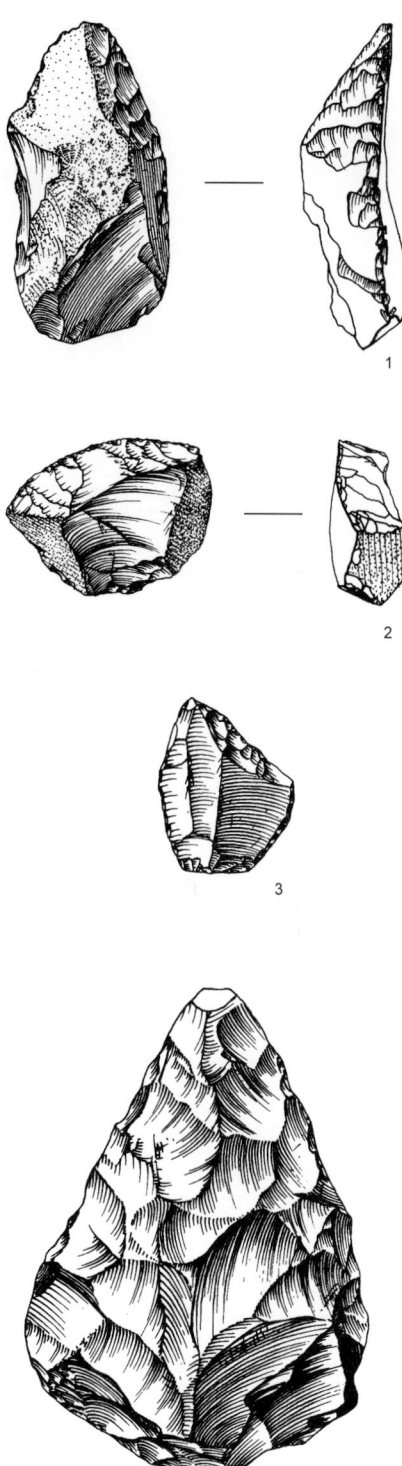

Finds from the ice-pushed ridges in the central part of the Netherlands
Somewhat less informative are the many thousands of Middle Palaeolithic finds that have been discovered by amateur archaeologists since the second half of the 1970s in various sand and gravel quarries in the central part of the Netherlands, in particular near Rhenen and Veenendaal (fig. 5.9). Those flint artefacts come from fluviatile deposits pushed up by the Saalian ice sheets and consequently have a clear *terminus ante quem*: they must date from before the Saalian glaciation, *i.e.* from before 150,000 years ago. Remains of this so-called Rhenen industry seem to occur at all outcrops of the coarse fluviatile deposits of the Urk formation.[25] The flint finds include Levallois flakes, blades and cores, scrapers and a small number of hand axes (plate 8B). A few choppers and chopping tools were made on quartzite pebbles from river gravels. The greater part of the Rhenen industry however consists of flint debitage, washed away from 'workshops' on the former banks of the Rhine and Meuse. An important question concerns the number of different geological phases spanned by these Rhenen artefacts. It would seem that this question cannot yet be satisfactorily answered. Many of the artefacts were found embedded in coarse-grained sediments which also contained fossil mammal remains. Those remains included both 'cold' and 'warm' elements. Typically 'warm' animals are for example straight-tusked elephant (*Elephas antiquus*) and hippopotamus (*Hippopotamus* sp.), while the 'cold' elements include mammoth (*Mammuthus primigenius*), woolly rhinoceros (*Coelodonta antiquitatis*) and musk ox (*Ovibos* aff. *moschatus*). The biostratigraphic contexts of the different species confirmed that faunal remains from different periods had become mixed. The great majority of the remains seem to date from the Saalian, but the remains of hippopotamus and the beaver *Trogontherium cuvieri* must date from an earlier (warmer) phase. Just as the faunal sample constitutes a mixture of remains from different chronological units, so too may the Rhenen industry be the result of different occupation phases, washed together by the river and turned into a large palimpsest spanning many tens of thousands of years in the gravelly sand matrix of the Urk formation.

fig. 5.9
Artefacts recovered from ice-pushed ridges.
Scale 1:2.
1 end-scraper made on a flake
2 large side-scraper
3 truncated flake
4 hand axe

MIDDLE PALAEOLITHIC 'LIFESTYLES'

One of the most important tasks of Palaeolithic archaeologists is to combine the information from such widely divergent sites so as to obtain an impression of the life of the Middle Palaeolithic people who, during their movements across Europe, roamed across the Netherlands, too. For such a synthesis we cannot re-

strict ourselves to the narrow confines of the Netherlands and its immediate surroundings, but must expand our view to encompass the whole of Europe. Much of
present-day Palaeolithic research focuses on three subjects: the natural environment and the great changes it underwent, settlement systems and subsistence. In
the current scenarios for the role of the environment in the evolution of mankind,
the natural surroundings are always the driving force behind changes: those surroundings are thought to determine human behaviour and inspire innovations.
Early humans were considered as slaves to nature, constantly engaged in a strug-
gle for survival. Nature to a large extent determined what resources were available
where and when, and the settlement system ensured that those resources were
exploited as efficiently as possible. The primary aim of special task groups was to
exploit the natural surroundings and it was for this purpose, too, that camps were
moved from one area to another. At odds with this view is a more cultural-anthro-
pological approach based on the assumption that the lives of *present-day* groups
of hunter-gatherers are governed primarily by their relations with other groups
and moreover by a fundamentally different contact with nature, which is often
conceived quite differently than as the supplier of protein of the model described
above. A good example of such a different conception of nature is provided by
the Australian Aborigines' well-known Dreamtime view of their surroundings. In
that Dreamtime, mythic beings shaped the landscape, as it were, leaving behind
conspicuous tangible evidence of their forces. Those traces of their actions still
play an important part in present-day Aboriginal belief. They for example serve
as landmarks in the 'songlines' that guide the Aborigines through their animate
surroundings. It should incidentally be borne in mind that such an outlook is ultimately rooted in the ability to symbolize, a capacity which many experts regard
as unique to modern humans and which Neanderthals and earlier hominids are
believed to have lacked.[26]

NATURAL ENVIRONMENT AND OCCUPATION

The natural environment plays an important part in the discussions about the history of the occupation of northern Europe, a region in which the climatic fluctuations of the Pleistocene had a major impact on the physical world.[27] As already
briefly mentioned in chapter 3, extremely cold (full-glacial) or warm (interglacial)
phases were actually rare in the Pleistocene. The Pleistocene was predominantly
characterised by 'intermediary' conditions that favoured lush steppe vegetations
and large herds of grazing animals, a unique interaction of flora and fauna which
has been described as a 'mammoth steppe'.[28] These intermediary conditions are
thought to have been ideal for pre-modern humans, as large herds implied large
quantities of game for groups who in these northern regions obtained their livelihood from a combination of hunting and scavenging. The proportion of plant
food is believed to have been far smaller in these regions than further south. In the
more extreme phases, activities had to be far more efficiently planned owing to
changes in the range of available food resources. In the coldest phases of the Pleistocene the great biotic diversity of the mammoth steppe declined to some extent,
while the extremely low temperatures implied further difficulties for the occupants
of the northern regions. No large herds of game were to be found in the dense
interglacial forests and the successful 'harvest' and storage of plant resources in
such an environment demanded efficient planning of activities and the integration
of large groups of individuals. According to many experts, only modern humans
are capable of such behaviour. They believe that this is demonstrated by the history

of the occupation of northern Europe, which seems to have been uninhabited in interglacials until modern humans made their appearance. In their opinion the large number of Holocene findspots prove that it was only in the Mesolithic that man managed to successfully adapt to forested environments.

Some however disagree with this view and maintain that various northern European sites convincingly demonstrate that there are no good grounds for assuming major differences in ecological tolerance between 'modern' and 'pre-modern' hominids. There are interglacial sites dating from the very first time of occupation onwards that falsify the above view, such as the aforementioned Boxgrove site, while a few Middle Pleistocene sites demonstrate that these regions were also occupied under extremely cold conditions. The evidence from these sites seems to show that early hominids were familiar with a broad ecological range, but this of course does not necessarily mean that their way of life, for example in forested environments, was comparable with that of modern humans. As we shall see below, archaeological evidence indeed shows that their lifestyle differed in important respects from that of Upper Pleistocene and Holocene hunter-gatherers.

In spite of the considerable ecological tolerance of the Lower and Middle Palaeolithic groups, the plains of northern Europe were not continuously occupied. Settlement showed a kind of ebb and flow pattern: at the beginning of extremely cold phases these regions were gradually abandoned (their occupants moving further south?), to be recolonised by new groups when the climate ameliorated. Only the southern parts of Europe were probably more continuously occupied.

SETTLEMENT PATTERNS

Camps

Palaeolithic archaeology has always concentrated more on the analysis of individual sites than on the way in which early hunter-gatherers wandered across the landscape. That is not so surprising, considering the specific nature of the archaeological evidence. A prerequisite for integrating individual sites within a wide spatial framework is some understanding of such factors as the contemporaneity of sites and, at the level of the site itself, the problem of palimpsests, i.e. the possibility that artefacts found lying close together at a particular site were actually left behind there in different phases and are consequently not contemporary. Archaeological 'time' is entirely different from the concept of time of for example anthropologists, who are able to observe living groups.

Many well-preserved Middle Palaeolithic sites represent short phases of episodic use of locations. At sites such as the aforementioned Boxgrove and Belvédère, short-term activities can sometimes be reconstructed, but no sites have provided evidence for more long-term consistent use of a location as a base camp with dwellings from which a group operated for some time. As already mentioned above, the spatial behaviour of many Lower and early Middle Palaeolithic groups can best be characterised as brief, episodic and highly mobile. We have virtually no indications of structures such as hearths and/or huts for these groups. The scarce features of structures all date from the later phases of the Middle Palaeolithic. This almost complete absence of unambiguous evidence for structures is in marked contrast with the relatively large amount of such evidence that is available for the Upper Palaeolithic. This considerable difference cannot be exclusively attributable to differences in site preservation. A spectacular Middle Palaeolithic exception is Molodova I, in the Russian Plain, where excavators discovered an arrangement of mammoth bones enclosing an oval area measuring 8 by 7 metres, which they interpreted as the remains of a dwelling.[29] This interpretation has however been disputed, one of the grounds being the fact that fifteen hearths were found within and inside the wall of the presumed dwelling. What those hearths do prove beyond doubt is that this site was used on several occasions. Another possible exception is the site Buhlen, near Marburg in Germany, where a ring of dolomite blocks with a diameter of about five metres was discovered in a late Middle Palaeolithic layer. At the centre of this circle was a hearth, which the excavators claim was used at the time when the structure was occupied. In an independent analysis of this structure Stapert recently arrived at the conclusion that the remains indeed represent a 'hut', which in various respects even bore a surprisingly close resemblance to the hut known from the (much later) Magdalenian site Gönnersdorf near Neuwied.[30]

Mobility

Whereas in the past individual sites tended to attract more attention than settlement systems, in the course of the past decade a number of studies have shifted the emphasis more towards 'landscapes'. Data have become available on the distances over which, in the course of the Pleistocene, raw materials were transported from their sources.[31] From the still scarce data from Western and Central Europe we may infer that groups travelled over distances ranging from 80 to more than 100 kilometres in the early phases of the Middle Palaeolithic (fig. 5.10). These distances are based on straight lines, drawn between an artefact's findspot and the source from which the flint was obtained. Such raw material lines run from, for example, the flint area of southern Limburg and Belgium to the Neuwied Basin near Koblenz, i.e. from the *Mittelgebirge* to the edge of the vast North European Plain. Similar raw material lines connecting two different geographic units are known in central Europe too, some covering distances of no less than 200-400 km, for example from the southern edge of the Polish Plain to the mountains in the north of Hungary.[32] The fact that the transport distances in Central Europe are greater than those further west may be attributable to differences in climatic conditions between the two regions and their consequences for the spatial distribution of food resources and hence for the distances covered by hunter-gatherers.[33]

fig.5.10
Tools made of flint from the southern part of Limburg that were found in the Neuwied Basin near Koblenz. Such finds show that during the penultimate glacial, more than 150,000 years ago, groups were already migrating within territories with a diameter of at least 100 kilometres. The illustrated artefacts were found during an excavation in the *Schweinskopf*, the crater of a former volcano. The fills of the craters of the extinct volcanoes in the Eifel region have yielded many Middle Palaeolithic finds. Actual size.

Such raw material lines give us a vague impression of the size of the 'territories' in which people lived. Within those territories certain locations were repeatedly visited, over periods that sometimes spanned thousands of years. La Cotte de St. Brelade (Jersey)[34] and Biache-Saint-Vaast (northern France)[35] are but two examples of the many sites at which assemblages from different occupation phases have been found. Biache is a rich site from the temperate beginning of the penultimate glaciation, a little younger than Belvédère, and like Belvédère well-preserved in the higher parts of fine-grained calcareous fluviatile deposits, in this case of the Scarpe, a tributary of the Scheldt. The site has yielded a vast abundance of flint and bone from different levels, indicating that this location was frequently visited.

An unusual site is La Cotte de St. Brelade, in the southwesternmost tip of the Channel Island Jersey. La Cotte is a T-shaped crevice in a 50-metre-high granite headland projecting into the sea. The fill of this crevice yielded tens of thousands of artefacts which together span almost the entire Middle Palaeolithic. The site's environmental situation was greatly dependent on the sea level, which varied considerably throughout the alternating glacials and interglacials. In most of the interglacials Jersey was an island, as it is today, but when the sea level dropped 15 to 20 metres, the surrounding land emerged from the sea and the island became a peninsula. When the sea level was even lower, La Cotte lay at the centre of a vast plain, several kilometres from the coast. The distance to the coast was very important with respect to the availability of raw materials for the manufacture of stone tools. During interglacials, fresh flint was constantly washed from the surrounding deposits, but in cold phases flint had to be imported from sources 10 to 15 kilometres away. The fill of La Cotte, formed over many tens of thousands of years, clearly shows how the occupants responded to these fluctuations in the availability of raw materials, for example by intensively resharpening used tools in periods in which fresh flint was scarce.

A debatable question is whether such frequently visited sites constituted well-known, fixed points in a settlement system: locations that were known to people, to which they kept returning for specific reasons. The latter seems to have been the case with La Cotte de St. Brelade. It could even be argued that the knowledge about the raw materials in the site's surroundings was passed down from generation to generation, so that every new group knew where they could obtain their flint. That is not so surprising in itself: we know of several sites where many hundreds or even thousands of cores show that sharp flakes that were intended for use elsewhere were produced on a massive scale (i.e. over long periods of time).[36] Such flint procurement sites were undoubtedly fixed, well-known points on the mental maps of early hominids. If some of the other sites were indeed also fixed dots on such 'maps', well-known places within a large area, then it would be logical to assume that people knowingly planned and undertook journeys between these points, for reasons which we will never be able to fully apprehend. Knowledge about the food and raw material resources within the area would be an obvious reason for the adherents of the 'economic' model, but for those who believe that Middle Palaeolithic humans saw their landscape rather like the Dreamtime landscape of the Australian Aborigines, the end point of the raw material lines extending from southern Limburg to the Neuwied Basin could be an interesting source of inspiration: in the latter area the flint artefacts that had been transported over such long distances ended up in the fills of extinct volcanoes, some of which still dominate the surrounding landscape today.[37]

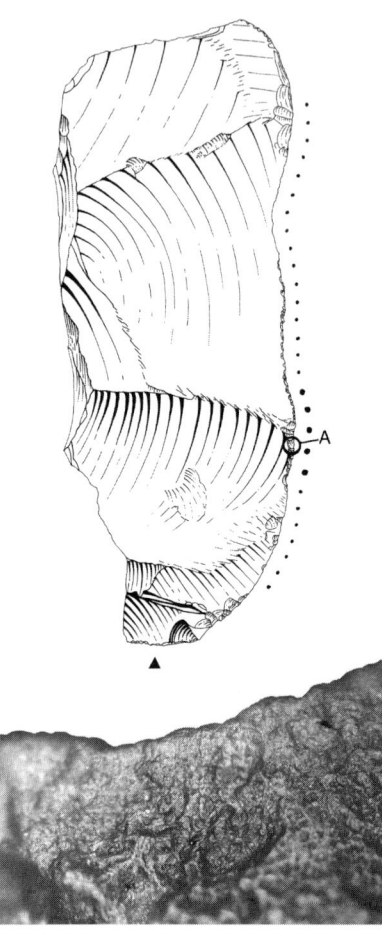

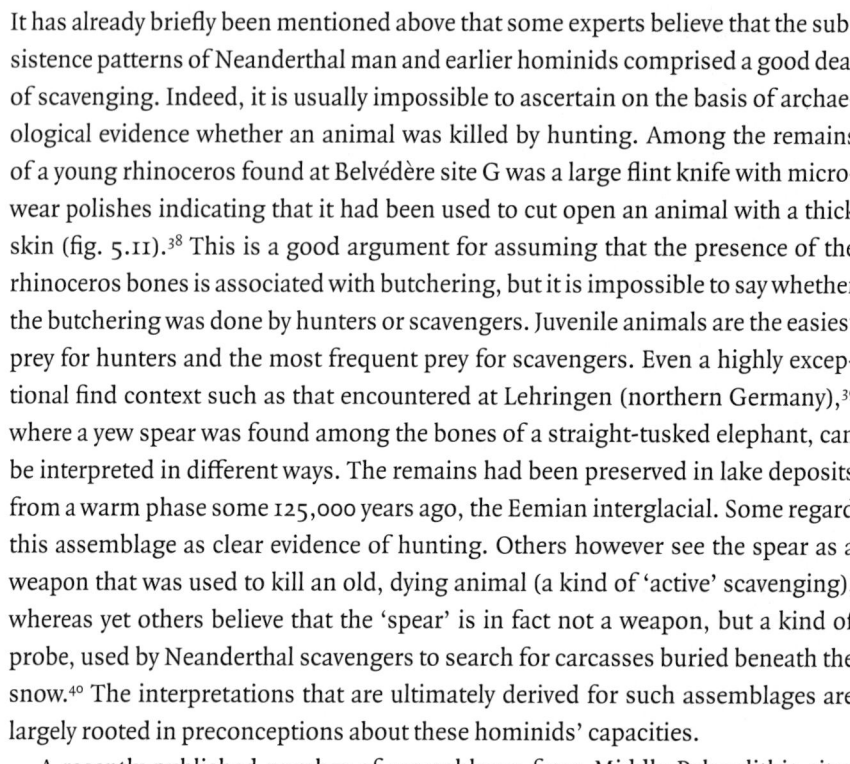

fig. 5.11

A large backed knife (scale 1:2) that was found during the excavation of site G, Maastricht-Belvédère, showing use-wear traces possibly formed in slaughtering a pachyderm. A photo indicating the use-wear traces is shown below (200x enlarged).

It has already briefly been mentioned above that some experts believe that the subsistence patterns of Neanderthal man and earlier hominids comprised a good deal of scavenging. Indeed, it is usually impossible to ascertain on the basis of archaeological evidence whether an animal was killed by hunting. Among the remains of a young rhinoceros found at Belvédère site G was a large flint knife with microwear polishes indicating that it had been used to cut open an animal with a thick skin (fig. 5.11).[38] This is a good argument for assuming that the presence of the rhinoceros bones is associated with butchering, but it is impossible to say whether the butchering was done by hunters or scavengers. Juvenile animals are the easiest prey for hunters and the most frequent prey for scavengers. Even a highly exceptional find context such as that encountered at Lehringen (northern Germany),[39] where a yew spear was found among the bones of a straight-tusked elephant, can be interpreted in different ways. The remains had been preserved in lake deposits from a warm phase some 125,000 years ago, the Eemian interglacial. Some regard this assemblage as clear evidence of hunting. Others however see the spear as a weapon that was used to kill an old, dying animal (a kind of 'active' scavenging), whereas yet others believe that the 'spear' is in fact not a weapon, but a kind of probe, used by Neanderthal scavengers to search for carcasses buried beneath the snow.[40] The interpretations that are ultimately derived for such assemblages are largely rooted in preconceptions about these hominids' capacities.

A recently published number of assemblages from Middle Palaeolithic sites throws a surprising new light on those capacities. The assemblages of these sites, among which are Wallertheim (Germany), Mauran (France) and Ils'kaya (Ukraine),[41] are dominated by the remains of many dozens of bison which were indisputably killed by human activities. At Mauran, in the foothills of the French Pyrenees, excavators found the bones of 83 bison concentrated within an excavated area of only 25 m². This assemblage showed a remarkable resemblance to assemblages known from various North American bison kill sites.[42] It seems that the majority of the animals were driven over a natural cliff in late summer or autumn, after which the animals were butchered in a fairly standard manner. In the 1000 m² still to be investigated the excavators expect to find the bones of about 4000 more bison, the remains of repeated use of this natural trap.

The sites mentioned above all date from the last glaciation: Wallertheim from its earliest phase, while Mauran is probably about 40,000 years old. But we also know of older sites for which recent research has yielded convincing evidence of hunting. The approximately 200,000-year-old site Biache-Saint-Vaast in northern France, for example, yielded numerous bones of bear, aurochs and rhinoceros bearing many cut marks which show that these bones ended up at this site as a result of human activities, most probably active hunting considering the predominance of remains of juvenile-adult animals.[43] The excavators are of the opinion that the composition of the bear remains indicates that these animals were hunted for their fur. Whereas it is often difficult to make sound statements about the involvement of hominids in the formation of faunal assemblages at Lower Palaeolithic sites, we know of many Middle Palaeolithic sites whose bone assemblages provide clear evidence for human activities in the form of cut marks and indications of the deliberate splitting of bones. Together with earlier finds like those from Lehringen, the approximately 350,000-year-old wooden spears that were recently found at the German site Schöningen show with what kind of – archaeologically virtually undetectable, for highly perishable – weapons large mammals may have been hunted (fig. 5.12).[44]

fig. 5.12
In the years 1995-'99 some unique objects came to light in the large lignite quarries near Schöningen, in the easternmost part of Lower Saxony: six complete javelins with lengths of between 1.8 and 2.5 m and two parts of such weapons, all made of pinewood. They were found among the remains of slaughtered horses in 400,000-year-old lacustrine deposits. The weapons were made not from a branch, but from the hardest wood of the tree-trunk, and were well-balanced and beautifully designed. These advanced spears came as a shock to our views on humans in those days.

TO CONCLUDE: ARCHAIC VERSUS MODERN

When we lump together the scarce evidence from 500,000 years of occupation in an attempt to typify 'the' Lower and Middle Palaeolithic we arrive at an 'episodic' use of locations and, at least from the Middle Palaeolithic onwards, a high mobility combined with a broad ecological range and sound indications of the systematic hunting of large mammals. Raw material transfers show that by the Middle Palaeolithic, if not earlier, people were covering large distances, probably between known, fixed points on the hominids' mental maps. The distances over which the raw materials were transported were however much smaller than in some phases of the Upper Palaeolithic, in which for example Mediterranean shells made their way to sites in the German Rhineland. The great distances covered in the Upper Palaeolithic most probably reflect contacts between groups within exchange networks that embraced vast areas. The lack of evidence for such contacts in the Middle Palaeolithic has led some specialists to assume that Middle Palaeolithic humans led a more 'local' existence, in fairly closed communities.[45]

A point that should be borne in mind with respect to what has been said above is that such comparisons can only be made by lumping together the relatively scarce Middle Palaeolithic data from many tens of thousands of years, gathered over vast areas, and setting them alongside the record of 'Upper Palaeolithic humans', who, like their Middle Palaeolithic predecessors, were also active in diverse contexts, over a period of 30,000 years in Europe alone. The American archaeologist M. Conkey coined the term 'spatiotemporal collapse' for such an approach.[46] She pointed out the risk involved in it: by subordinating what were undoubtedly substantial diachronic and synchronic variations within Middle and Upper Palaeolithic communities to a way of thinking in simple contrasts like Middle versus Upper Palaeolithic, 'archaic' versus modern, such pigeonholing in fact sustains our periodisations. The aforementioned divisions are indeed nothing more than working hypotheses, aids in ordering data and presenting archaeological evidence, means for obtaining a better understanding of unknown periods of many thousands of generations ago. Discussions of this kind are all the more emotionally charged in the case of such early periods, because at the end of the day the aforementioned contrasts revolve around one of the most important conceptual differences within our Western culture, namely the difference between human beings and animals, which each time raises questions not only about the past, but also about our own identity.[47]

NOTES

1 Warren 1920.

2 See for example Toth 1991.

3 Swisher *et al.* 1994; Lewin 1994.

4 For a discussion of this issue see Meltzer 1994.

5 For example Rolland 1991; Gamble 1993.

6 See for example various contributions in Bonifay/Vandermeersch 1991.

7 Roebroeks 1994; Roebroeks/Van Kolfschoten 1994; Dennell/Roebroeks 1996.

8 The recently published palaeomagnetic data for the Atapuerca-TD sequence (northern Spain) suggest, however, that the abundant human remains from what is known as the TD6 layer are to be placed *below* the Brunhes-Matuyama boundary, *i.e.* that they are older than about 780,000 years (*cf.* Carbonell *et al.* 1995; Parés/Pérez-González 1995). Earlier palaeomagnetic research had placed the change in polarity much deeper in the sequence and had yielded a date of around 500,000 years BP for the TD6 layer. The great similarity between the fauna of this layer and that of approximately 500,000-year-old sites in other parts of Europe strongly suggests that TD6 was formed around this time (*cf.* Roebroeks/Van Kolfschoten 1995b; Dennell/Roebroeks 1996. The latter publication also contains a detailed discussion of the finds from the surroundings of Orce in the extreme south of Spain, which are allegedly more than one million years old, *cf.* Gibert *et al.* 1994).

9 For speculative answers to this question see *e.g.* Gamble 1995.

10 Boxgrove: Roberts *et al.* 1994; Gamble 1994. Atapuerca: see note 8.

11 Roberts *et al.* 1994.

12 Cordy 1980 and 1981; Cordy/Ulrix-Closset 1981.

13 According to Roebroeks and Stapert (1986), it is extremely doubtful that these stones are artefacts. There is moreover a straightforward, natural explanation for the stones' shapes. They may very well come from an older deposit known from other parts of the Ardennes, which has in the past already yielded many impressive pseudo-artefacts. The stones recovered from the cave fill were found in secondary association with the faunal remains.

14 De Heinzelin 1977; Roebroeks 1989.

15 Peeters *et al.* 1988 have presented a series of finds that allegedly date from earlier phases, but in the author's opinion those finds are a curious combination of pseudo-artefacts and artefact assemblages that have been assigned too early dates.

16 Roebroeks 1980 and 1981; Wouters 1980.

17 See Stapert 1976 for a survey of such natural surface transformations.

18 Ulrix-Closset 1975.

19 Otte 1990.

20 Franssen/Wouters 1978; Stapert 1981 and 1987.

21 See *e.g.* Thieme 1981; Thieme *et al.* 1981.

22 See Roebroeks 1988; Roebroeks *et al.* 1993; De Loecker 1992; Van Kolfschoten/Roebroeks 1985; Vandenberghe *et al.* 1993.

23 1 Kyr or 'kilo year' = 1000 years.

24 This topic is discussed in Roebroeks *et al.* 1992.

25 Stapert 1987; Van Kolfschoten 1981 for faunal remains.

26 See for example Chase/Dibble 1987; Gamble 1993.

27 For a survey of these discussions see Roebroeks *et al.* 1992 and the comments of other workers appended to this *Current Anthropology* article.

28 See *e.g.* Guthrie 1990.

29 See *e.g.* Klein 1973.

30 Stapert 1992a.

31 Geneste 1985 and 1988; Roebroeks *et al.* 1988; Rensink *et al.* 1991; Féblot-Augustins 1993.

33 See *e.g.* Roebroeks *et al.* 1988; Stringer/Gamble 1993.

34 Callow/Conford 1986.

35 Tuffreau/Sommé 1988.

36 An example is the quartzite findspot Reutersruh in Hessen (Germany), published by Luttropp and Bosinski (1971). The 'De Hej' findspot near Sint-Geertruid was probably a similar, smaller-scale, flint procurement site.

37 See *e.g.* Bosinski *et al.* 1986.

38 Van Gijn 1989.

39 Thieme/Veil 1985.

40 Gamble 1987.

41 Gaudzinski 1995; Farizy 1994; Hoffecker *et al.* 1991, respectively.

42 Farizy/Jaubert 1994.

43 See *e.g.* Auguste 1988.

44 Thieme 1997.

45 See *e.g.* Gamble 1992 and 1993.

46 Conkey 1985.

47 See *e.g.* Roebroeks 1994. Since the writing of this chapter a large number of studies have appeared dealing with two important issues

discussed here, 1) the debate on the earliest occupation of Europe and 2) the subsistence strategies of Lower and Middle Palaeolithic hominids. For an up-to-date review of these two topics the reader is referred to Roebroeks 2001, with abundant references to the most recent relevant literature.

6 The first 'modern' humans Upper Palaeolithic

Eelco Rensink and Dick Stapert

THE TRANSITION FROM THE MIDDLE TO THE UPPER PALAEOLITHIC

Around the middle of the last glaciation the climate was a little less cold for a time span of more than ten thousand years; geologists call this period the Middle Pleniglacial. Pollen research has shown that three temperate phases can actually be distinguished within this period in the Netherlands, namely the Moershoofd, Hengelo and Denekamp interstadials, which are separated by colder phases or stadials.

Some time during the Middle Pleniglacial, approximately 35,000 years ago, Neanderthal man became extinct in Northwestern Europe. The first representatives of the present human species, Cro-Magnon man, had arrived in Europe at least five thousand years earlier. Their cultural tradition, which included works of art, is known as the Aurignacian. For a long time, archaeologists presumed more or less *a priori* that the distinctly different Mousterian and Aurignacian cultures were connected with the two anatomically different forms of man (Neanderthal man and 'modern' Cro-Magnon man). However, the transition from the Middle to the Upper Palaeolithic proves to have been a more complex event than originally assumed: there is no simple correlation between anatomy and culture; 'cultural historical' descriptions consequently elucidate only one aspect of this event.[1] Anatomically modern humans had been living in Africa and the Near East for more than 50,000 years already, but as far as we know they did not produce art. The *Homo sapiens sapiens* skulls of Quafzeh and Skhul in Israel (*c.* 90,000 years old) were moreover found in association with a Mousterian industry.

It is likely that acculturation processes played an important part in the transition from the Middle to the Upper Palaeolithic; the last Neanderthals and the first modern humans probably adopted some flint techniques and tool types from each other. One of the explanations for the extinction of the Neanderthals in Europe is that they ultimately proved unable to compete with the socially and communicatively more advanced newcomers. Interesting in this context is that modern man's colonisation of Europe approximately coincided with the appearance of the earliest works of art, some 40,000 years ago. This 'art' is conceived as the material expression of an extensive and complex system of abstract concepts, probably connected with their understanding and explanation of the surrounding world. The newcomers were apparently able to communicate with each other in a more advanced way, by means of a more developed language.

In southwest Europe the Châtelperronian marks the transition from the Middle to the Upper Palaeolithic. From the skull that was discovered at Saint-Césaire we may infer that this was a Neanderthal tradition.[2] In addition to Middle Palaeolithic artefact types, this tradition also includes Upper Palaeolithic types, but no convincing works of art have been associated with it.[3]

In northern and Central Europe the transition is represented by different leaf point traditions.[4] Generally speaking, the bifacially worked leaf points of the 'Mauern type'[5] can be said to be characteristic of the last Middle Palaeolithic in-

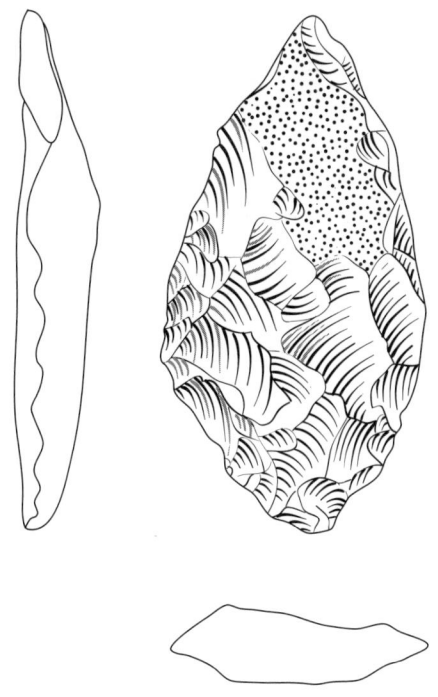

fig. 6.1

The bifacial leaf point dating from the end of the Middle Palaeolithic, *c.* 40,000 years ago, that was found on Leusderheide near Amersfoort. Actual size.

fig. 6.2

Fragment of a unifacial Jerzmanowice leaf point dating from the beginning of the Upper Palaeolithic found on the Aardjesberg near Hilversum. Actual size.

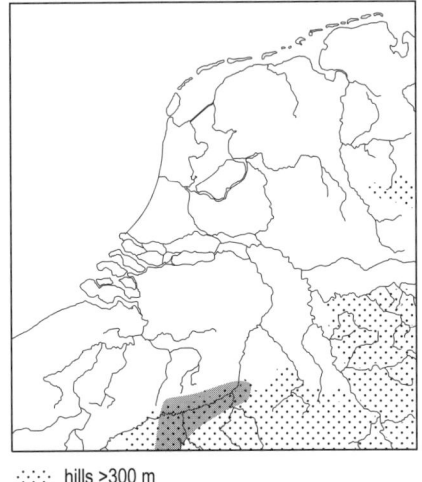

::::: hills >300 m

█ Aurignacian

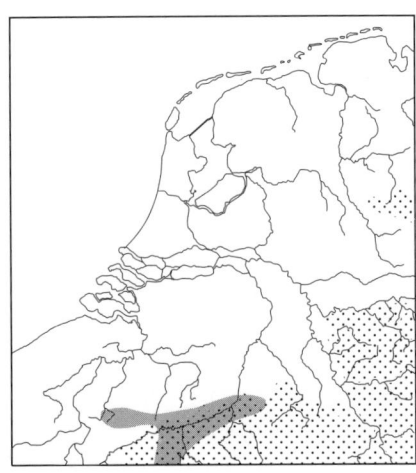

::::: hills >300 m

█ Upper Perigordian

fig. 6.3

Distribution of the Aurignacian and the Upper Perigordian in the Netherlands and its environs.

dustries. By this time, hand axes had become rare; the prevailing artefacts in this tradition are different types of side-scrapers. In the Netherlands, three bifacial leaf points have so far been found: at Eindhoven and Emmen and on the Leusderheide near Amersfoort (fig. 6.1).[6] The earliest Upper Palaeolithic industries include unifacial leaf points made on blades. This type, which we could call the 'Jerzmanowice type', is usually found in association with Upper Palaeolithic types like burins and scrapers. It is well-represented in Germany, Poland, Belgium and England.[7] Only one example is known from the Netherlands: a fragment from the Aardjesberg near Hilversum (fig. 6.2).[8]

In typological terms, the transition from the Middle to the Upper Palaeolithic is consequently characterised by Mauern and Jerzmanowice leaf points. It is, however, tempting to assume, by analogy with the Châtelperronian, that the industries including Jerzmanowice leaf points were still produced by Neanderthals. The fact that leaf points, mostly bifacially worked, have been found at a number of Aurignacian sites in Eastern Europe suggests that the acculturation process may have had a mutual effect.[9]

The four Dutch leaf points are badly weathered: they undoubtedly lay at or near the surface during the cold Upper Pleniglacial. The points indicate that the Netherlands was occupied during the Middle Pleniglacial, roughly between 50,000 and 35,000 years ago. The Jerzmanowice leaf points probably date from the Hengelo interstadial.[10]

The first Upper Palaeolithic tradition 'proper' after this transitional phase, the Aurignacian, is known from the Belgian Ardennes and the German Rhineland, but no convincing evidence for this tradition has yet been found in the Netherlands (fig. 6.3 left). The nearest sites are the Balve cave in the Ruhr area, the loess site Lommersum, to the west of Bonn and some caves in the Ardennes, along the river Meuse, of which Spy near Namen is the most renown. The Netherlands seems to have been situated to the north of the inhabited world. The same caves have been used in the subsequent Upper Perigordian and we know of some open-air sites in Hainaut, like Maisières-Canal, covered by several metres of valley floor deposits (fig. 6.3 right).These find conditions illustrate how many surface sites must have been eroded and silted over under the later periglacial conditions. One or more tools may be datable to an early stage of the Perigordian (Denekamp interstadial). Characteristic of this tradition are the large Font Robert tanged points.[11] The best example of such a point was found at Venray.[12]

During the subsequent Upper Pleniglacial, with the Weichselian glacial maximum, northern Europe was uninhabitable. In this period the Scandinavian ice cap extended to the German Plain and the adjacent areas were polar deserts, unfit for human occupation. The first Upper Palaeolithic communities arrived in Northwest Europe only about 15,000 years ago.[13] Their material remains are grouped into three traditions: the Magdalenian, the Hamburgian and the Creswellian (fig. 6.4).

THE MAGDALENIAN

Introduction

The Magdalenian was named after the French findspot La Madeleine near Tursac in the Dordogne. At the beginning of the twentieth century the French archaeologist H. Breuil divided the Magdalenian into six phases (I-VI).[14] His classic framework is based on the occurrence of certain types of bone points and harpoons.

Artefacts from phases I-III (between approximately 18,000 and 15,000 years ago) have been found mainly in caves and rock shelters in Spain and southern France. The walls of some of these caves are decorated with beautiful paintings of animals and human figures. The caves of Lascaux and Altamira are particularly well-known for their paintings.[15]

No occupation remains from the early phases of the Magdalenian have been found in the Netherlands. Only the southwestern part of Europe was occupied by Magdalenian groups in this period; the climate in the areas further north was probably too cold for permanent occupation. It was not until the end of the Upper Pleniglacial and the beginning of the Late Glacial that hunter-gatherers began to move into parts of Central and Northwest Europe. A number of Magdalenian sites associated with this colonisation phase have been found in the loess region to the north of the Eifel and the Belgian Ardennes: Orp-le-Grand and Kanne in Belgium, Mesch, Sweikhuizen and Eyserheide in the Dutch province of Limburg and Alsdorf in the adjacent German Rhineland. Owing to the absence of organic remains we have no ^{14}C dates, but typological characteristics of the lithic material indicate that the tools were produced in the late phases of the Magdalenian, approximately 15,000-12,000 years ago. These sites all lie along the northwestern periphery of the Magdalenian distribution area.[16]

Magdalenian research in Northwest Europe started in the 19th century. Between 1865 and 1870, E. Dupont investigated several caves containing Magdalenian occupation layers in the valley of the Lesse in the Belgian Ardennes.[17] The richest findspot in this area is Chaleux, where thousands of flint artefacts and bone fragments testify to the cave's long-term and/or frequent use (fig. 6.5). The presence of Magdalenian hunter-gatherers in the middle Rhine region in Germany was first demonstrated by Schaafhausen at Andernach, near Koblenz, in 1888.[18] At a distance of only two kilometres from Andernach, on the other side of the Rhine, lies Gönnersdorf, which was excavated between 1968 and 1976. This site yielded a great accumulation of finds, including hundreds of engraved schist slabs.[19]

The excavation, in 1974, of the site at Alsdorf near Mönchengladbach[20] marked the beginning of Magdalenian research in the loess region. The next sites to be excavated in this region were Orp-le-Grand and Kanne to the west of the Meuse in Belgium.[21] In the Netherlands, the first Magdalenian site was excavated in 1982-'83 near Sweikhuizen.[22] The sites at Mesch (1986) and Eyserheide (1990-'91) were to follow shortly afterwards;[23] they also lie in the hilly region of southern Limburg. The first Magdalenian artefacts discovered in the Netherlands were however not found in Limburg, but in North Brabant. It was in this province, in the 1950s, that artefacts were collected which were later classified as Magdalenian.[24] The site in question, in the Peel region near Griendtsveen, is the only Dutch Magdalenian site that has so far been discovered in the sandy region to the north of the loess.

Tools and raw materials

The Magdalenian sites in the Netherlands have yielded only a faint reflection of the rich material culture that characterises this tradition in southwest Europe. Bone and antler, for example, have not survived in the decalcified loess soils of the Dutch sites. That means that we don't know what animals were hunted in the surroundings of the camps or what types of points and harpoons the hunters used. Also conspicuous is the absence of engravings in stone, which are such a characteristic

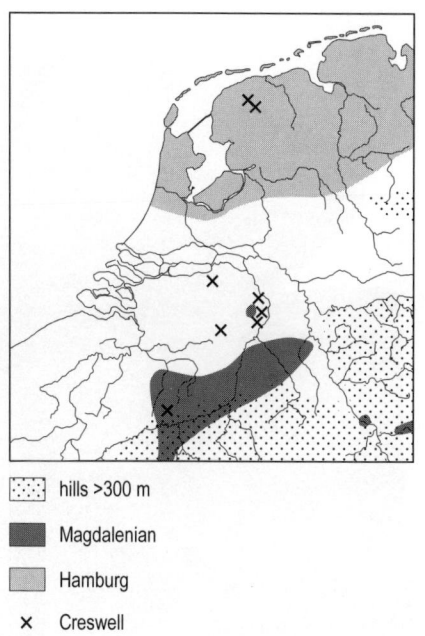

- ⠿ hills >300 m
- ▓ Magdalenian
- ▒ Hamburg
- × Creswell

fig. 6.4

Distribution of the Magdalenian, the Hamburgian and the Creswellian tradition in the Netherlands and its environs.

fig. 6.5

Slab of slate found at Chaleux (Ardennes) showing an incised aurochs and a reindeer or red deer in the background. Total width 80 cm.

Engraved animals and highly stylised female figures are known from several 'large' Magdalenian sites. They are thought to have played a part in rituals, for example during assemblies of different groups at 'aggregation camps'. Such camps are common among present-day hunter-gatherers.

element of the cultural evidence at French and German Magdalenian sites. Our knowledge of the Dutch Magdalenian is consequently based almost exclusively on what can be inferred from the site locations and the flint artefacts.

In the chalk region of southern Limburg, where the sites of Mesch and Eyserheide were found, good-quality flint could be relatively easily collected from colluvial deposits and river terraces. Four types of local flint were used for tool manufacture at Eyserheide, including what is known as 'Simpelveld flint' (fig. 6.6).[25] This laminated flint has its source in a small area to the south of Heerlen; small quantities of artefacts made from this flint could also be collected at Mesch and Sweikhuizen. The greater part of the flint that was used at Mesch came from the gravel deposits of the Voer. At Sweikhuizen, some 10 kilometres to the north of the chalk region, flint was collected mainly from a nearby Meuse terrace. The flint that was used at the open-air sites in the adjacent parts of Germany and Belgium was also mainly of local origin. The flint will have been collected during hunting expeditions or brief explorations of the camps' surroundings.

Besides this local flint, flint of non-local origins was occasionally also discarded at the camps. The assemblages of Sweikhuizen and Griendtsveen were found to include a small number of tools made from exotic fresh-water quartzite, which is most likely to have come from the German Rhineland.[26] Some of the artefacts found at Alsdorf are of Baltic flint from the ground moraine deposits (boulder clay) of the Saalian ice sheets, others were made from *Hornfels* from the surroundings of Mainz; these raw materials were transported over distances of 70 and 200 km, respectively.[27] Also exotic are the more than one hundred pieces of haematite or red ochre that were recorded at Sweikhuizen. At Eyserheide a few stone fragments were found to be covered with this pigment. Exactly where this ochre came from we do not know. It may have been collected in the Meuse region in Belgium (surroundings of Namur) or in the German Eifel during annual migrations.[28]

At the camps the flint nodules were reduced to cores, from which long, regularly shaped blades were struck. The blades were then retouched to form burins, end scrapers, borers and steeply retouched bladelets (fig. 6.7). These types, which are characteristic of Magdalenian assemblages, were encountered at all of the sites in varying numbers. Unfortunately, the patina on the surface of the flints precludes microwear analysis. Only a few artefacts of a black flint that were recovered at Eyserheide showed traces of use. They indicate that the artefacts had been used on antler and dry skins, among other things.[29] Refitting showed that tools like burins and end scrapers were often made, used and discarded at one and the same location. The steeply retouched bladelets, however, formed part of the hunting equipment; they were taken along on hunting expeditions, hafted in arrow shafts.[30]

Site types

The Dutch sites are relatively small, comprising small numbers of tools and no features or other remains of large dwellings or hearths. The only site at which such remains were found is Sweikhuizen-Groene Paal, where hundreds of lumps of quartzite, the largest forming a circular structure with a diameter of three to four metres, were found at the centre of the find scatter.[31] The large stones prob-

fig. 6.6
The Magdalenian site Eyserheide yielded this core of banded Simpelveld flint, to which several flakes and blades could be refitted. Total length of the composition is 20.3 cm. The flint was brought to several sites over distances of 20 km or more, showing that the hunters went to great effort to procure a good supply of high-quality raw materials at their camps. Eyserheide itself is, however, situated close by the source.

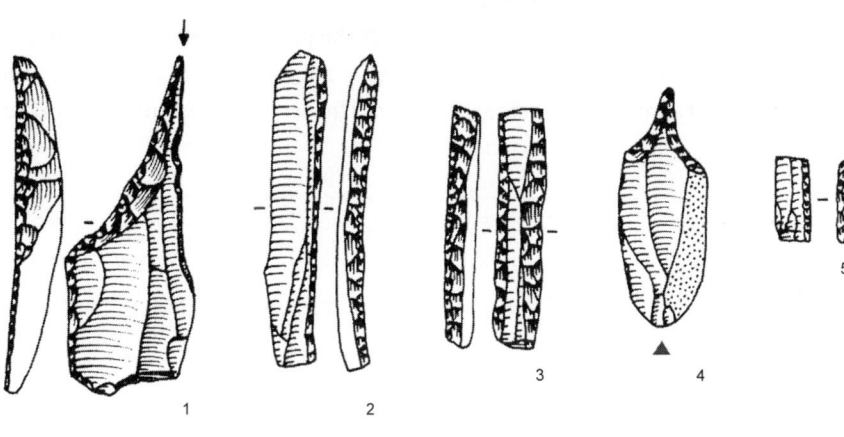

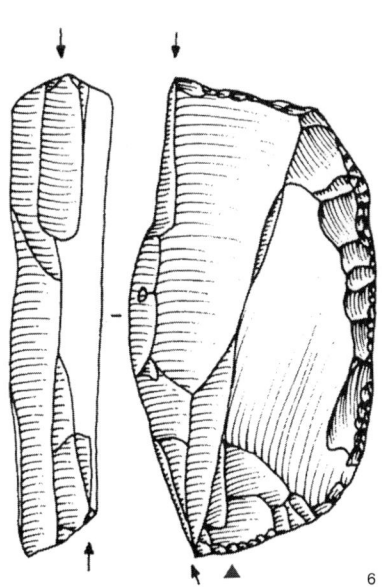

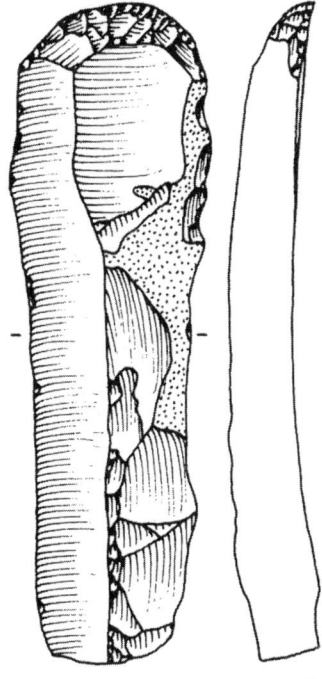

fig. 6.7
Typical Magdalenian artefacts found at Sweikhuizen-Groene Paal (Nos. 1-4, 6-8) and Griendtsveen (No. 5). Actual size.
1 burin on truncation
2 one-sided backed blade
3 two-sided backed blade
4 borer
5 microlithic backed blade
6 double burin
7 end-scraper made on a core preparation blade

ably marked the perimeter of a small tent of skins, whose edges they held down (fig. 6.8). The tent's entrance was probably in the east, where there was a gap in the stone circle. Fragments of a sandstone slab showing traces of burning were found near this entrance. This slab probably indicates the position of the hearth. The distribution of the finds shows that tool manufacture took place predominantly near the entrance, close to where the hearth is assumed to have been. Several steeply retouched bladelets were also recorded in the vicinity of the hearth. They were probably removed from the arrow shafts in order to be replaced by new ones. Relatively few finds came to light in the northwestern part of the stone circle; this may have been where the occupants slept. A concentration of tools found near one of the sides of the tent may represent a storage area.

The excavation at Sweikhuizen yielded information on a Magdalenian settlement that is of great importance in the Dutch context. This is further emphasised by the discovery of two more Magdalenian assemblages 400 metres to the west (Sweikhuizen-Oude Stort) and 200 metres to the east (Sweikhuizen-Koolweg) of the first site.[32] It was found that some flint artefacts from the latter site could be refitted to lithic material from the excavated site. That is an indication that several families camped near Sweikhuizen at the same time.

An isolated site of an entirely different nature was excavated in 1986 to the south of Maastricht near Mesch, at the edge of the plateau above the valley of the Voer, near the Dutch-Belgian border (fig. 6.9).[33] This site yielded a large amount of debitage and some seventy retouched tools. The occurrence of roughly worked

fig. 6.8

Stone circle at the Magdalenian site of Sweikhuizen-Groene Paal. The stones are thought to mark the edges of a tent dwelling. It is assumed that the stones were collected in the surroundings to hold down the edges of skin tents. Different activity areas can be inferred from the distribution of the artefacts. Such reconstructions can be made only if a site is reasonably intact and the positions of the finds are recorded three-dimensionally during the excavation. Scale 1:50. Cf. fig. 6.18.

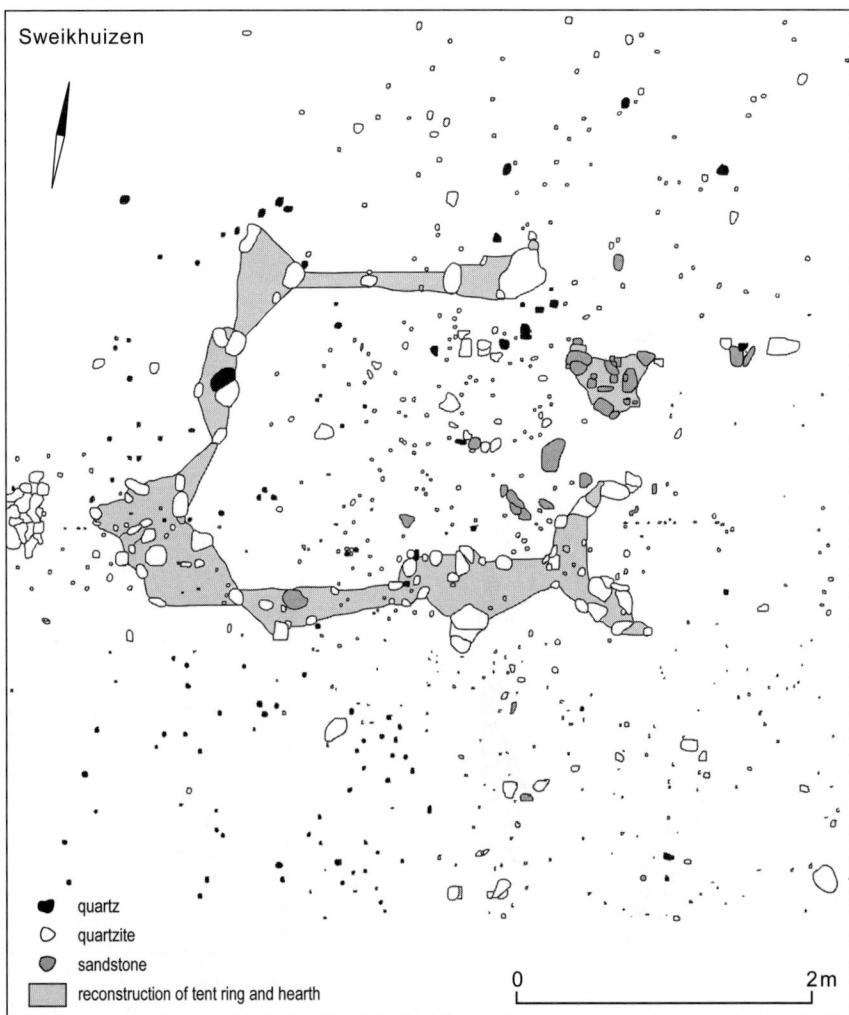

Sweikhuizen

- ● quartz
- ○ quartzite
- ◉ sandstone
- ▨ reconstruction of tent ring and hearth

0   2m

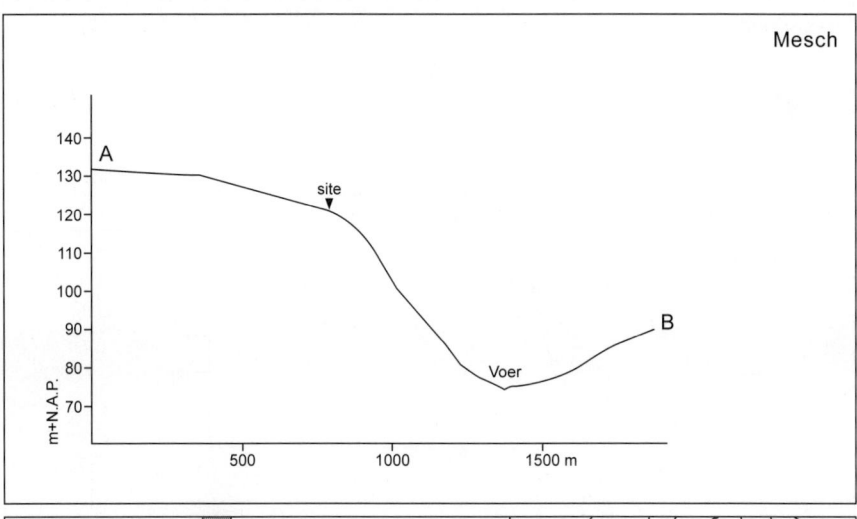

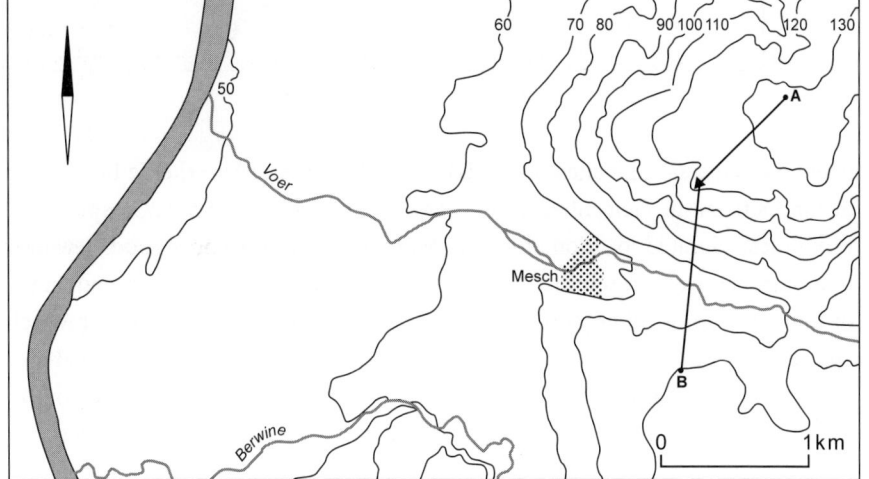

fig. 6.9
Position of the site of Mesch at the edge of a loess plateau approximately 50 metres above the valley floor of the river Voer. It is thought that Magdalenian hunters used this site as an observation stand. Scale 1:50,000.

cores and large flakes with cortex suggests that this was a flint procurement site. Most of the flint was carried up to the site from the valley of the Voer below. Rather conspicuous is the small number of tools in comparison with the large amounts of debitage. This indicates that the tool manufacturers concentrated mainly on the production of blades for future use at other locations, possibly at hunting camps in the valley of the Voer or the valley of the Meuse a little further away.

The excavation at Eyserheide, to the southwest of Heerlen, yielded information on a third type of site.[34] Within a total area of 150 m² two small concentrations of flint artefacts and a zone of more scattered finds came to light. The most important concentration (A) was more or less circular; besides flakes and blades it included some twenty retouched tools. Refitting shows that at least fifteen flint nodules were knapped here, mainly in the western part of the concentration, where the majority of the retouched tools were found (fig. 6.10). Fragments of stones, some showing evidence of burning, were recorded at the centre. These stones may have formed part of a small hearth. The second concentration (B) measured only 1.5 x 0.8 m and yielded relatively few artefacts. Some of those artefacts could be fitted to flints from the first concentration, which probably means that the two concentrations are contemporary. No evidence of a dwelling was found in the excavated part of the Eyserheide site. The finds are probably the remains of a small hunting camp, used by a small number of hunters for a short period of time.

The Magdalenian sites excavated in the hilly landscape of Limburg are all sit-

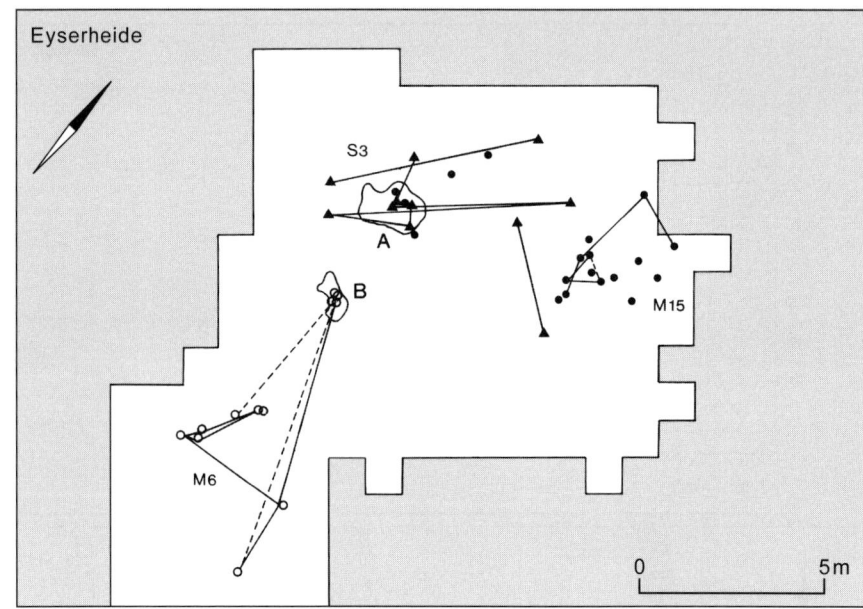

fig. 6.10

Plan of the excavation of the Eyserheide site indicating the recorded artefacts belonging to raw material units M6 and M15 (Meuse flint) and S3 (Simpelveld flint). The artefacts were classified as belonging to these raw material units on the basis of properties of the flint itself (such as colour, inclusions, cortex) and the results of refitting. Refitted artefacts are linked by lines in the figure; the dashed lines connect refitted broken pieces. The plan shows that the cores concerned were knapped in different parts of the excavated area. Scale 1:200.

uated on plateaus. The sites of Sweikhuizen, Mesch and Eyserheide lie at short distances from the Geleenbeek, the Voer river and a deep dry valley, respectively. From these elevated locations the occupants of the camps had a good view over large parts of the surrounding hilly terrain. They will have been able to spot herds of reindeer and/or other game at considerable distances. The location at Mesch appears to have been selected primarily because of the good view it afforded over the Voer valley. That is at least what is suggested by the site's position relative to its surroundings and the archaeological evidence indicating that flint was transported from the valley of the Voer to the edge of the plateau, and that selected blades were then taken to other locations: if this site was indeed an 'observation stand' then the manufacture and use of tools will have been of minor importance there.

The aforementioned sites tell us relatively little about the settlement system. It is likely that there were also camps in the valleys of rivers like the Meuse, the Gulp and the Voer, whose remains now lie buried beneath thick layers of sediment or have disappeared as a result of fluviatile erosion. This view is supported by evidence obtained at a site near Kanne in Belgium, to the southeast of Maastricht,[35] where Magdalenian flint artefacts were discovered in situ in the valley of the rivulet the Jeker during digging operations in 1979. Such chance discoveries are of great importance for our understanding of the diversity of Magdalenian site types. It could well be that there were also camps on the flat parts of the plateaus, whose remains, buried beneath thick layers of loess, have so far remained unobserved.

Subsistence

For a reconstruction of the subsistence economy in the late phases of the Magdalenian we must turn to the faunal evidence from German, Belgian and French sites. At Gönnersdorf the remains of one small dwelling (comparable with that of Sweikhuizen) and three large dwellings were excavated.[36] These remains lay buried beneath a 1.5-2-m thick layer of volcanic ash from the Laacher See volcano, which erupted in the south of the Eifel about 11,000 years ago. Analysis of the faunal sample showed that the occupants had hunted mainly horse and arctic fox. Remains of reindeer, woolly rhinoceros and red deer were found too. Besides food in the form of meat and marrow, these animals will also have yielded skins for clothing and tents. Birds (goose and swan) and fish (trout and burbot) were caught along the Rhine at a short distance from the site. The occupants consequently exploited a broad spectrum of resources. Radiocarbon dates and palynological evidence show that the Gönnersdorf site was occupied in the Bølling interstadial, between approximately 13,000 and 12,300 years ago.[37]

The availability, during the Bølling interstadial, of a wide range of resources in the Late Glacial steppe is confirmed by the results of research that was carried out in the Belgian Ardennes in the 19th century. There the excavator Dupont found large amounts of faunal remains in the cave of Chaleux. As at Gönnersdorf, horse was well represented, but the occupants of this cave had also hunted bovids, fox and reindeer.[38] The ^{14}C dates obtained for Chaleux fall within more or less the same range as those of Gönnersdorf.[39]

Since 1964, well-preserved concentrations of Magdalenian flint artefacts, hearths and bones have been excavated at Pincevent, on the banks of the Seine in the Paris Basin.[40] Instead of the wide diversity of animal resources represented by the faunal remains of Gönnersdorf and Chaleux, the bone spectra of these sites show a marked dominance of reindeer.[41] The camps at Pincevent were occupied in the autumn, in which season the hunters could kill large numbers of reindeer as they passed through that area on their annual migrations. The fact that assemblages were found at different stratigraphic levels shows that people frequently returned to this particular location to intercept the migrating herds. This and the origins of the exotic flint found at Pincevent point to a certain regularity in the communities' annual mobility pattern. As the research in the Paris Basin has concentrated mainly on hunting camps in river valleys, little information has so far been obtained on the resources that were exploited in the other seasons. The sites at Pincevent have been dated to the Older Dryas (approximately 12,200-11,800 years ago), to a phase characterised by climatic deterioration, which may have had an adverse effect on the diversity of the fauna.

The Northwest European context

The geographic situation of the Dutch Magdalenian sites, along the northwestern periphery of this tradition's distribution area, could be termed 'marginal'. Nevertheless, these sites do not form a separate, isolated group. As already mentioned above, similar camps have been excavated in adjacent parts of the loess zone across the Belgian and German borders. Research into the sources of the raw materials has moreover revealed a connection between this northern group and the Magdalenian sites in the middle Rhine region in Germany, about 100-120 km to the southeast: the occupants of the camps at Gönnersdorf and Andernach made extensive use of flint from Limburg, while Sweikhuizen and Griendtsveen yielded a few artefacts of fresh-water quartzite which were probably imported from the German Rhine region.[42] A plausible explanation for these raw material links is that both regions formed part of the annual territory of the same groups of people. They may have lived in the middle Rhine region in some seasons and have exploited regions further north, including the loess region to the north of the Belgian Ardennes and the Eifel, in other parts of the year. This exploitation pattern may have revolved around only one season, possibly on account of a temporary, seasonal, decrease in the amounts of game available in the middle Rhine region.

Noteworthy in this context is that there is a great difference between the types of sites found in these two regions. The – fairly small – sites found in the northern loess region yielded no remains of large dwellings or works of art, whereas both, in particular large numbers of engraved slabs showing animals and highly schematised female figures, were found at Gönnersdorf and Andernach.[43] The explanation for this difference is an important topic for future research. One possibility is that the excavated sites of Gönnersdorf and Andernach are 'aggregation sites', i.e. camps where larger groups of people lived together for certain parts of the year. Such camps are a common phenomenon of present-day hunter-gatherer communities; they are often characterised by the presence of large amounts of refuse. Unfortunately it is not easy to verify whether Gönnersdorf and Andernach were indeed aggregation sites. Both sites were probably used for a long time and/or on several occasions, making it very difficult to make a distinction between finds deposited during one and the same occupation phase.

THE HAMBURGIAN TRADITION

Introduction

In the Netherlands, the line separating the distribution areas of the Magdalenian and Hamburgian cultures coincides roughly with the course of the major rivers, the Hamburgian tradition being the northernmost (fig. 6.4). Hundreds of sites of this 'reindeer-hunting culture' lie, concentrated in five or six groups, within a zone with a width ranging from 200 km to 300 km, extending from the Netherlands, via Germany and Denmark, into Poland. The total distribution area covers between 300,000 and 600,000 km². The Hamburgian tradition must have originated in the middle Magdalenian of Western and Central Europe.[44] This is indicated by for example the results of typological studies of flint, in which shouldered points and other 'northern types' were identified at French Magdalenian sites.[45] The findspot Poggenwisch moreover yielded a decorated antler showing a carved mask-like face,[46] for which the best-known parallels come from Magdalenian (IV) sites in the Pyrenees.[47]

The first Dutch findspot of the Hamburgian tradition to have been identified as an Upper Palaeolithic site is Elspeet on the Veluwe.[48] Of great importance for our understanding of this tradition were the excavations which Alfred Rust carried out in the Ahrensburgian tunnel valley from the 1930s onwards. His publications discussing the sites of Meiendorf, Stellmoor and Poggenwisch[49] are still our best sources of information on the Hamburgians' way of life because they are the only sites with excellent organic preservation. Rust found hundreds of reindeer bones and antlers, but hardly any remains of other animals. He also found many different types of bone and antler tools.

In the 1940s and 1950s a number of Hamburgian sites were excavated in the Netherlands: Gasselte, Havelte-Holtingerzand, Ureterp and Duurswoude.[50] Since the 1970s a whole series of new sites has been excavated in the northern part of the country. The most important of these sites are Oldeholtwolde in Friesland and Luttenberg in Overijssel.[51] Among the others are Sassenhein, which lies a short distance to the south of the city of Groningen, Oosterhesselen, Rolde and Diever in Drenthe and Kolderwolde in the region known as Gaasterland. More than seventy Hamburgian sites are now known in the Netherlands. Ten are situated in the Veluwe, the others lie on the northern boulder clay plateau and its extensions. No remains that can be indisputably associated with this group have been found in the southern part of the Netherlands.

Oldeholtwolde is the only site in the Netherlands for which we have a few ^{14}C dates, obtained from charcoal from the hearth. They are fairly 'young' compared with the dates obtained for sites in Germany and Poland.[52] The best estimate of Oldeholtwolde's ^{14}C age is the average of the three dates that were obtained at Oxford using accelerator mass spectrometry: 11,650 ± 65 BP.[53] This date agrees quite nicely with that previously obtained at Groningen with the aid of the conventional dating method: 11,540 ± 270 BP (GrN-10,274). The standard ^{14}C time scale that has so far been used for the Late Glacial[54] places this date in the first half of the Allerød interstadial, but the stratigraphy of the coversand matrix dates the site to the last part of the Older Dryas. However, new series of radiocarbon dates obtained for pollen samples from sections at Usselo and Achterberg have recently shown that the atmosphere's ^{14}C content varied during the Late Glacial, too, which means that some ^{14}C dates cover long time spans. The radiocarbon dates of Oldeholtwolde may consequently point to dates in the Older Dryas as well as in the Allerød.

Material culture

None of the Dutch sites presented the excellent preservation conditions of Alfred Rust's sites. In the Netherlands, all organic remains (with the exception of charcoal) have disappeared without trace in the sandy soils. But as no research specifically aimed at the recovery of organic remains has so far been carried out in more promising places in the Netherlands, for example in the deposits formed in pingo remnants, organic remains may very well still come to light in the future. Several Hamburgian sites have been discovered on the ramparts of collapsed pingos. Oosterhesselen is an example of such a site in Drenthe.[55]

Typical of the Hamburgian culture are tanged and shouldered points. Such 'northern point types' are usually totally absent or represented by only a small number of artefacts at Magdalenian sites, except at a few very late sites of that tradition. In addition to those points, most flint assemblages of Hamburgian sites contain scrapers on blades, which were used for hide-working,[56] burins, borers and notched flints (fig. 6.11), all of which are also encountered at Magdalenian sites. The asymmetrically pointed Hamburgian borers are usually referred to as *Zinken*. Many archaeologists regard these boring tools as type fossils of the Hamburgian tradition, like the shouldered points, but in actual fact it is virtually impossible to distinguish between *Zinken* and the *becs* (solid borers) of the Magdalenian.

So far, no exotic flint has been found at Hamburgian sites in the Netherlands; all the employed flint was obtained from local boulder clay. We may assume that people set out on expeditions with the specific aim of collecting this flint; we know that they went to considerable effort to select high-quality flint, because most of the flint in the boulder sand had been affected by frost weathering, as a result of which large, intact lumps were fairly rare. As the occupants of these sites used only moraine flint from the boulder clay, we are unable to distinguish between local and imported flint on the basis of raw material properties as at the Magdalenian sites. We can however study the question of import to some extent in an indirect manner, namely by means of refitting, which entails attempting to put matching artefacts back together again. It is from evidence obtained by means of refitting that we know that the points of Oldeholtwolde were not produced at

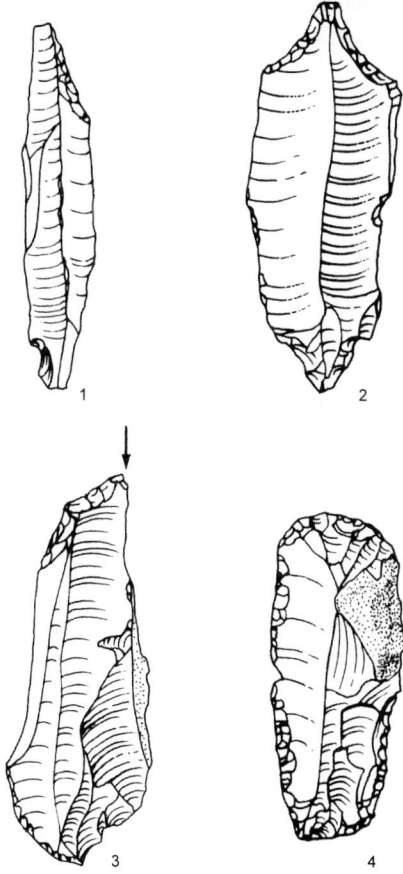

fig. 6.11

Typical Hamburgian tools found at Sassenhein (Gr.). Actual size.

1 shouldered point

2 double *Zinken*

3 burin

4 end-scraper

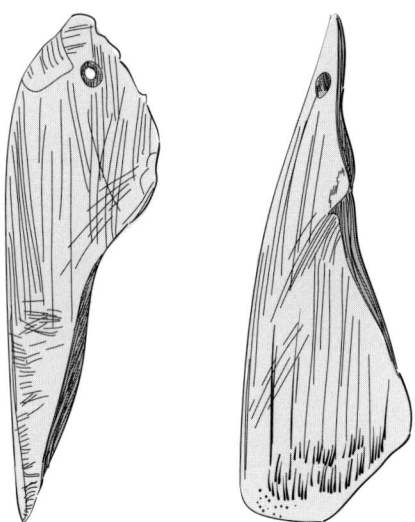

fig. 6.12
Piece of red ochre found at the Hamburgian site of Ees-Vledderveen. It appears to have been deliberately shaped. It has a biconical perforation and may have been used as a pendant. Actual size.

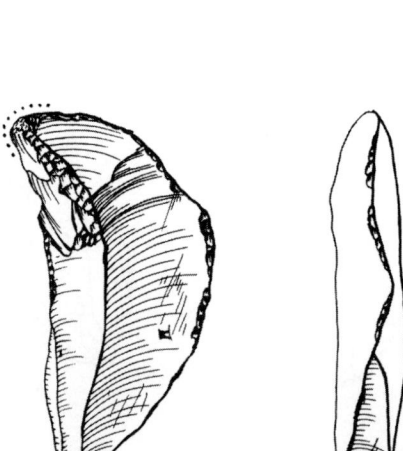

fig. 6.13
Flint flake found at Oldeholtwolde. The rounded edges and other use-wear traces indicate that it was used as a strike-a-light. Actual size.

the site itself, but were all imported from elsewhere.[57] This is also true of many of the scrapers and larger blades. Apparently, the nomadic Hamburgians always took a collection of good tools and blades along with them on their expeditions, in particular tools that were important for hunting. When they settled at a new site they then continued to use their tools for some time until they eventually replaced them by new tools manufactured from locally collected flint. Most borers, burins and notched flints appear to have been made, used and thrown away all at the same site (at least at Oldeholtwolde). They were used mainly for working bone, antler and hides.

Virtually all the other types of stone, such as different types of sandstone and granite, were obtained from local boulder clay and/or boulder sand deposits. As for two other, very rare, categories of materials – amber and ochre – things are somewhat more complex. Amber has been found at at least five Hamburgian sites. The best-known amber object is that which was found at Meiendorf: a small disc with a diameter of about 5.5 cm and a biconical hole in the centre.[58] There were many scratches on the disc, among which Rust claimed to have identified the outlines of a horse's head.[59] In the Netherlands, amber has been found at Ureterp and Ees-Vledderveen.[60]

In principle, this amber may have come from three sources: the former coast,[61] boulder clay deposits or, via exchange, from other (Hamburgian) groups in Sleswig-Holstein and Denmark. The smooth disc of Meiendorf may well have been found along the coast. The find from Ureterp had a weathered surface, which precluded the identification of its source. Amber from the Baltic has also been found at the Creswellian site of Gough's Cave in England.[62]

Most larger Hamburgian sites have yielded a few small lumps of red ochre. Some show one or more rubbing surfaces with subparallel scratches of the kind observable on the illustrated specimens from Ees-Vledderveen and Oldeholtwolde (fig. 6.12). A few lumps of ochre are also known from Havelte-Holtingerzand.[63] The ochre was apparently ground to a powder, which was probably rubbed into reindeer hides to improve their durability.[64] But it may well have been used for other purposes, too, for example to help organic adhesives set.[65] Although ochre, which is a product of weathering that is formed in the soil, can be collected in many areas, it has often been suggested that the larger lumps may have been imported from the Belgian Ardennes, which would imply contacts with the Magdalenian occupants of that area.

Finally, we have some evidence relating to the question as to how the Hamburgians struck fire. As their successors in later prehistoric periods, they probably struck sparks from flint and pyrite. The flints that were used for this purpose can be recognised by their rounded ends. Two such 'strike-a-lights' are known from Oldeholtwolde (fig. 6.13).[66]

Site locations and site types

All of the sites that have been discovered in the northern part of the Netherlands lie in coversand areas: at the surface of or buried within layers of sand deposited by the wind during dry phases (stadials) of the Late Glacial. There must however have been sites in boulder clay areas, too. We know that the Hamburgians obtained their flint from boulder clay and from its residual deposit, boulder sand. Many of the cores that were knapped at the camps must have been partly prepared at the flint procurement sites. Hardly any flintpreparation sites near flint sources have so far been found in the Netherlands, but there must be many.[67] Such sites will generally be poorly recognisable as sites belonging to, for example, the Hamburgian tradition as they will consist predominantly of debitage and will include no or very few diagnostic tools.

For the Hamburgians the most important factor in choosing a location for their camps was the presence of water and brushwood near a natural elevation. An elevated location presented the advantage of good visibility over the surrounding terrain, which was very important for hunters. Most of the known sites were situated on coversand ridges along the edges of valleys, as at Oldeholtwolde (near the rivulet the Tjonger) and Sassenhein (near the rivulet the A in Drenthe). A smaller number were situated on the low ridges of collapsed pingos, as at Oosterhesselen. That this criterion generally implied locations at some distance from boulder clay deposits was apparently not so important. Flint and other lithic material usually had to be carried over distances ranging from a few hundred metres to several kilometres.

The proximity to water implied many advantages besides the availability of drinking water. From the heat-cracked pot boilers that have been found at the sites we may infer that water was also used for cooking; quartz pebbles were often used for this purpose. River and stream valleys moreover attracted thirsty animals, including herds of game during their seasonal migrations. Ideal sites for large-scale reindeer hunting were the places where herds swam across a river. Many examples of Upper Palaeolithic sites of this type, with remains of butchered reindeer, are known, such as the Magdalenian sites of Pincevent in France and the sites in the Ahrensburgian tunnel valley.[68] The reindeer may have been hunted from boats made from reindeer skins.[69] A large portion of the meat may have been dried and stored for consumption during the meagre winter months. The aforementioned sites were probably occupied in the autumn. Another advantage of the edges of valleys was that coppice and brushwood grew in such areas; firewood will have been scarce elsewhere.[70] And, finally, the possibility of fishing will also have been an important consideration for camping near streams and rivers.

Different types of Hamburgian sites are known, but so far no large settlements have been found of the type represented by the Magdalenian site of Gönnersdorf in Germany,[71] whose remains also included numerous works of art. As large sites with remains of dwellings and works of art are well known from other traditions, too, for example the sites of Dolní Vestonice and Mezin, it is odd that no such sites of the Hamburgian tradition have yet come to light. Hamburgian sites are small or medium-sized. A good example of the latter is Oldeholtwolde. At the centre of this site was a hearth (fig. 6.14) consisting of a configuration of stones with a diameter of about 1.5 m, lying in a shallow depression. A conspicuous feature of this hearth, which was otherwise quite similar to many late Magdalenian hearths, such as those of Pincevent[72] was the fact that it had been built from carefully selected thin flat stones. Spatial analysis suggested that the Oldeholtwolde hearth had probably lain out in the open air instead of inside a tent. The same holds for the many hearths at Pincevent.[73]

Small sites often show indications of 'specialisation' in the sense that one or two tool types are dominant while other types are not or virtually not represented.[74] One particular type of small site is characterised by a dominance of points. Such sites may have been hunting camps, where the implements required for hunting were repaired. The somewhat larger sites appear to have been occupied by families; Oldeholtwolde, for example, yielded convincing evidence for the presence of at least one man and one woman as well as at least one child.[75] The same holds for most of the scatters of Pincevent.[76] Some small camps of both the Magdalenian

fig. 6.14

The central part of the hearth at Oldeholtwolde. At the centre was a shallow pit (next to the section) with a diameter of 35 x 50 cm The floor and walls of the pit were lined with flat stones (mainly sandstone) with an average thickness of around 2 cm. Charcoal was found predominantly under the stones in the central pit, which suggests that the stones were heated to grill meat or fish on them.

and the Hamburgian tradition seem to have been occupied by members of one sex only (for example, hunting camps only by men). But gender patterns research is still in its infancy and involves many uncertainties.

Subsistence

Rust's excavations led to the impression that the Hamburgian and Ahrensburgian groups had to an extreme extent specialised in reindeer hunting. This is however rather unlikely. The occupants of the sites in the Ahrensburgian tunnel valley may indeed have been primarily reindeer hunters, for at those sites reindeer were hunted as they passed through that area during their seasonal migrations, in the spring and/or the autumn. The hunting expeditions will not always have been successful because reindeer populations show dramatic, short-term fluctuations. There will hence have been years in which only few animals were killed, even during their seasonal migrations.[77] There are indeed indications suggesting that the Hamburgian occupants of Meiendorf suffered food shortages: at that site the killed reindeer had been extremely intensively exploited.[78]

What should also be borne in mind is that very little is known about subsistence patterns in the other seasons (winter and summer). It would seem obvious that other animals besides reindeer were hunted. Fishing was probably far more important than is often assumed. The site at Meiendorf indeed yielded a few fish bones. No bones have been preserved at the Dutch sites. On some of the flint artefacts from Oldeholtwolde (a few blades, an obliquely truncated blade and a few notched pieces) microwear patterns indicate that those artefacts had been used to process fish.[79] Plant food and fowl will have been consumed too. At Oldeholtwolde, for example, a dense concentration was found of some hundred small round stones which are believed to be gastroliths: stones from birds' stomachs.[80]

The employed hunting techniques have been a source of much speculation over the years. Besides individual stalking, communal hunting will probably have been practised; perhaps large-scale drives were organised, too, especially in the spring and autumn. The Hamburgian hunters certainly had throwing and thrusting spears as well as harpoons. We know for sure that the Ahrensburgian hunters used bows and arrows, but whether the Hamburgians did, too, is less certain.[81] We have some indirect evidence for the last phase of the Hamburgian tradition, the Havelte phase, which is not represented at Rust's classic sites. The range of projectiles used in this phase included tanged points. The site at Luttenberg yielded two 'arrow shaft polishers': sandstones containing approximately 1-cm-wide grooves that are assumed to have been used to smoothen arrow shafts (fig. 6.15). If these objects were indeed used for that purpose this would mean that the bow and arrow were invented in the Older Dryas already. Further indirect evidence is provided by the stray points that have come to light in many places, such as the (broken) tanged point from Slochteren: arrows were more frequently lost than spears.

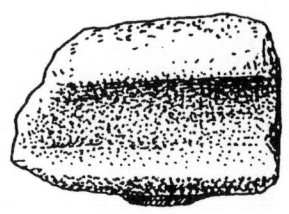

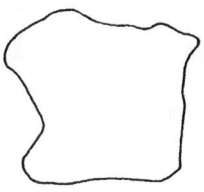

fig. 6.15
Piece of sharp sandstone found at the Hamburgian site Luttenberg. The stone contains three grooves with a width of about 1 cm, which may have been used for smoothing arrow shafts. Actual size.

The Northwest European context

The sites of the Hamburgian tradition have been divided into regional or chronological groups in different ways.[82] The evidence available in the Netherlands does not allow us to distinguish more than two phases: the Ureterp phase and the Havelte phase. The Ureterp phase can be roughly dated to the Bølling interstadial on the basis of the dates obtained for comparable sites in Germany.[83] Tanged points were rare in this phase; most of the points are different variants of shouldered points. In the later Havelte phase other types of points started to be used, as well, such as tanged points, Creswellian points and Tjongerian/Gravettian points.

The excavations at Oldeholtwolde and Luttenberg have yielded evidence with respect to the dating of the Havelte phase. On stratigraphic grounds this phase can be placed in the Older Dryas.[84] In this stadial, which lasted for only a few centuries, conditions were too dry, rather than too cold, to allow a forest to develop.[85] Coversand (Younger Coversand I) was deposited over the whole of the North European Plain and it is in that coversand that the artefacts of Oldeholtwolde and Luttenberg were found.

This evidence implies that the Hamburgian people lived in the Netherlands not only during an interstadial, but also during a stadial. Until recently it was always assumed that northern Europe was unfit for occupation during the Older Dryas, but this was apparently only true in the eastern half of the distribution area of the Hamburgian culture, as sites from the Havelte phase have been found only in the westernmost part of that area. The climatic conditions may have been more favourable – less dry and less continental – in the west than further east.

As only part of the distribution area of the Hamburgian tradition is known, it is difficult to place the Dutch Hamburgian sites in a Northwest European context. In the period in question the sea level was at least 50 m lower than it is today and the southern part of the North Sea basin was dry. The coastline must have run somewhere near the northern point of Denmark. It is very likely that bearers of the Hamburgian tradition lived in parts of the North Sea basin that now lie submerged beneath the sea. The northwesternmost site of this tradition found in the Netherlands lies on the island of Texel.[86] The Danish sites, such as Jels,[87] support

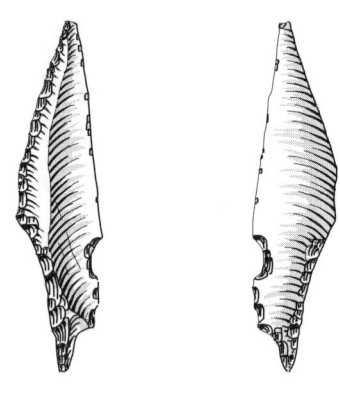

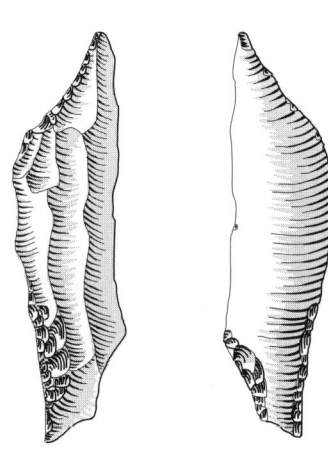

fig. 6.16
Two points from Luttenberg; a notched tanged point above, and a tanged point below. Hamburg culture. Actual size.

the conclusion that the North Sea basin was once occupied. It is quite possible that more inaccessible sites lie buried beneath the Holocene deposits in the clay regions in the northern and western parts of the Netherlands or beneath the water of the IJsselmeer.

Part of the Hamburgian population may have moved around according to a pattern of seasonal migration rather like that known from many Eskimo groups, for example living in the interior in the summer and along the coast in the winter. The Dutch sites, however, suggest that this is not likely to have been the case in the Netherlands. With most subrecent hunter-gatherer communities that practised such a system of seasonal migration the distance between the summer and winter habitation areas was less than 200 km, usually around 100 km.[88] The distance between the Dutch sites and the former coast is much greater, although we should allow for the possible existence of deep inlets. For the time being the most likely conclusion is that the Hamburgians whose camps have been found in the northern part of the Netherlands lived in the interior the whole year round, just like for example the Nunamiut Eskimos.

We have very little information as to whether – and, if so, how – Hamburgian groups maintained contacts with Magdalenian groups. There is little evidence for the exchange of materials. If the ochre found at Hamburgian sites indeed came from the Belgian Ardennes it could be an indication of exchange. The small lumps of amber that have been found at a few Magdalenian sites may also point to contacts between the two groups. Some archaeologists are of the opinion that while some Hamburgian groups migrated westwards when the climate became dryer and colder in the Older Dryas, others moved south in search of a better environment. Of relevance in this context are some Magdalenian sites dating from around this time have been found to the south of the area of the Hamburgian tradition, for example Marsangy[89] and Cepoy[90] in northern France. These sites, which date from the last phase of the Magdalenian, yielded point types that are usually associated with the Hamburgian and Creswellian traditions: shouldered points, tanged points and Creswellian and Cheddarian points. They may reflect an influx of people from the Hamburgian area into the Magdalenian area during the Older Dryas.

The composition of the assemblages from the aforementioned Dutch sites from this period may also present indications of mobility. The assemblages of the Havelte phase for example show a wider range of point types than earlier assemblages. Moreover, considerable differences in point styles are observable between sites which differ only little from one another in chronological terms. The artefacts from Oldeholtwolde, for example, include many tanged points and a few Tjongerian/Gravettian points, whereas those from Luttenberg include the same types plus a few Creswellian points and also unusual artefacts combining traits of shouldered points and Creswellian points (fig. 6.16).[91]

There is also evidence suggesting the movement of people in the opposite direction, i.e. northwards, around the end of the Older Dryas. That would imply that when the Low Countries became forested again, at the beginning the Allerød interstadial, the people of the Havelte phase followed the reindeer north. Sites like Jels in Denmark, where tanged points were the chief 'projectiles', could very well date from the early phase of the Allerød interstadial. In that region the people of the Brommian tradition[92] will then have continued to use tanged points during the remaining part of the Allerød, while the groups then living in the Netherlands started to use Tjongerian points and similar artefacts.

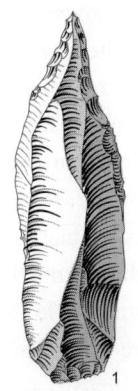 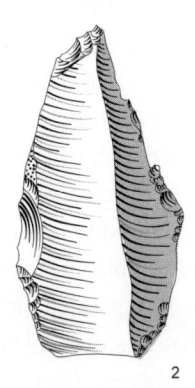 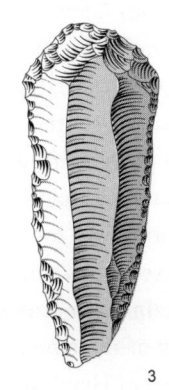 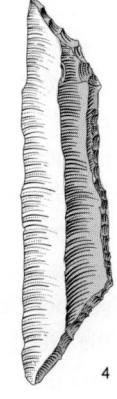

fig. 6.17

Typical Creswellian tools found at the Zeijen site. Actual size.

1 borer
2 burin
3 end-scraper
4 Cheddar point

THE CRESWELLIAN TRADITION

The Creswellian tradition, which is represented mainly in England, was largely contemporary with the Hamburgian tradition.[93] This tradition seems to have originated in the middle Magdalenian, too. And, like the Hamburgian tradition, it can be split into two phases. The earliest phase, datable to the Bølling interstadial, is characterised by the frequent occurrence of points with two obliquely truncated ends known as Cheddarian points. These points gradually went out of use in the later phase (Older Dryas and probably the first half of the Allerød), when points with one obliquely truncated end, known as Creswellian points, and other types

Zeijen

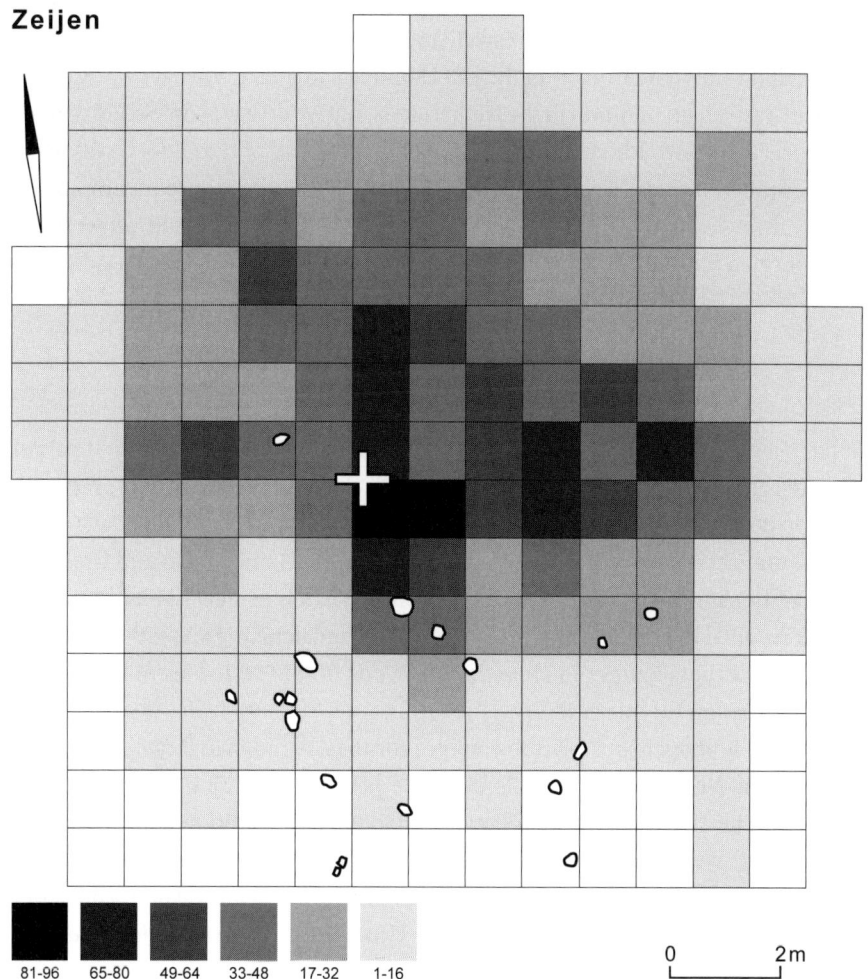

| 81-96 | 65-80 | 49-64 | 33-48 | 17-32 | 1-16 |

0   2m

fig. 6.18

The Hamburgian site of Zeijen consisted of a concentration of flint artefacts (in numbers per m²) next to a ring of large stones (white). Although some of the stones appear to have been moved, their distribution suggests that they held down the edges of a tent with a diameter of about 3.5 m. The cross indicates the approximate location of a hearth. *Cf.* fig. 6.8.

became more common. A few sites found in the Netherlands and Belgium could be ascribed to this tradition, although some archaeologists associate them with the *Federmesser* (or Tjongerian) tradition.[94] In the Netherlands these sits are 'Op de Hees' near Tienray in the southern part of the country[95] and Siegerswoude,[96] Emmerhout and Zeijen in the northern part.[97] The lithic material from these sites is clearly of a different nature than that from the *Federmesser* sites in those same areas; it shows more affinities with the Hamburgian tradition. Most of the assemblages for example comprise mainly scrapers made on blades; some also include tanged scrapers. They contain no or only very few Tjongerian points. Also remarkable is the excellent quality of the type of flint that was used to manufacture the tools. The same can be said of Hamburgian assemblages, but the flint of *Federmesser* assemblages is on the whole of poorer quality. Siegerswoude and Emmerhout are small, specialised sites with a predominance of points. Sites of this kind may have been hunting camps. Zeijen is a medium-sized site which yielded over 4000 artefacts representing a more 'normal' tool kit. The range of point types is interesting as it includes Cheddarian points besides Creswellian points and long B points (fig. 6.17). If we compare this evidence with the sequence set up for England, Zeijen could be one of the oldest Creswellian sites in the Netherlands, because in England the early phase of the Creswellian culture is characterised by a predominance of Cheddarian points. Zeijen is moreover one of the very few sites in the Netherlands to have yielded reasonably convincing evidence for a tent in the form of a ring of large stones which probably served to hold down the tent's skin coverings (fig. 6.18).[98] The densest artefact concentration lay 1 to 2 m outside this tent ring.

In the Netherlands, the Creswellian phase probably lasted for only a short period. As already mentioned above, some of the sites of the Havelte group, such as Luttenberg, yielded a few Creswellian points. That would suggest that the Creswellian sites date from after the last Hamburgian phase. We have no ^{14}C dates for the Creswellian tradition in the Netherlands, but we do have some stratigraphic evidence. Siegerswoude cannot date from before the end of the Older Dryas while Emmerhout can probably be dated to the Allerød. These sites consequently appear to date from the first half of the Allerød, immediately after the Havelte phase of the Hamburgian tradition and just before the appearance of the *Federmesser* tradition.

CONCLUSION

It has been suggested above that the Older Dryas and possibly also the first part of the Allerød were characterised by a considerable degree of mobility. The great variation in point types at different sites and the relatively rapid changes in their stylistic features seem to indicate that some groups of the Hamburgian and Creswellian traditions living in the Netherlands went in search of new habitation areas, which resulted in contacts and exchange with Magdalenian groups.[99] At present, the rather abrupt changes in climatic conditions in this period seem to offer the best explanation for this mobility.

A far more homogeneous picture emerges for the Allerød over large parts of Europe. In the Netherlands, the Allerød is the period of the Tjongerian tradition, which will be discussed in the following chapter. That tradition shows close affinities with what is in other parts of Europe known as the Azilian (France) or the *Federmesser* tradition (Germany). The trend towards greater cultural uniformity over a large area, for which we do not yet have a satisfactory explanation, is sometimes referred to as the 'Azilinisation process'.

NOTES

1 Mellars/Stringer 1989; Mellars 1990.

2 For example Léveque/Vandermeersch 1980; for a discussion see Mellars 1989.

3 Bosinski 1987.

4 Allsworth-Jones 1986.

5 For example Bohmers 1951.

6 Eindhoven: Roebroeks 1986b; Emmen: Beuker/Niekus 1994; Leusderheide: Stapert et al. 1993.

7 Chmielewski 1961; Hülle 1977; Jacobi 1990; Otte 1985.

8 Stapert 1992b.

9 Oliva 1990.

10 The best ^{14}C date was obtained for Jerzmanowice 6: 38,500 ± 1240 BP (GrN-2181); see Vogel/Waterbolk 1964.

11 Otte 1984a; Haesaerts/de Heinzelin 1979; Günther 1964; Hahn 1974.

12 Driessens 1982.

13 Burdukiewicz 1986; Rensink 1993.

14 Breuil 1912.

15 Leroi-Gourhan 1982.

16 Arts/Deeben 1987a; Rensink 1993.

17 Dupont 1872.

18 Schaaffhausen 1888.

19 Bosinski 1979.

20 Löhr 1979.

21 Vermeersch et al. 1985, 1987.

22 Arts/Deeben 1987b.

23 Rensink 1986, 1991, 1992.

24 Wouters 1983.

25 Arora/Franzen 1987.

26 Arts/Deeben 1983, 1987b, 63-66.

27 Löhr 1979.

28 Bakels 1978; Arts 1988.

29 M. van Poecke, pers. com.

30 cf. Leroi-Gourhan 1983.

31 Arts/Deeben 1987b

32 Arts/Deeben 1987b; Wouters 1985.

33 Rensink 1986, 1991.

34 Rensink 1992.

35 Vermeersch et al. 1985.

36 Bosinski 1979.

37 Brunnacker 1978.

38 Dewez 1987.

39 Charles 1993.

40 Leroi-Gourhan/Brézillon 1966, 1972; Audouze 1987.

41 Audouze/Enloe 1991.

42 Floss 1990.

43 Bosinski/Fischer 1980 ; Rensink 1993.

44 Burdukiewicz 1987.

45 For example Kobusiewicz 1983.

46 Rust 1951; 1958.

47 Bosinski 1978; 1982. The harpoon with a single row of barbs from Meiendorf has also often been interpreted as based on Magdalenian examples, but this is probably incorrect (Julien 1982). The harpoon may in fact belong to the Ahrensburgian tradition (Tromnau 1992).

48 Popping 1931.

49 Rust 1937; 1943; 1958; 1962. The 'Ahrensburg tunnel valley' is a valley, scoured in the subsoil by meltwater below the edge of the Weichsel ice cap. There are ponds in the valley fill, which probably originate from large ice blocks (so-caled Toteislöcher).

50 Gasselte: Van Giffen 1948. Havelte-Holtingerzand: Voerman 1937; Van Giffen et al. 1951. Ureterp: Bohmers 1947. Duurswoude: Bohmers/Houtsma 1961.

51 Oldeholtwolde: Stapert 1982; Stapert et al. 1986. Luttenberg: Stapert 1986b.

52 Fischer/Tauber 1986; Burdukiewicz 1986.

53 Stapert 1992a.

54 For example Lowe/Gray 1980.

55 Stapert 1985a. With 'collapsed pingos' or 'pingo ruins' round lakes, surrounded by a low sand bank, are indicated, being the remains of pingos in the Weichselian glacial period. These are rather numerous on the Drenthe Plateau.

56 Moss 1988.

57 In the case of Oldeholtwolde a total of about 60 kilos of lithic material will have been carried to the site (Stapert/Krist 1990).

58 Rust 1937; Burdukiewicz 1986.

59 According to Bosinski (1982), however, it is not certain whether a figurative representation can be identified.

60 Beuker 1983.

61 Waterbolk/Waterbolk 1991.

62 Leroi-Gourhan/Jacobi 1986.

63 A small lump of ochre from Havelte-Holtingerzand shows a fossil shell impression; that means that this ochre, which consists of goethite/limonite, must have come from a sedimentary formation (G.J. Boekschoten, pers. com.).

64 Keeley 1978; but see also Moss 1983.

65 See e.g. Musée de préhistoire d'Ile de France 1987.

66 Moss 1988; Stapert et al. 1986; Stapert/Krist 1990. Several (at least four) of such strike-a-lights were found at Sassenhein. A Zinken has been used secondary as such in view of its two rounded ends.

67 Arts 1984; Beuker 1981.

68 For example Bokelmann 1979; 1991b.

69 Tromnau 1984.

70 Charcoal from willow bushes was recovered from the hearth at Oldeholtwolde (Casparie, pers. com.; the branches were at most 1 cm thick). See Stapert 1982.

71 Bosinski 1981.

72 Leroi-Gourhan/Brézillon 1966; 1972; Julien 1984.

73 Stapert 1992a.

74 Stapert 1985a.

75 Stapert 1992a; Stapert/Krist 1990.

76 Level IV-20. *Habitation* 1 seems to have been occupied by men only; see Stapert 1992a.

77 Amsden 1977; Burch 1972; Spiess 1979.

78 Grönnow 1987.

79 Moss 1988; Microwear polishes resulting from use on fish are however difficult to identify and may consequently be underrepresented (Van Gijn 1986).

80 Bottema 1975; Stapert *et al.* 1986.

81 Unfortunately, microwear analysis of a flint point cannot provide a definitive answer to the question whether it was hafted in a spear or an arrow.

82 Burdukiewicz 1986; Tromnau 1975a.

83 Fischer/Tauber 1986.

84 Stapert 1986b.

85 Van Geel/Kolstrup 1978; Kolstrup 1982.

86 Stapert 1981c.

87 Fischer 1991; Holm/Rieck 1983; 1987.

88 Campbell 1977.

89 Schmider 1979; 1984; 1989.

90 Allain 1989 classes this site even as Hamburgian.

91 De Vries 1988. In his MA thesis he postulates a 'dwelling' at Luttenberg, but in the opinion of the author (D.S.) there is not sufficient evidence for such a conclusion.

92 For a recent survey see Fischer 1991.

93 Campbell 1977; Jacobi 1991. See chapter 7.

94 For example Arts 1988.

95 Stapert 1979a.

96 Kramer *et al.* 1985.

97 Emmerhout: Stapert 1985b; Zeijen: Stapert/Johansen 2001.

98 The existence of a tent at Sweikhuizen could not be confirmed by research using the 'ring and sector' spatial analysis method (P. Folkersma, pers. com.).

99 *Cf.* Wiessner 1983, 1984.

A A lost craft
Flint tool manufacture in prehistory

Jaap Beuker

If there is one rock that deserves to be called 'Stone Age steel' it is flint. In the Palaeolithic and Mesolithic flint was used more frequently than any other rock for the manufacture of tools. Flint is a very common raw material that possesses a number of unique properties. It has a hardness of 7 on Mohs' scale and is hence even harder than steel. Besides being hard, it is also brittle, as a result of which it splits easily. It is a highly isotropic material, which means that its properties are the same in all directions. This is a great advantage to the flint knapper, whose work is hence not limited by any lamination in the stone. There are, however, differences in isotropy between individual nodules: chalk and fossil inclusions, which are quite common, can affect a nodule's isotropy.

Flint working is based on the principle that energy (generated by a blow or by pressure) produces shock waves that propagate conically through the rock. Sufficient energy will cause the rock to crack along the edges of the cone.[1] This usually only happens when a piece of flint is struck near its edge. The fragment that is thus removed is called a flake; its edges are often very sharp (fig. A1). The flint core from which the flake has been struck shows a flake removal scar.

The shape and size of a flake can be influenced by varying the striking instrument or the force, angle or position of the blow. They are, moreover, dependent on the shape and structure of the flint nodule from which the flake is struck. There are essentially two different techniques for the manufacture of flint tools. First of all, flakes can be removed that have such sharp cutting edges that they do not require further flaking. Such flake tools may however be slightly retouched before use if so desired. Secondly, it is possible to remove flakes from a nodule in a reduction process that finally results in a core implement of the desired shape. The latter technique was used for the production of, for example, hand axes in the Palaeolithic.

Reconstructing a lost craft

There are several complementary ways of determining the flint-knapping techniques used in prehistory. First of all, the flake removal scars observable on flint artefacts, in particular on finished tools and on blanks, provide a wealth of information from which the flint-working technique can be inferred in general terms. Sometimes a very precise picture of the different stages of the knapping process can be obtained via a technique known as 'refitting', which entails putting flakes and cores 'back together again'. An entirely different source of information is ethnography. The stone-working technique that peoples like the Australian Aboriginals and the North American Indians used until well into the twentieth century must have greatly resembled that practised in our regions in prehistory. And, last but not least, there is experimental archaeology. The experiments that have been carried out over the past few decades have without doubt proven the most helpful in reconstructing the ancient flint-knapper's craft. These knapping experiments enable archaeologists to answer specific questions such as:

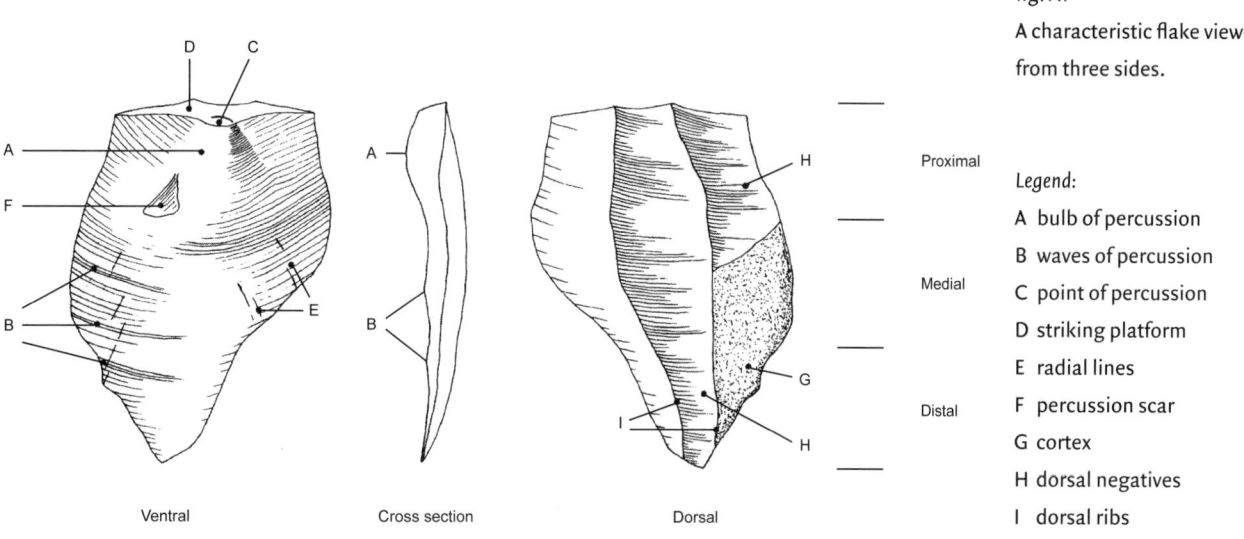

fig. A1
A characteristic flake viewed from three sides.

Ventral   Cross section   Dorsal

Proximal

Medial

Distal

Legend:

A bulb of percussion

B waves of percussion

C point of percussion

D striking platform

E radial lines

F percussion scar

G cortex

H dorsal negatives

I dorsal ribs

how was a particular type of tool made? How long did it take to make such a tool? What materials were most suitable for use and what are the effects of different materials and different techniques?

Knapping techniques

There were essentially three different ways in which flakes could be produced, namely via direct percussion, indirect percussion or pressure. Since the effects of these three techniques differ, more than one technique was sometimes used to produce a particular implement. The production of polished stone tools did not start until some time in the Neolithic, around 4000 BC. In the case of direct percussion a distinction is made between hard and soft percussion. The simplest form of hard percussion was to hurl a nodule onto an 'anvil' to obtain what would hopefully be usable fragments. This fairly rough mode of production was really only suitable for cracking large lumps of flint. The effect of *striking* a nodule onto an anvil could be controlled somewhat better. The form of hard percussion that could be controlled best was to strike the flint with a hard stone hammer (fig. A2). Rocks like quartzitic sandstone or quartzite were most suitable for use as hammers, being more tenacious than the flint that was to be knapped.

In the case of soft percussion use was made of a hammer of antler or hardwood. The base of the antler of a red deer, elk or reindeer was most suitable for use as a soft hammer.

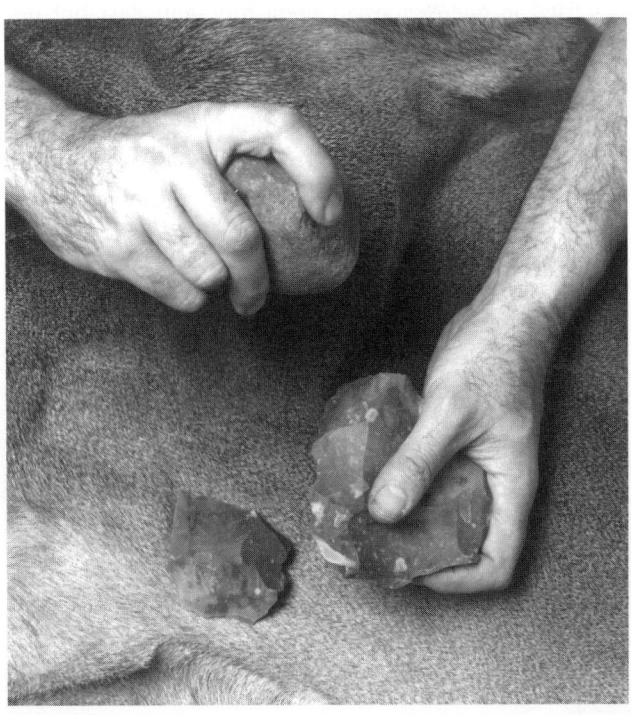

fig. A2
Hard percussion using a hammer.

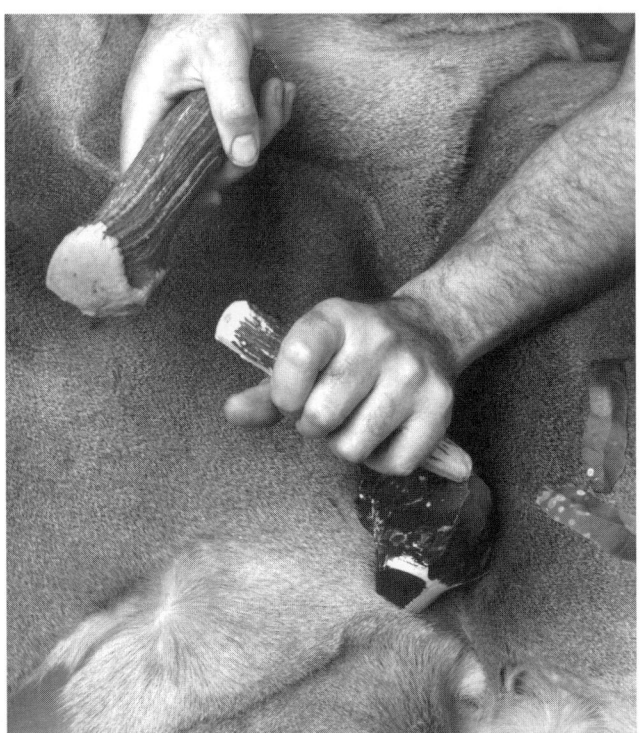

fig. A3
Indirect percussion using an antler punch.

Indirect percussion involved the use of a punch of antler, bone or stone, which was placed on the core platform and then struck with a hammer (fig. A3). With a second form of indirect percussion, the so-called *contre-coup* method, the nodule was placed on an anvil and was then struck.

With the pressure technique a pointed piece of antler, bone, flint or stone was used as a tool. The point was positioned on the nodule in the desired place and at the desired angle and then a flake was removed from the nodule by exerting pressure on the tool. Sometimes the nodule was placed on an anvil.

Hard percussion usually results in fairly thick flakes that left deep scars on the core. It was used mainly for the primary knapping of flint nodules, which involved the removal of large flakes and irregularities. In soft percussion thinner flakes were removed, which left shallower scars on the core. This technique, in which fewer vibrations were produced, was more suitable for finishing a tool and for producing flakes with thin, sharp edges. The same applies to an even greater extent to indirect percussion. With this technique the effects of a blow could be fairly accurately predicted because the angle and the point of percussion could be precisely determined.[2] This was also the case with pressure flaking, a technique with which only small flakes could be produced. Because of this, pressure flaking was particularly suitable for trimming or 'retouching' edges.[3]

The following examples serve to illustrate the manufacture of a number of different tools.

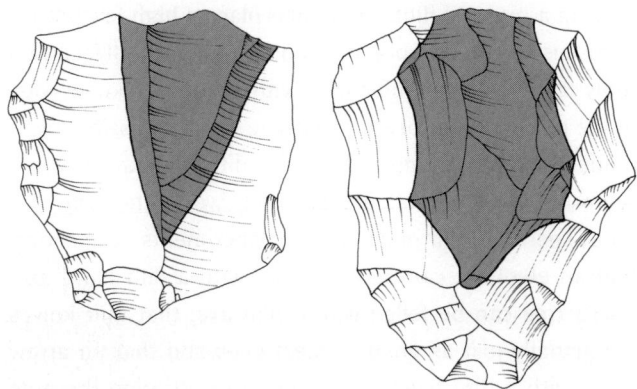

fig. A4
Schematic representation of the Levallois technique for the production of flakes (right) and points (left).

Hand axes and the Levallois technique

A large flake or a, preferably flat, nodule could be used to produce a hand axe. A relatively sophisticated hand axe was manufactured in two main stages. First of all a number of large flakes were alternately removed from two sides of the nodule with the aid of hard percussion. During this process the flint knapper remained seated and kept turning the nodule from one side to the other so that one flake removal scar could serve as the striking platform for the next removal. In this way the outline of the hand axe was roughed out from the nodule. Parts of the skin or cortex of the nodule remained in the middle. At this stage the edge of the implement was still very irregular and had an angle of 55-75 degrees.

The second stage involved the use of soft percussion. The flakes that were removed in this stage were longer, extending right up to the middle of the implement. The remaining cortex was thus removed and the implement became thinner. The shallower scars left by the flakes that were removed in soft percussion resulted in a more regular cutting edge with an angle varying from 40 to 60 degrees. In the process described above up to eighty large and five thousand small flakes were removed.

The aim of the Levallois technique, which marks the transition from the Lower to the Middle Palaeolithic, was to produce flakes or points of a predetermined shape from a carefully prepared core, called a 'tortoise core' (fig. A4).[4] The flake that was removed after this reduction process was thin and had a roughly oval shape, like the core from which it was detached.

A Levallois point was obtained by first producing a triangular pattern of ribs on a core. The flake that was then struck from this core had the same triangular shape.

Blades, burins, flake axes and 'microburins'

Blades are regularly shaped, parallel-sided flakes. Their length is at least twice their width. They were obtained by first shaping a striking platform on a nodule (fig. A5). Next, small flakes were removed to obtain a straight rib from the platform downwards. This stage is known as core preparation. The first blade that was struck from the core followed the rib and was hence long and straight. The scar that this core preparation blade left on the core showed two ribs, along which the next blades could be detached. This core reduction sequence could be described as 'peeling'.[5] Blades could be produced using either direct soft percussion or indirect percussion.

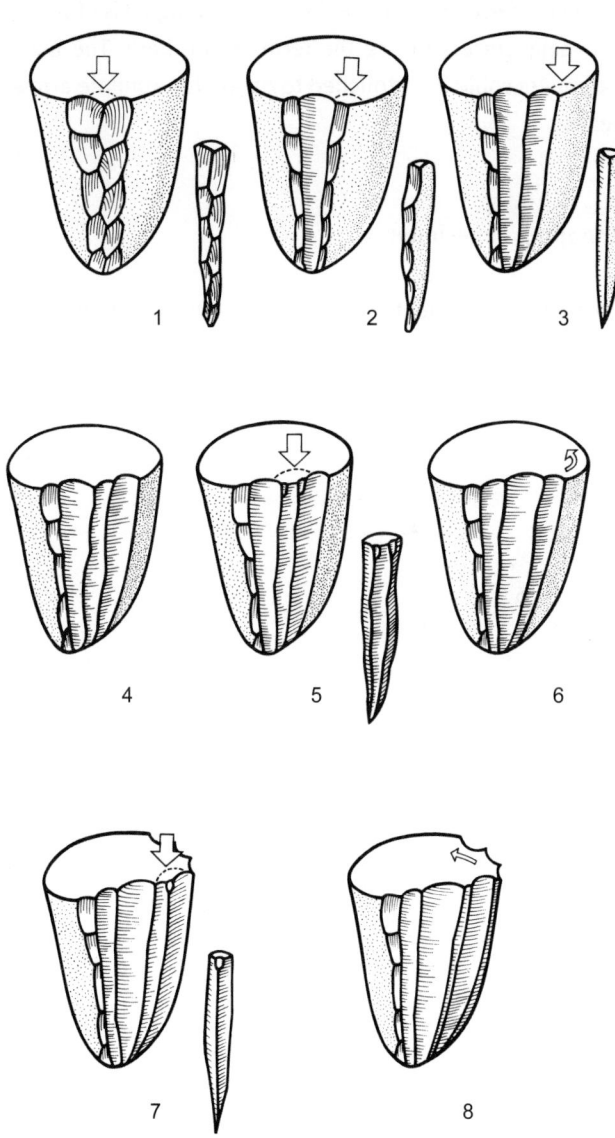

fig. A5
Schematic representation of the production of blades.

Legend:

1-3   core preparation

4-6   production of two-ribbed blades

7-8   production of one-ribbed blades

The manufacture of burins and so-called flake axes is comparable with that of blades. By removing a bladelet along the edge of a blade, flake or other flat piece of flint, a chisel-shaped tool was obtained that was a very suitable gouging instrument.[6]

The cutting edge of a flake axe was produced by using a narrow side of a blank as a striking platform. A bladelet was then detached obliquely from the edge of the blank.[7] In both cases, the burins and the flake axes, the ultimate purpose is not the detached flake, but the negative left on the tool.

In the Mesolithic some tools were made on blades. This was often done by breaking the blades: a notch was made in the blade,[8] after which the blade was broken in one well-aimed blow. Because one half of the blade resembles a burin it is also referred to as a 'microburin', although it is of course not really correct to use the term 'burin' here. The blade fragments could be retouched to obtain for example arrow-heads.

Knapping experiments

Knapping experiments have made it quite clear that flint tool manufacture involves a good deal more than simply striking a piece of flint. In the first place a high level of expertise is required to obtain good results. Secondly, certain tools can only be manufactured with a thorough knowledge of the production process and of the various possible techniques. Flint knapping is far more difficult than it would seem but the products are definitely worth the time and effort spent in their manufacture: experiments have shown that an elephant can be butchered with a flint hand axe, that a tree can be felled with a flint axe, that flint knives are actually just as good as steel ones and that an arrow fitted with a flint head is capable of penetrating the hide of a deer.

Notes

1   Beuker 1983, 30.
2   Crabtree 1972, 13.
3   Crabtree 1972, 15.
4   Tixier et al. 1980, 44-51.
5   Crabtree 1972, 43.
6   Tixier et al. 1980, 76.
7   Crabtree 1972, 96.
8   Beuker 1983, 60.

7 From tundra hunting to forest hunting Later Upper Palaeolithic and Early Mesolithic

Jos Deeben and Nico Arts

HISTORY OF RESEARCH

This chapter discusses the last phase of the Upper Palaeolithic and the Early Mesolithic; in ^{14}C years that corresponds to the period between 11,800 and 8200 BP. This time span saw major changes in the natural environment. In geological terms these changes mark the transition from the Pleistocene to the Holocene. Archaeologists have taken this transition, which in the Netherlands took place between 10,250 and 10,000 BP, to define the line between the Palaeolithic and the Mesolithic.

For the first half of the twentieth century the Mesolithic was regarded as a period of decline in man's cultural evolution. This view was based mainly on comparisons of the cultural remains of the Mesolithic with those of the preceding Upper Palaeolithic and the succeeding Neolithic. This 'degeneration' was primarily attributed to the changes that took place in man's natural environment, such as the disappearance of the steppe-tundra along with the herds of reindeer that roamed them and the appearance of a varied forest fauna.

Nowadays, however, more and more emphasis is being placed on the continuity observable in the material remains of the Upper Palaeolithic and the Mesolithic, because it has been found that many cultural traits, such as the various stone, bone and antler technologies, including that of microliths,[1] which were in the past interpreted as specifically Mesolithic, can in fact be traced further back in time, into the Upper Palaeolithic. One of the consequences of this discovery is that it has become very difficult to define the Mesolithic in archaeological terms. Many archaeologists nowadays therefore use the term 'post-glacial adaptations' when referring to this period.[2]

Over the past fifty years a considerable amount of information on the last phase of the Palaeolithic and the beginning of the Mesolithic has been obtained in the Netherlands. It is thanks to this information that – up to a point – we are now able to present a picture of the various Upper Palaeolithic and Early Mesolithic societies and their material equipment, their settlements and the ways in which they exploited their natural environment.

It was only in the 1920s that the first Upper Palaeolithic and Mesolithic remains were identified in the Netherlands. Systematic research into these periods was not started until some twenty-five years later. At first it was mainly the Department of Biology and Archaeology of Groningen University that showed an interest in these periods. Between 1945 and 1964 A. Bohmers, a member of that department, supervised the excavation of the remains of dozens of sites. Much of this fieldwork was done in close cooperation with amateur archaeologists, who also discovered many new findspots themselves. In the southern part of the Netherlands in particular, Bohmers often worked with the amateur archaeologist A. Wouters. Together, they laid the foundations for a typological synthesis. Unfortunately, a survey of their work was never published. The study of the Palaeolithic and Mesolithic by Dutch professional archaeologists reached an impasse after 1964, which, as far as the periods discussed in this chapter are concerned, lasted until about 1975.

In the Netherlands, a large proportion of the research into the Upper Palaeolithic and Early Mesolithic has been done by amateur archaeologists. Especially since 1964, in the absence of professional support, they have followed a course of their own, published their own journals[3] and formed independent interpretations. The past decades have seen an explosive growth of interest in the Stone Age in amateur circles. The number of amateur archaeologists has increased considerably, and so have the numbers of their discoveries and publications.

Groningen University resumed its research around 1975, concentrating almost exclusively on the northern provinces. In 1981 the Department of Pre- and Protohistory of Amsterdam University launched a research project in the southeast of the Netherlands.

As a result of the intermittent development of the research into the Upper Palaeolithic and Early Mesolithic and the emphasis on the northern and southeastern parts of the Netherlands and the adjacent sandy part of Belgium in the work of P.M. Vermeersch in particular, a somewhat distorted picture has emerged of the number of sites and their distribution.[4] Until recently, hardly any systematic research had for example been carried out in the sandy central part of the Netherlands.[5] Things have started to change over the past few years, but the results so far obtained do not yet allow detailed analysis. In the western part of the Netherlands and in the river valleys the picture is further distorted owing to the geological processes that have taken place there; in those parts, much evidence has disappeared due to erosion or now lies buried beneath thick Holocene deposits.

Owing to the various factors outlined above the following synthesis is therefore based largely on evidence from the coversand regions in the northern and southeastern parts of the country, which together cover about one-third of the total area of the Netherlands.

CLIMATIC AND ENVIRONMENTAL CHANGES

At the end of the Pleistocene the landscape of Northwest Europe was affected by changes in climatic conditions (see chapter 3). After the relatively dry Older Dryas stadial, conditions became wetter from around 11,800 BP onwards, the beginning of the Allerød interstadial, while the temperature remained virtually un-

fig. 7.1
Section of an Usselo horizon from the Allerød period in a coversand stratification near Wierden (Overijssel). The dark band containing charcoal particles is an old litter horizon. The projections are the features of digging beetle tunnels. The underlying pale band is an eluvial horizon.

changed: on average about −17 °C in January and about 14 °C in July.[6] These new environmental conditions were to remain relatively stable for almost a thousand years, until c. 10,900 BP. This is evident from, for example, the formation of organic deposits (peat and *gyttja*) in damp areas and the development of podzols, the so-called Usselo soils, as a consequence of leaching in some parts of dryer areas (fig. 7.1). These soils have been found to contain small charcoal particles in many places. They are generally believed to indicate extensive forest fires caused by a volcanic eruption, some 11,000 years ago, in the area of the Laacher See in the German Eifel.[7]

Around 10,900 BP, at the beginning of the Younger Dryas, the climate started to deteriorate. Mean July temperatures dropped to about 11 °C, mean January temperatures to around −20 °C. These rapid environmental changes led to the replacement of the pine forests of the Allerød by a more open, herbaceous vegetation. About halfway through the Younger Dryas, from c. 10,500 BP onwards, conditions became dryer and possibly also a little warmer, enabling the forests to expand again.[8] In periods of sparse vegetation, coversand (Younger Coversand II) started to drift again in the Younger Dryas. The greater part of this sand came from parts of the river plains that periodically dried out.[9]

Around the beginning of the Holocene, c. 10,250 to 10,000 BP, conditions became warmer again, enabling the vegetation to expand at a relatively fast rate. The temperature rose at a steady rate, reaching mean values of 17 °C in the summer and 0 °C in the winter by the end of the Pre-Boreal (c. 9000 BC). The higher temperatures soon resulted in a further expansion of the forest vegetation. At first this forest consisted mainly of birch and pine, later on it also comprised hazel, oak and elm.[10] Another consequence of the higher temperatures was the gradual melting of the Scandinavian ice cap, resulting in a relative rise in sea level. Around 8300 BP the Atlantic Ocean and the North Sea merged.[11] Although the rise in sea level brought the Netherlands within the direct range of a rapidly expanding North Sea, it is assumed that the climate remained continental and relatively dry until the end of the Boreal.[12]

The Netherlands and the adjacent parts of Belgium and Germany cannot be said to have constituted an environmentally homogeneous area in this period.[13] We are to see the development of the vegetation as the gradual movement in a northerly direction of different vegetational zones characterised by fine-meshed microregional patterns. Palaeobotanical research in the south of the Netherlands has shown that the development of the vegetation was different in different areas around the close of the Pleistocene and in the Early Holocene varied from the one area to another.[14] These differences appear to be related to variations in landscape, for example between river valleys and coversand regions; we may assume that watersheds, such as the Peelhorst, were also partly responsible for this spatial diversity. Although no comparable research has yet been carried out in the central and northern parts of the Netherlands and surrounding areas, it is likely that similar differences were to be found there, too.[15]

CHRONOLOGY AND CULTURAL SEQUENCES

It is generally accepted that the Upper Palaeolithic B and Early Mesolithic sites of the northwestern part of Continental Europe can be divided into at least three groups, referred to as *Federmesser*, Ahrensburgian and Early Mesolithic (fig. 7.2).[16] They are primarily distinguishable on the basis of typological criteria, in the south moreover on the basis of the raw materials used. Some – mostly excavated – sites

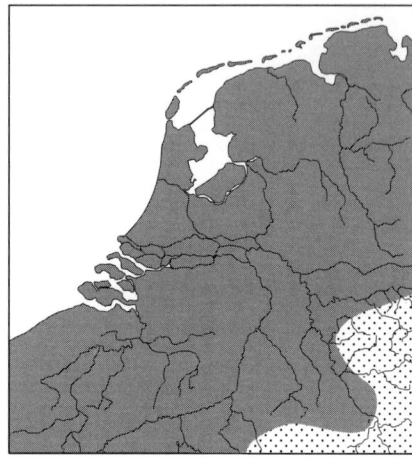

hills >300 m

Federmesser tradition

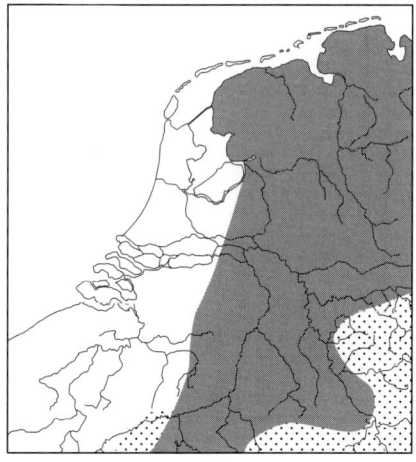

hills >300 m

Ahrensburgian culture

fig. 7.2
Distribution of sites of the Ahrensburgian culture and the *Federmesser* tradition in the Netherlands and its environs.

have also yielded stratigraphic evidence and palaeobotanical and/or radiometric dates.

These groups are assigned cultural, functional or chronological meanings, depending on the researcher's theoretical starting points and the employed criteria. The earliest tradition is called *Federmesser*;[17] in the Netherlands it is sometimes also referred to as the 'Tjongerian' culture.[18] The second group, the Ahrensburgian culture, is so called after the famous sites in the Ahrensburgian tunnel valley.[19] The third group is simply referred to as 'Early Mesolithic'.

At first, these groups were arranged according to a chronological framework which linked cultures directly to Late Glacial phases and the associated environmental conditions.[20] Over the past years, however, the correctness of such sequences has been the object of discussion, because more and more evidence suggests that different groups co-existed for two or more Late Glacial phases.[21] Moreover, several researchers have distinguished another tradition besides that of the *Federmesser*, namely the Creswellian tradition.[22] But so far, the assumption that this tradition existed in the Netherlands is based solely on the occurrence of one or possibly two point types – the Creswellian and Cheddarian points – and the quality of the employed flint.[23] It is hence not justifiable to distinguish a separate, Creswellian tradition in the Netherlands on the basis of typo-morphological affinities with the remains of the *Federmesser* tradition.[24]

At some excavated sites the find horizons of the distinguished groups can be related to geological deposits, with the Usselo horizon serving as a useful guide. The material remains of the *Federmesser* tradition were found beneath, in and just above this horizon (fig. 7.3). Ahrensburgian and Early Mesolithic remains were both found in the coversand horizon (Younger Coversand II) overlying the Usselo horizon. The fact that these sites were incorporated in coversand indicates that sand was still drifting in the Pre-Boreal. Research at Late Glacial settlements that were reused in the Early Holocene has shown that it is possible to stratigraphically distinguish different find horizons by accurately recording the individual finds' contexts, such as their depths.[25]

The lack of an unambiguous chronological framework for the Netherlands as a whole is due partly to problems concerning the ^{14}C dates. About one-third of the dozens of ^{14}C dates obtained for archaeological finds from Upper Palaeolithic and Early Mesolithic sites in the Netherlands and Belgium is considered unreliable.[26] Most of those dates are (much) younger than would be expected on the basis of typological evidence. The deviations are probably due to the poor associations of the samples, many of which were taken in badly documented excavations. Most of the dated charcoal samples moreover come from Holocene deposits, in which younger organic matter may have become mixed with older sediments as a consequence of bioturbation and the formation of new soils. Lately, materials whose associations are above doubt, such as human skeletal remains, artefacts of bone and antler, game bones and resin, are increasingly being used for dating purposes to circumvent the problem of the unclear association between samples taken for radiocarbon analysis and the artefacts found with them.[27]

Federmesser sites have been found in all areas of Pleistocene deposits in the Netherlands. They form part of a distribution area that extends roughly from the southern and central parts of Britain in the west[28] to the Ukraine in the east and to northern France[29] and southern Germany in the south and Denmark in the north. The available dates suggest that the *Federmesser* tradition was to be found in this region at least from the Older Dryas until in the Younger Dryas.

Important *Federmesser* sites have been excavated in the central and northern parts of the Netherlands, at Usselo in Overijssel, Haule V and Siegerswoude in

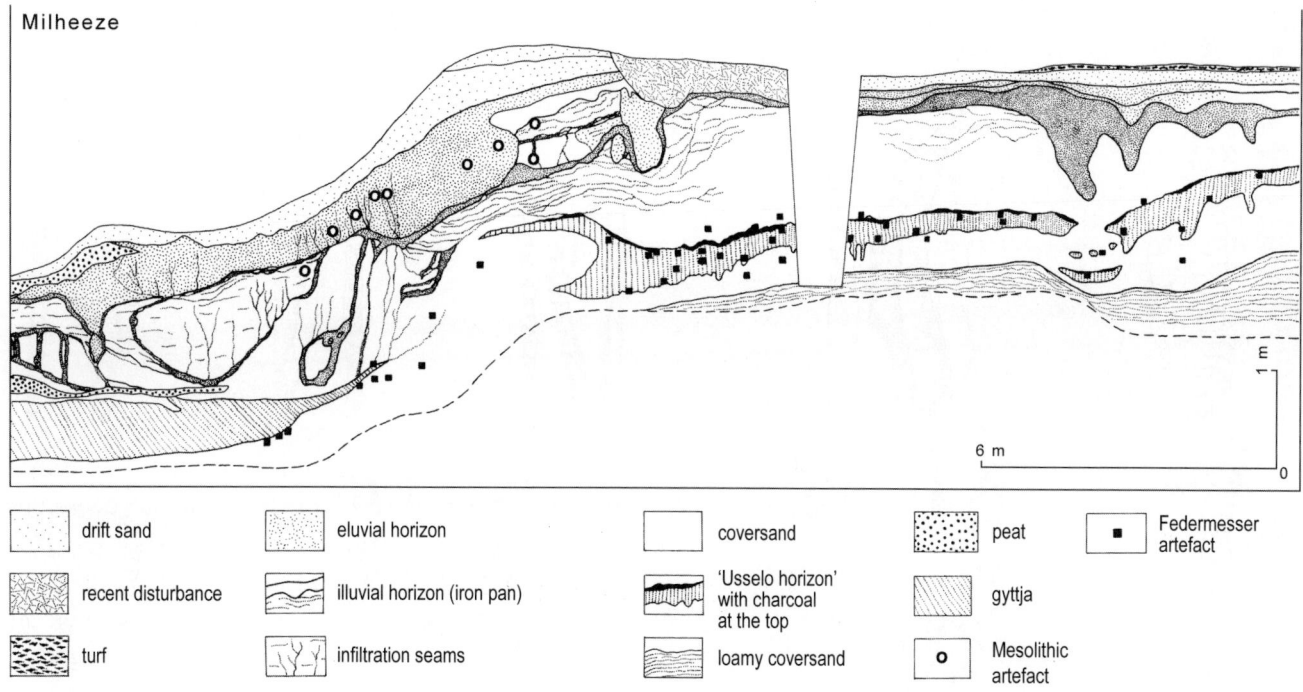

Milheeze

	drift sand		eluvial horizon		coversand		peat	▪	Federmesser artefact
	recent disturbance		illuvial horizon (iron pan)		'Usselo horizon' with charcoal at the top		gyttja		
	turf		infiltration seams		loamy coversand	○	Mesolithic artefact		

Friesland and on the Hoornse Veld in Drenthe.[30] Milheeze, Budel II and Geldrop III-4 in North Brabant and De Banen-Nederweert in Limburg can be mentioned for the south of the country.[31] But all these sites were excavated at an early date and many are poorly documented.

For a long time it was assumed that the distribution of Ahrensburgian sites was restricted to the southern part of the Netherlands.[32] However, it was recently found that it in fact covers the whole of the country. This conclusion is based on new evidence obtained from surface findspots[33] and from an excavated site at Oudehaske in Friesland.[34] In the southern part of the Netherlands Ahrensburgian sites have been excavated at, for example, Vessem and Geldrop.[35] The Dutch Ahrensburgian sites form part of a distribution area that covers the Netherlands, Luxembourg, central Germany and Russia and extends up to southern Norway and Sweden in a northerly direction.[36] The dates obtained for the Ahrensburgian culture range from the beginning of the Younger Dryas until the beginning of the Pre-Boreal.[37]

Characteristic of Early Mesolithic sites is the great typo-morphological similarity of artefacts in an area extending from England to Poland and from France and Switzerland to Norway.[38] In the Netherlands, Early Mesolithic sites have been excavated at Nijnsel, Geldrop, Swalmen and Gramsbergen.[39] During the Early Mesolithic, regional differences started to appear in the material culture. On the basis of these differences, around 8200 BP, approximately at the beginning of the Boreal, a *Nordwest Kreis* in the northern part of the Netherlands and a *Rhine Basin Kreis* in the southern part of the country have been distinguished.[40] This regional differentiation marks the beginning of the Middle Mesolithic. An increase in the number of point types and, in the southern part of the Netherlands, a marked increase in the use of Wommersom quartzite and the first use of surface retouch distinguish the Middle Mesolithic flint assemblages from those of the Early Mesolithic.

fig. 7.3
Stratigraphic position of a *Federmesser* site associated with an Usselo horizon and a Mesolithic site on Younger coversand at Milheeze (province of North Brabant). Horizontal scale 1:150. The height has been enlarged twice for the sake of clarity.

143

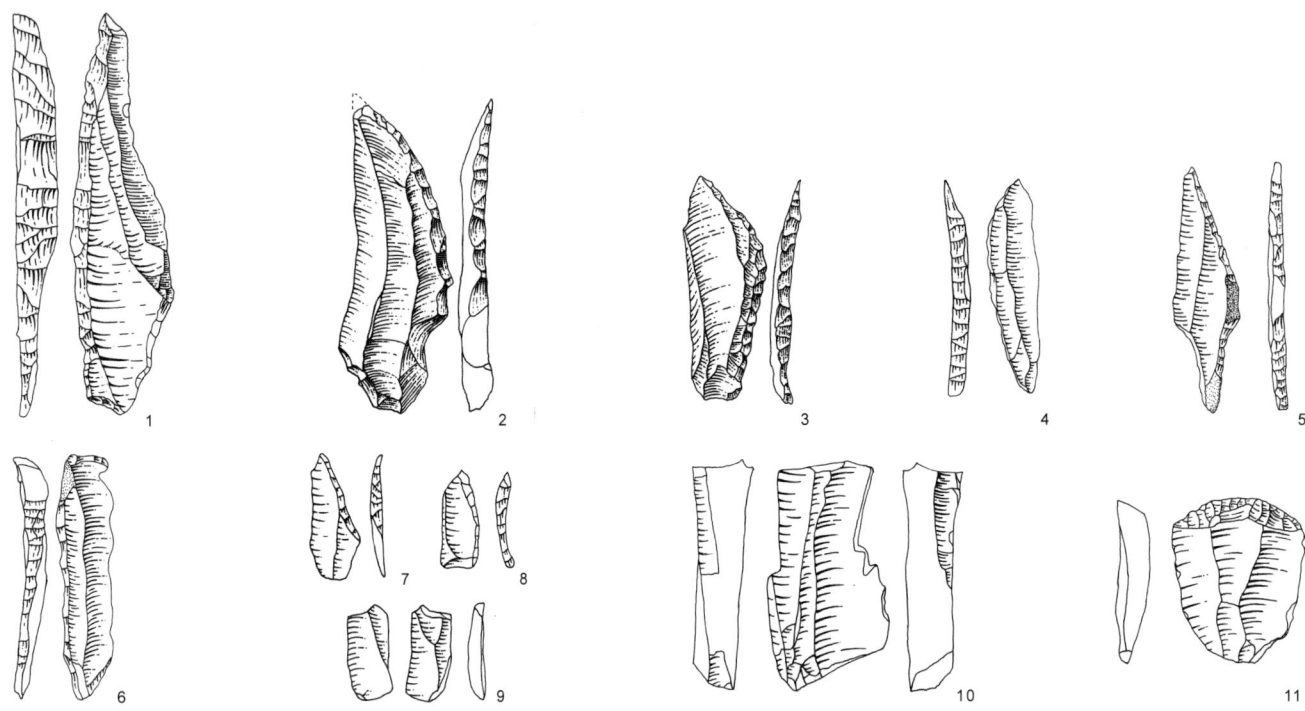

fig. 7.4

Typical *Federmesser*, Ahrensburgian and Early Mesolithic artefacts from different sites. Actual size.

1 Gravettian point
2 Tjongerian point
3 Creswellian point
4 Azilian point
5 tanged point
6 steeply retouched blade
7 B-point
8 A-point
9 'microburin'
10 burin
11 scraper

MATERIAL CULTURE

Preservation

The remains from the period discussed here undoubtedly present a very biased picture of the contemporary material culture. The finds recovered from the individual findspots consist largely of flint artefacts plus a few artefacts made from different types of stone.

With the exception of charcoal and, in one case, calcinated bone fragments, no organic remains have been found among the flint scatters. Artefacts of bone and antler dating predominantly from the Upper Palaeolithic and the Early Mesolithic have on the contrary been found in dredging operations in the rivers area and in the Meuse plain.[41]

The virtual absence of organic matter in the sandy regions is due to the fact that most of the sites are situated on soils deficient in lime, in which uncarbonised plant and animal remains are rarely preserved. Moreover, most of the excavations of these sites focused on concentrations of flint and stone artefacts. So far, no systematic research has been carried out in the low-lying surroundings of those sites, which sometimes contain calcareous *gyttja* deposits and/or peat layers. Any organic matter that was discarded in those low-lying areas may have survived; however, in spite of the greater attention that has recently been given to such areas, no organic waste has so far come to light.

Flint

The typo-morphology of stone artefacts on the basis of which *Federmesser*, Ahrensburgian and Early Mesolithic assemblages can be distinguished from one another shows a great deal of variation (fig. 7.4). A number of typological sequences have been set up for the Netherlands which in many respects correspond to one another: usually the presence or absence of certain types of points is considered diagnostic.[42] In the past, phases or subgroups were often distinguished within the three groups discussed above on the basis of qualitative and quantitative aspects of certain types and variations in flint technology.[43]

The flint points that are characteristic of the *Federmesser* tradition are Tjongerian and Gravettian points and to a lesser extent also Kremsian, Creswellian, Cheddarian and Azilian points. They are all relatively large, so-called 'steeply retouched' points. Common types of tools are end scrapers, burins, truncated blades and steeply retouched blades, the latter often occurring in relatively large numbers.

Characteristic – and often diagnostic – Ahrensburgian artefacts are tanged points, which are frequently found in fragmented condition. The aforementioned steeply retouched points are also encountered in Ahrensburgian assemblages, while the large numbers of obliquely truncated points (B points) mark the beginning of the microlithic trend that was to continue in the Mesolithic. Also common are truncated blades, scrapers and burins. The occurrence of large unworked blades (*Riesenklingen*) is often considered characteristic of the Ahrensburgian culture.[44] In actual fact, however, such blades are only rarely encountered; what's more, they are found not only at Ahrensburgian sites, but also at *Federmesser* and Early Mesolithic sites. The presence of long blades should hence be seen not as a cultural characteristic, but as an indication of the amount of raw material available and its quality.

Owing to the small number of diagnostic point types, the Early Mesolithic is poorly recognisable; A and B points are characteristic, while triangles are also to be found in Early Mesolithic assemblages. Scrapers, and to a lesser extent burins, remained common throughout the Early Mesolithic; the number of burins decreased substantially in later phases of the Mesolithic.

The reduction in the size of points can be followed at sites of the Ahrensburgian culture. This development coincided with the introduction of a technique for producing microliths by notching and snapping blades, represented by the appearance of micro- or pseudo-burins.[45] Microliths, retouched blades or fragments of such blades were used predominantly as arrowheads and barbs in hunting weapons. Microwear analysis has shown that microliths were also used on plant materials.[46]

Different kinds of flint were used to manufacture artefacts. Most of the flint will have been obtained from fluvial deposits or boulder clay. Some artefacts were made from kinds of flint that do not occur naturally in the Netherlands and are therefore considered exotic. Examples of such kinds of flint are the Helgoland flint that has been found in the north of the Netherlands[47] and a fine-grained, usually brownish black to grey flint with red inclusions from Obourg in Hainaut (Belgium). The latter kind of flint has been encountered mainly at *Federmesser* sites in the southern part of the Netherlands. Another remarkable observation made in the south of the country is that the same types of flint had been used at the various Ahrensburgian sites. Other types of exotic flint, which were likewise used mainly in the southern part of the country, may have been obtained from the North Sea basin, which was then still dry. So far, no systematic petrological research has been carried out to determine the sources of the different types of flint.

Other artefacts

In the absence of ^{14}C dates, the tools of bone and antler that are recovered in dredging operations can be dated only approximately; however, they do give us an impression of the great diversity of the organic component of the material culture of this period. They enable comparisons with similar artefacts found elsewhere, in

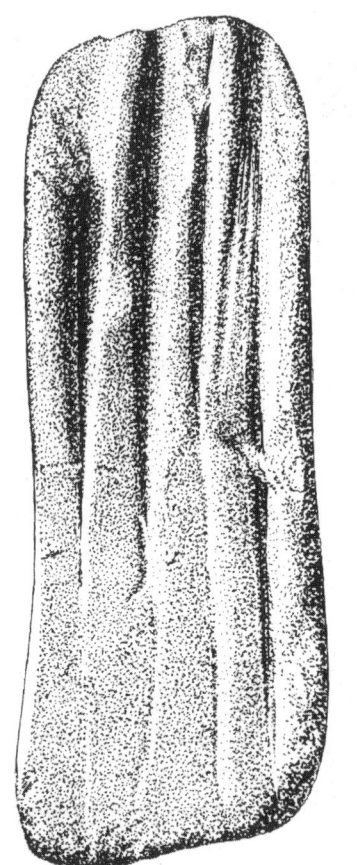

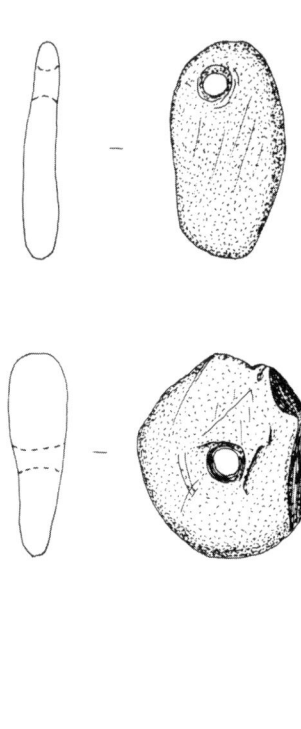

fig. 7.5
Two lydite pebbles perforated for use as
pendants and a piece of fine sandstone with
wide grooves that was used for finishing
arrow shafts, awls, needles and the like.
Found at the Ahrensburgian site of Vessem-
Rouwveen. Actual size.

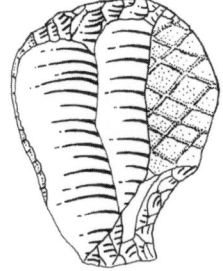

fig. 7.6
Flint scraper with engraved cortex found at
the *Federmesser* site Budel II. Actual size.

the wide surroundings of the Netherlands,[48] which comprise denticulated points, harpoons and hacking implements of elk and red deer antler and a few decorated reindeer antlers.[49]

The other types of stone that were used besides flint are mainly quartz, quartzite and sandstone; in the north use was also made of stones transported by the ice sheets, such as different kinds of granite. A number of pierced, polished stone pendants, many of lydite, are known from Ahrensburgian sites (fig. 7.5). So-called retouchoirs were also often made from lydite. 'Arrow shaft polishers' of coarse-grained sandstone with a groove down one side, which are believed to have been used to smoothen arrow shafts, have been found in assemblages of all three groups. The same holds for 'needle polishers', also made from sandstone. Small and larger lumps of ochre, often showing traces of grinding, have been found mainly at *Federmesser* and Ahrensburgian sites and to a lesser extent also at Early Mesolithic sites in the south of the Netherlands; some of the lumps were pierced.[50] Features consisting of patches of ochre powder have been found at a few excavated Ahrensburgian sites.[51]

Many sites have yielded Upper Palaeolithic artefacts decorated with engravings. The meaning of these engravings, which have been observed in flint cortex and in other types of stone, still eludes us (fig. 7.6). Many show geometric motifs: lozenges, zigzags and 'ladder motifs'.[52] Noteworthy are the stylistically similar engravings of human figures found at Geldrop and Wanssum.[53]

SETTLEMENTS

Basic data

The Dutch *Federmesser*, Ahrensburgian and Early Mesolithic sites consist of scatters of artefacts amongst which features are only rarely observed. There where they are

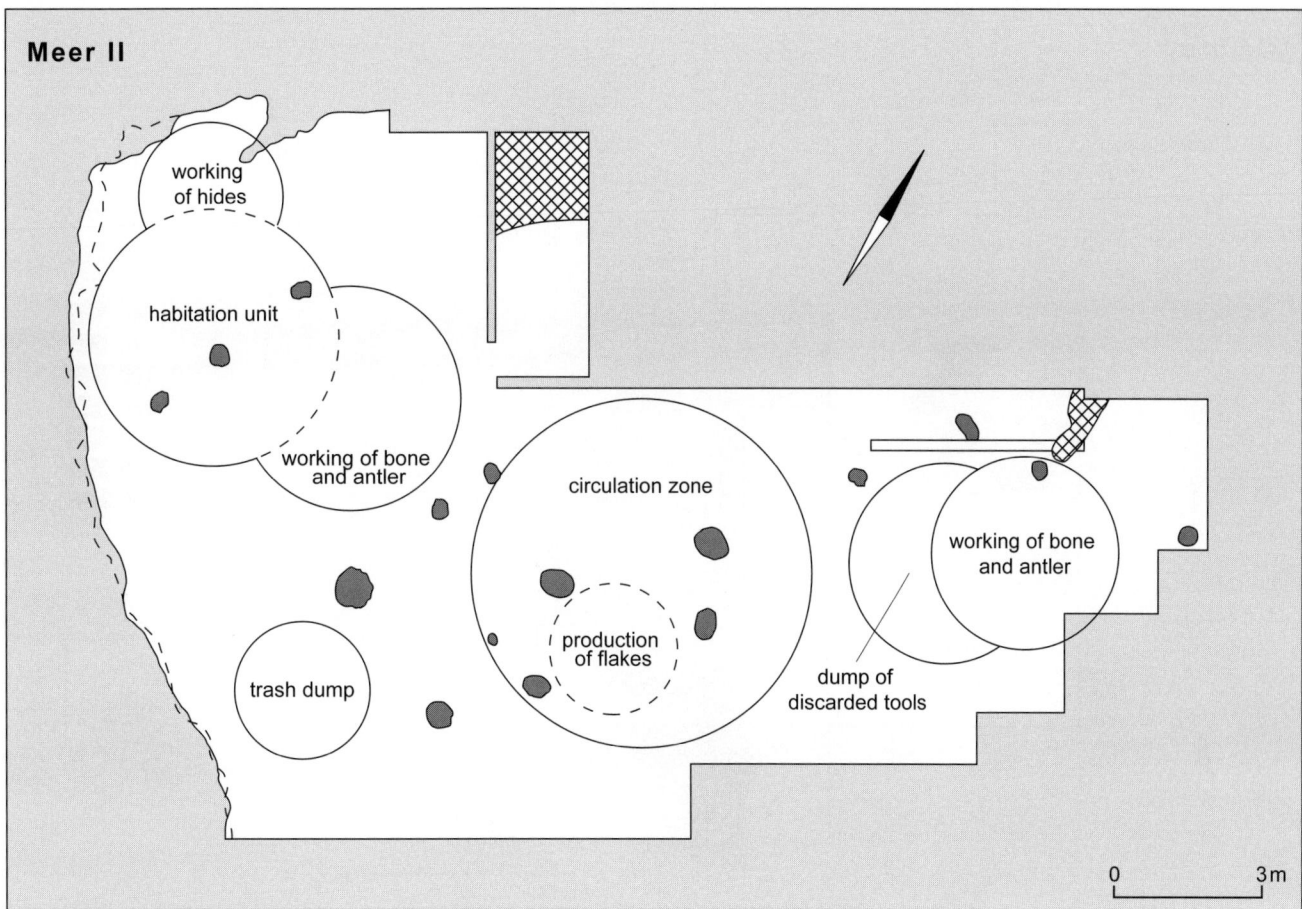

Meer II

working of hides

habitation unit

working of bone and antler

circulation zone

production of flakes

trash dump

working of bone and antler

dump of discarded tools

0   3m

found they comprise isolated pits, discolourations that are believed to be postholes, patches of ochre and concentrations of charcoal, sometimes in depressions. The association between these features and the stone artefacts scattered around them is not always clear. Many features are the consequences of natural processes or of reuse of the site.[54] Features that can be unambiguously interpreted as evidence for the existence of houses, huts or tents in the period discussed here have not been found in the Netherlands. From research at sites with good preservation conditions in surrounding countries we have some idea of the nature of the structures that were built in this period. The peat bog of Duvensee in Sleswig-Holstein for example yielded the remains of an Early Mesolithic platform built from bark.[55]

In the absence of remains of concrete structures it is often assumed that scatters of artefacts reflect the size of the settlements. Analyses of the organisation of sites are based on this assumption. Direct, visual interpretations of scatters are combined with statistical methods[56] and – increasingly – refitting experiments.[57] Sometimes the aim of spatial analyses is to identify specific activity areas. This was for example the aim of the analysis of the *Federmesser* site of Meer in Belgium, which was reconstructed by integrating the results of microwear analysis, refitting experiments and visual inspections of the flint scatter. The settlement was found to have comprised a living area, several activity areas and zones where waste was discarded (fig. 7.7).[58]

A site's size and the composition of its find assemblage can also provide insight into a cultural unit's settlement system and land use. Stapert has distinguished five categories of Upper Palaeolithic sites chiefly on the basis of the numbers of artefacts measuring more than 1.5 cm and their nature:[59]

1) Sites consisting of a single stray find, such as a point, which may have been lost during a hunting expedition.

fig. 7.7
Activity areas reconstructed on the basis of the results of refitting efforts and microwear analysis of flint artefacts at the *Federmesser* site of Meer, Belgium. The clearly defined, small find scatters and the distinct distribution patterns imply that this 12 x 15 m site represents the remains of a base camp that was used only once. Later research has incidentally shown that the excavated scatters form part of a series of sites on an elongated coversand ridge. Scale 1:150.

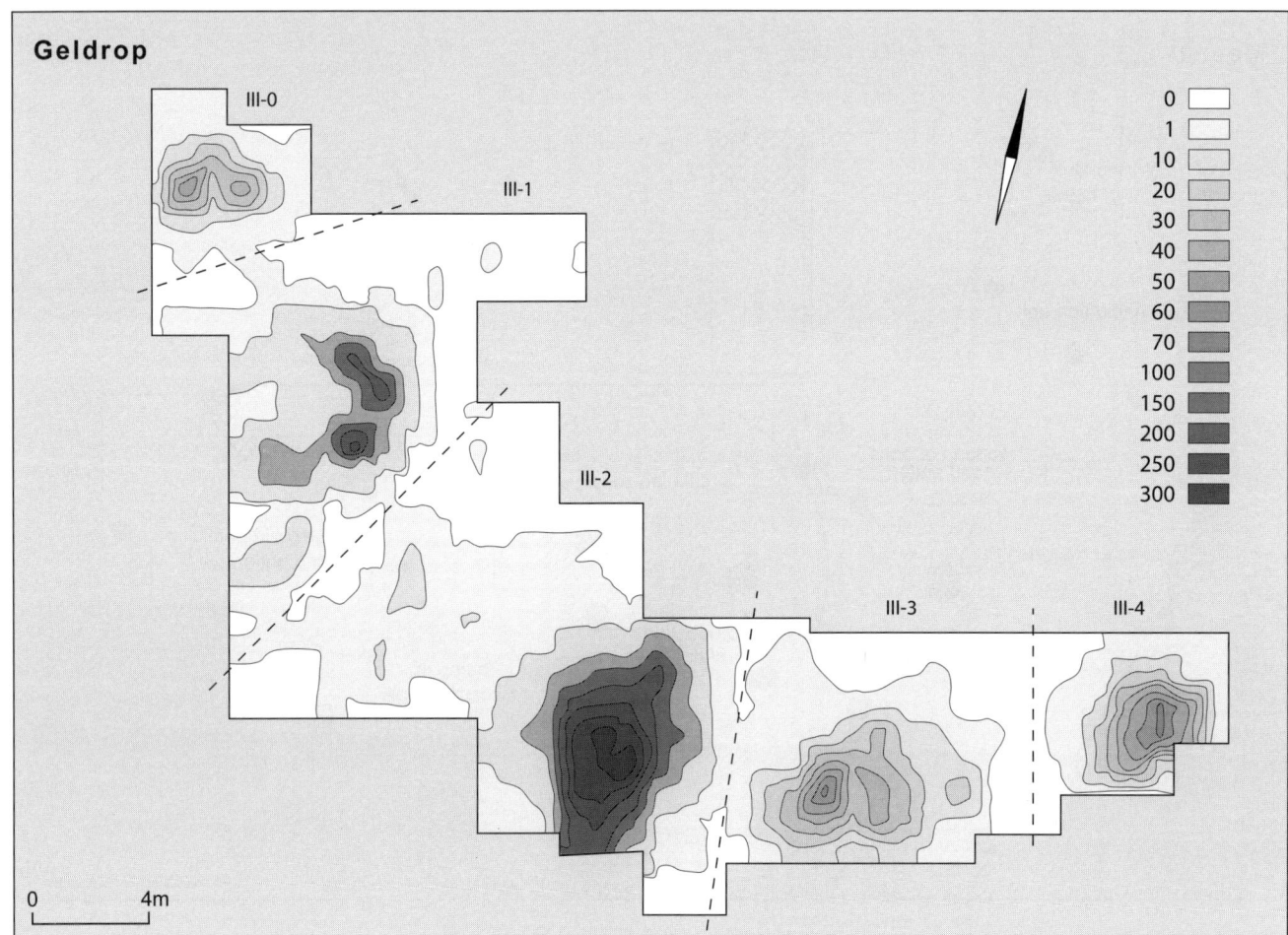

Geldrop

III-0 III-1 III-2 III-3 III-4

| 0 |
| 1 |
| 10 |
| 20 |
| 30 |
| 40 |
| 50 |
| 60 |
| 70 |
| 100 |
| 150 |
| 200 |
| 250 |
| 300 |

0   4m

fig. 7.8
Reoccupied area at Geldrop with closely
spaced *Federmesser*, Ahrensburgian and Early
Mesolithic sites. Densities in numbers of
artefacts per m². Five ¹⁴C dates obtained for
the Ahrensburgian sites indicate several
phases of occupation between 10,600 and
9970 BP. Scale 1:250.

2) Flint procurement sites, which are characterised by high percentages of debitage and few finished artefacts. Such sites are usually found in the vicinity of
flint outcrops; in the Netherlands they have been found at Uffelte in Drenthe
and at Waubach in Limburg.[60]

3) Small sites comprising fewer than 1500 artefacts, where a particular tool type
is predominant. Examples of sites of this kind are the *Federmesser* sites Haule
V, Geldrop III-4 (fig. 7.8) and Siegerswoude.[61] Stapert assumes that such sites
were used for specific activities, such as the butchering of killed game.

4) Medium-sized sites with between 1500 and 5000 artefacts where the majority
of the different types of tools are represented in more or less the same proportions. Such sites are believed to have been the base camps of one or more
families, about 5-20 individuals (fig. 7.9). An example of such a site is the Tjongerian settlement of Meer.

5) Large and very large sites with more than 5000 and 20,000 artefacts, respectively. In the Netherlands only very large sites of the *Federmesser* group are
known. According to Stapert, such large artefact concentrations represent
sites that were used for a long period of time or were reused on several occasions.

Newell has distinguished various categories of Mesolithic occupation sites, three
of which are relevant with respect to the Early Mesolithic.[62] His classification is
based on:
  – the length and width of the artefact concentration as defined by the distribution
    of retouched tools;
  – the shape of the concentration;
  – the number of tools and the amount of debitage;

148

– the density of the tools;
– the nature and distribution of associated features.

The first type of site is more or less trapezoidal and has average dimensions of 24.2 x 19.4 m. The number of retouched tools ranges from 153 to 400 and the features all lie within the limits of the tool scatter. All tool types are represented at these sites, which indicates that a wide range of activities was carried out.[63] The second type is oval and has average dimensions of 8.3 x 4.2 m. The number of tools varies from 34 to 40 and the features again lie within the distribution area of the debitage. The average dimensions of the third type, which is more or less round, are 3.4 by 2.4 m. The number of retouched tools varies from 6 to 37. At sites of this type the artefacts are distributed in one, two or three concentrations. Sites with two concentrations often contain a hearth at the centre. The tools of the second and third types frequently indicate specialisation. According to Newell, this, com-

fig. 7.9

In 1983 a small site was excavated in a sandpit at Helchteren-Sonnisse Heide (Belgian province of Limburg). The site comprised a thin scatter of flint artefacts surrounding a small concentration of sandstone plates, which – as shown by evidence of burning – formed part of a hearth. The size of the site, the relatively small number of archaeological finds and the distinct pattern of the finds suggest that this was a camp that was used once, for a short period of time. Scale 1:50.

Helchteren-Sonnisse Heide

0   2m

⟍⟍ disturbance   ❙ backed blade   ▪ core   ▲ scraper
• debitage   ▲ point   ◆ burin   ⊘ sandstone

149

bined with the small size of the sites, suggests that specific activities were carried out by a small number of the members of the social unit. He assumes that there is a functional relationship between the distinguished site types, the sites of types 2 and 3 having been subordinate to those of type 1, which were the primary subsistence units' base camps.

Interpretation problems

The problem with these classifications is that they are based on the results of investigations, which were on the whole primitively executed and poorly documented and in which neither the size of the site nor the number of artefacts was accurately determined. In most cases the excavation stopped where the artefact scatter ended or became less dense; the excavators assumed that they had then investigated the entire site. Excavations of larger areas, such as at Rekem in Belgium[64] and Niederbieber in Germany,[65] have shown that several artefact concentrations of one and the same cultural unit are often to be found at short distances from one another. This raises the question whether – and if so, how – the individual scatters of such complex composite sites are related. Small concentrations including specialised tools or large numbers of flakes from one or a few flint nodules may reflect activities that were carried out at some distance from the actual camp or base. Alternatively, different concentrations may reflect the simultaneous use of the site by different households or different instances of repeated use of the site. Excavators try to solve this problem by finding out whether artefacts from different concentrations can be refitted; if so, the scatters represent simultaneous, but spatially separated activities.[66] Another possibility involves the use of residual lithic material brought along from a different site. A classic example of research into these alternatives is that which was carried out at the aforementioned Tjongerian site at Meer.

One way in which questions regarding contemporaneity can sometimes be answered is by means of pollen analysis. Recent research at Milheeze revealed recurring minima in the values of pine pollen in the diagrams obtained for the organic sediments in the vicinity of a number of *Federmesser* sites. Each of these minima was succeeded by a regeneration phase with a vegetation characteristic of clearances. It is not unlikely that these cyclic disturbances in the vegetation were caused by human activities. If this interpretation is correct, we may regard this as evidence that the site at Milheeze was repeatedly occupied[67] and as further support for the conclusion that (very) large find concentrations represent sites that were used on several occasions: the knowledge that important resources were available at a particular location would have been a reason for returning there.

Site location

The sites are not randomly distributed throughout the landscape, but according to a specific pattern. The proximity of water (a pool, lake, river or a cut-off meander) was clearly an important condition for settlement. Many sites lie on the (south)eastern slopes of coversand ridges; those natural elevations probably provided shelter against the then prevailing (north)westerly winds.[68]

The fact that well-drained coversand ridges were repeatedly occupied implies that they played important parts in the Upper Palaeolithic and Early Mesolithic settlement systems (fig. 7.10). However, as already mentioned above, our picture

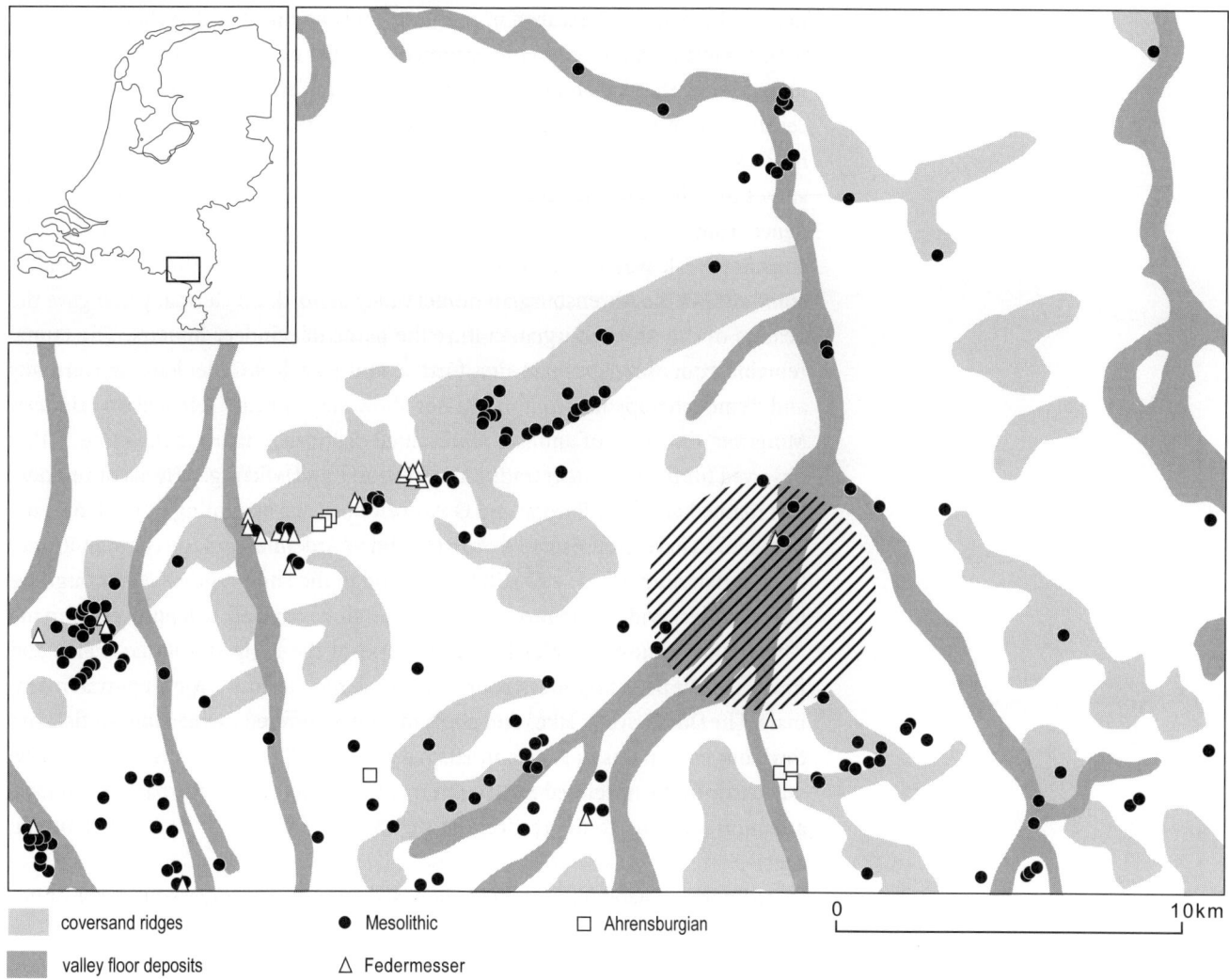

▨ coversand ridges	● Mesolithic	☐ Ahrensburgian	0 10km
▨ valley floor deposits	△ Federmesser		

of those settlement systems is biased owing to the fact that large parts of the old land surface now lie buried beneath thick Holocene deposits. In theory, with their wealth of different resources, the wide valleys of the major rivers will have been attractive foraging areas, while the edges of those valleys have offered ideal settlement conditions for Upper Palaeolithic and Early Mesolithic groups. It is only in the last decade that some information on this matter has come to light in the form of objects of organic material and flint scatters.[69]

SUBSISTENCE

In the Netherlands, virtually no factual information is available on subsistence patterns and the relative importance of hunting, fishing and gathering. Likewise, little or nothing is known about the functions of sites or the season of occupation. The sparse organic remains that are found during excavations, from which such information could theoretically be derived, are frequently burned and very fragmentary. Bones are often stray finds or they are recovered from layers in which their association with lithic artefacts is not certain.

For information on subsistence patterns we must therefore turn to evidence from countries surrounding the Netherlands. There, too, the available data presents a biased picture of the resources exploited by the prehistoric occupants. This is due mainly to differences in the state of preservation of occupation re-

fig. 7.10

Distribution of Late Palaeolithic and Mesolithic sites in the Kempen region around Eindhoven in the province of North Brabant. The sites reveal a pronounced preference for locations on the large southwest-northeast oriented coversand ridges, visible on the present-day soil map as relatively dry ('high'), poor and fine sandy soils which originally contained podzol horizons. Hatched area: Eindhoven. Scale 1:200,000.

mains, the employed excavation methods and the unequal distribution of sites with organic remains across the occupied area. For example, the sample does not include sites that lay along the former coastline.[70] Apart from that, it is almost certain that not all the different types of sites of the former settlement systems have yielded organic remains. *Federmesser* evidence from the German Rhineland shows that the main animals hunted were elk, red deer, auroch and beaver.[71] Evidence from northern Germany and Great Britain suggests that reindeer was also consumed.[72] It was the large amounts of reindeer remains that were found at some sites in the Ahrensburgian tunnel valley in northern Germany that gave the bearers of the Ahrensburgian culture the name of reindeer hunters. The faunal remains from Ahrensburgian sites further south, such as Callenhardt in Germany and Remouchamps in Belgium, do not show such a heavy reliance on reindeer. Moreover, the range of animals represented by those remains is the same as that observed for the *Federmesser* tradition, plus horse and wild pig.[73] Herds of reindeer still roamed northern Europe and Great Britain at the beginning of the Holocene but seem to have disappeared from the Belgian Ardennes and the German Rhineland by that time. Horse was still to be found in the latter regions.[74] Although we have no direct evidence to prove it, the impression is that elk disappeared from the Netherlands almost completely in the course of the Early Mesolithic.[75] Fish and fowl will have been important sources of food, too, besides large terrestrial mammals. The Dutch rivers, lakes and pools must have offered a wide range of fish and fowl, but no remains of such animals have come to light at the sites. This may be due partly to the unrefined excavation methods employed in the past, when little attention was paid to the recovery of the skeletal remains of such small animal species.

Although palaeobotanical research has shown that an increasing range of ed-

fig. 7.11
Around the end of the last glacial, dogs were the first animals to be domesticated in different parts of the world, to assist in hunting. Dating from between 9000 and 8000 BC, this dog skull from the Pre-Boreal Early Mesolithic site of Bedburg-Königshoven (Rhineland) constitutes the oldest known dog remains found in the Lower Rhine Basin. The skull is 19.5 cm long.

ible fruits and plants became available around the end of the Pleistocene and the beginning of the Holocene, we have only very little direct evidence that they were actually consumed. Our evidence from the Early Mesolithic consists largely of carbonised hazelnuts. Hazels were so common in the open pine forests of the Boreal that this period was in the past sometimes referred to as the 'hazel-pine period' in Germany. Apparently grateful use was made of the vast abundance of hazelnuts. Some British researchers have interpreted the marked decrease in tree pollen in pollen diagrams and the observed increase in charcoal in peat bogs as indications of Mesolithic man's interference with the environment.[76] Clearances are attractive habitats for certain animal species; they are also believed to have played an important part in increasing the productivity of plant resources, as in the case of the pioneering hazel. Activities of the kind that affected the natural environment in Great Britain[77] have, however, not been attested in the Netherlands as yet. Hearth pits at Early Mesolithic sites may have been used for processing plant food besides being sources of heat.[78]

What may also be regarded as an indication of human activities affecting the natural environment is the appearance of domesticated dogs; they will have been kept both as pets and as hunting assistants. Remains of dogs have been found in Upper Palaeolithic contexts, for example at Oberkassel, Döbritz and Saalfeld in Germany and at Remouchamps in Belgium,[79] and at Early Mesolithic sites, such as Star Carr (England) and Bedburg-Königshoven in Germany (fig. 7.11).[80]

Faunal remains, the results of determinations of the season of occupation and ecological and anthropological models have together given rise to the view that the distribution patterns of sites reflect settlement systems that were determined largely by seasonal differences in activities and migration patterns. The aforementioned models are to a great extent based on the cultural remains of the Ahrensburgian hunters and gatherers, on account of their assumed reliance on reindeer.[81] So far, however, hardly any efforts have been made to apply these models to new or previously unused archaeological evidence in order to test their validity.

Ethnographic parallels and ethno-archaeological observations have led some researchers to assume the existence of large base camps. For this assumption, however, no or only very little archaeological evidence exists.[82] The explanation that is often advanced to account for the fact that no such camps have yet been found is that they must have been situated along the former coastline, in what are now submerged parts of the North Sea basin, or in river valleys and deltas, from where they have disappeared owing to erosion or where they now lie buried beneath thick layers of Holocene deposits. The question, however, is whether the analogies derived from (sub)recent societies of hunter-fisher-gatherers on which this assumption is based hold for prehistoric situations, too.

CONCLUSIONS

The Late Glacial and Early Holocene occupation remains that have come to light in the Low Countries form part of a vast body of archaeological evidence, with a distribution area covering large parts of northern Europe, relating to communities of hunters, fishers and gatherers with a similar material culture. This archaeological evidence from the last phase of the Upper Palaeolithic and the Early Mesolithic points to continuity of occupation. The material culture of the last phase of the Upper Palaeolithic closely resembles that of the beginning of the Mesolithic; the observed differences (for example the appearance of microliths) are more likely to be the consequences of developments than of actual changes. Stylistic changes in the material culture from the period in question allow us to distinguish three groups: *Federmesser*, Ahrensburgian and Early Mesolithic. It is not so easy to interpret these groups in socio-ethnic terms. Units like the Ahrensburgian culture could perhaps be correlated with a 'maximum band' or dialect tribe of the kind distinguishable among subarctic societies of hunter-fisher-gatherers in the interior of Canada and Alaska.[83]

The evidence relating to the exploited animals is greatly biased as a result of different kinds of formation processes and shows numerous hiatuses. Nevertheless, it seems to indicate that the representatives of the *Federmesser* tradition exploited predominantly uniformly distributed, relatively immobile species. The Ahrensburgian people exploited the same kinds of animals, but in some seasons and/or areas reindeer also formed an important part of their diet. The territories of sedentary game were probably smaller in the Younger Dryas than they had been in the preceding Allerød. The mobile species, especially reindeer, which are well capable of coping with a sparsely vegetated environment, gradually disappeared in the Early Holocene. The range of sedentary game species increased, but so did the density and distribution of these animals across the landscape. Fish, fowl and plant resources were probably increasingly exploited, too. The occurrence at some sites of remains of animal species favouring open environments alongside species favouring forested habitats reflects the diversity of the natural environment and the wide range of ecological zones that were exploited.[84]

The increasing diversity and more uniform distribution of resources led to changes in subsistence activities, for example a greater use of bows and arrows and – probably – the use of dogs as hunting assistants. These developments not only enabled more efficient hunting techniques but also allowed the hunters to supplement their diet with new species which had probably been difficult to exploit with less sophisticated technologies in the past. The transition from the Upper Palaeolithic to the Mesolithic is but a phase in the gradual process of adaptation to a changing environment, a phase which is at present moreover very difficult to follow in the archaeological record of the Low Countries.

NOTES

1 See Newell 1984, 71 for a survey.

2 See Price 1987 for a discussion of this problem.

3 *Archeologische Berichten* (1977-1987), *Archeologie* (since 1989), *APAN-Intern* (1986-1991) and *APAN-Extern* (since 1992).

4 Of the Prehistoric Laboratory of the Catholic University of Louvain, Belgium (Vermeersch 1982b, 1984).

5 The maps shown in Van Es *et al.* 1988, 63-65, give an impression of the unequal distribution of Upper Palaeolithic and Mesolithic sites in the Netherlands.

6 The temperatures are from Bohncke 1991, 96. The summer temperatures were inferred from palaeobotanical evidence and remains of beetles, the winter temperatures from the occurrence of periglacial phenomena such as frost cracks.

7 Bosinski 1992, 52.

8 Bohncke 1991, 104.

9 Koster 1992, 91.

10 The colonisation rates of the various species at the beginning of the Holocene are thought to have differed from those in comparable phases at the beginning of the Late Glacial (*e.g.* the Bølling interstadial). The difference was probably due to the continuous presence of certain plant communities in specific landscape features (such as river valleys) at the beginning of the Holocene.

11 Zagwijn 1986, fig. 26.

12 Bohncke 1991, 98.

13 The Netherlands (for example Bohncke *et al.* 1988); Germany (such as Bunnik *et al.* 1993, Ursinger 1985) and Belgium (for example Cordy 1991).

14 Van Leeuwaarden 1982.

15 Bohncke 1991.

16 Street *et al.* 1994; Vermeersch 1984.

17 *Federmesser* is the German word for penknife. It refers to the shape of the type of point that is considered characteristic of this culture. For a survey of the sites of the *Federmesser* tradition see Schwabedissen (1954); there is no recent survey.

18 The Tjongerian culture or Tjongerian group is named after the rivulet the Tjonger in Friesland (Bohmers 1947, 53).

19 For the Ahrensburgian tunnel valley see chapter 6, note 49 and Rust 1943.

20 For example Arts 1988, 1990.

21 Deeben 1988.

22 Stapert 1979b, 1985; Kramer *et al.* 1985.

23 Stapert 1985b, 54-55.

24 Arts 1988, 304; Paddayya 1971, 266. For a discussion of this matter see Stapert 1985b, 54-56, and the chapter written by Rensink and Stapert in this volume.

25 This was for example possible at a settlement at Westelbeers (province of North Brabant), which was excavated between 1967 and 1989. At this site, with its area of some 3000 m², an Upper Palaeolithic and a Mesolithic find layer were found to partly overlap one another spatially.

26 Gilot 1984; Lanting/Mook 1977.

27 Since 1983 dating programmes have been carried out at Oxford and other research centres, in which use has been made of Accelerator Mass Spectrometry (AMS). With this method only small amounts (approx. 250-500 mg) of bone or antler are required to date an object (Housley 1991). Housley (1991, 27) also mentions ^{14}C dates obtained for charcoal from the *Federmesser* sites of Neerharen (Belgium), which vary from 9900 to 2230 BP, and the date obtained for the resin/mastic adhering to a Tjongerian point. The latter sample yielded a date of 11,350 ± 150 BP, a date that would be expected for a *Federmesser* site.

28 Campbell 1977; Smith 1992.

29 Fagnart 1988.

30 Usselo (Stapert/Veenstra 1988); Haule V (Houtsma *et al.* 1990); Siegerswoude (Kramer *et al.* 1985; those authors however class Siegerswoude as a Creswellian site); Hoornse Veld (Musch 1974).

31 Milheeze (Heesters/Wouters 1970; Rozoy 1978); Budel II (Wouters 1990); Geldrop 3-4 (Deeben 1988); De Banen-Nederweert (Bohmers 1956; Beerenhout *et al.* 1990).

32 Arts/Deeben 1981.

33 Van Noort/Wouters 1987.

34 Stapert 1989.

35 Vessem (Arts/Deeben 1981); Geldrop (Bohmers/Wouters 1962; Deeben 1990, 1994).

36 The indicated distribution area is based on the occurrence of Ahrensburgian tanged points. For a survey of the distribution of points of this type see Taute (1968). It has however recently been found that the limits of his distribution area should be moved much further eastwards (Zalieznjak 1989).

37 Fisher/Tauber 1986; Lanting/Mook 1977. The early date (10,960 ± 85 BP) obtained for the Ahrensburgian site Geldrop 1 is open to doubt; it is likely that the charcoal sample which yielded the date for (what is currently) the earliest site of the Ahrensburgian culture came from a layer of Usselo soil drifted from elsewhere (Deeben 1994).

38 Jacobi 1976; Newell 1973, 420.

39 Nijnsel (Heesters/Wouters 1968); Geldrop (Deeben 1988, 1994); Swalmen and Gramsbergen (Stapert 1979). Elsewhere (Stapert 1989, 20), Gramsbergen has been dated to the last phase of the Ah-

rensburgian tradition, the so-called 'epi-Ahrensburgian', on the basis of Upper Palaeolithic characteristics of the flint.

40 Newell 1973.

41 Arts 1988; Verhart 1988.

42 Arts 1988; Bohmers 1956; Bohmers/Wouters 1956; Newell/Vroomans 1972.

43 For example Schwabedissen (1954) for the *Federmesser* tradition; Bohmers (1956) for the Tjongerian culture and Taute (1968) for the Ahrensburgian culture. See the comment made above with reference to the Creswellian group.

44 *Riesenklingen* are longer than 15 cm at a minimum width of 2.5 cm, or longer than 12 cm at a minimum width of 5 cm (Taute 1968, 16).

45 Bordaz 1970.

46 Clarke 1976; Dumont 1988.

47 Beuker 1990.

48 Dewez 1987. Unusual Early Mesolithic finds are what are described as 'deer antler masks': skulls of deer with or without antler that may have been used as a form of disguise in hunting or as a headdress during rituals (Street 1989b, 49). Antler masks have been found in Germany (Bedburg-Königshoven, Hohen Viecheln) and Great Britain (Star Carr).

49 Arts 1988, fig. 11; Louwe Kooijmans 1970; Verhart 1988, 1990.

50 Odé 1990.

51 Geldrop 1 (Wouters 1957; Deeben 1994), Geldrop/Mie/Peels 1985 (Deeben 1990).

52 Arts 1988; Wouters 1991.

53 Geldrop 3-1 (Bohmers/Wouters 1962), Wanssum (Verhart/Wansleeben 1990).

54 Newell 1980; see also the problems involved in the dating of charcoal samples discussed above.

55 Bokelmann 1991a.

56 See for example Newell/Dekin 1978; Stapert 1992.

57 Cziesla *et al.* 1990.

58 Van Noten 1978; Cahen *et al.* 1979.

59 Stapert 1985b, 57 ff.

60 The Uffelte site probably dates from the Mesolithic (Beuker 1981; Price 1975), that of Waubach from the Upper Palaeolithic and the Mesolithic (Arts 1984).

61 Haule V (Houtsma *et al.*, 1996), Geldrop 3-4 (Deeben 1988), Siegerswoude (Kramer *et al.* 1985).

62 Newell 1973.

63 Newell (1973) regards primary subsistence units as functional social units; on the basis of ethnographic evidence it is assumed that such units comprised 20 to 25 individuals.

64 Lauwers 1988.

65 Loftus 1984; Loftus 1985; Winter 1986; see also Bolus 1992.

66 Arts 1988, 307.

67 Bos/Janssen 1996.

68 Arts 1988, 308-309.

69 *E.g.* Arts 1987a.

70 *E.g.* Andersen *et al.* 1990.

71 Deeben 1988.

72 Campbell 1977.

73 Deeben 1988. But evidence for the exploitation of horse by the *Federmesser* group, too, has recently been found in the German Rhineland (Bolus 1992).

74 E.g. Street 1991.

75 Andersen *et al.* 1990.

76 Mellars 1976; Simmons *et al.* 1989.

77 E.g. Bush 1988; Smith *et al.* 1989.

78 Groenendijk 1987, 99.

79 Dewez *et al.* 1974.

80 Clark 1954; Street 1989a.

81 See for example Arts/Deeben 1981; Bokelmann 1979; Sturdy 1975 and Van Noort/Wouters 1987.

82 E.g. Arts 1990; Houtsma *et al.*, 1990, 1996; Stapert 2000.

83 Arts/Deeben 1981.

84 As observed at the site Bedburg-Königshoven in particular (Street 1989b, 1991).

B A drowned land
Mesolithic from the North Sea floor

Leo Verhart

North Sea

One afternoon in September 1931 a large lump of peat fell from the fishing nets to the deck of the British trawler Colinda, where it broke in half. The fracture surface revealed a yellow elongated object. Back on shore, the master of the ship consulted an archaeologist, who identified the object as a barbed bone point dating from the Mesolithic.

This discovery meant that it was possible to recover remains of the occupants of the originally dry North Sea Basin. At the end of the last glacial period large amounts of water were stored in the ice caps of Scandinavia and other areas, as a result of which the sea level at the beginning of the Mesolithic (10,000 BP) was some 65 m lower than it is today (fig. B1). The Netherlands formed an 'inland' part of an area whose coast lay to the south of what are now the Channel Islands and some 300 km from the present town of Den Helder in the northwest. The coversand landscape of this area was inhabited by hunter-gatherer communities. The improvement of the climate after the last glacial period, however, had disastrous consequences for their occupation area. In 2000 years the sea level rose almost 40 m and the water submerged the entire North Sea Basin, an area of 180,000 km². The original occupants must have witnessed drastic changes in the coastline during their lives: with each new generation the coastline moved several kilometres further inland, the islands became smaller and large inland seas were formed.

The rise in sea level made the occupation remains from this period inaccessible to archaeologists via normal research methods, but a favourable consequence is the exceptionally good preservation conditions for organic remains. Stray artefacts have regularly been washed ashore, for example the Whitburn point,[1] or have been dredged up, such as the point from the Leman and Ower Banks[2] and the picks and axes from the Brown Bank (fig. B2).[3] Large numbers of finds were, however, recovered during the creation of the artificial sand plain the 'Maasvlakte' and the raising of the shoreline as a means of protection against the sea.

Maasvlakte, Europoort

In the mid-1970s several amateur archaeologists started to comb the Maasvlakte beach of Europoort in search of Pleistocene bones. Their first finds were a few points of bone and antler, a small axe and an small sleeve.[4] In the early 1980s a change in tidal currents along the coast improved the chances of finding Mesolithic implements: in a relatively short time more than 500 points were collected (fig. B3). The complete lack of worked flint among the thousands of fragments of flint is remarkable.

The large number of finds and the new ¹⁴C dating method based on mass spectroscopy (AMS) have made it possible to study these stray finds and to draw conclusions regarding

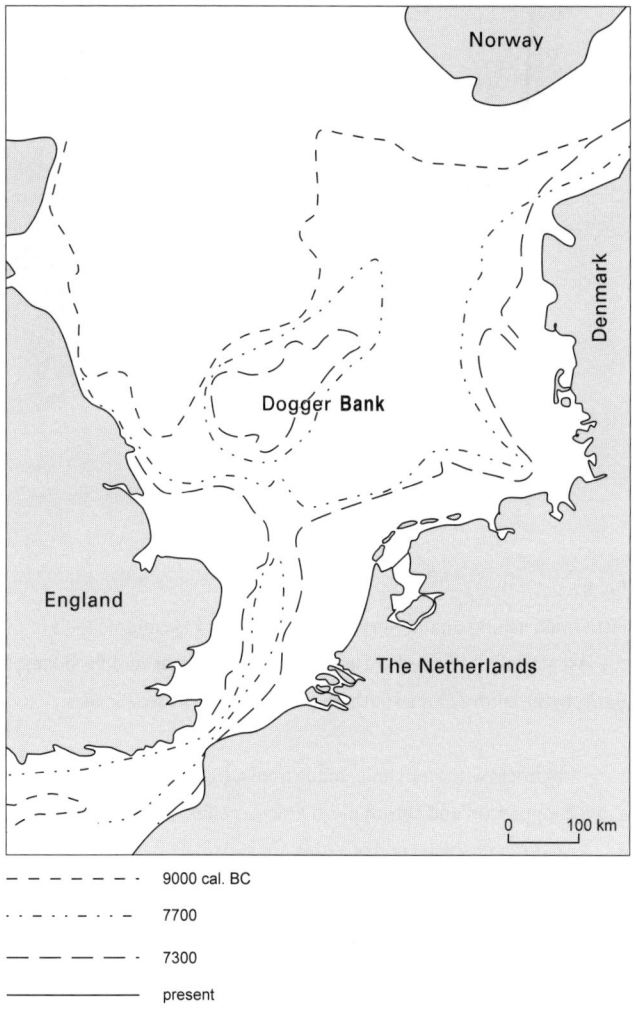

fig. B1

Coastlines during the submersion of the North Sea basin between *c.* 9000 and 7000 cal. BC. The coastlines are based on the combination of the well-established sea level data and the contour lines of the sea floor. The connection between the Channel and the North Sea was a saltwater tidal area, completely different from the present situation.

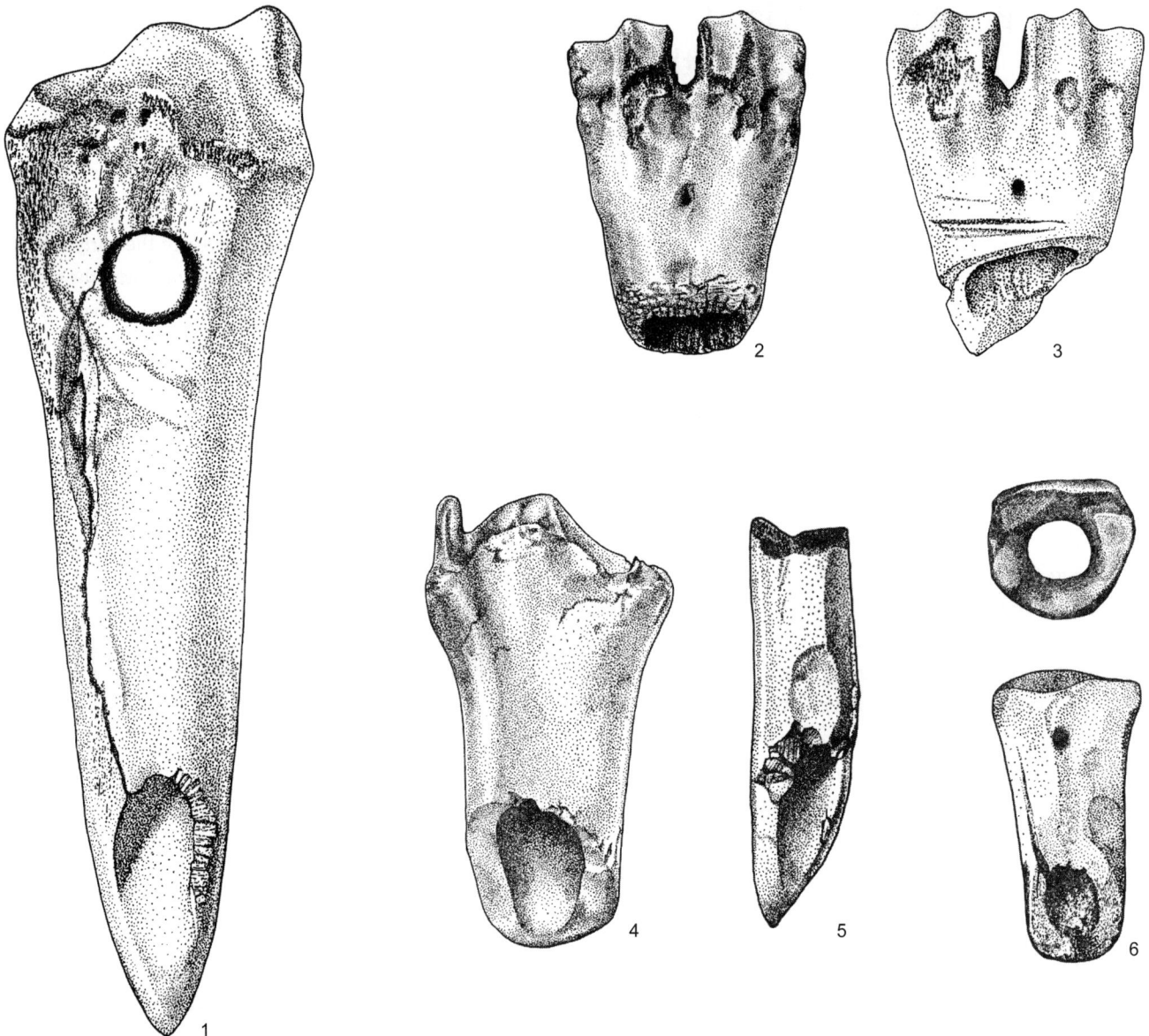

fig. B2

Fishermen fishing on the North Sea regularly find Mesolithic tools in their trawling nets, mixed up with mammal bones from the last glacial. Illustrated are implements made from aurochs bones, fished up from a deep gully, adjacent to the Brown Bank, in the centre of the southern part of the North Sea. Scale 1:2.

1   'mattock' with shaft hole, made from a right radius

2, 3   chopped-off and cut-off distal articular ends, refuse of tool production

4   axe from the distal end of a tibia

5   pointed axe from the shaft of a metapodal

6   socketed axe on the proximal end of a metapodal

their context, age and function. The finds from the Maasvlakte also gave rise to a study into the occurrence and use of bone and antler points in Northwest Europe in general.[5]

On the basis of the results of a statistical analysis of the finds, a comparison of associations of such artefacts with the animals hunted in the rest of Europe and the study of traces of use and wear on the points themselves, three classes of points with different functions have been distinguished: harpoons, points for spears or lances and arrow heads.[6] The composition of the group of finds from the Maasvlakte and the great similarities in the manufacturing methods used initially suggested a closed assemblage of finds, possibly dating from a fairly short period. The ^{14}C dates obtained for four of the points, however, indicate a period of use from

9950 to 8060 BP, which made the hypothesis that the finds all belonged to one and the same assemblage no longer tenable. The harpoons and the large points for spears or lances date from the Early Mesolithic, whereas the small (arrow) points are younger. The virtual absence of the manufacturing waste and other (flint) artefacts that are usually found at settlement sites suggests that the bone and antler points represent the remains of special activities. All these data show that the artefacts were used in a wet area in which animals were hunted over a long period of time. The lack of settlement waste may indicate that the area was a lake or a swamp. A change in hunting strategy appears to have taken place at some time: in the early phase spear points dominate, whereas in the later phase the emphasis was more on hunting with a bow and arrow.[7]

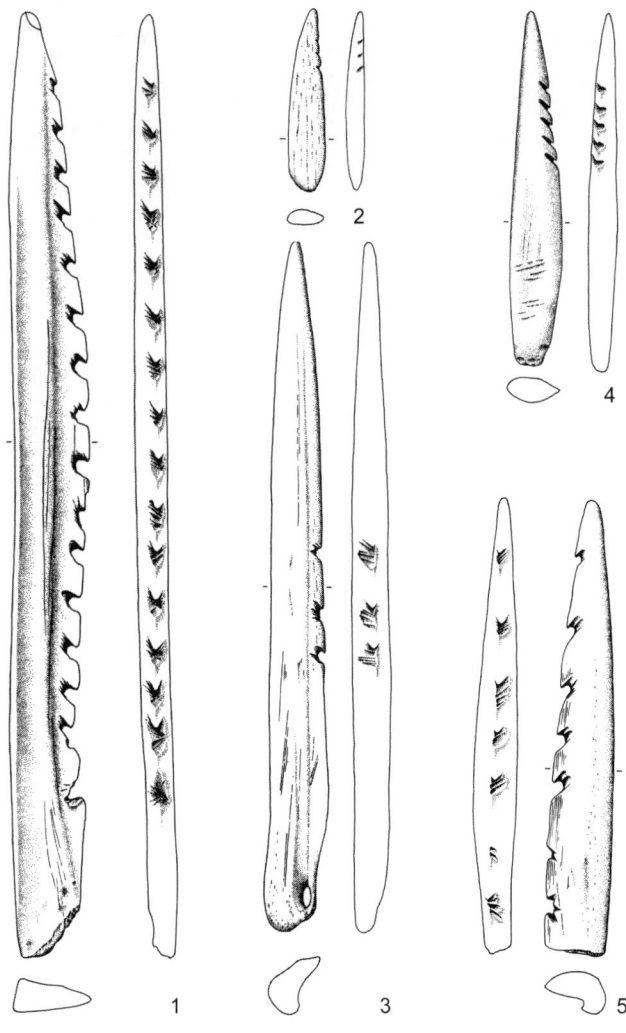

fig. B3

Some of the bone and antler barbed points, dating from the Late Palaeolithic and the Early and Middle Mesolithic, dredged up in Europoort. The large points have been used as harpoon or javelin tips, the small specimen as arrow heads. Scale 2:3.

Recent finds from outside the area that yielded the points of the Maasvlakte present a different picture. These finds comprise a number of antler axes that came to light during coastal protecting works near Hoek van Holland and Scheveningen and a few bone points and a flint scraper were found in the sand suppletion of the beach of Monster. They indicate that the settlements, of which only the 'poor' flint remains are found in the dry part of the Netherlands, must have lain in the direct vicinity of the lakes or swamps. That makes it likely that the remains of many such settlements have been preserved on and in the floor of the North Sea.[8]

North European groups

The large number of points recovered from the Maasvlakte also gave rise to a study of the typology and distribution of such artefacts over the whole of Northwest Europe.[9] The finds from the Maasvlakte can be divided into two main groups on typological grounds: points with fine barbs spaced close together and points with coarser barbs spaced further apart. The first group has a wide distribution area. The points of this group were fairly common throughout the entire period from 11,000 to 5000 BP. The points of the second group present a more striking picture: they prove to have been used for only a short period of time in a remarkably small area. The available dates indicate that the points of this second group were used in the Late Palaeolithic and the Early Mesolithic.

Although the distribution pattern of Northwest Europe as a whole is to some extent determined by preservation conditions the area can be split up into three parts: points with widely spaced barbs in the west, points with a double row of barbs in the central part and points with a single row of barbs in the east (fig. B4). This spatial and stylistic division may be the result of several factors: the artefacts may have been used for different purposes, they may have been used for hunting specific kinds of animals or they may have been used by different cultural groups. The most likely explanation is that the stylistic differences express differences in the cultural backgrounds of different groups of peoples. In that case the distribution areas of the three types of points may represent social territories in the transitional period between the Late Palaeolithic and the Early Mesolithic.

Notes

1   Mellars 1970.
2   Burkitt 1932.

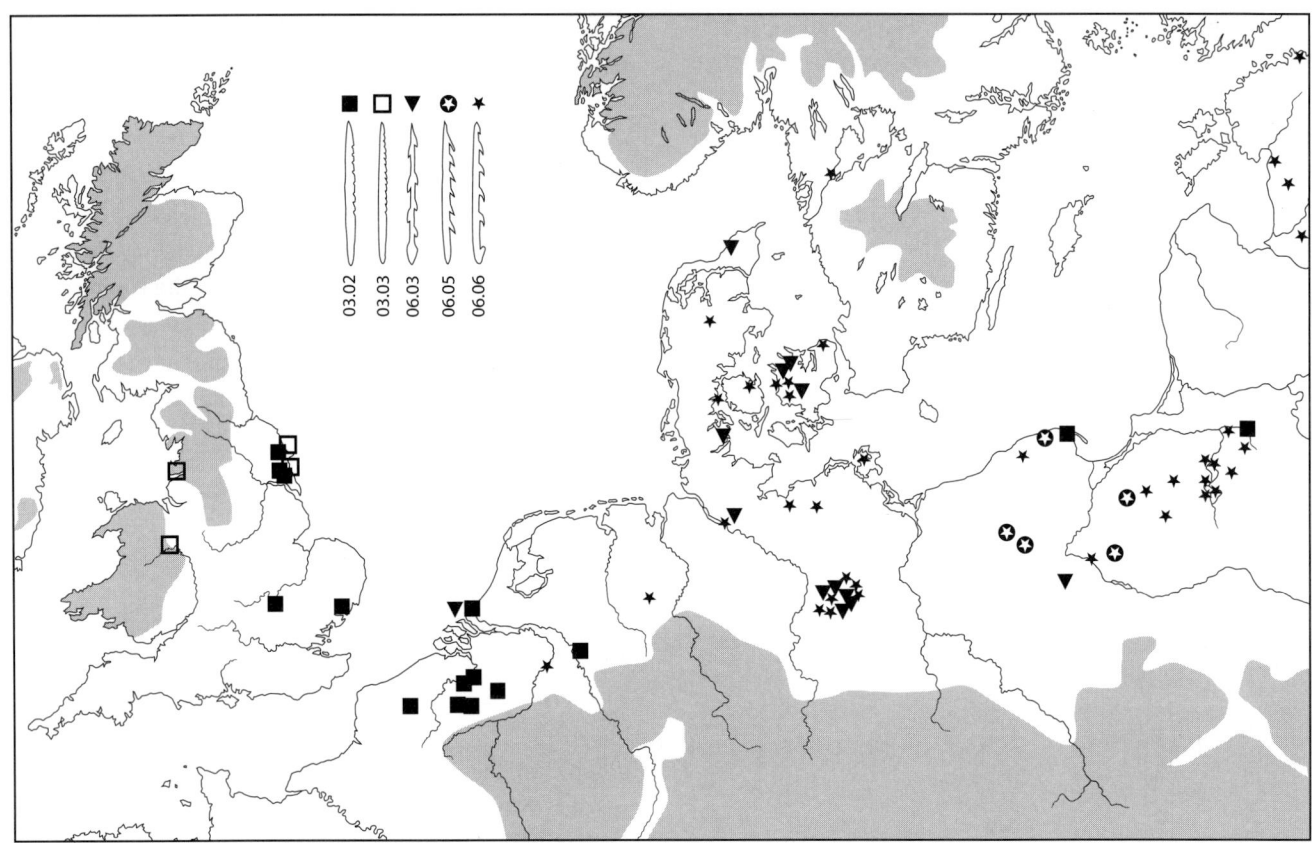

fig. B4

Distribution of the different types of points used in Northwestern Europe between 10,000 and 7500 cal BC.

3   Louwe Kooijmans 1970-'71; Stolzenbach/Stolzenbach 1991; Verhart 2000b.

4   Louwe Kooijmans 1970-'71.

5   Verhart 1990, 1995.

6   Verhart 1988, 1995.

7   Verhart 1995.

8   Verhart 2000b.

9   Verhart 1990.

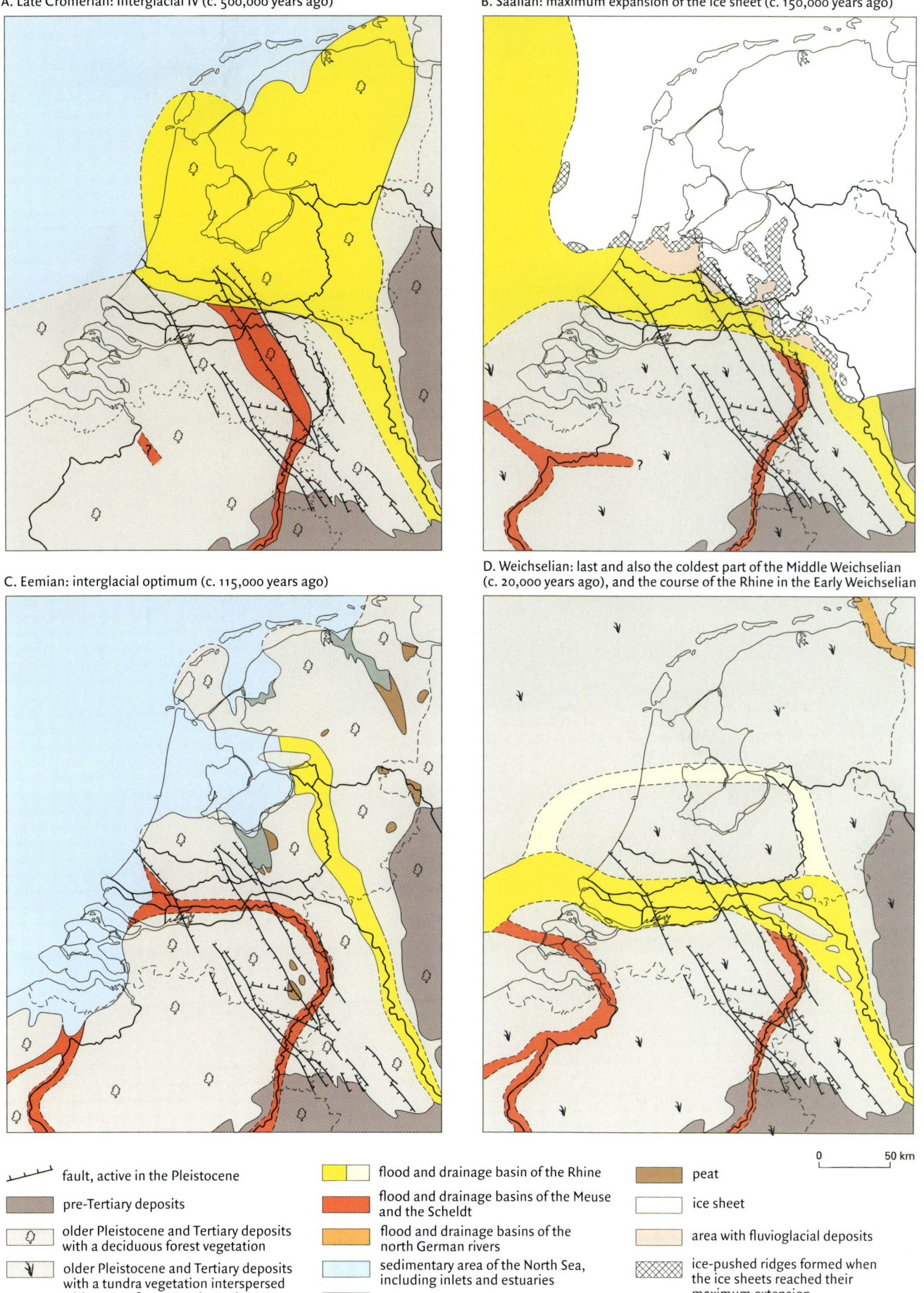

A. Late Cromerian: Interglacial IV (c. 500,000 years ago)

B. Saalian: maximum expansion of the ice sheet (c. 150,000 years ago)

C. Eemian: interglacial optimum (c. 115,000 years ago)

D. Weichselian: last and also the coldest part of the Middle Weichselian (c. 20,000 years ago), and the course of the Rhine in the Early Weichselian

0   50 km

fault, active in the Pleistocene	
pre-Tertiary deposits	
older Pleistocene and Tertiary deposits with a deciduous forest vegetation	
older Pleistocene and Tertiary deposits with a tundra vegetation interspersed with areas of coversand (northern part of the Netherlands) and loess deposits (southern part of the Netherlands)	

flood and drainage basin of the Rhine

flood and drainage basins of the Meuse and the Scheldt

flood and drainage basins of the north German rivers

sedimentary area of the North Sea, including inlets and estuaries

salt marshes and tidal flats

peat

ice sheet

area with fluvioglacial deposits

ice-pushed ridges formed when the ice sheets reached their maximum extension

pl. 1 Reconstruction of the most important sedimentary areas and vegetations in the Netherlands in various phases of the Middle and Late Pleistocene. Some of the original sediments have disappeared due to erosion, in particular in the German and Belgian border areas, where the ground has subsided less than in the rest of the Netherlands. In the central part of the Netherlands the formation of deep glacial basins caused a good deal of erosion in the Saalian. During the interglacials some of the sediments disappeared as a result of erosion by the sea. Inferred limits of sedimentary areas are marked by dashed lines, actual limits by solid lines.

0   50 km

pl. 2-6 Palaeogeographic maps indicating the different natural landscapes occurring in five phases of the Holocene. The focus is on the development of the large sedimentary area between the coastline and the Pleistocene sand. The many rivulets and streams with their alluvial deposits that intersected the sandy areas are not indicated on the maps.

pl. 2 The Netherlands in the Early Atlantic / Late Mesolithic, around 5700 BC, at the end of the formation of the Calais I deposits. The Rhine and the Meuse flowed into the sea via a – still incised – joint valley approximately 50 km to the west of the present coastline. The old river dunes lay in the plain as large high islands. The area of North- and South Holland was a large expanse of tidal flats bordered by a relatively narrow strip of fen peat. The convex coastline to the west of the present province of North Holland and the islands Texel and Vlieland resulted from two relatively high Pleistocene elevations which supplied sediments to the concave coasts further north and south and the tidal basins behind them. The geography of the North Sea basin is somewhat hypothetical.

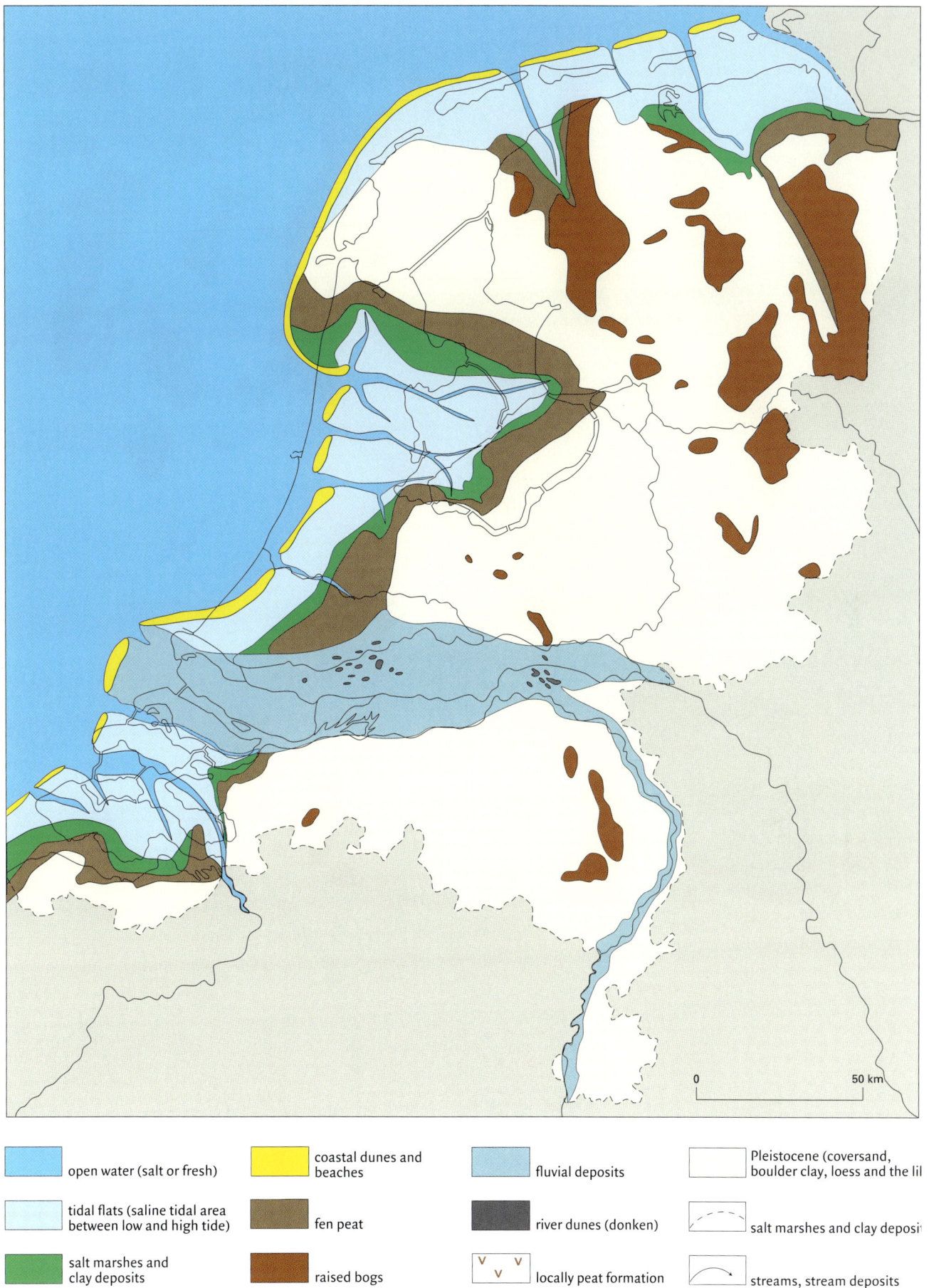

	open water (salt or fresh)		coastal dunes and beaches		fluvial deposits		Pleistocene (coversand, boulder clay, loess and the lil
	tidal flats (saline tidal area between low and high tide)		fen peat		river dunes (donken)		salt marshes and clay deposi
	salt marshes and clay deposits		raised bogs		locally peat formation		streams, stream deposits

pl. 3 The Netherlands in the Late Atlantic / Middle Neolithic A, around 4200 BC, at the end of the formation of the Calais II deposits. The decrease in the rate at which the sea level rose led to the end of the inland movement of the coastline. By this time, large quantities of sand of the Rhine-Meuse delta had been carried away on either side of the delta. The cliff coast of the province of North Holland had meanwhile become much shorter and lower. The tidal basins were almost entirely filled with sediments. All the landscape zones had moved towards the east. In this period the marine and tidal influences reached their furthest extension inland. Large raised bogs developed in the sandy areas.

0   50 km

pl. 4 The Netherlands in the Early Subboreal / Middle Neolithic B, around 3000 BC, at the end of the formation of the Calais IVa deposits. The belt of coastal barriers had been rapidly expanding on the seaward side, especially along the coast of North- and South Holland, on either side of the Rhine estuary. This meant that the sea could penetrate the coastal plain only via the tidal inlets. The coastal plain was consequently transformed into a vast peat bog, with intertidal zones in the IJsselmeer basin and the province of Zeeland. The northern coastal plain was much less protected.

![blue]	open water (salt or fresh)	![yellow] coastal dunes and beaches	![light blue] fluvial deposits	Pleistocene (coversand, boulder clay, loess and the lil...
![light blue2]	tidal flats (saline tidal area between low and high tide)	![taupe] fen peat	![dark grey] river dunes (donken)	salt marshes and clay deposi...
![green]	salt marshes and clay deposits	![brown] raised bogs	locally peat formation	streams, stream deposits

pl. 5 The Netherlands in the Late Subboreal / Middle Bronze Age, around 1250 BC, the end of the formation of the Dunkirk 0 deposits. The coast in the west had become an almost uninterrupted straight barrier. This coastline protected the hinterland so well as to allow peat to grow almost everywhere, ultimately even on the high sedimentary deposits in the tidal inlet of Bergen, in the area of what is now Westfrisia. Only the estuaries were still open. Vast raised bogs developed in parts of the coastal plain not affected by marine or fluvial influences. A more open situation was to remain permanently in the north. Wave action may well have been less effective for the landward transport of sand in this area.

■ open water (salt or fresh)	■ coastal dunes and beaches	■ fluvial deposits	□ Pleistocene (coversand, boulder clay, loess and the lil
■ tidal flats (saline tidal area between low and high tide)	■ fen peat	■ river dunes (donken)	salt marshes and clay deposi
■ salt marshes and clay deposits	■ raised bogs	ᵛ ᵛ ᵛ locally peat formation	streams, stream deposits

pl. 6 The Netherlands in the Early Subatlantic / Middle and Late Iron Age, between approximately 400 and 100 BC, at the end of the formation of the Dunkirk I deposits. In spite of the slow rise in sea level, storm surges created large gaps in the natural defence barrier bordering the sea. Large areas of peat were consequently drained to varying degrees. The subsequent subsidence of the surface allowed the deposition of extensive layers of clay. Clay meanwhile continued to be deposited in the north, too, resulting in the formation of salt marshes. The part of the coast that was to provide access to what was later to become the Zuiderzee had by this time become weak.

c

b

a

pl. 7 Typical stratigraphy in the area of the Younger and Older Dunes near Velserbroek. A soil formed on top of the Older Dunes was frequently under cultivation (a, ard marks).This soil was covered by thin layers of drift sand alternating with peat (b), implying a groundwater level at or just above the surface. In a later stage a somewhat thicker layer of Younger Dune sand (c) was deposited by the wind, after which the Breesaap dune valley formed here. The blast furnaces visible in the background lie in the northern half of the former Breesaap valley.

pl. 8 Three handaxes recovered from varying contexts in different parts of the Netherlands. Scale 1:2.

A. A handaxe found at Wijnjeterp in 1939 was for a long time the only evidence showing that the northern part of the Netherlands was occupied in the Middle Palaeolithic. The characteristic orange patina and gloss are the result of soil processes during the Weichselian. The same features are observable on other Middle Palaeolithic artefacts from the residual soil at the top of the boulder clay, the layer known as 'boulder sand'. The artefacts' stratigraphic positions imply that they postdate the Saalian ice expansion.

B. Handaxe from a gravel pit near Rhenen, found in fluvial deposits that were pushed up to the Utrecht ridge of hills around the end of the Saalian. This means that the axe predates the period of ice expansion that occurred around 150,000 years ago, but it is hard to say exactly how old it is. Buried so deep beneath the surface, this artefact has survived the ravages of time in fairly good condition.

C. Handaxe from the high terrace remnant known as 'De Hej' near Rijckholt, presumably from outcropping terrace deposits beneath Weichselian loess. Long-term exposure at the surface has led to the formation of a pronounced white patina on one side of the axe.

pl. 8D Rescue excavation of a Middle Palaeolithic site in the Belvédère quarry near Maastricht. The site has been saved as an island by the quarry owner, while the gravel and loess was dug away around the site to allow the excavation.

pl. 9A Aerial view of the excavation of an Early Mesolithic campsite near Posterholt. The entire area of the camp was excavated in units measuring 25x25 cm; the peripheral zone was sampled in a 1x1 m grid. Finds were collected by sieving the excavated soil; visible at the centre are three sieving installations surrounded by heaps of excavated soil.

pl. 9B Life at a Mesolithic camp. The huts have been left out of this artist's impression as we still know too little about them. People lived in a rich environment and exploited a wide diversity of food resources. In the drawing, we see fish being caught with traps and with spears from a canoe, a hunter and his son returning from a deer-hunting expedition and children picking wild apples. Activities like the scraping of animal skins and the smoking of fish were carried out at the periphery of the camp.

pl. 10A Four microliths made from Wommersom quartzite from various sites in the southern part of the Netherlands. On the left is a *feuille de gui*; next to it are two leaf-shaped points en to the right a broad trapeze, made on a regular blade with two parallel ribs, a so-called Montbani blade. 2x enlarged.

pl. 10B Section of one of the Late Mesolithic burial pits found at Mariënberg. The bottom part of the fill shows a red discolouration caused by ochre. The higher parts have been disturbed by animal and root action. Later soil formation led to the creation of thin, irregular illuvial horizons of iron compounds which are known as 'fibers'.

pl. 11A Excavation of a Late Mesolithic site on the Hardinxveld-Polderweg river dune in a pit measuring 16x28 m with steel sheet piling and deep drainage. On the left is the edge of the dune, on the right the former swamp. After the period of occupation the dune was covered with clay and peat deposits with a thickness of 4-8 m due to the rise in groundwater level.

pl. 11B Hardinxveld-De Bruin, complete tree-trunk canoe dating from the Late Mesolithic, approx. 5400 cal BC. The canoe was made by hollowing out the trunk of a lime tree; it is 5.5 m long, 42-29 cm wide and 2-4 cm thick. It was moored at the former edge of the river dune.

pl. 12 Two views of the Late Mesolithic community at Hardinxveld, around 5400 BC. Above: women are involved in domestic activities in front of one of the huts, children play at the water's edge. Below: the off-site activities. Man and boys are fishing pike. The crank canoes and the dogs played a central role in their lives.

pl. 13A Well in a *Bandkeramik* settlement at Kückhoven in the German Rhineland. The well was about 15 metres deep. The entire timber lining of the bottom eight metres has survived. It was built from segments of split oak trunks with lengths of approx. 3 m and widths of approx. 40 cm and with interlocking wood-joints at the corners. The tree that yielded the timber was felled in 5090 BC. The well was repaired on two occasions by inserting smaller lining structures in it, but it was also used as a refuse pit. Several objects of wood and other organic materials survived in the fill.

pl. 13B Part of a model of an idealised *Bandkeramik* settlement in the National Museum of Antiquities in Leiden. The settlement lies in a large clearing in the wood. A dense hedge has developed along the edge of the wood. The fields are fairly small and lie partly in the shade. The settlement itself consists of yards with houses of varying sizes. Clay pits are visible next to the houses and between the houses are kitchen gardens.

pl. 14A Plan of the tripartite house 13 in the early *Bandkeramik* settlement of Geleen-Janskamperveld; total length 21 m. Visible at the front are the double posts of the southeastern part. The roof supports in the central part are arranged in a distinct Y pattern. Only the walls of the northwestern part were set in a foundation trench. It is a plan of type 1b. The dead-straight edge of the clay pit on the left may be attributable to rainwater dripping from the roof.

pl. 14B Triangular feature of a split tree-trunk that was used as a wall post in a house in the *Bandkeramik* settlement of Stein.

pl. 15A One of the galleries of the Rijckholt flint mines. The galleries were at most 80 cm high. A thick horizon containing large nodules of dark flint stands out clearly from the surrounding paler lime. The miners dug under the flint so as to be able to free the lumps by breaking them or wresting them from the lime. They left sufficient – but not too thick – roof supports: production and safety were evidently both important concerns.

pl. 15B Tool marks made by mining implements in a wall of one of the Rijckholt flint mines. The lengths of the marks (many longer than 10 cm) indicate that the flint picks were mounted in or on a handle.

pl. 15C A deposit of flint picks in the Rijckholt mines. The flint was used to produce not only axes and blades, but also the implements needed for the mining operations. Such supplies of picks have been found at the bottom of shafts in several places, but many more came to light in the fills of the corridors.

pl. 16A Flint mine gallery exposed in the Geul valley slope near Valkenburg, along Plenkertstraat, which have been dated to the second half of the 4th millennium, the Middle Neolithic B. In earlier times people will have obtained flint from colluvial deposits. The mine corridors came to light in the early 20th century when the road was built here, but they were not identified as such until 1992. See also plate 21B.

pl. 16B In the Middle and Late Neolithic people ground their flint axes with hard quartzite, using sand as an abrasive. They took profit from large blocks of quartzite, which occurred naturally in the southern part of Limburg, such as this polishing stone from the valley of the Geul near Slenaken.

8   Living in abundance
Middle and Late Mesolithic

Leo Verhart and Henny Groenendijk

INTRODUCTION

Mesolithic research started late in the Netherlands. As it was always carried out by only one researcher or a small number of researchers it is characterised by periods of intensive activity alternating with periods of stagnation.

At first, it was mainly amateurs who did all the research; professional archaeologists followed later.[1] The early phase was dominated by typology. The arrival of a number of American researchers in the Netherlands in the mid-1960s gave the research a new impetus. These archaeologists, trained in the tradition of the New Archaeology, introduced an entirely new approach, involving such research methods as intra- and intersite analysis and the economic and social analysis of hunter-gatherer communities.[2] The research in Belgium also received a new impetus in those years.[3]

In recent years Mesolithic research has been placed in a regional context, with the emphasis on environmental, economic and social topics.[4] The first results of this research will be discussed in the following sections.

NATURAL ENVIRONMENT

The gradual improvement of the climate in the Holocene had consequences for the vegetation and the fauna. The open Pre-Boreal forest slowly gave way to a dense deciduous forest in the Atlantic period. Finds discovered abroad, in particular in Denmark, and ethnographic data have shown that Mesolithic hunters and gatherers intensively exploited trees and plants as sources of raw materials and food. From wood they made implements like canoes, paddles, sleighs, arrows, bows and spears; their dwellings will also have been made mostly from wood. Bark was used to make sleeping mats and to cover hut floors; adhesive was also extracted from it. Evidence, exclusively in the form of carbonised remains recovered from hearths, indicates that for example hazelnuts, cherries, acorns and water chestnuts were consumed.[5]

A major problem in the reconstruction of the fauna is the virtually complete lack of animal remains. Our information on the fauna comes from excavations in Denmark in the first place and, to a lesser extent, from north Germany, England, Belgium and France.[6] It is based mainly on the remains of mammals: elk, aurochs, red deer, horse, roe, wild boar, bear, beaver and otter, and also wolf, lynx, hare, squirrel, badger, marten and fox. The similarities in such a wide area around the Netherlands and the virtually identical environment make it likely that the same animals were hunted here, too. There is also evidence for fowling and fishing. The dog was the first – and for some time also the only – animal to be domesticated in these regions already at the beginning of the Mesolithic.

As large parts of the area occupied in the Mesolithic now lie submerged in the North Sea or are covered by several metres of sediments, we do not know what part the sea and the animals living in it played in the subsistence of the occupants of the Netherlands. Coastal regions are among the richest biotopes in the world[7] and we may therefore assume that their exploitation played an important part in the economy. This is corroborated by the results of site research and the analysis of skeletal remains in Denmark and Sweden.[8]

THE ARCHAEOLOGICAL EVIDENCE

Find patterns

The information on the past of the Netherlands is distorted by a large number of factors, some of which are specific to the study of the Mesolithic. The first of these concerns the geological development of the Netherlands. In the regions of the Pleistocene deposits in the east and south of the country the former Mesolithic surface lies at ground level. Virtually all of the finds recovered in the Netherlands – all of which are of imperishable materials – come from those areas. Until the discovery of the Hardinxveld sites (feature D), hardly any remains of Mesolithic occupation were found in the western part of the Netherlands, where the former surface is covered by Holocene deposits.[9] Our picture of Mesolithic society is hence virtually entirely based on one source of information: the lithic artefacts discovered in the dry parts of the Netherlands. Animal and vegetable remains relating to subsistence activities, which are so important for the reconstruction of the economy, are extremely scarce.

The second distortion is attributable to human activities in the (sub)recent past. Mesolithic man appears to have dug little at the sites occupied, with the exception of hearth pits. Because of this the refuse that was left behind could not be covered up. The activities affected mainly the top 30 cm of the soil profile, the very same layer that has been disturbed by ploughing, sod cutting, digging and draining. The only Mesolithic sites that can still provide information are those covered by layers of medieval *essen* (*Plaggen soils* and refuse accumulated around historical village sites) or remnants of peat and possibly sites buried beneath layers of drift sand or sites situated in the rare Dutch nature reserves.

The third distortion concerns the area investigated and the intensity of the research: the factors which largely determine the distribution pattern and the density of sites. The parts of the Netherlands that have been intensively investigated are the eastern part of Groningen, the province of Drenthe and parts of the south of the Netherlands. Large areas of the central part of the Netherlands and the western part of North Brabant have hardly been investigated, in spite of the fact that the Mesolithic remains are well accessible in those areas.

The fourth major distortion has an archaeological background. For the recon-

fig. 8.1
Finds typical of the Middle Mesolithic of the southern part of the Netherlands and Belgium are microliths with surface retouch. They incidentally constitute only small proportions of the microlith assemblages. Provenance: Steenven near Netersel. Actual size.

1, 2 leaf points

3, 4 mistle leaf points, also known as *feuilles de gui*

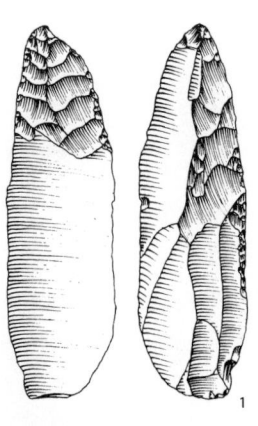
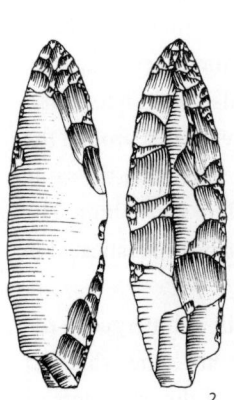
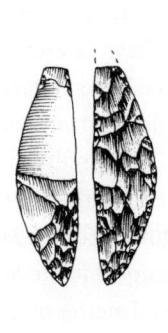
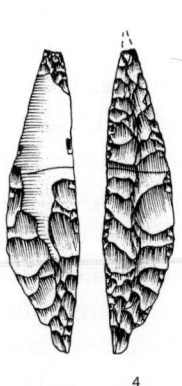

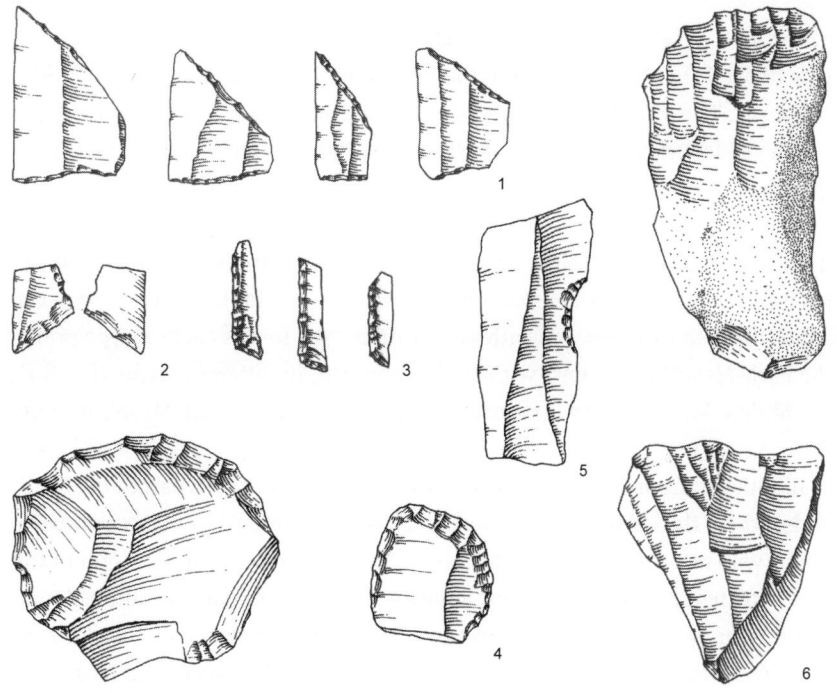

fig. 8.2
Late Mesolithic tools from Merselo-Haag
(L.). Actual size.
1 broad trapezes
2 point with *Bandkeramik* features
3 backed knives
4 scrapers
5 notched blade
6 blade cores

struction of the society and for the determination of the chronology it is important that sites can be studied at which activities were carried out for short periods of time. The majority of the Mesolithic sites prove to be the results of repeated use in different periods that are sometimes far removed from one another in time. The inability to separate areas of activity in terms of time and space is a major problem in establishing typological sequences and in studying different types of sites.

Chronology

There are several typological sequences for the Netherlands and its immediate surroundings. They are based on data which in some respects should be approached more critically. In the Netherlands, no use has been made of assemblages from stratified contexts for the simple reason that there aren't any. An alternative was typological seriation of flint assemblages coupled with ^{14}C dates obtained for the same sites.[10]

Some objections can be made to this approach on the basis of recent research data. First of all, the majority of the sites prove to have been used more often and for longer periods than regularly assumed.[11] In the past only a small part of a site was usually excavated, often only one concentration of finds. Research on a larger scale has shown that most sites consist of a succession of such small concentrations which represent different activities, sometimes separated in time, too.[12] Secondly, the ^{14}C dates rarely yield one moment of use. Research into the dates of large numbers of hearths has shown that the dates of the hearths of one and the same site often cover a long period.[13] This also means that it is difficult to place an assemblage in a chronological sequence.

All this implies that no detailed statements can be made as yet. However, the development and the use of points that were subject to changing fashions can yield a general typological sequence. A good sequence based on evidence from stratified contexts is available for south Germany,[14] into which also the sites of the Rhineland can be fitted.[15] The Early Mesolithic remains of this region are domi-

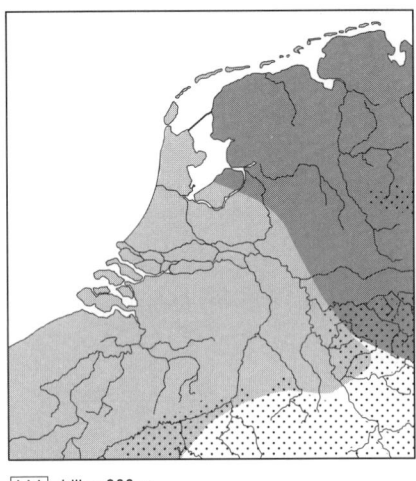

fig. 8.3

Distribution areas of the Northwest group and the Rhine Basin group, to the north and south of the Rhine, respectively, in the Middle Mesolithic in the Netherlands and its environs.

nated by steeply retouched points which resemble the Dutch A points. Characteristic of the Late Mesolithic, from the Beuronien D period onwards (7700 BP), are trapezes. The Middle Mesolithic is less clear; Beuronien B layers (9000-8300 BP) have yielded triangular points with some surface retouch. Surface retouch is more apparent in assemblages from the Ardennes which can also be dated to this phase.[16]

This very limited sequence resembles Newell's five-phase typological sequence on the whole. His division into five phases should, however, be reduced to a division into three phases with one or more type fossils each: A-type points in the Early Mesolithic, points with surface retouch, in different forms (fig. 8.1), in the Middle Mesolithic and trapezes predominantly in the Late Mesolithic (fig. 8.2).

A slightly different development is observable in the northern part of the Netherlands, where the Early Mesolithic evidence is characterised by a predominance of points with retouched edges, in particular represented by B points, A points and to a lesser extent isosceles triangles. Points with surface retouch are almost completely absent in this region, which means that there is no clear type fossil for the Middle Mesolithic. Newell and Price assume that C points were used frequently in this phase,[17] whereas the Middle Mesolithic in north Germany is characterised by a predominance of triangles.[18] As in the southern part of the Netherlands, the (broad) trapeze is the type fossil of the Late Mesolithic.

Newell has distinguished the 'De Leien-Wartena' complex (DLW), which he regards as a western representative of the Oldesloe group, at the end of the Late Mesolithic.[19] The definition of the DLW is not unambiguous. Typological characteristics are important, but so are the size of a site, the occurrence of Maglemose and Svaerdborg points and the introduction of core and flake axes. The much larger site size, however, appears to be mainly the result of the activities carried out at the site, the number of instances of use, the number of persons who used the site and the period of use. Maglemose and Svaerdborg points had already been used in Denmark for 1500 years by then; their occurrence may also indicate that the sites in question were used for a long time. Moreover, the assumption that core and flake axes were introduced as new types of artefacts in this last phase of the Mesolithic is no longer tenable.[20] It is true that they are late elements but they cannot be attributed to a specific cultural group. We therefore prefer to distinguish a Late Mesolithic as the youngest phase in the northern Netherlands, having as its most characteristic artefacts narrow trapeze-shaped points and, to a less extent, wide trapeze-shaped points and core and flake axes.

Artefacts and raw materials

The introduction of points with surface retouch – with the *feuille de gui* or mistle leaf point as the most prominent type – marks the beginning of the Middle Mesolithic. Two cultural areas can be distinguished in the Netherlands in this phase (fig. 8.3).[21] To the north of the Rhine a *Northwest Group*, which forms a continuation of a northern European (Maglemose/Kongemose) tradition, and in the south the *Rhine Basin Group*, also known as the Rhine-Meuse-Scheldt complex,[22] which is a continuation of a Western European (Sauveterre/Tardenoisien) tradition. The two cultural areas differ in artefact typology but also in the use of resources. There are however many similarities too.

Trapezes are the most important projectile points used in the Late Mesolithic; core and flake axes appear to have become more popular in that phase. Although

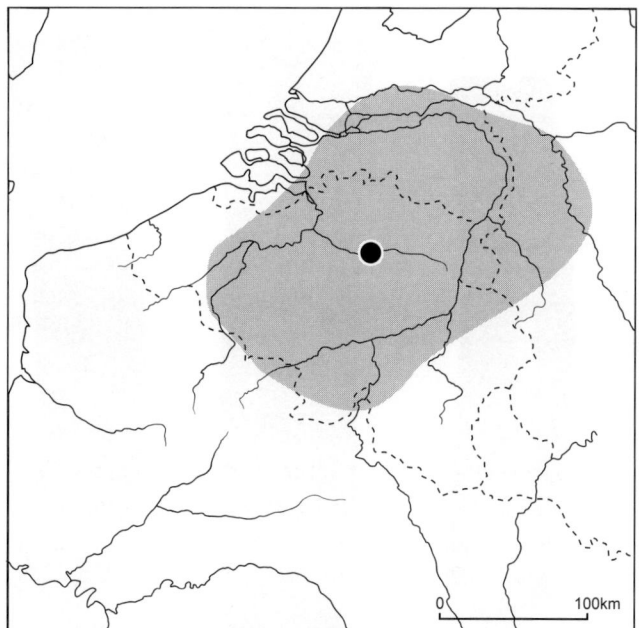
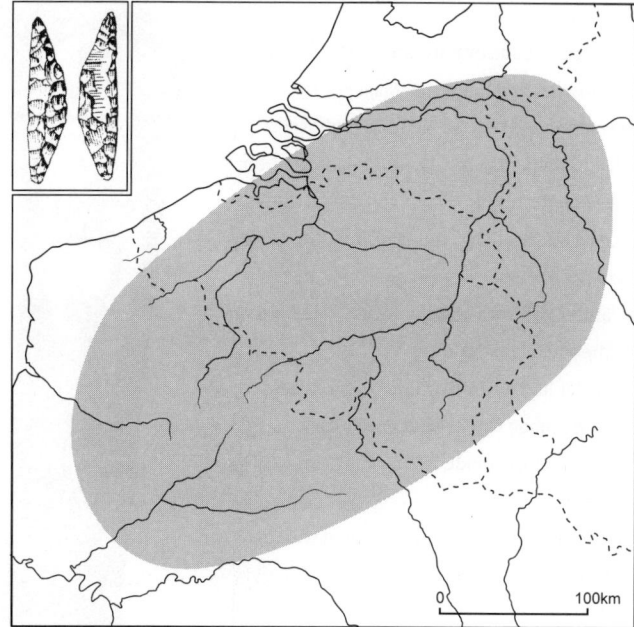

the core and flake axes found in the south of the Netherlands have been interpreted as indications of the presence of the DLW complex in this area,[23] the majority of these core and flake axes were recovered from mixed Mesolithic/Middle Neolithic sites. These axes may very well be datable to the Middle Neolithic, in particular the Michelsberg phase.

Stone working was aimed at the production of blanks in the form of blades, on which the characteristic small geometric tools were then made: microliths, knives, borers, scrapers and burins. On the basis of English and Danish finds it may be as-

fig. 8.4

Left: area in which Wommersom quartzite was used as a raw material for tools in the Middle and Late Mesolithic. The point marks the quartzite's source.

Right: distribution area of *feuilles de gui*, the type fossils of the Middle Mesolithic Rhine Basin group.

fig. 8.5

By the Mesolithic, people had mastered the art of perforating hard types of stone, in particular quartzite, by means of pecking. This technique they used to manufacture implements known as *Geröllkeulen* (1 and 2) and *Spitzhauen* (3). Damaged edges and wear in the biconical perforations indicate that these tools were used as striking implements, and that the hole contained a handle. Fine evidence of this is provided by a specimen with a preserved wooden handle that was found at Friesack (Brandenburg). This find moreover demonstrates that this technique was being used in the Pre-Boreal already. The illustrated examples are all stray finds from Overijssel. Scale 1:3.

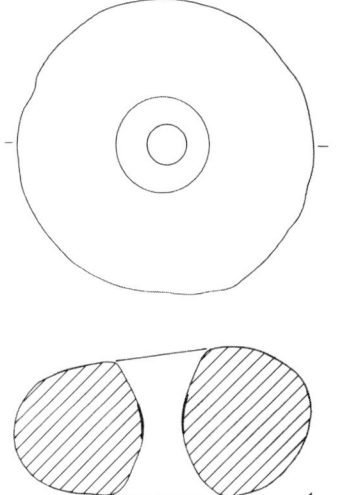
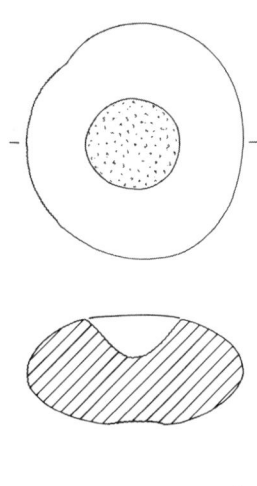
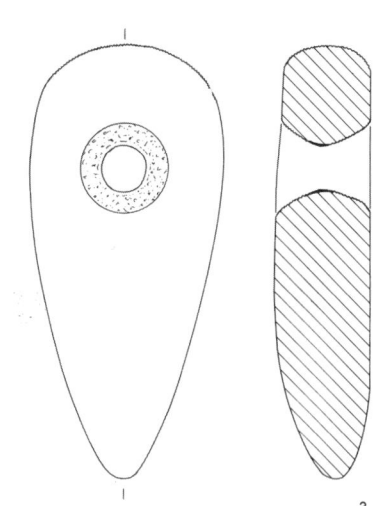

1 2 3

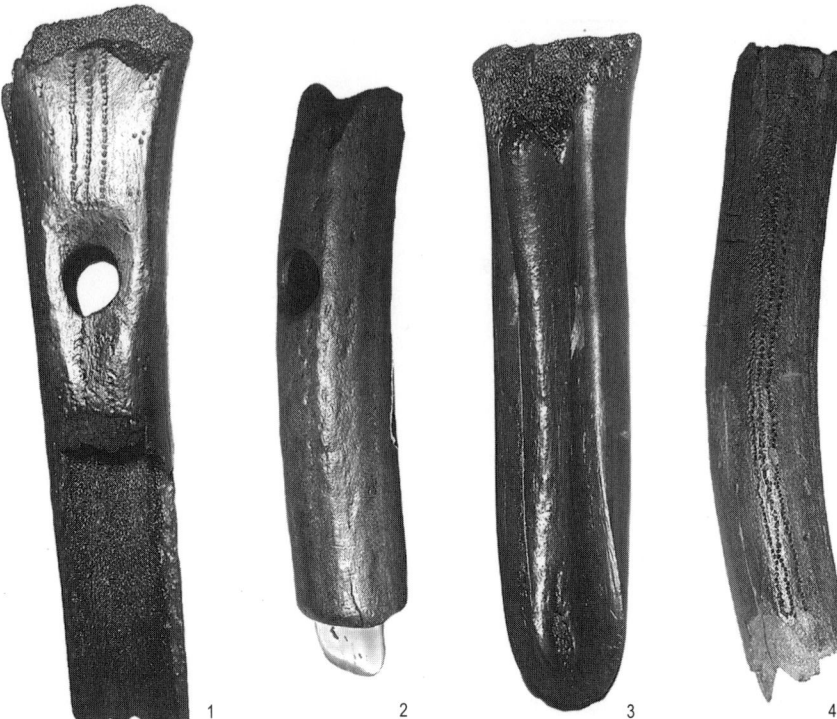

fig. 8.6

Four tools made of bone and antler recovered during the digging of the 'Maaspoort' recreational lake near 's-Hertogenbosch. The implements are all assumed to date from the Late Mesolithic on typological grounds (based on parallels from Hardinxveld). Scale 1:2.

1 antler haft with shaft hole decorated with the *pointillé* technique

2 antler haft with shaft hole and a chisel blade made from a wild boar's tusk

3 sturdy chisel made from an aurochs metatarsal

4 part of an antler beam decorated with the *pointillé* technique

fig. 8.7

The pine canoe of Pesse, dated to the Boreal.

sumed that scrapers, burins, borers and knives were used for the manufacture of all kinds of utensils from organic materials such as antler, bone and wood and from plant material like grasses and rushes, while microliths served as insets of composite tools.[24]

Flint that was collected in the immediate surroundings was used as raw material. In the northern part of the Netherlands flint (of poor quality) could be found in the sand; in the south it was collected from river beds and terrace deposits. In addition to this flint there were the types of stone (and flint) which had been transported here from sources far away. The best known of these is the Wommersom quartzite, a type of stone which could be worked extremely well and which occurred in primary contexts exclusively around the small town of Wommersom in Belgium (plate 10A). The distribution pattern of this material underwent several changes in time but it appears that this type of quartzite was have been hardly used to the north and east of the Rhine (fig. 8.4, left).[25] Feuilles de gui have a very similar distribution. They mark the area of the Rhine Basin Group (fig. 8.4, right). Another easily recognisable type of stone, which was used somewhat less commonly, is phtanite, which outcrops near Ottignies and the nearby Céroux-Mousty.[26] At the odd site, such as the Middle Mesolithic site Steenven-Netersel in North Brabant,[27] phtanite was the main raw material used.

Remarkable changes took place in the use of raw materials in the southern part of the Netherlands during the Mesolithic. In the Early Mesolithic several good flint types – Zevenwegen, a variety known as 'light grey Belgian' flint, and a variant of the Rijckholt type – were used alongside pebble flint. A radical change took place in the Middle Mesolithic, when the proportion of Wommersom quartzite increased and flint from Hesbaye went out of use almost completely. In the Late Mesolithic the proportion of Wommersom quartzite increased even further, in particular in the areas to the west of the Meuse, while the proportion of materials from local sources, usually pebble flint, also increased. Other exotic raw materials were rare in this phase. We are less well informed about the situation in the north of the Netherlands due to the lack of easily recognisable exotic types of flint and stone.

An unusual type of stone frequently encountered at Mesolithic sites and in graves is ochre. This material occurred, usually in the form of lumps of haematite, in secondary contexts in Rhine and Meuse gravels and in a primary context near Namur (Belgium).[28] The stone implements comprise grinding stones, rubbing stones and hammer stones for working flint and for processing food. The so-called *Spitzhauen* and *Geröllkeulen*, usually oval to round stones with an hourglass-shaped perforation,[29] were produced in the Middle and Late Mesolithic (fig. 8.5). *Geröllkeulen* are commonly interpreted as weights for digging sticks.[30] The distribution pattern of this implement shows that it belongs in the northern tradition. They are fairly rare in the south.[31] A unique find, discovered near Tilburg, is an elongated flat object of lydite with a hole at one end, which was probably used as a bullroarer.[32]

Implements of bone and antler are rare owing to the poor preservation conditions. In the past few years, however, quite a few antler and bone implements have come to light. The majority of these have been recovered from rivers, a few have been found in peats. In addition, several artefacts are known from the North Sea and from the Europoort area (see feature B).[33] They are all dated to the Mesolithic on typological and/or technological grounds. Curious are the many finds recovered from a dredging pit near 's-Hertogenbosch (fig. 8.6). They include awls, a chisel, polished and decorated elk antlers, a chisel blade made from a wild boar's incisor mounted in an axe shaft, an antler and a pierced axe shaft with stippled decoration.[34] Parallels of the latter object have been found in the north of France.[35] Finally, a few wooden objects are known from the Netherlands: the famous Pesse canoe (7500 BC, fig. 8.7) and a figurine recovered during the construction of the Volkerak locks near Willemstad (5300 BC, fig. 8.8).[36]

MESOLITHIC SOCIETY

Organisation and demography

It is not easy to reconstruct the social organisation of the mobile hunter-gatherers of the Mesolithic. The models that are used for this purpose, which are often of a generalising character, are largely based on the results of recent anthropological research into subrecent and present-day hunter-gatherer communities.[37] It must be borne in mind that these models are greatly distorted by the fact that virtually all these recent communities exploit what we – in our western perception – will consider relatively marginal areas. In the Mesolithic, however, the greater part of the Netherlands had a rich environment with less extreme differences between the seasons. This means that the mobility characterising present-day hunters and gatherers will have been less in the Mesolithic. The Mesolithic societies of Europe were to a great extent original societies, without clear parallels in (sub)recent communities.

The recent groups of hunter-gatherers are characterised by social hierarchy.[38] The smallest unit is the *nuclear family*, consisting of a father, a mother and their children. Another form is the *extended family*, which also includes uncles, aunts and grandparents. A number of families often join forces in hunting, fishing or gathering food. Such a group, which is called a band or a microband, comprises about fifty individuals. In biological terms it is unwise for all members to select their partners from such a small group[39] and that is why hunter-gatherers select their partners from a larger group, a macroband or tribe, which consists of a number of bands and includes between 200 and 500 individuals. These macrobands in turn

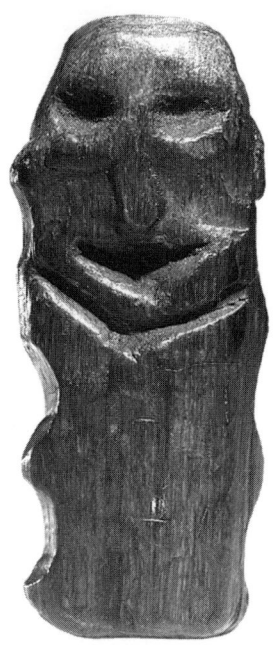

fig. 8.8
Oak human figurine found during the construction of the Volkerak locks near Willemstad, dated c. 5300 BC. Height: 12.5 cm (2/3 of actual size).

form part of an even wider unit whose members all speak the same language or dialect and which is therefore known as a dialectic tribe. They may count 500-2000 people.

For archaeological parallels it is very important that the dialectic tribes, and possibly also the macrobands, are not only characterised by kinship and social contacts but also by a more or less uniform material culture. The study of this material culture can then provide insight into the geographical and chronological development of the social organisation.[40] A good example of this is the distribution and the use of Wommersom quartzite. The exchange networks that can be inferred from the distribution pattern are based on ethnographic examples. An exchange network proves to be deeply embedded in the system of social relations, usually kinship relations, of groups and individuals.[41] The distribution pattern of Wommersom quartzite shows clear limits to the north: virtually no Wommersom quartzite has been found to the north and east of the Rhine, while a clear decrease in the proportion of this type of stone is observable in the area between the Meuse and the Rhine. The distribution area may be regarded as the territory of a dialectic tribe.[42]

One way of studying the lower levels of the social organisation and the demographic development is through the analysis of sites. The diversity, the size and the number of sites are the archaeological correlates required for this purpose. Large Late Mesolithic sites, for example, are interpreted as aggregate camps, where a large number of families camped in periods in which food was available in abundance.[43] Increases in the size and the number of sites are taken as indications of the growth of the population.[44] We must be careful here, though: an increase in the size of a site may indeed be the result of an increase in the size of the group camping there, but it may also reflect a longer period of use by one and the same group. The degree of mobility and the exploitation strategy followed are important factors in this respect. A second explanation for the large number of artefacts could be that the site was specifically suited for the exploitation of certain sources of food and that the same group of people therefore kept returning there time and time again.[45] Although the group may have camped there for only short periods at a time, the repeated use of the site will have led to an accumulation of settlement waste.

Hardly any traces of dwellings have been found at these sites. What have been interpreted as the remains of huts or shallow occupation pits were often natural features caused by, for example, uprooting.[46] It is even doubtful whether the Bergumermeer hut plans have been correctly interpreted. It is very unlikely that secondary or sometimes tertiary soil formation of the kind encountered there are the consequence of compaction of the soil inside a Mesolithic hut or a tent. If the observed evidence of infiltration of humus and leaching of iron were indeed associated with compaction it will be encountered far more frequently at Mesolithic sites and this is not the case. The plans that have been interpreted with certainty as the remains of shelters or resting places show how perishable these structures were, varying from a simple mat of pine bark[47] to very simple structures consisting of a floor of birch bark and a few thin posts.[48] Such insubstantial dwellings will have left very few or no traces behind in the dry, acid Dutch soil.

Most hunter-gatherer groups were egalitarian communities. Recent research into Mesolithic cemeteries in Scandinavia has shown that there may have been differences between groups and sexes in that area in the Late Mesolithic; there also appear to have been individuals with a higher status.[49] In the Netherlands and its immediate surroundings indications of social ranking are rare. What may point in that direction are the 'exotic' objects or raw materials which are sometimes encountered at the youngest Mesolithic sites or in graves, such as *Bandkeramik* adzes and Rössen *Breitkeile*.[50]

Ritual and ideology

Statements on ideology are the most difficult for archaeologists, on the one hand because the basic data usually allow only technological, economic and social models, on the other hand because of the problems involved in determining what particular artefacts meant to Mesolithic man. Because of this, an artefact or a combination of artefacts that cannot be directly related to everyday life are sometimes interpreted as ritual objects. From ethnographic studies, however, we know how closely ideology, rituals and economy are linked.

Some examples of objects which are in this way assigned a ritual-ideological significance are the wooden figurine from the Volkerak locks near Willemstad, a group of decorated antler implements from 's-Hertogenbosch, engraved stones (fig. 8.9), a bullroarer from Tilburg and masks of red deer antler from Bedburg-Königshoven (fig. 4.11), just across the German border.[51]

Another aspect of the ideology of Mesolithic man is the handling of the deceased. The earliest burials known in the Netherlands date from the Mesolithic: what are thought to be two isolated graves at Dalfsen and Oirschot[52] and a small cemetery containing six burials near Mariënberg (see feature C). The first two presumed graves both contained cremation remains and the burials of the cemetery are all inhumations, some of which are accompanied by grave goods. The formal burial of the deceased and the fact of burial in a cemetery are regarded as indications of decreased mobility and the formation of group territoria.[53]

Subsistence

Owing to the lack of organic remains, so important for the reconstruction of the economy, research into the subsistence activities in the Middle and Late Mesolithic concentrated on the analysis of the different site types and the settlement pattern.[54] The imperishable finds recovered from the sandy soils constituted the point of departure. This has hardly changed since the 1970s. Stray finds recovered from the Europoort, the North Sea and the western part of the Netherlands indicate that there are also sites in the parts of the Netherlands that have been submerged by the North Sea or have been covered by Holocene sediments, where organic remains have been preserved. However, the finds recovered from these sites have not fundamentally increased our knowledge of the food economy. The Mesolithic implements can be typologically identified but the unworked bones of the hunted animals can rarely be dated to the Mesolithic as they are usually mixed with older and younger finds. This situation may improve in the future. The results of recent research in Germany, for example at Bedburg-Königshoven and Gustorf,[55] make it likely that organic matter will also come to light in Dutch river valleys, backswamps and the lakes, resulting from former pingos.

The first theories on Mesolithic economy were strongly grafted on the results of the research at Star Carr in England and of excavations in south Scandinavia, which led to the assumption that in the Netherlands, too, Mesolithic sites were to be found chiefly along the banks of rivers and the shores of lakes.[56] This was associated with an economy based on hunting, with a strong emphasis on fishing.

fig. 8.9

Pebble engraved with a dancing (?) figure found at Wanssum (northern Limburg). Enlarged twice.

The above assumption was based on the presence of large numbers of microliths, which were interpreted as parts of fishing spears. However, the recent research in eastern Groningen, the Meuse valley and De Kempen shows that the 'interior' was more intensively exploited than originally assumed.

Secondly, the proportion of plant food sources was often underestimated on account of the small amounts of botanical matter compared with the quantities of animal remains.[57] At many sites, however, carbonized remains of hazelnuts have been found, suggesting that hazels were intensively exploited in the relatively open environments in which they thrived.[58] Cherries and water chestnuts were also consumed. If the *Geröllkeule* are indeed to be interpreted as weights for digging sticks, they reflect the importance of root vegetables and possibly insects and larvae in the diet. Only by chance do we obtain information about the use of food sources that left no traces behind: rock carvings found in eastern Spain depict the use of baskets and the gathering of honey.[59]

The promising analysis of use-wear traces on flint tools may tell us more about the use of the various tools and their relation to the economy. Serious obstacles, however, are mechanical wear and patination, in particular in the analysis of tools from the coversand areas, the areas which already yield so little information on the economy. The first results have shown that the tools were not only used for working bone, antler and wood, but also for processing plant material in manufacturing all sorts of implements and for preparing food.[60]

Remains of animal food are also scarce. Hearths have yielded fragmentary bones, which only give an impression of the small animals that were hunted. At Weelde-Paardsdrank, for example, burned bones of fox and deer have been found.[61] A few Mesolithic tools made from the bones of large mammals such as aurochs and red deer have been preserved.

The many hearths found at the sites served both as sources of heat and for the preparation and conservation of food. The sunken hearths in particular may be associated with the preparation of food,[62] as indicated by the numerous heat-cracked 'potboilers'. The hearths vary from structures consisting of stacks of stones and carefully dug pits to hearths that were lit simply at the surface.[63]

SETTLEMENTS IN THE LANDSCAPE

Settlement systems

Newell and Price have attempted to reconstruct Mesolithic economy and the associated settlement form from the scarce archaeological evidence available.[64] Basing himself on the evidence from excavated sites, Newell distinguished three types of sites, differing from one another in size and in the numbers and the nature of the artefacts found. Comparable evidence led Price to five types of sites. These he placed in a wider context, after which he applied his site typology in a regional study. He related the differences between the five types of sites to differences in subsistence activities.[65] In the Netherlands, where no organic matter has been found, bone assemblages found in the neighbouring countries have to be used as points of departure in reconstructing the economy. That evidence leads to an annual cycle comprising five seasons. The main problem is how to relate the different types of sites to the reconstructed subsistence activities.

The above site typologies are actually the result of an overoptimistic point of departure. The objection that in many investigations only one concentration of finds was excavated, which was moreover often the result of repeated use of the site, was raised earlier in this context. Another objection to these typologies is that they are based on sites that were selected at random across the southern and northern parts of the Netherlands, without allowance for the fact that those sites form part of a smaller, independent, regional settlement pattern.

The economic models formulated by Binford and Jochim have been applied to the Dutch evidence only rarely so far.[66] An exception concerns the study of the Drenthe plateau by Price. The absence of organic matter and the limited number of intensively excavated sites makes it very difficult to make any well-founded statements. Another matter of much debate is the seasonal character of the sites. At present it appears to be impossible to say in which season a camp in the Netherlands was used.[67] A regional approach seems to be the best way of arriving at statements about the settlement form and the surrounding landscape. Two examples of this will be given below.

Hunters and gatherers in the Meuse Valley

A large number of Mesolithic sites are known in the southeast of the Netherlands; some of these are now being studied in the Meuse valley project (fig. 8.10),[68] a regional project focusing on the reconstruction of the economy.

In one central region with an area of some 150 km², largely coinciding with the territory of the present municipality of Venray, 89 Mesolithic sites have been found (fig. 8.11). Geologically this region can be split up into three major landscape features: in the east is a narrow zone of Late Pleistocene and Holocene Meuse deposits, in the centre are coversands and in the west is the now largely excavated peat district known as De Peel. Two streams flow from De Peel eastwards into the Meuse.

On the basis of the typological development outlined above the sites can be classified as follows: fifteen Early Mesolithic sites, nine Middle Mesolithic sites and thirty Late Mesolithic sites; it is not possible to say from what periods the remaining thirty-five date. The finds of the majority of the sites were mixed with older or

fig.8.10

Distribution of Mesolithic assemblages in the Meuse valley that have been dated on the basis of flint typology.

1 Early Mesolithic

2 Middle Mesolithic

3 Late Mesolithic

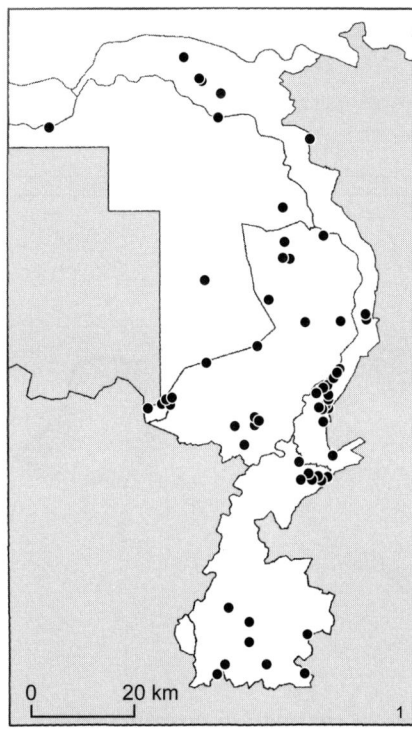
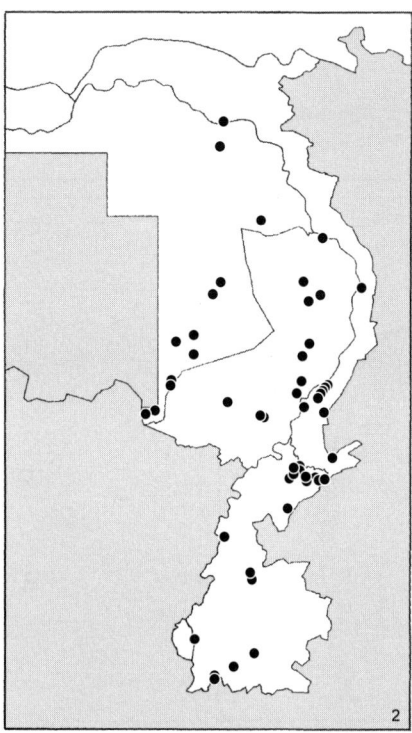
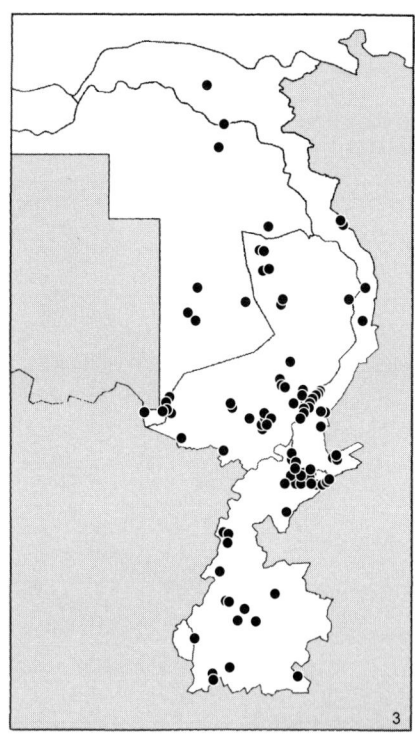

younger Mesolithic finds and/or with Neolithic artefacts. The lack of organic matter meant that a special research strategy had to be adopted to enable statements to be made on the economy. The point of departure was the assumption that such statements may be based on the range of tools encountered at the individual sites, the environmental situation and the distribution pattern of the sites.

A small area was selected for further research near the source of the Loobeek, at the transition of two of the major landscape features: the coversands and the wet De Peel district. Twenty sites were located during field surveys. The marked similarity in the situation of the sites indicates that the locations were selected with some aim in mind, possibly a specific function. However, the mostly small

fig. 8.11

Distribution of Mesolithic assemblages in the 'Venray core region' investigated in the context of the 'Meuse valley project'. Scale 1:250,000. Both the Early and the Late Mesolithic are represented by two complementary clusters, one on the bank of the Meuse, the other near the sources of the streams at the periphery of the Peel peat bogs. Merselo-Haag lies in the northwestern concentration of map 4.

1 all sites
2 Early Mesolithic
3 Middle Mesolithic
4 Late Mesolithic

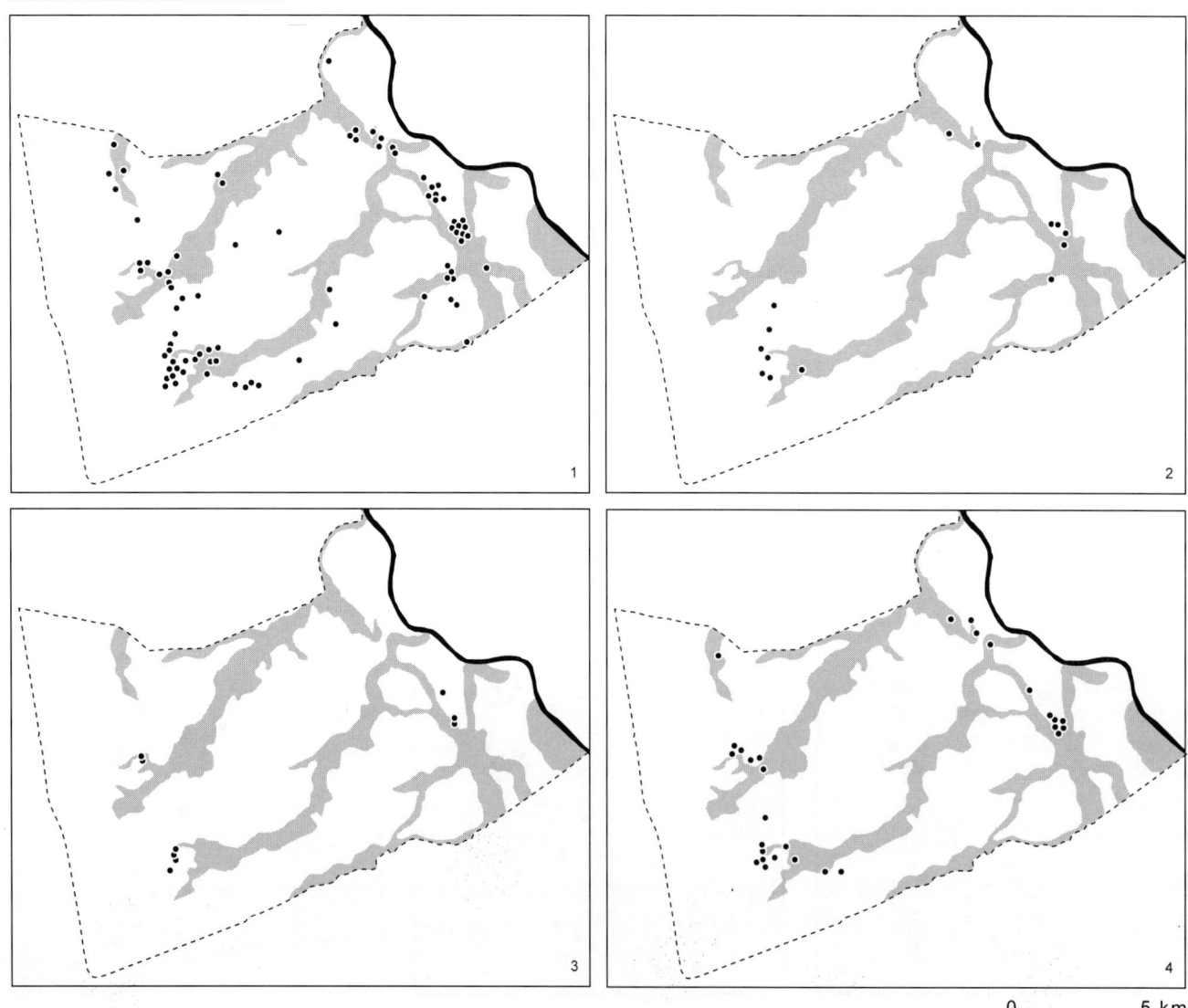

0   5 km

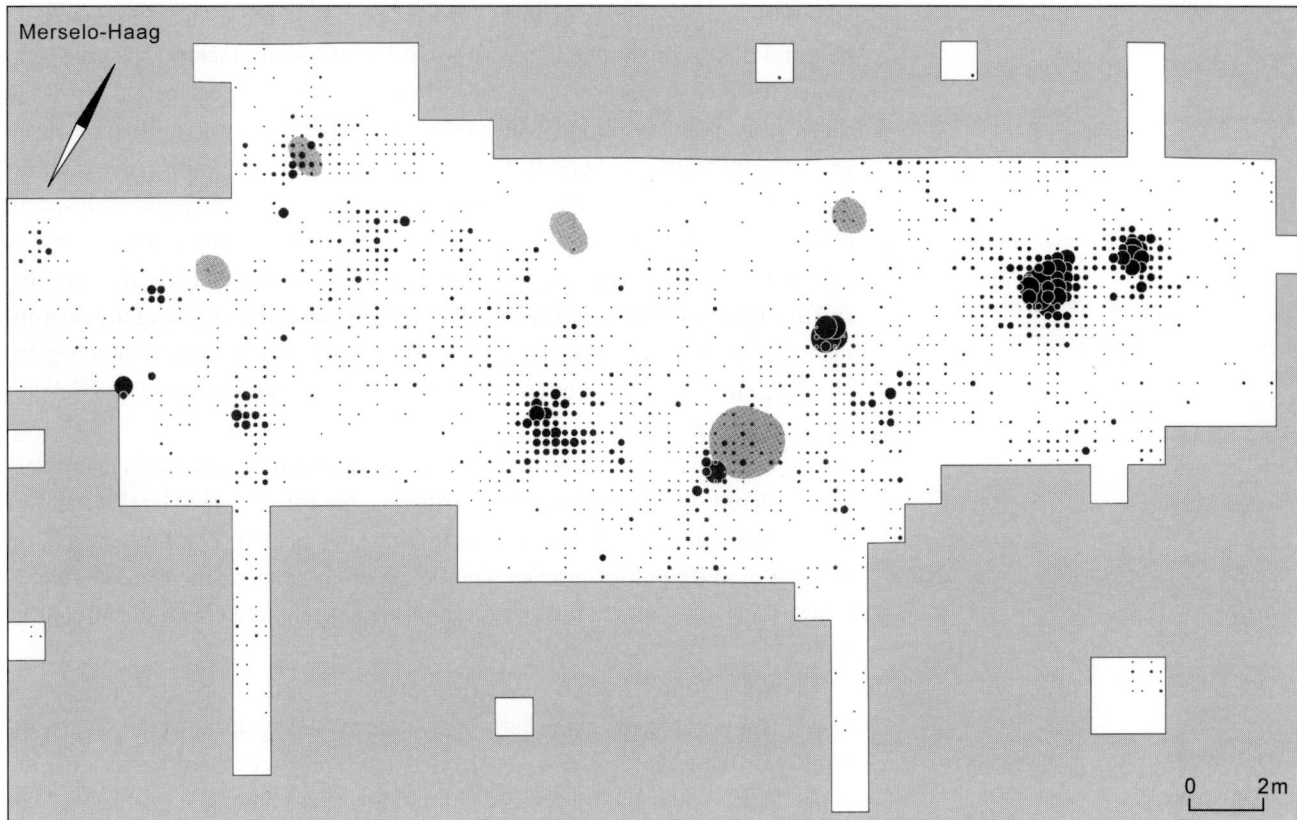

Merselo-Haag

0 2m

fig. 8.12

Merselo-Haag consists of a group of small assemblages, each representing a short period of occupation on a narrow ridge of sand bordering a stream valley. Find densities are indicated in numbers of flint artefacts per unit of 25 x 25 cm (maximum number = 32). Scale 1:200.

number of surface finds can tell us very little about the activities that were carried out there. One site, Merselo-Haag, was selected for excavation to obtain a clearer picture of the evidence. Three small concentrations were distinguished at this site, which had a low find density (fig. 8.12). The composition of the artefacts of two of these concentrations was virtually identical. The many small flakes and cores and the small number of tools indicate that they were small flint-working sites. The third concentration contained a relatively large number of tools, such as retouched flakes and blades, trapezes, scrapers and a remarkably high percentage of backed knives. This site is therefore most probably to be interpreted as a camp.

If Merselo-Haag is representative of the other sites discovered near the source of the stream, then this area contained only small transit camps and no larger base camps. Fairly few finds were recovered at these sites, but they did include a relatively high proportion of points, which further supports the assumption that hunting played an important part in the economy of this area. Tools commonly associated with household activities, such as scrapers, knives and burins, were not numerous. The larger camps lay elsewhere, possibly in the zone along the Meuse. No sites have been investigated in that area yet, but the diversity in the range of tools in the assemblages of surface finds suggests that they may very well have been base camps.

Occupation and environment: an example from eastern Groningen

Since 1982 the BAI has been carrying out research into the Mesolithic occupation of the peat district of Groningen. In the mid-Atlantic period this region, with its area of some 130 km² , was covered with a layer of peat, which was only removed

300 years ago. Remnants of this peat have preserved the underlying coversand here and there, which, together with two other important factors, has greatly favoured research in this area. The first of these factors is that peat started to grow in this region in the Mesolithic, which means that the finds have not become mixed with remains from later periods. Secondly, the region is very uniform in a geomorphological respect: as the environment is virtually the same everywhere consistent observations can be made over a large area. Stream valleys, for example, are only to be found at the edges of the peat district. These three factors make this area very suitable for research into the relation between Mesolithic camps and the environment. Key questions in this research are: when did the first groups of hunter-gatherers appear in this area, why and how long did they remain here and why did they ultimately leave?

Little sand drifted in the peat district in the Late Dryas period and in many places the Allerød surface is exposed. Nevertheless, the percentage of late Palaeolithic sites is not high; on the contrary, Mesolithic sites prevail. The finds which, on grounds of tool typology, artefact size and use of material, do indicate late Palaeolithic camps are spatially and stratigraphically not separated from the Mesolithic finds.

The typological characteristics of the flint tools indicate that the Groningen peat district was occupied from the Early Mesolithic to the beginning of the Late Mesolithic. The many ^{14}C dates, obtained from ten different sites distributed across the entire district, yield a more detailed chronology. These dates were virtually all obtained from charcoal recovered from hearth pits. It has been found that with such dating material the risk of contamination with older or younger material is small because the hearth pits were deep and the bottoms of the pits have been well preserved. It has been assumed that digging shaft-shaped pits for hearths was a fixed custom, deeply rooted in Mesolithic tradition.[69] This makes evidence from hearth pits very suitable for determining the period of occupation of the coversand. Four of the 34 samples analysed yielded dates between 9470 ± 70 and 9045 ± 45 BP and thirty yielded dates between 8490 ± 50 and 7275 ± 70 BP. This means that most activities took place in the Boreal period.

Geological and hydrological factors were studied to obtain an impression of the appeal of the area in the Boreal period. The point of departure was that a uniform coversand area with an endless succession of low dunes and depressions must have contained sensitive gradients. Minor local differences can play an important part in transitional zones between dry and wet soils. This viewpoint constituted the basis for a search for deposits capable of (temporarily) retaining rain water and an analysis of the former groundwater table. Here and there in the low-lying parts of the area were deposits of a loess-like soil. There were no podzols in those parts; they prove to have been the wettest parts of the area, from which peat started to grow in the mid-Atlantic period. It is noteworthy that the camps, which were always on top of low dunes, were all situated in the vicinity of such loam deposits (fig. 8.13). This leads to the assumption that these low-lying parts were indeed wetter, which will have had consequences for the flora and fauna. A study of peat profiles in these depressions revealed that the groundwater table has never been more than 1-2 m below the surface since the Late Glacial period, which further emphasises the aforementioned 'sensitive gradients'. These loamy depressions will hence have formed a contrast with the dryer areas surrounding them in the Pre-Boreal and Boreal periods. The substantial size of some sites, undoubtedly the consequence of frequent use, indicates that the environment in these areas was, at least periodically, very attractive. However, the environmental 'equilibrium' was unstable and was easily disturbed by the slight-

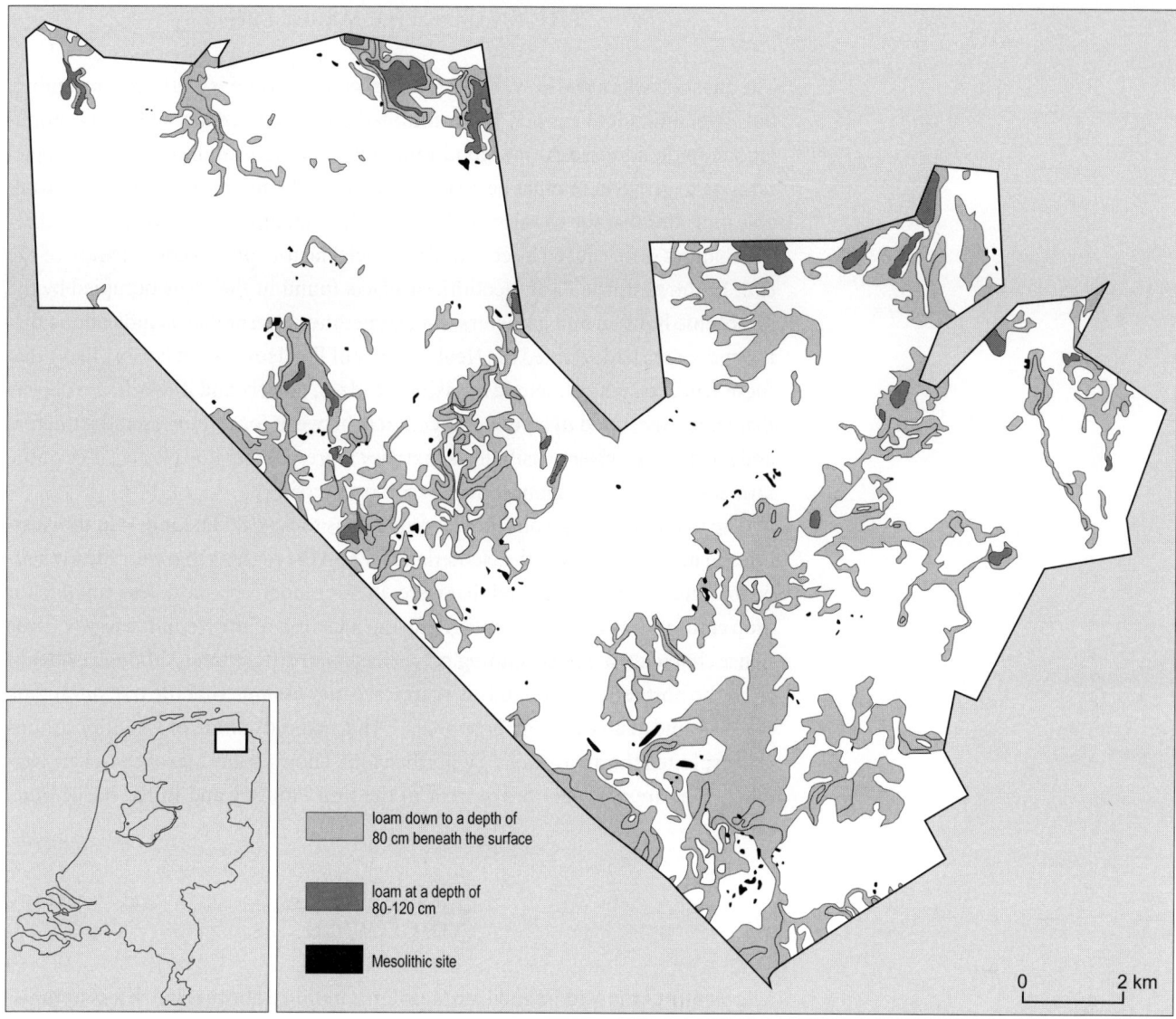

loam down to a depth of
80 cm beneath the surface

loam at a depth of
80-120 cm

Mesolithic site

0   2 km

est changes. After c. 6500 BC settlement started to shift towards stream valleys. Peat did not start to grow in this area until around 5000 BC, so that cannot have been the cause of this shift. The increase in the range of deciduous tree species in the charcoal from the younger Mesolithic hearth pits indicates that a so-called Atlantic climax vegetation started to develop on the – originally poor and later moreover leached – substrate around the end of the period of occupation. These considerations lead to the tentative conclusion that the area was not abandoned because it became wetter but because the Atlantic forest on the leached substrate grew denser. This environmental explanation[70] is not the only hypothesis put forward; similar shifts on a supra-regional level have also been attributed to social changes.

The research in the Groningen peat district has shown that the results of palaeographical reconstructions are always dependent on the research level. Correlations between environmental developments and human behaviour are often discovered on a regional level, whereas questions of a higher order are at issue on a supraregional level.

fig. 8.13

The Mesolithic landscape in southeast Groningen was preserved by the peat that formed over it. It was brought back to light by peat-digging operations in the 18th and 19th centuries. The majority of the Mesolithic sites lie at the transition from coversand ridges (white) to lower parts, where loam deposits can be associated with wet conditions at the time of occupation. Site dimensions have been slightly enlarged to enhance the sites' visibility.

The question when and how the Mesolithic came to an end is extremely intriguing, but as yet difficult to answer. The common theory that the entire Mesolithic population rapidly adopted the new food-production methods of the first (*Bandkeramik*) farmers to arrive here must be revised. The limited amount of information available indicates that the changes took place only gradually. It is still unclear whether the changes were caused by economic or social factors or by a combination of the two. In the past, the Early Neolithic artefacts found in the areas occupied by the Mesolithic hunters and gatherers were sometimes interpreted as indications that the entire area had adopted the Neolithic way of life. However, it is more likely that these artefacts, which include *Bandkeramik* adzes, pottery and *Breitkeile*, are objects that were exchanged in a period of contacts between local hunters and gatherers and farmers. Another possibility is that they represent small-scale activities of the farmers of the loess regions, outside their own territory.

The transition to a Neolithic economy seems to have taken longest in the western and northern parts of the Netherlands, *i.e.* in the regions that were ideally suited to hunting and fishing and that were, in our modern opinion, less suitable for crop cultivation and cattle keeping. The introduction of the Neolithic way of life is hence characterised by chronological and regional differences. Although evidence from the northern Netherlands is scarce, we may assume that the transition took place around 4800 cal BC in those areas.[71] The material culture of Neolithic groups that exploited the area around Swifterbant still shows many Mesolithic characteristics; they are particularly apparent in the flint industry and in the burial practice.[72]

CONCLUSION

The picture of the Middle and Late Mesolithic outlined above is much less optimistic than pictures presented in the past. Future research will have to be of a regional character. There is little sense in attempting to fill the gaps in our knowledge via research into individual sites randomly distributed across the whole of the Netherlands. Research of sites in relation to a region seems to be the most suitable option. Collections of surface finds will continue to play an important part in this research. Much attention will have to be paid to the clear definition of regions, the excavation of sites in their entirety, the performance of sound spatial analyses and the detailing of the typological sequences.

Of an entirely different character is the need for sites yielding organic finds. This organic component is indispensable for the reconstruction of subsistence activities. It must be possible to investigate such sites in a regional context so that general statements can be made. A Mesolithic site yielding organic finds that cannot be placed in such a context will provide no new information because the evidence for hunting will be the same as that already obtained in Britain and Scandinavia.

Its fairly unappealing Mesolithic evidence will seem to make the Netherlands a relatively unimportant contributor to international research. However, we will like to look into the future with some optimism, too: the scarcity of finds may also have an important positive effect. In the study of the Dutch evidence attention is not diverted by more sensational categories of finds such as wooden and bone tools and beautifully preserved settlements. The Netherlands can play a part in the research of flint, the material that has been found in such abundance. Interesting research projects could be detailed regional studies into the use of different types of raw materials and into the underlying exchange networks, the nature and distribution of stylistic differences in flint tools, the analysis of intra- and intersite patterns and the functional interpretation of site types.

NOTES

1 Amateurs, notably: Oppenheim 1928; Popping 1929b; Siebinga 1944; Wouters 1952-'53. Professionals: Bohmers/Wouters 1956; Bursch 1928; Hamal-Nandrin/Servais 1909.

2 Newell 1970a, 1970b, 1970c, 1973, 1975, 1980, 1984; Newell/Vroomans 1972; Price 1975, 1978, 1980; *Price et al.* 1974.

3 Vermeersch 1982a, 1989.

4 Arts 1987b, 1989; Arts/Deeben 1977, 1981; Beuker 1989; Groenendijk 1987, 1988, 1997; Groenendijk/Smit 1984-'85, 1990; Verhart 2000a; Verhart/Wansleeben 1990, 1991a, 1991b; Wansleeben/Verhart 1990.

5 Hazelnuts: Arts 1989; Groenendijk 1987. Cherry pits and acorns: Newell 1973; Vermeersch *et al.* 1974; Vermeersch *et al.* 1980. Water chestnuts: Casparie 1991.

6 Aaris-Sørensen 1988; Andersen *et al.* 1990; Petersen 1973; Gob 1976; Clark 1954; Schwantes 1958; Street 1991.

7 Rowley-Conwy 1983.

8 This research focuses on the relation between ^{12}C and ^{13}C in the bones. A high ^{13}C content indicates a high proportion of marine components in the diet, whereas a high ^{12}C content indicates a primarily terrestrial diet. Denmark: Fischer 1987. Sweden: Larsson 1983, 1990. Skeletal research: Price 1989; Tauber 1981.

9 Louwe Kooijmans 1985; Verhart 1988.

10 Especially Newell 1973; Arts 1989; also: Arora 1976; Bohmers/Wouters 1956; Gendel 1984; Gob 1981; Narr 1968; Rozoy 1978; Taute 1973-'74; Vermeersch 1984.

11 Lanting/Mook 1977; Waterbolk 1985.

12 Creemers/Vermeersch 1986; Price *et al.* 1974; Verhart/Wansleeben 1991a, 1991b.

13 Groenendijk 1987.

14 Taute 1973-'74.

15 Arora 1976.

16 Gob 1981.

17 Newell 1970a; Price 1975, 1980.

18 Bokelmann 1971.

19 Newell 1970a, 1970b, 1970c, 1973, 1975.

20 Harsema 1978.

21 Newell 1970a, 1973; Price 1975.

22 Gob 1985; Kozlowski 1975.

23 Newell 1970a, 1970b.

24 See *e.g.* Andersen 1985, 1987; Clark 1954.

25 Arora 1979; Gendel 1982, 1984.

26 Caspar 1984.

27 Arts/Deeben 1977.

28 Coninx 1984. Haematite is not known from erratic boulder sources in the northern Netherlands. It is however possible that iron concentrations occurring there were converted into haematite as a result of heating (pers. com. H. Kars).

29 Hulst/Verlinde 1976.

30 Broadbent 1975-'77.

31 For the north: Hulst/Verlinde 1976; Tackenberg 1970. For the south: Hoof 1970. A few new sites are Loon op Zand (Verwers 1988), St.-Oedenrode (Heesters 1971), Tilburg-Kraaiven (Arts 1986) and a small number of sites in the Meuse valley.

32 Arts 1987b.

33 For rivers and peats: Arts 1987a; Bosscha Erdbrink 1982; Elzinga 1962. For the North Sea: Clark 1936; Louwe Kooijmans 1971-'72, Stolzenbach/Stolzenbach 1991; Verhart 1988.

34 Arts 1987a; Verhagen 1991.

35 D'Acy 1893; Blanchet/Blanchet 1977.

36 Pesse: Van Zeist 1957. Willemstad: Van Es/Casparie 1968.

37 Ingold *et al.* 1988; Leacock/Lee 1982; Lee/De Vore 1968.

38 An excellent list of further references is to be found in Newell *et al.* 1990.

39 Wobst 1973.

40 Gendel 1984, 1987, 1989; Newell *et al.* 1990; Verhart 1990.

41 Healey 1990; Sahlins 1972.

42 Gendel 1987, 1989.

43 Newell 1973; Price 1975; 1978.

44 Arts 1987b; 1989; Newell 1975.

45 Forsberg 1985.

46 Heesters 1971; Musch 1981; Newell 1980.

47 Bokelmann 1981; 1986; 1990.

48 Andersen, K. *et al.* 1982.

49 Albrethsen/Petersen 1976; Petersen 1988; Larsson 1989; 1990; Price/Brown 1985.

50 Gassel: Brounen/De Jong 1988. West Germany: Breest 1988. For *Breitkeile* see Van der Waals 1972.

51 Street 1991; Verhart/Wansleeben 1990.

52 Dalfsen: Verlinde 1974. Oirschot: Arts/Hoogland 1987.

53 Price/Brown 1985.

54 Newell 1973; Price 1975, 1978.

55 Arora 1974; Street 1991.

56 Newell 1970a, 1970b; Waterbolk 1985.

57 Clarke 1976.

58 Bokelmann 1981, 1986, 1990; Bokelmann/Averdieck/Willkomm 1981, 1985.

59 Obermaier 1925.

60 Gendel *et al.*1985; Jensen 1986; Jensen/Petersen 1985.

61 Van Neer 1982.

62 Groenendijk 1987; Groenendijk/Smit 1990.

63 Scherpenseel (Arora 1976); Opglabbeek-Ruiterskuil (Vermeersch/Munaut/Paulissen 1974); Groenendijk 1987.

64 Newell 1973; Price 1975, 1978, 1980.

65 Largely on the basis of the model formulated by Jochim (1976).

66 Binford 1980; Jochim 1976.

67 Huiskes 1988; since the text of this chapter was written new evidence has led to a more balanced vision: see feature D on the Hardinxveld excavations.

68 Verhart/Wansleeben 1990; 1991a; 1991b; Wansleeben/Verhart 1990. This text is based on preliminary data. See Verhart 2000 for the final report.

69 Groenendijk 1987, 1997.

70 Waterbolk 1985.

71 This is based on a Swifterbant pot from Bronneger (Lanting 1992).

72 Deckers 1982.

C Mesolithic along the Overijssel Vecht
Camp sites and burial pits at Mariënberg

Ad Verlinde

During the levelling of an extensive area of medieval arable land (a so-called *es*) around the village Mariënberg in the period 1975-1985, archaeological discoveries were made over an area of some 350 x 50 m. The ROB, in close cooperation with the owner of the site, carried out systematic excavations at this site, situated on a prominent Late Glacial coversand ridge along the valley of the Vecht river in Overijssel. Here the remains of three small urnfields from the Late Bronze Age and a few flat graves of the single-grave culture of Late Neolithic date were found. The most striking discoveries, however, were the large numbers of Mesolithic features which, in addition to the usual, small round 'hearths pits', included a group of six pits that are unique in the Netherlands and its surroundings; they are probably to be interpreted as graves, in which the deceased had been buried seated, with their knees pulled up. Thanks to the *es* cover, which had preserved these features, we now have a good picture of a Mesolithic site that was used intensively over a long period of time.

Hearth pits

Hundreds of hearth pits were observed within the investigated area of about 1 hectare (fig. C1). In the eastern part of this area the hearths lay further apart than in the western part: about 4 metres as opposed to only 1 metre. However, there were only few intersections, which implies that the hearths had remained recognisable, either as shallow pits or as patches with a different vegetation, for a long time after their use. The only pattern that appeared to be distinguishable in the widely scattered pits was that of a circle formed by a number of lightly coloured features. They were found to surround a podzolised disturbance caused by tree roots, which, on account of this context, probably dates from the same period as the hearth features surrounding it.

The round to oval hearths almost all had diameters of 0.5-1 m; they extended to depths of only 5-40 cm beneath the exposed surface, which lay in the B-horizon of a humus-iron podzol, ploughed in the Middle Ages. Stratigraphic evidence indicated that the pits were originally 25 cm deeper, in other words, that their maximum depth had been 65 cm.

The fills of the pits were homogeneous and unleached. A distinction could be made on the basis of the colour of the fills between pits with dark fills containing large amounts of (powdered) charcoal and pits with light fills containing

little charcoal. Analysis of charcoal samples revealed that the light fills contained chiefly charcoal from pine while the darker ones contained charcoal from oak or both. There turned out to be a chronological difference between the two types of hearths. [14]C analysis yielded early Mesolithic and Boreal dates for the light group and late Mesolithic and Atlantic dates for the dark group. The types of wood used reflect the differences between the forests of the two periods. However, other types of wood were also attested. It is not so easy to

Mariënberg

● hearth-pit, dark coloured fill		▨ grave, Late Mesolithic
○ hearth-pit, light coloured fill		⟨ᵖ⟩ tree root disturbance
▧ grave, Late Neolithic		

0   2 m

fig. C1

Part of the plan of the excavation near the sheep pen of Mariënberg.
Scale 1:400.

explain the difference in colour between the features. It is possible that the oak was burned in a damper condition and hence produced more (powdered) charcoal. Another possibility could be stronger – and in any case longer-lasting – erosion processes in the case of the older features.

The fills of the hearths contained only little Mesolithic settlement waste: a few fragments of pot-boilers, flint flakes, many of which were fragmented or burned, small blades and a very small number of flint implements were found. One of the youngest hearths contained part of a sandstone 'arrow-shaft polisher'. With the exception of the charcoal, almost no finds of organic matter such as (burned) bones or (carbonised) seeds were recovered. In spite of this it was for a long time assumed that butchering refuse or food remains had been deposited in the pits because of the light brownish green hue of the less dark fills, which could indicate the presence of certain phosphate compounds. However, this could not be confirmed through chemical analysis, on the contrary. The aforementioned hue is probably attributable to brown forest soil or to a *moder podzol*, which we assume overlay the coversands in this area in the Atlantic period.

The number of flint flakes found around the hearths was also small. Apparently, specific activities for which fairly deep wood or charcoal fires were required were carried out on a large scale here. Hearths of this kind were introduced at the beginning of the Mesolithic. Experiments have shown that they were very suitable for certain activities requiring a steady amount of heat over a long period, such as the preparation or preservation of food or the curing of hides. Because of their limited heat radiation, they will have been unsuitable as hearths at the centre of a hut, tent or camp.[1]

A question still remaining is whether these hearths were associated with a camp. The hundreds of flint artefacts, collected from the arable, together with the large number of hearth pits (600 at least) and the 2500 year time span are arguments in favour of the interpretation of the site as a base camp.

Burial pits

In one place six distinctly larger pits spaced between 1 and 4 m apart were found among the hearth features. The different shape, colour and contents of these pits distinguished them from the hearths. Although the features lay close together in this particular area, none of the pits intersected any of the hearths, which suggests that the two groups of features are contemporary. [14]C dates obtained for samples from five hearths lying beside and between the larger pits indirectly dated the latter to the end of the Mesolithic, i.e. around 6200 BP.

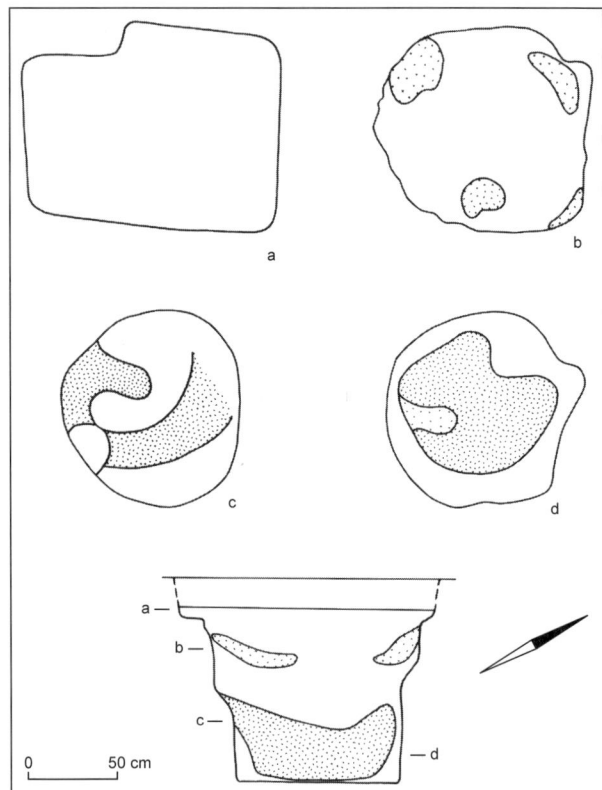

fig. C2
Horizontal and vertical sections of the Late Mesolithic grave No. 55.
The dotted areas represent soil mixed with ochre. Scale 1:40.

Although no traces of any burials were found, there are indications suggesting that these unusual pits are to be interpreted as graves. The pits were cylindrical and had flat bottoms. The three deepest pits widened in their upper parts; their contours at the top were oval or rectangular with rounded corners. They had diameters of 65-140 cm and depths of 30-130 cm, calculated from the exposed surface, which means that they extended to depths of 55-155 cm beneath the former ground level (fig. C2).

The pits had apparently been backfilled with the soil dug from them: their fills consisted of a light greenish soil, which probably came from the former forest soil, or of a yellow sand from a deeper horizon. The base of the fill had a striking deep red colour, attributable to red ochre mixed with the sand (plate 10B). The red ochre surrounded the individual grains of sand as iron membranes. Apparently ochre powder, whether or not mixed with sand, had been sprinkled over the bottom of the pit before the latter was filled in or the pit was filled with natural red sand. Pedological processes had later caused the ochre to be deposited around the grains of sand in the form of iron membranes. As far as we know, the closest sites from which (red) ochre (usually referred to as haematite) could be obtained lay in the Eifel and the Ardennes. This by no means common raw material must have

180

been imported from more than 200 km away; it is possible that it was mixed with sand for reasons of economy.

In addition to 'normal' settlement waste, each of the six pits yielded one or more unusual finds which are considered grave goods. All of these unusual finds were recovered from the ochre layer. The settlement remains were distributed throughout the fill; they were small and often burned and fragmented. In the ochre layers were several larger objects, a few of which were arranged in a certain order. Most of these were of good-quality flint showing red patches caused by the ochre: relatively large blades and flakes, some of which had been flaked to obtain a knife or some other implement, but also nodules and unknapped lumps of flint and hammer stones.

The ochre layers of two of the pits each contained three sandstone artefacts that have been interpreted as (arrow-shaft) polishers: elongated stones having one flat side with a longitudinal groove down its centre (fig. C3). Two of these stones placed with their flat sides against one another could very well have been used to smoothen arrow-shafts *etc*, but they may of course also have been used singly. The equally sized stones lay next to one another with their flat sides facing downwards above the bottom of the ochre layer. This specific position indicates deliberate, structured deposition. The discovery of half of such a stone in one of the hearths supports the assumption that the two types of features are contemporary. So-called arrow-shaft polishers are a rare type of artefact as a burial gift in the overall prehistory of Northern Europe and in the Netherlands. They have been encountered mainly in Beaker contexts; a few have been found in older contexts but none have so far been found in association with Mesolithic remains.[2]

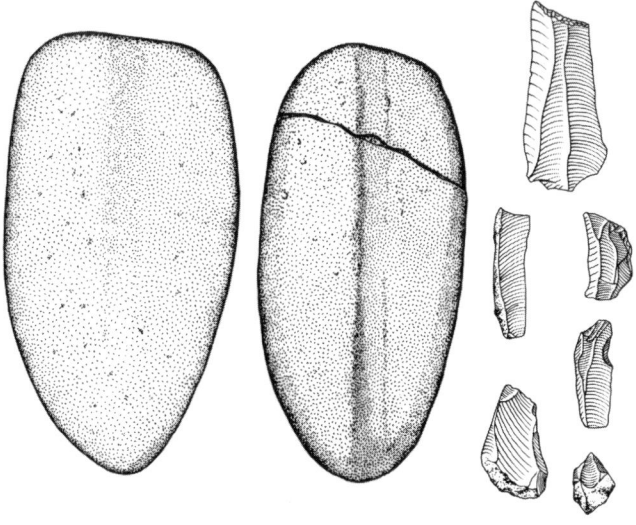

fig. C3
Flint grave goods and an 'arrow-shaft polisher' found in the Late Mesolithic graves. Scale 1:2.

From the above it will be clear that we are dealing with something quite exceptional for the Mesolithic. The shape of the pits, the composition of their fills, the use of red ochre and the deposition of specific artefacts together led to the interpretation of these features as burial pits. The lack of any traces of the deceased can be entirely accounted for by the acid soil conditions. The dimensions and the shape of the pits suggest that the dead were buried seated, with their knees pulled up, as observed in the case of a few burials from an earlier phase of the Mesolithic in southern Scandinavia.[3] This is further supported by patterns observed in the ochre layers in three of the six pits, which could indicate the positions of the bodies and legs in the graves when the sand and ochre were sprinkled over them. The six pits from Mariënberg are well-connected to the nine so-called sitting graves, known from the West European Mesolithic.

It is of course curious to encounter a small cemetery among hearths at a site at which the preparation and/or preservation of food or other activities will have taken place. A possible alternative interpretation is that the pits were used for some very special activity which involved the use of red ochre and polishing stones instead of fire. This may have been the preservation and working of hides,[4] in which case the polishers may have been used for bone piercers and needles instead of arrow shafts. Most pre-industrial communities cure hides outside the settlement site because of the stench involved.

Mesolithic graves are scarce in the Netherlands and its wide surroundings. At two sites in the Netherlands human cremation remains have been found in Mesolithic contexts: in a hearth at Dalfsen (Overijssel) and in a cremation burial at Oirschot (North Brabant).[5] In neither of these cases indisputable evidence was found of the deliberate deposition of cremation remains. In the area under consideration the dead were apparently seldom buried in the Mesolithic. This changed at the end of that period. A few graves and cemeteries from the end of the Mesolithic have been found in southern Scandinavia in particular. They are still rare, though, and are associated with increased sedentism and territorial competition.

Unlike Neolithic graves, Mesolithic burials in Europe never contain arrow-shaft polishers. The deposition of such implements in graves is actually a Neolithic custom. We may speculate that the persons who were buried at Mariënberg had become acquainted with Neolithic customs. Buried in the area occupied by their ancestors, they had apparently accepted this Neolithic custom in their burial rite, a first step in a virtually unknown acculturation process.[6]

If the discoveries made at Mariënberg are to be interpreted as evidence of a small cemetery, we are dealing with a rather exceptional combination of burial rite and grave goods. The interpretation according to which the pits were used for some special activity implies an equally unusual phenomenon. What we know for sure is that the features dating from the last period of use of the site at Mariënberg are attributable to communities for which we have very few concrete data: the hunter-gatherers of the sandy soils to the north of the *Bandkeramik* farmers on the loess.

Notes

1 Groenendijk 1987.
2 Louwe Kooijmans 1974, 299.
3 In 1998 such a Late Mesolithic seated burial with well-preserved skeletal remains was excavated at Hardinxveld-De Bruin (Louwe Kooijmans 2001b, see feature D).
4 Van de Velde 1973.
5 Verlinde 1974, 1982a; Arts and Hoogland 1987.
6 Final publication: Verlinde/Newell forthcoming.

D Hunting camps in the swamps
The river dunes near Hardinxveld

Leendert Louwe Kooijmans

From extensive coring research it had for quite some time been known that the old river dunes in the river district had been occupied not only in the Neolithic, but even in earlier times. Unfortunately, the high costs involved in excavation had precluded further research into the occupation sites. The discovery, during prospecting for the new Betuwe railway line in 1994, of two new river dunes, both with evidence of Late Mesolithic occupation, near Hardinxveld-Giessendam did therefore not come as a major surprise, but was indeed a stroke of luck (fig. D1). It was found that the sites would be disturbed by the creation of the body of sand needed to construct the railway, so they would have to be excavated. This took place in 1997-'98. To save time and for financial reasons excavations were at both sites restricted to a single, large section of the periphery of the settlement site that was assumed to be representative of the entire periphery plus part of the adjacent swampland (fig. 4.9, plate 11A). The excavations yielded a wealth of new evidence and information.[1]

As in most other parts of Europe, our understanding of the Mesolithic was hitherto based almost entirely on the flint scatters of former camps. Only very few wetland sites are known with preserved organic remains from which so

much extra information can be obtained: Star Carr in England, Noyen-sur-Seine in France, Friesack in Meckelenburg (Germany). Wetland sites dating from the *Late* Mesolithic are however known only from southern Scandinavia and the Baltic countries. They have governed our understanding of this period to such an extent that the European Mesolithic may be considered a clone of the Danish Mesolithic. So from this perspective the two Hardinxveld sites are particularly valuable.

The sites were located on two small river dunes, known as Polderweg and De Bruin, whose tops lay 5 and 4 m below NAP, respectively. Both dunes were first occupied around 5500 BC. People continued to live on the dunes until the rise in the water level caused them to disappear beneath peat and clay, the first around 5000 BC and the second around 4450 BC. The short distance of about one kilometre between them suggests that the two dunes were islands in the immense surrounding swamps affording dry living areas for one and the same community (plate 12).

The settlement sites themselves lay at the tops of the dunes. Large, shallow, flat-bottomed pits dug in those parts are assumed to be the features of sunken huts. This is also

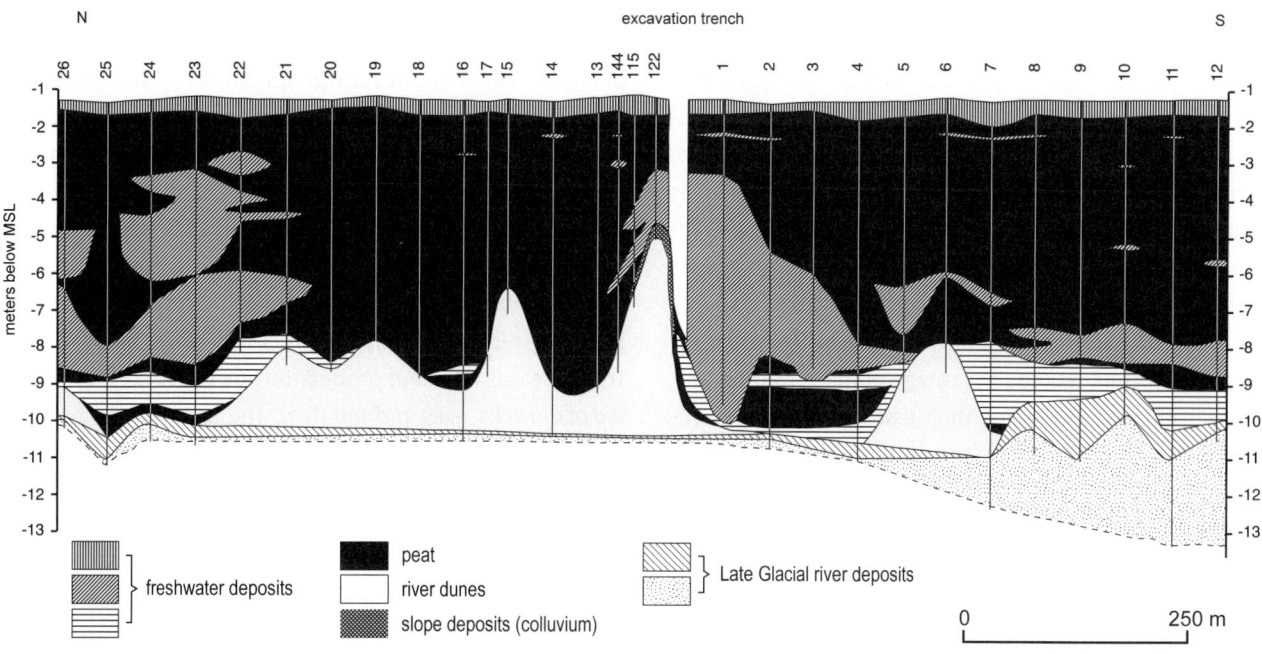

fig. D1

Section based on cores of part of the buried river-dune landscape of the Alblasserwaard region
with the Polderweg dune at the centre. Horizontal scale 1:8000, elevation 40 times enlarged.

suggested by postholes with fairly small diameters, the deepest of which still contained the remains of a 6-cm-thick post. On both dunes deceased members of the community were in the first centuries of use buried at the occupation site, and so were the occupants' dogs, with which they evidently had a close bond (fig. D2). One of the deceased was a woman of about fifty (fig. 9.4). Human bones, some deriving from young children, were also found among the refuse. This evidence, along with the sites' dimensions (lengths of 80 and 50 m), shows that the dunes were not just hunting and fishing stations, but base camps for entire households. This is indeed confirmed by the broad range of bone and antler artefacts found at the sites and by the results of microwear analysis of the flint artefacts.

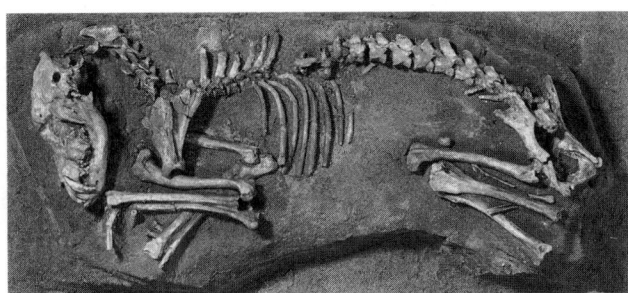

fig. D2

Polderweg, burial of a dog, phase 1, c. 5400 BC.

The thousands of animal bones show that beaver, wild boar, red deer and otter were the most important hunted animals. The beavers and otters were caught with traps, the deer and boars were actively hunted. Roe deer and furred animals – European wildcat, pine marten and polecat – were also killed in small numbers. The hunters killed large quantities of waterfowl: many mallards, but also typical winter visitors such as the red-throated diver, goosander, goldeneye, wigeon, Bewick's swan and whooper. White-tailed eagles will have been shot for their feathers and possibly also for prestige. The tremendous amounts of fish remains suggest that fish, in particular pike, was the most important source of food. Pike is indeed so prominently represented as to imply that the occupants took advantage of the spawning season, when the fish overcome their usual timidity and venture into shallow waters. That is in the second part of winter, around February. Besides the represented bird and fish species, the parts of red deer antler found on the dunes also show that the sites were winter camps: 20% of the bases derive from killed animals, which must have been shot between September and January, and the other 80% are gathered beams, which will have been picked up in February and March. Water nuts (some of which showed signs of burning) and hazelnuts were collected in the early autumn. The complete absence of remains of young deer, young beavers

and typical summer fish such as sturgeon, salmon and thin-lipped grey mullet suggests that the camps were not occupied in the summer, at least not in phase 1 of the Polderweg site (fig. D3). We do have some evidence for summer use from the later phases: a few bones of the purple heron and young deer and remains of adult sturgeons. The sites' function seems to have changed in those phases, possibly as a result of the introduction of arable farming, which will have demanded more permanent residence on the sandy soils (see below).

The most spectacular artefacts are of course those of wood: large parts of two man-sized elm bows, four ash paddles, a unique axe handle, also of ash wood, and a complete, elegant 5.5-m-long canoe made from the hollowed-out trunk of a lime (fig. D4, plate 11B) plus parts of some other canoes and part of a fish weir. Split wood, a few half-finished products and some chips show that such artefacts were not only discarded, but also manufactured at the site itself, and that brings us to the varied range of bone and antler implements.

The hundreds of bone and antler tools represent a tool kit that varies considerably from those known from Scandinavia – not so much in functional respect, but more stylistically. The severely battered cutting edges suggest that the heaviest implements were used for primary wood-working operations and for felling trees, but this was surprisingly not confirmed by chopping experiments using axes similar to those found at the site. The axes concerned are primarily T-shaped antler axes without a shaft hole. Small chisel blades of wild boar teeth inserted in shafts, some of which were perforated, were used for finer wood-working. The site also yielded a varied range of axes and chisels made of parts of antler beams or tines. Large quantities of discarded bases and a few crowns show that these implements were also made at the site. Damaged and broken parts were repaired. Unique and highly characteristic of Hardinxveld are fine serrations at the cutting edges of axes that were no longer considered suitable for their primary function. Microwear analysis showed that they were granted a new lease of life as scraping implements. Besides this systematic 'antler industry' there was a second production line based on the *metapodia* of aurochs, elks and red deer. The bones of the first two species were used to make heavy socketed axes, while the red deer *metapodia* served as raw materials for various chisels and awls. A few special tools are decorated with rows of dots, finely hatched geometric motifs or groups of short hatched lines. An exceptional find is a blunt gouge-shaped awl made from the ulna of a mute swan that is decorated with rows of small hatched triangles. Although the overall range does show some similarities with contemporary Danish assemblages, its most conspicuous feature is nevertheless its great originality. This implies a high degree of cultural differentia-

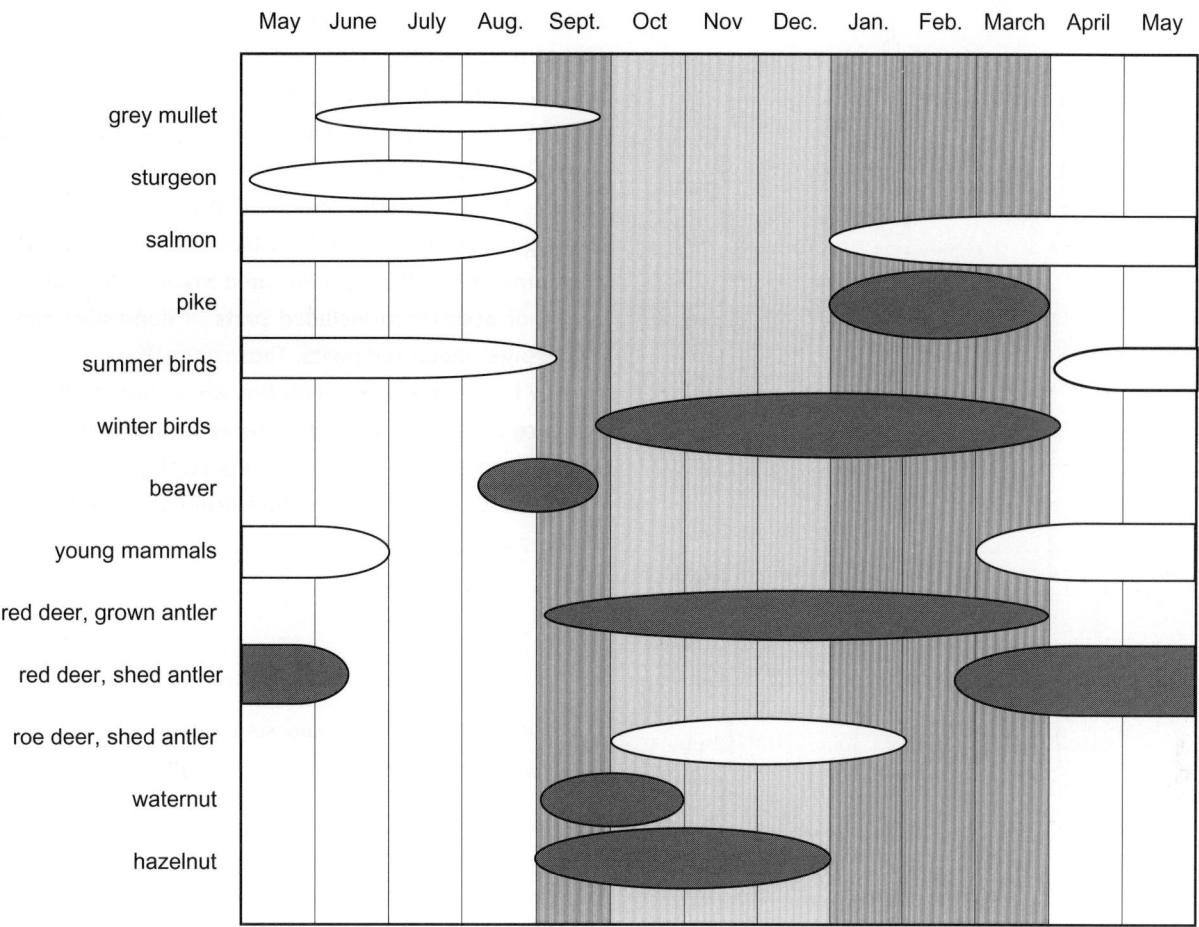

fig. D3

Polderweg, phase 1. Survey of absent (white) and represented (dark grey) seasonal indicators. There are two possible interpretations: occupation in two phases – early autumn and late winter (dark grey bands) – or throughout the autumn and winter (dark and light grey bands together). What we do know for sure is that the site was not occupied in the summer, which implies seasonal movement of the base camp within an annual territory.

tion, greater than would be assumed on the basis of the flint assemblages.

The hinterland of the Hardinxveld site hence lay not to the north, but to the south. This is evident from the provenance of the stone. From phase 1 date several blades of Wommersom quartzite (see chapter 8), but also a large block of Rijckholt flint that must have been imported directly from southern Limburg. A large angular lump of schist must have come from the Ardennes, and the same holds for a number of river pebbles. The Ardennes may also have been the provenance of a few small pieces of pyrite that were found among the refuse. They were probably used to light fires, along with tinder. The greater part of the flint will however have been picked up closer to the site, from the Meuse terrace deposits in the central part of Limburg, though some came from sources to the north. Generally speaking, Hardinxveld may

however be considered a northern, relatively late outpost of the 'Wommersom community' of the southern part of the Netherlands (see chapter 8). The obvious conclusion would be to suppose the complementary summer camp in the same southern direction. The hunters may have lived in the summer at the periphery of the sandy soils, from where they could exploit the game of the hinterland and the salmon and sturgeon of the rivers. Further evidence confirming this was provided by some bone and antler tools that came to light in dredging activities during the development of the new Maaspoort district of 's-Hertogenbosch.

The Hardinxveld camp sites were contemporary with the *Bandkeramik*, the culture of the first farmers in the loess zone more than 120 km to the south, with which region the hunters seem to have been in contact. This is evident not only from the imported types of stone, but also from a typical *Band-*

keramik point from phase 1, from Blicquy pottery from phase 2 and from a few very large blades of Rijckholt flint knapped according to the Michelsberg tradition from phase 3. Around 5000 BC people began to produce pottery at the Hardinxveld sites. This is taken to mark the beginning of the Swifterbant culture. To what extent the sites' occupants engaged in farming is difficult to say in the case of such winter camps in a swamp. Votive offerings deposited towards the end of the period of occupation included parts of domestic animals: cattle, pigs, sheep and goats. Those animals were evidently already being kept elsewhere. But we do not yet have any evidence of cereals, which are known from the Hazendonk site near Molenaarsgraaf 500 years later. This shows that the transition to the Neolithic in the North European Plain was indeed a hesitant process.

Notes

1 See the contributions of many specialists in Louwe Kooijmans 2001a, 2001b and 2003.

fig. D4
Polderweg, phase 1, wooden artefacts. Scale 1:8.

1, 2 blades of ash paddles

3 one half of a bow, elm wood

4 axe handle, ash wood

9 Hunters and gatherers: synthesis

Jos Deeben and Annelou van Gijn

INTRODUCTION

Over the past few decades the number of Palaeolithic and Mesolithic finds has increased tremendously, both in the Netherlands and elsewhere. There is however much disagreement about the meaning of the finds. The debate revolves essentially around two issues: the nature and quality of the archaeological evidence and the way in which we are to interpret the Palaeolithic and Mesolithic remains.

The Palaeolithic and Mesolithic occupation remains are predominantly lithic artefacts. As many of these remains are surface finds, their quality is fairly poor. Only a few of the discovered sites have been excavated. The methods employed in their excavation and the size of the investigated area moreover varied considerably. A revision of site formation processes has led to doubts about the meaning of a concentration of stone artefacts in terms of human behaviour,[1] and has also sparked off discussions about the artificial character of finds from before 500,000 BP. Until a few years ago, most experts assumed that Europe was colonised around a million years ago. But arguments have now been presented that support a different view – at least for the northern part of Europe – based on what is known as the 'short chronology'. One of these arguments is that it has proved to be impossible to establish the artefactual nature of finds of more than 500,000 years old, because none of those finds derives from primary deposits. All the sites that have been found in fine-layered, primary deposits date from after 500,000 years ago. The finds that have been assigned dates before 500,000 BP are all individual finds, selected from large quantities of lithic material, whereas those from *after* this date consist of excavated knapping floors. Another important argument supporting the 'short chronology' is the absence of human skeletal remains of more than 500,000 years old.[2]

Until the 1960s, archaeological evidence was gathered and interpreted predominantly from a cultural-historical perspective. In the 1960s, however, the processual approach, with its strong emphasis on the use of anthropological models and functional interpretation, attracted progressively more attention. Fearing that present-day hunter-gatherers would rapidly 'modernise', some workers started to carry out ethnoarchaeological fieldwork themselves. It was assumed that such fieldwork would yield an appropriate framework for interpreting excavated settlements, camp sites and land use. This development went hand in hand with a growing interest in the Palaeolithic and Mesolithic, to which many of the newly developed anthropological models seemed directly applicable. Upper Palaeolithic communities in particular were pictured as counterparts, as it were, of the Nunamiut in Alaska, which Binford described in such vivid terms (fig. 9.1).[3]

Over the past decade, doubts have been expressed about this approach, too. The main points of criticism are the theoretical basis of processual archaeology, in particular the assumptions of evolutionist anthropology, the limited applicability of ethnographies of (sub)recent communities of hunter-gatherers[4] and, finally, the often strictly economic principles. The debate has not yet crystallised into a new approach.[5] In anticipation of the development of an unambiguous theoretical framework,[6] Palaeolithic and Mesolithic research is meanwhile focusing on the accumulation of a high-quality data base. In some respects the cul-

fig. 9.1
A rack full of reindeer meat being dried on a thawing tundra at a site of Nunamiut hunters where a summer camp will soon be set up. Studies of the settlement systems of present-day hunter-gatherers can be of use in interpreting archaeological patterns. The American Lewis Binford to this end studied the migration patterns of the Nunamiut (Alaska) and the way they handle the game caught on their hunting expeditions.

tural-historical approach seems to be winning ground again, especially when we consider the great attention that is again being paid to refining the chronological framework.

Our understanding of the Palaeolithic and Mesolithic occupation of the Netherlands is very incomplete, so it is very difficult to interpret the available evidence in any detail. Nevertheless, an attempt will be made to draw some general conclusions on environment and occupation, society, subsistence and technology on the following pages. It goes without saying that this tremendously long time span, from c. 500,000 years ago until c. 5300 BC, saw several drastic changes; we will therefore also review the processes that brought about those changes. The chapter will be concluded with a survey of possibilities for further research.

ENVIRONMENT AND OCCUPATION

The Pleistocene and Holocene saw radical changes in climatological conditions, which had a major impact on the landscape in the various archaeological periods. The information available on the environment is of a very general, supraregional, character in the earliest periods and becomes progressively detailed as we approach the present. So far, only little attention has been paid to regional variation in the development of the natural environment. On the whole, the available reconstructions of the environment offer only a very general framework for interpretation. Integrated archaeological, geological and ecological research projects on local and site levels are only rarely organised; in the Netherlands, such projects have been carried out at, for example, Maastricht-Belvédère, Geldrop, Milheeze and Venlo.[7]

Until in the Upper Palaeolithic, the occupation of northern Europe showed a kind of ebb and flow pattern: in extremely cold phases settlement moved further south, to spread northwards again when the temperatures rose. The small number of finds recovered *in situ* makes it very difficult to interpret the settlement patterns of the Middle and early Upper Palaeolithic in the Low Countries. Our understanding of this issue is still too strongly determined by preservation conditions and the intensity of research. In the Netherlands, the ebb and flow pattern seems to have come to an end around 13,000 BP; from then onwards the area appears to have been continuously occupied. The high density of occupation remains from this date onwards forms a marked contrast with the evidence from preceding periods, even when we allow for the problem of preservation.

The majority of the Middle Palaeolithic 'sites' were created during only short periods of time; features of structures are entirely absent. Settlement seems to have been characterised by a high degree of mobility. This changed in the Upper Palaeolithic and Mesolithic. Features representing dwellings, windbreaks, hearths

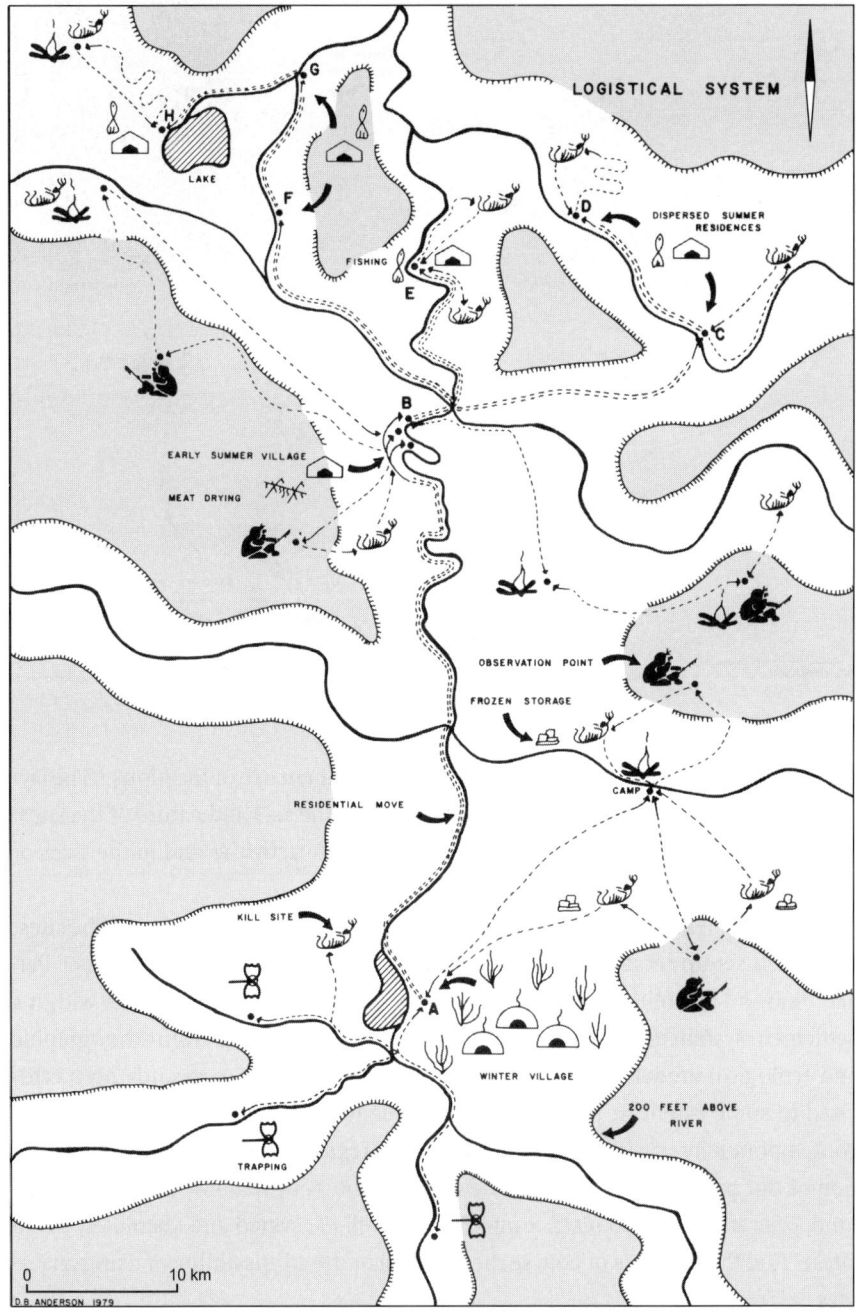

fig. 9.2
Model for the settlement system of *collectors* with *logistical mobility*, based on a study of Nunamiut reindeer hunters. Collectors tend to move their base camps only two to three times a year. Small task groups are sent out to obtain food and raw materials. This form of organisation results in a differentiated range of site types, comprising base camps and specialist 'field stations'.

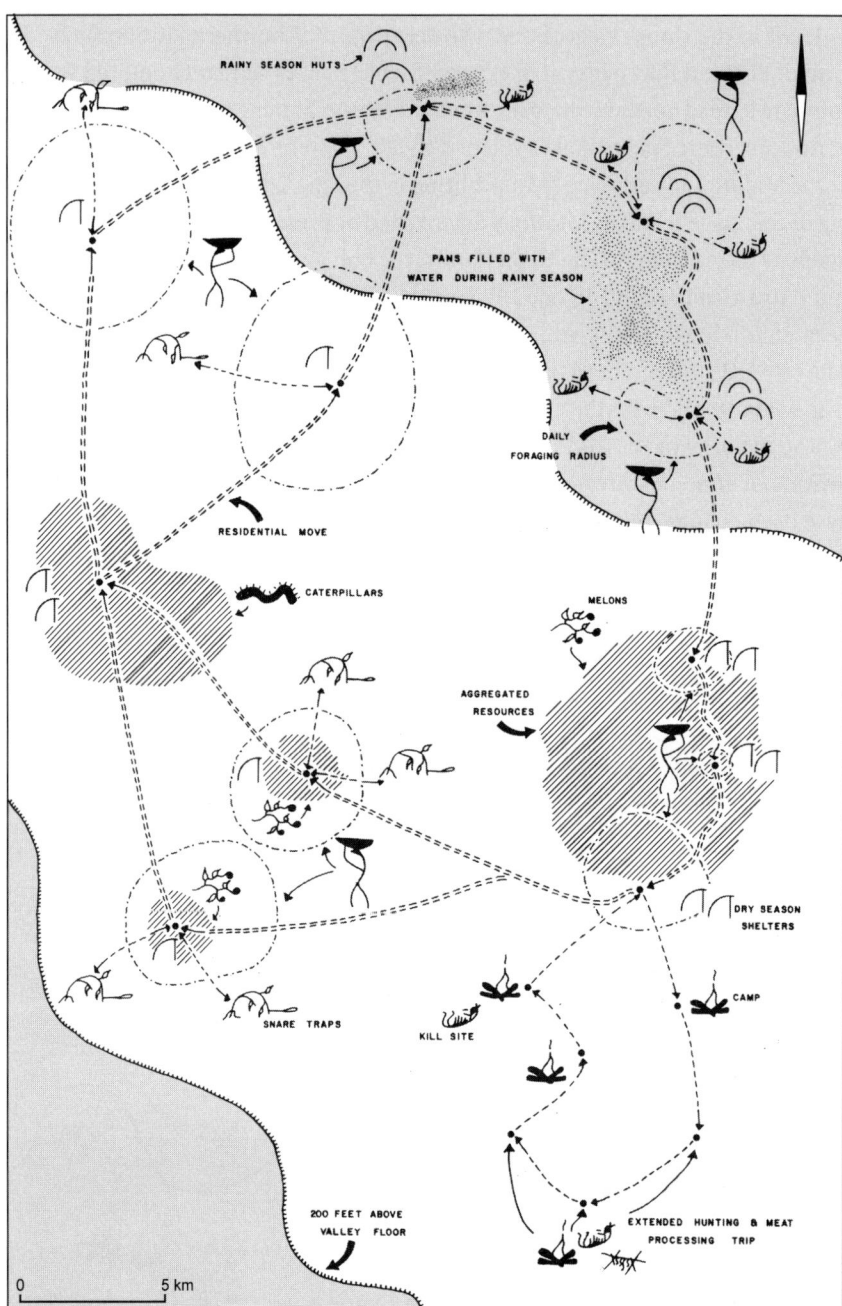

fig. 9.3
Model for the settlement system of *foragers*, with *residential mobility* based on a study of G/wi San Bushmen. Foragers move on to a new site when they have exhausted the resources in the vicinity of their base camp. So the entire group moves to a different site several times a year. There are no specialist field stations or camps briefly occupied by small task groups. This system of residential mobility consequently results in a less varied range of site types.

Within the figure, the following labels appear: RAINY SEASON HUTS, PANS FILLED WITH WATER DURING RAINY SEASON, DAILY FORAGING RADIUS, RESIDENTIAL MOVE, CATERPILLARS, MELONS, AGGREGATED RESOURCES, DRY SEASON SHELTERS, CAMP, SNARE TRAPS, KILL SITE, 200 FEET ABOVE VALLEY FLOOR, EXTENDED HUNTING & MEAT PROCESSING TRIP, 0 5 km, D.B. ANDERSON 1979

and cooking and storage pits point to a more permanent use of locations.[8] The layouts of the individual sites vary considerably, as do the size and nature of the sites. This variation is attributable to differences in on-site activities and in the sizes of the groups living at the sites.

Several settlement typologies, based on the shape and composition of the sites, have been set up in attempts to define the settlement pattern in the Upper Palaeolithic and Mesolithic.[9] How the different sites related to one another within a settlement system of mobile hunter-gatherers is often inferred from ethnographic and ecological models (fig. 9.2 and 9.3).[10] This approach has recently been criticised to some extent. It is, for example, virtually impossible to demonstrate the contemporaneity of sites, even within a microregion. The chronological resolution of our present data base is believed to be too poor to allow research of this kind, even if we were to restrict ourselves to well-excavated and absolutely dated sites.[11] And then there is of course the problem of the admissibility of using analogies.

The existence of large Mesolithic find scatters has led some experts to assume that the degree of inter-site differentiation increased with time: some sites are considerably larger than others in terms of find density and surface area.[12] However, the large sites may also reflect long-term reuse of a particular location, in other words: they may be palimpsests of archaeological remains, accumulated over long periods of time during the Upper Palaeolithic and Mesolithic, when little sedimentation took place. The reason why Palaeolithic and Mesolithic humans kept returning to the same locations must be that they knew, from previous visits to the area or through exchange of information with other groups, what resources were available there.[13]

Most sites lie on well-drained soils, in the vicinity of open water. Dutch Palaeolithic and Mesolithic research has so far paid only little attention to the topic of site location. A tentative conclusion that could be drawn from the currently available evidence is that in the Upper Palaeolithic and Early Mesolithic sites tended to be clustered, whereas they were more uniformly distributed across the landscape in later phases of the Mesolithic.[14] This development may have been brought about by changes in hunting strategies connected with a changing environment, *i.e.* a transition from interception tactics to the stalking of sedentary game.[15]

We must bear in mind that an important facet of the former settlement pattern is missing: the domestic and procurement camps in the North Sea Basin and those in stream and river valleys. The fact that so many sites were located in precisely these ecologically varied environments in Scandinavia suggests that something similar would have been the case in the Low Countries, too. This supposition is supported by the impressive Upper Palaeolithic findspots that have been discovered in the Paris Basin, such as Pincevent and Verberie, the objects that have been trawled from the Brown Bank region in the North Sea and the Mesolithic sites that have come to light along rivers, such as Bedburg-Königshoven and Noyen-sur-Seine.[16]

SOCIETY

Archaeologists distinguish different chronological units within the Palaeolithic and the Mesolithic (a Lower, Middle and Upper Palaeolithic and an Early, Middle and Late Mesolithic), but they also distinguish different 'cultures', 'groups' or 'traditions'. The latter divisions are traditionally, and in the absence of alternatives, based on differences in the manufacturing techniques and shapes of flint artefacts, coupled to absolute or relative dates. Such divisions enable us to order our evidence in geographical (distribution maps) and chronological (sequences) terms.[17] If we assume that specific similarities between artefacts reflect social and cultural links between people, we can assign the distinguished groups a social meaning. However, ethnographic studies of (sub)recent hunter-gatherers have shown that we should not attach too much importance to the cultural areas thus established. The distribution patterns of exotic raw materials and unusual objects like ornaments show that the territories of the assumed ethnic units (dialect tribes) may be tremendously large,[18] and that there were contacts between the individual units.[19] In the southern part of the Netherlands and Belgium, for example, the distribution of the characteristic Wommersom quartzite clearly points to interaction between the Mesolithic groups (bands).[20]

The territories of the cultural groups distinguished in the Netherlands have been defined largely on the basis of the aforementioned cultural-historical criteria. In our country, territorial units are clearly visible only from *c.* 13,000 BP on-

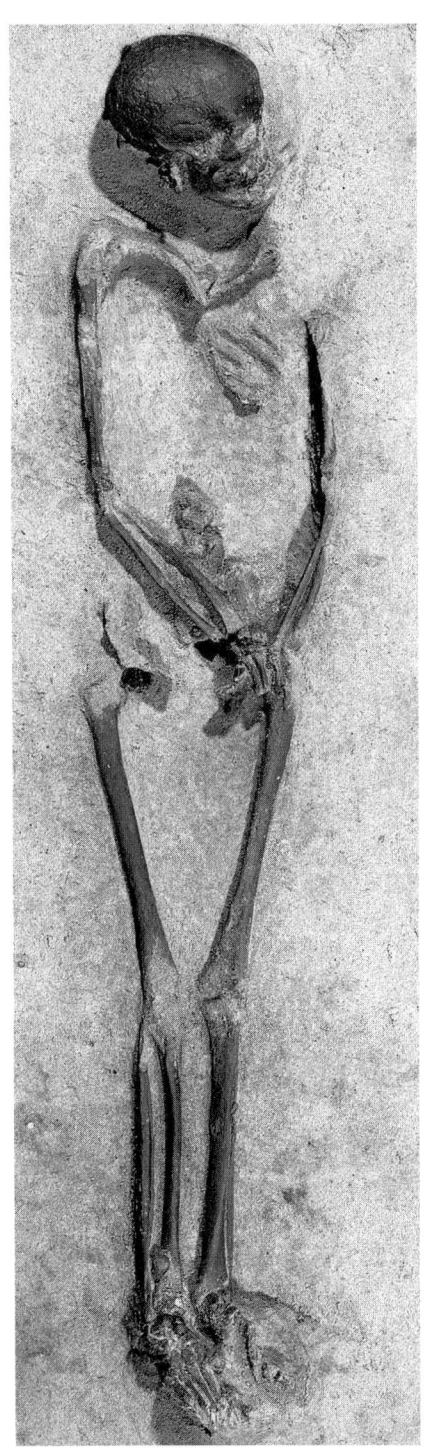

wards. We then see the boundary between the northern Hamburgian tradition and the southern Magdalenian running across the central part of the country. These two traditions both form part of large cultural areas, extending far beyond the Netherlands.[21] The distinction between the northern and southern parts of the country disappeared in a later phase of the Upper Palaeolithic, but the cultural areas remained extensive, largely owing to a low population density and a high degree of mobility.[22] In the Middle Mesolithic the territories clearly decreased in size.[23] In the Netherlands we can again distinguish two different cultural areas in this period: the Northwest Group in the north and the Rhine Basin Group in the south.[24] Generally speaking, the information networks that can be inferred from the distances over which raw materials were exchanged were smaller in the Mesolithic than they had been in the Upper Palaeolithic.[25] This could be attributable to a change in economy, from a system based primarily on the exploitation of migrating animals in the Upper Palaeolithic to one based predominantly on stationary animals, with a wider diversity of exploited food resources, in the Mesolithic. The more stable ecological conditions in the Holocene implied fewer risks and hence less need to keep moving to different regions. Moreover, if it is true that the size and density of the population increased in the Mesolithic, social units of the same size would have occupied smaller territories than previously at the end of the glacial period.

Although the assumed link between the number of sites per chronological unit and the size of the population is now a heavily debated issue, there does seem to have been a slight increase in population in the *Federmesser* period, followed by a relative decrease in the Ahrensburgian period and the Early Mesolithic and another increase in the Middle and Late Mesolithic.[26]

The Late Mesolithic in northern Europe was characterised by population growth,[27] a reduction in the size of the occupied territories and increased sedentism. The latter is apparent from, for example, the cemeteries that have been found in association with settlements.[28] The occurrence of formal cemeteries in the Late Mesolithic in particular is regarded as an indication of an important change in social organisation.[29] In some cemeteries the grave goods and burial rite are no longer exclusively dependent on age and sex.[30] Some regard this as evidence for the emergence of a form of social stratification. It should be added that only little, incidental, evidence for the treatment of the dead and no cemeteries whatsoever have been found in the plain to the west of the Elbe (fig. 9.4).

SUBSISTENCE

Mobility is the key concept in the Palaeolithic and Mesolithic communities' exploitation of their surroundings. The distribution, the seasonal availability and the density of the food resources largely determined the frequency of the movements and the distances they covered, and also the composition of the groups, which ranged from small task groups to large, aggregate social units like bands. In the Low Countries, our understanding of the exploited resources, the activities in the different seasons and the functions of the sites is severely limited by the lack of organic remains. Most of our information on food resources comes from surrounding countries. Another, perhaps even greater impediment with respect to our understanding of the logistics and the settlement system of the entire period is the absence of coastal and other wetland sites, as a result of which we know virtually nothing about the exploitation of the Dutch littoral.

The subsistence strategies of Lower and Middle Palaeolithic groups are still a

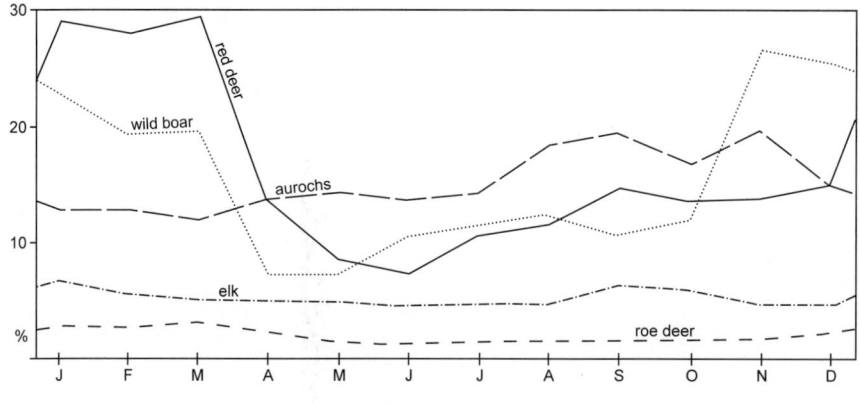

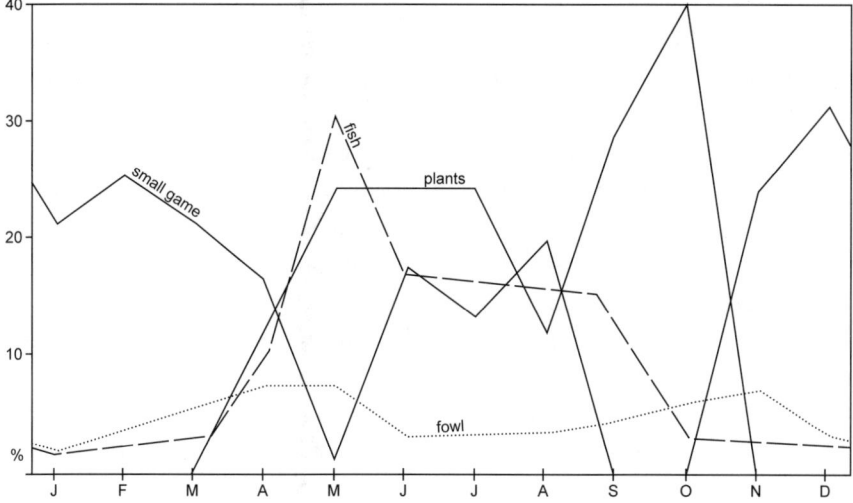

fig. 9.5
Availibility of various (groups of) plants and animals throughout the year in temperate Europe based on the weight, mobility, density and other characteristics of these subsistence resources. In the past, models for Mesolithic subsistence strategies have been formulated on the basis of such evidence. But those models are nowadays viewed with scepticism as many of the assumptions on which they are based, such as optimisation, proved to be incorrect.

matter of some controversy, though recent finds (*e.g.* Schöningen) seem to indicate that the earliest occupants may have been capable hunters of large game in various ecological settings. [31]

Large mammals living in herds and showing a high degree of mobility (seasonal migrations) constituted the main source of (animal) food in the Upper Palaeolithic, too. The trend towards the exploitation of a single species suggested by evidence from some Middle Palaeolithic sites seems to have intensified in the Upper Palaeolithic. [32] In Western Europe the species in question was often horse or reindeer in the latter period. [33] This trend shows that humans had chosen to exploit a single, widely available food resource whose (migratory) behaviour they were evidently able to predict, [34] for dependence on a single species implies a risk and this risk had to be covered, for example by means of a 'safety net' of social alliances. As the forest expanded towards the end of the Weichselian, the degree of specialisation came to depend on the nature of the landscape. In tundra-like environments of the kind that were to be found in northern Germany during the Hamburgian and Ahrensburgian periods the emphasis remained on a single dominant species: the reindeer. In areas further south, for example in southern France during the Azilian, people exploited mainly forest animals. For a large part of this period the Netherlands constituted a kind of transitional area between open and more closed landscapes, whose boundaries shifted in the alternating stadials and interstadials.

In the Mesolithic the consumption of plant food, fowl and fish increased and the economic system evolved into what is known as a broad spectrum economy (fig. 9.5). The evidence for fishing, the hunting of marine mammals and the gathering of shellfish in this period for the first time demonstrates the importance of the coastal zone in the exploitation patterns of the prehistoric hunter-gatherers of Northwest Europe. The Mesolithic may have seen two kinds of adaptations: an adaptation to varied landscapes with wide ranges of resources, such as coasts, lakes and rivers, and an adaptation oriented more towards inland environments. The more varied ecological zones offered more food for larger groups of people. It is indeed in these environmental zones that, in a later phase of the Mesolithic, we find the first cemeteries and indications of a more complex social organisation.

TECHNOLOGY

The Lower and Middle Palaeolithic are characterised by a relatively long use of the same basic technologies. A distinctive tool in Lower Palaeolithic assemblages is the well-known hand axe, a bifacial implement that was probably used for a multitude of tasks. Around 300,000 years ago the Levallois technique made its appearance: a complex knapping technique of which there were many variants (see feature A). Refitting studies of the lithic material from Maastricht-Belvédère have shown that the technical intelligence of Middle Palaeolithic flint tool manufacturers was not far removed from that of modern man (fig. 9.6).[35] In later phases of the Middle Palaeolithic use was made of a variant of the Levallois technique that enabled the systematic production of blades.

The transition from the Middle to the Upper Palaeolithic was for a long time regarded as a major turning point in prehistory.[36] One of the reasons for this was that the systematic production of blades and various technological innovations were seen as distinctive features of the Upper Palaeolithic, the period in which modern man made his appearance. Nowadays it is however believed that the contrast between these two periods is actually less sharp than previously assumed. As we have seen above, man was already producing blades and using fairly complex hunting strategies in the Middle Palaeolithic, as attested by the carefully finished 2.5-m-long wooden spear that was found at Lehringen in association with the skeleton of a straight-tusked elephant dating from the Eemian and the even older and more advanced javelins found at Schöningen.[37] Even so, the blades did become increasingly regular and smaller with time. Upper Palaeolithic assemblages also show a greater diversity of stone tool types, the majority of which were specifically intended for particular functions, and a progressive increase in the number of tools and objects made of wood, bone, ivory and antler. Two important Upper Palaeolithic innovations are the spear thrower and the bow and arrow. Another

fig. 9.6
Refitting small flakes to an 80,000-years-old scraper (right) from Maastricht-Belvédère Site J showed that this tool acquired its ultimate shape in different phases of use and resharpening (reduction).

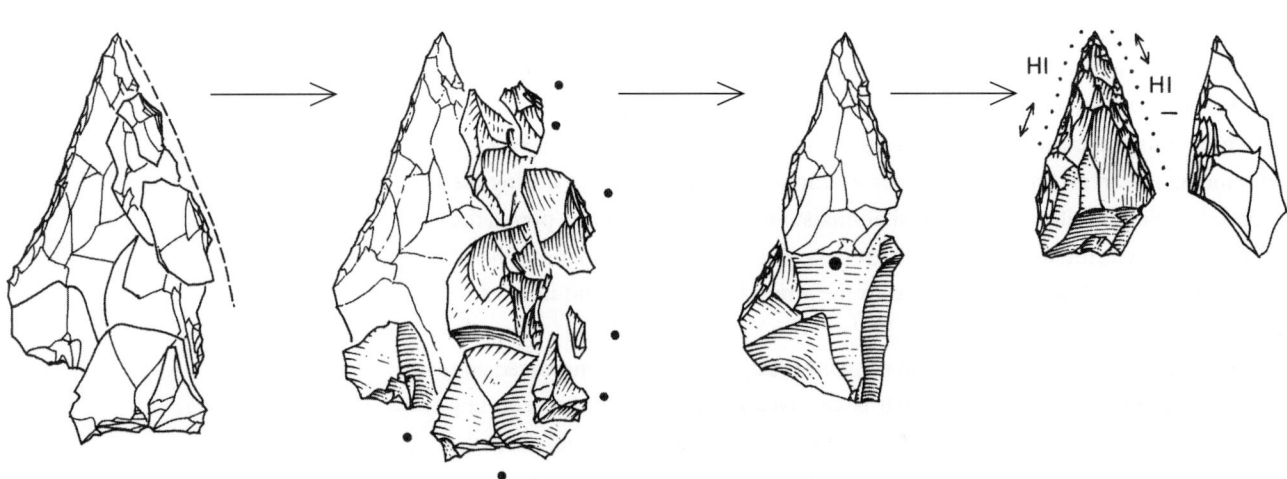

noteworthy aspect of Upper Palaeolithic assemblages, finally, is the observable reduction in the size of the stone tools, which is probably connected with hafting. In the Lower and Middle Palaeolithic, the basic technology had remained unchanged for long periods of time, over large areas with different environmental conditions. The Upper Palaeolithic, on the contrary, is characterised by a wide range of stylistic developments and greater diversity and complexity, as also attested by the appearance of more specialised tools. So all in all, there is indeed a major difference between the tool kits that were used for obtaining a livelihood in the Lower and Middle Palaeolithic on the one hand, and the Upper Palaeolithic on the other hand.[38]

The trend of technological innovation continued in the Mesolithic.[39] New elements can be related to more intensive subsistence strategies. They include storage (for example in bark baskets and containers), greater mobility (canoes, snow shoes, skis) and more efficient hunting, involving untended facilities[40] like traps and nets. The greater variation displayed by the microlithic points, finally, can in part be related to the need to be able to respond quickly, flexibly and efficiently to 'chance' encounters with prey. At the end of the Mesolithic pottery started to be produced in many parts of Europe, under the influence of nearby farming communities. This technological innovation marks the beginning of a new era.

PROCESSES OF CHANGE

Archaeologists traditionally distinguish three large-scale changes in the Palaeolithic and Mesolithic of Europe. The first is the transition from the Middle to the Upper Palaeolithic, the second the transition from the Upper Palaeolithic to the Mesolithic and the third is the transition from the Mesolithic to the Neolithic. For many years, developments in the way of life during the Palaeolithic and Mesolithic were explained largely in terms of changes in environmental conditions. Nowadays, however, such ecological explanations are being met with increasing scepticism. Ethnographic information on present-day hunter-gatherer communities shows that people have many ways of coping with changes in the landscape and even catastrophes. They include diversification of food resources, mobility, storage and exchange.[41] The 'contingency plans' are often expressed in oral traditions, describing events of hundreds of years ago.[42] The extent to which the hominids that preceded *Homo sapiens sapiens* were able to solve problems is difficult to ascertain on the basis of archaeological evidence. This issue is currently the subject of a heated debate.[43] The evidence seems to suggest that the social organisation increasingly came to serve as the 'safety net' for unforeseen events in the course of the (Upper) Palaeolithic, while the environment in principle merely determined the limits of what was feasible.[44] On the other hand, however, there is evidence for efficient organisation and planning in the Middle Palaeolithic, too, whereas there were periods in the Upper Palaeolithic, for example during the Weichselian glacial maximum, when the environment became so inhospitable as to force the occupants of the North European Plain to move to more favourable regions further south.[45] Some experts are of the opinion that the landscape was by this time already 'filled up' to such an extent that large-scale migration to areas already occupied would have been possible only if there was a network of alliances between the different groups.[46]

The great ingenuity with which prehistoric man coped with changing conditions is also evident in the Late Mesolithic, when the rise in the sea level and the thickening of the forest in the Holocene led to a decrease in the number of lo-

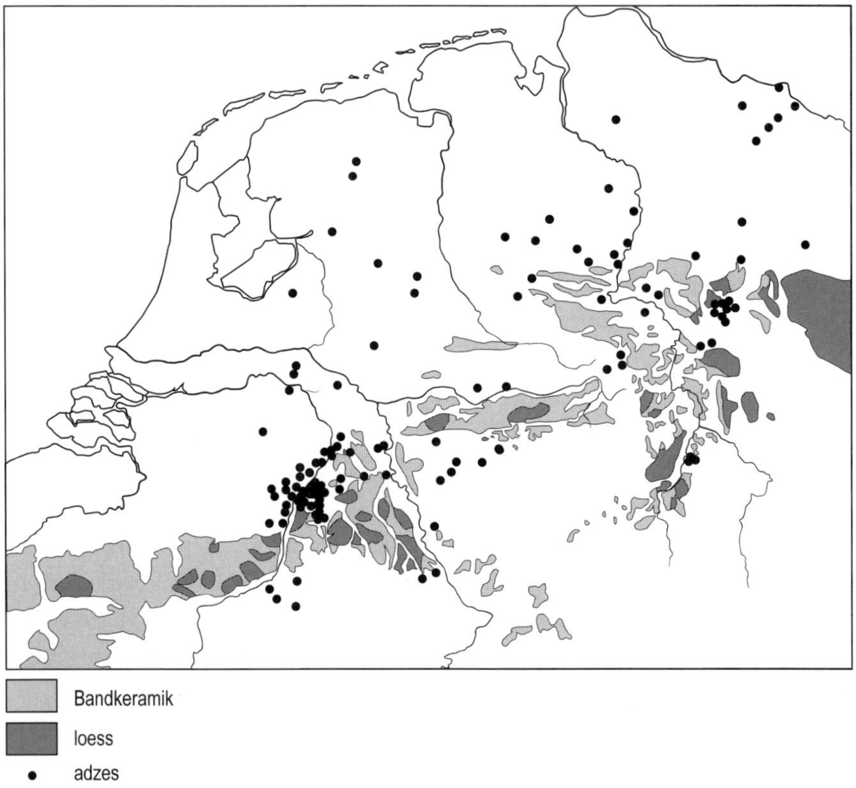

fig. 9.7

Many *Bandkeramik* adzes have been found outside the loess region, the occupation area of the *Bandkeramik* farmers. These finds are thought to be prestige objects acquired by the Mesolithic hunter-gatherer population of this area through exchange.

Bandkeramik

loess

• adzes

cations suitable for occupation. Possibly in response to these trends,[47] man began to exploit a more diverse range of resources, a development made possible by a change in the physical environment itself.[48] The exploitation of new food resources necessitated the development of new strategies, which entailed several technological innovations, one of which was probably forest clearance by means of burning, which resulted in increases in the productivity of the vegetation and faunal density.

In some optimum areas mobility decreased as sedentism grew. There we also find evidence for an increased sense of territory.[49] The cemeteries contain the bodies of individuals who met a violent death, as is testified by arrowheads.[50] If we exclude the possibility of hunting accidents, this may point to intensifying social conflicts. In parts of Europe outside the Low Countries there is evidence for increasing social complexity towards the end of the Mesolithic. The degree of differentiation within a community may have played a part in the adoption of Neolithic elements such as pottery production, the grinding of axes and ultimately domestication: some of the novelties may well have been regarded as prestige goods, which the social 'elite' could use to mark and secure their position (fig. 9.7).

In the last phase of the Mesolithic the first contacts were established with farming communities in the south. Denmark has yielded sound evidence showing that the people of the last Mesolithic culture in that country, the Ertebølle culture, produced pottery, but did not cultivate crops or keep cattle. Whether this was also the case in the Low Countries is still unclear. Several Mesolithic sites with pottery have been reported, but in each case the association between the pottery and the flint artefacts is not entirely certain.[51] So the existence of a 'ceramic Mesolithic' remains a matter of debate. Another controversial issue is the nature of the relation between the early farmers and the Mesolithic hunter-gatherers. There seem to have been virtually no contacts whatsoever between the *Bandkeramik* colonists and the Mesolithic groups. The few *Bandkeramik* adzes and arrowheads that have been found outside the loess area may be regarded as remains left behind by the farmers during small-scale activities outside the loess, or as products of exchange.

WHAT NEXT?

The greatest problem as far as the Palaeolithic and Mesolithic are concerned is the deficiency of the data base, especially in the Lower Rhine Basin. This is partly attributable to a relatively poor professional interest in these periods and partly to specific geological processes like deposition and erosion, which have made it very difficult to locate and excavate sites in large parts of the Low Countries. There is hence a great need for systematic surveys specifically aimed at detecting Lower and Middle Palaeolithic sites with *in situ* remains, and research into such sites. One of the aspects to which close attention will have to be paid in that research is the sites' formation processes. Much useful information, in particular on Upper Palaeolithic and Mesolithic sites, could be obtained in large-scale research into settlements in different ecological zones. So far, predominantly small-scale research has been carried out, mainly in the high, dry areas; only recently have specific efforts been made to find sites with preserved organic remains along rivers and on lake shores.

Methodically innovative and more reflective research projects have been launched for the purpose of obtaining as much information as possible from the known sites. The newly developed methods and techniques and those borrowed from other disciplines have turned Palaeolithic and Mesolithic research into a more serious scientific enterprise and have opened new avenues for interpretation. Most of the innovations relate to material research, but the past few years have also seen the development of new methods enabling more accurate dating of finds that are too old for ^{14}C analysis. Major advances have been made in the theoretical field as well, in particular by Lower and Middle Palaeolithic experts. They have had important consequences for the development of archaeological theory in a more general sense.

Experts on the Palaeolithic, especially the Upper Palaeolithic – the period to which anthropological models initially seemed so ideally applicable – have begun to question the value of anthropology for archaeology.[52] They maintain that anthropological information can be of a heuristic value at most, in other words, it can serve only as a source of ideas. The growing awareness of the importance of an understanding of the processes involved in the formation of the archaeological record with respect to the formulation of interpretations has led to an increasing demand for a more empirical, archaeological approach.[53] A major problem, however, is that the chronological resolution of our evidence is often insufficient to enable us to present synchronous pictures, for instance of a settlement system. But the archaeological record does contain a wealth of information for the study of the long-term processes of occupation and change.

The studies that are currently being carried out into the provenance of raw materials and objects like ornaments with a view to obtaining a better understanding of group mobility and exchange show that Palaeolithic and Mesolithic research is gradually losing the parochialism which dominated it for so long.[54] The congresses that have been organised over the past few decades, for example on the Mesolithic,[55] have been very beneficial in this respect. They have given rise to far more complex questions, demanding approaches on higher, supra-site levels. The employed spatial levels now vary in accordance with the problems involved. Most research into settlement systems, for example, seems to take place on a lower (regional) spatial level than that into the functioning of exchange systems (supra-regional). Both levels are however important for gaining an understanding of occupation and change.

In the past century, the periods discussed in the preceding part of this book have always been associated with the transition from 'savagery' to 'civilisation'.[56] The Mesolithic, in particular, was in a sense taken to mark the boundary between the civilised Neolithic with its farming communities and the Palaeolithic 'hordes' or 'troops'. As our appreciation of the aesthetic value of Magdalenian cave art and mobiliary art increased, we however came to see the Upper Palaeolithic as 'modern'. The modernity of Neanderthal man is currently a topic of debate.[57] Our views on these matters, and those on Neanderthal man in particular, are strongly dependent on our definition of what distinguishes 'us', modern humans, from 'primeval man'. Another, similar debate is that revolving around the distinction between 'human' and 'not quite human' around two million years ago. Palaeoanthropologists are playing an important part in this debate because it is they who determine to what extent physical features, such as an upright posture, brain size and many other morphological skeletal characteristics, are 'human' or – in the discussion about *Homo sapiens neanderthalensis* versus *Homo sapiens sapiens* – 'modern'. Prehistorians, on their part, are contributing towards the debate by providing evidence, obtained in their studies of artefacts, camp sites and burials, on issues like behaviour, planning and levels of cultural and intellectual development. Questions like language capability and the degree of articulated speech are arousing speculation among both archaeologists and palaeoanthropologists. But of all the definitions of a human being so far proposed, not one has been found to be watertight in every respect: time and time again features that were initially taken to be typically human or 'modern' proved not to be so after all. A striking observation in retrospect is that whenever such a definition proved to make insufficient distinction, it was immediately adjusted so as to secure the unicity of (modern) man: a clear case of 'policing the boundary'.[58] As the distinction between human and animal also has moral implications, the findings and statements of palaeoanthropologists may in a certain respect be regarded as *myths*, legitimising our control of nature.[59] These myths can be 'exposed' only from the perspective of the history of science, via a reflective approach in which attention is paid to the sources of the concepts employed and the socio-historical context in which they originated. Such an approach demands the cooperation of specialists in different disciplines: historians, philosophers, biologists, palaeoanthropologists and archaeologists.[60]

Our interpretations of the transition from the Mesolithic to the Neolithic are likewise strongly coloured by our views of the world and our preconceptions. Seen from the common (almost subconscious) evolutionistic perspective of our Western outlook, the transition to a farming existence was a logical and almost inevitable step. It was primarily anthropological considerations that induced us to take a fresh look at the neolithisation process and to pay more attention to such important aspects as the emergence of social differentiation and, hence, prestige and power.[61]

1   See for example the discussion in Stapert 1985, 58, on the possible meaning of large find scatters.

2   Roebroeks/Van Kolfschoten 1994, see also Roebroeks 2001.

3   Binford 1978a, 1978b.

4   Wobst 1978 and the so-called revisionists' debate (*e.g.* Lee 1992; Lee/Solway 1990; Schrire 1984; Wilmsen/Denbow 1990).

5   See for example Bettinger 1981 for a discussion.

6   See Rensink 1995 and the comments on this article by T. Murray and C. Gamble.

7   Maastricht-Belvédère: Roebroeks 1989, Geldrop, Milheeze and Venlo: Bos 1992; Deeben/Bos 1989.

8   Until recently, only little evidence on the use of such early sites was available in the Netherlands, but this is rapidly changing now that more and more information is being obtained in research and analyses (see chapters 6-8).

9   Newell 1973; Price 1975; Stapert 1985. These are ideal models of the settlement system, for it is difficult to demonstrate the contemporaneity of sites owing to the limited amount of chronological evidence available.

10 Binford's ethnoarchaeological fieldwork (in particular the article which he published in 1980) among the Nunamiut in Alaska has greatly influenced interpretations of the settlement systems of prehistoric hunter-gatherers. Jochim (1976) used predominantly ecological models; particularly influential was his research into the differentiation of Mesolithic settlements in southern Germany.

11 See Rensink 1995.

12 For example Newell 1984.

13 Exchange of information between groups was also important for arranging meetings and for preventing the risk of areas being 'doubly' exploited.

14 Bonsall 1980; Jacobi 1973; Meiklejohn 1978.

15 Myers 1989.

16 Bedburg-Königshoven: Street 1989; Noyen-sur-Seine: Mordant/Mordant 1992.

17 For a critical discussion of this approach see *e.g.* Newell/Dekin 1978; Gamble 1986.

18 The results of the different studies vary from 298 to 801,309 km², with an emphasis on estimates between 10,000 and 100,000 km². For a survey see Constandse-Westermann/Newell 1989. Nowadays anthropological information and data on analogous ethnographic communities are used in attempts to distinguish smaller social units, such as bands, within the territories of dialect tribes (Newell *et al.* 1990).

19 Newell *et al.* 1990; Rensink 1993.

20 Gendel 1984.

21 Arts/Deeben 1987, fig. 1.

22 It should however be added that the known distribution areas of archaeological remains are static units. They are the sum totals of a large number of annual territories which need not all have been used simultaneously.

23 See *e.g.* Kozlowski 1975; Newell *et al.* 1990; Gendel 1984; Vang-Petersen 1984; Verhart 1990. In imitation of Price (1981), Verhart (1990) has calculated the following areas: Upper Palaeolithic/Early Mesolithic approx. 230,000 km², Middle Mesolithic approx. 80,000 km² and Late Mesolithic 30,000 km².

24 Newell 1973.

25 This conclusion, which probably holds for the Netherlands too, is based on evidence (works of art and molluscs) from Magdalenian sites in Germany and Belgium (see Rensink 1993). See also the work by Newell *et al.* 1990 for developments during the Mesolithic.

26 Newell (1973) for the Mesolithic and Arts (1989) for the Upper Palaeolithic and Mesolithic. Calculating the size of a population on the basis of the number of sites in a particular area involves problems. A change in the number of sites may also be the consequence of a change in settlement pattern, the number of sites reflecting the ways in which the environments were exploited. Moreover, a sound understanding of chronology is needed to calculate relative increases in population, *i.e.* the beginning and end of a particular period must be accurately known.

27 Newell (1973) found a proportionally greater increase in population in the Late Mesolithic, of three times that in the preceding period.

28 Neeley/Clark 1990.

29 Clark/Neeley 1987; Newell 1984. This change, which is observable in coastal regions in particular, may possibly be interpreted as a transition from a socio-political organisation on a band level to one on a tribal level.

30 See *e.g.* O'Shea/Zvelebil 1984.

31 Roebroeks 2001.

32 See *e.g.* Gaudzinski 1995 for Middle Palaeolithic, Mellars 1973 and White 1982 for the Upper Palaeolithic.

33 Jochim 1983.

34 Gamble (1986) is of the opinion that Middle Palaeolithic Neanderthal man cannot be seen as a systematic hunter (see also Stringer/Gamble 1993).

35 Schlanger 1994.

36 Mellars 1973; White 1982.

37 Thieme/Veil 1985.

38 Mithen 1994, 34 ff.

39 This is not to say that some of the new elements were not present in the Upper Palaeolithic already; generally speaking, Mesolithic sites are better preserved.

40 Oswalt 1976.

41 Halstead/O'Shea (eds.) 1989; Minc/Smith 1989.

42 See Minc 1986 on 'contingency plans' expressed in the mythology of the Eskimos of North Alaska.

43 See Stringer/Gamble 1994 and the comments on that work.

44 Gamble 1983; Ingold 1981.

45 Otte 1990.

46 Gamble 1983.

47 There is much discussion in the literature as to whether population growth is a cause or a consequence of processes of change (cf. Hassan 1981).

48 Hayden 1981.

49 Newell 1984.

50 Albrethsen/Brinch-Petersen 1976; Larsson 1983.

51 For example Weelde-Paardsdrank (Huyge/Vermeersch 1982), Swifterbant S21-24 (Price 1981) and Melsele (Van Berg/Van Roeyen/Keeley 1991). See also the above comment on the limited possibilities of stratigraphic research. The start of local pottery production in the western Netherlands has been firmly dated to 5000 cal BC at Hardinxveld (feature D).

52 Wobst 1978; Rensink 1995 and the comments by Murray in particular. It is precisely in Australia, with its seemingly great continuity between present and past, that Binford's proposition 'archaeology is anthropology or it is nothing' is being criticised (see *e.g.* Murray 1988). The reasons for this however have more to do with politics than with science.

53 Gamble 1986, 60.

54 Gamble 1986; Neeley/Clark 1990.

55 The proceedings of the congresses have been published in several volumes: Kozlowski 1973; Gramsch 1980; Bonsall 1989; Vermeersch/Van Peer 1990.

56 Corbey 1989.

57 Mellars/Trinkaus 1989; Roebroeks 1990; Stringer/Gamble 1993; Trinkaus 1989; Trinkaus/Shipman 1993.

58 Roebroeks 1995.

59 Cartmill 1990.

60 Corbey/Roebroeks 2001.

61 The 'Ape, man, apeman: changing views since 1600' symposium (Corbey/Theunissen 1995) is a good example of such interdisciplinary reflection.

62 Bender 1985; Thomas 1986, 1991.

Part II

The first farmers

The Neolithic comprises the last period of the Stone Age, a period in which technology was still entirely based on stone, but in which man slowly exchanged his hunting and gathering existence for a way of life based on crop cultivation and stock keeping. This was one of the most momentous transitions in the history of the development of human society. The increasing dependence on crop cultivation led to changes in the relationship between man and his environment, from one of dependence and equality to one in which man gained increasing control over nature. The era in which man had lived solely on what nature offered him was over. Man and nature came to oppose one another to an increasing extent. Crop cultivation and stock breeding also enabled population growth, with all its positive and negative consequences. Many technological innovations took place and social organisation became increasingly complex.

Farming originated in the Near East some 10,000 years ago, in developments in the area known as the Fertile Crescent. From there, the new knowledge and the associated way of life gradually spread to other areas, over a period spanning several thousands of years. The first farmers arrived in southern Limburg around 5300 BC. Their arrival marked the beginning of a period of confrontation and transformation of two communities that differed from one another in many respects: the farmers in the south and the native hunter-gatherers in the north. These communities established contacts with one another and influenced one another. In a lengthy process, which was to reach a conclusion only at the end of the Neolithic, the northern communities adopted the farming way of life. This process is also known as 'Neolithisation'.

Our understanding of this period is based mainly on evidence obtained in settlement research over the past forty to fifty years, in particular in the loess region in Limburg and in the Dutch wetlands. This is, however, also a period in which imposing monuments were built, such as the hunebedden, the burial chambers of the first farmers on the northern sandy soils. New technological developments took place at the end of this era, marking the start of a new epoch: the Bronze Age.

10 Early and Middle Neolithic: introduction

Annelou van Gijn and Leendert Louwe Kooijmans

THE ORIGINS OF FARMING

The Neolithic was first defined in 1865, as the era of polished stone tools, to indicate the difference with the chipped stone tools of the Palaeolithic.[1] Later on, three more criteria were introduced, namely agriculture (crop cultivation and stock keeping), the sedentary existence it implies and pottery production. Over the years it became clear that these criteria are not inextricably linked. For example, we now know of hunter-gatherers who produced pottery (what is known as the 'Ceramic Mesolithic', e.g. the Ertebølle culture in Denmark) and of farmers who did not (Aceramic Neolithic, e.g. the 'Pre-Pottery Neolithic A and B' in the Levant). Nowadays, food production is regarded as the most distinctive feature of the Neolithic; this is now the only criterion used in practice.

The broad-spectrum economy of the Late Mesolithic in the Low Countries has been described in the previous chapter; in various regions it was possible to live an almost sedentary existence based at a location strategically positioned between different ecological zones offering an abundance of food resources. But mobility remained important for exploiting certain essential resources, although it was often only a small proportion of the community that temporarily left the settlement for this purpose. In the Near East a similar development took place towards a more settled mode of life with a broad-spectrum economy. There, the seeds of wild large-grained grasses (various wheat species and barley) constituted an important source of food. They presented the great advantage that under the prevailing relatively dry climatic conditions they could be easily stored for later consumption, in particular in seasons in which food was in short supply. That offered the people living in those areas an excellent basis for a sedentary existence. As cereal happens to be an ideal staple food it is not surprising that a form of 'management' of the wild grain fields gradually emerged (fig. 10.1). The earliest archaeological

fig. 10.1a

Ears of emmer (left) and einkorn (right).

fig. 10.1b

A wild einkorn field in the Zagros mountains in Iran. On the slopes of the mountains in the 'fertile crescent' in the Near East wild cereal species were an important source of food around the end of the last glacial. Shortly afterwards, they were to constitute the basis for the development of agriculture.

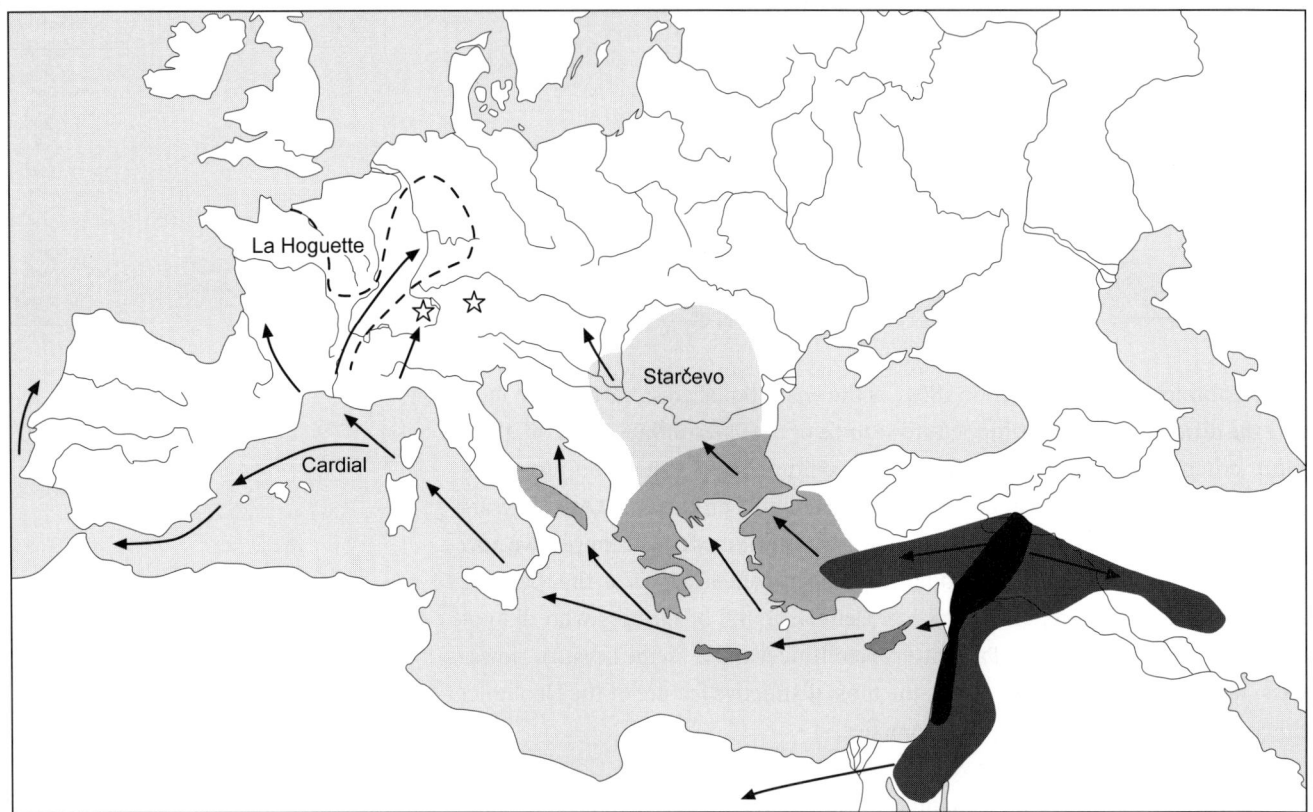

La Hoguette

Starčevo

Cardial

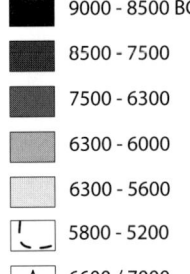

■	9000 - 8500 BC
■	8500 - 7500
■	7500 - 6300
▨	6300 - 6000
☐	6300 - 5600
☐	5800 - 5200
☆	6600 / 7000

fig. 10.2

The origins of agriculture and its spread to Europe prior to 5500 BC. Until around 6000 BC agriculture and animal domestication were restricted to the Near East. After that time the new form of subsistence gradually spread westwards via two routes: via the coasts of the Mediterranean ('Cardial culture') into Western Europe ('La Hoguette') and via the Balkan to southeast Europe (Starčevo complex). The early pollen evidence from Switzerland at present however appears to be inconsistent with this pattern.

evidence for the domestication of these plants dates from the 10th millennium BC. The first plants to be domesticated were barley and emmer; various legumes followed shortly after. Sheep and goat were domesticated around the same time or possibly a little later.[2]

Our parts of Europe, with their wet climate, lacked a suitable equivalent of wild cereal. The occupants of these areas were therefore strongly dependent on a system of seasonal exploitation of diverse food resources that had to be consumed immediately. This necessitated greater mobility. Nevertheless, it is now increasingly often argued that farming evolved endogenously in these parts, too, via a certain degree of management of essential resources. The most important large wild animal, red deer, was hunted with such evident care that we may speak of 'selective cropping'. It has recently been suggested that the same can be said of certain plants, too.[3]

One of the questions that archaeologists ask over and over again is *why* people started producing food. In the past, this question was hardly ever asked, because it was implicitly assumed that prehistoric man aspired to a 'better existence'. In that evolutionistic outlook hunter-gatherers were inferior to farmers. In the 1960s, however, it was realised that some hunter-gatherers had in fact enjoyed a stable economy, supported by abundant resources, which invalidated the evolutionistic interpretation.[4] All kinds of reasons have been postulated for why people started practising crop cultivation and stock keeping. As far as the Near East is concerned, it is now generally believed that the cereal-harvesting hunter-gatherers of Natufian and related groups gradually started producing their food as they adopted a more settled way of life. The facilities for storing and processing the cereals had to be managed and maintained, which entailed social integration and possibly also social differentiation; the local permanent population expanded, but as it grew, it also became increasingly vulnerable to unforeseen food shortages. The transition from the management of wild cereals to their cultivation will then have been a logical step, as it led to greater control over food resources. In economic terms, this can be seen as risk reduction. In this context it has been proposed that crop cultivation may have originated in areas where wild cereals did not occur in large quantities. But this is less likely, as the earliest evidence for domestication seems to come mainly from the primary zones. An important aspect of food production is that it enabled increasing social stratification; in that respect it laid the basis for the development of the later complex societies of the Near East.[5]

As for the origins of food production in Europe, it was for many years assumed that the 'enlightened' ideas on food production were spread in a westerly direction by colonists: the *Ex Oriente Lux* hypothesis. According to this view the Neolithisation of Europe was the consequence of the immigration of farmers who more or less forced the native occupants to accept the new, 'superior' form of subsistence. But there is actually little concrete evidence to support this colonisation model. Nowadays, archaeologists are therefore far more in favour of a combination of small-scale – and hence archaeologically virtually invisible – incursions and acculturation of Mesolithic hunter-gatherers. This may have been the case with, for example, the earliest *Bandkeramik* in Central Europe. The same arguments as those proposed to explain the origins of farming in the Near East can be used to support the adoption of a farming existence via acculturation, *i.e.* risk reduction and prestige, possibly with population growth as an impetus. Migration and the colonisation of new regions, whether or not already exploited by hunter-gatherers, can be related to stress in the colonists' area of origin, for example caused by a sense of 'overpopulation' and territorial competition, and the availability of a suitable new settlement area.

Whether or not this view is correct, it is certain is that farming gradually spread westwards from the Fertile Crescent via Anatolia and the Balkans, to the Danubian plain and then on to the Lower Rhine Basin on the one hand, and across the entire Mediterranean on the other hand (fig. 10.2). During this process of expansion, novel elements were added to the agricultural system along the way, for example in Anatolia and southeast Europe. Among these novel elements were pig and cattle. Around 5500 BC a new culture evolved in the western part of the Hungarian Plain, at the periphery of the contemporary farming communities: the *Bandkeramik*. Exactly how this culture spread across the whole of Central Europe is still poorly understood. The *Bandkeramik* farmers who lived in the Netherlands definitely came from elsewhere. They settled on the loess soil of southern Limburg around 5300 BC. There seems to have been no acculturation of the Mesolithic occupants of the Netherlands in this first phase; the first signs of agricultural activity to the north of the loess are of a much later date. There, the transition from a hunting-gathering way of life to a fully-fledged farming existence was a lengthy process that spanned almost the entire Neolithic (see chapters 14 and 15). An economy based predominantly on crop cultivation and stock keeping seems to have been fully established there only by the Late Neolithic. But the products of hunting and fishing and – to a lesser extent – foraging continued to supplement the diet, as they indeed still do today.

CLIMATE AND LANDSCAPE

In contrast to the preceding transition from the Palaeolithic to the Mesolithic at the beginning of the Holocene, the transition to the Neolithic was not characterised by major changes in environmental and ecological conditions. The *Bandkeramik* farmers spread across Europe and settled on the loess of southern Limburg in the middle of the Atlantic, a period in which temperatures in Europe were a little higher than they are today, possibly 2 °C on an annual basis. That may not seem very much, but as far as the plant and animal life – and hence also farming – are concerned it was a substantial difference. The relatively mild climate will have influenced the *Bandkeramik* expansion towards the north and west, but we should not go so far as to see it as the prime cause of the migrations.

The transition from the Atlantic to the Sub-Boreal has been dated around 3500 BC on the basis of changes in the vegetation. In the past it was generally believed that the climate became a little drier in the Sub-Boreal, but this view has been modified to allow for the influence of the early farming communities on the primeval forests: the creation of clearances and the consequences for the hydrological regime. The Neolithic also coincides with the transgressive phases in which the Calais I-IV deposits were formed (chapter 3). By the beginning of the Neolithic the sea level had risen to about 9 m below the present Mean Sea Level and what is now the western part of the Netherlands had changed into a vast sedimentation zone. At first this zone was largely a tidal-flat area, protected from the open sea by a series of narrow coastal barrier islands separated by wide tidal inlets. On its landward side this tidal-flat area was bordered by a zone of tidal deposits and a peat belt.

From 3500 BC onwards the coastal barriers gradually consolidated, enabling the salt marshes and the peat to expand over the tidal flats, which they turned into clearly distinct tidal areas behind the major tidal inlets. Generally speaking, the environmental diversity of the coastal plain increased and the area as a whole became more attractive for settlement and exploitation. The coastal area must also have become more accessible in this period. As the delta comprised so many different ecological zones, it contained several types of vegetation. The dunes supported a mixed forest containing oak, elm and lime, with hazel stands in the more open parts. Alder carrs will have grown in the backswamps, while belts of reeds and sedges bordered the open water.

In the course of the early Holocene a rich brown forest soil formed beneath the lush forest vegetation of the higher sandy areas. It would probably not be correct to describe these regions as poor and marginal by analogy with present conditions, but they will have been vulnerable to crop cultivation without manuring. The forests in these areas will have consisted predominantly of oak; many alder stands were to be found in the valleys. An important environmental change was the formation of vast raised bogs, in particular in Drenthe, Overijssel and the eastern part of North Brabant. Together with the peat expanding from the coastal zone, these raised bogs, especially those in the northern part of the country, greatly reduced the area of land suitable for occupation.[6]

The Late Glacial relief of the loess zone had by this time consolidated as a result of forestation. We must assume that the weathering of hill slopes and the formation of colluvial deposits started with the creation of the first clearances in the Neolithic, although we have little concrete evidence to support this. What is still a topic of debate is the question as to whether water flowed through what are now dry valleys before the hills were deforested, and if so, how much water. As deciduous forest has a much higher evaporation rate (400 mm/year) than open (grass)land (200 mm/year) this is not very likely. A second unsolved question with respect to the environment concerns the nature and degree of soil formation. There are convincing arguments for assuming that the formation of the Grey Brown Podzolic soils, characteristic of the loess, began already during the *Bandkeramik* period. The reconstruction of the vegetation of the loess zone is a difficult issue; it is generally assumed that a lime forest grew on the plateaus and a mixed deciduous forest with a high percentage of oak in the valleys.[7]

Our knowledge of the fauna in the Neolithic is based on reconstructions of the former landscape and vegetation on the one hand, and on the faunal remains recovered in excavations on the other. The great ecological diversity of both the lowlands and the higher sandy soils with their many stream valleys and varied deciduous forest suggests that large amounts of game were to be found in these regions. The only areas where this was not the case will have been the loess region, with its impenetrable deciduous forest and its small amount of undergrowth, and of course the raised bogs. The excavated remains of large terrestrial mammals include aurochs, elk, red deer, roe deer, wild boar and brown bear. There were also many smaller fur animals, such as marten, polecat, beaver and otter. Marine mammals like common and grey seals, bottle-nose dolphin and porpoise were to be found along the coast. Remarkable birds among the many common species are Dalmatian pelican, flamingo, crane and white-tailed eagle, which suggests the presence of large stretches of open water. Conspicuous fish, besides the currently known freshwater species, are sturgeon and European catfish.[8]

fig. 10.3
Chronological-geographical scheme of the Neolithic cultures in the Netherlands and its wider environs.

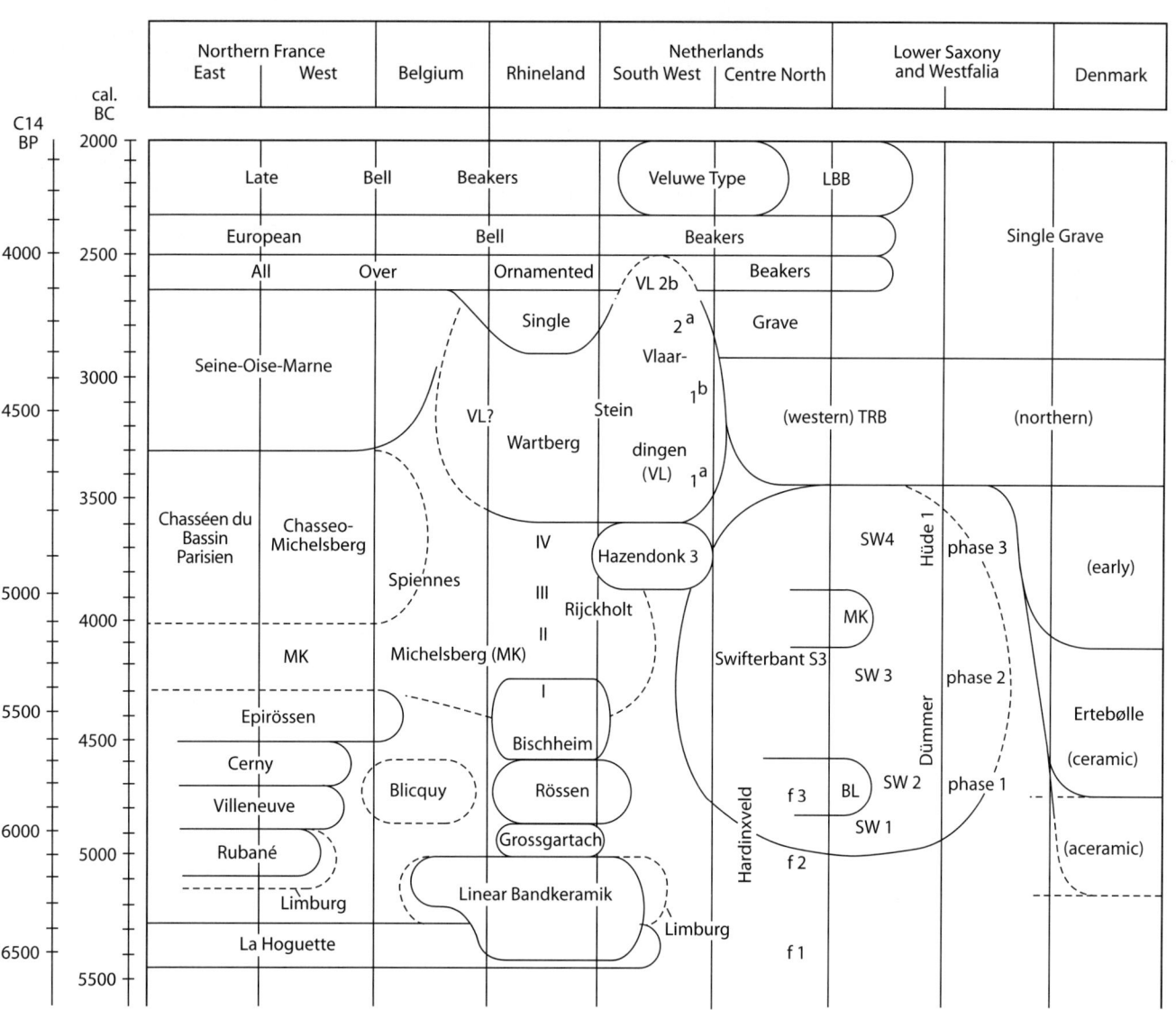

fig. 10.4
View of the 1991 excavation of the Middle Neolithic site Brandwijk in the peat district of South Holland. Drainage by well points and a stepped trench enabled people to work safely and dry a few metres below groundwater level.

CULTURAL UNITS

The Dutch Neolithic spans the period from 5300 until 2000 BC, *i.e.* the period from the arrival of the first farmers in southern Limburg until the first use of bronze. It would be convenient if we were able to set up a uniform chronological and cultural framework for the whole of the Netherlands and its surrounding areas. But unfortunately the Netherlands is dissected by the boundary of two major cultures which existed before, during and after the Neolithic. Throughout the whole of prehistory there were close relations between the southern part of the Netherlands and Belgium, with the Rhineland and, via the latter region, Central Europe. The south of the Netherlands is one of the regions where agriculture was first introduced (what is known as the 'primary Neolithic'). There were also contacts in a westerly direction, with England. The northern part of the Netherlands, on the contrary, was oriented towards Westphalia and Lower Saxony, and northern Europe in a more general sense. Farming was not introduced in this northern glacial plain until much later. The way of life and the development of the material culture in these two distinct parts of the Netherlands differed considerably and there are therefore major differences in their periodisations (fig. 10.3).

The Early Neolithic A is the period of the *Bandkeramik* (see chapter 11) and of the somewhat enigmatic groups who used the La Hoguette and Limburg pottery, roughly from 5300 BC onwards. Because of the great uniformity and the novelty of the *Bandkeramik* as a whole, we assume that this culture was introduced into the loess zone of the Netherlands and Belgium by colonists, notably from the Rhineland. The areas north of the loess zone were inhabited by predominantly spatially separated Mesolithic hunter-gatherers. The nature of the relationship between the *Bandkeramik* people and the Mesolithic groups living in their surroundings is still poorly understood. It seems that the *Bandkeramik* culture had little influence on the way of life of these hunter-gatherers; there is no clear evidence to suggest the existence of exchange networks between the two communities either. But we should be careful in drawing such conclusions as only very few contemporary Late Mesolithic sites have so far been found.

A later phase of the *Bandkeramik* saw the first signs of the disintegration of this population into smaller social units: the material culture reflects increasing regionalisation. Around the same time, *Bandkeramik* society seems to have become less egalitarian: indications of social stratification have been found in both the settlements and the cemeteries of the later phases of the *Bandkeramik*.[9] These changes may be connected with an increase in the density of the population of the most favourable area, the fertile loess zone.

The process of regionalisation continued in the Early Neolithic B in the Rhineland, in the Grossgartach and Rössen cultures, successively. Only the latter culture is represented in the Netherlands, notably in southern Limburg. Belgium clearly lay in a different, French, sphere of influence in this period. There, the Omalian (a local variant of the *Bandkeramik*) evolved into the *Groupe de Blicquy* in the Hainault. The distribution area of the so-called *Rössener Breitkeile*, which extends all the way into Denmark, suggests that contacts with the neighbouring hunter-gatherers

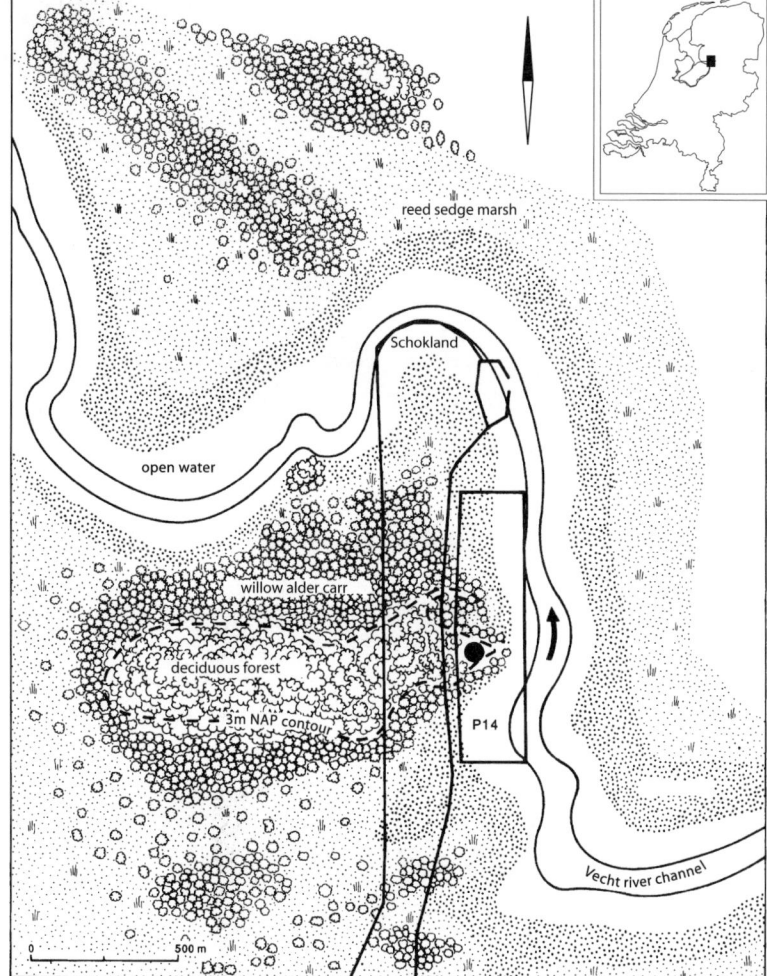

fig. 10.5
Settlement P14 in its reconstructed environmental setting. The site was situated on a boulder clay outcrop measuring about 0.5 km² with a deciduous cover in a vast swamp intersected by a former course of the river Vecht.

had intensified since the *Bandkeramik*. Only one Rössen settlement has so far been excavated in the Netherlands: the site of Maastricht-Randwijck, which included no house plans, only pits.

Until recently, little was known about the period of the Rössen culture in the northern zone. However, finds from Drenthe and Flevoland have now shown that between 4900 and 4600 BC this area was definitely inhabited by pottery-producing groups, who may be regarded as the immediate predecessors of the occupants of the settlements on the levees near Swifterbant (Swifterbant 1 and 2). But we do not yet have any information on the economy in this early phase.

Our understanding of the history of the occupation of the northern part of the Netherlands remains poor up to 4200 BC, the beginning of the Middle Neolithic A, the period of the sites on the levees near Swifterbant which gave the Swifterbant culture its name (phase 3). It is believed that in the higher sandy areas occupation concentrated in and along the stream valleys in this period. The people of the Swifterbant culture seem to have maintained contacts mainly with people further east, but there are also indications of contacts with the Rössen communities.[10] The sites that have come to light on river dunes in the western coastal zone, such as Hazendonk (phase 1) and Brandwijk, are also classed as belonging to the Swifter-

fig. 10.6

The rescue excavation, in 1983, of the Heveskesklooster *terp* near Delfzijl led to the chance discovery of a megalithic monument. The structure is not a *hunebed* 'proper', but only a fairly small funerary chamber or 'dolmen' built on a sandy elevation. The monument was first covered by peat, after which the *terp* was built on top of it. That ensured its excellent preservation. Two conspicuous features of the dolmen are that it was not covered with an earth mound and that it was disturbed at some time in the past, possibly already in the Beaker period.

bant culture (fig. 10.4). Cereals have been found both at Swifterbant and Hazendonk, but they were probably not grown locally. It is believed that the occupants of the sites on the higher sandy soils exploited the natural resources of the delta. According to the present views, hunting and fishing were still very important in these communities' broad-spectrum economy, although they had begun to supplement their diet with the products of agricultural activities.

The southern part of the Netherlands was in this period occupied by a new 'Northwest Group' of the Michelsberg culture and its successors, the Hazendonk 3 group. Their remains seem to indicate that the Neolithisation process had reached a much further stage in the south than further north. This is also the period of the first systematic flint (shaft) mining activities in the chalk regions (see feature E). Well-known mining sites from this period are Rijckholt in the Netherlands and Spiennes in Belgium. A large number of Michelsberg sites fortified with earthworks are known in the Rhineland and in Belgium. Many smaller sites have been found on the loess and on the sandy soils in the Netherlands. The settlements on the sandy soils were probably also inhabited by farming communities, but in the coastal area in this period some sites were still used predominantly for the exploitation of natural resources, such as the aforementioned Hazendonk.

Until recently, no sites dating from 4000-3500 BC were known in the northern part of the country. In other words, regarding chronological counterparts of the later Michelsberg sites in the south there appeared to be a hiatus in this part of the Netherlands. However, an assemblage has now been found at site P14 in the Noordoostpolder, which shows close stylistic affinities with an early phase of the TRB culture in Schleswig-Holstein known as Fuchsberg. This material has provisionally been called 'pre-Drouwen' or 'Swifterbant 4' ware (fig. 10.5).[11]

Although the Neolithisation process can be said to have started in the Swifterbant 3 period in the north of the Netherlands, we cannot really speak of true Neolithic societies until the time of the emergence of the TRB communities of the Middle Neolithic B, after 3400 BC. The origins of the TRB culture are still unclear. Some see clear indications of continuity in the pottery of the Swifterbant culture, that of the pre-Drouwen phase and that of the TRB.[12] The TRB pottery of the Drouwen phase however shows unmistakable signs of northern influence.

In the Netherlands, the TRB culture is best known for the *hunebedden*, which were built until approximately 3200 BC, but remained in use until the end of the TRB period (fig. 10.6). The oldest flat graves date from the early TRB period, but they are still few in number; with time, however, interment in a flat grave gradually came to be the predominant form of burial. The TRB settlements that have so far come to light in the Netherlands consist of nothing more than artefact scatters.

The later phases of the TRB coincide with the period of the Vlaardingen group in the coastal area, which is closely related to the Stein group in Limburg and the Wartberg culture in Hessen.[13] The sites of the Vlaardingen group show considerable functional differentiation. Some of the sites were indisputably bases for fishing, large-game hunting, trapping and fowling. These sites, which formed part of the settlement system of people with southern origins, indicate that hunting, fishing and gathering were still being practised alongside agriculture.

The transition from the TRB to the Single Grave culture has been taken to mark the beginning of the Late Neolithic. According to current views, the Single Grave culture (which used to be known as the Protruding Foot Beaker culture in the Netherlands) was predominantly a native development and not, as previously assumed, a culture introduced by belligerent nomadic tribes.[14] The transformation of the Vlaardingen group into a 'Beaker culture' seems to have been a slightly later – and

site	Wateringen 4	Bergschenhoek	Swifterbant s3	Hazendonk 1-3	Gassel
date	3600 BC	4100 BC	4000 BC	4000 - 3600 BC	(3600 BC)
'culture'	Hazendonk 3	Swifterbant 3	Swifterbant 3	Swift 3 - Haz 3	Hazendonk 3
geography	coastal dune	peat margin	gulley - levee	rivierdune (donk)	cover sand margin
grain pres/abs	+	-	+	+	- quern stones
% dom.animals	50%	0%	50%	10%	-
flint	coastal + terrace	-	erratic	terrace + Rijckholt	terrace + Rijckholt
time span	short (years)	short (years)	long (decades)	long (3x decades)	short (years)
season	(year round)	winter	summer	var. seasons	-
function	permanent	hunting/fishing camp	summer settlement	hunting/fishing camp	campsite

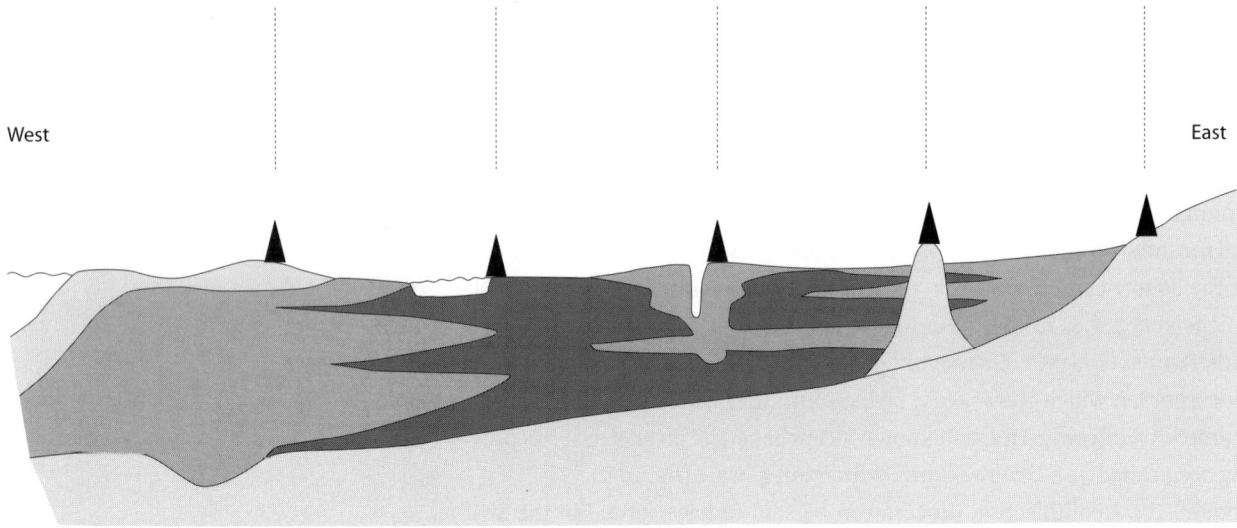

West   East

fig. 10.7

West-east cross-section of the Netherlands showing the typical locations of Neolithic settlement sites in different phases of the Neolithic. The sites differed substantially in size, length of occupation, subsistence strategies and type of hinterland as reflected by the types of flint used. The sites are therefore interpreted not as the settlements of isolated groups of 'delta occupants' but more as wetland hunting camps of communities whose bases lay on the sandy soils.

possibly also more gradual – development. A few early Single Grave artefacts have been found at Vlaardingen, but elsewhere this transition took place in the phase of the 'All-Over-Ornamented beakers'.

THE REPRESENTATIVITY OF THE EVIDENCE

Two general processes have distorted the archaeological record of this period. In the Early Neolithic the sea level was still rising at a high rate. As a result, archaeological remains in the lowlands rapidly became buried beneath thick sediments in some places or were washed away in others. What were then the peripheries of the higher sandy soils constituted relatively favourable occupation areas with high groundwater levels and good access to the ecologically varied delta, but it was the coversand surface of precisely this zone that was covered with organic and clastic sediments, which rendered it inaccessible to normal methods of archaeological research. The old land surface now lies at depths of between 9 and 3 m below NAP, the average sea levels in 5200 BC and 2900 BC, respectively. In discussions of Neolithic occupation insufficient allowance is made for the 'invisibility' of this zone, which is quite wide in some parts of the flat coversand area.[15] In the higher sandy areas the main problem is on the contrary the absence of sedimentation, owing to which occupation remains from different periods have become mixed and many objects have decayed or have been fragmented (fig. 10.7).

Three aspects are of importance with respect to the question of the representativity of the evidence. In the first place, no sites whatsoever are known from certain periods and certain areas. This is for example true of the entire Early Neolithic: we have virtually no information on the Late Mesolithic hunter-gatherers who lived in the areas outside those containing the *Bandkeramik* settlements. A second problem is whether we may regard the sites that are known from a particular period as representative of the whole range of site types and, if so, whether they accurately reflect the activities of their prehistoric occupants. For example, for some archaeological cultures we have settlement remains but no burials, whereas for others we have burial evidence but few settlement remains. We may, moreover, assume that the settlements themselves varied considerably, from permanent settlements to extraction camps, because people still frequently practised hunting, fishing and gathering besides agriculture. A complicating factor is that we do not have much information on off-site activities either, as little research has been carried out in areas beyond the limits of the find scatters.

The third aspect concerns the representativity of the material culture. In the delta, organic remains, such as wooden and bone objects, have survived beneath the groundwater level. Such objects tell us more about technology and the use of raw materials than can be inferred from inorganic remains alone. Analyses of the wood, seeds and pollen that have been preserved at the sites in this area, moreover, enable us to reconstruct these sites' former environment in great detail, while archaeobotanical and archaeozoological remains provide insight into subsistence activities, from which a site's function in the overall settlement system can sometimes be inferred. The situation in the delta hence forms a marked contrast with that on the sandy soils, where only pottery (often severely eroded), flint and stone remains have survived.

HISTORY OF THE RESEARCH

Being so conspicuously visible above the surface, the *hunebedden* and barrows were the first Neolithic remains to attract attention. They were described in 1660 already, by Johan Picardt.[16] Many *hunebedden* and barrows have been robbed, or were excavated in what we would now term a careless manner. Between 1910 and 1955 Van Giffen investigated and restored a large number of *hunebedden*. Since the Second World War, *hunebed* D26 and the newly discovered *hunebed* beneath the Heveskesklooster *wierde* in the province of Groningen have been excavated (the former in 1968-1970), and a few monuments have been re-investigated, but otherwise very little fieldwork has been carried out into these monuments. Instead, research has concentrated on different aspects of the pottery from the *hunebedden*.[17]

With the exception of the *hunebedden* relatively little research has been carried out into Neolithic burial practices. A spectacular discovery was the *Bandkeramik* cemetery that was found at Elsloo, but otherwise we know of only small cemeteries like those of Swifterbant and plot P14 in the Noordoostpolder, or of cremation burials such as those of the Vlaardingen site Hekelingen III. For the TRB culture we have, besides *hunebedden*, a few flat grave cemeteries, such as that of Allardsoog. Flat graves are often found by chance during settlement research. A different kind of funerary monument, which also came to light during the excavation of settlement remains is the burial chamber of Stein. Such chance discoveries provide insight into other, less conspicuous, types of burial.[18]

Around 1925 settlement research, in particular research into settlement layouts, slowly began to attract attention. A good example is Holwerda's excavation (1926-1930) of the site Maastricht-Caberg, which in 1925 had yielded the first

Bandkeramik finds in the Netherlands. More settlement remains were found near Stein (1926) and Geleen (1933). A great surprise was the discovery of settlement remains in the wet lowlands in the west, at Zandwerven;[19] they showed that this region had also been occupied. It was after the Second World War that settlement research really began to make progress. Inspired by the discoveries made by Buttler and Haberey at Cologne-Lindenthal (1929-1932), Dutch archaeologists began to organise large-scale rescue excavations of Bandkeramik sites on the loess of southern Limburg that were soon to disappear beneath new estates. The excavation of these sites – Elsloo, Sittard, Geleen and Stein, all of which lie along the peripheries of the large middle terrace of Graetheide[20] – had a profound international influence. The research at Rosmeer and Darion in Belgium and the large-scale Aldenhoven Plateau Project (1965-1980) in the Rhineland loess region have also contributed much to our understanding of Bandkeramik settlements in the lower Rhine region.[21]

Over the past few decades more and more settlement research has been carried out in the delta, too. Hekelingen was partly excavated in 1948.[22] In the early 1960s an entirely new approach was adopted in the excavations of Vlaardingen, Voorschoten and Leidschendam, which were investigated on a smaller scale, per square metre. As no clear house plans were found, attention focused on material objects and their distributions. Pioneering stratigraphic research was carried out in the excavation of Hazendonk (1974-1976). Around that same time the excavations at Swifterbant had a profound influence on settlement research. A key question in the latter investigation was whether crop cultivation and cattle keeping had been practised locally; many ecological samples were taken and vast volumes of soil were sieved for the purpose of finding an answer to this question.[23] The Swifterbant project is the earliest example of a large-scale interdisciplinary project. Something that all the aforementioned wetland sites have in common is that the excellently preserved organic remains amply compensate for the scarcity of features. The delta research in the western and northern Netherlands and the way in which the sites were excavated attracted much international interest, for these sites are important not only with respect to our understanding of Dutch prehistory, but also for their uniqueness from a European viewpoint (fig. 10.8).[24]

fig. 10.8
Block diagram of the lower courses of the rivers of the river district showing the *donken* (river dunes). The dunes that have been investigated by means of manual coring are indicated in black. Also indicated in the cross-section are the ^{14}C dates obtained for the Mesolithic and Neolithic occupation horizons. They show that the river dunes as a group were systematically used as settlement sites from at least 5200 BC (the greatest depth reached in the coring) until the Beaker period. See also feature D.

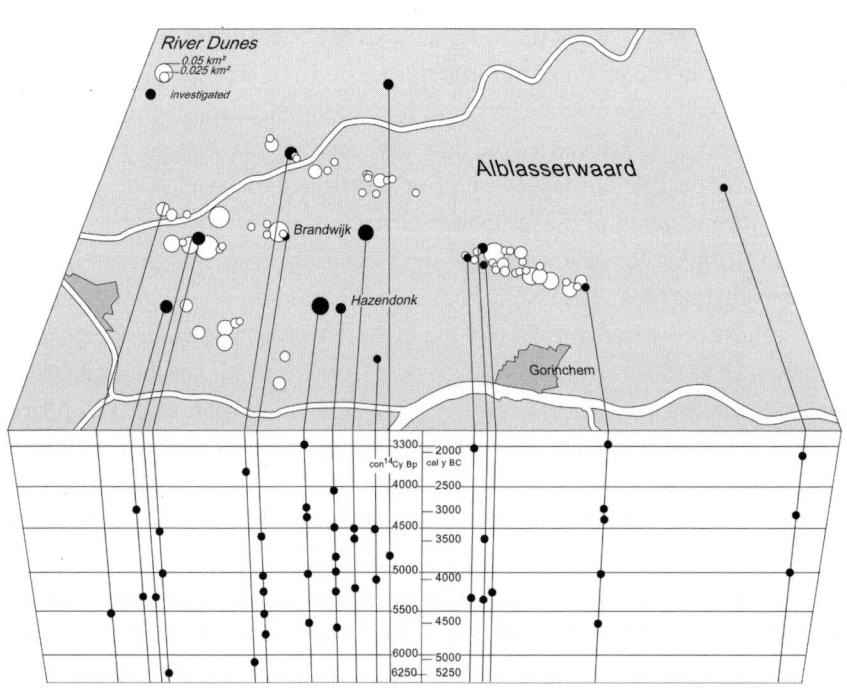

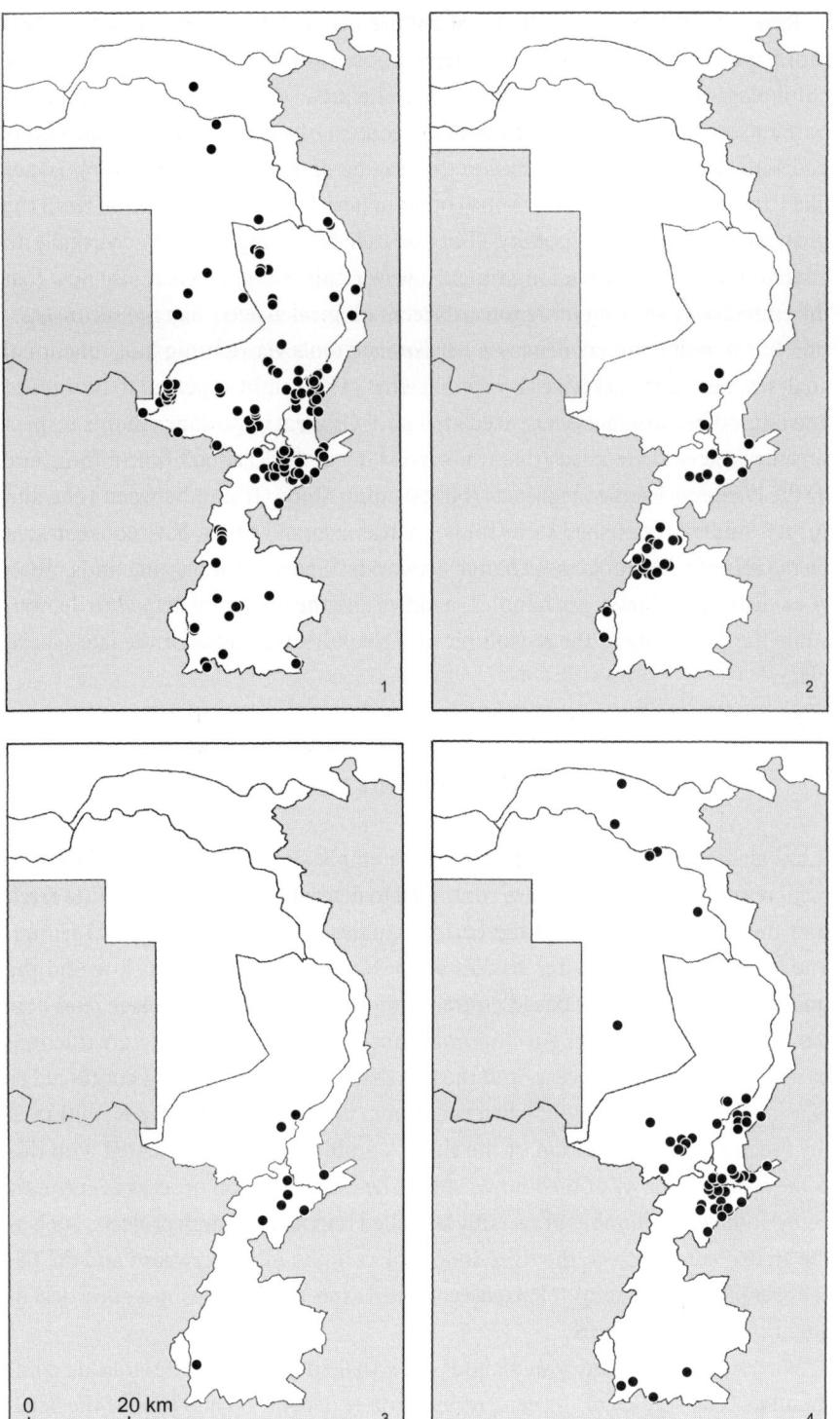

fig. 10.9
Distribution of findspots, interpreted as
settlement sites, from the Late Mesolithic
and three phases of the Neolithic in the area
surveyed in the Meuse valley project. In the
periods of the *Bandkeramik* and the Rössen
culture occupation was restricted to the
southern part of this area, the peripheral
parts of the loess zone. The Neolithic way of
life was to spread to the rest of the area only
in the period of the Michelsberg culture.
1 Late Mesolithic
2 *Bandkeramik*
3 Rössen
4 Michelsberg

Other Neolithic settlement research has been less spectacular. Only one Rössen settlement and a small number of sites of later Neolithic cultures like the
Michelsberg and TRB cultures have been investigated. With the spectacular exception of the multiple palisade of Anloo, no features came to light in those investigations. House plans of the TRB culture have been unearthed in the adjacent part of
northern Germany, though.

To conclude, the settlement research in the coastal region (the wetland sites)
and on the loess has led to methodical innovations, both in the field and in the
later processing of the finds and other data. The evidence obtained in the research
in the delta, in particular, has been of major importance for our understanding of
the Dutch Neolithic.

Research into aspects of material culture originally focused on cultural-historical questions: type fossils, in particular pottery, were studied to determine the chronological sequence of the findspots. The 'new' pottery proved to be an important source of inspiration, both in the context of cultural-historical questions and with respect to the information that can be derived from it regarding issues like (ethnic) identity.[25] Research into other materials suffered somewhat from the great scientific interest in pottery. Flint research, for example, received virtually no attention whatsoever for a long time. However, this is rapidly changing now that the emphasis is shifting more towards technological aspects like the reconstruction of the reduction sequence of *Bandkeramik* tools via refitting and functional analyses. Such analyses have shown that what at first sight appeared to be unused and unmodified artefacts were used after all.[26] Of great importance in this respect was the large-scale research that was carried out at the Rijckholt flint-mining site by the *Werkgroep Vuursteenmijnbouw* (Flint-Mining Study Group) between 1964 and 1972.[27] Studies of polished stone tools, such as axes and adzes, have concentrated on the role of these tools in exchange networks.[28] Spectacular organic finds, finally, such as traps, bows, axe handles, paddles and the like, have helped to demonstrate the continuity of the Mesolithic and Neolithic traditions of the late-glacial plain.

CURRENT RESEARCH TOPICS

It has already been outlined above how the emphasis gradually shifted to settlement research. Settlements have continued to determine the direction of research over the past few years, only the current studies are of a more regional nature. The key issue in present-day studies is the Neolithisation process: how did the transition to an economy based entirely on food production take place, and how did this differ per region? An important question, considering the great length of the Neolithisation process, and the fact that hunting and fishing continued to play important parts in the subsistence system throughout the entire Neolithic, is the functional differentiation of the sites. A problem closely associated with this is the representativity of the known sites. The Neolithisation process is currently being studied in a number of recently launched regional research projects, such as the Meuse valley project, the river dune project in the Alblasserwaard and the IJsselmeer project (fig. 10.9).[29] Palaeo-ecological aspects are receiving a good deal of attention in these projects.

We are still poorly informed about the social structure of the Neolithic communities. The studies of the cemeteries, pottery decoration and flint of the *Bandkeramik* culture have provided some insight into this matter[30] and much has been written about the role of the *hunebedden* in TRB society.[31] As far as the other Neolithic phases are concerned, an analysis of raw material procurement strategies could yield information on mobility and social networks.[32]

Although our understanding of the Neolithic in the Low Countries is steadily widening, a number of important questions still remain unanswered. One of these questions concerns the great homogeneity of the *Bandkeramik*. This is usually explained by assuming that the bearers of this culture were colonising pioneers. But if so, how did this colonisation come about in such a short time span, what sort of relationship existed between the colonists and the native population, why did such a colonisation take place and how did the pioneers retain their identity? These are but a few of the questions that can be asked with respect to the *Bandkeramik*. Of importance in this context is the meaning of the Limburg and La Hoguette pottery,

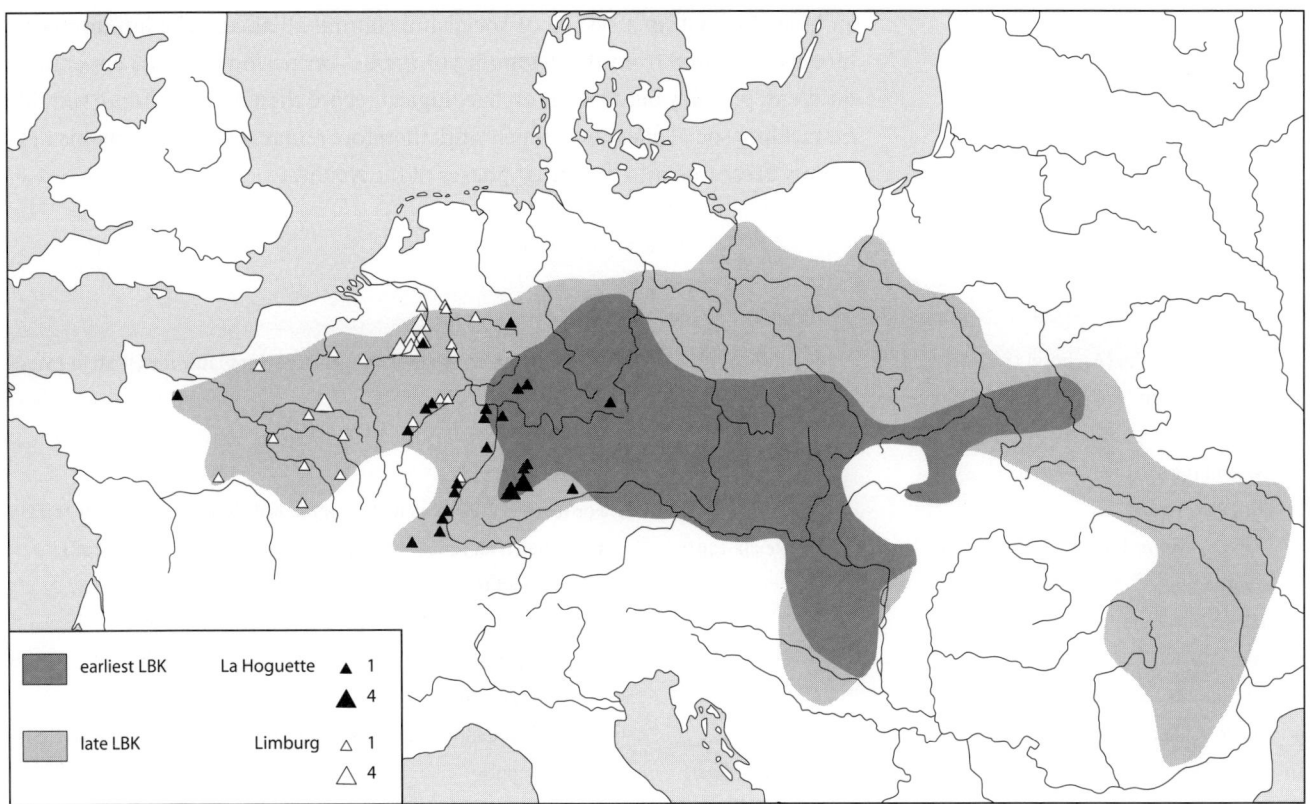

earliest LBK La Hoguette ▲ 1
                           ▲ 4

late LBK   Limburg   △ 1
                           △ 4

which has been found outside the loess, too. Are we to interpret this as pottery produced by Mesolithic groups or does it reflect, for example, specific activities of people belonging to the *Bandkeramik* culture (fig. 10.10)?[33] The abrupt end of the *Bandkeramik* is also an intriguing topic.

Another current research topic is the transition from the Swifterbant culture to the TRB culture: when did the Neolithisation process start in the north of the country and how are we to envisage the communities that lived there before this process started? The research that is currently being carried out in the IJsselmeer polders may throw some light on this issue. Something else that is not yet entirely clear is whether the TRB culture reflects the colonisation of the sandy soils or is instead to be regarded as the outcome of the acculturation of local hunter-gatherers.

Thanks to intensive, detailed research in the various regions we are now slowly gaining more insight into a crucial phase in the development of prehistoric society: the transition from a hunting-gathering way of life to farming. Besides the obvious logistic consequences, in particular the adoption of an entirely sedentary existence, this transition also implied tremendous changes in terms of social organisation. Food production gave a community – or at least some of its members – the possibility of creating a surplus. If control of this surplus was an exclusive right, it may have been used to acquire a higher status within the community and reduce other members of the community to a position of dependence. The transition to food production, moreover, led to an entirely different relationship with nature, from a relatively equal relationship to one in which man enjoyed greater control over nature. Apart from that, it also laid the basis for the emergence of social differentiation. Although our knowledge of the subsistence system is steadily expanding, we are unfortunately still insufficiently informed about social structure and social organisation, partly because these are not important topics in the theoretical context within which much Neolithic research is carried out.[34] Neolithic man is still seen predominantly as a food consumer, and too little as

fig. 10.10

Distribution of the earliest phase of the *Bandkeramik* in Central Europe from around 5500 BC onwards, and its later expansion to the west, north and east after 5300 BC. The 'western Neolithic', which is characterised by La Hoguette and Limburg pottery, is known almost exclusively from *Bandkeramik* pit fills.

an individual within a system of social and cultural alliances. The interpretation models employed from the beginning of the Beaker period onwards are entirely different, possibly because the archaeological record then becomes more suitable for tackling social questions. Much work therefore remains to be done in this field in future research into the earlier phases of the Neolithic.

NOTES

1   Lubbock, sir John (Avebury) 1865. See also Daniel 1967: 118-124.
2   O.a. Anderson 1992; Harris/Hillman 1989; Reed 1977; Zohary 1992.
3   Zvelebil 1994.
4   Lee/DeVore 1965.
5   See a.o. Binford 1968; Braidwood/Willey 1962; MacNeish 1991; Moore 1989.
6   Griede/Roeleveld 1982; Roeleveld 1974.
7   Bakels 1978.
8   For example Louwe Kooijmans 1993a.
9   Van de Velde 1979a, 1979b.
10 Ten Anscher forthcoming; Deckers et al. 1982; Van der Waals 1972.
11 Ten Anscher forthcoming.
12 Ten Anscher forthcoming.
13 Louwe Kooijmans 1983.
14 Fokkens 1986, 1998b; Van der Waals 1984.
15 An exception is for example Fokkens' study of the plateau of Friesland and Drenthe (1991a, 1998a).
16 Picardt 1660.
17 Bakker 1979; Brindley 1986; Voss 1982.
18 Elsloo (Van de Velde 1979a); Swifterbant (Meiklejohn/Constandse-Westermann 1978); Hekelingen III (Hoogland 1985); Stein (Modderman 1964).
19 Van Giffen 1930.
20 Modderman 1985.
21 For Rosmeer, excavated 1952-1966, see Roossens 1962; for Darion see Cahen et al. 1986; for Aldenhovener Platte see Lüning 1982.
22 Modderman 1953.
23 See Deckers et al. 1980.
24 For example Louwe Kooijmans 1987; Waterbolk 1981.
25 Voss 1982; Hodder 1982.
26 Reductiesequenties en refitting: De Grooth 1987; functional analysis: Van Gijn 1990.
27 Felder 1980.
28 For example Bakels 1978, 1987a; Van der Waals 1972.
29 IJsselmeerproject (Hogestijn 1992; Hogestijn et al. 1995; Ten Anscher/Gehasse 1993); Alblasserwaard (Verbruggen forthcoming); Maas Valley Project (Wansleeben/Verhart 1990).
30 Van de Velde 1979a, 1979b, 1990; De Grooth 1987, 1991.
31 For a summary see Bakker 1992.
32 For example De Grooth 1991.
33 Brounen 1985; Lüning et al. 1989.
34 An exception is the research carried out by Van de Velde (1979).

11 Colonists on the loess?
Early Neolithic A: the *Bandkeramik* culture

Marjorie de Grooth and Pieter van de Velde

INTRODUCTION

Traces of the oldest agrarian groups in the Netherlands are only found in the province of Limburg. The material remains of these groups are known as the *Linear-bandkeramik* Culture, often referred to as *Bandkeramik* for brevity's sake. The abbreviation used most commonly both within and outside the Netherlands is LBK.[1] The name, which was coined by Klopfleisch as early as 1883, refers to the ribbon-shaped patterns composed of lines which decorate much of the pottery.

The Limburgian LBK is the northwestern offshoot of a large complex spanning the oldest Neolithic period in the temperate zones of Europe (fig. 10.10 and 11.1). *Bandkeramik* occupation remains are now known from near the Black Sea in eastern Rumania to the English Channel in Normandy and from the Danube to the Baltic in the Polish-German border region.[2]

Geographical environment

LBK settlements are found predominantly on loess, one of the most fertile soils in large parts of Europe. They reveal a clear preference for sites at the edges of the loess plateaux, near open water.[3]

Most of the findspots in Limburg lie in the Graetheide region, an area covering some 10 x 5 km between the Geleenbeek and the Meuse (fig. 11.2). Large-scale

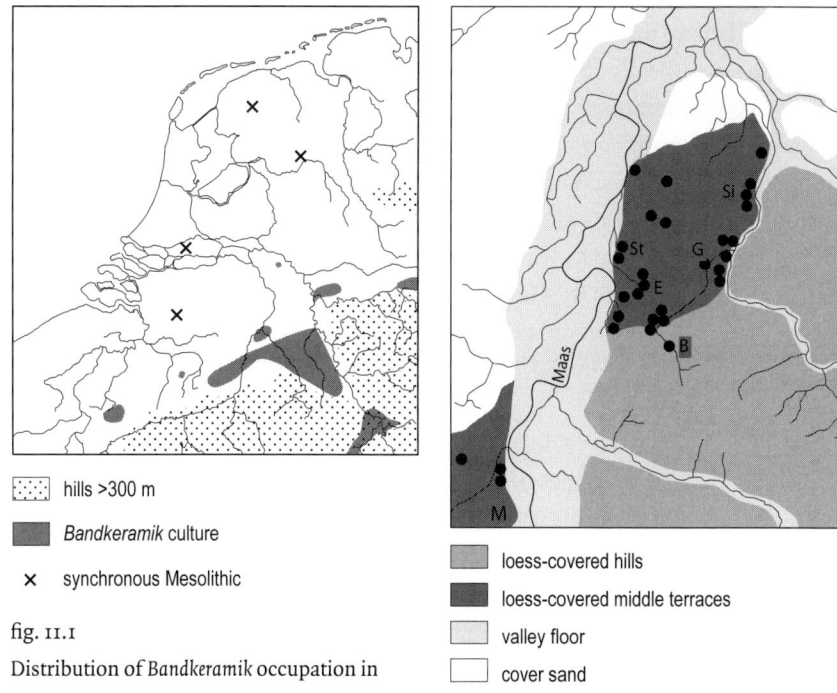

hills >300 m

▓ *Bandkeramik* culture

× synchronous Mesolithic

fig. 11.1
Distribution of *Bandkeramik* occupation in the Netherlands and its environs.

loess-covered hills
loess-covered middle terraces
valley floor
cover sand
● Bandkeramik settlement

fig. 11.2
Bandkeramik settlement cluster on the Graetheide plateau. Most of the settlements lie at the edges of the loess plateau, close to the Meuse valley floor and the valley of the Geleenbeek. Similar clusters can be made out elsewhere. They seem to represent the highest level of social organisation.

B = Beek
E = Elsloo
G = Geleen
M = Maastricht
Si = Sittard
St = Stein

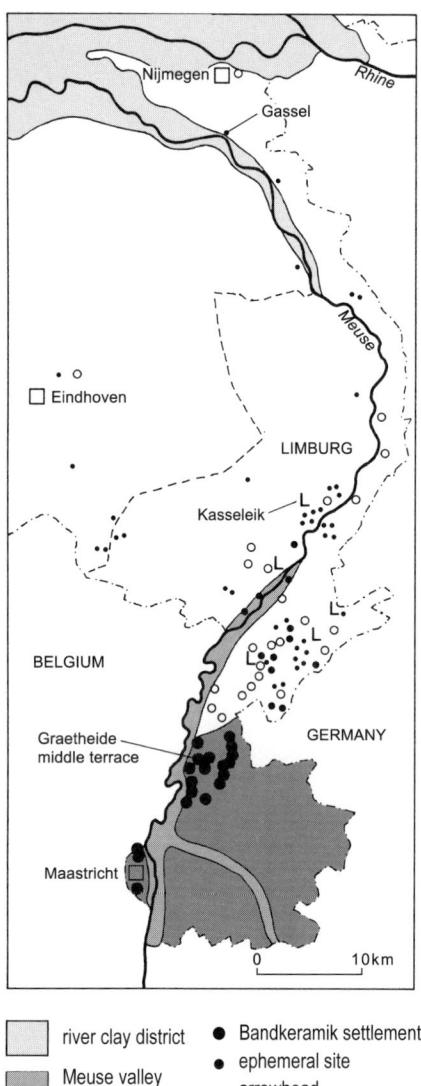

fig. 11.3

The occupation area of the northwest group of the *Bandkeramik* was restricted to the loess zone in the southern part of the province of Limburg. Isolated *Bandkeramik* artefacts found further north indicate that the sandy area was also exploited, possibly for hunting and the herding of cattle.

Legend:

- river clay district
- Meuse valley floor deposits
- loess
- ● Bandkeramik settlement
- ● ephemeral site
- · arrowhead
- ○ adze
- L Limburg pottery

excavations have been carried out here, for example in Geleen, Sittard, Stein and Elsloo in the 1950s and 1960s and at Stein-Sanderboutlaan and Geleen-Janskamperveld in the early 1990s.[4] The findspots on the west bank of the Meuse are the northern offshoots of a group of settlements along the river Jeker (referred to as the Geer in the Walloon provinces of Belgium) extending into Hesbaye in Belgium. In that area the site of Darion has been fully investigated.[5] The nearest findspots in the east are to be found on the Aldenhoven plateau, between Aachen and Jülich, where systematic research has been carried out since 1965 in connection with the large-scale extraction of brown coal. In a 1.3 km long strip of land on either side of the Merzbach all *Bandkeramik* settlements and one cemetery have been completely excavated (plate 12).[6] Scattered LBK finds are discovered outside the loess zones all over Europe, in areas which, however, do not appear to have been permanently occupied. This is for example the case in the Roer basin in central Dutch Limburg (fig. 11.3).[7]

Background

Almost all researchers agree that the LBK was not an indigenous development in these regions, but arrived as a ready-made package from Central Europe. The hypothesis of immigration of people with this tradition is usually preferred to that of the adoption of knowledge and ideas by the original occupants of these regions. The LBK was not geographically isolated. In the neighbourhood evidence for other groups with pottery has been found: Limburg and La Hoguette, while there were probably also groups with a late Mesolithic way of life further away.

Dating problems

Most ^{14}C dates for the 'classic' LBK, as we know it from the Rhineland and the Graetheide region, lie between 5300 and 4900 BC. On the basis of typological and stratigraphic evidence an older phase (the 'Oldest' LBK) is distinguished to the east of the Rhine, which is limited to a smaller area than the classic LBK. Some researchers believe that this oldest phase in fact even lasted for 400 years, but there is as yet no scientifically obtained chronological evidence to corroborate this.[8]

The LBK is traditionally divided into phases on the basis of, in particular, changes in the decoration of the pottery. Usually three or four main phases are distinguished: the Oldest, Old, (Middle) and Young LBK.[9] The typochronological classification proposed by Modderman, which is based on the decoration of the pottery, stratigraphic evidence and details of house plans, proves to be still largely valid for and applicable to the Graetheide region (even though it lacks formal logical consistency). Modderman's classification distinguishes two main phases, an old and a young phase (I and II), each of which is divided into four subphases (fig. 11.4).

Phase I comprises the Oldest (Ia in this classification), the Old (Ib) and the Middle LBK (Ic, Id). No traces of the Oldest LBK have been found to the west of the Rhine. The pottery of this phase was made from clay tempered with chaff and decorated with shallow grooves in wavy or spiral patterns. These motifs were to remain popular throughout the entire LBK.

The Old LBK is characterised by pottery decorated with narrow bands, sometimes with adjacent rows of dots.[10] From this phase onwards the clay of the pottery was tempered with grog. At the beginning of the Middle LBK the rims of the pot-

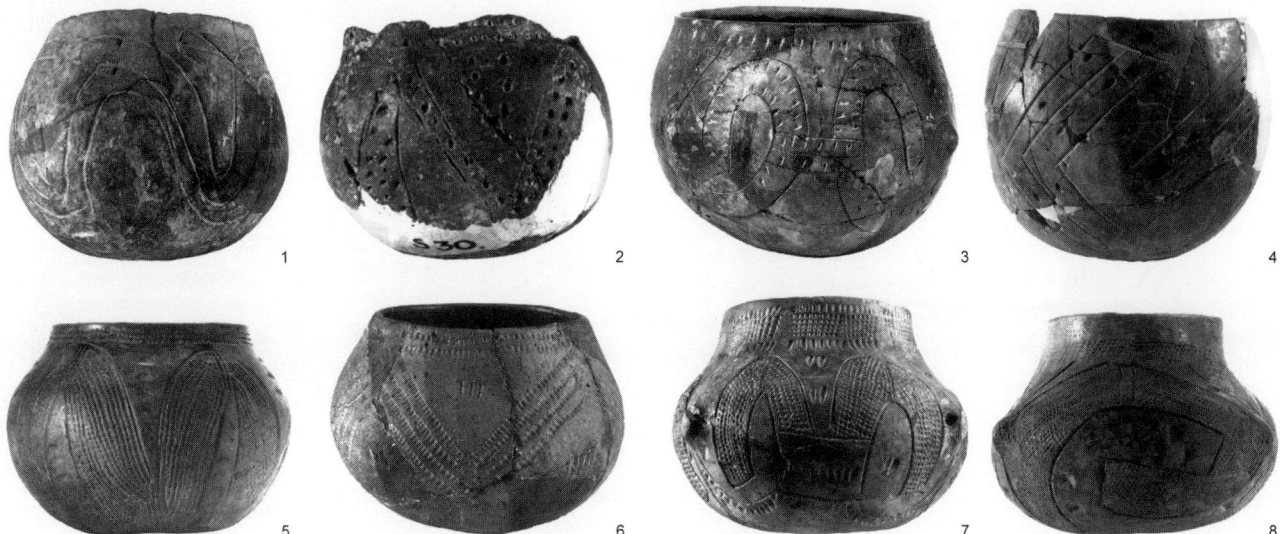

tery started to be decorated, too, first of all with a simple line or a row of dots, later on with more complex motifs.

In the Young *Bandkeramik* (phase II) the bands on the pottery were filled with rows of dots, lines or hatchings in increasingly varied patterns. Besides the main motifs secondary forms of decoration were used to fill the bands. In the youngest phase (IId) the dots used to fill the bands were no longer placed one at a time, but were made with the aid of a toothed spatula, a kind of comb (fig. 11.5). Sometimes the bands were no longer defined by lines but consisted exclusively of rows of dots. The beginning and end of this development have probably been fairly accurately determined but there are no ¹⁴C dates to verify the classification into the phases or the order of the phases. This need not be surprising. At best, a ¹⁴C date has a standard deviation of 25 to 30 years, which means that the 'resolution' is only a century. Most samples from Limburg have standard deviations of at least 80-100 years, which means that the 95% reliability of the determination is in the order of the overall duration of the LBK in this area.

The dating of the timber lining of a well at Kückhoven near Erkelenz in Germany, which was excavated in 1991, provides a good example of the problems encountered (plate 13A, fig. 15.8). Ironically, the dendrochronological evidence first presented a choice of two equivalent options, notably *c.* 5303 or *c.* 5100 BC. The calibrated ¹⁴C date for the wood was 5200 ± 50 BC, so that did not provide a solution. On the basis of the traditional pottery chronology the excavator preferred the youngest date. The dendrochronologist has since then obtained evidence to corroborate this.[11]

SETTLEMENTS AND CEMETERIES

Settlements

Large numbers of soil discolourations are usually found in excavations of *Bandkeramik* settlement sites. Regular, elongated patterns are recognisable in the jumble of features, which since about 1950 have been interpreted as house plans (plate 14A). Characteristic are the five parallel rows of heavy posts set in deep holes or, along the outsides, in bedding trenches.

Immediately beside the house walls are elongated pits, which were originally dug to obtain the loam used to coat the walls and the possibly slightly raised floor

fig. 11.4

Bandkeramik pottery from Elsloo, Maastricht-Caberg and Sittard showing the various decorative patterns. Upper row: Older LBK, lower row: Younger LBK. From left to right: curvilinear arc; rectilinear arc; curvilinear spiral, rectilinear spiral. *Cf.* fig. 11.15.

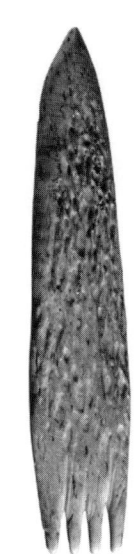

fig. 11.5

Four-toothed bone spatula, presumably used for decorating pottery, from the *Bandkeramik* settlement at Liège, Place St.-Lambert. Actual size.

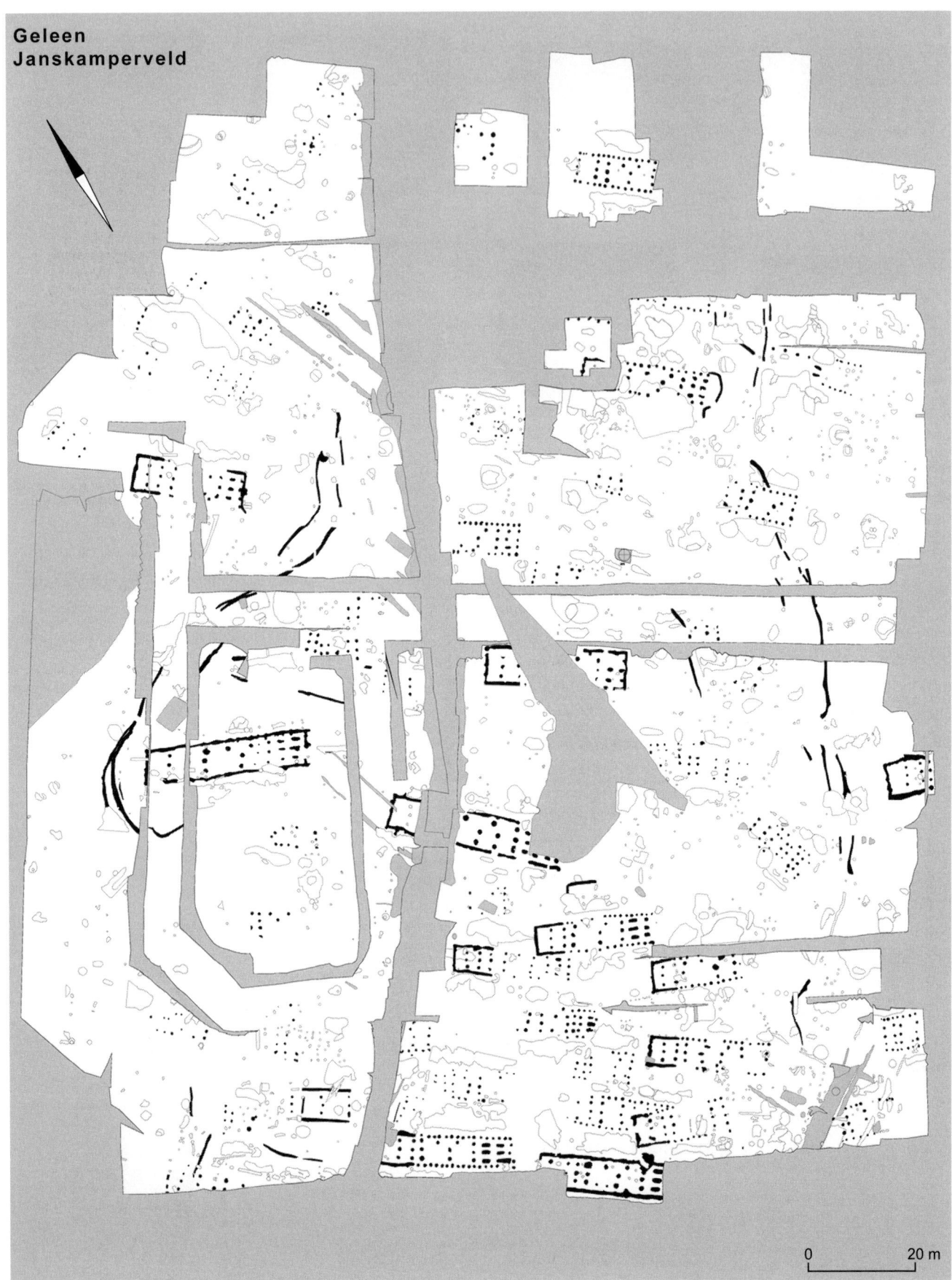

**Geleen
Janskamperveld**

0   20 m

fig. 11.6

In 1991 a settlement dating from the early *Bandkeramik* was excavated almost in its entirety at the Janskamperveld site

in Geleen. Unfortunately, about a quarter of the site has over the centuries been disturbed by the construction of a

road and buildings and the digging of loess quarries. The site was only occupied during the early *Bandkeramik* period

(Modderman's phases 1b/c). The greater part of the settlement was enclosed by a narrow trench, which probably held

a palisade. The settlement comprised three to four house generations. Scale 1:1000.

and which were later filled up with refuse. Further away from the house are cylindrical or pouch-shaped pits which are thought to have been storage pits. Also encountered at *Bandkeramik* settlement sites are large complexes of pits, some of which mark areas where specific activities were carried out, and, in some regions, split-shaped pits which may have been used in tanning. Kilns have been found in some of the pits.[12]

Long, shallow ditches of the kind encountered in Sittard or at Geleen-Janskamperveld may have marked the limits of yards (fig. 11.6). Sometimes, in the youngest LBK in particular, the settlements were surrounded by deep ditches and banks with special entrances (Darion, Köln-Lindenthal). In the Rhineland earthworks with deep V-shaped ditches and palisades were constructed outside the settlements around this time.[13]

The features found at most sites are not contemporary but reflect long periods of occupation in which successive houses were built on more or less the same spot. The traditional chronological framework comprising seven or eight phases presents an insufficiently differentiated picture of the history of occupation. This has led to the development of other methods, based on a detailed description of the assemblages of decorated pottery found. The following two major assumptions served as points of departure. First, the way in which a pot was decorated was at least partly a matter of fashion, and was hence subject to change: new elements were cautiously introduced, after which they increased in popularity and then gradually lost their former appeal. Second, like all other refuse, the decorated sherds ended up in the loam pits near the houses while the latter were occupied. Statistic comparison of the contents of these pits can hence reveal contemporaneity. In the end, this approach can show which houses in a settlement, and even in a region, were simultaneously occupied. It can also reveal the history of the occupation of individual house sites.[14]

Burials

It was probably fairly customary to bury the deceased, in particular the children, in pits within the settlement. In the Netherlands, where organic matter has been very poorly preserved in the decalcified loess, such burials are only recognised by chance. In the Graetheide region one separate cemetery has been discovered, which has been excavated almost in its entirety (113 graves). It dates from the youngest phases (IIc and d) of the settlement of Elsloo (fig. 11.7). Only one cemetery has been found on the Aldenhoven plateau, too, namely that of Niedermerz, which comprised at least 108 graves dating from phases Ic to IIc. In both cemeteries both inhumation and cremation burials were found. Hardly any of the graves intersected one another, which means that they were probably marked by a mound or perhaps some sign of perishable material.

The majority of the deceased were accompanied by grave goods. In the Netherlands only objects that are resistant to decalcification have been preserved in the graves; elsewhere ornaments of different materials are regularly found, such as neck and head decoration of snail shells, bone combs and especially beads, pendants and buckles of *Spondylus*, a mother-of-pearl-like shell from the eastern Mediterranean. In the northwestern part of the LBK distribution area both women and men were accompanied by decorated pots. Quern stones, associated with food preparation, were also often placed in the graves of women. Moreover, red pigment (haematite), probably a symbol of life, was sprinkled over them (fig. 11.8). Men's graves regularly yield undecorated pots and the remains of adzes and bows

Elsloo

0   10 m

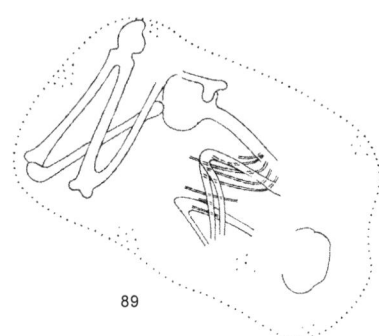

89

👁   inhumation burial with corpse silhouette

🐛   burial with traces of haematite

∿   cremation remains

fig. 11.7

Plan of the Elsloo cemetery from the youngest phases of the LBK (IIc/d). Scale 1:500. The cemetery, which has been excavated almost in its entirety, comprised 113 burials, both inhumations and cremation burials. All the skeletal remains had decayed as a result of the decalcification of the loess. The only remaining evidence encountered were occasional corpse silhouettes, such as that in grave 89. The dead were buried on their sides, with their knees drawn up.

fig. 11.8

Elsloo, grave goods from grave 89. The composition of the grave goods – a small decorated pot (h. 10 cm), a quern and a lump of haematite – suggests that this is a burial of a woman.

and arrows, associated with tree felling and woodworking, hunting and fighting.
Similar patterns, but varying in details, are observed elsewhere (fig. 11.9).[15]

MATERIAL CULTURE AND TECHNOLOGY

The LBK has a remarkably varied material culture, in terms of both the number of
categories and the raw materials used.[16] The majority of these raw materials were
available in the immediate surroundings of the settlements but some important
types of implements were obtained from distant regions (fig. 11.10).

Houses and building material

The evidence regarding the materials used in house construction is mostly indirect. The best structural timber comes from oak trees, which grew in the stream
and river valleys. From the features we know that cleft posts and planks were also
used, besides entire posts (fig. 11.11 and plate 14B). Lumps of burned daub bearing
the impressions of twigs indicate that the walls were of wattlework coated with
mud on either side. The roof was probably covered with straw.

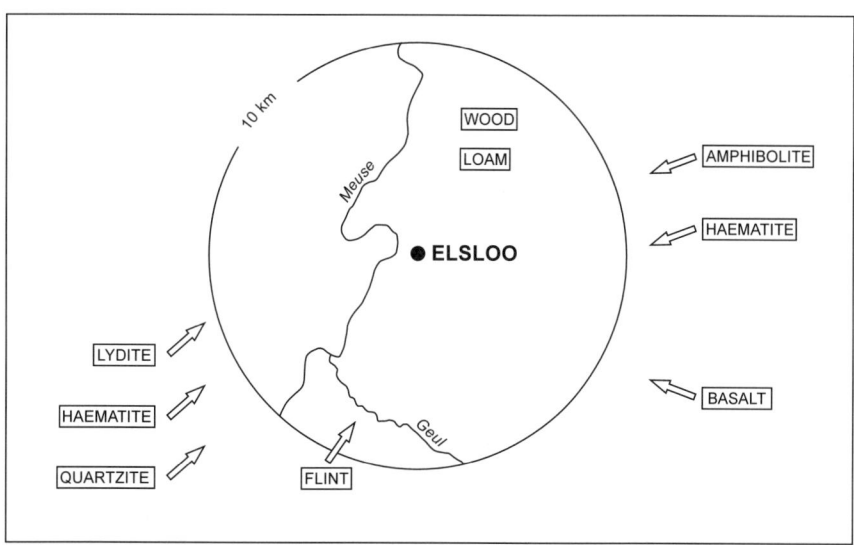

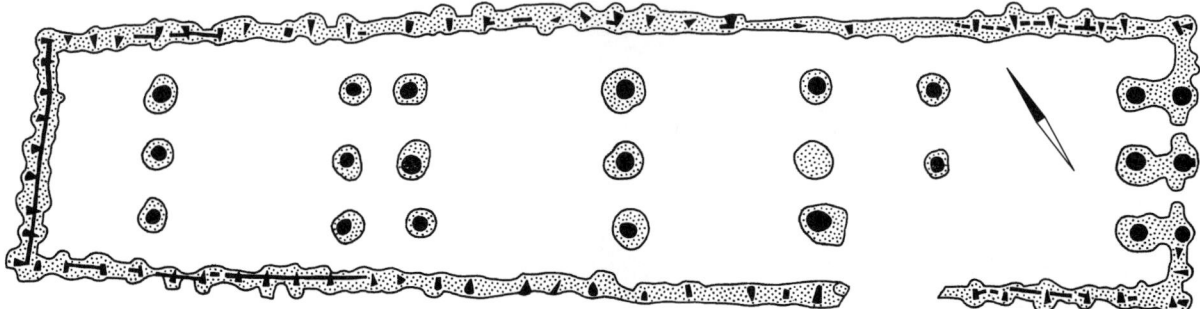

fig. 11.11

The plan of one of the largest Bandkeramik houses in South Limburg, house 29 at Stein, which was of type 1a and 32 m long. The features are of exceptionally good quality, showing that the walls were built from cleft trunks and planks. Scale 1:200.

fig. 11.12

Survey of the different types of Bandkeramik house plans. Top row: younger Bandkeramik, bottom row: older Bandkeramik. The main difference between the two types concerns the arrangements of the posts in the central part of the house. The smallest houses (type 3) consisted of only one part with wattle walls. The plans of type 2 include an extra unit added in the northwest, usually with plank walls. The buildings of type 1 also had an extension to the southeast, characterised by extra posts that may have supported a loft. Type 1a houses had plank walls all round.

The farm houses were between about 8 and 35 metres long and between 5 and 8 metres wide. An estimated wall height of about 1.50 m and a pitch of 45° yields an overall height of over 5 m for the largest houses. The estimated life of these houses is 25-35 years. Until recently, it was assumed that only extremely simple timber joints had been used. The well found at Kückhoven, however, shows that this assumption needs adjusting. The perfectionist manner in which the lining had been composed and finished exceeded all expectations: tongue-and-groove joints, unit construction and oakum proved to have been used much earlier than had ever been thought.[17]

The houses of the northwestern LBK were oriented northwest-southeast, with their main entrances in the southeast. Modderman has distinguished three types of house plans (fig. 11.12). Plans of type 1 consist of three parts: a *central part*, in all probability the living area, a *northwestern part*, whose function is still unclear but which almost always had a wall made of planks, and a *southeastern part*, which often had a double number of posts which are assumed to have supported a storage loft. Plans of type 2 have no southeast part while plans of type 3 have neither a southeastern nor a northwestern part. A further distinction is made in type 1 on the basis of the composition of the outside walls: houses of type 1a had walls made of planks on all sides whereas with type 1b only the outside walls of the northwest part were made of planks. House plans of type 1a appear to be limited to the northwestern LBK. The same holds for a remarkable – though puzzling – structural detail in the central part of houses from period I, where the posts were arranged in a Y pattern.[18]

Flint and stone

In the immediate vicinity of the settlements, namely in the gravel banks of the Meuse, stones could be collected which without much further trimming could be used as querns for grinding corn and as polishers for the manufacture of, for example, wooden arrows or bone awls.

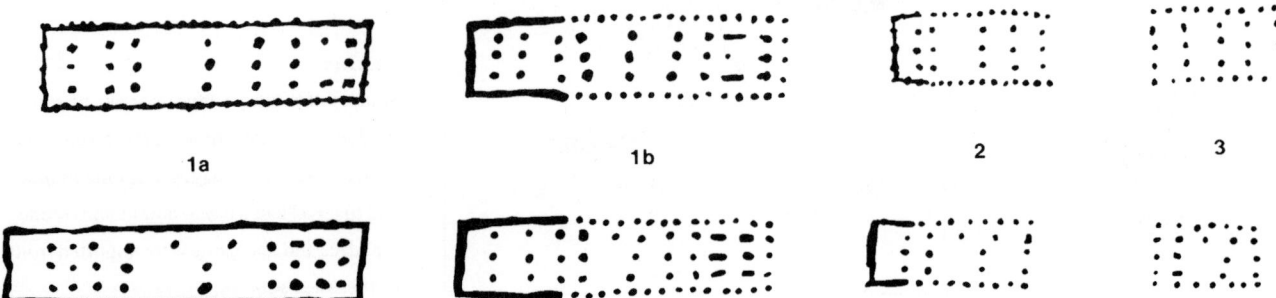

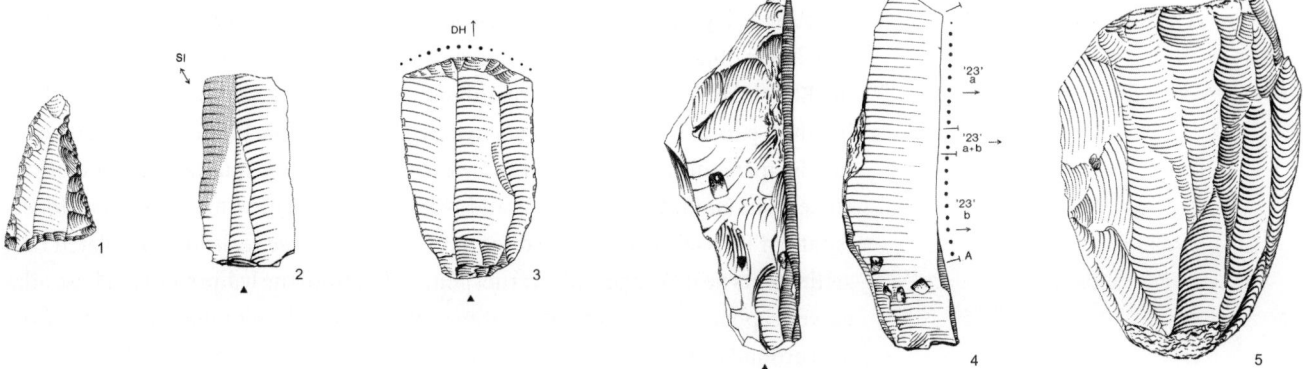

Most of the preserved tools or parts of tools are made of flint. The raw material was collected at the bottom of slopes in an area 10-15 km to the south of the Graetheide region, on the other side of the river Geul, where chalk containing flint seams outcrops.[19] By refitting flint from two refuse pits at Beek-Kerkeveld the production process could be reconstructed. The greater part of this process, which was aimed at the production of blades with lengths of some 10 cm, took place in the settlement. The cores were prepared in a simple manner and were regularly rejuvenated during the production process, which was not characterised by any economy of raw material. Exhausted cores were used as hammerstones or hammers. Almost all pits contained debitage, which means that, in principle, every household has made its own tools. At Elsloo, however, evidence has been found for part-time specialists in the presence of refuse pits which yielded too much debitage in proportion to the number of tools they contained.

End scrapers, borers and arrowheads had standardised shapes (fig. 11.13). In addition, all kinds of blades had been used as knives. Some of these show a well-developed gloss. Set in a wooden or bone handle in groups of three or four, they formed part of sickles. In the younger phases in particular all kinds of less standardised implements were also used: notched and denticulate fragments and the rare 'orange segments', recognised in Belgium in particular, which often show traces of an as yet unidentified use.[20]

The main tree-felling and woodworking implements were polished stone axes, whose asymmetrical shape indicates that they were hafted as adzes (i.e. with the cutting edge at right angles to the handle) or as chisels (fig. 11.14 and 15.8). They

fig. 11.13

Some characteristic tool types from the Beek-Molensteeg settlement which have been subjected to use-wear analysis. 2/3 of actual size.

1 point with impact damage at the tip
2 'sickle blade', blade fragment showing the gloss formed in cutting cereal
3 end-scraper made on a blade which was used for scraping dry hide
4 so-called orange slice showing a typical gloss ('23') formed in an as yet unidentified activity
5 core that has been used as hammer stone

fig. 11.14

Various adze blades found at Elsloo and Maastricht-Caberg made of amphibolite and lydite. Three main types can be distinguished: small, tall adzes, large, tall adzes and flat adzes. Hafted, the small, tall adzes may have been used as chisels. The other two types are thought to represent different types of implements. This assumption is partly based on the observation that whenever a deceased was accompanied by more than one adze, these always were of different types.

were made from tenacious types of stone which do not occur in the vicinity of the Graetheide region. In the Old LBK virtually all adzes were made from amphibolite, which was obtained from as yet unidentified outcrops in Central Europe (possibly the Bohemian Massif or the Carpathians). In periods IIa and IIb use was made of basalt in particular (from the Siebengebirge or the Eifel). In the youngest phases, finally, material imported from the west was also used: quartzite from Horion-Hozémont (southwest of Liège) and lydite from the environs of Céroux-Mousty (south of Brussels). Adzes of lydite were made on a large scale in two isolated LBK settlements near Wange and Overhespen, 35 km from the lydite source. These adzes were apparently exchanged for flint and other goods with the occupants of the area around Darion (on the upper reaches of the Geer). Amphibolite and quartzite could be shaped by splitting and sawing (using a thin sheet of sandstone), while basalt and lydite were worked in the same manner as flint.[21] Another imported material was haematite, an iron compound that was used as a red pigment and possibly as a tanning extract. It was obtained from the valley of the Lahn in Germany and from the Belgian Ardennes.

Organic matter

Hardly any objects of organic matter have survived, which is why the aforementioned beautifully preserved timber well of Kückhoven is so invaluable. Among the objects recovered from its fill were wooden tools (two different types of digging implements with separate handles and a spade), a bucket made from bark and remains of rope.[22] From areas where the loess still contains chalk, implements of bone and antler are known: in particular awls, chisels and small combs.

There are some rare indirect indications of the way in which hides, wool, bark and vegetable fibres were processed, for example traces of use on flint tools[23] and a few earthenware spindle whorls. In some graves, for example at Aiterhofen in Bavaria, clasps and pendants of worked *Spondylus* shell were found in the area of the hips of the deceased, which suggests that the latter wore some kind of tunic that was held together by a belt.

Pottery

The find category most frequently encountered is pottery. The numerous sherds belonged to cooking pots, tableware, storage pots and bottles.[24] The raw material was local loess or loam, which was tempered with grog in particular. The pots were produced by hand, either from a single ball of clay or from several slabs of clay; they were hence *not* shaped from coils. Their dark, blackish-grey colours indicate that they were fired in a reducing atmosphere. Most of the pots were simple open types with round bases. Small lugs were arranged in zigzag patterns on the walls of the pots; strings could be threaded through or round these lugs so that the pots could be suspended. The thin-walled tableware especially was decorated with incised or impressed ornamentation before firing. As already mentioned in the introduction, the decoration consisted essentially of ribbon-shaped motifs composed of lines. The range of decorative motifs was limited: all *Bandkeramik* patterns are composed of two basic motifs, an arch and a spiral, which, in rectilinear or curvilinear form, were repeated and/or mirrored (fig. 11.15). Only one type of motif was used per pot. The basic motifs are separated by partition marks or are emphatically coupled, either by means of small linking motifs or by means of

fig. 11.15

The structure of the decoration on *Bandkeramik* pots. There are two basic motifs: an arc and a spiral. They were both used to create curvilinear or rectilinear patterns by rotating or mirroring them around horizontal and/or vertical axes of symmetry. *Cf.* fig. 11.4.

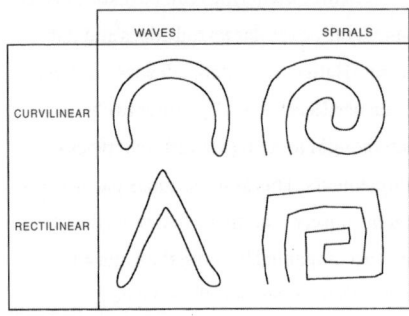

entwining or interweaving. Sometimes remains of a white or red filling are found encrusted in the grooves.

RELATIONS WITHIN THE SETTLEMENTS

So far, we have given a fairly basic description of the archaeological evidence. In order to be able to interpret this evidence in terms of social organisations, the data must be supplemented and classified. An interpretation of the aforementioned kind must be based on what Braudel, referring to the fact that social structures usually span long periods, described as 'quasi-constants': habits of behaviour and thought, ways of grouping and organising people, in which the members of a community are brought up and which they – usually unconsciously or semi-consciously – 'reproduce' themselves and pass on to the next generation. This reproduction process comprises more than imitation and upbringing; the way in which the environment is arranged also affects the development of habits, while, conversely, existing habits lead to reproduction of the environment in the way that for example houses are rebuilt in an accustomed manner and new fields are laid out in the same way.[25]

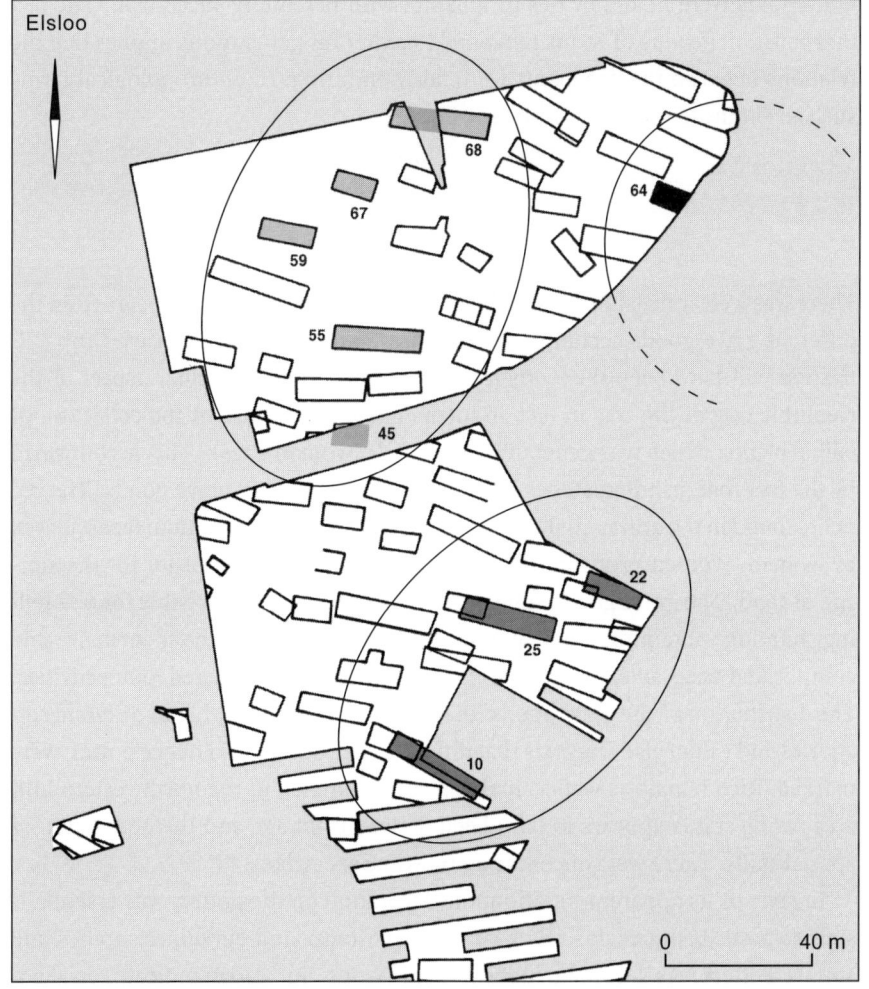

fig. 11.16
Excavated part of the Elsloo settlement showing several wards with houses simultaneously occupied in the third occupation phase. Three groups of house plans have been distinguished, each comprising one large tripartite farm house and a few smaller ones. These wards were often used for long periods, during which houses were rebuilt at more or less the same spot. Scale 1:2000.

Location and structure

The settlements were almost all situated along the edges of plateaux, above valleys. The settlement density increased with time, in particular the areas between older settlements were gradually filled in. In the Graetheide region five settlements are known from phase Ib as opposed to about twenty from phases IIc and IId. Less favourable environments were also selected for occupation only in the youngest phases.[26]

The settlements were usually open. Only rarely did the ditch-and-bank systems of the Young LBK have a clearly defensive function; they are usually interpreted as cattle pens and/or as religious or symbolic monuments.[27]

The settlements had a modular ('segmentary') structure. Contemporary houses were grouped in wards of two to five farms (fig. 11.16). Larger settlements, such as Elsloo, Langweiler 8 and Köln-Lindenthal, were composed of between two and five of such wards, with totals of 10-20 dwellings. They were occupied for about fourteen house generations of an average of 25-35 years each, i.e. for a total of some 350-500 years.

The smaller settlements were often occupied for shorter periods than the large ones; they were founded later, as though they were subsidiary villages of a primary settlement, and were sometimes abandoned earlier, too. Isolated houses are rare: in the Graetheide region Stein provided an example of an isolated house, on the Aldenhoven plateau an isolated house plan was found at Langweiler 16.[28] The above implies that the chief social relationship in LBK society was not that of the household or of the village but that of the ward, the relationship between the individual households of such a group of dwellings. It may be assumed that these households were linked by ties of kinship, with hereditary succession. The fact that constant groups of farms remained together for generations implies that the relations between the occupants were fairly enduring. In anthropological terms such an enduring group is known as a lineage.

Social positions

There was a clear division of tasks between women and men, as appears from the different grave goods accompanying the two sexes in the cemeteries. Crop cultivation will have been the women's domain since this particular aspect of the Neolithic way of life was in fact an intensified continuation of the collection of edible plants, which was generally considered a woman's task. This is confirmed by the fact that grinding stones were characteristic female grave goods. The red ochre found in the graves could furthermore indicate some ceremonial part played by women. Women probably also produced the pottery, important for the storage of food. The grave goods suggest that the men were responsible for tree felling, hunting, obtaining raw materials and tending cattle. Labour-intensive and complicated tasks such as house construction may be considered joint activities. The distribution of the grave goods (in terms of quantity, number of different categories and value) also suggests that differences in status, and hence power, were marked. Rich female as well as male graves are known in the northwestern LBK area, while status appears to have been derived from age and the possession of special skills. There were of course no full-time specialists.[29]

In spite of its apparent variation, the decoration on the pottery was essentially stereotypical, being exclusively based on rectilinear and curvilinear arches and spirals. Pottery was decorated for aesthetic reasons, but also to indicate social po-

sitions, as a kind of name plates. The distribution of decorations within the settlement and the cemetery of Elsloo appeared to be fairly structured rather than arbitrary. We are unable to interpret most distribution patterns with the exception of
one: women's graves never contained both rectilinear and curvilinear decorations,
while some men's graves did and others didn't. Both types are however always
found together in the refuse pits in the settlements. It has been concluded on this
basis that descent was traced through the maternal line (matrilineage) whereas
the place of residence was that of the man's family (patrilocality).[30] Another interesting aspect is that the oldest decoration, executed at a time when occupation was
concentrated in isolated hamlets in the forests, includes isolated motifs. The motifs on younger pottery are intertwined, just like the way the settlements expanded
towards one another.

Social differentiation

The wards usually consisted of one tripartite and several smaller houses, all of
which had central parts. At Geleen-Janskamperveld this pattern was recognisable
already in the oldest phase (Ib). The small houses at this site had been founded
less deep than the others; under less favourable conditions elsewhere (more erosion, a deeper leached A horizon, a poorly legible soil) they would probably have
been less readily recognised, which could explain the rather small proportions of
this type of house plans observed at other settlements. The variation in the areas
of the central (residential) parts and in the pottery decoration in the associated
refuse pits at Elsloo has led to the conclusion that the households in the Graetheide region consisted of couples of successive generations with their children
and possibly a few additional adults: what are known as extended families. Households are usually assumed to have consisted of three to five adults and a number of
children, at most about ten individuals. This would mean that the wards had 20-50
inhabitants while large settlements like that of Elsloo were inhabited by at most
100-200 persons. In the earliest period of occupation about 100-200 and at most
(in phases IIc and IId) 1000-2000 people will hence have simultaneously inhabited
the Graetheide region.[31] A group of some 500 members is often mentioned as a
basic demographic unit; normally this number includes sufficient marriage partners to secure the survival of the group.[32] In the Graetheide region it took several
generations before this number was reached.

The considerable and invariable differences in the types of houses indicate social differences between the individual households of the wards. In the northwestern part of the LBK distribution area this differentiation is more apparent than
elsewhere because of the presence of tripartite houses with walls composed entirely of planks (type 1a). It is estimated that it took only 5% more time, but 15%
more trees, to construct a house of this type than a house of type 1b. In view of the
scarcity of good building timber, especially in the young LBK, such a house was
especially costly.[33] The various types of houses do not only differ in the number of
modules; the size of the individual modules also differs: the rooms of the more
complex houses were considerably larger than those of the simple ones. In this
respect, too, type 1a is at the top.

At Elsloo only one house of type 1a in an associated group of wards appears to
have been inhabited at a time, although this house was not each time situated in
the same place.[34] A similar pattern is recognisable in the Merzbachtal, although
there two houses of type 1a were sometimes occupied at the same time. The refuse
associated with the houses of type 1a at Elsloo does not indicate that more or other

things were produced and discarded in these houses than in the others. In view of the shifting location, the community function reflected by this type of house was linked with a female line of descent. What could be considered in this context is an intermediary (male or female) between the visible and the invisible world, whose importance extended beyond the ward itself.[35]

The proportion of cereals in the food economy was high. Estimates range between 65% and 80%. This means that good storage technology was very important. The control of the cereal supplies of a ward appears to have been in the hands of the occupants of the large tripartite houses. On the Aldenhoven plateau far more threshing remains were found in the yards of houses of type 1 than in those of the smaller types of houses, while the numbers of grains recovered were more or less the same. If this difference proves to be structural (*i.e.* if it is also encountered at for example Geleen-Janskamperveld), it can be regarded as indicative of unequal access to the means of production, which would further corroborate the theory regarding the structural inequality of the households within a ward. Cereal could only be harvested once a year and therefore good storage technology was needed to form a significant surplus, which could be used to obtain goods, services and partners from elsewhere. Concentrated storage enables vertical differentiation of the community.[36] As far as the LBK is concerned, a possible explanation for the clear and relatively large vertical differences could lie in the mode of existence: throughout the entire LBK period, with the possible exception of the last phase, there was an almost constant abundance of land and hence a shortage of manpower to till that land. In such a situation internal competition may be expected to have been aimed at recruiting more workers, not only from among the permanently present women, but also in the form of 'foreign workers', *i.e.* members of other groups in the neighbourhood who came to lend a hand in the field.[37] This could help to explain the equal status of men and women suggested by the grave goods: if the women tilled the fields and labour was scarce, women (and the work they did) will have been highly esteemed. Ties of kinship within the community and between neighbouring groups will also have been useful in this context (neighbourly help). Heads of families had an interest in large wards, from which more workers could be recruited than from smaller ones.[38]

RITUALS

All agrarian communities communicate with heaven and earth and with the beings inhabiting them via all kinds of rituals. Things will have been no different in the northwestern LBK area, where, leaving aside the evidence for burial rites, only few material remains of ritual acts have been found, with the possible exception of miniature pots. In the Central European LBK area earthenware statuettes of enthroned females and of domestic animals testify to a fertility cult. The skeletal remains found in the Jungfernhöhle near Tiefenellern (Bavaria) show that human sacrifices and cannibalism also played a part in the rituals.[39]

There is a considerable discrepancy between the numbers of LBK occupants and the numbers of graves. In total, some 5000 people must have inhabited the Graetheide region during the LBK period, whereas fewer than 150 graves have been found.[40] Even with due allowance for the possibility of a substantial number of shallow graves having been destroyed by ploughing, the same discrepancy was apparent along the Upper Rhine and on the Aldenhoven plateau, where the intensive systematic research carried out makes it unlikely that large numbers of graves were 'overlooked'. This leaves only one possible conclusion: by no means all of the occupants were buried in an archaeologically visible manner; most 'disappeared', for example because the survivors threw them into a river, sent them into the forest, hung them from a tree or burned them and then scattered their ashes. This kind of ritual fits in with a *Weltanschauung* based on continuity, in which the deceased and death do not affect the continuity of life. The sudden, local and short-lived custom of interring the deceased in a clearly visible manner, close to the settlement, is typical of an atmosphere of crisis. The territorial and ancestral ties are to be visualized. Moreover, in such a crisis death is more clearly felt to be a definitive end and is therefore 'rendered innocent' as in the metaphor of 'death as a journey after which life continues as before'. In this perception the grave goods can be seen as an extensive packed lunch for the journey or as the attributes that are needed to be able to show the other world who and what one is.[41]

CONTACTS WITHIN THE BANDKERAMIK WORLD

There were fairly close relationships between the hamlets within a group of settlements. These contacts were aimed at the exchange of information and manpower and not at that of products, because there were hardly any economic differences within a region. Everybody was related; with the numbers of occupants being far too small, the individual hamlets were unable to provide sufficient suitable marriage partners, like spouses in previous generations they also had to come from other hamlets.

On the Aldenhoven plateau a certain degree of specialisation and mutual dependence is apparent in the way the flint was worked. The same applies to the working of flint and the production of fine pottery on the upper reaches of the Geer. In the latter area even pots produced by one and the same potter in different settlements have been recognised, but that does not necessarily indicate specialisation: alternative interpretations could be based on mobility of the potter or of the pot on account of its contents or symbolic value. The construction of the fortifications around Darion must have involved the cooperation of the occupants of several hamlets.[42] Help from outside the small, personal ward may have been welcome in the case of more civil tasks, such as the construction of a house, because some 2500 man-hours were required for the construction of a tripartite house (type 1b).[43]

This all does not mean that the contacts within the LBK world were always peacefully. The clearest evidence for the contrary was found at Talheim (in Baden-Württemberg), where the entire population of a *Bandkeramik* village had been slaughtered with *Bandkeramik* adzes, robbed and thrown in a mass grave. Similarly, the 67 (LBK) victims of an (LBK) attack had been dumped in the ditch around their village at Aspern (Austria) without any apparent ceremonial.[44] There is also a relatively large number of graves containing (typically *Bandkeramik*) arrowheads which are to be considered the cause of death rather than grave goods: two graves of females and three of males out of a total of 113 graves in the cemetery of Elsloo are probably to be classified in this category.[45] Some scholars interpret the concentration of fortified settlements in Hesbaye, at the edge of the former LBK world, as a reaction to a hostile outside world, populated by shepherds of the Limburg group (see below) or late Mesolithic hunters.[46]

Contacts with other *Bandkeramik* groups, in different regions, were much less intensive, as appears from the clear differences in pottery decoration between, for example, the Graetheide region and the Aldenhoven plateau. In the overall LBK area all kinds of regional groups are identifiable which differ from one another not only in the development of pottery decoration, but also in the types of crops cultivated and the ratios of the various crops, in the types of tools used, in details of house construction and in the composition of the settlements. From this it can be concluded that the LBK by no means constituted a supra-regional unit, but was in fact characterised by substantial differences in behaviour, social rules and organisation. There were, however, efficient extensive networks via which raw materials, tools and ornaments, some of which possibly also having a symbolic or prestigious value, were exchanged over large distances (at least 1000 km): the occupants of areas in Germany poor in flint had obtained blanks and finished tools of Limburgian flint while adzes made of amphibolite from the Bohemian Massif or the Carpathians and basalt from the Eifel were used in the Graetheide region.[47]

EXTERNAL CONTACTS

LBK refuse pits regularly yield sherds of foreign-made, differently shaped and decorated pottery. Similar pottery is sometimes found at sites which cannot be considered LBK findspots, outside the loess zones. At present two groups of this foreign pottery are distinguished: La Hoguette and Limburg.

La Hoguette

La Hoguette pottery was described as an independent tradition in 1983.[48] Characteristic of this kind of pottery are the egg-shaped pots with pointed bases and inverted rims. They were composed from strips of clay, which was usually tempered with crushed burned bone and well fired in an oxidizing atmosphere. Some pots are decorated with cordons applied in festoons flanked by double rows of dots, impressed with the aid of a toothed spatula. As far as the decoration is concerned (but not the shape and the type of temper used), this pottery bears some resemblance to that of French offshoots of the Mediterranean Early Neolithic culture, the Cardial culture.

fig. 11.17
Sherds of La Hoguette pottery from Sweikhuizen (municipality of Geleen), 2/3 of actual size. The site lay at the edge of the Upper Terrace, which afforded a broad view across the valley of the Geleenbeek. It is one of the northernmost sites with pottery of this kind (see fig. 10.10). Sweikhuizen is moreover one of the very few sites where this type of pottery has been found independently, not associated with *Bandkeramik* finds. The site seems to have been a lookout post of the *Hoguettiens*, preceding the arrival of the *Bandkeramik* farmers.

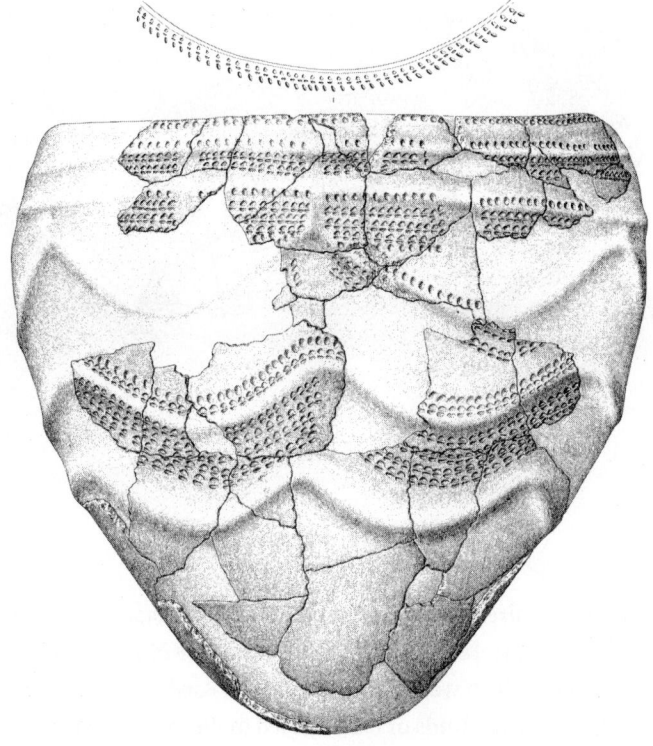

At the findspot in Normandy, from which this pottery derives its name, the
sherds had been preserved on a buried surface beneath a megalithic funerary monument. The greatest concentration, however, was found much further to the east.
To the east of the Rhine La Hoguette pottery is regularly found in refuse pits from
the Oldest LBK. In the Alsace, along the Moselle and in the Rhine-Meuse area, the
finds are not only associated with the Old LBK, but also with later material. One La
Hoguette findspot lies, high above the Geleenbeek, within sight of a *Bandkeramik*
settlement, near Sweikhuizen (municipality of Schinnen, fig. 11.17).[49]

Virtually nothing is known about the people who used La Hoguette pottery. The
lack of concrete evidence for crop cultivation in permanent settlements led some
researchers to regard them as 'hunters or shepherds with pottery' who had become
acquainted with the new technology in the southwest, in the area of the aforementioned southern French Neolithic culture.[50] The shapes of the pots themselves, in
particular the curious egg-shaped bases (fig. 11.18), resemble those of the oldest
pottery of several other groups with a transitional economy between purely hunting and gathering and a full agrarian existence (such as Ertebølle, Swifterbant,
Dümmer). They suggest a different, more limited range of functions than that of
the more varied pottery of agriculturists. Discoveries made in the zoo of Stuttgart-
Bad Cannstatt seem to support this hypothesis. There, in a well-sealed context, La
Hoguette pottery was for the first time found together with settlement refuse from
its makers. The first analysis revealed a predominance of domesticated sheep/goat
in the bone spectrum and a lack of cattle and pig bones. The flint-working method
used and the type of flint arrowheads bear resemblance to those of the Late Mesolithic culture of southern Germany. The same applies to a few fragments of harpoons of deer antler.[51]

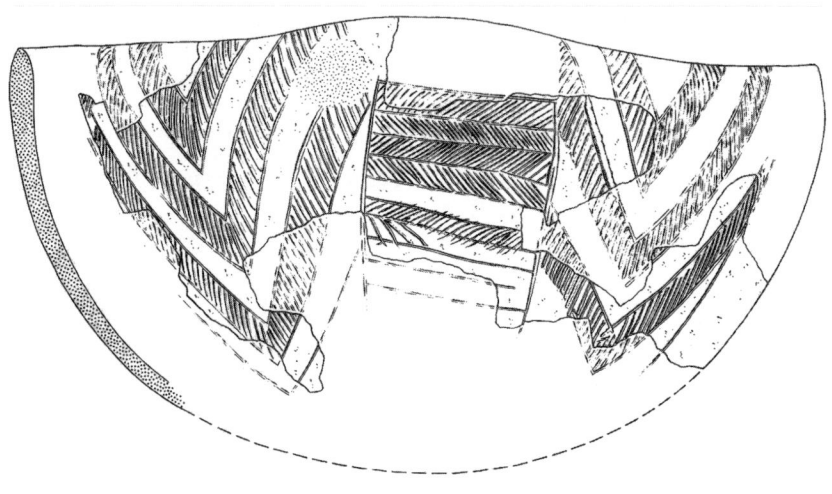

fig. 11.19
Large bowl of Limburg pottery from
Kesseleik on the bank of the Meuse in middle
Limburg. Scale 1:4. This site was chosen
as eponymous for this type of pottery on
account of the fact that the vessel was not
associated with *Bandkeramik* finds, in spite
of the findspot's marginal position in the
distribution area (fig. 10.10).

Limburg pottery

Limburg pottery had already been recognised as *Fremdkörper* and termed 'Import-gruppe I' by Buttler and Haberey in their excavation of Köln-Lindenthal. Finds recovered in Kesseleik, which were the first outside a *Bandkeramik* context, although without any accompanying finds or features, led to the presentation of this pottery as an independent tradition in 1970 (fig. 11.19).[52]

Limburg pottery was also composed from strips of clay tempered with crushed burned bone and also has a yellow/brown/red colour. However, the fabric is much softer and more brittle than that of La Hoguette (and LBK) pottery. Characteristic of Limburg pottery are tall, open bowls and large open dishes with rims thickened on the inside. The incised decoration covers the entire area of the pot and often consists of hatched zigzag bands or rectangles, sometimes combined with herringbone patterns or horizontal triangles. An interesting example was found at Geleen-Haesselderveld, where an otherwise empty pit contained a *Bandkeramik* adze and an intact pot of Limburg pottery; the pit was probably a grave. *Bandkeramik* contexts, both Old and Young, including Limburg pottery have only been encountered to the west of the Rhine, in an area extending into northern France.[53]

fig. 11.20
Besides thousands of purely Mesolithic
artefacts, the Late Mesolithic Weelde-
Paardsdrank site also yielded arrowheads
bearing a slight or strong resemblance to
those of the more or less contemporary early
Bandkeramik. Were they obtained through
exchange, gathered or imitated, or were
things indeed the other way round and did
the western *Bandkeramik* people borrow the
shape of their arrowheads from that of their
Mesolithic neighbours?

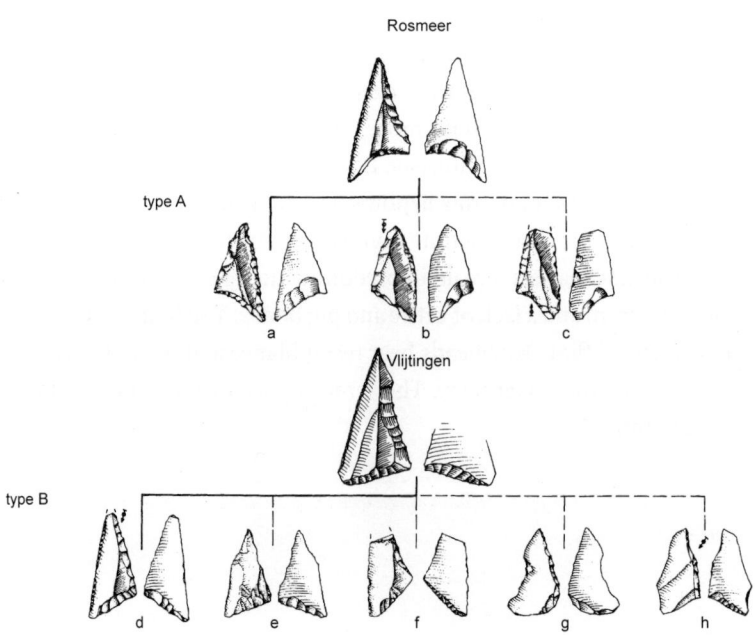

The discussion about the place and the meaning of the two pottery traditions is by no means concluded. The latter is for example apparent from finds recovered at Gassel: the sherds were originally published as Limburg pottery but in the meantime identified as La Hoguette pottery. However, they also bear a striking resemblance to finds recently discovered at Wettolsheim-Ricoh (Alsace), which are associated with a newly defined 'Rhone Valley Early Neolithic culture'. The place of two pot fragments from Ede which bear some resemblance to the latter finds is also still unclear.[54]

As long as the virtual lack of well-dated, closed assemblages outside the context of LBK settlements persists, we can really only speculate about the relations between the LBK, La Hoguette and Limburg traditions. This is particularly unfortunate because a whole range of interesting questions concerning the contact finds awaits answers: Were traditions like La Hoguette and Limburg indigenous, i.e. acculturation phenomena, or were they imported by migrants? Was La Hoguette already present to the east of the Rhine when the fully Neolithic way of life started to be adopted there? Were there at that time already Hoguettiens to the west of the Meuse, too, or did they (or only their way of life?) not reach areas so far north until later? Did they play an active part in introducing the Neolithic way of life to the loess zones? What part did this group play in the LBK's contacts with the southwest (apparent from the use of poppy seed)? May we regard the use of a toothed spatula in the youngest northwestern LBK as inherited from La Hoguette? What relations existed between the La Hoguette and Limburg traditions? Was the latter a product of the former or were they independent developments?[55]

The relations with nearby Mesolithic hunter-gatherers are also still unclear. All that we do know is that *Bandkeramik* adzes and allegedly *Bandkeramik* arrowheads are occasionally encountered at findspots that also yield Mesolithic finds (fig. 11.20).[56] In view of the fairly great differences in the two modes of existence we may perhaps not expect much more: what was there to offer one another besides the odd daughter, some game or a basket of cereal?[57]

THE ORIGINS OF THE LBK

The presumed great age of the aforementioned exchange networks leads to a closer consideration of, on the one hand, the origins of the *Bandkeramik* way of life or tradition and, on the other, the *Bandkeramik* people.

Until recently, the LBK people were generally regarded as colonists from the region of the Starčevo-Körös-Criş complex in the northern Balkans, which had already adopted the Neolithic way of life some time earlier. It was believed that the pioneer situation in an uninhabited area with land in plenty for all encouraged a very rapid population growth, which was not absorbed by expanding existing settlements but by founding subsidiary settlements, as also happened in the Wild West in the 19th century.[58]

There are certain problems attached to this hypothesis. Firstly, there are only some 100-150 years between the earliest dates obtained for Central Europe and the Flomborn phase in the west. This means that the migrants must have covered a distance of 1000 km, from Transdanubia (Hungary) to the Meuse, within four to six generations. A maximum nett population growth figure of 3% per year has been documented for groups in comparable situations; in that case the population doubles every generation and there is a sufficient surplus for new settlements.

However, even under these conditions the theoretical distance of 150-250 km between each primary and subsidiary settlement and the implied purposiveness of the movements are rather inconceivable. Secondly, in research on *Bandkeramik* skeletons, physical anthropologists have found a great genetic heterogeneity, which is difficult to reconcile with the migration model.[59] Thirdly, mass migrations are no longer popular as explanatory models, particularly when coupled with the idea of *Ex Oriente Lux* (see chapter 10):[60] for virtually all other cultural changes in the past acculturation/adaptation appears to provide a more satisfying explanation.

In the past years an alternative explanation has been proposed, which solves many of these problems.[61] According to this interpretation, the LBK is an independent culture representing the transition to an agrarian way of life, based on ideas and knowledge derived from nearby Neolithic communities in the Balkans, of the local 'late Mesolithic' population of a large area in Central Europe, namely that area where traces of the Oldest LBK phase are encountered. This transition was a very gradual process, following a general trend in the Mesolithic towards a greater proportion of plant food, less mobility and expansion of the settlements. The adaptation may also have taken a long time (even some 500 years has been suggested) but there is as yet no chronological evidence to either support or contradict this: the Early Neolithic did not become archaeologically visible until people with LBK pottery started digging LBK pits and constructing LBK houses. It is certain that the development was slow at first, with a gradual increase in population and little change in pottery decoration and in the range of types. Infilling of and expansion in all directions from this large area of origin did not take place until in a later phase (Flomborn). In the west, a third expansion phase, in which Hainault and northern France were reached, was to follow in the Younger LBK.

Several arguments can be adduced to support this interesting hypothesis: when we compare the Oldest LBK with the culture of the Neolithic neighbours in the Balkans we see that the Oldest LBK shows an independent development of precisely non-functional elements like pottery decoration and the grouping of people in houses and of houses within settlements. The technology and the arrowheads (the hunting weapons) of the oldest flint industry (as for example encountered in Bruchenbrücken in Hessen)[62] show Mesolithic elements, whereas the material culture associated with the new way of life was adopted unaltered, or at most adjusted to the different environment and different climatic conditions. The main crops (including field weeds) and domestic animals are the same as those in the Balkans, just like the harvesting and woodworking implements and the principles of house construction; this hypothesis has also been used to determine the origins of the pottery types and the basic form of decoration, but the question is: how many possible alternatives are there? In the Oldest LBK settlements the quantitative composition of the range of crops and domestic animals was not uniform. This can be explained by experimentation with a new technology.[63] Agriculture might have become attractive for these people because of a presumed drastic change in the climate and vegetation. At the present stage of research it is not possible to make a definitive choice between the two models: migration or acculturation.

However, we believe there is no reason to opt for acculturation instead of migration as an explanatory model for the Flomborn phase. The entire material culture was exported as a ready-made package and relations with relatives in the home country were maintained for generations via exchange networks. This would explain the small regional differences at first. Moreover, in this phase

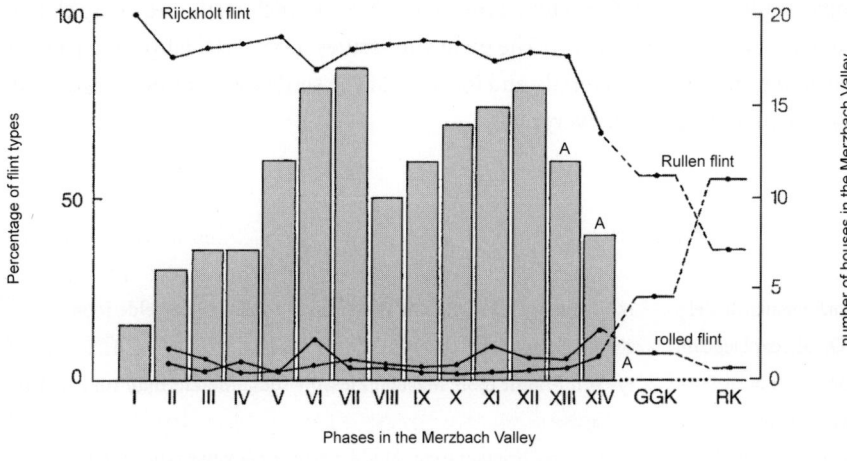

fig. 11.21

Development of the population density in the Merzbachtal on the Aldenhovener Platte: the number of simultaneously occupied houses initially increased steadily until phase VIII, which saw a first abrupt decline followed by new growth. The population density decreased rapidly from phase XIII onwards. By the end of the occupation period the valley was devoid of houses and contained only an earthwork. Also indicated is the ratio of the three types of flint used in the different phases.

GGK = Großgartach Kultur
RK = Rössen Kultur

we do seem to recognise the characteristics typical of the arrival of pioneers, *i.e.* rapid population growth and rapid expansion over and infilling of a large area.[64] In this case the distance from the area of origin to the Graetheide region was only 200 km. It is quite conceivable that the pioneers had already become acquainted with the new areas beforehand, while grazing their cattle in peripheral areas, searching for raw materials like flint, or possibly also via traditional exchange networks.[65]

CRISIS AND CHANGE

For generations the LBK farmers managed to keep going, undefeated by the precariousness of their farming existence. In the area under consideration they successfully overcame at least one crisis. In the Merzbachtal (and possibly also at Elsloo) this crisis is apparent from a sudden decrease in the number of farm houses around the transition from the Old to the Young LBK (fig. 11.21).[66] The number of settlements peaked in phases IIc and IId in both regions. After that the Graetheide region appears to have been suddenly abandoned. The Aldenhoven plateau was depopulated in a more gradual and less definitive manner. The succeeding Großgartach and Rössen settlements, however, show a preference for a different kind of location, on the upper reaches of streams and at the centres of plateaux.[67] It is possible that the final crisis was already foreshadowed in phase IIc, by a disturbance in the traditional exchange networks: in that period the occupants of the Aldenhoven plateau had difficulties in obtaining flint. In the Graetheide region a relative decrease in the amount of Rijckholt flint is apparent, while the amphibolite used as raw material for the adzes was partly replaced by quartzite and lydite from Belgium.[68] The literature mentions numerous possible (partial) causes of the crisis, for example exhaustion of the soil, deforestation (resulting in a shortage of structural timber and firewood), severe drought, social unrest due to overpopulation, increasing tension due to hierarchical tendencies, pressure from outside (remember the fortifications and the earthworks) or an epidemic.

This crisis was not a pan-*Bandkeramik* phenomenon: further to the southwest the LBK continued and may have integrated with the Limburg group, from which the Blicquy and all kinds of late *Bandkeramik* and post-*Bandkeramik* groups may have evolved in northern France. In Central and eastern Europe changes in LBK pottery and houses that were so substantial as to be indicative of new archaeological cultures, like Hinkelstein, Großgartach, *Stichbandkeramik* and Lengyel, had already taken place earlier on. The great similarities in material culture, means of existence, use of raw materials and location of the settlements indicate a gradual change in those areas, however.[69]

NOTES

1 From the German: *Linearbandkeramik* or *Linienbandkeramik*; in Belgium it is often still called Omalien, after the site Omal near Liège in Hesbaye, or (like in France) *Rubané*; in England the term Linear Pottery Culture (LPC) is sometimes used instead of the loan word from German; in older literature it is often still referred to as Danubian (*Danubien, Donauländisch*), a term which refers to the assumed region of origin.

2 Fundamental, general literature: Bakels/Lüning 1990; De Grooth/ Verwers 1984; Lüning 1988a, 1988b; Lüning/Stehli 1989; Modderman 1985, 1988.

3 Bakels 1978 and chapter 14.

4 Geleen: Waterbolk 1958-'59; Sittard: Modderman 1958-'59; Elsloo, Stein: Modderman 1970; Geleen-Janskamperveld: Louwe Kooijmans *et al.* 1992, 2003; Schute 1992.

5 Cahen *et al.* 1985; Jadin/Cahen 1992; Keeley/Cahen 1989.

6 Boelicke *et al.* 1988a; Dohrn-Ihmig 1983b; Kuper *et al.* 1977; Lüning 1982a; Stehli 1989a.

7 Bakels 1978b, 1982a; Bogucki 1984; Kalis/Zimmermann 1988; Louwe Kooijmans 1998; Wansleeben 1987.

8 Breunig 1985, 1987; Lüning 1988b. A series of seven recent ^{14}C dates obtained for a settlement from the Oldest LBK phase at Bruchenbrücken (Hessen) indeed centres around a date that appears to be slightly earlier than the western dates: between 5400 and 5200 BC (Gronenborn 1990b). In a recent, critical review of the available radiocarbon dates a shorter duration for the Dutch LBK is opted for: 5230-5000 instead of the traditional dating to 5300-4900 BC (Lanting/van der Plicht 1999-2000).

9 Dohrn-Ihmig 1973, 1979; Meier-Arendt 1966; Modderman 1970.

10 The Old LBK is known as the Flomborn phase, after a cemetery near Worms (Germany).

11 Schmidt 1992; Weiner 1992a, 1992b.

12 Boelicke 1988a, 1988c; Modderman 1970; Von Brandt 1988.

13 Bernhardt 1986; Buttler/Haberey 1936; Keeley/Cahen 1989; Louwe Kooijmans 1993b; Lüning 1988a; Modderman 1958-'59; Schwellnus 1983.

14 Boelicke *et al.* 1988b; Stehli 1982, 1989a, 1989b; Van de Velde 1979a, 1979b.Van de Velde and Stehli use different approaches. Stehli first used *seriation* and later *correspondence analysis*, Van de Velde uses *principal components analysis* (which somewhat resembles correspondence analysis). The basic data also differ: Stehli uses what is essentially a more complex version of Modderman's pragmatic chronotypology, while Van de Velde uses a newly developed logically consistent (aprioristic) system of classification. The two researchers' results are to a great extent comparable.

15 Extensive references in Modderman 1988; Van de Velde 1995.

16 Bakels 1978; De Grooth/Verwers 1984.

17 Von Brandt 1988; Masuch/Ziessow 1985; Modderman 1972; Startin 1978.

18 Meyer-Christian 1976; Modderman 1970; Von Brandt 1988.

19 This flint is generally referred to as Rijckholt flint, after the location of the Middle Neolithic flint mines which exploited the same flint seams (see feature E).

20 Cahen *et al.* 1986; Van Gijn 1990; De Groot 1987b; Zimmermann 1988.

21 Arps 1990; Bakels 1987; Schneider & Schwarz-Mackesen 1983. Lydite and phtanite are synonyms for a dense silicoclastic type of rock.

22 Weiner 1992a.

23 Van Gijn 1990.

24 Dohrn-Ihmig 1974; Sainty *et al.* 1983; Stehli/Zimmermann 1980.

25 Bourdieu 1972; Braudel 1966; Hillier/Hanson 1984.

26 Bakels 1978, 1982a with additions. Two newly discovered early sites, however, testify that the 'interior' of the Graetheide was reclaimed in an early stage as well (Hendrix 1999; Van de Velde/Bakels 2002).

27 Keeley/Cahen 1989; Lüning 1988b; Modderman 1988.

28 Bernhardt 1986; Lüning 1982; Lüning/Stehli 1989; Modderman 1988; Stehli 1989a; Van de Velde 1979b, 1990.

29 Dohrn-Ihmig 1983b; De Grooth 1987; Storch 1985; Van de Velde 1979a, 1997.

30 Van de Velde 1976, 1979a, 1979b.

31 Bakels 1982a, 39; Modderman 1985, 74-79; Van de Velde 1979b, 140, 150.

32 Birdsell 1973; Kosse 1990; Wobst 1976.

33 These percentages can be inferred from the calculations in De Grooth/Verwers 1984: 30-32. See also Bakels 1978, 1992; Startin 1978.

34 Louwe Kooijmans *et al.* 2003.

35 Boelicke *et al.* 1988a, 1988b; Stehli 1989a; Van de Velde 1990.

36 Bakels 1982b, 1992c; Boelicke 1982, 1988a; Testart 1982.

37 Chapman 1988.

38 As far as the description of heads of families is concerned, two distinctions are important: formal versus informal power and matrilineage versus patrilineage. Formal power is exerted by the person who, according to tradition, is entitled to it: the head of the family. Informal power is the power of a person who actually exerts this power, if necessary indirectly (via the head of the family). In the ethnographic literature it is almost always men who are credited with the formal power over families; this is by no means true of informal

power. With matrilinearity descent is traced through the maternal line and the brothers of the oldest women formally act as head of the family. With patrilinearity descent is traced through the paternal line and the oldest man is the titular head. Both 'oldest' and 'family' are moreover manipulatable notions: some relationships may be emphasized, others concealed; in this way informal power can often be made to coincide with formal power.

39 Höckmann 1972; Wamser 1980; also Van de Velde 1995.

40 In addition to Elsloo a cemetery is presumed by Modderman (1970, 78) at Stein, while three graves have actually been found at Geleen-Haesselderveld (Vromen 1982). A second cemetery has been discovered and excavated on the Aldenhovener Platte as well (Graiewski/Rupprecht 2001).

41 Charbonnier 1961; Criado Boado 1989; Lévi-Strauss 1962.

42 Van Berg 1987b; Cahen et al. 1990; Jadin 1990; Zimmermann 1982.

43 De Grooth/Verwers 1984, 30-31; Startin 1978.

44 Wahl & König 1987; Windl 1996.

45 Van de Velde 1979a, 1979b.

46 Cahen et al. 1990.

47 Bakels 1983, 1987a; De Grooth 1990; Lech 1990; Willms 1985; Zimmermann 1991.

48 Jeunesse 1986; see also: Brounen and Vromen 1990; Jeunesse 1987; Lüning et al. 1989; Van Berg 1990. For the northwestern Cardium culture see e.g. Roussot-Larroque 1990.

49 Van Geel 1980; Modderman 1987; Van Berg 1987a.

50 Van Berg 1990; Jeunesse et al. 1991.

51 Schütz et al. 1991; Strien/Tillmann 2001.

52 Modderman 1970, 1974.

53 Van Berg 1990; Constantin 1985; Cahen et al. 1981-'82.

54 Van Berg 1990; Brounen/De Jong 1988; Jeunesse et al. 1991; Schut 1988.

55 Aimé/Jeunesse 1986; Cziesla 1992.

56 Gronenborn 1990b; Vermeersch 1990; Wansleeben/Verhart 1990.

57 Verhart 2000.

58 Ammermann/Cavalli-Sforza 1973; Bogucki 1988; Hamond 1981; Hodder 1990; Kreuz 1991; Whittle 1985.

59 Modderman 1988, 128-130.

60 It should be commented here that the search, at all costs, for an indigenous development can lead to something smacking of nationalism.

61 Bakels/Lüning 1990; Lüning 1988a; Lüning/Stehli 1989.

62 Gronenborn 1990a.

63 Kreuz 1991.

64 Mesolithic population densities are about 10-200 times lower than Early Neolithic ones (Butzer 1971). Expansion and infilling of the occupied area through autonomous growth at a maximum (average) percentage of 3% per year would require between four and ten generations, or between 100 and 300 years. The growth of the number of settlements in some regions (by a factor of 70) reported by Lüning (1988, 38, 48) and his assumed duration of the Oldest LBK (500 years) are in the same order of magnitude. These observations describe a kind of demographic limiting symptoms (not conditions) for this phase.

nett growth	time required for doubling	time required for a 10-fold increase in density	time required for a 200-fold increase in density
3%	25	100	200
2%	35	140	300
1%	70	280	600
0.5%	140	560	1200

65 In Hessen 'western' flint types were already being used in the Oldest LBK; cf. Gronenborn 1990a, 1990b.

66 Lüning 1988b, 63.

67 Schwellnus 1983.

68 Bakels 1987a; De Grooth 1987b; Zimmermann 1988.

69 Bogucki 1988; Kruk 1980; Starling 1985.

E   Mines in the marl
The flint extraction at Rijckholt

Marjorie de Grooth

Introduction

The Neolithic saw an increase in the demand for good-quality raw materials for axes to be used for felling trees and for woodworking. In the Early Neolithic, the period of the *Linearbandkeramik* and Rössen cultures, polished adzes and axes made from scarce tenacious rocks such as amphibolite, basalt and lydite were transported to the Netherlands over large distances. The people of the Michelsberg culture showed a preference for axes made from flint, a raw material that was available in large quantities in the chalk deposits of south Limburg and Belgium.

The first flint axes that were produced in the aforementioned regions, examples of which have been found at the settlement sites of Thieusies in Hainault, were very simple tools whose cutting edges were produced by means of two intersecting flaking negatives. Sometimes the cutting edge was resharpened by striking off new flakes. Very soon, however, more carefully polished axes started to be produced that had cutting edges that stayed sharp for a longer time.[1] The main characteristics of these 'western' Neolithic axes are their oval cross-sections and their narrow tips.

The earliest axes had been made from nodules that had been simply picked up from the surface, where they lay exposed in secondary contexts, for example in alluvial and colluvial deposits and in clay-with-flints. The flint implements of the Michelsberg culture, however, are the results of a more intensive, large-scale exploitation of flint resources. The representatives of this culture also used less accessible 'fresh' flint from chalk deposits deep beneath the surface, which, depending on the geological situation, was obtained via open-cast mining, for example on the Lousberg near Aachen just across the German border, or via shaft mining. This was of course not a regional development: throughout the Neolithic and the Bronze Age flint was mined all over Europe at sites where it was found to be of good quality. Well-known extraction sites are for example Krzemionki in Poland, Grimes Graves, Cissbury and Harrow Hill in England, Jablines, St.-Mihiel and Le Grand-Pressigny in France and Spiennes, Obourg and Jandrain-Jandrenouille in Belgium.[2]

At many sites in southern Limburg large amounts of waste material in the immediate vicinity of flint resources indicate that flint was systematically exploited in this area. Flakes that are entirely or largely covered with cortex, abandoned blanks, useless cores and nodules that were apparently considered unfit for use have been found at for example Banholt, Cadier-en-Keer, Mheer, Simpelveld and at several sites near Valkenburg (plate 16A). Evidence for flint mining has been found at Valkenburg, where shafts with short galleries were investigated in 1991 and 1992,[3] and near Rijckholt in particular.

The mines of Rijckholt-Sint-Geertruid (plate 15)

Since 1881 research has been carried out on the evidence for the exploitation and working of flint observed between Rijckholt and Sint-Geertruid, on the slopes between the Meuse terrace and the loess plateau, which are now covered with the forest Savelsbos, and on the plateau itself (fig. E1). For many years the research concentrated on the two most conspicuous discoveries made in this area: what is known as the Grand Atelier, a quarry of some two thousand square metres which was gradually filled up with an approximately 1.5-m-thick layer of waste, and the marl walls of the Schoone Grub, a deep dry valley, in which the entrances to short galleries were visible. In 1964 an investigation by the *Biologisch-Archaeologisch Instituut* of the University of Groningen supervised by Professor Waterbolk revealed the existence of shafts too. Unfortunately it appeared to be impossible to investigate the shafts, some of which were twelve metres deep, by means of the usual archaeological excavation methods, starting from their entrances at the surface.

A group of amateur archaeologists with professional mining expertise came up with a solution. With an official permit to 'reuse a prehistoric flint mine' the members of the Prehistoric Flint Mining study group dug a tunnel with a length of over 150 m into the marl at a level at which, on the basis of the results of the research carried out by Van Giffen, they expected to encounter prehistoric galleries. A total of 73 shafts with radiating galleries were investigated in this underground excavation, in which an area of some 3000 m² was covered (figs. E2-3). The excavators discovered that the prehistoric miners had concentrated on the best-quality flint. This was to be found in flint seam 10 in the Lanaye Chalk, which forms part of the Upper Cretaceous Gulpen formation.

The shafts ranged from 1 to 1.5 metres in diameter and varied in depth from 4 metres on the slope to 12 metres on the

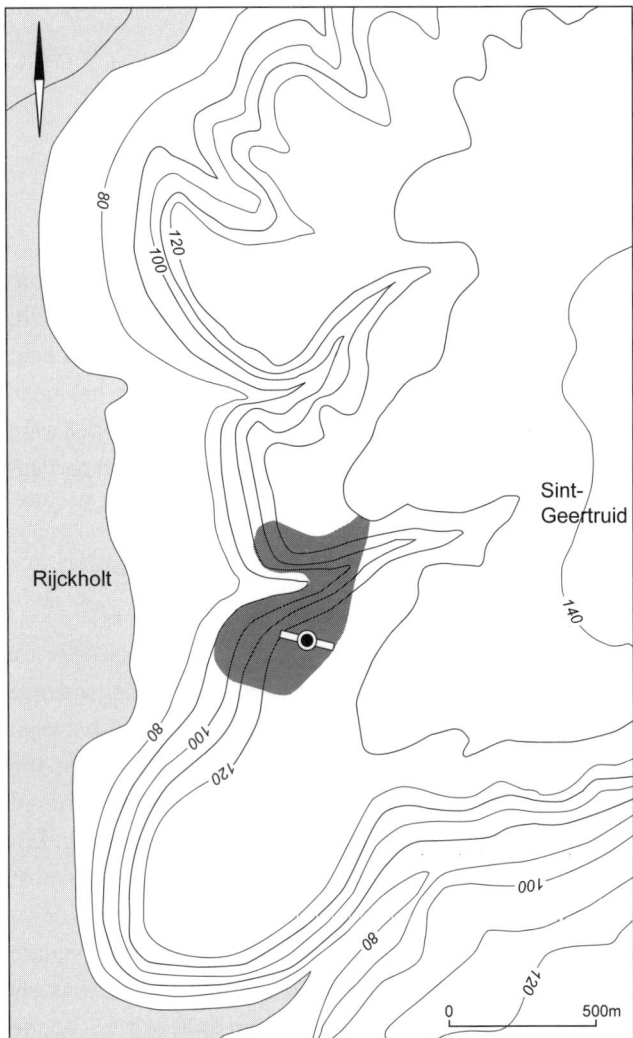

fig. E1
Situation of the mining field at both sides of the small and narrow valley called 'Schoone Grub', between the villages of Rijckholt on the edge of the Meuse valley floor (grey) and Sint-Geertruid on the terrace plateau. Indicated are the constructed tunnel and the location of the illustrated plan (fig. E2). Scale 1:25,000.

plateau (fig. E4). The distance from the floor to the ceiling of the galleries was 60-80 centimetres, which, when compared with the average height of some recent coal-mine galleries, is not as little as it may seem. The flint nodules were situated approximately midway between the floor and the ceiling. The main mining implement was a pick with a flint axehead set in a wooden handle. The manufacture of the wooden handle will have been a fairly time-consuming task but the flint axeheads could be made in less than no time above the ground. An axehead that was found to be too blunt for further use was therefore not sharpened underground but was discarded and replaced by a new one. More than 10,000 of such worn axeheads were found during the excavation (plate 15C). Antler picks and heavy stone hammers (*Schlägel*) were used only rarely at Rijckholt.

Exhausted galleries and shafts were backfilled with rubble from new galleries. At some points a stretch of gallery between two mines had been left open to serve as an escape route or as a ventilation channel.[4] There were no indications of artificial lighting, such as traces of soot or large amounts of charcoal; presumably the daylight coming from the shafts was sufficient to enable the miners to distinguish between the dark hard flint and the light-coloured soft chalk. The excavators were impressed by the very safe and efficient mining techniques of their prehistoric predecessors. It is estimated that there were some 2000 mines in the Rijckholt area. The area of the investigated mines ranges from 5 to 56 m², with an average of about 25 m². This average mine will have yielded an estimated 8000 kg of flint. Calculations based on experimental results suggest that it will have taken a team of three miners about a month to exploit a mine of that size.[5]

The tremendous amounts of debitage found at the surface of the mines and in their immediate surroundings suggest that the initial shaping of the tools was done at the site of the mines. Further away from the mines, at distances of one day travel by foot or more, only finished tools and blanks have been found: axes and long, retouched *Spitzklingen* or 'daggers' but also larger blades and flakes on which all kinds of tools could be made, such as knives, scrapers and arrowheads.

Period of use

It is difficult to determine the exact period of use of the mines because virtually no pottery or other datable finds were found at the site. Some ¹⁴C dates obtained for samples from the western part of the mining site lie between 5090 ± 40 BP and 5000 ± 40 BP, i.e. between approximately 3940 and 3750 BC, which is around the beginning of phase III of the Michelsberg culture. In 1923 Van Giffen found a base fragment of a vessel produced by the Stein group, datable to between 3500 and 2600 BC, in a shaft on the plateau, in the eastern part of the mining site, where the deepest mines had been sunk. The contexts from which some of the finished flint products have been recovered confirm the time range that can be inferred from the above evidence: flint implements have been found among the remains of Michelsberg settlements at sites situated up to about 180 kilometres from the mines, in the valley of the Meuse, in the German Rhineland, in the river area in the east of the Netherlands and in Westphalia, also in Germany. Some of the flint recovered from Hazendonk contexts in the river area in the west of the Netherlands probably came from Rijckholt, too, although the possibility that it came from Spiennes in Belgium cannot be excluded: it is not (yet) possible to

RIJCKHOLT

shaft with the serial number of the mine

inaccessible connection, known as a 'breach'

sink hole, filled with terrace gravel

chalk, not mined

tectonic fault

0   5m

fig. E2

Plan of a part of the investigated mine galleries at Rijckholt / Sint-Geertruid.

fig. E3
One of the galleries during the excavation. The lumps of dark flint are
clearly visible in the wall. The chalk pillar served as a buttress.

distinguish between these two types of flint. Mined flint of
the Rijckholt type has also been found at the few sites that
have so far been identified as settlements of the Stein group
of the Vlaardingen culture. Rijckholt flint continued to be
transported over large distances in the Middle Neolithic period B as we know from the blades of flint of the Rijckholt
type that have been found in a number of stone cists of the
Wartberg group in Westphalia and Hessen that are dated to
that period. The above evidence leads to the conclusion that
flint was mined at Rijckholt for at least 500 years, possibly
even 1300 years. With an estimated total of 2000 mines this
means that at most four and at least two mines must have
been exploited per year.[6]

The different kinds of raw materials encountered in settlements show that flint was being mined at several sites
at more or less the same time. The Michelsberg settlement

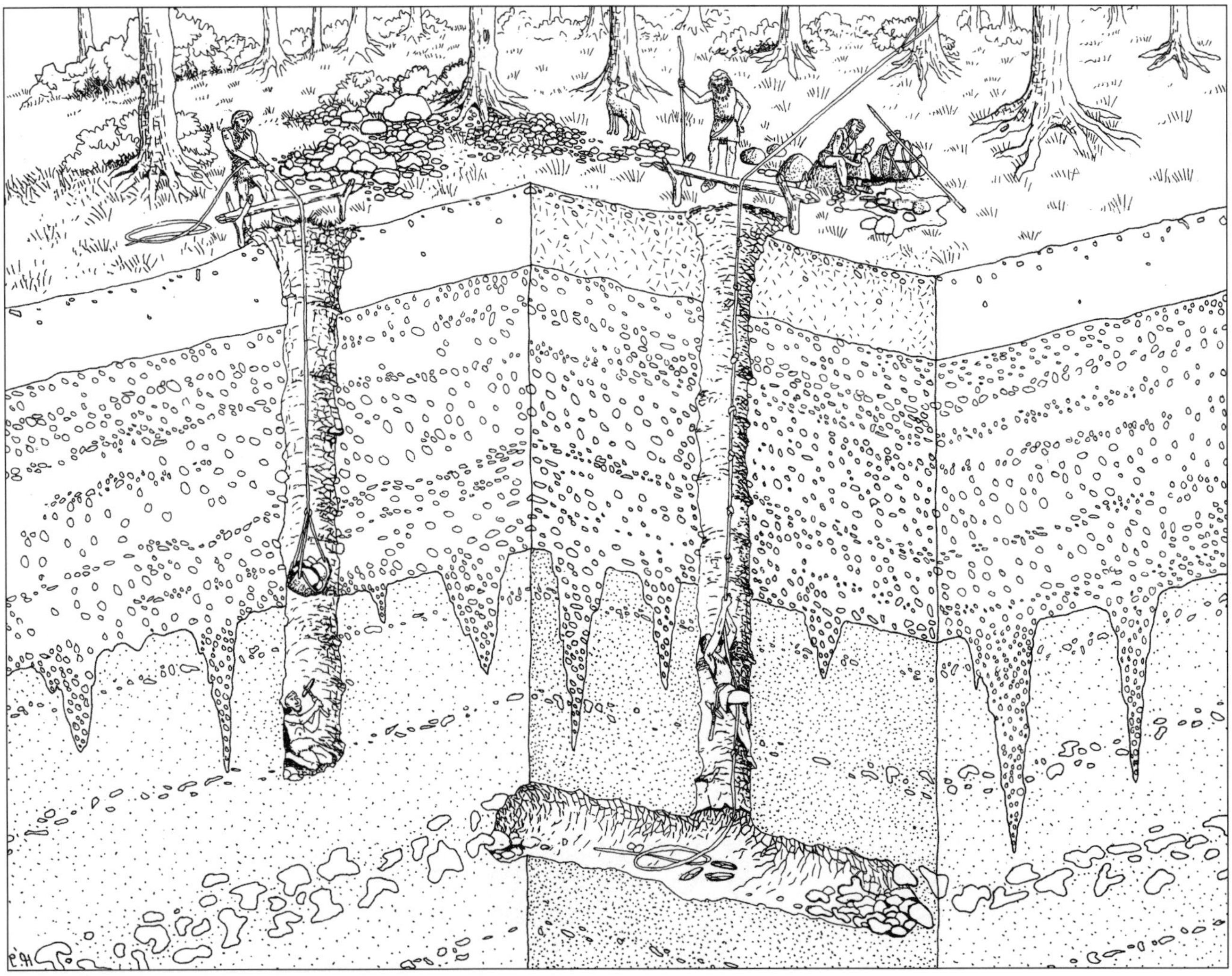

fig. E4
Two mine shafts in production. The shafts have been dug through the cover of terrace gravel and measure only 1
m in cross-section. The galleries are less than 1 m high, which means that the miners had to work in a recumbent
posture. A mining team consisted of no more than three miners. The extensive mining field is the outcome of
many centuries of such a small-scale exploitation.

Kraaienberg, near Groot Linden, in the river area in the east of the Netherlands, for example, yielded mined flint from Rijckholt as well as flint obtained from other extraction sites in south Limburg and in the adjoining part of Belgium (fig. E5).[7]

Exploitation and distribution

Several different models have been developed for the ways in which the flint was exploited and distributed. Unfortunately, our insufficient knowledge of the socio-economic structures of the groups involved and the fact that different mechanisms are often indistinguishable in the archaeological record make it impossible for us to say at this stage which of these models applies to Rijckholt.

Some researchers assume that the mines were accessible to anyone and that the users of distant regions mined their own flint. Others are of the opinion that the flint was mined and worked by a group of local professional full-time miners who exchanged their products on the spot for basic food products. As far as the available evidence is concerned, both options are possible. Miners from distant regions could have done some knapping at the site of the mines to lighten the burden to be transported back to their settlements. Without a trademark, flint axes and blades can tell us nothing about the relations between producers and consumers. However, the territoriality reflected by the earth works of the Michelsberg culture and the distinct regionalism of the Michelsberg culture, Wartberg-Stein-Vlaardingen complex and Seine-Oise-Marne culture make the option of free access less likely. On the other hand, full-time specialists do not fit in with our current concept of the socio-economic structure of these societies. Moreover, it would have been rather difficult for a full-time miner to provide a living for himself in lean years when there were sufficient alternative sources of flint available to the consumers.

It is most likely that the flint was mined on a part-time, seasonal basis by local groups of miners, whose products were distributed via a down-the-line exchange system. We do not know of any durable commodities for which the flint products may have been exchanged but besides brides there is a whole range of perishable goods imaginable that may have appealed to the occupants of the ecologically fairly unvaried loess regions, such as salt, sealskin cloaks, caviar and smoked sea fish.

Good examples of this model are known from ethnographic studies of groups that exploited flint or other rocks in comparable socio-economic systems. In many of these cases mining was not just an economic activity, but connected with all kinds of rituals. And the products of this activity were not always regarded or traded as mere utilitarian commodities.

fig. E5
Three fitting blades of mined Rijckholt flint with fresh cortex, as found in a Michelsberg culture settlement site on the so-called Kraaienberg, near Groot-Linden, more than 100 km to the north of the flint mines. Scale 1:2.

For example, in some areas axes were highly valued parts of dowries and in others long-distance expeditions to special extraction sites formed part of initiation rites. There are indications that similar non-material factors played a part in the mining and distribution of flint in the Neolithic. For example, a skull (without the lower jaw) was found to have been carefully deposited behind a wall at the end of one of the galleries of Rijckholt. Secondly, much time and effort appears to have been spent on trimming some axes to a degree of perfection which (in our opinion!) would not have been required for normal use. Some of these axes are moreover too large for normal use; they can only have been made by highly skilled experts. Such showpieces are definitely to be interpreted as prestige objects.

Notes

1   Vermeersch 1980.

2   Weisgerber *et al.* 1980.

3   Brounen/Ploegaert 1992; Brounen 1995a.

4   A 'mine' is here understood to be one shaft and the galleries radiating from it.

5   Felder 1980.

6   Calculations adjusted on the basis of a corrected extent of the mined area. See also De Grooth 1991 with an extensive bibliography.

7   Louwe Kooijmans/Verhart 1990.

8 Two volumes of the final publication of the investigations of the Rijckholt mines have appeared since this feature was closed: Felder et al. 1998 and Rademakers 1998, with a survey of all flint exploitation points in the southern part of Limburg (Felder 1998).

12 Hunters become farmers
Early Neolithic B and Middle
Neolithic A

Leendert Louwe Kooijmans

INTRODUCTION

The end of the *Bandkeramik* culture was followed by a long period for which we have less complete and less abundant evidence of the activities of the farmers on the loess. Our understanding of the northern communities, on the contrary, is constantly improving, thanks especially to the evidence from the wetland sites in the western coastal plain.

This long period was characterised by a high degree of interaction and exchange: the exchange of goods and, inevitably, also knowledge and ideas. The influence of the 'southerners' in the north is clearly visible in the archaeological record: the hunter-gatherers gradually borrowed the farmers' material equipment, including their pottery, axes and querns, and augmented their subsistence system with crop cultivation and stock keeping. This has been called the 'Neolithisation process'. To what extent these contacts were conversely responsible for the drastic changes that took place in the farming settlements on the loess is difficult to say, but they were certainly an influential factor.[1]

As recently as the 1950s our knowledge of this entire period was still exclusively based on evidence from sites on the loess in Belgium and the German Rhineland; the only site known in the Dutch part of the loess belt were the Rijckholt flint mines. The northern plain was *terra incognita*, except for the site of Hüde I on the peat surrounding lake Dümmer.[2] The following survey is based entirely on discoveries and research over the past forty years.

Almost all of our knowledge of this period is based on settlement sites and on stray finds which can be dated to this period on typological grounds, in particular

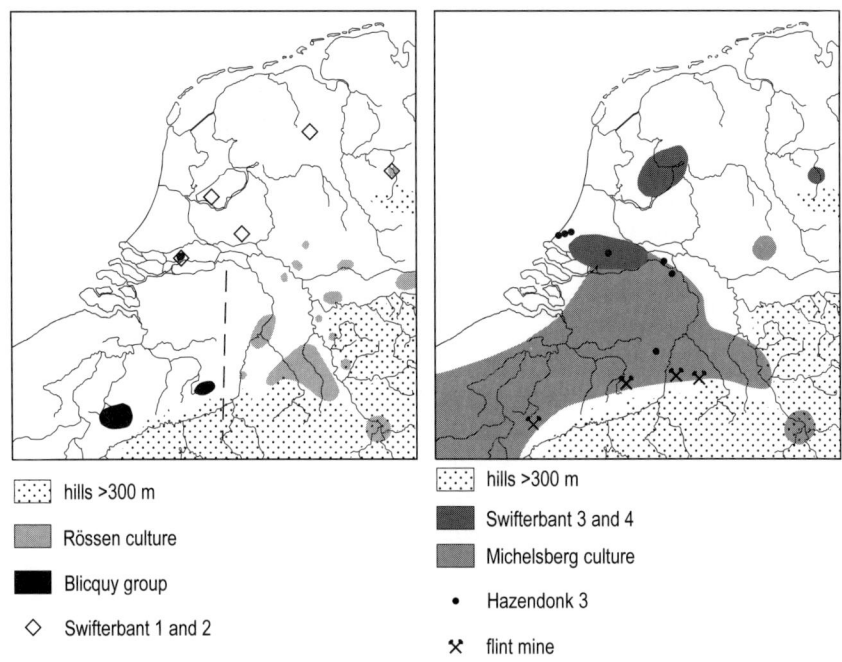

▦ hills >300 m	▦ hills >300 m
▨ Rössen culture	▨ Swifterbant 3 and 4
■ Blicquy group	▨ Michelsberg culture
◇ Swifterbant 1 and 2	• Hazendonk 3
	✕ flint mine

fig. 12.1

Distribution of the various culture groups during the Early Neolithic B (left) and the Middle Neolithic A (right) in the Netherlands and its environs.

axes. There are no visible monuments, no hoards and only very few burials. The flint mines are spectacular exceptions.

In the following sections the available evidence will be discussed according to geographical regions. We will first consider the farmers of the Rössen and Michelsberg cultures in the loess zone and their cultural developments. Next, we will concentrate on their interaction with the occupants of the southern sands, after which we will conclude with the Swifterbant culture of the delta and the northern part of the Netherlands (fig. 12.1).

FARMERS IN THE LOESS ZONE: THE RÖSSEN AND MICHELSBERG CULTURES

Chronology and geography

A chronological sequence has been set up for the lower Rhine region on the basis of stylistic changes in the pottery, which are observable over a much wider area. This sequence comprises the Rössen and Michelsberg cultures, both of which have been divided into phases (fig. 10. 3). Each of these phases is represented by one or more settlements that have been investigated in large-scale excavations. The scarce evidence available for the Netherlands can be placed in this Rhineland sequence.[3]

Belgium lies outside the area of the Rössen culture. In the period in question the *Groupe de Blicquy* developed in Belgium. Settlements of this group have been found in Hainault, but also in the Hesbaye, in the surroundings of Liège (Darion, Vaux-et-Borset), not more than 25 km from the westernmost Rössen settlement of Maastricht-Randwijck. The two cultural regions hence seem to be separated by a fairly sharp line. It is tempting to assume that this line separates two communities with distinct identities.[4]

By the Middle Neolithic this distinction had disappeared. The Michelsberg culture is the successor of both the Rössen culture and the *Groupe de Blicquy* of the Belgian loess zone.

Settlements

Rössen
Around 4900 BC occupation at all the *Bandkeramik* settlements came to an abrupt end. In the Rhineland the settlements of the succeeding Grossgartach phase lie in the same territories, but at different locations. They were fortified with earthworks and large V-sectioned ditches comparable with those known from the last phase of the *Bandkeramik*.[5]

Rössen settlements consisted of a small number of longhouses, arranged fairly close to one another. Many of the settlements were surrounded by a palisade. The houses were up to no less than 53 m long and tapered towards their ends.[6] In technical terms, these buildings were far more advanced than those of the *Bandkeramik*: the weight of the roof was supported mainly by the walls, which were built entirely of posts and split beams. This meant that far fewer internal roof supports were required and the houses consequently contained a wide, open hall. At the broad end of the house was an open area beneath the projecting roof. One or more annexes, usually polygonal, stood near to or abutted the main building; they are believed to have been storage facilities (fig. 12.2). No quarry pits have been found along

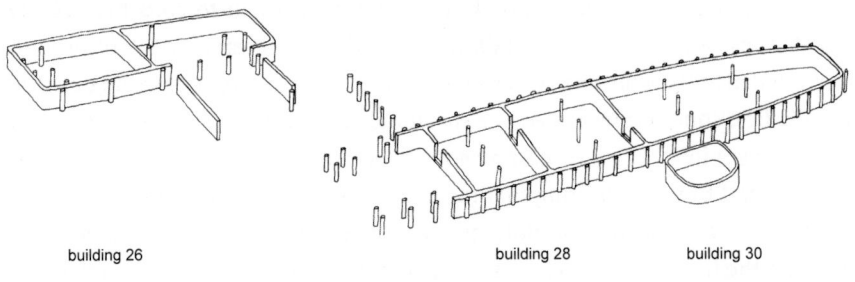

building 26   building 28   building 30

fig. 12.2
Perspective view of a Rössen house plan with two annexes at settlement Inden 9 on the Aldenhovener Platte (Germany) to the east of south Limburg. Including its forecourt, the large house (No. 28) had a length of 44 m and, we assume, will have had room enough to accommodate several households or possibly an extended family.

the walls; the clay for the walls was probably obtained from some large clusters of pits that have come to light at the peripheries of the settlements. Within the settlement were cylindrical pits, presumably used as silos or storage pits for cereals. The settlements were consequently smaller, less open and more compact – and hence easier to defend – than those of the previous period. The ditches and palisades with which they were often surrounded show that defence was indeed an important consideration, probably because of mutual rivalry and threats.

The structure of the settlement and the settlement system differed markedly from those of the preceding *Bandkeramik*. The settlements were shifted more frequently: each settlement represents only a few generations of houses, spanning at most 150 years. This could mean that the occupants went in search of new soils for their crops more frequently. Secondly, the Rössen settlements cover a somewhat larger distribution area, comprising not only the left bank of the Rhine, but also the floodplain and the right bank and the sandy soils further north; a few Rössen settlements have even been found in the valleys of the Eifel. This reflects greater flexibility in the choice of environments for agricultural activities. The former marked distinction between small and large houses has disappeared. The Rössen longhouse appears to be the counterpart of the cluster of houses of the *Bandkeramik* settlements, in which case it may be interpreted as the dwelling of several nuclear families or of one extended family. At Bochum-Hiltrop the plan of a longhouse was documented, with a length of 64 m and an adjoining enclosure measuring 38 x 48 m which was surrounded by a sturdy fence. Here the entire (village) community may have lived together in one building.[7]

Until recently, no remains whatsoever of the successors of the large *Bandkeramik* community had been found in southern Limburg, in spite of the intensive surveys conducted in this area.[8] In 1987, however, digging activities at Maastricht-Randwijck brought to light the remains of a settlement, which was investigated in a rescue excavation in 1988 before the site was built over. The settlement lay in the valley floor of the Meuse, on the lowest river terrace, at a point where the terrace was transected by a small gulley. Owing to fluctuations in the local water level the site had been severely eroded, but it had ultimately been covered with a layer of clay, which had preserved what then still remained: the bottom parts of seven round pits with diameters of 1-2 m. The pits appeared to have been storage pits; they yielded typical settlement refuse (pottery, flint, querns, carbonised grain), which showed beyond doubt that this was an 'ordinary' permanent settlement.[9] This discovery seems to have partly solved the problem concerning the successors of the *Linearbandkeramik* communities in southern Limburg: apparently they built their settlements on valley floors, where settlement remains are only very rarely discovered. But why they moved away from the Graetheide plateau is still a mystery.

Michelsberg
With the emergence of the Michelsberg culture the settlement system underwent new changes. The agricultural communities in Belgium and the Rhineland, like

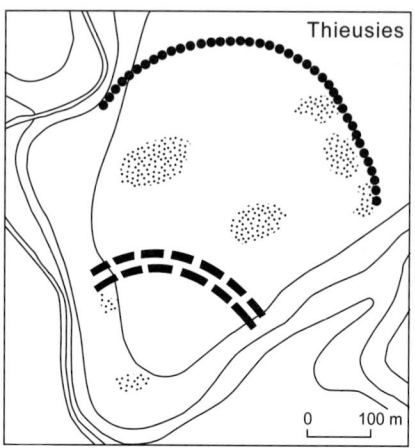

fig. 12.3
Schematic plan of the 'central site' of the Michelsberg culture at Thieusies, Hainault (Belgium). Two successive palisades (dotted lines) and two ditches protected a projecting area.

those elsewhere in Western and Northern Europe, began to construct 'central sites'. These are enclosures with dimensions of up to several dozens of hectares surrounded by flat-bottomed wide ditches and banks built from the earth dug from the ditches, some accompanied by substantial palisades of split tree-trunks.[10] The ditches were interrupted by narrow entrances. Some of these entrances were rebuilt several times, indicating that the enclosures were used for long periods of time. They were situated on hilltops, in areas enclosed by deep meanders (fig. 12.3), at the foot of hills or even at locations without distinct geomorphology, for example on the Aldenhoven plateau.[11]

The function of these 'causewayed enclosures' or 'interrupted ditch systems' has been, and still is, the subject of much discussion. In some countries (Great Britain, Denmark) evidence has been found which indisputably indicates that they were used primarily for some ritual purpose, involving unusual forms of burial.[12] All that can be said about the monuments in the Lower Rhine Basin and Belgium is that they were not settlements, but central sites that were used by larger social units, such as tribes or subtribes, and that they had a multiple, complex function. On account of their size, the many finds they have yielded and their high chances of discovery (also on aerial photographs!) they dominate the archaeological record.

So far, 'ordinary' settlements have largely escaped our notice, either because they are smaller or because they have suffered slope erosion or have become buried beneath colluvial deposits. Several settlements have been discovered in surveys, but only few have been excavated. Consequently, we know very little about Michelsberg houses or settlement layout. At Thieusies (Belgium) the plans of small, rectangular houses were recorded and at Mayen (near Koblenz in Germany) the features of small square huts with a sunken floor and a central roof support were unearthed. Quite spectacular are the large plans of Mairy (near Sedan, French Ardennes).[13]

No Michelsberg earth works has so far been found in southern Limburg, but more and more sites of this culture are being identified there. Large amounts of flint datable to the Middle and/or Late Neolithic have been found on a number of loess-covered valley spurs in the eastern part of this area. A Michelsberg site was excavated in the Klinkers quarry on the Caberg, to the north of Maastricht, in 1989. Owing to slope erosion little more than a few assemblages had survived, but it was clear that the settlement had not been surrounded by ditches. The early Michelsberg settlement remains in the valley of the Meuse at Maastricht-Vogelzang show that valley floor settlement location continued into this later period.[14]

Burials

So far, no cemeteries from this period have been found in the loess zone. The only noteworthy burial is a Blicquy grave that was found at Darion (Hesbaye). The silhouette of the deceased, who had been buried in crouched position on his/her side, was outlined in the floor of the pit. Powdered red ochre appeared to have been scattered across the pit. The deceased had been accompanied by a typical Blicquy vessel and no fewer than eight of the slate bracelets that are characteristic of this group.[15]

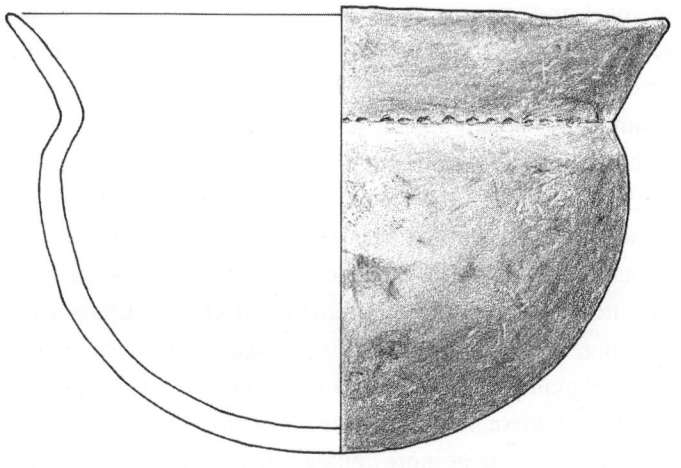

fig. 12.4
Wide round-bottomed beaker characteristic
of the earliest phase of the Michelsberg
culture from the Maastricht-Vogelzang
settlement. Scale 1:2.

Material culture

Pottery

The earliest Rössen or 'Grossgartach' pottery did not evolve from the late *Linear-bandkeramik* earthenware found in the Lower Rhine Basin, but shows stylistic affinities with the pottery of the late *Bandkeramik* Hinkelstein group of the upper Rhine plain.[16] That must hence have been a dominant area. So the pottery stiles may be seen to reflect these social relationships.

The pottery is of excellent quality: it is hard, thin-walled, smoothly finished and very regular in shape. Unlike the pottery of the *Bandkeramik*, it comprises a wide range of functionally different types. This typological differentiation was to become even more pronounced in the phase of the 'evolved Rössen' ware. The earliest Rössen ware comprises for example globular beakers, (cooking) pots, storage vessels, dishes, pedestal bowls, flasks and strainers. New is the frequent use of a spatula with two teeth for the impression of decorative patterns of impressions, which were filled with a white paste (plate 17B). These patterns formed a marked contrast with the vessel's black surface. The linear decoration has given way to a form of decoration consisting of filled bands and repeated squares and triangles arranged in panels. The 'evolved Rössen' ware differs in that it comprises new types and the decoration is arranged in larger panels. In the 'Bischheim' phase, finally, the lavish decoration gradually disappeared until only a single row of impressions remained.

In Belgium in this period, the *Groupe de Blicquy* evolved from the local late *Bandkeramik* ware. The vessels have uniform shapes; they are tempered with crushed burned bone (like the Limburg ware) and are often overall decorated with zigzag motifs arranged in panels. The contrast between fine, decorated ware and coarse, undecorated vessels that characterised the *Bandkeramik* pottery has disappeared.[17]

The pottery of the Michelsberg culture is a direct continuation of the preceding Bischheim ware. In the absence of decoration, the chronological and geographical classifications of this pottery are based entirely on morphological developments and are hence less refined and more difficult to use. Lüning[18] set up a sequence comprising five phases (MK I-V). MK I is rare and in fact differs little from 'undecorated Bischheim' ware. It was in the next phase that the 'classic Michelsberg' ware was developed. This Michelsberg II pottery is characterised by tulip-shaped beakers, large jars with pierced lugs, storage pots with flaring rims and a coarsely smeared surface, spoons and flat discs ('baking trays').[19] It has a wide distribution area, covering parts of Belgium and extending to the Paris Basin. In 1994-'95 pottery from this early period, datable to around 4100 BC, was excavated at

Maastricht-Vogelzang, at a site along the edge of a former gulley where a large number of pots, including misfires, had been discarded. Characteristic are wide bowls with round bases and relatively low, projecting rims (fig. 12.4). Flint flake axes found among the pottery and the use of flint as temper point to relations with Belgium, while large blades made from the distinctive brown/white banded flint from Romigny-Léhry, near Reims, betray contacts with communities living in the Paris Basin some 200 km away (plate 29).[20] At a contemporary site at Koslar near Aachen this same flint was found in association with some unusual pottery types, namely decorated *vase supports*, a characteristic of the French Chasséen.[21]

The following, late Michelsberg (MK III) phase is characterised by considerable regional differentiation. In the loess zone a classic lower Rhine group and a northern French/southern Belgian Chasséo-Michelsberg group have been distinguished.[22] MK IV and V are of more limited geographical significance; they have not yet been encountered in the lower Rhine region.

Flint

At the same time that the pottery was undergoing this conspicuous stylistic development changes were also taking place in the flint industry: in the types of raw materials used, the basic technology and the typology of the tools.[23]

From the very beginning of the Grossgartach phase onwards the Rössen communities exploited a new source of flint: the eluvial deposits of Rullen in the Voer region. This flint is recognisable by yellow patches and orange veins, caused by iron oxides absorbed from the soil. It may well be that a special value was ascribed to this flint (plate 17A). Half of the artefacts were however still made from colluvial flint of the Rijckholt type. The basic technology and most of the tool types were still the same as in the *Bandkeramik* period. The only new elements are the large, triangular point types and the obliquely truncated blades.

Conspicuous elements in the flint industry of the Blicquy group are very fine, long, thin blades. They were used to manufacture various types of burins, an uncommon tool type in the Neolithic.[24]

Great changes took place in the flint industry at the beginning of the Michelsberg culture. For the first time use was made of flint that had been obtained from shaft mines (feature E). Tool manufacture focused on the production of axes and (very) large blades, on which the typical Michelsberg tool kit was made: large perforators, *Spitzklinge* and various types of end scrapers. Large flakes were used to produce heavy, round 'horse-shoe scrapers' (fig. 12.5). Many of the arrow points are triangular, fairly thick and asymmetrical when viewed from the side, but very fine, long, leaf-shaped points were also produced.[25]

Flint was mined at many other places in the chalk region besides at the two

fig. 12.5
Michelsberg toolkit made from mined flint of the Rijckholt variety found at the settlements on the Kraaienberg near Groot-Linden (1-3, 5) and Gassel (4, 6, 7), 120 km north of the flint mines. Besides these tools imported from a distant source there were also small flakes made from flint which the occupants picked up on the Meuse terraces in the settlements' immediate vicinity. 2/3 of actual size.

1-3 points
4   piercer
5   scraper made on a flake
6   end-scraper made on a blade
7   axe fragment

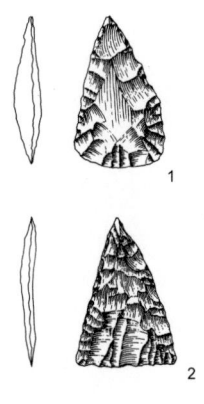

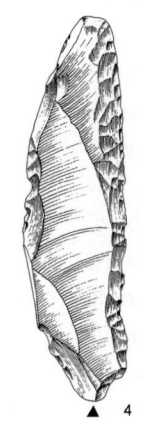
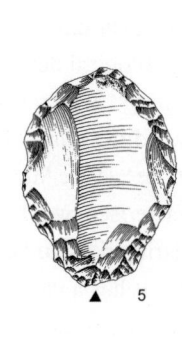
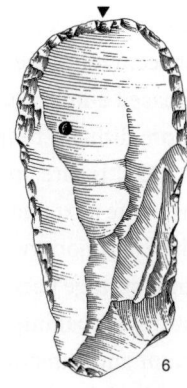
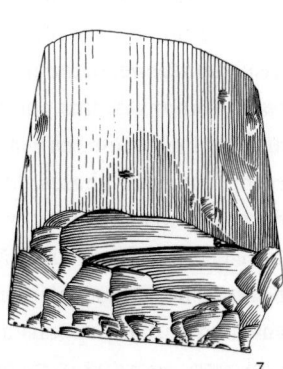

aforementioned sites. Some of the mined flint cannot be distinguished from the Rijckholt flint (the flint from Mheer and Banholt for example), whereas other flint types, for example those from the Lousberg near Aachen, Simpelveld and Valkenburg, show very distinctive features.[26] The mines that yielded some of the flint types encountered in the settlements have not yet been found, for example those in the Belgian Hesbaye that yielded a light grey flint. Some types (in particular that from Lousberg) were exploited most intensively in a later phase of the Neolithic, but started to be used at a much earlier date already (fig. 15.7).

Until recently it was assumed on simple functionalistic grounds that the excessive use of flint and the extraordinarily large sizes of the tools (compared with those of the preceding and succeeding periods) were related to a substantially increased demand for flint tools required for felling trees and crop cultivation. However, this argument no longer seems tenable. In the period of the *Bandkeramik* and Rössen cultures blade tools of quite small dimensions had been satisfactory, while people in the Late Neolithic even managed very well with a distinctly narrow range of small tools. Moreover, only very little land was actually taken into cultivation on the loess and it was not until the end of the Neolithic, in the Beaker period, that large clearances started to be created in the forests.[27] The opinion that is finding more and more acceptance nowadays is that the main reason why people went to such great efforts to mine flint from the mother rock and made predominantly conspicuous, large tools is that they attributed a symbolic value to this specific flint. Whether this interpretation is correct or not, the fact remains that large tools are a distinctive feature of the Michelsberg culture. Via exchange, large quantities of mined flint were distributed over a wide area, extending up to the Dutch delta and the Münster basin in the north and to Hessen and incidentally even Lake Constance in the south. This distribution area can be seen to reflect a sphere of interaction extending beyond that represented by the various pottery styles.[28]

Axes

In the period discussed in this chapter different types of axes, made from varying types of stone, were used for different purposes. These axes reflect important developments in stone technology.[29]

At the end of the *Bandkeramik* the technique of perforating stone, *i.e.* of providing adzes with a shaft-hole, was developed. These shaft-holes were probably made with the aid of a bow-operated hollow drill of bone or wood, using water and sand as grinding agents.[30] The tenacious types of stone that were used to produce the axes could also be sawn with the aid of thin plates of sandstone. At the end of the *Bandkeramik* flat adzes started to be perforated perpendicular to their cutting edge. From the Grossgartach phase onwards heavy, thick adzes were perforated transversely, parallel to the cutting edge, to obtain perforated 'shoe-last celts'. In the evolved Rössen phase, finally, the asymmetric cross-section disappeared and a new kind of tool, called a 'perforated wedge' (fig. 12.6),[31] started to be produced. The damage suffered by these heavy 'wedges' shows that they were used to split tree-trunks. We assume that the majority of these tools, which were made from exotic types of stone such as amphibolite, basalt and selected types of quartzite (phtanite, lydite), were manufactured elsewhere and made their way into the Netherlands via exchange. But a rare find from the Rössen settlement of Maastricht-Randwijck shows that some were produced locally. This site yielded a piece of diabase or diorite collected from the local river gravels, hammered into shape and provided with two deep saw cuts: a blank for two (perforated) Rössen wedges, one large and one small. Apparently a corner of the stone had broken away in an

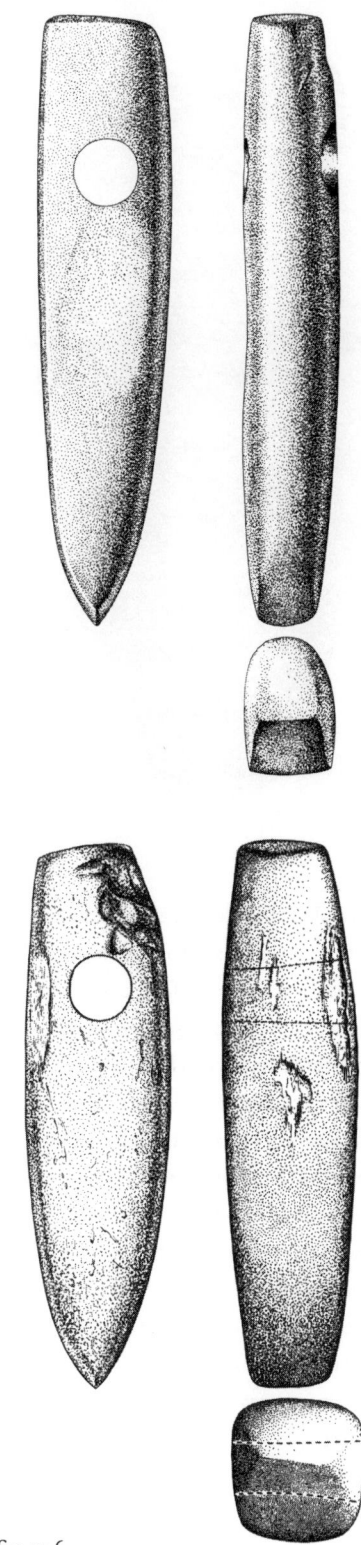

fig. 12.6

Perforated amphibolite wedges, which Swifterbant people obtained from the Rössen communities living in the loess zone. Scale 1:3.

Top: thick perforated *Schuhleistenkeil* (with an asymmetric cross-section) found near Bargererfscheidenveen, to the southwest of Emmen.

Bottom: *Breitkeil* (with a more or less symmetric cross-section) from Megen, to the north of Oss.

fig. 12.7
Large diabase pebble shaped by hammering.
The stone, which has deep saw cuts on
two sides, was recovered from one of the
settlement pits of the Rössen culture at
Maastricht-Randwijck. It is assumed to
represent an intermediate phase in the
manufacture of two (perforated) axes
or wedges. The sawing was evidently
discontinued when a corner of one of the
intended products broke off. This blank
shows that axes were not exclusively
distributed via exchange networks, but that
some were produced on site, using stones
that were in one way or another imported.
Scale 1:4.

attempt to split the blank, after which it was discarded, even though it could still be used (fig. 12.7).[32]

These heavy perforated wedges disappeared in the Michelsberg period. They were replaced by simple stone axes made of blades, which were inserted into a socketed handle. The earliest of these axes, made from quartzitic stone types, are found in Rössen context. Around the transition to the Michelsberg period an important technical innovation took place: the extremely hard flint started to be polished. This was done with the aid of quartzite grinding stones, probably using sand and water as grinding agents. Small, portable grinding stones were used, but also immobile large blocks of quartzite, such as the large grinding stones known at Slenaken (plate 16B).[33] The flint axes show great diversity in their shapes, but they are all variants of the 'western type', with an oval cross-section, sometimes with flattened sides, and a pointed or wide, thin butt. As the many thousands of axes that have come to light are all stray finds, very little can be said about their cultural context; nor can they be accurately dated.

Besides the axes of local flint and other types of local stone there are also axes made from exotic types of stone, in particular green jadeite (plate 20A), which occurs only in the western Alps. The first 'battle axe' – the 'flat hammer axe', whose shape appears to have been inspired by copper prototypes from southeast Europe – also dates from the Michelsberg period.[34] All the evidence indicates that great value was attached to such axes; they may be regarded as showpieces and hence as status markers. They were preferably manufactured from exotic stone types and were obtained via exchange networks. Great attention was paid to their design and finish.

Other indications of social differentiation among the Rössen communities, besides axes, are pendants and strings of beads made from shells. No such shell ornaments have however been preserved in the decalcified soils of the Low Countries. Ornaments that have survived in this region are the aforementioned slate bracelets of the Blicquy group.

Conclusion

The fifteen centuries discussed in this chapter saw constant changes in the material culture of the farming communities of the loess zone. Periods of very gradual developments alternated with phases of more or less abrupt changes, which appear to reflect social disturbances: a first crisis at the transition from the *Bandkeramik* to the Grossgartach phase, a second at the Bischheim-Michelsberg transition and a third at the end of the latter period, when the causewayed enclosures went out of use.

So far, archaeologists have failed to explain the cause of the relatively abrupt transition from the *Bandkeramik* to the Grossgartach culture. The fortifications suggest that this transition involved threats and armed conflicts, but we do not know whether they were the consequences of tensions between different *Bandkeramik* communities or between *Bandkeramik* and other communities. What we do know for certain is that the successors of the *Bandkeramik* people had an entirely new 'culture', including pottery of a southern (Grossgartach) style, more defensively organised settlements, a wider range of site locations and a different range of crops.[35]

The Grossgartach-Rössen-Bischheim period was a time of very gradual developments, while the transition to the Michelsberg culture was again marked by fairly drastic changes. The crisis appears to have been less acute, but its outcome was a new society with a different culture, characterised by central sites, a new pottery style, shaft mining and the attribution of a greater value to the flint that was obtained at such great effort, and new (rare) prestige goods, such as axes of jadeite, Romigny-Léhry flint and hammer axes. The regional styles distinguishable within the Michelsberg pottery could reflect the emergence or intensification of regional organisations, such as tribal associations. The area covered by these styles, for example, has similar dimensions as the Mesolithic Wommersom quartzite distribution area, for which a similar interpretation has been suggested. The causewayed enclosures can be seen to represent smaller social units within this area. No such social hierarchy appears to have existed in earlier periods. If one of the purposes of these central sites was defence, they imply an increase in the scale of armed conflict. Tribal warfare, either of a ritual nature or in the form of raiding, must have been endemic from the beginning of the Neolithic, if not earlier. We should not expect to find many other indications of such warfare besides modest, incidental fortifications and sporadic evidence of violent death in graves. The only – but very significant – indications of tribal warfare found in the Lower Rhine Basin are the fortified sites and the 'battle axes', that is, if that is indeed what the unusually shaped hammer axes were.[36]

The last crisis, finally, which marks the transition from the Middle Neolithic A to B, around 3400 BC, was characterised by a conspicuous break in cultural developments and the replacement of old traditions over large parts of Northwest Europe.

fig. 12.8

The Hazendonk, one of the Late Glacial river dunes in the Alblasserwaard region, was used as a settlement site at least seven times in the Neolithic. The rising groundwater level and constant deposition of peat and fluvial sediments led to the gradual burial of the dune's slopes, and the dune consequently became progressively smaller and lower. The refuse of the successive occupation phases has survived in seven occupation levels in the natural Holocene stratification dating from 4000 to 2200 BC.

No.	culture	date
7	late Bell Beaker	2200 BC
6	Vlaardingen 2b	2600-2500
5	Vlaardingen 1b	3200-3000
4	Vlaardingen 1a	c. 3400
3	Hazendonk 3	3700-3600
2	Swifterbant phase 3	3900-3800
1	Swifterbant phase 3	c. 4000

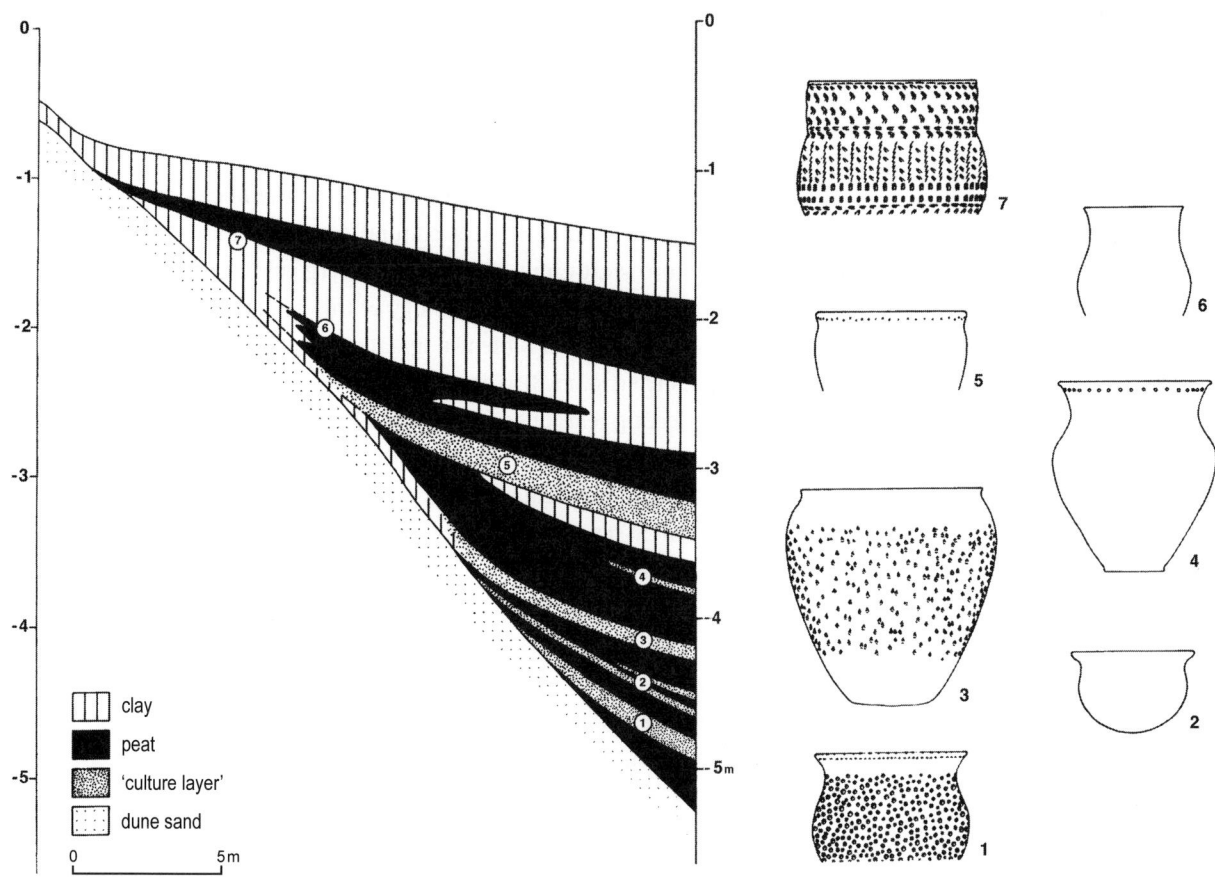

clay
peat
'culture layer'
dune sand

0   5m

257

Chronology and settlements

We assume that the sands to the north of the loess were still occupied by hunter-gatherers at the beginning of this period. The excavations carried out in the Meuse Valley Project, especially those in the Merselo region near Venray, have shown that their remains consist of flint assemblages comprising the products of a simple flake industry for which locally collected gravel flint was used, and small blades made on imported, southern types of flint and Wommersom quartzite. By this time the typically Mesolithic microlithic element had almost completely disappeared. Future research will hopefully show whether these assemblages are to be ascribed to the earliest phase of the Swifterbant culture or whether they are to be classed as a separate group.[37]

From several small assemblages containing Rössen pottery and flint that have been found on the sandy soils, within a zone extending to about 25 km outside the loess region, we know that the Rössen farmers also exploited these areas, just like their predecessors had done.[38] The most obvious interpretation is that these assemblages represent the remains of cattle herders' camps or small hunting stations. At Echt-Annendaal, in the Roer region, such a site was located at the upper slope of a valley, from where the occupants had a good view across the valley of the Vlootbeek. Bandkeramik and Michelsberg pottery showed that the site was also used in previous and later periods, which implies a marked continuity in the settlement system.[39] The activity area of the Rössen people did not extend beyond that of their Bandkeramik predecessors. The few findspots that have been found outside this activity area point to longer expeditions or to exchange with the local population. That such exchange indeed took place, even with people living far away, is apparent from the perforated Rössen axes that have been found in some quantities across the entire north German plain and even in Denmark, i.e. in the areas of the Swifterbant and Ertebølle cultures. Although these tools must have been of great value to the Rössen farmers, it was apparently fairly easy for the hunters to obtain possession of them.[40]

Major changes took place in the course of the Michelsberg period: the native hunter-gatherers underwent a cultural transformation, the outcome of which was the northwest group of the Michelsberg culture, a truly Neolithic group. Of great importance for the chronology of this period is the stratigraphic sequence at the Hazendonk near Molenaarsgraaf, where three successive assemblages were distinguished (fig. 12.8). That of Hazendonk 1 (4000 BC) is a Swifterbant assemblage reflecting relations with the Bischheim group. Further evidence supporting such relations was provided by a small assemblage showing Bischheim characteristics found at Ven-Zelderheide, near Gennep. Hazendonk 2 (3800 BC) is also a Swifterbant assemblage, which however contains a number of typologically and technically different vessels that must originate from the northwest group of the Michelsberg culture. The Hazendonk 3 remains (3600 BC), finally, include an original and easily recognisable kind of pottery which, we assume, must have evolved from the preceding Swifterbant ware. But on account of the many differences between the two styles the former may be regarded as a separate pottery group (fig. 12.9). Around 3400 BC this style was succeeded by early Vlaardingen types.[41]

On the whole, Michelsberg sites can be easily recognised by the presence of characteristic, large tools made on mined Rijckholt flint. The sites' distribution pattern and the site locations in the Meuse valley in Limburg are the same as those

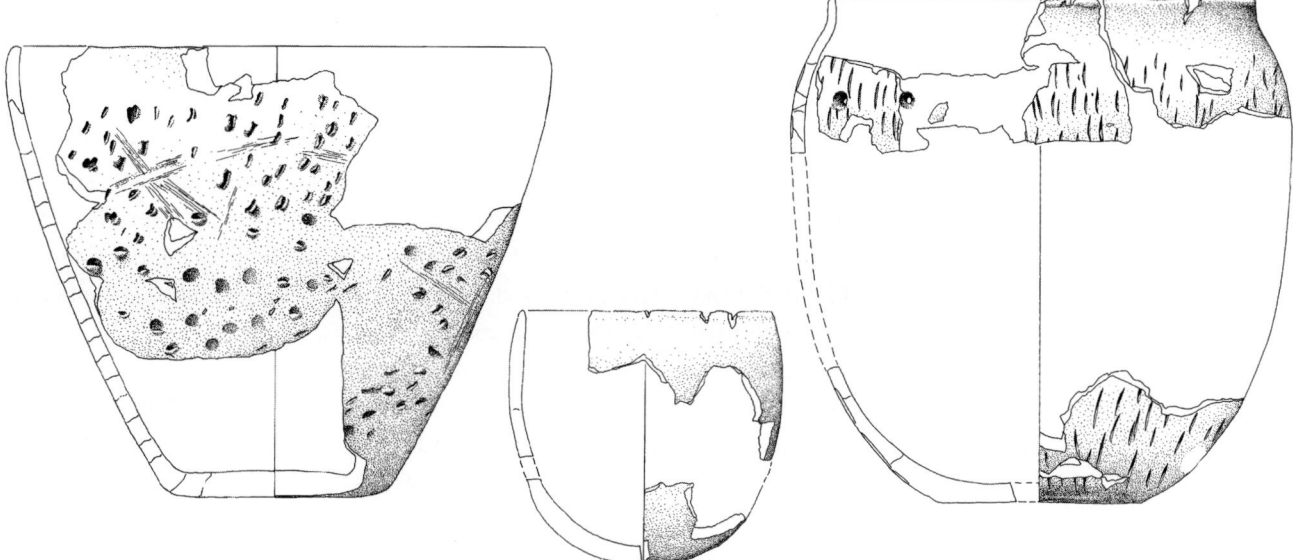

of the Late Mesolithic, but differ from those of the *Bandkeramik* and Rössen farmers.[42] Much of our information on the sandy soils comes from the buried sites in the region between Grave and Cuijk, which yielded pottery in association with flint and stone tools. Even more evidence has been obtained at the lowland sites in the west of the Netherlands, *i.e.* Hazendonk, Wateringen, Rijswijk and Ypenburg.[43]

The northwest Michelsberg group covered an area extending into the Münster basin and up to the river district in the central part of the Netherlands.[44] A small number of Hazendonk 3 sites have been recorded in the southern part of the Netherlands and in the adjacent parts of Belgium. In that phase the southern part of the delta, up to the North Sea coast, is incorporated in the southern sphere of influence.[45]

fig. 12.9

Pottery from the Hazendonk, Hazendonk 3 occupation level, assumed to represent the last development of the southern group of the Swifterbant culture, *c.* 3600 BC. Characteristic are the bucket shapes, the 'wobbly bases', the coiled build-up and the simple wall decoration comprising fields filled with various impressions and grooves. Scale 1:4.

Material culture

The pottery of the northwest Michelsberg group comprises a distinct range of types, in which many 'classic' Michelsberg elements are scarce or altogether absent. Characteristic of this pottery are sharply carinated wide bowls, sometimes with one or two rows of pin-pricks at the carination, for which exact counterparts are known in the contemporary Early Neolithic Grimston bowls in Britain. Typical Michelsberg vessels are large pots with roughened walls and collared rims and vessels of fine earthenware with wide necks, carefully finished thin rims and smooth inside and outside surfaces. In some respects, however, this pottery differs from the 'Michelsberg proper' known from the loess zone. For example, it does not include clay discs and spoons, and the 'functional types' are less striking.

The pottery of the Hazendonk 3 assemblages consists largely of bucket-shaped pots tempered with crushed white quartz, sometimes mixed with grog. The vessels have rough walls and were built from thick, poorly joined coils of clay. Many of the pots were found to have broken along the joints between the coils. A large proportion (approx. 30%) of the pottery is decorated with impressions made with finger tips, fingernails or various objects, extending over the entire surface of the pot with the exception of narrow bands at the base and beneath the rim. Some show deeply incised sets of lines. This form of 'decoration', without motifs, applied to pots of all sizes, can be regarded as a form of rustication, resembling that found on the storage pots of the previous phase.

259

The flint artefacts of all the northwest Michelsberg and Hazendonk 3 assemblages, including those in the delta, comprise the products of a simple flake industry made on small flint pebbles derived from river gravels and the aforementioned imports in Michelsberg style. We recall that the assemblages of the previous period had included imported bladelets and tools made on blades. The small flakes (up to 4 cm) show little retouch; few tools were made on those flakes. The number of tools made from (mined) Rijckholt flint varies considerably, from a few specimens to remarkably large numbers. Noteworthy are the frequent occurrence of broken flint axes and their use as flake cores. All the dated assemblages containing such axe fragments fall between 4100 and 3400 BC.[46]

The occurrence of small fragments of querns together with heavy, facetted hammer stones made on quartzite derived from river gravels in Michelsberg and Hazendonk 3 contexts at Kraaienberg and Gassel, respectively, indicates that these communities consumed cereal products, which implies that they grew crops.

Way of life

In the sandy region in the south of the Netherlands the transition from the Mesolithic to the Neolithic consequently coincided with the early phase of the Michelsberg culture. It is however still unclear to what extent the occupants of this area switched to a farming way of life. The locations of the sites in the Meuse valley in Limburg provide no clues in this respect. From the quern fragments and the sickle gloss on some of the flint tools we know that crop cultivation was practised. On the whole, microwear analysis of flint tools has revealed no fundamental differences in activities between the sandy soils and the loess, which is an argument for assuming that the lifestyles of the occupants of the two regions were very much the same.[47]

Very interesting are the Hazendonk 3 sites that were discovered in the coastal

fig. 12.10

Small two-aisled house plan of the Hazendonk 3 group found at the Wateringen 4 settlement on a low coastal dune in the coastal area of South Holland. Scale 1:100.

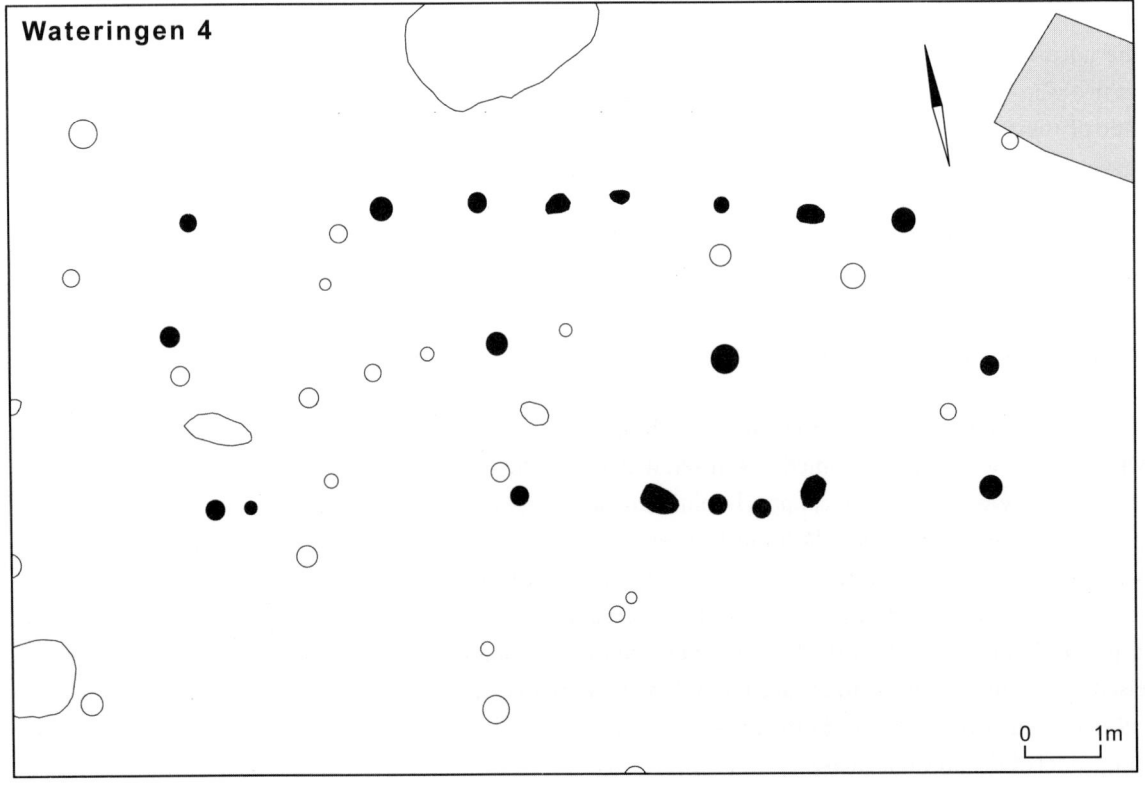

Wateringen 4

0   1m

district in 1993; they are the oldest sites known in that region.[48] The evidence obtained at the sites is very similar. The occupants lived on low dunes, along whose edges they dug pits, possibly to tap the fresh water in the dune. At Wateringen the plan of a small, rectangular house was recorded (fig. 12.10). The Ypenburg site yielded a spectacular cemetery (feature F). The bone spectra showed that the occupants had combined cattle keeping with hunting (red deer) and fowling (aquatic birds). This evidence supports the suggestion that the Michelsberg and Hazendonk 3 settlements along the margins of the river district between Grave and Cuijk were pasturing camps.[49] More in general, the evidence for agriculture found at these coastal settlements strongly suggests that the occupants of the southern part of the Netherlands had by this time switched to a farming way of life. However, they apparently continued to use the river dunes in the peat region – in particular the Hazendonk – as bases for hunting and fishing. This clearly shows that they are to be seen as the heirs to the native Swifterbant culture.

THE NORTHERN LOWLAND PLAIN: THE SWIFTERBANT CULTURE[50]

Chronology and geography

Our knowledge of the Swifterbant communities in the northern part of the plain is based largely on evidence obtained from sites on the Holocene deposits and the odd wetland site outside that area, in particular Hüde I on the shore of lake Dümmer. The sites in the delta lie predominantly in the zone of marshes, lakes and freshwater tidal creeks, where preservation conditions are of course much better than in the more dynamic ecological zones like the fluvial clay regions and the

fig. 12.11
Palaeogeography of the northern part of Flevoland around 4000 BC based on the results of a soil survey. Settlements of the Swifterbant culture were found on the tops of former river dunes and on levees of freshwater creeks. Scale 1:50,000.

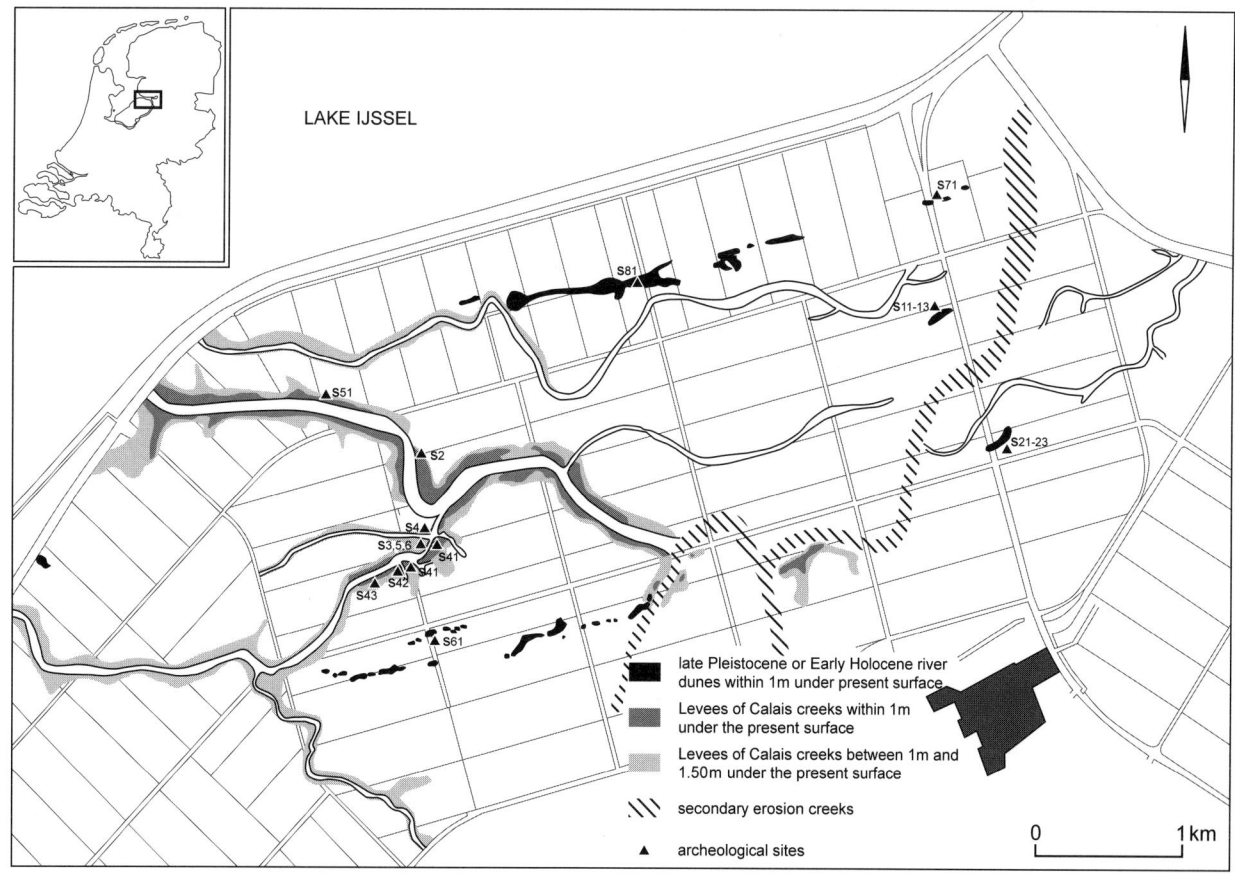

LAKE IJSSEL

S71
S81
S11-13
S51
S21-23
S2
S4
S3,5,6
S41
S42
S43
S61

late Pleistocene or Early Holocene river dunes within 1m under present surface

Levees of Calais creeks within 1m under the present surface

Levees of Calais creeks between 1m and 1.50m under the present surface

\\\\ secondary erosion creeks

▲ archeological sites

0   1 km

coastal plain. The sites cluster in two regions: the IJsselmeer basin and the Alblasserwaard region. In the IJsselmeer basin the process of sedimentation came to an end when the IJsselmeer came into existence in historical times. Later on, when large parts were reclaimed, the river and creek deposits of Calais II age became accessible for archaeological research. Settlement sites on levees and dune tops have been excavated at Swifterbant, in the north of the Flevoland polder (fig. 12.11 and plate 18B).[51] In the south of the Noordoostpolder large-scale research has been carried out in plot P14, where a boulder clay outcrop capped by coversand bordered what was in prehistoric times the lower course of the Vecht (fig. 10.5).[52]

In the western part of the river district a total of 61 sites covering the period 5500-2500 BC were discovered on 20 of the 25 surveyed river dunes; 31 of those sites date from the period discussed in this chapter (fig. 10.8).[53] Many more settlements must still lie buried beneath the surface because the sea level – and consequently also the groundwater level and the old land surface – was then between 7 (at first) and 4 m lower than it is today (see feature D).

No Swifterbant sites are known on the upland (with the exception of Hüde I on lake Dümmer). That will be due mainly to the poor recognisability of the flint artefacts, which do not include proper type fossils. In the northern part of the Netherlands only a few assemblages in stream valleys have been identified as Swifterbant sites on the basis of pottery or tools of bone or antler.[54]

The Swifterbant culture has been divided into four phases (Sw 1-4) on the basis of some stylistic changes in the pottery, stratigraphic evidence and the absolute ages of assemblages found in the IJsselmeer basin. The majority of the sites, including those on the levees of the Calais II creek system in Flevoland, date from a relatively short period: 4350-3950 BC. This 'classic' phase has been classed as Sw 3.[55]

The succeeding Sw 4 phase is best known from the research in plot P14 in the Noordoostpolder (fig. 10. 5). There, along the bank of a former meander of the Vecht, three successive layers were found to contain both Swifterbant pottery and early TRB pottery dating from shortly before 3400 BC, which has for the time being been termed 'pre-Drouwen'. There are numerous parallels between this ceramic and the younger pottery of Hüde I. A small assemblage of the same date was found at Nagele (also in the Noordoostpolder).[56]

Sw 1 and 2 were distinguished exclusively on the basis of stratigraphic evidence and absolute dates. The transition from a Late Mesolithic to Early Swifterbant has been well-documented by the excavations at Hardinxveld (feature D). These early phases are, moreover, represented by the oldest pottery from Hüde I and by a few assemblages found in Flevoland and the Noordoostpolder for which ^{14}C dates of 4500-4300 BC have been obtained. At the Hogevaart site in the southern part of Flevoland, comprising a coversand elevation along the former course of the Eem, pits, flint, pottery and (burned) bone were found at a depth of about 6 m below Normal Amsterdam Level. Their stratigraphic position shows that they must date from the middle of the 5th millennium. Radiocarbon dates concentrate in the period 4800-4600 BC.[57]

A noteworthy, early earthenware find is a pot, unfortunately without its base, which came to light during dredging operations near Bronneger (Drenthe) in 1990, together with two large red deer antlers. Carbonised remains encrusted on the pot yielded a ^{14}C date of c. 4800 BC. The remarkable composition of this assemblage suggests that it represents a ritual deposit.[58]

The assemblages of Bergschenhoek, Brandwijk and Hazendonk 1 and 2 found in the southern part of the delta have been dated to Sw 3. The oldest layers at the surveyed sites may well contain Sw 1 assemblages. In phase Sw 4 this region clearly came under southern (Hazendonk 3) influence.

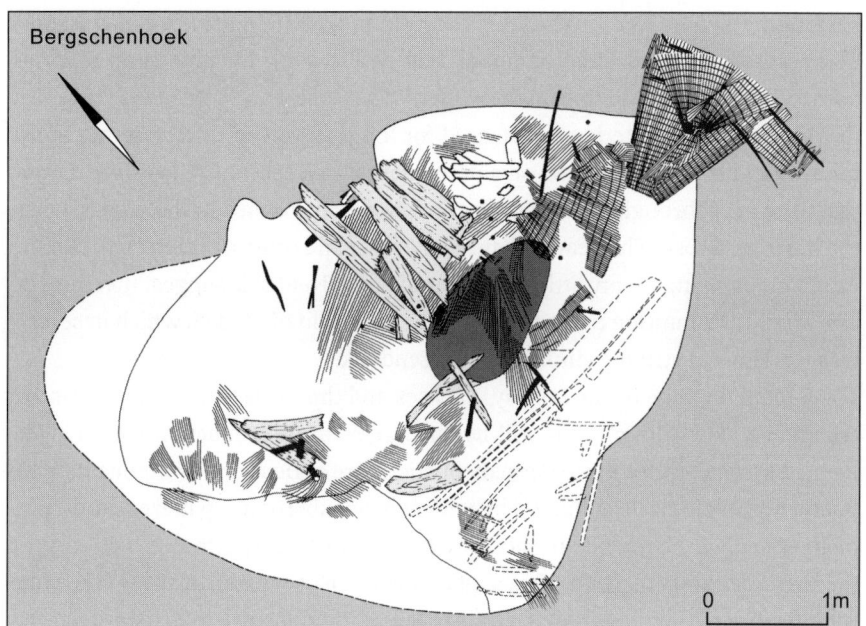

Bergschenhoek

peat
clay (formerly open water)
bundles of reeds
planks

0   1m

fig. 12.12
Plan of the small winter camp at Bergschenhoek, c. 4200 BC. The peat ground was
reinforced with reed bunches, remains of
an old fish trap and planks from a discarded
dug-out canoe. Scale 1:60.

Settlements and way of life

The Swifterbant settlements in the delta lay at the mouths of the major rivers, on
top of semi-submerged dunes, on the levees of creek systems or on the shores of
lakes (plates 18B, 19A). Reconstructions of the former landscape suggest that the
choice of these locations was not dictated by agricultural interests, but this is only
partly confirmed by the botanical and zoological evidence. Almost all the Swifterbant phase 3 sites yielded carbonised cereal remains (including chaff), but it is
unlikely that this cereal was grown locally. The proportion of domestic animals
represented in the bone spectra varies from 0% (Bergschenhoek) and about 10%
(Hazendonk) to 50% (Swifterbant-S3). Apparently the occupants found pastures
for their cattle even in the swamps, or else on the salt marshes in the wider surroundings. The substantial differences in subsistence activities between the sites
in the different environments raise questions concerning the function of these
wetland sites: were they occupied on a permanent or a temporary, possibly seasonal, basis, and how did they relate to the settlements in the upland? These are, in
other words, questions concerning the 'settlement system'.[59]

The settlements are not very large. Most vary from 500 to 3000 m². In this respect
they do not differ from those of the Late Mesolithic De Leien/Wartena group.[60]
From stratigraphic evidence, the thickness of the occupation layers and ^{14}C dates
we may infer that the individual sites were not occupied for much longer than a
century, although locations that were particularly suitable for occupation, such as
the river dunes, were often re-occupied. Within these periods the sites were used
intermittently or continuously. The pollen diagrams of Hazendonk show true
landnam phases, each followed by a regeneration phase. Although some evidence
suggests that the occupants of Swifterbant S3 occasionally left their site for one
or more seasons, the superimposed hearths point to permanent occupation, possibly even to the existence of permanent huts. But no huts could be reconstructed
from the hundreds of posts found at the site. The site appeared to have been raised
with bundles of reeds as a countermeasure against floodings.[61] Evidence indicating the use of bundles of reeds for the same purpose was found in combination
with superimposed hearths at Bergschenhoek, too (fig. 12.12, plate 19A).

It is difficult to say in which season or seasons the sites were occupied. On the

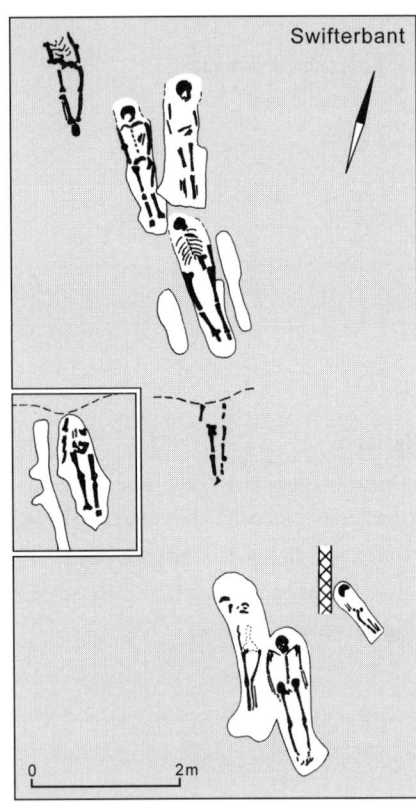

Swifterbant

0   2m

basis of the aquatic birds in the faunal sample and other evidence we may assume
that Bergschenhoek, which lay among bog pools, was a fowling camp that was
used for short periods of time in the winter.[62] The cemetery of site S2 indicates that
the levee sites of Swifterbant were used for long periods of time, but that is not
to say that they were occupied on a permanent basis: they may have been camps
that were used throughout the summer and were abandoned in the winter, when
the water level rose. The heavy reliance on beaver and otter at Hazendonk and the
fact that this changed very little until the end of the Neolithic suggest that this site
was primarily a hunting camp.[63] The same can be said of Hüde I, which in several
respects shows a striking similarity to Hazendonk.[64]

All in all, in spite of the pottery, the axes and the cattle, the wetland sites are
remarkably 'Mesolithic'. This will be due largely to their function within a settlement system whose more permanent and more agricultural components have
poorer archaeological visibility. The evidence for subsistence patterns and settlement system in the period around 4000 BC is in many respects similar to that of
the later Vlaardingen group. This suggests that the occupants of these sites were
very attached to their traditional, familiar way of life and stuck to that until the end
of the Neolithic. But we should bear in mind that this period is less well-documented than the later Vlaardingen period because much evidence has disappeared
owing to erosion, while other remains are inaccessible due to the thickness of the
overlying sediments.

Burials: the cemeteries of Swifterbant and P14

Three cemeteries were discovered near the settlements in the northern part of
Flevoland, two on top of dunes (S11 and S21-23) and one on the levee of a wide
creek (S2, fig. 12.13)[65] The cemetery in plot S2, which was excavated in its entirety,
comprised nine graves. In plot H46 the two ends of a 200-m-long dune top were
investigated. Seven and six graves were unearthed at the northern (S21) and southern (S22) ends, respectively. It is not clear whether they represented the two ends
of a single, elongated cemetery or two separate, small cemeteries. These graves
are our only source of information on the burial rites in the period discussed here.
The deceased had all been buried on their backs, in extended position. This tradition betrays the Swifterbant group's Mesolithic origins. The deceased included
men, women and children, which shows that the Swifterbant settlements were occupied by complete households. We may moreover conclude that these sites were
important, stable elements in the settlement system. There are modest indications
of social differentiation. One woman in the cemetery of S2 had for example been
buried with a few small amber beads, while a man had an ornament consisting
of large perforated pieces of amber on his forehead, a perforated flat pebble in or
near his right ear and a boar's tooth with several perforations on his chest (plate
18A). The amber may have been found in the Netherlands – along the coast or in
ice-pushed Tertiary clay in the eastern part of the country – but the larger lumps
may also have been 'imported' from Denmark.[66]

A small cemetery came to light in P14, too. Three or four of the graves may date
from phase Sw 4. They contained the remains of deceased who had been buried
on their backs, in extended position, without grave goods. The graves also yielded
evidence for the secondary burial of older skeletal remains, in particular skulls.[67]

In addition to these formal burials in a separate cemetery, fair amounts of disarticulated human remains were also found inside the settlements at Swifterbant.
They probably point to some different treatment of the dead which did not com-

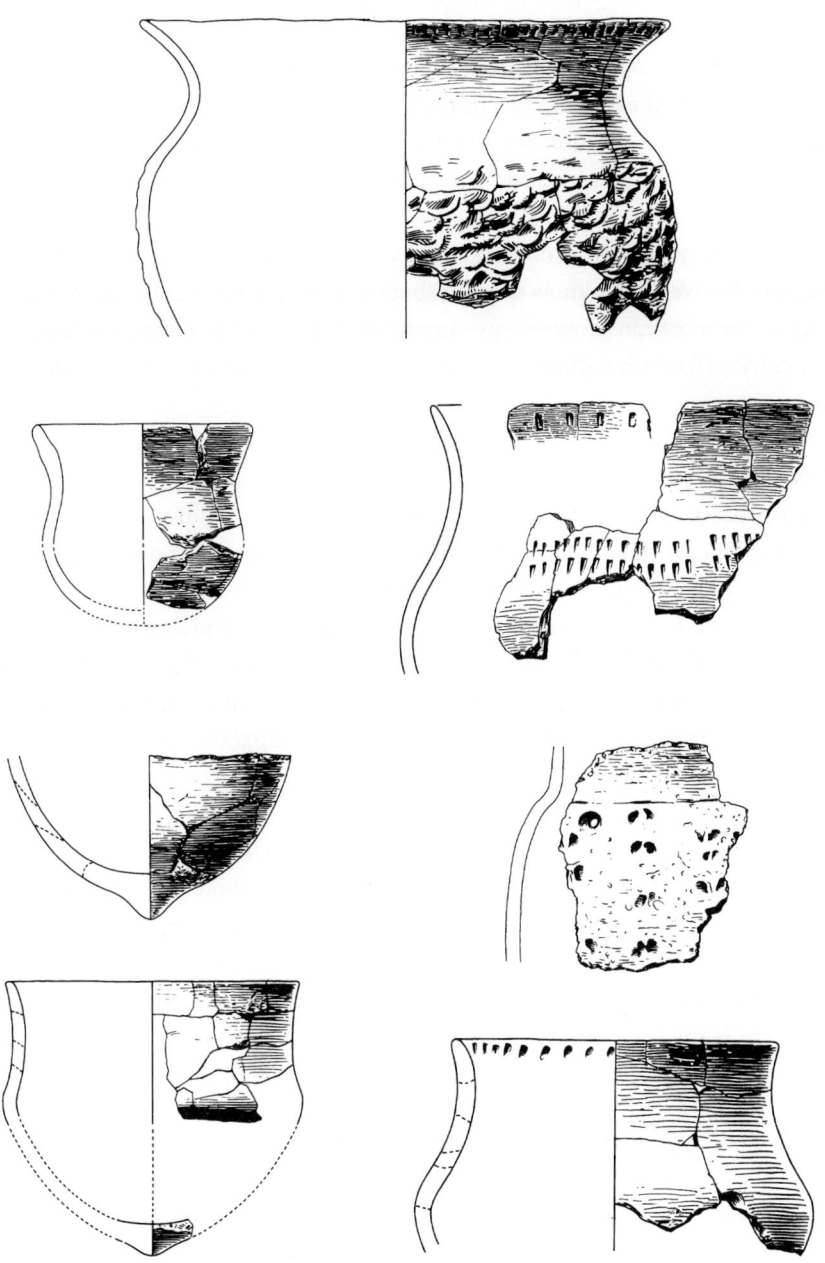

fig. 12.14
Pottery from the Swifterbant settlement S3, representing the 'classic' phase of the Swifterbant culture, around 4100 BC. The pointed bases and flaring rims are typical of this phase, but the simple shoulder decoration is known mainly from the IJsselmeer area. Scale 1:5.

prise interment. Of course, this does not necessarily hold for the milk teeth, which may simply have been lost when they were replaced by permanent teeth.

Material culture

Pottery (fig. 12.14)

Although the pottery of the Swifterbant culture was probably inspired by that of the Rössen and Michelsberg communities, there are considerable differences between the two. The Swifterbant pottery comprises only one type, with an S-shaped profile and a tall, widely flaring rim, which was often notched with the aid of a spatula. The pots have a globular body and pointed or round bases, some with a bump of clay. The clay was tempered with short parts of plants or with finely crushed crystalline rock. The pots were built from thin coils of clay. Some of the pots show a modest form of decoration comprising rows or scatters of impres-

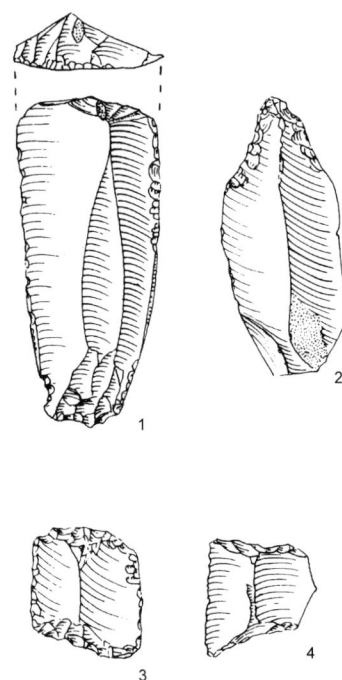

fig. 12.15

The flint of the Swifterbant sites (in this case site S2) in the IJsselmeer basin shows clear evidence of its Late Mesolithic origins in the small, regularly shaped blades and the broad trapezes. Actual size.

1 end-scraper

2 borer

3 double scraper

4 broad trapeze

sions made with the finger tips, spatulas or some pointed instrument, in particular on the shoulder, but sometimes extending over the entire surface of the pot. The pottery ranges from fine, thin-walled vessels to coarse, thick pots, and varies in size from the dimensions of a beaker to those of a storage vessel, without there being any clear connection between the size of the vessel and its fabric. This description applies to the 'classic' Swifterbant ware from the period around 4100 BC.[68]

The pottery that was produced in phases Sw 1 and 2 seems to have been quite similar, but we do not know enough about it to be able to distinguish any differences. The most conspicuous types among the pre-Drouwen pottery of phase Sw 4 are collared flasks and (funnel) beakers decorated with incised vertical lines on the belly.[69]

Flint (fig. 12.15)

On the basis of the study of the flint from Swifterbant S2 in particular we may assume that the flint tradition was a direct continuation of that of the Late Mesolithic.[70] The technique focused on the production of fairly small, regularly shaped blades with a maximum length of only 6 cm. The range of tools was very limited, including only long and short end scrapers, borers and small symmetrical trapezia. At first sight, the tool kit seems to resemble that of the pre-Michelsberg sites in the southern part of the Netherlands, but no comparative study has yet been carried out.[71] We do not know to what extent this Mesolithic micro-blade tradition continued in phase Swifterbant 4.

A noteworthy feature of the southern Swifterbant sites on the river dunes, for example that of Brandwijk, is that their flint traditions show more affinities with those of the southern Netherlands. They moreover all yielded artefacts made from flint mined at Rijckholt, indicating that they formed part of the exchange network of that flint type.[72] The combination of Swifterbant pottery and flint from southern Limburg is the first indication that in the southern part of the Netherlands the northwest Michelsberg group was indeed preceded by a Swifterbant phase.

Axes and other heavy implements

The start of the production and use of polished axes can be dated to the phase Sw 3 of the Swifterbant culture on the basis of the absence of fragments of such axes at Hogevaart and the presence at Bergschenhoek and at later sites. Characteristic of this period are axes with a round or oval cross-section and a pointed or rounded butt, which were made from quartzitic stone using the hard-hammer technique.[73] In addition, various types of perforated axes were imported from the Rössen communities in the south. Flint axes with a pointed butt are known from settlements from phase Sw 3 onwards.

The discovery at Hazendonk of a broken biconically perforated pebble hammer shows that such hammers were still being used in this period. Biconically perforated pointed implements were also used.[74]

The conspicuous absence of (fragments of) querns links these sites with Mesolithic sites and distinguishes them from most Neolithic settlements. This is a clear indication that the consumption of cereal products – and consequently the cultivation of cereals – was of subordinate importance.

Bone and antler (fig. 12.16)

Only a few bone and antler tools have been found at the settlements in the delta, but nevertheless sufficient to give us some idea of the types of tools that were manufactured from these raw materials. That antler was also a very important raw ma-

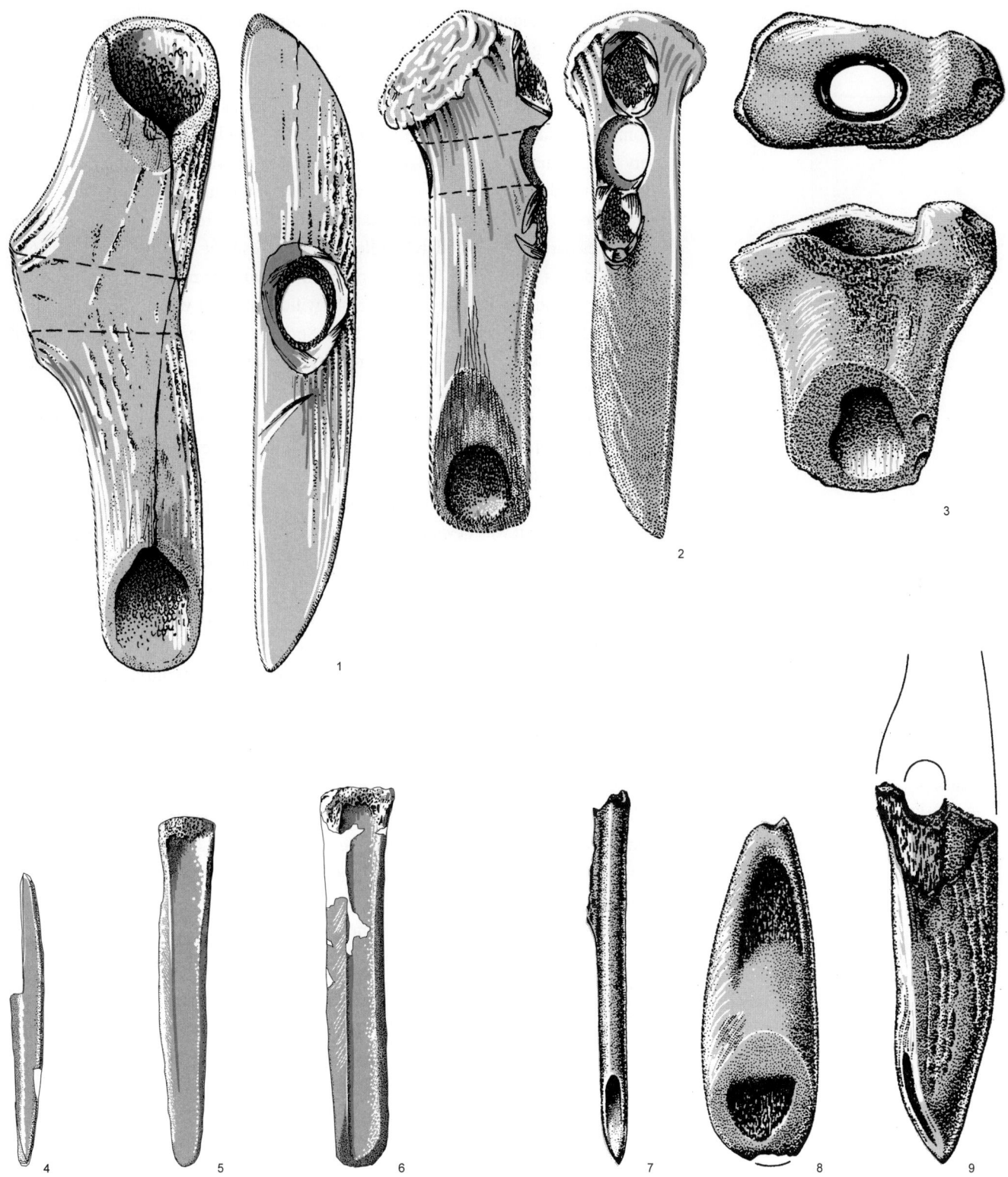

fig. 12.16

Bone and antler tools dating from the Middle Neolithic A found at various sites. Scale 1:2.

1	double T-shaped axe
2	base axe
3	socketed axe made from the radius of a domestic ox
4	bone awl
5, 6	chisels made from metatarsals
7	awl made from the long bone of a large bird
8	axe blade made from red deer antler
9	beam axe, red deer antler (broken)

sites:

1-2	Spoolde
3	Swifterbant
4-6	Hazendonk
7-9	Bergschenhoek

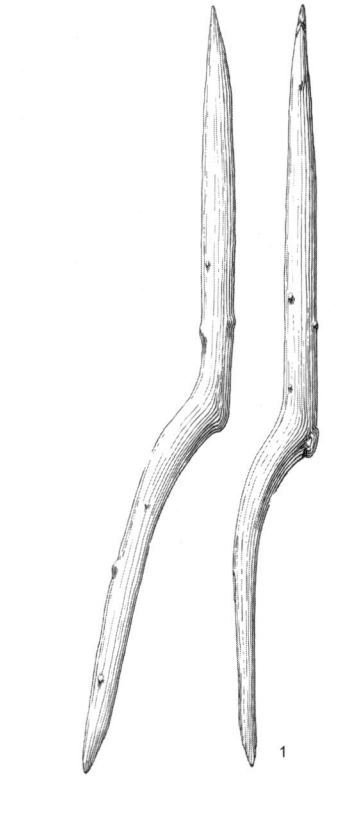

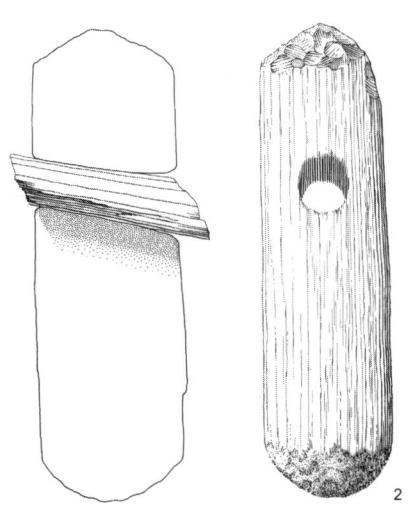

fig. 12.17
Wooden implements of the Swifterbant culture have also survived in wet contexts. Scale 1:4.

1 Bergschenhoek, two parts of eelspears
2 Hazendonk, phase 1, wooden hammer made of apple wood with part of its ash handle preserved

terial is clearly illustrated by the spectacular discovery of several dozens of antler artefacts during dredging operations at Spoolde near Zwolle.[75]

The beams of the antlers of red deer were used to produce what are known as 'base axes' and 'T-shaped axes'. Axes of the former type were in common use from the Middle Mesolithic until the end of the Neolithic. T-shaped axes were very popular across the whole of Central and Northern Europe in the 5th millennium. A third type of axe has the brow time as handle and the cutting edge made on the beam. We also know of imitations in antler of stone blade axes. In a few rare cases parts of the wooden handles of these axes have survived: 13 of the 96(!) T-shaped axes from Hüde I had been preserved with (remains of) their wooden handles. These handles were made from willow or alder wood; they were fairly short and remarkably thin. The finds from Spoolde represent a wide range of tool types and the waste formed in the manufacture of those tools. Although some earlier and later material might have been mixed up in this assemblage, it does seem to reflect some special activity carried out at one or more sites, but exactly what that activity was, is not clear. One possibility is the manufacture of canoes from tree-trunks.[76]

The articular ends of heavy, long bones were used to manufacture socketed axes, a tool type that was developed early in the Mesolithic. Knives were made from ribs. The metapodials of red deer – the most solid bones available – were systematically used as raw materials for the manufacture of chisels and awls. The awls made from bird bones reflect a similar efficient and selective use of bone. These antler and bone industries are in every respect continuations of the earlier Mesolithic traditions, insofar as the latter are known to us. They continued in the succeeding Vlaardingen period.[77]

Wood and rope (fig. 12.17)
Thanks to their excellent preservation conditions, the wetland sites have also provided a glimpse into the skilful use of wood. We may assume that wood was in common use as a raw material in this period. Roughly sharpened posts have been found at Hüde, Swifterbant and Bergschenhoek. The fill of a creek at Swifterbant 3 yielded two carefully finished ends of axe handles made from hazel and ash wood. A wooden hammer of apple wood and part of its ash handle were found among the remains of level 1 at Hazendonk and a 4.6-m-long part of a tree-trunk canoe came to light at Hüde I.[78] At Bergschenhoek an old canoe made from a heavy alder tree-trunk had been broken into pieces and reused to make a platform. Near the camp were a number of wooden arrow shafts, a pair of stakes with sharpened ends and two conspicuous branches sharpened at both ends, which may have formed part of eelspears or leisters. Lengths of rope of different thicknesses made from entwined fibers were also found embedded in the clay. The most spectacular finds, however, were three almost complete fish traps and a series of fragments of traps (plate 19B; fig. 12.18).[79]

Ornaments
Modest ornaments were found at Swifterbant, both among the settlement remains and in the graves: pieces of jet, small and larger pieces of amber, flat quartzite pebbles and canine teeth of predators and dogs. These teeth, which were pierced, had been worn as beads or pendants or they had been sewn onto clothing. The range of ornaments is a little wider than that of the preceding Mesolithic, but it does not differ markedly from that of the later Vlaardingen group.

CONCLUSION

In conclusion, the period discussed above can be *geographically* characterized as an era in which two markedly different communities were confronted with one another. On one side were the sedentary farmers on the loess soils, whose roots lay in Central Europe, on the other were the more mobile native communities with an economy based on gathering, fishing and hunting. For a long time these communities were divided by a fairly sharply defined frontier, which first extended along the northern perimeter of the loess zone and later shifted to the southern margin of the river district.

In *chronological* terms it was a transitional period, a long phase of incomplete and hesitant 'Neolithisation'. This process took the most time to the north of the major rivers, where it was not yet completed by the end of this period. The communities to the south of the river district were apparently in closer contact with the farmers of the loess zone; they switched to the Neolithic way of life at an earlier stage. On the grounds of their pottery and their use of mined Rijckholt flint they can be classed as 'Michelsberg', while the sickle blades and fragments of querns to some extent classify them as 'agricultural'. At some stage the (Swifterbant) communities living on the river dunes were incorporated in the 'Rijckholt flint network' (Brandwijk). They ultimately developed a new pottery style of their own (Hazendonk 3). However, they continued to use the river dunes in the same way as their predecessors had, *i.e.* as bases for hunting and fishing.

Major social changes were however also taking place among the agricultural communities on the other side of the 'frontier'. These changes were not gradual developments but crises, involving drastic transformations in the communities' culture. It is tempting to associate some, if not all, of these changes with the confrontation, contacts and exchange of knowledge with the northern native population, although we cannot specify these contacts in any greater detail. The outcome was a 'Neolithic' that was apparently acceptable to the native population of large parts of Northern Europe, from Great Britain to southern Scandinavia, but oddly enough not to the occupants of the region between the Rhine and the Elbe.[80]

fig. 12.18

One of the Bergschenhoek fish traps. Detail of the funnel-shaped entrance, showing that the osiers were tied together in the coils of an unknotted rope, which was evidently twisted from fibres during the manufacturing process. The photo shows the staggered transition between two coils. See also plate 19B.

NOTES

1   For surveys focusing on this problem see Bakels 1992a; Louwe Kooijmans 1993b, 1998.

2   Many short reports, specialist articles and monographs have been published on the excavations of Hüde I. For preliminary reports see Deichmüller 1969; pottery and synthesis: Kampffmeyer 1983, 1991; flint: Stapel 1988; subsistence: Hübner *et al.* 1988.

3   Dohrn-Ihmig 1983a and Jürgens 1979 for the Rössen sequence, Lüning 1968 for the Michelsberg sequence.

4   Blicquy-sites: Cahen/Docquier 1985, Caspar *et al.* 1993, Jadin *et al.* 1989, Jadin/Cahen 1992. Although the authors assume that Blicquy and the *Bandkeramik* are contemporary phenomena, as suggested by the ^{14}C dates, they are here discussed as though they succeeded one another. The available evidence allows this far less complicating option. Randwijck: Louwe Kooijmans 1988.

5   Associations: Stehli 1974, 1989a for the synchronism of the final phase of the *Bandkeramik* and the Grossgartach phase; site locations: Schwellnus 1985; earth works: Langweiler 10-12 (early Grossgart-

ach) measured approx. 5000 m² and was surrounded by a 3-m-wide and 2.5-m-deep V-sectioned ditch; Hambach 260 (late Grossgartach) measured approx. 7000 m² (Dohrn-Ihmig 1983a).

6   See Dohrn-Ihmig 1983a, 18-43 for a survey of Rössen settlements and house construction. Rössen settlements are still modelled on the settlement of Inden 1, which was excavated almost in its entirety: Lüning 1982b, *Abb.* 11, 12. For various settlements on the Aldenhoven plateau see *Bonner Jahrbücher* 171-182 (1971-1982): Untersuchungen zur neolithischen Besiedlung der Aldenhovener Platte 1970-'82.

7   K. Brandt 1967. This site apparently consisted of a single, isolated house.

8   The chance of Rössen sites being discovered at surface level is fairly small because they comprise far fewer pits filled with remains and consequently fewer finds come to light in ploughing. However, in the lignite mining area, where nothing escapes attention, Rössen sites were found to outnumber *Bandkeramik* sites (Schwellnus 1985).

9   Louwe Kooijmans 1988; Oude Rengerink 1991; Bakels 1990b, Bakels et al.1993b.

10 Vermeersch 1987-'88 mentions ten such monuments in Belgium, of which the one at Thieusies (Vermeersch/Walter 1980) is probably the best documented.

11 On the Aldenhoven plateau: Inden 9 (Kuper et al. 1975), Kreuzwein-garten (Bakels 1992, 75) and Jülich (Amtmann/Schwellnus 1987).

12 For causewayed camps in general see Thomas 1991.

13 Vermeersch 1987-'88; Vermeersch/Walter 1980.

14 Brounen 1988, 1995b; Thanos 1995; Schreurs 1992, 1994.

15 Jadin et al. 1989; Jadin/Cahen 1992.

16 Dohrn-Ihmig 1983a, 6-17.

17 Cahen/Docquier 1985.

18 Lüning 1968.

19 In general, the German terminology is used: Tupfenleisten, Schlickrau-hung, Schöpfer.

20 Brounen 1995b.

21 Koslar 10: Lüning 1978, 317.

22 Louwe Kooijmans 1980, 172-198.

23 For surveys see: Fiedler 1979. Various factors make it very difficult to date the many surface assemblages: the number of diagnostic ar-tefact types characteristic of a particular culture is very small, the types were usually used for a longer period of time and very many assemblages are mixed or they are contaminated with younger or older remains. For a discussion of these problems see: Löhr 1972-'77; Wansleeben 1987.

24 Cahen/Docquier 1985. A beige-chocolate flint which could be mined at Baudour in the Hainault was preferred for the long blades and the burins (id. 103-108). The burins that have been found in Belgian Michelsberg contexts (Vermeersch 1987-'88) may have been derived from these tools.

25 Many of the points were made on flakes with a pronounced bulb of percussion. The large blade tools are the most conspicuous, but on the whole, the technology seems to have focused on the production of flakes. For the Michelsberg flint industry and the use of flint see: Schreurs 1992, 1994 and forthcoming.

26 Valkenburg flint: Brounen/Ploegaert 1992, Brounen et al. 1993; Brounen 1995; Lousberg: Weiner 1980; Gronenborn 1992.

27 Clearances: Kalis 1988; Kalis/Meurers-Balke 1988.

28 For the organisation of mining and the distribution of flint, see feature E. Blades of Rijckholt flint have been found in Neolithic contexts at great distances from the mines, for example on Lake Constance. A similar 'interaction sphere', overlapping that of the Rijckholt flint, is that of the conspicuous brown-banded Romigny-Léhry flint (Polman 1993).

29 The Netherlands has no tradition of comprehensive axe studies. For surveys see: K.-H. Brandt 1967; Hoof 1970; Schut 1987, 1991.

30 The string of the bow of a bow-operated drill was twisted round the (vertical) drill. The drill could then be set in motion by moving the bow to and fro. Such drills are known from ethnographic sources. The only archaeological evidence for such drills consists of bored cylinders.

31 The German terms for these tools are: Plattbolzen, hohen durchlochte Schuhleistenkeil and durchlochte Breitkeil (Van der Waals 1977).

32 Oude Rengerink 1991.

33 Modderman 1960-'61. A second specimen was found in 1983 at Mechelen, also in the Geul valley.

34 Schut (1987, 47) mentions five flachen Hammeräxte from the Nether-lands; Schut et al. 1987; Brandt 1971.

35 Bakels 1990b; Bakels et al.1993.

36 See also feature J and the discussion in Jadin/Cahen 1992.

37 Merselo-Haag: Wansleeben/Verhart 1995. Assemblages like those of Ede-Frankeneng (Schut 1988) and Melsele (Van Berg et al. 1991) may date from this period. In the case of Ede there are only typo-logical arguments; in the case of Melsele the association with (Late) Mesolithic flint is not entirely certain. De Roever (1986) disputed such a relation for Swifterbant S11. Even older is the claim regarding the pottery of Weelde-Paardsdrank (Huyge/Vermeersch 1982). On the one hand the Mesolithic substrate in the southern part of the Netherlands (Rhine basin group) differs from that to the north of the major rivers (northwest group), on the other hand this differ-ence seems to have largely disappeared by the end of the Mesolithic. Moreover, the earliest assemblages found on the river dunes in the Alblasserwaard, dating from c. 4200 BC, show clear Swifterbant characteristics.

38 Bloemers 1972; Hinz 1974, 197-199, 215; Schut 1987, 55; Lüning 1982b, Abb. 3; Louwe Kooijmans 1993b.

39 Brounen 1985.

40 Van der Waals 1972.

41 Louwe Kooijmans 1976a, 1967b, 1993b; Ven-Zelderheide: Mooren 1993; The study by Raemaekers et al. 1997 has led to a drastic revision of, in particular, the interpretation of the Hazendonk 2 assemblage as presented here. The new evidence shows that it is not correct to refer to the northwest Michelsberg group as 'Hazendonk 2'.

42 Wansleeben/Verhart 1990, 1995, Verhart 2000.

43 Hazendonk: Louwe Kooijmans 1993a, Zeiler 1991; Wateringen: Rae-maekers et al. 1997; Rijswijk: Koot 1994, 16-21; Ypenburg: zie inter-mezzo F.

44 Münster Basin: Coesfeld, Osterwick (Willms 1982; Wilhelmi 1972) and Nottuln (Eckert 1986); Cuyk region: Kraaienberg (Louwe Kooij-mans/Verhart 1990). Belgian sites: Lüning 1968.

45 Hazendonk 3: Het Vormer (Louwe Kooijmans 1980), Gassel (Ver-hart/Louwe Kooijmans 1989), Grave (Verhart 1989), Meeuwen (Bel-gian Limburg, Creemers/Vermeersch 1989) and at some sites in the Meuse valley, as far south as southern Limburg.

46 The earliest assemblage containing Rijckholt flint is the Swifter-bant 2 assemblage of Brandwijk (4100 BC, Van Gijn/Verbruggen 1992). This flint type appears to have gone out of use by the time of Vlaardingen 1a (Hazendonk, 3500 BC). The use of broken axe fragments as a raw material is a conspicuous feature of the later Vlaardingen assemblages.

47 Schreurs 1992, 1994, forthcoming; see also Bienenfeld 1988.

48 Raemaekers et al. 1997; Koot 1994; Koot/Van der Have 2001.

49 Verhart/Louwe Kooijmans 1989, 108.

50 Kampffmeyer (1991) and Gehasse (1995 quoting Ten Anscher forthcoming) speak of a 'Hüde-Swifterbant culture'.

51 Many specialist articles have been published on Swifterbant; a series of 'Swifterbant Contributions' in *Helinium* (1976-'85), a series of final reports in *Palaeohistoria*. The most important are: Ente 1976, Casparie *et al.* 1977, Meiklejohn/Constandse-Westermann 1978, Constandse-Westermann/Meiklejohn 1979, Deckers 1979, De Roever 1979, Van der Waals 1977, Zeiler 1986, 1987, 1991, Van Zeist/Palfenier 1981. For a summary, see Deckers *et al.* 1980.

52 Ten Anscher/Gehasse 1993; Gehasse 1995; Ten Anscher forthcoming.

53 Verbruggen 1992a, 1992b, forthcoming Three of the sites date from before 4900 BC, 27 are from later periods, mainly the period of the Vlaardingen group.

54 For example De Gaste and Heemse (Van der Waals 1972).

55 Hogestijn (1990) previously proposed the terms 'Dronten phase' (= Sw 3) and 'Nagele phase' (= Sw 4). We have used the sequence set up by Ten Anscher (forthcoming; see also Gehasse 1995, 199), which is based largely on ¹⁴C dates and signs of (weak) influences: Rössen, Bischheim, Michelsberg and TRB, respectively. Ten Anscher emphasises the absence of stylistic changes in the Swifterbant pottery itself and the intersite variability.

56 Hogestijn 1990; Ten Anscher forthcoming

57 Hogestijn *et al.* 1995; Hogestijn/Peeters 2001. Part, at least, of the fragmentary pottery may be classified as 'Swifterbant'. No data are yet available on agricultural aspects.

58 Kroezenga *et al.* 1991. The two antler beams were still attached to parts of the frontlet. The ¹⁴C dates were published a year later: OxA-2908 5890 ± 90 BP for the encrusted remains and OxA-2909 5720 ± 90 and OxA-2910 5970 ± 90 for the antlers (Lanting 1992).

59 See also chapter 14. For reconstructions of the landscape see Van der Woude 1981; Ente 1976.

60 Louwe Kooijmans 1993a, 88; Newell 1973. The existence of the postulated De Leien/Wartena group is now a matter of debate. It has been found that flake axes encountered in mixed assemblages in the Meuse valley can be associated with the Michelsberg culture. Moreover, many large flint scatters are to be regarded as palimpsests, formed over many centuries or even millennia of use of a particular site. An example is the scatter of Koningsbosch (Van Haaren/Modderman 1973).

61 Van der Waals 1977; Van Zeist/Palfenier 1981.

62 Louwe Kooijmans 1986, 1987; Clason/Brinkhuizen 1993. The site was originally interpreted as a camp on a floating peat island, but serious mechanical and stratigraphic objections have arisen against this interpretation. It is more likely that the site lay on the shore of a pool and that the peat was torn away from the shore at some later date. This would mean that the site may have been used for a longer period of time and that it may also have been larger. Some finds from Schiedam and an antler axe from Krimpen aan de IJssel probably come from similar sites (Louwe Kooijmans 1974, 19, 36).

63 For the evidence and detailed interpretations see chapter 14; Zeiler 1986, 1987; Bakels 1981; Louwe Kooijmans 1993a.

64 The bones of domestic animals account for no more than 5% of the faunal remains. Other similarities between the two sites are the wetland location, the size (approx. 2000 m²), the very long period of use, the combination of local and 'imported' objects, of both pottery and flint. Taphonomic differences have however resulted in different archaeological records. Kampffmeyer 1983, 1991; Hübner *et al.* 1988.

65 Meiklejohn/Constandse-Westermann 1978; Constandse-Westermann/Meiklejohn 1979.

66 Waterbolk/Waterbolk 1992.

67 Ten Anscher/Gehasse 1993, 36-37. A settlement and a cemetery with 10 individuals in 8 graves was excavated in 1997 at Urk-E8, Noordoostpolder (Peters/Peeters 2001). Radiocarbon dates show a wide range, but all remains have a *terminus ante quem* of 3400 BC on palaeogeographical (water level) arguments.

68 De Roever 1979; Kampffmeyer 1983. Hüde I yielded vessels with pointed and round bases made from local clays, which closely resemble the pottery of Swifterbant, but also several Rössen and Bischheim beakers made from loess.

69 Ten Anscher/Gehasse 1993; Ten Anscher forthcoming; Hogestijn 1990.

70 Deckers 1979.

71 For example Merselo-Haag (Wansleeben/Verhart 1995), Weelde-Paardsdrank (Huyge/Vermeersch 1982). The assemblages of Brandwijk and Hazendonk I comprised a small proportion of blades.

72 Van Gijn/Verbruggen 1992.

73 The German terms are: *Walzenbeile*, *Felsrundbeile* and *Felsovalbeile*. See K.-H. Brandt 1967, Schut 1987, 1991; Fokkens 1991a, 91-97.

74 *Geröllkeule* and *Spitzhauen*, respectively. For a discussion of their functions see chapter 8. Hulst/Verlinde 1976, 1979.

75 Spoolde: Clason 1985; a smaller, but nevertheless comparable assemblage was found at Donkerbroek-Zwembad, Friesland in 1933 (Fokkens 1991a, 97, 197, site 268).

76 Assemblages of a similar composition and size were found in settlement contexts at Ringkloster (late Ertebølle, Andersen 1973) and Hüde I (Deichmüller 1969).

77 Hazendonk: Van den Broeke 1983; Bergschenhoek: Louwe Kooijmans 1985, 1987; Swifterbant: Clason 1985.

78 Swifterbant: Casparie *et al.* 1977; Hazendonk: Louwe Kooijmans 1985; the ¹⁴C date of the Dümmer canoe is 4895 ± 80 BP = *c.* 3600 BC (Kampffmeyer 1991, 63-64).

79 Bergschenhoek: Louwe Kooijmans 1985, 1986, 1987. For eelspears see Meurers-Balke 1981.

80 These considerations are discussed in greater detail in Louwe Kooijmans 1998. Raemaekers 1999 discusses the part played by the Swifterbant group in the Neolithisation process.

F   Stone Age farmers along the North Sea
The Rijswijk-Ypenburg cemetery

Hans Koot

Until 1993 we had very little evidence for Neolithic occupation before the period of the Vlaardingen group in the coastal area of the western Netherlands. Most of the settlements known from that early time lay on the belt of coastal barriers between Monster and Voorschoten, with only a few elsewhere, such as Haamstede-De Brabers in Zeeland (chapter 13). Some unexpected discoveries made in 1993 in a pit dug for the construction of national motorway No. 4 in the Hoekpolder, Rijswijk, changed this picture. At a depth of just over three metres beneath the surface were the remains of two settlements situated on old, buried coastal deposits. Features of pits and other structures were observed in the old soil strata. Finds consisted of pot sherds, animal bones, flint flakes, wood, *etc.* dating from 3650-3400 BC.[1] A few comparable sites from the same period came to light in the vicinity in the following years: Wateringen 4, Ypenburg and Schipluiden-Harnaschpolder.[2] These settlements all lay on low dunes, some 10 kilometres to the east of the present coastline, but they will originally have been situated close to the coast and the estuary of the Meuse. On the whole, the remains were well preserved; even some organic remains had survived.

In 1998 a remarkable discovery was made at Ypenburg site 4: a cemetery containing the remains of 42 individuals, including 25 almost complete skeletons, whose bones had survived in excellent condition. The deposits covering the cemetery had been removed shortly before discovery of the findspot by the Explosives Clearing Service (the site was a former airport!), as a result of which the burials lay virtually at the surface and the skeletons were exposed to the weather. The cemetery could not be preserved *in situ*, since the area containing the site was designated for new development. It was therefore excavated.[3]

How can it be that these former coastal sites have come to light at such a distance from the present coastline? We should realize that temperatures began to rise at the beginning of the Holocene, causing the polar ice caps to melt and the sea level to rise. The plain between the European continent and England was gradually submerged and became what is now the North Sea. In the process, the coastline of the western Netherlands moved in an easterly direction. Around 4100 BC it reached its most inland position. By then, the rise in sea level had decreased to such an extent and sand was being deposited in such large quantities, that the coastline could not move any further inland. There was even sufficient sand for dune formation, resulting in a coastline with low dunes on tidal deposits. The coastline was still open, allowing the sea to penetrate far inland via wide tidal

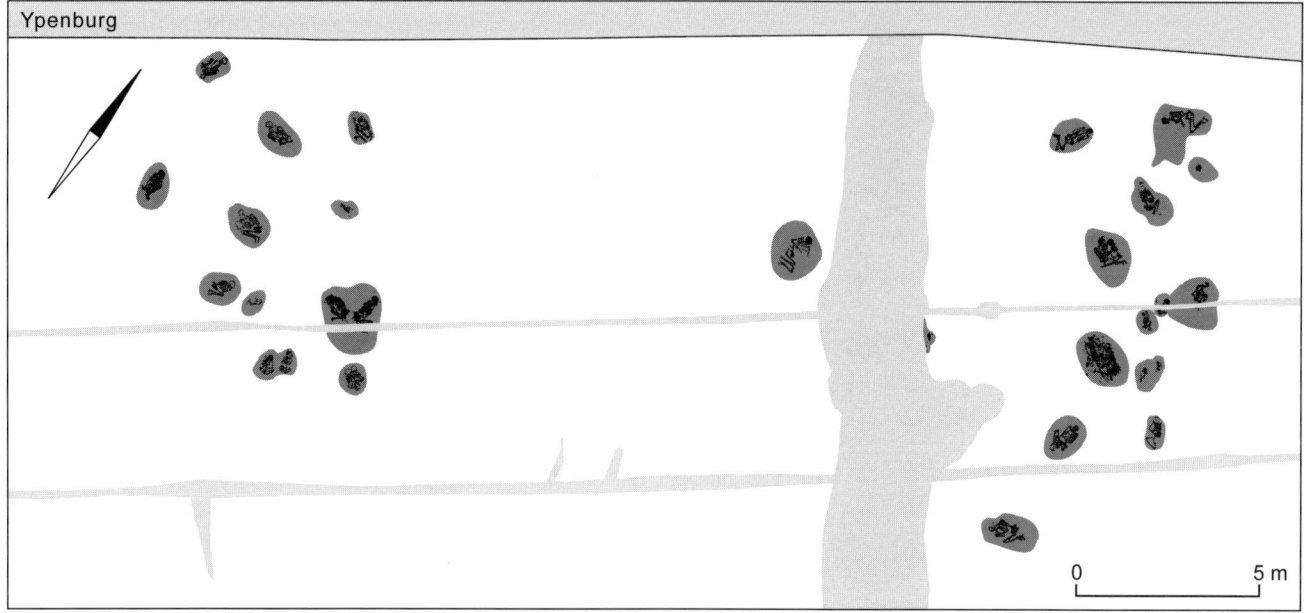

Ypenburg

0   5 m

fig. F1

Plan of the Ypenburg cemetery, which clearly comprises two clusters of burials. Scale 1:200.

channels. The Ypenburg site demonstrates that people visited this dynamic coastal landscape and even settled there in the period when the dunes were being formed. Thin clay deposits on the dune sand show that the dune was initially still flooded from time to time, but once it had acquired a certain height it continued to grow only through the deposition of drift sand. Between the layers of drift sand on the Ypenburg dune were several layers of occupation remains, showing that people lived there over a fairly long period. The period of occupation has been dated between approximately 3800 and 3200 BC. The settlements were probably permanent. Numerous postholes have been found on the dune and even the plan of a two-aisled rectangular building with a length of at least ten metres and a width of 3.80 m. The occupants kept livestock, but still supplemented their diet with the products of hunting and gathering. No evidence of crop cultivation has been found at the site itself, but cereal did form part of the diet.

For a limited period of perhaps two centuries the occupants also buried their deceased on the dune. The cemetery concerned yielded important information on the community living on the dune. In total 31 burials, containing the remains of 42 individuals, have been found.[4] The graves were

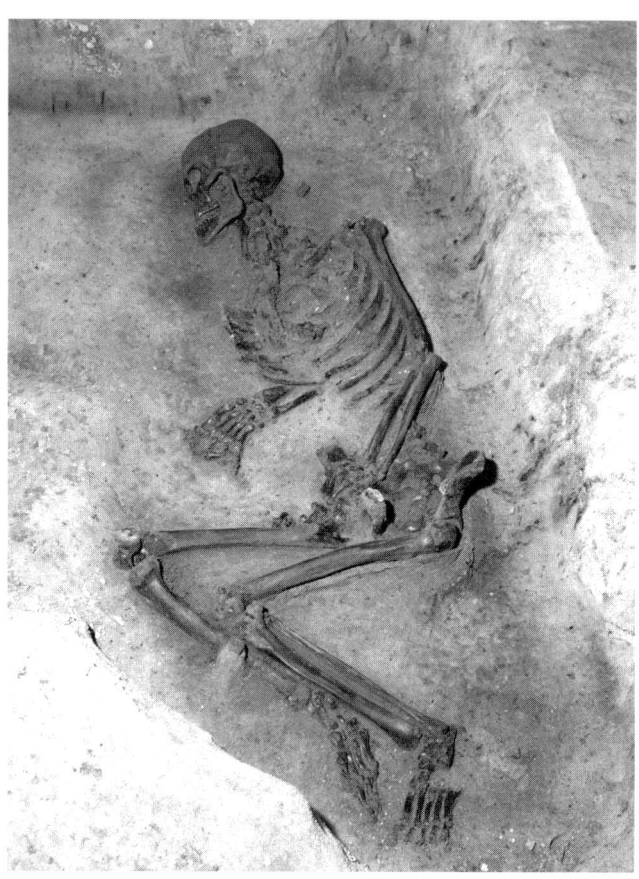

fig. F3
Ypenburg, burial of a male adult.

arranged in two clusters spaced some ten metres apart (fig. F1). Both adults (aged from twenty onwards) and younger individuals were buried here, and both men and women (fig. F2-3). Adult men and women were buried here in almost equal numbers: eight men and ten women; the sex of four individuals could not be determined. Most of the adults were aged 35-44; only a few had lived to a greater age. Almost half of the individuals had died at an early age, before they had reached twenty. No fewer than sixteen infants of less than seven years old were buried here, the youngest a foetus of only four months. The people were fairly short, with average lengths of 160 cm for men and 153 cm for women. The well-preserved bones show that several of the adults had worn joints, indicating physical strain. The teeth were fairly worn, possibly as a result of the type of food consumed and/or the use of the teeth as a 'third hand'.

Most of the graves contained single burials (23 individuals), but there were also some with multiple burials: five containing the remains of two individuals, one containing those of three and one those of four individuals. Insofar as still observable, the majority of the deceased were buried lying on their sides with their legs drawn up to their chests (fig. F2). There seems to have been no preference for the left or the right side; both positions were represented. Two indi-

fig. F2
Ypenburg, burial of a female adult with her legs drawn up close to her body.

274

viduals were buried on their backs, five were found lying on their backs with their legs drawn up. Whether the latter posture was deliberate is not certain; the body may have twisted somewhat when the grave was filled. There was no strict rule concerning the orientation of the grave; we observed only a slight preference for west-east and northwest-southeast orientations. The burials contained very few objects such as grave goods or parts of clothing. In total, ten amber and three jet beads were recovered. One child wore a bone ring round one of its fingers. Palynological and other analyses of soil samples yielded no evidence for grave goods, but perishable goods such as clothing or flowers may of course have been deposited in or on top of the graves.

So several burials contained the remains of more than one individual. Two children were buried in one of the graves. The way the two skeletons were arranged implies that the children must have died and been buried (almost) simultaneously. This was not the case with the individuals interred in various other graves, which had been reopened for later burials. The grave of an adult, for example, was at some stage opened for the burial of a child, at which time the adult's skeleton was moved aside to make room for the child's remains. Another grave was reopened at least four times for subsequent burials. The graves were not always reopened for another burial: a few cervical vertebrae of a young man were for example found alongside the rest of the skeleton elsewhere in the grave. His grave may have been reopened, perhaps for the purpose of removing something (beads?) from it, but the disturbance may also have had a different, natural, cause. A grave could be reopened only if people knew its exact location. That means that the burials must have been marked in some way, but no remains or other evidence of such markings were found during the excavation. The fact that graves were reopened, and the different forms of multiple burial reflect complex rituals for the handling of the deceased. We are well familiar with this from ethnographic studies. It reminds archaeologists that what they interpret as 'burial rites' are in actual fact nothing more than the outcomes, preserved in the soil, of complex rites of passage in which the deceased were transported from the world of the living to the realm of their ancestors and in which their relatives mourned their loss.

This cemetery greatly enhances our understanding of occupation in the coastal area of the western Netherlands in the Middle Neolithic. This area was occupied by communities consisting of both adults and children, and both men and women. The settlements were not temporary camps used for short periods of time by for example inland hunters visiting the coast for specific activities. The cemetery may perhaps have served to add weight to a group's claim on a territory at the coast.

Notes

1   Rijswijk: J.M. Koot 1994.
2   Wateringen 4: Raemaekers *et al.* 1997; Ypenburg: Koot/Van der Have 2001; Schipluiden: excavated in 2003, publication in prep.
3   Koot/Van der Have 2001.
4   Koot/Van der Have 2001.

G   Import from all quarters
Stone axes in the northern Netherlands

Jaap Beuker

The flint axes from the Mesolithic that are known to us are on the whole irregularly shaped, small implements with lengths of at most ten centimetres. They must have been used for felling trees and working wood. With the transition to the Neolithic way of life a need for larger and more efficient axes apparently arose. Neolithic axes are generally much longer than ten centimetres, some being no less than thirty centimetres long. They were symmetrically shaped and ground for optimum efficiency and to enable them to be shafted properly. Great care also went into the selection of the type of stone to be used. Flint, the material used most for tools throughout the entire stone age, was extremely suitable for making axes. Before the Neolithic, the flint that was to be found in the northern part of the Netherlands had apparently met the flint workers' requirements. This flint had been deposited there by glaciers during the Saalian (see chapter 3). The transport in the glacier ice and temperature effects had caused the flint to crack; by the time it was deposited in the Netherlands it had been reduced to mere fragments. No fragments but relatively large nodules of flint were needed for the production of a well-finished axe of the kind required in the Neolithic. The need for good-quality raw material that was readily available in the northern part of the Netherlands could be partly met by using the often very suitable tenacious and impact-resistant types of stone that were to be found in the boulder clay, for example gabbro, diorite and diabase. In addition, flint axes and axes made from other types of stone, including so-called flint geodes, were imported from other areas.

The import of flint

Relatively few of the axes that have been found in the northern part of the Netherlands are made of flint from the south, for example from the Lousberg near Aachen in Germany or from the mines near Rijckholt in the province of Limburg. The majority are made of flint that was imported from areas further north.

It is not so easy to determine the source of these northern imports. In Scandinavia, identical or very similar types of flint often occur at different sites or over wide areas. In the case of axes made from such flint types it is not possible to trace the flint back to individual outcrops within a restricted area. Moreover, good-quality Scandinavian (in particular Danish)

flint made its way into northern Germany in Weichselian moraines. Such factors often make it impossible to determine the exact origins of axes made from foreign types of stone.

The question which of the axes that have been found in the northern part of the Netherlands were made from local flint and which were imported has been the topic of much discussion.[1] In the past the size of the axe was always an important criterion in distinguishing between the two: only the large specimens, with lengths of over fifteen centimetres, were considered (indisputable) imports. However, the tool's finish and typological features should also be considered. Comparatively large roughouts were needed to produce the axes of the northern type, with their rectangular cross-sections. A number of poorly finished axes whose shape was clearly determined by the shape of the flint nodule have been found in the north of the Netherlands. Most of these axes are small and may be considered local products. No semi-fin-

Northern flint

■ primary sources

▨ secondary sources along the Sleswig-Holstein coast

— — westernmost limit of the Weichselian ice cap

Silica geodes

☆ primary sources

fig. G1

The natural sources of northern flint and of quartz geodes, as used for axe production in the Neolithic.

277

ished axes have been found so far. This, and the poor quality of the flint available in the northern part of the Netherlands, suggests that virtually all of the axes found in this area are imports.

Schleswig-Holstein

For a long time it was assumed that the flint axes that have been found in the northern part of the Netherlands came from outcrops in Denmark. This is, however, not so likely as it first seemed. Large amounts of flint nodules of excellent quality can be collected at the foot of the cliffs along the eastern coast of Schleswig-Holstein, where they were deposited by the aforementioned Weichselian moraines (fig. G1). Carried over shorter distances and deposited in a more recent past, these flint nodules are larger and of a better quality than those found in the north of the Netherlands. Many roughouts have been found near the cliffs, in particular at the foot of the steepest cliffs, where the amounts of flint released as the sea eroded the matrix containing them were greatest. They show that axes, and other implements, were produced in large numbers here. It is quite possible that many of the middle and late Neolithic axes that have been found in the Netherlands were imported from this area and not from

Denmark. Schleswig-Holstein lies some three hundred kilometres away, whereas the Danish outcrops lie a good two hundred and fifty kilometres beyond that. However, it is very difficult to find irrefutable evidence for the importation of flint from Schleswig-Holstein. About ten different types of flint occur at that site. The axes that have so far come to light in the Netherlands indeed include specimens made from some of these flint types. Further evidence is sometimes provided by hoards of axes (plate 20A): some hoards were found to contain combinations of different types of flint which can be collected along the eastern coast of Schleswig-Holstein without any difficulty today.[2]

Helgoland

The only northern flint imports that can be traced back to their source with certainty come from outcrops in the vicinity of the island of Helgoland, in the German Bay. Five different types of flint occur in this area, three of which are suitable for making axes. The most easily recognisable is the rare red flint. The other two types are both grey; one occurs as longitudinal nodules, the other as sheet-like bodies. The latter can sometimes be distinguished from other northern types. We know for sure that the distribution area of the flint of Helgoland, in particular the red variety, is limited to the island and its immediate surroundings. Moreover, we may assume that none of this flint, or at most very small amounts, was carried to the Netherlands in moraines. So far, artefacts made of the red flint have been found at a total of fifty-six findspots in Northwest Europe. Twenty-one of these are axes or fragments of axes. Fourteen of the latter category were found in the provinces of Drenthe and Gelderland; one came from the province of Limburg in the south of the Netherlands (fig. G2). However, this distribution pattern is without doubt distorted, because more research has so far been carried out in the northern part of the Netherlands, in particular in Drenthe, than in the southern part.

One of the finest finds is a roughout that was found near Een, in the municipality of Norg (plate 20B).[3] The flint finds recovered in the northern part of the Netherlands also include six flakes which were probably formed in the production of axes. These flakes and the roughout suggest that some of the axes were imported as roughouts. The find from Een formed part of a hoard consisting of a ground axe, a partially ground axe, two sheet-shaped nodules and two longitudinal nodules (fig. G3). The partially ground axe of grey flint is certainly from Helgoland. The typical shapes of the four nodules and the fact that they were recovered from the same context imply that they, too, came from Helgoland.

The axes of red Helgoland flint are all datable to the mid-

fig. G2
Distribution of finds made from the red Helgoland flint in the Netherlands.

axe

flake

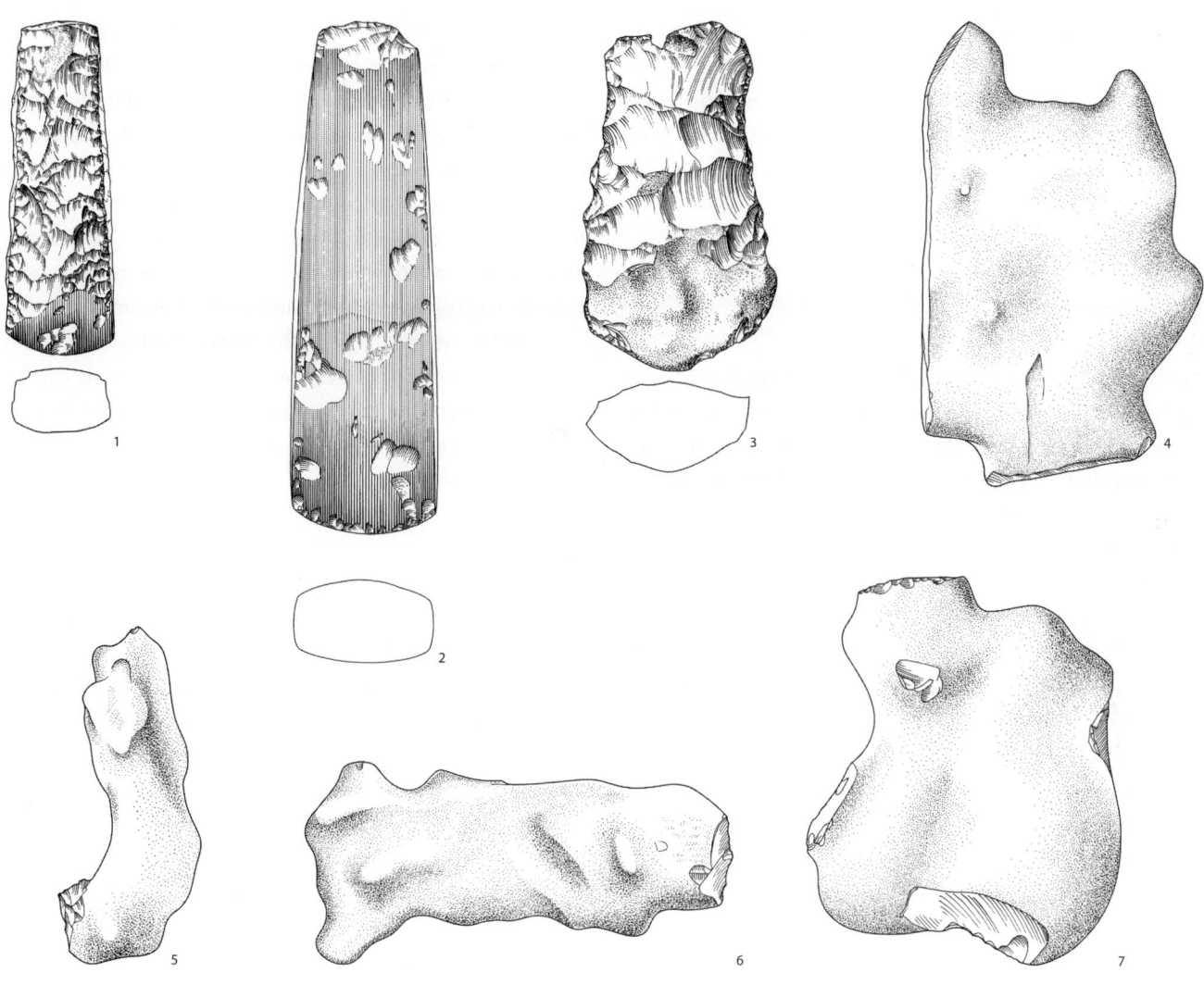

fig. G3

Hoard found at Een, municipality of Norg, in 1940, comprising three axes in different production stages (1-3) and four nodules (4-7). The blank No. 3 is made from Helgoland flint (*cf.* plate 20C).

dle or late Neolithic. Most of the finds are associable with the Funnel-Beaker (TRB) culture. The fact that the high-quality sheet-like grey flint occurred in large amounts on Helgoland would suggest that this type of flint was imported more often than the red variety, which was much rarer and, moreover, was often found in pieces that were too small for the production of axes. On the other hand, it is possible that the red variety was much in demand for its exotic character or for aesthetic reasons, as suggested by the artefact that was found in Limburg, within the distribution area of other flint types. The simple grey kind of flint could probably more easily be obtained from Schleswig-Holstein. In prehistoric times the flint could be collected at the foot of the chalk cliffs which then still existed to the east of what is now the island of Helgoland. Originally, Helgoland formed part of the mainland but it became an island in the course of prehistory. In the Neolithic, the flint probably already had to be transported by sea.

The distribution pattern of flint axes shows that the flint that occurs in northern Germany, for example near Hemmoor and Lüneburg, was not used for the production of axes. Presumably that flint was situated too far beneath the surface for prehistoric exploitation.

Silica geodes

A number of axes have been found in Lower Saxony and in the northern part of the Netherlands that are made of a dense, black type of stone that can be worked like flint. Microscopic analysis has shown that these axes were made from so-called silica geodes, which must have been obtained from the Wiehengebirge in Germany. The area around Bramsche near Osnabrück is a very likely source,[4] although the greatest number of axes made from such geodes were found some fifty kilometres further southeast. These geodes were fairly easily obtainable; they could be collected from, for example, stream beds. Axes made from geodes have been found in Friesland, Drenthe and Overijssel. Most of these finds date from the middle and late Neolithic. Usually, only small axes could be made from geodes because of the many cracks that they contained.

Future research

The types of stone that were used for the production of axes in the northern part of the Netherlands are well known. We know that several types, such as flint and flint geodes, were imported from elsewhere. It is unlikely, but not altogether impossible, that the axes made from stone types such as gabbro, diorite and diabase were also imported. Future research into the sources of flint axes will concentrate mainly on the flint types occurring in Schleswig-Holstein and on the island of Helgoland. Microfossil research and chemical analyses will probably enable us to differentiate between some of the flint types from Helgoland and those from other northern outcrops. However, it is very unlikely that they will reveal any differences between the flint from Schleswig-Holstein and that from Danish sources, as they are both of the same type. It is even less likely that we will ever be able to determine the sources of the axes made from rocks such as gabbro, diorite and diabase, which can even be found in the Netherlands, in the form of erratic boulders.

Recently, a few rare imported jadeite axes (plate 20A) have been discovered in the northern part of the Netherlands. Moreover, axes of a black type of quartzite have been found, which were probably also imported from elsewhere. These discoveries show that there is a possibility of axes of stone types not yet encountered in the Netherlands being found in the future. But in view of our present knowledge we may safely assume that the number of axes of new stone types that may come to light will be extremely small.

All of the data available on the (indisputable) imports will have to be carefully studied before any conclusions can be drawn regarding the size and nature of the distribution patterns of the axes and any mechanisms that may have played a part in shaping them.

Notes

1 See Bakker 1979a, 80.
2 Good examples are a hoard that was found at Een, municipality of Norg, some time before 1898 (Van den Broeke 1979) and the hoard from the Wildeveen, municipality of Zuidlaren (Drents Museum, Assen, inv. no. 1923/XI 3 a-b; not published).
3 Harsema 1979b.
4 Büchner 1986, 168. The rock type is also known as *Wiehengebirgslydit*. Whether the term 'silica geode' is formally correct is doubtful. 'Septarian nodule' would be more correct (A.P. Schuddebeurs, oral communication).

13 Megalith builders and sturgeon fishers Middle Neolithic B: Funnel Beaker culture and the Vlaardingen Group

Annelou van Gijn and Jan Albert Bakker

INTRODUCTION

The best-known archaeological monuments in the Netherlands, the *hunebedden*, belong to the Funnel Beaker culture or *Trichterbecher Kultur* (TRB). The distribution area of this culture covers the whole North European Plain, extending to Poland and the western Ukraine towards the east, southern Sweden towards the north, and Slovakia towards the south. Within this vast area a number of regional groups can be distinguished, including what is known as the West Group in the Netherlands and northwest Germany.[1] Remains of this group have been found mainly in the sandy parts of the plain to the north of the Rhine, but also along the banks of the Hunte in the Dümmer fen peat region (Lower Saxony) and in the wetlands bordering the North Sea coast. The artefacts and burials of the West Group are very similar to those of the North Group in southern Scandinavia and northern Germany.

The delta of the Rhine and the Meuse has yielded remains of a quite different culture group that has been called the Vlaardingen group. These remains, which have been found in different ecological zones within the coastal region, bear a close resemblance to finds from the sands and loess of Limburg and the adjacent part of Belgium, which are attributed to the Stein group, a well-known funerary monument of the latter group. The contents of the burial chamber of Stein, in turn has some affinities with that of the *Galeriegräber* of the Wartberg group in Hessen (Germany), suggesting links in that direction, too. In view of the many similarities between the pottery of the Wartberg, Stein and Vlaardingen groups, such as the almost complete absence of surface decoration, the vessels' S-shaped profiles or straight walls, the flat bases and the occurrence of collared flasks and lugs,[2] it has been suggested to use the term 'Wartberg-Stein-Vlaardingen complex' for these groups.[3] Besides there are several similarities to the Seine-Oise-Marne culture of Belgium and northern France (fig. 13.1).

The material evidence available for the different archaeological cultures and groups varies considerably, largely due to differences in the environments in which the remains have been found. The TRB culture is known predominantly from its burial monuments, *i.e.* the *hunebedden* and flat graves. Although we also know of many TRB settlement sites, most of these sites consist of nothing more than scatters of flint and pottery; they very rarely include features. Also very rare are unburned organic remains; among the exceptional sites where such remains have been preserved are the 'Huntedorf' on the shore of lake Dümmer (Germany) and Slootdorp in the Wieringermeerpolder (North Holland).[4]

The same holds for organic remains of the Stein group in Limburg. The interpretation of the evidence of this group is complicated by the fact that the archaeological remains of most Stein sites were mixed with finds from other periods. The sites of the Vlaardingen group are an entirely different matter. Like the Swifterbant sites, they were situated in wet environments, where organic remains have been much better preserved. Consequently, we are well informed about the settlements

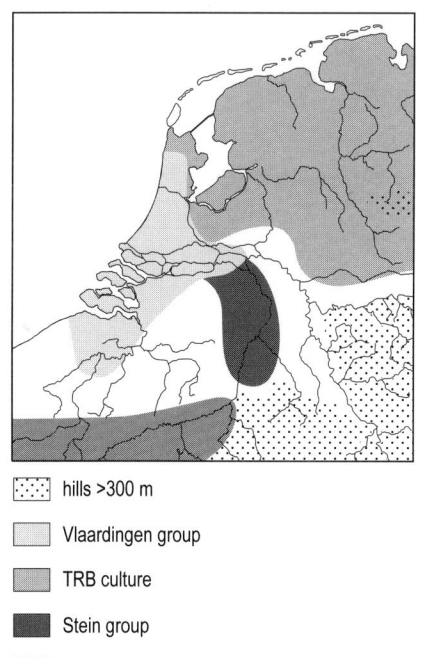

hills >300 m

Vlaardingen group

TRB culture

Stein group

Seine Oise Marne culture

fig. 13.1

Distribution of the various culture groups during the Middle Neolithic B in the Netherlands and its environs.

of this group. Without this 'wet component', the Vlaardingen group would however differ very little from the southern Stein group. Unfortunately we know very little about the burial rites of either of these groups as only few burials have been found. The Stein burial vault is an exception.

The aforementioned differences in the available evidence to a great extent dictate the kind of archaeological research that can be carried out into these groups. Because of the large amount of information available on the burial rites and the regional differentiation of the pottery of the TRB culture, research into this culture has focused largely on the communities' social structure. Much less is known about the subsistence activities and the economy of this culture or about any functional differences between the settlements. With the Vlaardingen group it is precisely the other way round: the best-known aspects of this group are the locations of the sites and the subsistence system.

THE TRB CULTURE

Setting aside the possibly semi-agricultural, but still poorly known groups of the Middle Neolithic A, we may regard the western group of the TRB culture as the first agricultural community in the central and northern parts of the Netherlands. In Denmark, clear signs of continuity are observable between the Ertebølle culture and the TRB culture in terms of site location and economy; hunting and gathering remained important for these early farmers.[5] The resemblances observable between the late Swifterbant culture and the early TRB culture in the Noordoostpolder suggest a similar continuity in the Netherlands.[6] The farmers in these regions probably practised an extensive method of cultivation known as 'slash-and-burn' cultivation, which implied periodically creating clearances in different parts of the forest and allowing the forest to regenerate before clearing it again. The cattle foraged in the woods.[7] Major innovations introduced in the TRB period are the *ard* (the precursor of the plough) and wheeled vehicles.[8]

Material culture

Pottery

Our main source of information on the material culture of the TRB is pottery, which has been found in large quantities in the *hunebedden* and flat graves in the Netherlands and northwestern Germany. This pottery is characterised by a specific style of decoration known as *Tiefstich*, or stab-and-drag, which consists of motifs that were deeply incised in the polished surface of the vessel using an obliquely held bone or wooden rod or a bird's quill.[9] After the vessel had been fired, the incisions were filled with a mixture of grease and burned bone. In the rare cases in which this paste has survived it is yellowish white, but it is possible that other colours were used, too. Characteristic types are collared flasks, funnel beakers, jars, tureens, amphorae, shouldered bowls, buckets or pails, bowls and dishes. The settlement pottery was less lavishly decorated and also included large storage vessels and round disks, that perhaps were used as lids but mostly are called 'baking plates', which are rarely encountered in graves.

The pottery underwent marked changes in shape and decoration with time. Van Giffen's[10] successive Drouwen and Havelte styles were later subdivided and detailed by others (fig. 13.2).[11] Although we will use the old terminology in the following discussion, it should hence be understood that we are actually referring to a continuous

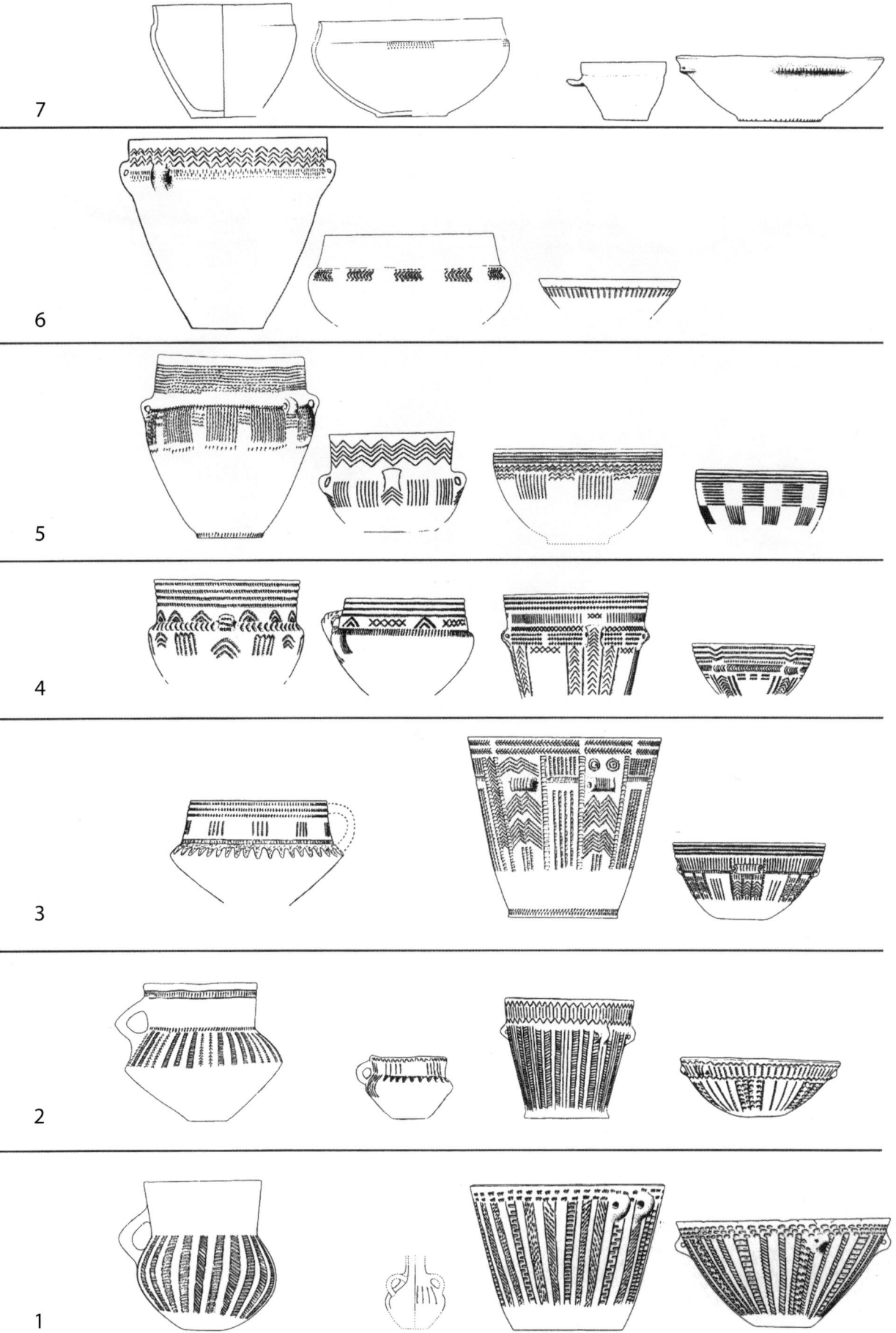

fig. 13.2

Typochronological sequence of the TRB Westgroup after Brindley. The 'horizons' or phases 1-4 correspond to Drouwen, 5-7 to Early, Middle and Late Havelte, respectively.

fig. 13.3
Pottery from the Havelte phase of the TRB culture (fig. 13.2; phase 5). Grave goods from flat graves excavated in the early 20th century by J.H. Holwerda near the Uddelermeer.

fig. 13.4
Collared flask from the Drouwen *hunebed* D19. Scale 1:2.

development. In general terms, the Drouwen style can be said to be characterised by a wide range of types, lavishly decorated with alternating horizontal and vertical patterns. Early Havelte pottery shows less variation; the main types are bowls and tall and squat amphorae, and the decoration, simplified to horizontal bands and blocks, covers a smaller area of the pot (fig. 13.3). Late Havelte ware is hardly decorated at all and shouldered bowls and shallow dishes have replaced the amphorae and globular bowls of the early Havelte phase. Collared flasks (fig. 13.4) and 'baking plates' were common in all phases. Recently, very early TRB pottery, from before the period of the *hunebedden*, has been discovered at site P14 in the Noordoostpolder (province of Flevoland).[12] This pottery, which is still very poorly known, has provisionally been termed 'pre-Drouwen ware (phase 0)' (see chapter 12).

It is often assumed that in communities that were essentially egalitarian – which we presume was also the case with the TRB communities – the women produced the pottery. The results of research into a pedestalled bowl from *hunebed* D26 (Drouwenerveld, Drenthe) confirm this assumption: the widths of the nails of thumb and index-finger impressions on fracture surfaces were found to be narrower than those of male nails. The pottery was in all probability produced on a household level. Each lavishly decorated pot shows a unique combination of common motifs. Most of the 'services', the sets of pots of the same workmanship that were collectively placed in a *hunebed*, are not paralleled in other graves.[13]

Flint and hard stone

The largest find category after pottery is that of artefacts of flint and other types of stone, the most conspicuous being flint axes with rectangular cross-sections (see feature G). The majority of these axes will have been used for felling trees and building houses. Some are however more than 20 cm long. In view of this exceptional length, most of those which have survived intact and unworn are probably

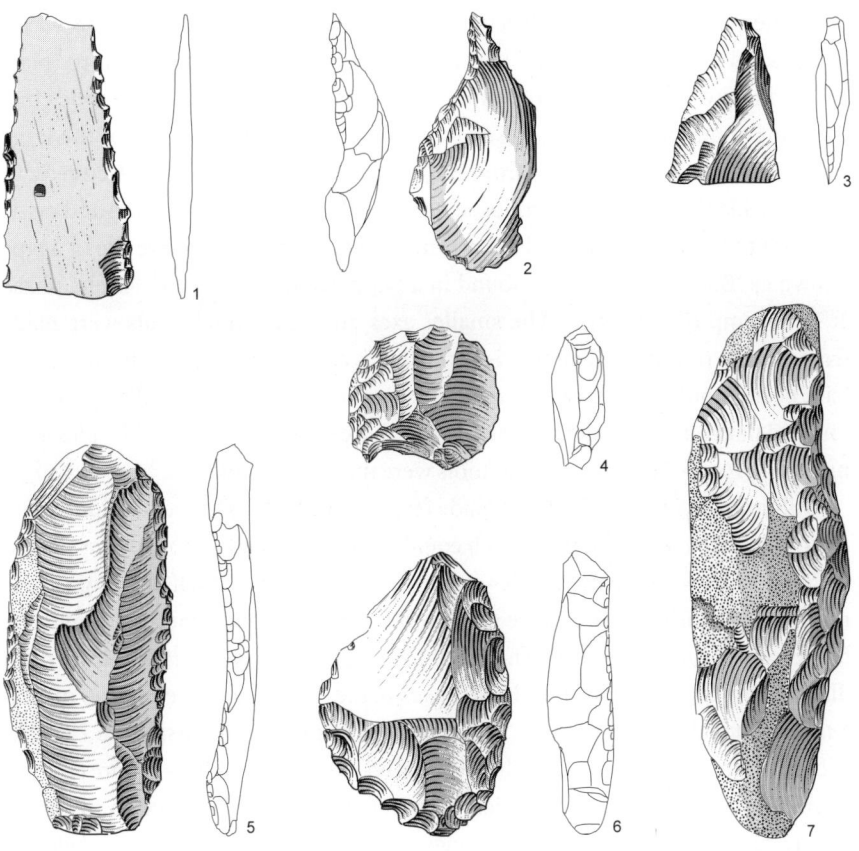

fig. 13.5

Flint tools of the TRB culture from the settlement at Anloo. Actual size.

1, 3 transverse arrowheads

2 borer

4-6 scrapers

7 pick (strike-a-light)

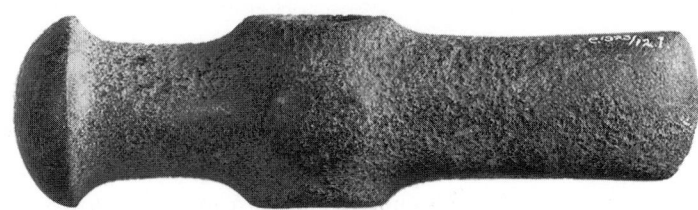

fig. 13.6

Knob-butted axe made of diabase from Wapenveld near Heerde. Scale 1:2.

fig. 13.7

Simple, bowl-shaped granite quern with a rubbing stone, found as a stray find at the Anloo settlement. Scale 1:6.

fig. 13.8
Characteristic Neolithic grinding stone made of quartzitic sandstone with bowl-shaped grinding surfaces on all four sides, found at Weper (Fr.). Scale 1:6.

to be interpreted as prestige objects. We know of many finds of one or more axes of this kind that were deposited in watery environments as votive offerings (plate 20C).[14] Many of the deposits containing such axes also included nodules and chisels. Flint of a high quality was used to manufacture the tools. Most of the large axes and chisels were imported from Helgoland, Schleswig-Holstein, Denmark or Rügen as blanks or finished products.[15] Axes with an oval cross-section and made from southern flint types are also known. A good example is a large axe of a type known as 'Buren axe' that was found in a flat grave from the Late Havelte phase at Denekamp (fig. 13.23).[16] The smaller axes and other small tools were made from local, erratic flint. Characteristic tool types are transverse arrowheads, which have been found in the *hunebedden* in large numbers, scrapers, so-called pics,[17] retouched flakes and bladelets, some showing sickle gloss (fig. 13.5). The pics were made on prepared cores, the other tools were made on flakes.

Utilitarian axes were also often made from locally available types of stone, such as diorite, diabase and gneiss, which could be collected from boulder-clay deposits. Axes made from quartz geodes were imported from the Wiehengebirge to the north of Osnabrück (see feature G). Knob-butted axes and other representative battle axes found in the northern part of the Netherlands were made mostly from diabase (fig. 13.6). A few knob-butted axes made their way to the plateau of Brabant and the valley of the Semois (in Lorraine in Belgium), far outside the TRB distribution area, via exchange.[18] Other lithic artefacts found at TRB sites are concave querns, usually of granite, in which the ground grain accumulated in the cavity (fig. 13.7). The associated rubbing stones are rarely encountered; they are believed to have been round.[19] The stone axes were polished on large, immobile grindstones of Dala sandstone, quartzitic sandstone and quartzite. Most querns and grindstones were found as site furniture at settlements, for example at Anloo (Drenthe) and Laren (North Holland); a few came to light as stray finds (fig. 13.8).[20]

Ornaments
Amber beads are often encountered as grave goods in *hunebedden*. Hunebed D26 (Drouwenerveld), for example, yielded dozens of amber beads, possibly from one and the same string. Less common are amber pendants and beads or pendants of quartz, jet or pierced gravel fossils (ammonites).[21] We may assume that numerous beads made of animal teeth and other organic materials have not survived. Amber could be picked up along the coast in the north of the Netherlands,[22] the jet may have come from southern Belgium or northern France.

The *hunebedden* of the western group have also yielded small discs, beads, strips and tubes of sheet copper, which may have formed part of necklaces or have been sewn onto clothing. They probably came from southeastern Europe.[23]

Settlements

Settlement remains have been found at many TRB sites in the sandy region. In addition to the decorated *Tiefstich* pottery known predominantly from the graves, the refuse that was discarded in and around the dwellings also included sherds of typical settlement types like clay discs, large storage funnel beakers and other large vessels. Other objects recovered from settlement sites comprise the axes and arrowheads that are also encountered in funerary contexts, plus scrapers, flint flakes and fractured querns, grindstones and hammers tones.

The areas of domestic refuse vary in size from approximately 5600 m² (Laren, middle Drouwen phase) to 50,000 m² (Elspeet, Gelderland, early and middle Drou-

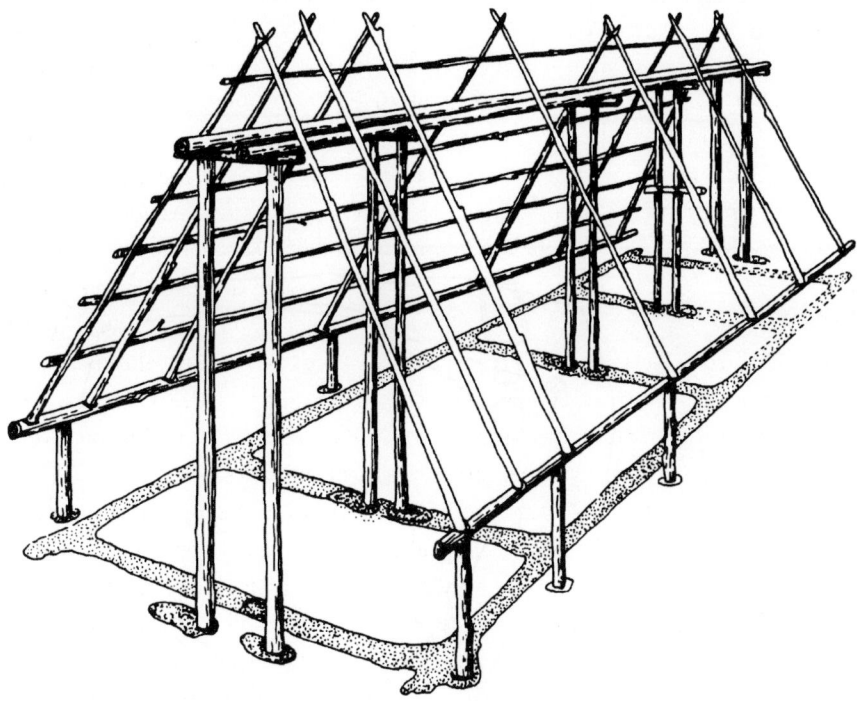

fig. 13.9
Reconstruction of a 12-m-long TRB house based on a plan documented in the excavation at Eekhöltjen, Flögeln (northeast of Bremerhaven). The house evidently comprised several rooms. The ridge pole was supported by pairs of roof supports.

wen phases). In the case of the latter site, which comprised a 1-km-long scatter of sherds on the banks of a dry stream bed into which wells had been dug, the settlement was probably gradually shifted, and was consequently smaller than suggested by the expanse of the refuse.[24] In view of the form of agriculture practised by the occupants, it is indeed very likely that the settlements were shifted from time to time. As most features have lost their colour as a result of soil formation processes, only a few house plans of the West Group are known. At Flögeln (near Cuxhaven), Penningbüttel (near Bremen) and Heek (Westphalia) the remains of identical two-aisled longhouses measuring 13 x 5 m were found (fig. 13.9).[25] The houses were situated in isolation or a few dozen metres from neighbouring houses and were not surrounded by a palisade.

Features of palisades have been found at Anloo and near the Uddelermeer (Gelderland). Although no house plans could be recognised, it was evident that the settlement of Anloo had lain inside this palisade (fig. 13.10). A study of the locations of monuments in relation to the surrounding landscape has shown that the palisade of Anloo was situated not at a randomly selected site, but along a major route along the low Hondsrug ridge.[26]

Conspicuously few TRB settlements have been found outside the dry sandy region. The remains of an entire hamlet, known as the 'Huntedorf', were found on the northern shore of lake Dümmer near Lehmbruch (Germany). Besides many organic objects, they included the excellently preserved wooden floors of thirteen houses enclosed by a fence.[27] A timber palisade and some pottery came to light at Schokkerhaven on the bank of the IJssel; if there was a settlement at this site, its remains have probably been washed away by the river. The other TRB settlements that have been found in wet environments are probably to be interpreted as extraction camps. At Slootdorp (Wieringermeerpolder), two relatively small (summer) camps were excavated on a salt marsh deposit.[28] The main activities practised at these camps were fishing in the North Sea, mollusc-gathering, hunting and cattle keeping. The pottery was made from local (marine) clay, which suggests that a relatively large proportion of the community lived at this camp for a fairly long time. The subsistence was similar to that of the later sites of the Single Grave culture found in this same area (see chapter 17 and feature J).

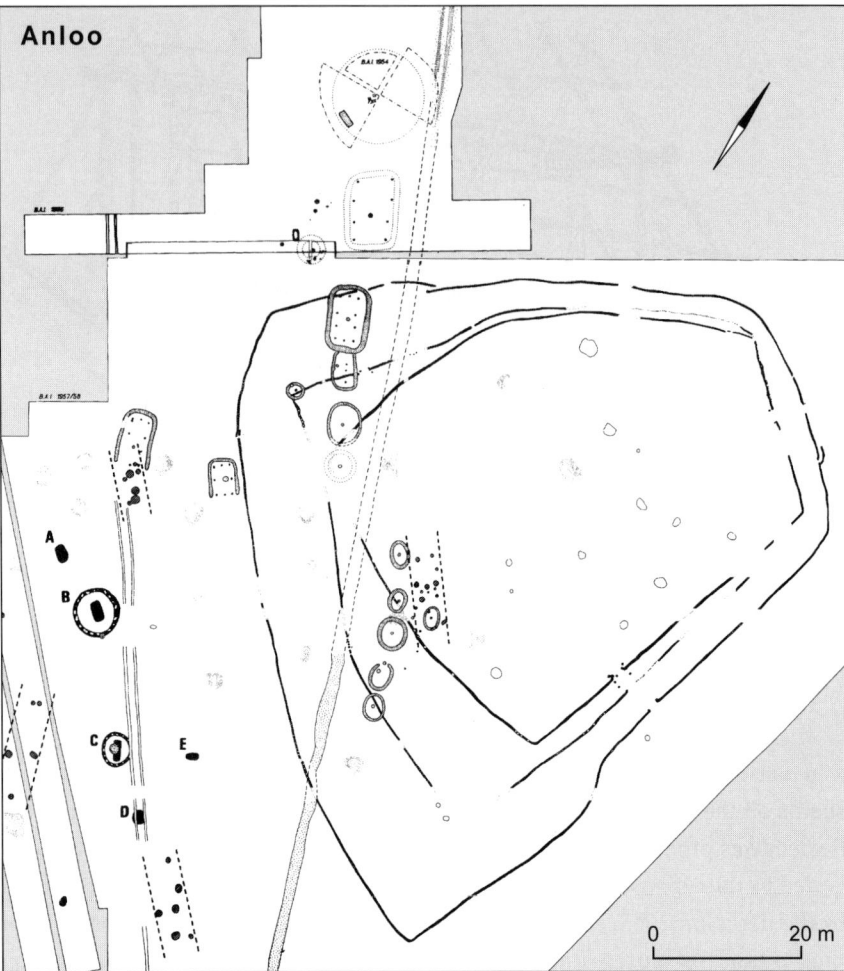

fig. 13.10
Three-phase palisade enclosure that was
excavated at Anloo (Dr.) in 1958. Associated
finds date the palisade to the Havelte style
phase of the TRB culture. This unique
enclosure has been interpreted as a cattle
pen on the basis of the absence of house
plans, but that could also be attributable
to soil processes. A possible alternative
interpretation is that it was a central meeting
point with a social function. Next to the
enclosure is a series of Beaker barrows. A
sandy track runs across the enclosure and
next to this track is a small Late Bronze Age
urnfield.

This scantily available evidence presents snatches of a differentiated settlement
system. Like the sites of the early phase of the northern TRB group,[29] the settlements of the pre-Drouwen phase lay in the vicinity of water. Good examples of
such settlements are the extraction camps that were discovered on the southern
shore of lake Dümmer.[30] The people of the Drouwen and Havelte phases preferably built their settlements in sandy areas, where they cultivated their crops; their
cattle they pastured in the oak-lime forests and in fallow fields. Ideal sites were
those where water could be obtained from a nearby stream, pit or collapsed pingo.[31] The hamlets, which consisted of five to fifteen widely spaced small houses,
were surrounded by palisades (Anloo, Lehmbruch), but there were also fairly isolated settlements consisting of only one to three houses (Heek, Flögeln, Laren).
The houses were repeatedly rebuilt at a new site. A proportion of the population
practised hunting and fishing and pastured cattle at seasonal camps.

Burial practices and ritual life

Megaliths and flat graves

The TRB communities buried their dead in different ways; besides communal burial in the spectacular burial monuments known as *hunebedden*, they also practised
individual burial, in stone cists and flat graves. The *hunebedden* (see also feature H
and plate 22) were built in the Drouwen phase (c. 3400-3050 BC). As the deceased
were buried as corpses and were not cremated, their remains have not survived
in the acid sandy soils. We do not know whether they were buried in the *hunebedden* immediately after death or some time later, after excarnation. We are better

informed about the grave goods, at least those of durable material. Besides large numbers of pots, which were probably filled with provisions for the deceased, they include stone (hammer) axes, flint arrowheads and axes and ornaments of copper, amber, jet and other unusual stones. Both women and men were buried with the ornaments they had worn in life (necklaces and beads sewn onto their clothing); the men were also accompanied by their weapons and hunting gear. It is thought that, over a period of 75 to 400 years, one body, accompanied by on average one to five pots, was buried in a *hunebed* every two to ten years. For a short time, around the transition from the middle to the late Drouwen phase, the known *hunebedden* were almost all in use at the same time; some of the monuments had then only recently been built whereas others were soon to go out of use.[32] No more *hunebedden* were built in Drenthe after the early Havelte phase, but the existing burial monuments continued to be used in the same manner as before.

Individual burial was practised in flat graves or stone cists, in which the deceased were interred accompanied by the same grave goods as those found in the *hunebedden*. The reason for the differences observable in burial practice is not clear. Perhaps the deceased were buried in extended position in the flat graves until the end of the Drouwen phase and from then onwards in crouched position, but the available evidence does not really justify such a generalisation. We also know of several flat-grave cemeteries from the early Havelte phase, for example at Heek in Westphalia, where excavators observed the silhouette of an individual who was buried in crouched position, on his or her left side.[33] In the middle and late Havelte phases cremation started to be practised. The cremated remains were buried in flat graves or *hunebedden*, accompanied by pots containing food and beverages.

The *hunebedden* played an important part in the ritual life of the TRB people. Sherds of pottery showing the same decoration as the pottery found inside the burial chambers have also been found in front of the tombs, from which we may infer that foodstuffs were offered at the entrances. The decorative motifs adorning a tureen that was found in the offering zone in front of *hunebed* D26 on the Drouwenerveld bore a remarkably close resemblance to those on a pot of the same type found inside the monument, suggesting that the two pots were made by the same woman or by relatives.[34]

Peat bog deposition

The TRB people also deposited pottery in peat bogs and other watery environments. A pot and a number of deer antlers discovered in the Voorste Diep near Buinen[35] indicate that this custom already existed at the time of the Swifterbant culture. Six pots that came to light during peat-cutting activities in different parts of the raised bogs in Drenthe and the north of Overijssel had been offered to supernatural powers, probably filled with foodstuffs or beverages, near rivulets like the Hunze, the Mussel-Aa and the Runde (fig. 13.11). At least four of these pots date from the Drouwen phase. One of the pots was probably found in association with remains of a deer and a pike. We know that the other TRB groups frequently offered pots containing foodstuffs in rivers, swamps, lakes and wells.[36] We may assume that the vast majority of the TRB pots that were deposited here escaped notice during the reclamation of the peat bogs in this area.[37]

Hoards of one or more axes are known from the entire distribution area of the TRB culture, in particular from regions where over the past hundred years greater concern has been shown for archaeological finds in peat-cutting and heath-reclamation work. Hoards of two or more often extremely large axes and chisels in different stages of completion are known from almost twenty sites in the peat lands

fig. 13.11

Large TRB 'tureen' with a large ribbon handle characteristic of the second phase of the West group of the TRB culture found in peat near Weerdinge. Depositing objects in peat bogs was an ancient north European cult-related custom. A wide range of objects were deposited in such contexts, including such pots, with or without contents.

of Drenthe and Groningen (plate 20C; feature G).[38] Being made of flint imported from northern Germany and Denmark, they must have been very valuable objects. Some hoards also included flint nodules and unpolished rough-outs which, unlike the hafted and worn axes known from a few Danish food deposits, were not yet ready for use. In Denmark, hoards of axes were usually deposited in bogs, whereas food offerings were deposited in open water.[39] A few hoards were found there buried in the ground, for example beneath or near a large stone. For a long time the possibility was left open that these hoards had been temporarily buried with the intention of recovery at some later time, like many of the hoards of coins and possibly also some of the hoards of bronzes known from later periods. However, in view of such factors as the deposits' isolated location in or at the periphery of bogs, most prehistorians nowadays agree that they are to be interpreted as ritual deposits. Many of the complete stray axes that have been found in peat or sand

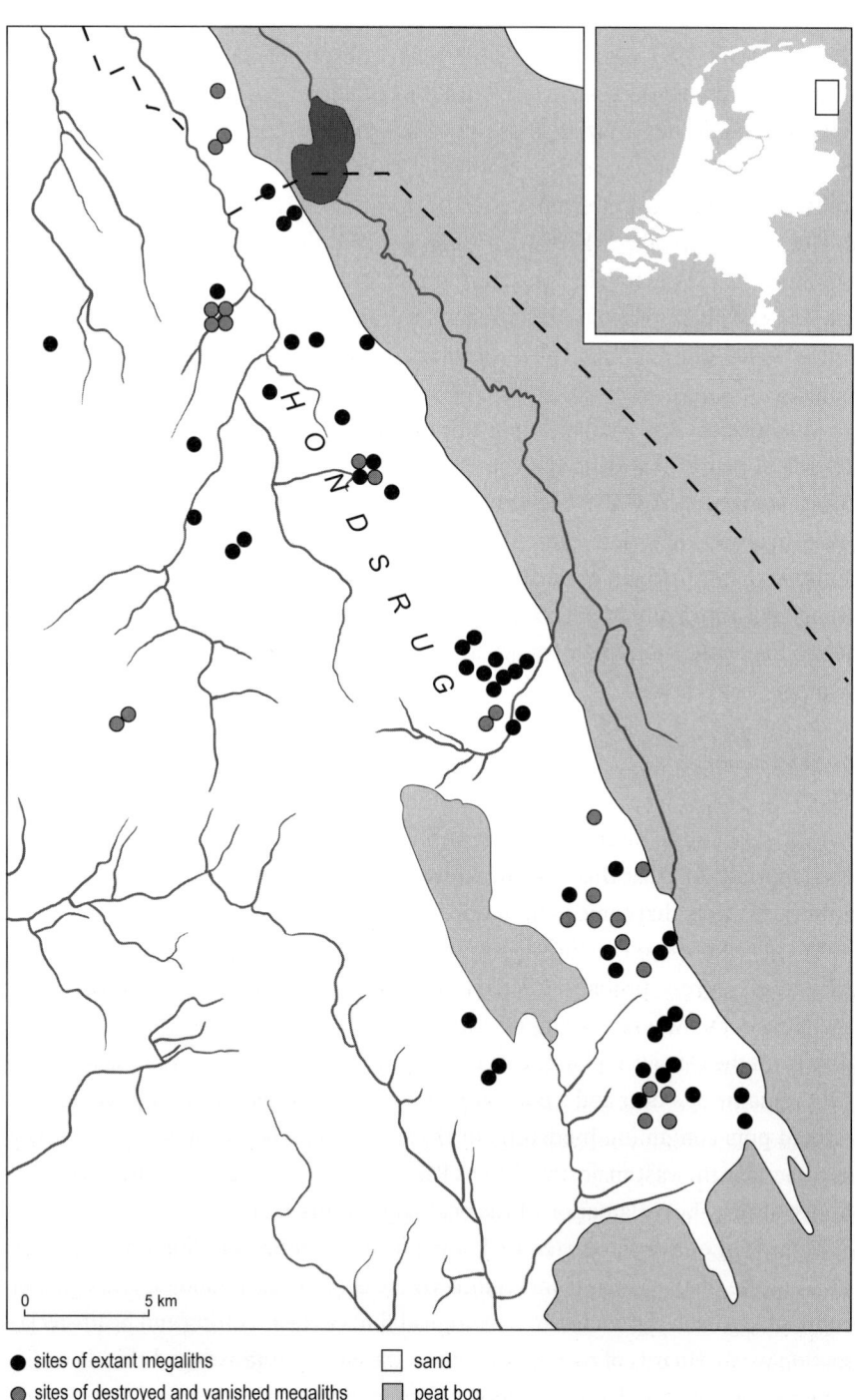

fig. 13.12

The low Hondsrug ridge in the east of Drenthe showing the sites of extant and vanished *hunebedden*. Is this remarkable concentration a result of the availability of large erratic boulders on this boulder clay ridge or could it (also) imply that this elevation in the landscape had a special significance?

● sites of extant megaliths □ sand

● sites of destroyed and vanished megaliths ▨ peat bog

may also be regarded as ritual deposits. Such stray finds are known from several sites to the north of the major rivers, also outside the plateau of Drenthe.

Some of the axes and chisels that have been found in hoards or as stray finds are of types typical of the later Single Grave culture. We also know of votive deposits, consisting of for example flint sickles and large scrapers, from the period of the Bell Beaker culture and from the Bronze Age and the Early Iron Age in both the northern and the southern parts of the Netherlands. The many perfect Buren axes and other ceremonial axes and chisels of southern flint that have been found in stream valleys in particular and during heath-reclamation activities in the southern part of the Netherlands may also be regarded as deliberately deposited offerings.

Social structure

Most of our information on the social organisation of TRB communities comes from the *hunebedden*. The construction of a *hunebed* was without doubt a communal effort in which the population of a large area participated. The planning and organisation of such an effort called for some form of leadership, probably based on proven skills in setting up such an enterprise. A supply of food was required to support the large group of people involved in the monument's construction; this had to be planned, and so did the transport and erection of the stones and the digging of the burial chamber.

The large numbers of *hunebedden* suggest that every community had one or more at its disposal. The pottery recovered from the *hunebedden* seems to differ somewhat from one monument to another. That is one of the reasons why it has often been suggested that *hunebedden* were territorial markers, symbolising the territories of specific social units, namely kinship groups of 50-100 people, who descended from one or more communal ancestors.[40] However, spatial analysis of *hunebedden* and other TRB finds with the aid of Thiessen polygons has failed to reveal unambiguous patterns that could point to the existence of such territories.[41] The *hunebedden* show an irregular distribution, with a high density in the Hondsrug hills and a relatively small number in western Drenthe (fig. 13.12). There are several possible explanations for this. The irregular distribution pattern could be attributable to differences in the availability of large boulders or to differences in the numbers of monuments that have been destroyed over the ages. A perhaps more attractive hypothesis, in the absence of a better interpretation model, is however that which associates the *hunebedden* with particular kinship groups, rather like the 'tomb groups' of Madagascar.[42]

There is no evidence to suggest any social hierarchy in the TRB period. Some distinction was made in burial rites in the sense that some members of the community were buried in *hunebedden* while others were interred in (what are in our eyes less prestigious) flat graves, but as no skeletal remains have survived we do not know whether this distinction was in any way related to the age or sex of the deceased. The grave goods recovered from the *hunebedden* and flat graves do not show any conspicuous differences in terms of 'richness' or number, so the meaning of the distinction between burial in a *hunebed* and in a flat grave remains a mystery. The pottery of the TRB communities has also inspired social interpretations. Voss, for example, concluded that the lavishly decorated Drouwen vessels are the products of small social units. In his opinion, the decrease in the amount of decoration in the late Havelte phase could reflect increasing social integration.[43] Hodder regards the recurrence of the horizontal and vertical decorative motifs

fig. 13.13

Palaeogeography of the southwestern part of the Netherlands in the Middle Neolithic B showing the locations of the sites of the Vlaardingen group. The sites lay on Older Dunes, behind the former coastline, along tidal streams in the Meuse estuary and on outcropping river dunes in the peat district. The almost complete absence of sites in Zeeland is attributable to later erosion and sedimentation.

A = Antwerp

B = Breda

D = Dordrecht

H = The Hague

L = Leiden

M = Middelburg

R = Rotterdam

U = Utrecht

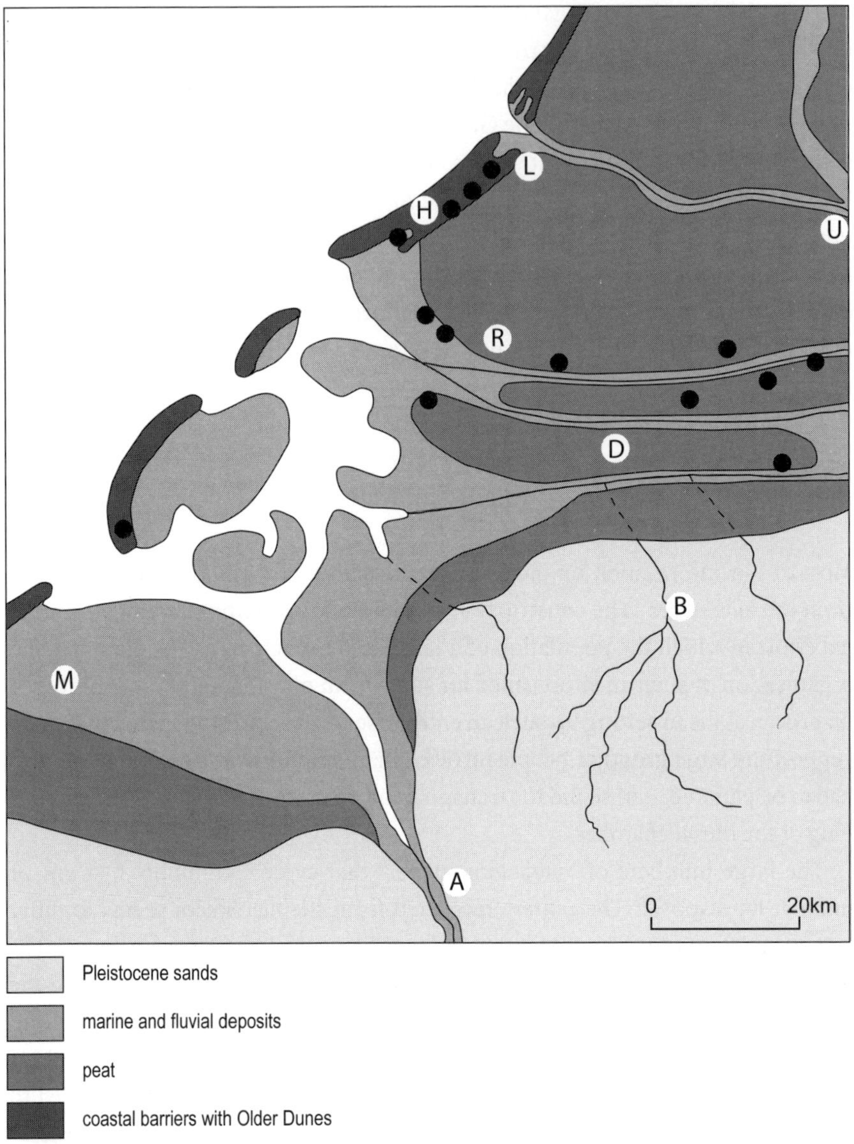

Pleistocene sands

marine and fluvial deposits

peat

coastal barriers with Older Dunes

characteristic of Drouwen pottery as evidence for the existence of different classes within the community. In his opinion the subsequent decrease in the amount of decoration points to a denial of the social distinctions and a trend towards a more egalitarian society.[44] The transition from the Drouwen pottery with its wide range of different types and lavish decoration to the simple late Havelte ware is of course a conspicuous and significant development, which may very well be attributable to social changes within the community, but Voss' and Hodder's interpretations of these stylistic changes are only speculative.

Summarising, it may be said that the TRB people lived in local kinship groups. Theirs was probably an egalitarian society, in which village chiefs, master builders, religious specialists and other members with specific tasks acquired their special positions through talent and experience.

THE VLAARDINGEN GROUP

The Vlaardingen group is known to us from some thirty sites, most of which lie in the Rhine/Meuse basin. The term 'Coastal Neolithic' was initially used for the first excavated sites of this group (Zandwerven and Hekelingen I), because of their

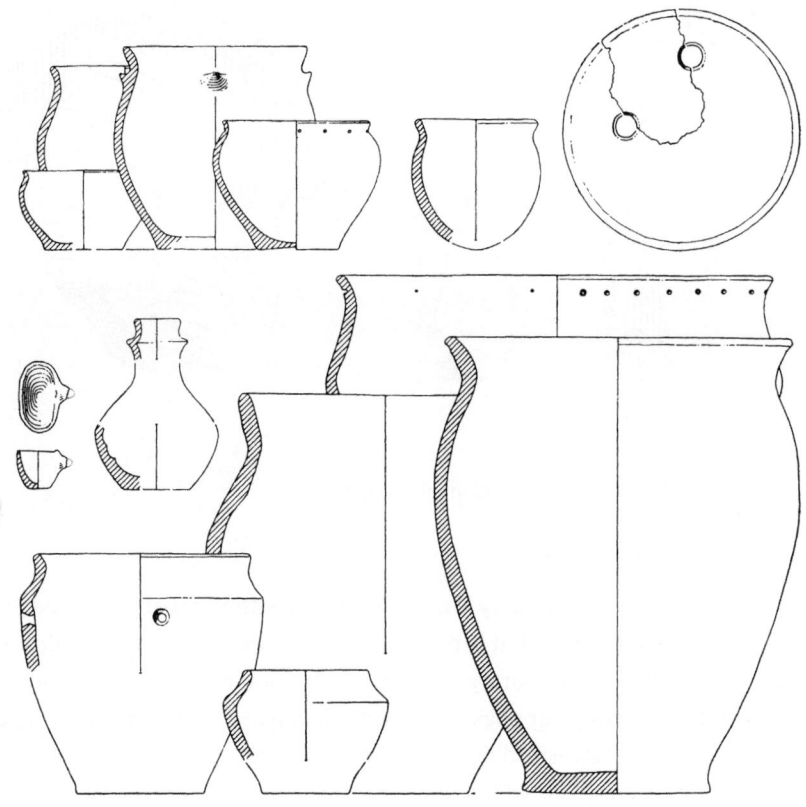

fig. 13.14
A representative selection of pottery from
Vlaardingen, datable to the middle phase of
the Vlaardingen group. Scale 1:6.

situation near the coast.[45] After the excavation of the site at Vlaardingen the term
'Vlaardingen culture' was used, but nowadays 'Vlaardingen group' is preferred.
Vlaardingen sites have been found in different ecological zones (fig. 13.13):
– on coastal barriers in the Older Dune area (Haamstede-Brabers, Leidschendam,
Loosduinen, Voorschoten-Boschgeest, Voorschoten-De Donk and Westbroek 3 in
the Velserbroek polder);[46]
– on stream ridges in the freshwater-intertidal zone (Vlaardingen, Hekelingen);[47]
– on river dunes in the peat region (Hazendonk);[48]
– on levees in the fluvial clay region (Ewijk).[49]
And, finally, there is also the above-mentioned site of Zandwerven, on a low dune in
the salt marshes of Westfrisia, which yielded remains of both the late Vlaardingen
group and the Single Grave culture.[50] A number of Vlaardingen finds have recently
come to light outside the coastal zone, too, for example in northern Limburg and
at Oudenaarde in the Scheldt basin.[51] The occurrence of Vlaardingen objects in
these regions supports the hypothesis that the area to the south of the major rivers is to be regarded as a single cultural area, between the distribution areas of the
TRB culture in the north and the Seine-Oise-Marne culture in northern France and
the Ardennes.[52] In the absence of pottery, it is still unclear where the line dividing
the Stein group and the Seine-Oise-Marne culture is to be drawn in Belgium and
the Netherlands.

A major problem with respect to the sites of the Vlaardingen group is that it is
very difficult to determine their nature. In spite of the large amount of ecological information available on these sites (see chapter 14), we do not really know
whether the individual Vlaardingen sites were permanent settlements or seasonal
camps. The evidence suggests that the Vlaardingen people grew crops and kept
cattle in the drier areas (on the coastal barriers and the wide levees of the fluvial
clay region) and practised hunting and fishing in the more marshy zones.

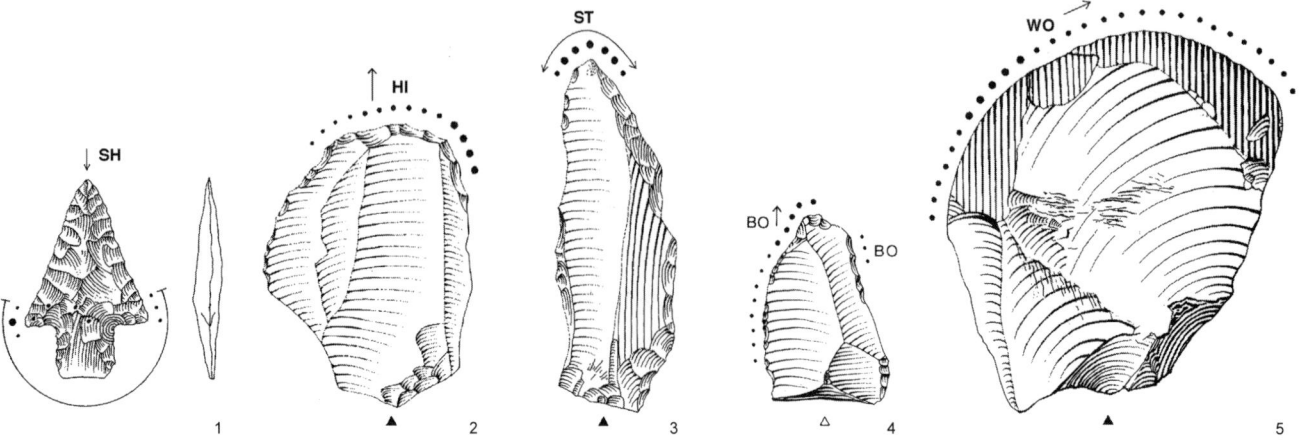

fig. 13.15
Flint tools characteristic of the Vlaardingen
group with codes indicating microscopic
traces of use, Hekelingen III. Natural size.

1 tanged arrowhead

2 scraper

3 borer

4 retouched flake

5 axe flake

Legend:

BO   bone

HI   hide

SH   shooting

ST   stone

WO   wood

Pottery

The relatively thick-walled pottery is rather uniform, with S- or barrel-shaped profiles and flat bases (fig. 13.14). It is predominantly tempered with quartz; decoration is almost absent. Noteworthy is the great variation displayed by the pottery
from the different sites. Four phases can be distinguished within the Vlaardingen
period on the basis of stylistic differences in the pottery:

– The pottery of phase 1a, which is built from coils, has been encountered at
Hazendonk only; it is characterised by pronounced S-shaped profiles and perforated rims.

– The pottery of phase 1b is tempered with quartz. The pots, many of which have
perforated rims, vary considerably in shape, from vessels with S-shaped profiles to
barrel-shaped types. The pottery of this phase also includes a few collared flasks,
'baking plates' and vessels with lugs.

– The pottery of phase 2a is characterised by the use of grit as temper and the
occurrence of more beaker-like types. The 'baking plates', collared flasks and vessels with lugs have disappeared.

– The pottery of phase 2b is very similar to that of phase 2a, except that it also
shows various distinct Single Grave features.[53]

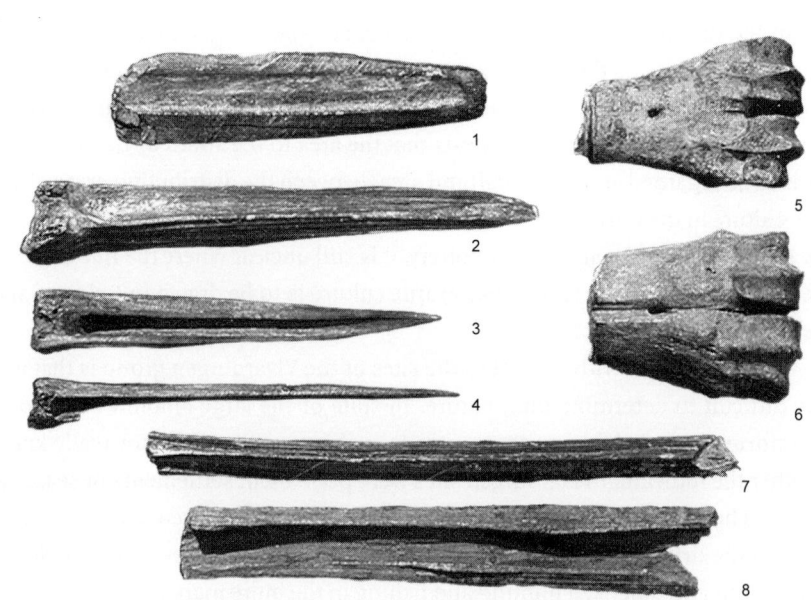

fig. 13.16
Characteristic bone tools made from red deer
metapodals and waste found at Hekelingen
III (Vlaardingen group). Scale 1:2.

1, 2   chisels

3, 4   awls

5, 6   cut-off distal articular ends

7, 8   split medial parts

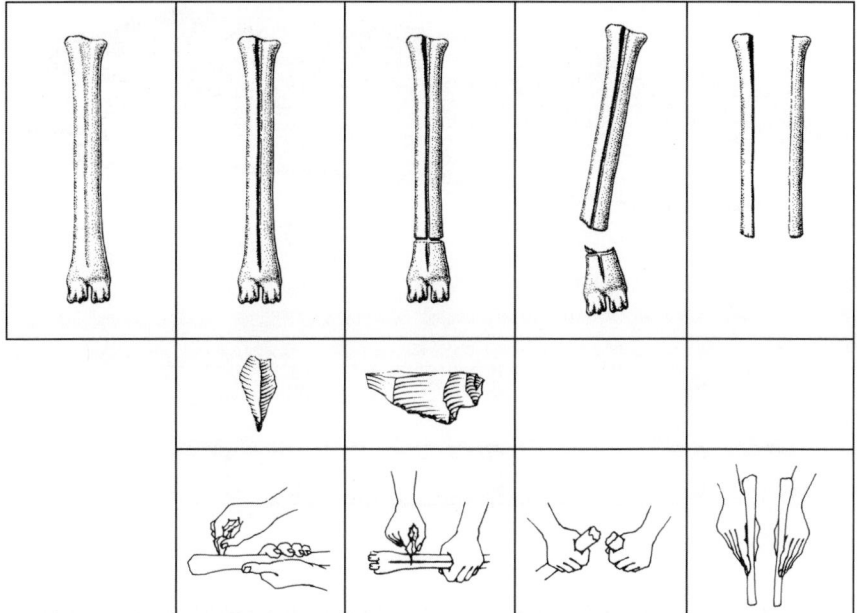

fig. 13.17
Diagram illustrating the production of
bone tools from metapodals in the Middle
Neolithic, based on the material recovered
at Hekelingen III. The groove naturally
occurring in a (red) deer metatarsal was
deepened with the aid of a flint implement.
The distal end was then sawn or broken off,
after which the bone was split into two halves
along the groove. Those halves could each
be turned into a tool, probably with the aid
of a sandstone grindstone, or be split for the
production of thin awls (cf. fig. 13.16).

Flint

The flint tools include predominantly transverse arrowheads, tanged points and a few leaf points, borers, many scrapers, including small 'thumb nail scrapers', and, finally, polished axes with oval cross-sections, among which are also Buren axes (fig. 13.15, 13.23). These axes were imported as finished products from the flint outcrops between Aachen and Boulogne-sur-Mer. The smaller tools were made from various types of flint. At the settlements on the coastal barriers (Voorschoten, Leidschendam and Haamstede-Brabers) much use was made of intensively rolled flint, which is why the tools found at these sites are rather small. The occupants of Hazendonk used predominantly flint from the Meuse gravels. Hardly any gravel flint was on the contrary used at Hekelingen III and Vlaardingen, where all the flint came from the south. One of the types of flint found at Hekelingen shows a marked resemblance to a type that is still to be found near Boulogne-sur-Mer today.[54] About 10-20% of the flint tools were made from fragments of broken axes, which apparently were secondarily used as a raw material for flake tools. Most of the tools were produced according to a flaking technology, often using a hard hammer. Blades are extremely scarce. A conspicuous aspect of the employed technology is the lack of care paid to the initial knapping: there is little or no evidence for the preparation of a striking platform or for the use of a systematic, well thought-out method for the reduction of the cores; the available flint was hence used in a highly inefficient manner.

Microwear analysis of flint from Vlaardingen, Hekelingen and Leidschendam revealed use-wear traces not only on the (retouched) tools, but also on many unretouched 'waste' flakes. The latter were used mainly to split stalks and twigs (for baskets or traps) or to produce bone awls and chisels.[55]

Artefacts made of organic materials

Thanks to the wet environments of the Vlaardingen sites, bone and other organic remains have survived in excellent condition. Many bone implements have been preserved, such as awls and chisels, and also large amounts of the waste that was produced in manufacturing these tools (fig. 13.16). From the marks observable on the tools and waste, archaeologists were even able to infer the various steps in the tools' production (fig. 13.17).[56] Many of the bone awls showed a distinct patina

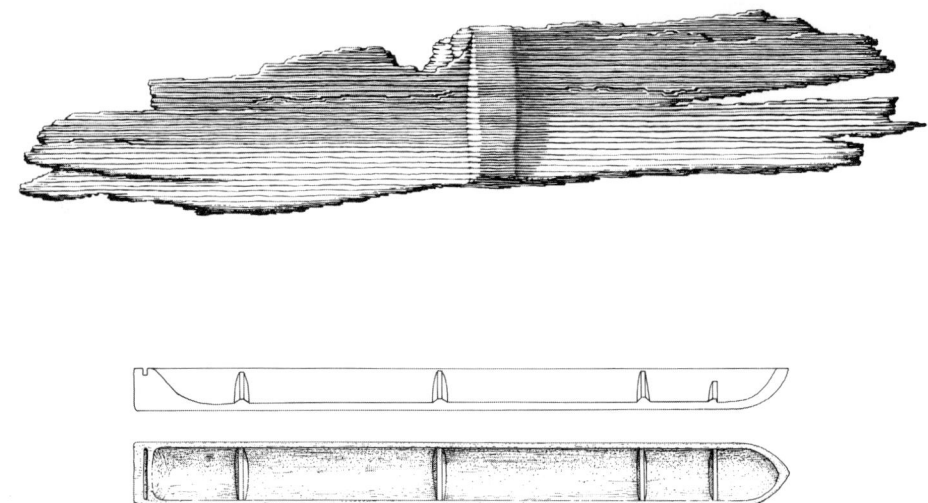

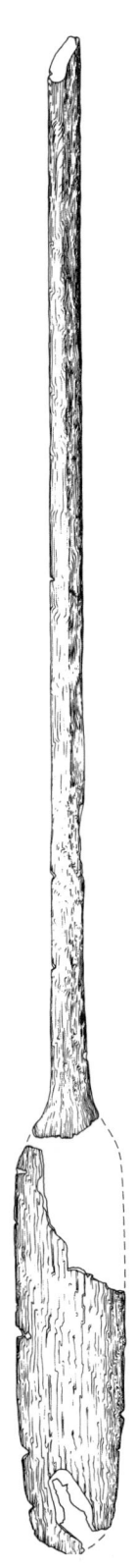

fig. 13.18

An almost complete paddle made of ash wood from the Hekelingen III site (scale 1:8) and the 2.5-m long central part of a dug-out canoe made of oak (scale 1:20) recovered from the Vlaardingen 1 level at the Hazendonk site. A canoe from the Federsee marshes (Bavaria) is shown for comparison.

and scratches indicating frequent use. Vlaardingen also yielded antler hammers with oval sockets; one of these hammers had been reinforced by hammering small points of antler into the tool's soft, spongy butt.

Objects of wood and other plant material had likewise been excellently preserved at the Vlaardingen sites. The finest example of a wooden object is the trap of Vlaardingen, which is of the same type as that which was found at Bergschenhoek (fig. 14.12, plate 19B). Vlaardingen also yielded fragments of string (as at Bergschenhoek of a two-strand variety), which most probably derive from fishing nets.[57] At this site excavators moreover found a net sinker, consisting of a few sherds rolled in birch bark, and an ash staff. An oak dug-out canoe, a paddle and an axe haft both made of ashwood are known from Hazendonk; Hekelingen III yielded a yew bow and an ash paddle (fig. 13.18). Microwear analysis of flint tools has shown that wood was worked at the latter settlement; the wooden tools were apparently made and repaired at the site itself.[58]

Other finds from Vlaardingen sites comprise pierced teeth (of bear, dog and other animals), which were worn as pendants, amber and jet beads, a single earthenware spindle whorl and clay net sinkers.[59] Vlaardingen itself also yielded fragments of querns and rubbing stones.

Burial rites

Only little is known about the burial rite of the Vlaardingen group. Burned human remains, some mixed with burned animal bones, were found in four places at Vlaardingen; they are probably the remains of deliberately cremated individuals. The remains had been deposited on the highest part of the levee, close to the houses.[60] Cremations are also known from Hekelingen III. One consisted of the remains of a man aged between 20 and 40 who had been cremated in seated posture, with his knees drawn up and his arms wrapped around his shins (fig. 13.19).[61] Unburned human bones were also found at this site, near the remains of a sturdy, six-posted oak structure. The deceased, an individual of over 21 years of age of unknown sex, may have been laid out on a bier.

These burials are difficult to interpret. At none of these sites did they form part of frequently used cemeteries of the kind usually encountered. Some prehistorians are of the opinion that the fact that the remains found at Hekelingen belonged to adult males indicates that this site was a base camp; they assume that adult males would have been granted a proper burial and would not have been buried at a camp that was visited for only a short period of time.[62] A more likely conclusion is that the small number of burials on the contrary points to seasonal occupation.

Settlements

Most Vlaardingen sites consist of find scatters and large numbers of postholes in which, however, no clear house plans can be distinguished. An exception is the site of Haamstede-Brabers, where at least three clear plans were identified. The finest and largest house (fig. 13.20) was oriented east-west and measured 9 x 4 m. Like most Neolithic house plans, the plans are two-aisled; the cattle stalls of the later Bronze Age and Iron Age plans are still absent. The clusters of postholes found at Leidschendam and the remains of posts preserved at Vlaardingen lay within the areas of refuse unearthed at those sites; at Vlaardingen they lay on the highest parts of the levees. Only few unambiguous house plans can be reconstructed from these postholes and post remains. It is thought that the settlement of Leidschendam consisted of two rectangular houses, which were constantly rebuilt, while that of Vlaardingen comprised at least three houses. There is no evidence to suggest the existence of round houses, as has been proposed for these sites.[63] The only unambiguous plan identified at Vlaardingen (that in excavation trench 15) differed from the plans of Haamstede. The structure in question had comprised sturdy posts arranged in two adjoining hexagons, which were surrounded by wall posts forming a rectangle. According to the results of a recent study, this was not a dwelling, but an open structure containing racks on which nets or skins were dried;[64] this however seems a less likely interpretation.

Hekelingen III differed from the aforementioned settlement sites in that it consisted of small concentrations of artefacts, many of which were grouped around one or more hearths. Clusters of thin posts were also observed. They probably indicate the positions of the former dwellings, which at this site were circular and very small, definitely not substantial structures. The dwellings are more likely to have been huts, as suggested by the narrow diameters of the posts and postholes. The analysis of the wood that was used at Hekelingen III did not yield any evidence to suggest the presence of substantial structures either: the range of wood types included no heavy building timber. No house plans whatsoever were found at Hazendonk and Ewijk in the peat and fluvial clay regions.

Little is known about the internal arrangement of the houses. In a few cases the features of hearths were found in and near the houses. Some consisted of discolourations containing charcoal, others – for example Hekelingen, subsite M1 – comprised successive thin layers of clay, suggesting that the hearths in question were used several times.[65]

In addition to house plans, features of a few other structures have been found, which have shed some light on the layout of the settlements. At Hazendonk, for example, part of the feature of a palisade came to light along the edge of the dune. The palisade appeared to have formed an enclosure in the eastern part of the dune, which the excavators interpreted as a cattle pen.[66] At Hekelingen III excavators found a row of posts at the mouth of a lateral creek which connected pools lying behind the stream ridge to the main creek. They are probably the remains of a fish weir, which may have been used to catch sturgeon as they made their way to their spawning area; a similar fish weir was found at Vlaardingen.[67] The sturdy six-posted platform of Hekelingen III that may have served as a bier has already been mentioned above. Rows of thin posts discovered at Vlaardingen and Hekelingen

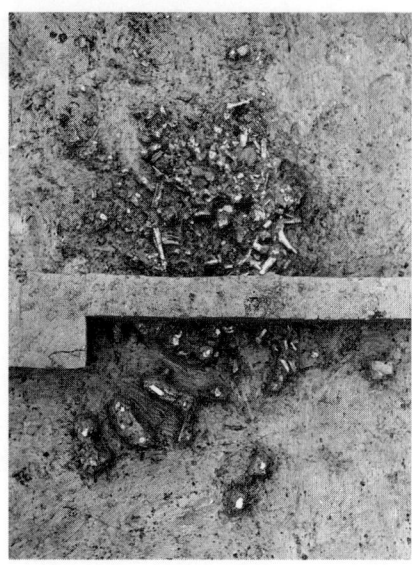

fig. 13.19
Careful excavation of a concentration of well-preserved cremated remains at Hekelingen III showed that an adult male had been cremated at the location in seated position.

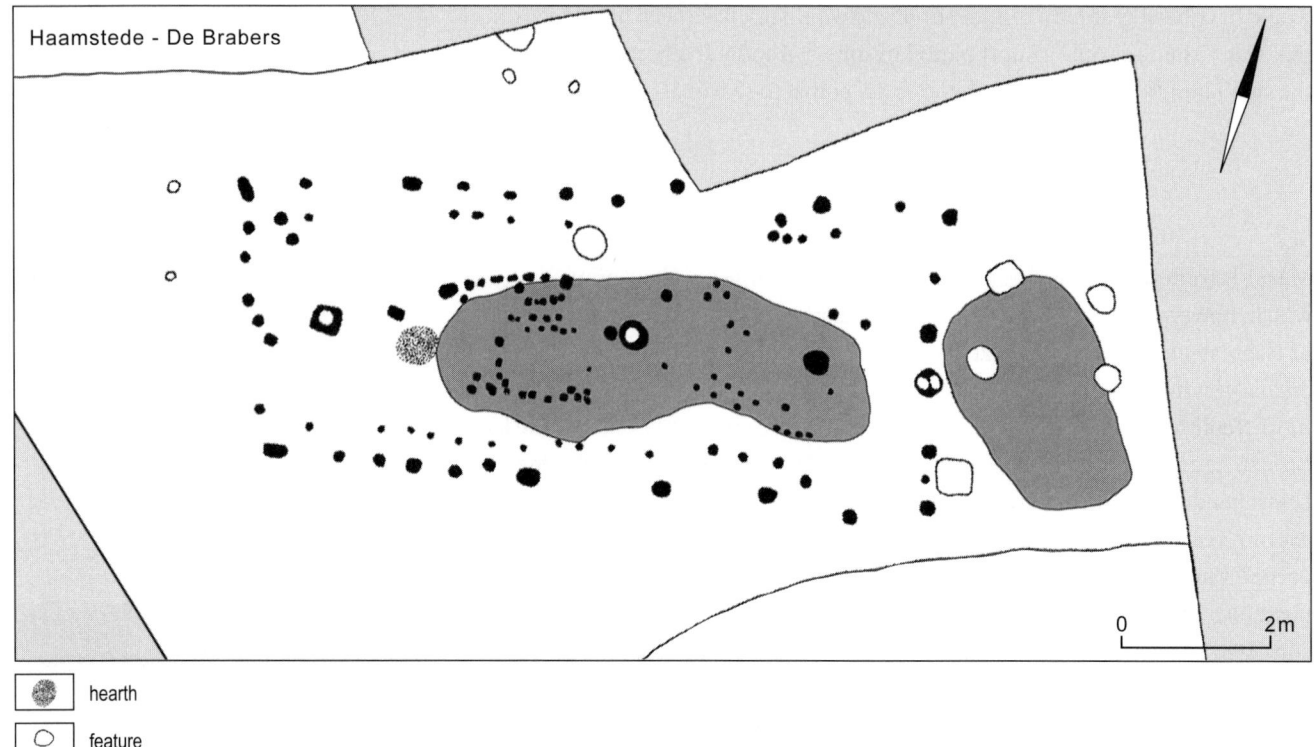

Haamstede - De Brabers

hearth

feature

posthole

pit fill

0   2m

fig. 13.20

One of the three house plans excavated at the Vlaardingen site Haamstede-Brabers. Scale 1:100.

III may be the remains of fences, windbreaks or racks for drying fish or other goods; some may represent some form of timber facing. Post rows in the gully fills at these sites have been interpreted as fish weirs (fig 14.13).

The Vlaardingen group: 'unity in diversity'?

The Vlaardingen sites are conspicuous for their seemingly great diversity. There are major differences in the sites' environments, which vary from dry coastal barriers to river dunes or levees in swamps, but also in their material culture. The inhabitants of the settlements on the coastal barriers used almost exclusively gravel flint, whereas the great majority of the flint found at Hekelingen III was imported from the chalk regions in Hainault and Pas-de-Calais. The occupants of Vlaardingen and Hazendonk used both types of raw materials, while those of Ewijk, finally, obtained most of their flint from the south. Even the pottery, which is fairly homogeneous in general terms, varies considerably in details. For example, the pottery from Vlaardingen is characterised by many lugs and few perforated rims, whereas the opposite holds for the pottery from Hekelingen. The features and the structures of the individual sites also differ. At Hekelingen III excavators unearthed sharply demarcated find scatters concentrated around hearths, whereas unmistakable house plans were found at Haamstede-Brabers. And, finally, there are also conspicuous differences in the bone spectra and the plant remains (see chapter 14).

How are we to interpret this variation? Up till the Vlaardingen group sites seem to have served different functions. Hekelingen III, for example, was probably a camp that was used to exploit specific food resources: sturgeon in the early summer, furred and other animals, especially red deer, in the autumn.[68] The faunal remains of Ewijk, on the contrary, show very little evidence for hunting and fishing; here, pig and cattle were the dominant species. The soundly built dwellings and the nature of the find scatters at Haamstede-Brabers and Leidschendam point to permanent occupation, whereas the 'huts' of Hekelingen III most probably reflect temporary use.

298

Over the years, several hypotheses have been advanced to explain these differences. It was first believed that all the sites were occupied on a permanent basis, by non-agricultural groups who specialised in the exploitation of the specific watery environments of the delta.[69] Later, most archaeologists came to favour the hypothesis that the sites outside the coastal barriers, such as Hekelingen III and Hazendonk, were occupied on a seasonal basis.[70] In this context it was also suggested that the Vlaardingen communities had contacts with related farming groups, with whom they exchanged certain goods, for example fur and fish for flint, grain and cattle.[71] These farming groups may have lived in the vast salt marshes of Zeeland, possibly in settlements like those whose remains have come to light in Westfrisia (the Vlaardingen site Zandwerven and the Single Grave sites Aartswoud, Kolhorn and Zeewijk).

A recently proposed hypothesis is that none of the Vlaardingen sites, not even those on the coastal barriers, were permanently occupied. This hypothesis is based on the absence of *ard* marks on the coastal barriers and on the large numbers of transverse arrowheads, associated with hunting, that were found at Haamstede-Brabers. Moreover, the specific locations of Haamstede and Voorschoten-De Donk, on the very edges of the coastal barriers, suggest a marine orientation, which could be another argument for assuming periodic occupation.[72] On the other hand, a large number of transverse arrowheads also came to light at Ewijk, whose bone spectrum includes predominantly domestic species. However, it is quite plausible that transverse arrowheads were used primarily for hunting water fowl, an activity that could well have been combined with farming. The fact that no *ard* marks were found at Leidschendam and Voorschoten need not necessarily imply that no crops were grown at these sites; the *ard* marks that were found at Zandwerven were so vague that we should not attach too much significance to their absence elsewhere.

The third, and most likely, possibility is that the settlements on the coastal barriers and in the fluvial clay region were permanently occupied, while those in the freshwater tidal area and the peat region were used predominantly on a seasonal basis.[73] That would imply that Hekelingen, and probably also Hazendonk, were periodically occupied camps. The presence of different types of southern flint at Hekelingen indicates that the freshwater tidal area was also visited by people from the southern sandy regions, the salt marshes of Zeeland and possibly even the surroundings of Antwerp.

The distribution patterns of the remains of the Vlaardingen group seem to reflect the activities of groups of people with a fairly flexible, expedient mode of existence, who moved around in a heterogeneous landscape. The binding element, from the viewpoint of the archaeological definition of cultural groups, is the typical, thick-walled, coarsely tempered Vlaardingen pottery. In terms of the location of their sites, their subsistence activities and the selection of their raw materials, the occupants of the region 'between TRB and SOM'[74] seem to have enjoyed considerable freedom. This freedom they owed largely to the many possibilities offered by the local landscape. The apparent heterogeneous character of the Vlaardingen group is hence largely attributable to friction between a tradition based on a particular environment (life in a coastal region with a considerable degree of functional differentiation between sites at different locations) and the employed definition of cultural groups based largely on pottery traditions (the typical Vlaardingen pottery). Although the occupants of the Vlaardingen sites were evidently primarily farmers, they also made much use of the resources available in the coastal zone. From their settlements, whether seasonal or permanent, they exploited fish, shellfish, marine mammals, large game, small furred animals and

fig. 13.21

The stone floor of the burial chamber discovered at Stein. Clearly visible are the chamber's tripartite plan and the positions of the large posts that formed part of the walls of the long sides. The collared flask is visible in *situ* in the rear.

a wide variety of plant resources (see chapter 14). In including these resources in their subsistence system they were actually continuing an old tradition, as testified by the clear signs of continuity observable in technology and lifestyle. There are for example remarkable similarities in the technique that was used for carving bone at the Vlaardingen sites and that which was employed at the Middle Neolithic sites of Brandwijk-Het Kerkhof and Hazendonk; such similarities point to strong links with the past, which can be traced back to Mesolithic traditions.

THE STEIN GROUP

During the excavation of the *Linearbandkeramik* settlement of Stein in 1963, a spectacular discovery was made: a Neolithic underground burial chamber. This and other, later, finds led Modderman to introduce the term 'the Middle Neolithic of Limburg' for these finds.[75] As already explained above, this is for several reasons a rather unlucky term; nowadays the sites in the Meuse valley and its surroundings are classed as belonging to the Wartberg-Stein-Vlaardingen complex.

The underground burial chamber of Stein measured 5.5 by 1.75 m. Its floor was paved with large and small stones and four thick posts supported its roof (fig. 13.21). The entrance was in the narrow eastern part. A pair of large, flat stones probably constituted two internal thresholds; the burial chamber hence comprised three compartments, like the *allées couvertes* in northern France.[76] The only human remains found in the chamber were of cremated individuals, but any unburned remains would not have survived in the decalcified loess soil. In the surrounding areas the deceased were usually buried uncremated; there, cremations are rare. The cremated remains of several dozen individuals had been deposited in two piles. The grave goods comprised a flask with a star-shaped collar, 96 transverse arrowheads and 11 bone points (fig. 13.22). Most of these finds showed traces of burning. A large vessel with an S-shaped profile was found in the northeastern part of the chamber.

A number of sites classed as belonging to the Stein group, among which are Koningsbosch (Dutch province of Limburg) and Geistingen (Belgian province of Limburg),[77] yielded finds from other periods, too, which could unfortunately not be stratigraphically distinguished from the Stein finds. On the whole, the material remains of the Stein group show a close resemblance to those of the Vlaardingen group. The clay for the pottery was tempered with coarse quartz grit, which was mixed with a little grog and, incidentally, sand. The surface of the vessels was smoothed and sometimes very lightly burnished, but it always remained a little irregular. Most of the pots have S-shaped profiles and flat bases and are devoid of decoration. A difference with respect to the Vlaardingen ware is the scarcity of lugs and perforated rims. Types like baking trays are entirely absent.

Koningsbosch is conspicuous on account of the large amounts of flint that were found at this site: tanged arrowheads, leaf points, transverse arrowheads

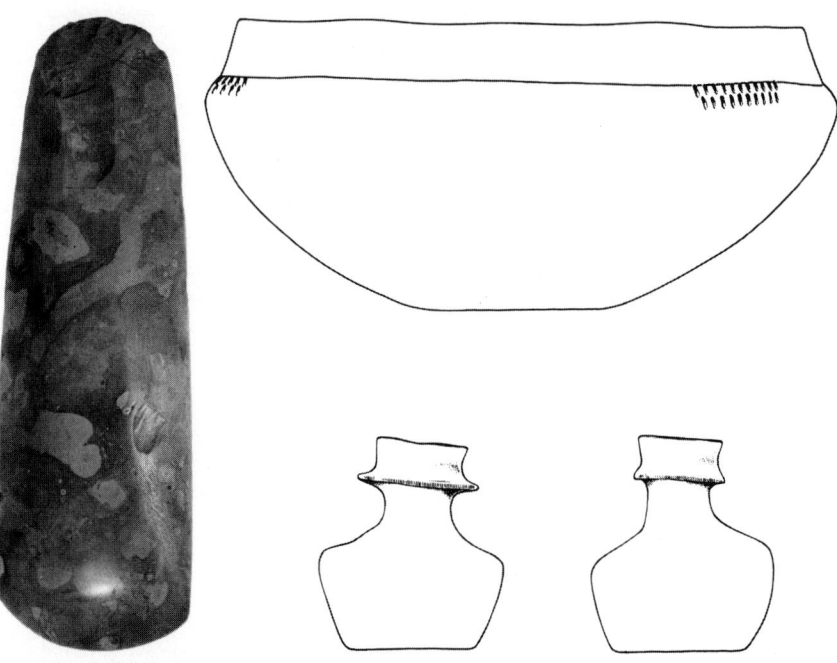

fig. 13.23
Inventory of a cremation grave, discovered near Denekamp in 1963. A bowl characteristic of the last phase of the TRB culture was associated with an equally characteristic axe of the Buren type that was produced somewhere in the central part of Belgium and exported from there to the northern part of the Netherlands. Two collared flaks complete this funerary assemblage.

and borers.[78] As in all Late Neolithic assemblages, scrapers prevail. Among these scrapers are also many thumbnail scrapers with diameters of less than 2 cm. In addition, many axes were found, mostly with oval cross-sections. Some of these axes were made from Lousberg flint (plate 21A).[79] Stein people may have been involved in the exploitation of flint mines.

Other find categories were not represented at the sites of the Stein group. As no plant remains or bones had survived in the acid soil, we are poorly informed about the subsistence system, but we assume that crop cultivation and cattle keeping were practised. No house plans or other features had been preserved either. The only exceptional discovery in this respect is that of a pit containing the remains of several almost complete pots which came to light at Groot-Linden-de Kraai-enberg (North Brabant). The pots had clearly been intentionally deposited in the pit. As there was no unambiguous evidence (no organic remains) suggesting that this pit was a storage or a burial pit, it was interpreted as a ritual pit.[80] We do not know much about the settlement system of the Stein group either, because only a small number of sites of this group has so far been found. Our interpretation of this group is further complicated by the fact that the northernmost Stein site, de Kraaienberg, lies only 10 km from the Vlaardingen site Ewijk, while Vlaardingen 1b remains have also been found at the nearby village of Grave.[81] This further supports the assumption that the Vlaardingen and Stein groups belonged to one and the same cultural complex, the Stein group being the 'dry' variant of the Vlaardingen group.

THE TRB AND VLAARDINGEN PEOPLES IN A REGIONAL CONTEXT

Recent research has shown that the TRB culture was a local development, which evolved out of the Swifterbant culture and was not, as previously assumed, rooted in the Scandinavian northern group.[82] The bearers of this culture had close contacts with people in Schleswig-Holstein and southern Scandinavia. The Drouwen pottery shows many affinities with the contemporary earthenware of the northern group, and many similarities are also observable in the burial and votive rites. The northern axe types that have been found in hoards in the TRB area likewise indicate direct or indirect relations. In the late Havelte phase the contacts with the north weakened considerably. Finds like the fragments of flint axes with oval cross-sections that have come to light at Laren (middle Drouwen phase) and the beautiful Buren axe that was discovered in a late Havelte flat grave near Denekamp (fig. 13.23)[83] suggest that the TRB people had closer contacts with the south in this phase.

Separation and contact

The Vlaardingen and Stein groups were oriented predominantly towards the south. Together with the Wartberg group, they constituted a link between the TRB culture in the north and the Seine-Oise-Marne culture in the south. No northern axes with rectangular cross-sections and only a few knob-butted axes have been found in the Vlaardingen and Stein areas. The Vlaardingen sites have yielded finds indicating that the occupants of those sites made use of raw materials or end products imported from regions far away. The jet beads, for example, are assumed to have come from northern France or southern Belgium. How these objects made their way to the Vlaardingen sites is difficult to ascertain. One thing that is certain, though, is that the Vlaardingen people were not 'backward swamp dwellers'. Finds like the aforementioned objects support the hypothesis that the coastal region was also exploited from the south, possibly by boat.[84]

The material remains of the TRB culture differ considerably from those of the southern Vlaardingen and Stein groups. The Tiefstich decoration that is so characteristic of the TRB pottery does not occur on Vlaardingen vessels. Although the decorated and undecorated 'baking plates' are identical, the shapes of the pots, including the collared flasks, are on the whole entirely different. Many differences are also observable in the ranges of flint tools: the assemblages of the Vlaardingen group contain no 'pics' and the transverse arrowheads are small. We know very little about the nature of the relations between the TRB people and the Vlaardingen group. Two sherds of decorated TRB pots were found mixed with the Vlaardingen remains at Hazendonk. As the clay was tempered with the local coarse sand, the pots must have been made on the dune itself or in its vicinity. Perhaps the pots were made by a TRB woman who married into a Vlaardingen family and continued to produce her own type of pottery for some time. We also know of Vlaardingen finds that have come to light in the TRB area, for example a complete, stray Vlaardingen pot that was found in the soil at Kootwijk. The Buren axes also point to relationships between the two groups. The Stein occupants of the Meuse valley probably played a role in the distribution of these southern axes throughout the TRB area. The four TRB knob-butted axes that came to light in the Kempen region and the specimen that was found in the valley of the Semois may reflect a network of alliances that covered a large area, including the southern part of the Netherlands, Belgium, western Germany and northern France. Most knob-butted axes are made of diabase. They were probably very much in demand and may have been exchanged for objects of equivalent value, possibly the Buren axes. Other objects that probably made their way into the Netherlands via down-the-line exchange are the simple copper pendants and beads that have been found in a few hunebedden. These copper ornaments came from the copper mines in southeast Europe, but their exact origins have not yet been determined. The same holds for the copper flat axes from TRB context.[85]

We should not attach too much importance to the substantial differences that seem to exist between the TRB culture and the Vlaardingen group, especially in the locations of their sites. At least some of these differences are attributable to differences in the available evidence. We must bear in mind that the sites of the Vlaardingen group are concentrated in the wetlands of the coastal zone, whereas the TRB culture is known to us predominantly from the dry sandy areas. A site like Slootdorp-Bouwlust, located in a salt marsh landscape, shows that the differences are indeed not as great as often assumed and that some TRB groups were also capable of surviving in the coastal region and were even familiar with the practice of offshore fishing. If we may indeed classify the Stein and Vlaardingen groups as belonging to one and the same cultural complex, then the 'dry' component must have been represented in the Vlaardingen area, too, and we should not see the Vlaardingen people exclusively as swamp dwellers.

An important question that still remains unanswered is why the material culture of the TRB differs so much from that of the Wartberg-Stein-Vlaardingen complex. The beautifully decorated pottery and the impressive *hunebedden* of the former form a marked contrast with the remarkably simple pottery and the lack of monuments in the Vlaardingen area. There is conspicuously little archaeological evidence of contacts between the two, though we should of course bear in mind that there may have been contacts which are not reflected in visible material remains. A second unsolved question is: why did these differences disappear into a pan-European uniformity with the emergence of the Single Grave culture? No unambiguous answers can yet be given to these questions.

The transformation into the Single Grave culture

In the TRB area the transition to the Single Grave culture took place within a remarkably short space of time of roughly 50 years. The explanations for this are based largely on social theories. In the past, the differences in burial rite and material culture between the TRB and the Single Grave culture were seen as signs of ethnic discontinuity. Nomadic invaders, armed with battle axes, were believed to have settled in TRB territory. Nowadays, however, most prehistorians stress the spatial continuity characterising the two cultures and the few similarities that are observable between them. The Single Grave finds that have come to light at the periphery of the sandy region, for example at the late Havelte sites of Bornwird, Steenendam and Oostrum (all in Friesland), also suggest a continuous development.[86] The same holds for a late Havelte flat grave near Angelslo which yielded an early beaker sherd.[87] The transition from the Vlaardingen group to the Single Grave culture was a far more gradual process. This is demonstrated by, for example, the battle axe and the Single Grave amphora that were found at Vlaardingen, the increase in the number of beaker-shaped pots observable in the pottery of the Vlaardingen 2b phase, and the Vlaardingen and Single Grave remains that were found together in the uppermost find layers at Voorschoten.

It is clear that major changes took place around the time of the appearance of the Single Grave culture. It has been suggested that these changes were initiated by the introduction of the plough, which took place in the course of the TRB period: the use of the plough meant that the soil could be used for crop cultivation on a more permanent basis, leading to stronger ties between the people and their land. This may have ultimately resulted in the dissolution of the old tribal associations, centred on the *hunebedden*, into smaller social units such as families. According to this view, this social transformation is reflected by the transition from collective burial to individual burial, *i.e.* from the *hunebedden* to the flat graves and the barrows of later times.[88] Objections that could be made against this line of reasoning are that burial in a flat grave was being practised at the beginning of the TRB period already, and that the number of flat graves does not seem to have increased in the late Havelte phase. Moreover, there is evidence suggesting that not only the plough but probably also wheeled vehicles had already been 'invented' and introduced during the TRB period. This was certainly the case in Denmark, where these technological innovations did not directly lead to any major cultural changes. The two viewpoints can be reconciled by assuming that the new technology reached the level of development which enabled the drastic reorganisation of farming practices with the associated consequences for social relationships only in the final stage of the TRB culture.

As the Single Grave culture is a pan-European phenomenon and there are no unambiguous explanations for its emergence, the invasion theory has recently been receiving attention.[89] But whichever hypothesis one prefers, it is certain that the transition to this culture was accompanied by major technological and sociocultural changes. These changes will be extensively discussed in the part on the Beaker cultures and the Bronze Age.

NOTES

1 Bakker 1979a, fig. l; Midgley 1992.

2 Schwellnus 1979.

3 Louwe Kooijmans 1983a.

4 Reinerth 1939; Hogestijn *et al.* 1991.

5 Madsen 1982; Skaarup 1973.

6 Hogestijn 1990: Ten Anscher *et al.* 1994; Gehasse 1995.; Ten Anscher forthcoming; Kampffmeyer 1991.

7 Madsen (1982) associates the rapid diffusion of the western group with the slash-and-burn system of agriculture. See also Bakker/ Groenman-van Waateringe 1988.

8 The exact beginning of the 'Secondary Products Revolution' – the use of milk, wool, traction power, dung – (Sherratt 1981) is a matter of debate. Some (Bakker 1992; Andersen 1993) place its beginning in the TRB period, others (Fokkens 1991a, 1998b) date these changes a little later, around the transition to the Single Grave culture (see also chapters 15 and 16).

8 Brindley 1986b.

10 Van Giffen 1925-'27.

11 Bakker 1979a; Brindley 1986a. Brindley's seven 'horizons' are a partial improvement on the nine (sub)phases proposed by Bakker (1979a). See also Bakker 1992, 42-45, tables 1-2, figs. 21-27.

12 Ten Anscher *et al.* 1994; Ten Anscher forthcoming.

13 Bakker/Luijten 1990.

14 Bakker 1979a; Van den Broeke 1979; Harsema 1979b; Jager 1982; Fokkens 1991a.

15 Beuker 1986, 1990; Bakker 1979a.

16 Bakker/Van der Waals 1973; Bakker 1982.

17 It is often assumed that the 'pics' served as strike-a-lights, but as this type of implement has not yet been subjected to microwear analysis this assumption remains uncertain.

18 Bakker 1979a.

19 Harsema 1979b.

20 For Laren see Bakker 1979a, 192. Stray finds from Friesland are presented in Fokkens/Schinkel 1990.

21 Bakker 1979a, 110; Knöll 1959, 35-36.

22 Amber can still be picked up in the Dutch Wadden Sea region today (Waterbolk/Waterbolk 1991).

23 Bakker 1979a, 127-131; 1992, 57. Whereas the copper objects of the northern group are made exclusively of arsenical copper, those of the western group are made of both arsenical and arsenic-free copper.

24 Bakker 1979a, 188-193.

25 For Flögeln: Zimmerman 1980; Penningbüttel: Assendorp 1987; Heek: Finke 1989, 1990.

26 Jager 1985. In accordance with contemporary views, Waterbolk (1960) assumed that the palisade of Anloo was to be interpreted as a cattle pen of the Protruding Foot Beaker culture (as the Single Grave culture was then still called); the bearers of this culture were in those days still regarded as nomadic cattle keepers who settled in the occupation area of the TRB people (see chapter 16).

27 It is not known whether all the houses were in use at the same time, because the pottery recovered at the site included middle and late Drouwen ware, late Havelte pottery as well pottery of the Single Grave and Bell Beaker cultures, and the stratigraphy was only summarily studied (Reinerth 1939). See Schirnig 1979a, Bakker/Van der Waals 1973, 30-32.

28 Schokkerhaven: Hogestijn 1991; Slootdorp: Hogestijn 1992, 1992, pers. com.

29 Specific hunting and fishing camps have also been found in Denmark and Schleswig-Holstein, for example at Hesselø and Sølager

(Skaarup 1973) and near Bistoft (Johansson 1981).

30 Kampffmeyer 1983, 1991.

31 Bakker 1982.

32 Brindley/Lanting 1991-'92, 137-140.

33 Bakker 1992, fig. 32.

34 Bakker/Luijten 1990.

35 Kroezenga *et al.* 1991.

36 Becker 1947; Bennike/Ebbesen 1986; Midgley 1992; Rech 1979.

37 They may have occurred at the peripheries of all the peat regions in the northern and central parts of the Netherlands.

38 Achterop 1960; Bakker 1959, 1979a and 1982; Beuker 1986: Beuker *et al.* 1992; Van den Broeke 1979; Harsema 1979b; Schut 1987 and 1991.

39 Bennike/Ebbesen 1986; Ebbesen 1993; Karsten 1994; Midgley 1992; Nielsen 1977; Rech 1979.

40 Chapman 1981; Madsen 1982.

41 Bakker 1980, 1982; Bakker/Groenman-van Waateringe 1988; Harsema 1988.

42 Bloch 1971, 1975a. For a more extensive argumentation see Fokkens 1991a, 1998b.

43 Voss 1982.

44 Hodder 1982a.

45 Modderman 1953, 10.

46 Haamstede-Brabers: Trimpe Burger 1977; Verhart 1992. Voorschoten-Boschgeest and Leidschendam: Glasbergen *et al.* 1967; Groenman-van Waateringe *et al.* 1968. Voorschoten-De Donk: Van Veen 1989. Westbroek 3: Ten Anscher pers. com.

47 Hekelingen III: Van Gijn 1990; Louwe Kooijmans 1986. For ecological information and references, see chapter 14. Vlaardingen: Van Beek 1990; Glasbergen *et al.* 1961; Van Regteren Altena *et al.* 1962-'63, 1964.

48 Louwe Kooijmans 1985.

49 Asmussen/Moree 1987.

50 Van Regteren Altena/Bakker 1961.

51 Van der Plaetsen *et al.* 1985.

52 Louwe Kooijmans 1983a.

53 Louwe Kooijmans 1976a.

54 Verhart 1983, 1992. In the sites on the coastal barriers predominantly Miocene beach pebbles were used. These washed ashore at, for example, Cadzand, Zeeland Flanders, but they are also found in lower percentages in the terrace deposits of the river Meuse. These so-called 'Meuse eggs' have their source in the Miocene deposits in the environs of Brunssum in south Limburg.

55 Van Gijn 1990.

56 Van den Broeke 1983 Maarleveld 1985.

57 Van Iterson Scholten 1977.

58 Van Gijn 1990.

59 Van Beek 1990.

60 Hoogland 1985.

61 Louwe Kooijmans 1986.

62 This is however based on Western views on burial rites and need hence by no means apply to the situation at Hekelingen III.

63 Van Beek 1990.

64 Verhart 1992.

65 Louwe Kooijmans 1985.

66 Louwe Kooijmans 1985.

67 Boddeke 1971.

68 For an extensive discussion of the term of occupation of Hekelingen III, see Van Gijn 1990, 128-132.

69 Modderman 1953.

70 Louwe Kooijmans 1985, 1993a.

71 Louwe Kooijmans 1983b.

72 Verhart 1992.

73 Van Gijn 1990; Louwe Kooijmans 1985, 1993a.

74 Louwe Kooijmans (1983a) has proposed that the Vlaardingen, Stein and Wartberg groups together constitute a major cultural unit between the TRB culture in the north and the Seine-Oise-Marne culture in the south.

75 Van Haaren/Modderman (1973) introduced this concept primarily on the basis of the assemblage from Koningsbosch.

76 The reconstructed plans of the dolmens of Wéris in the northern Ardennes are similar, but it is possible that these plans do not agree entirely with the excavation data (Modderman 1964).

77 Koningsbosch: Van Haaren/Modderman 1973. Geistingen: Heymans/Vermeersch 1983.

78 Van Haaren/Modderman 1973.

79 As this site also yielded a fair amount of Michelsberg remains, Louwe Kooijmans and Verhart (1990) have suggested that the Lousberg axes may also date from the Michelsberg period.

80 Louwe Kooijmans/Verhart 1990.

81 L.B.M. Verhart, pers. com. Vlaardingen objects have also been found at Herpen (Verwers/Beex 1978; Verwers 1981).

82 Kampffmeyer 1991; Ten Anscher forthcoming.

83 Laren (Bakker 1979, 192), Denekamp (Bakker/Van der Waals 1973).

84 Bakker 1982.

85 Arsenic copper objects from this period are rather common in south Scandinavia, Schlewig-Holstein and Poland, either as stary finds or in hoards (*e.g.* Bygholm, near Horsens (Brøndsted 1957, quoted in Ebbesen 1993).

86 Van der Waals 1964, 1984; Lanting/Van der Waals 1974; for ^{14}C wiggles see chapter 1.

87 Bakker/Van der Waals 1973; Fokkens 1982, 1991a.

88 Fokkens 1991a, 1998b.

89 Kristiansen 1991.

H   Funerary buildings from erratic boulders
The construction and function of the *hunebedden*

Jan Albert Bakker

Hunebedden, the ruins of the burial monuments of the TRB culture, are the oldest architectural monuments in the Netherlands.[1] They were built between 3400 and 3000 BC. Fifty-three of these monuments still survive, mostly in the province of Drenthe (see fig. 13.12). We also know of the sites of about twenty-five more monuments that have at some time in the past been destroyed.[2] The hunebedden in the Netherlands and northwest Germany are related to those of the northern group of the TRB culture in Schleswig-Holstein, Mecklenburg, Vorpommern and southern Scandinavia. The oldest megalithic monuments ('megalithic' means 'built from large stones') are to be found in Brittany and Portugal. They date from around 4700 BC. A conspicuous feature of megaliths is that they almost all lie at, or close to, the coast.

Virtually no megalithic tombs were built in Europe after 2500 BC. Many megalithic monuments are to be found in central Africa, India, Japan, Indonesia and Madagascar, where they still play a role in society today.[3]

Different types of hunebedden

A hunebed consists of chambers formed by series of 'trilithons', two upright stones known as 'orthostats' supporting a horizontal capstone. The end of each chamber is closed by a blocking stone. The chambers vary in height from 0.8 m to almost 2 m; their floors lie about 0.50 m below the ground surface. Most monuments are oriented roughly east-west.

fig. H1

Most *hunebedden* are situated on the Hondsrug, a low boulder clay ridge at the eastern edge of the Drenthe Plateau. Sometimes they are found close together, in small groups, like these two (D19 and D20) near Drouwen. They are well-known by the excavations of J.H. Holwerda in 1912 and eponymous for the Drouwen phase of the Funnel Beaker culture. See also fig. 13.12.

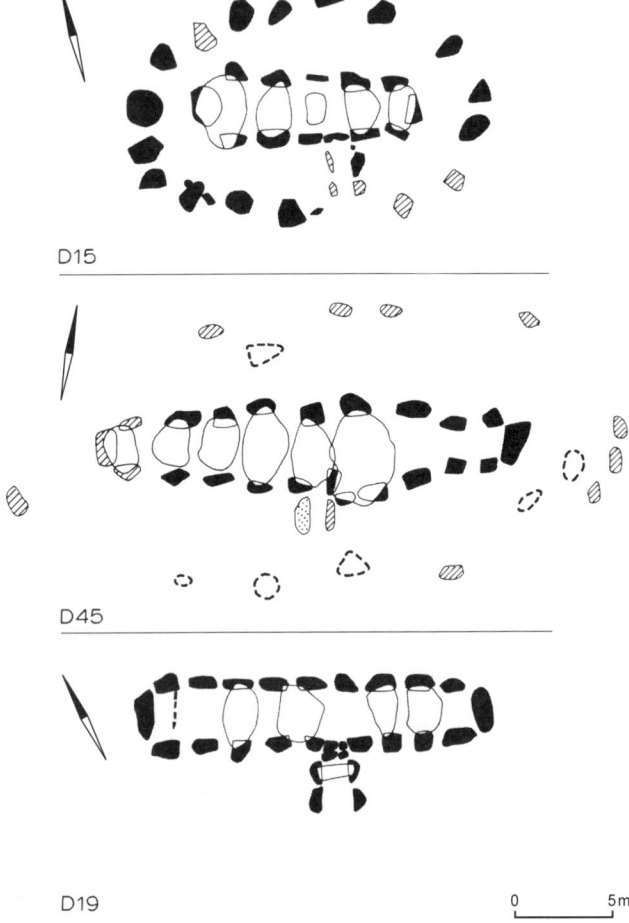

D15

D45

D19

0   5m

The length of the hunebedden in the Netherlands varies from two to ten trilithons, that is, 2.5-17 m, but much larger monuments are known elsewhere, such as the 40-m-long hunebed at Wechte in Westphalia.

Almost all the Dutch hunebedden are 'passage graves' (fig. H1-2, plate 22). Hunebedden of this type have an entrance in the middle of the long south or southeast side. This entrance consists of an opening between two orthostats, often flanked by one or two pairs of 'portal stones' on the outside. Four hunebedden differ somewhat from this common type:

- D43, a 'long barrow' near Emmen, consists of two fairly small, longitudinally linked passage graves covered by an earth mound with a length of 40 m and a width of 7 m. The periphery of the mound was marked by a kerb of large stones (fig. H3).
- D13, the 'stepped tomb' near Eext, has a stairway comprising three stone steps leading to the burial chamber (fig. H4).
- G5 is not a hunebed but a dolmen. It came to light in

1982, during the excavation of the Heveskesklooster terp in northeast Groningen. Dolmens always have an entrance in the narrow side. The Heveskesklooster dolmen consisted of three trilithons and one capstone (fig 10.6).
- D30a near Exloo was also a dolmen, insofar as can be inferred from the scanty remains of this completely destroyed monument.[4]

The interstices between the orthostats were filled with dry-stone walling of flat stones and clay, after which a mound of earth was erected over the monument. In the case of the long hunebedden the mound was often surrounded by a kerb of large upright stones and dry-stone walling. Half of hunebed D49, known as de Papeloze Kerk ('the Priestless Church'), at Noordsleen has been restored to its original state (plate 22B).[5]

The floors of the hunebedden were rather irregularly paved with cobbles, which were covered with a thin layer of burned crushed granite. From evidence obtained elsewhere we know that the monument was closed by a wooden or stone door.

fig. H4

The small *hunebed* of Eext (D13), with its unique stepped entrance, shortly after its discovery in 1756.

Burials and interments

The hunebedden were used for the burial of the deceased for many centuries. We do not know whether an individual was placed in a hunebed immediately after death, or whether his or her bones were deposited there some time later, after excarnation, because no unburned bones have been preserved. What has survived are the less perishable grave goods and offerings: between dozens and hundreds of pots, now scattered across the chambers in the form of small sherds, plus beads and pendants of amber, jet and copper, stone and flint axes, stone hammer axes and flint arrowheads and sickles. From objects that have come to light in front of the entrances we know that offerings were deposited there, too. This reflects the importance of ancestor worship. We are probably to interpret the hunebedden as family tombs. The monuments were built at locations where they were visible from some distance, for example on slopes and coversand ridges. They hence symbolised the territory of the kinship group (see chapter 13). Many moreover lay along important routes.[6]

Construction

For a long time it was believed that hunebedden were the works of giants (fig. 2.1), for how could ordinary human beings possibly have built such impressive monuments without cranes and pulleys? Experimental reconstructions of megaliths, observations made during the construction of megaliths in Madagascar, on Nias and the Sunda islands, geological research and the results of excavations of the hunebedden themselves have led to the following scenario.

The hunebedden were built from large boulders transported by glaciers. The large blocks that were used in Drenthe weighed several tonnes, the heaviest even 23 tonnes! A hunebed was preferably built at a location where sufficient large stones were to be found at the surface within a range of several hundred metres.[7] The stones were towed to the construction site on a sledge, a forked tree-trunk, over a rollway of thin tree-trunks with the aid of ropes and levers. It is possible that oxen were used, but even then, a large group of people was required to move the stones. Estimates vary from 100 to 125 men to move a 15-tonne stone (without the help of oxen).

The orthostats were probably installed first. They were carefully canted into previously dug foundation pits, with their flat sides sloping inwards a little. Then the floor of the chamber was dug out, after which the capstones were towed to the top of the structure over a ramp of thin tree-trunks and manoeuvred into the desired position. At this point the positions of the orthostats could be adjusted if necessary. Next, the interstices between the orthostats were filled in with dry-stone walling, after which the capstones were lowered onto the tops of the orthostats by chopping in two the timber posts bearing the ramp. Traces of these posts have been found in some hunebedden.

How such a major project was organised, and how the necessary people were assembled we do not know, but we get some idea of how this may have taken place from ethnographic evidence. For example, we know that the master builders of the 20th-century megalithic monuments on the Sunda islands and in Madagascar hope to win eternal fame for themselves by involving as many people as possible in the building work and treating them to a lavish eating and drinking feast that may last for several days.[8] In communities that are predominantly egalitarian, which we presume was also the case with the TRB communities, status and prestige are usually acquired through competence, rather than inherited. Organising a hunebed-building feast undoubtedly yielded considerable status and prestige. A prerequisite was the ability to accumulate a substantial surplus of foodstuffs (cereal, cattle). This is one of the reasons why megalithic monuments appeared only in the course of the Neolithic.

The future of the hunebedden

Many hunebedden were destroyed for the sake of using the stones to construct dikes. In 1731 the pile-worm (Teredo) suddenly multiplied substantially in saltwater and bored holes into the timber revetments of the dikes. This led to a serious threat of floods in the Dutch provinces of Zeeland, Holland, Friesland and Groningen and Ost Friesland in Germany. When in 1733 stone dike revetments started to be built, millions of tonnes of stone were transported to the coast from Drenthe, northwest Germany and Scandinavia. In Drenthe even ancient stone boundary markers were not spared. When a law was passed to protect these boundary markers the authorities also forbade the demolition of the hunebedden in this province, which, they had decided, were 'valuable monuments and famous memorials from days of yore that merited conservation' (1734-'35). The fact that so many hunebedden have survived in Drenthe we owe to this first Ancient Monuments Act.[9]

One of the best-known Dutch archaeologists, A.E. van Giffen, devoted a large part of his scientific career to excavating and documenting the hunebedden in Drenthe. He also made them accessible to the public. Over the years, the public, however, became a serious threat to the monuments. It has therefore been decided to remove the signposts calling attention to the hunebedden and to publish a guide containing directions and warnings to the public.[10] It is to be hoped that this will foster a greater responsibility towards our cultural heritage.

Notes

1 Bakker 1992; Van Giffen 1925-'27; Van Ginkel 1988; Mohen 1989; Schirnig 1979.

2 Bakker 1988, 1992. In 1992 one, or possibly two, sites of destroyed *hunebedden* were discovered near Schipborg.

3 Joussaume 1985; Mohen 1985.

4 Brindley/Lanting 1991-'92.

5 Van Giffen 1961.

6 Bakker 1978.

7 Bakker 1982; Bakker/Groenman-van Waateringe 1988.

8 Hoskins 1986; Ziegler 1990.

9 Bakker 1979b, 1992.

10 Van Ginkel 1988.

14 The fruits of the land
Neolithic subsistence

Corrie Bakels and Jørn Zeiler

INTRODUCTION

Not only hunter-gatherers, but farmers, too, had to adapt their subsistence activities to the ecological opportunities and constraints of their occupation areas, which varied considerably in the different parts of the Netherlands. In the following discussion a distinction will therefore be made between six types of landscape identified in the Netherlands:
- the loess of southern Limburg;
- the Pleistocene sands to the south of the major rivers;
- the Pleistocene sands to the north of the major rivers;
- freshwater swamps;
- saline and brackish environments; and
- coastal barriers and Older Dunes.

With the exception of the saline and brackish regions in the coastal zone and parts of the swamps, the land was covered with deciduous forests. The saline and brackish regions resembled the present beaches, tidal flats and salt marshes, only the salt marshes were much wider and higher in those days; since the construction of the dikes this landscape feature has largely disappeared. Parts of the freshwater swamps consisted of open water and reed marshes dotted with alder and willow carrs. The scarce dry areas in that landscape – the levees, river dunes and stream ridges – were covered with rich, mixed deciduous forests. The wet part of the Netherlands was hence a mosaic of different kinds of vegetation.

The woods on the higher grounds were dominated by lime, oak, elm and (to a lesser extent) ash (*cf.* fig. 22.1). Beech and hornbeam were not to be found in the Netherlands in those times. The precise composition of the forest varied according to the type of soil and the groundwater level. In the course of the Neolithic the vegetation was moreover increasingly affected by human activities. By felling trees or clearing large parts of woods and by grazing and feeding their cattle, the Neolithic occupants of these areas gradually changed the original forest into a more open woodland.

The available subsistence data will be dealt with per period and per natural landscape below. The sources on which the discussion will be based are first of all the remains recovered in excavations: animal bones and (often carbonised) plant remains. In the areas of the Pleistocene sands and the loess all bones have disappeared due to decalcification. Moreover, only carbonised plant remains or impressions of parts of plants in pottery have survived in those areas, which are hence much more poorly represented than the wet lowlands (fig. 14.1). The second source of information are pollen diagrams. The third and last comprises specific features: impressions of animal hooves in the prehistoric soil and the typical marks made by the *ard*, a kind of primitive plough that only made furrows and did not turn the soil. Artefacts such as querns and sickles will not be included in this chapter as their use is – though frequently – not exclusively associated with farming practices.

fig. 14.1
Wheat grain impression in a *Bandkeramik* potsherd. The grain itself was burned when the pottery was fired. 3x actual size.

The loess region

Crop cultivation and animal husbandry were introduced into the Netherlands by the people of the *Linearbandkeramik* (LBK), who brought along their crops, animals and technology from their area of origin. They settled in the loess region – at that time one of the most densely forested parts of the Netherlands. The loess soil itself supported mainly lime trees, which, being very shady, precluded the growth of much else in the forests. Lime was less dominant on the slopes along streams, but the most varied woods were to be found in the river valleys, where many oak trees grew, too. This landscape was not very attractive for hunting and gathering.

The LBK is one of the best investigated cultures in Europe, also in terms of subsistence. The Dutch settlements represent the northwesternmost extension of the LBK distribution area. In cultural terms they closely resemble the settlements of the German Rhineland and those of Hesbaye in Belgium. The following discussion will therefore be based on data from the area covered by all three of those regions. That way the difficulty of the lack of sufficient data, in particular bones, from the Dutch findspots will be overcome.[1]

Cattle were the principal stock, followed by sheep, goats and pigs. The crops were emmer and einkorn, pea, lentil, linseed and poppy (figs. 14.2 and 14.3). The flax which yielded the linseed was also grown for its fibre. The foundations for this subsistence system had been laid in the Near East, where most of the aforementioned plants and animals were to be found in the wild. It was there that they were first domesticated. From there, the agricultural way of life spread to the Balkans and other areas, and from the Balkans on to Hungary, the cradle of the LBK. Five of the crops and the sheep and goats descended almost directly from Near Eastern ancestors. As these species were not to be found in Central and Western Europe,

fig. 14.2
Carbonised emmer (the thicker kernels) and einkorn (the more slender kernels) from the *Bandkeramik* settlement Geleen-Urmonderbaan. 4x actual size.

fig. 14.3

The first farmers introduced not only cereals but other crops that had been cultivated in the Near East as well: lentils, peas and linseed. Poppy is the single crop that was not part of this 'classical package'. It must derive from the western Mediterranean, where we find the wild ancestors today.

1 charred pea, *Bandkeramik*, Geleen-Spaubeeklaan, 10x actual size,

2 charred lentils, Older *Bandkeramik*, Geleen-Janskamperveld, 10x actual size,

3 charred linseed, Younger *Bandkeramik*, Crisnée (Hesbaye, Belgium), 10x actual size,

4 poppy, used as a temper in Blicquy pottery, Vaux-et-Borset (Hesbaye), 20x actual size.

they could not be crossed with new genetic material. This was not the case with cattle and pigs. Excavated bones from, for example, Müddersheim in Germany constitute clear evidence of crossbreeding with aurochs and wild boar. Whether this was the result of human intervention we do not know. The lack of indisputable evidence of stalls or cattle pens suggests that the animals were allowed to roam around freely. Under such circumstances crossbreeding may have taken place naturally.

Poppy is a special case. The history of this crop is not well known; its wild ancestor is believed to have grown only in the countries of the western Mediterranean, which would imply that it must also have been brought into cultivation in that area. So far, moreover, poppy has only been encountered in the western part of the LBK distribution area, the highest concentrations having been found in the Netherlands and the adjacent part of Germany.[2]

Hunting and gathering do not seem to have been very important economic activities. The plant remains recovered from the settlements include only the odd fragment of a hazelnut, apple, elderberry or sloe and a few seeds of fat hen, the spinach of those times.[3] Less than 10% of the bones from Müddersheim were of hunted animals. However, at Liège-Place-St.-Lambert, a site which differs from the others on account of its situation on the river terrace of the Meuse, 15% of the faunal remains were of red deer, 10% of roe. Wild boar was also well represented

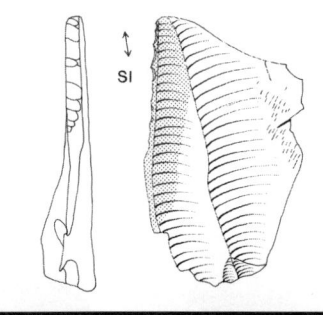

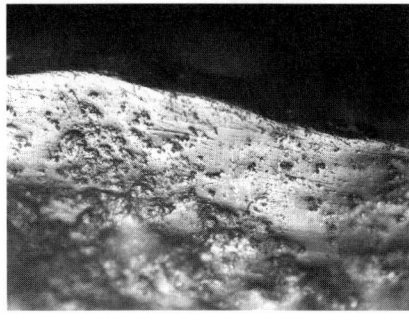

fig. 14.4

Bandkeramik sickle blade from Beek-Molensteeg. The distinct gloss along the cutting edge (grey hatched area) is the result of cutting cereal stems. The other part of the sickle was fixed in a handle. The photo shows a greatly enlarged part of the glossy cutting edge.

at that site.[4] The occupants had moreover supplemented their diet with a wide range of fish.[5]

As already mentioned above, the cattle, or at least the majority of the cattle, were not stalled, not even in the winter. Very little forage for the animals was to be found in the dense lime woods surrounding the settlements. Only the valleys and the woods outside the loess regions contained sufficient fodder. That means that the animals must have been pastured far away from the settlements for part of the year at least, which could explain the odd find of LBK features outside the loess region.[6]

The farms themselves were permanently occupied. They lay within the loess region, probably on account of their vicinity to the fields. Although no traces of fields have been found in excavations, it is assumed that the crops were cultivated on the loess. The weeds that were brought into the farms along with the grain indicate that the crops were grown in a fertile soil in a clearance. We know that the fields were shaded for part of the day, possibly by the trees of the forest, and it is therefore believed that they were quite small. They were used more or less permanently, in the sense that they were not left fallow every few years as is common practice in tropical jungles. Slash-and-burn cultivation was not practised. Experiments have shown that there was no need for such an approach in the loess region. Moreover, the settlements lay so close together that there was no room left for swidden farming.

Calculations of the dietary requirements of these farmers led to figures of 0.6-2.3 ha of cultivated land per household. How the land was tilled is not clear. With the exception of the flint knives of sickles, no agricultural implements have been found (fig. 14.4). Analysis of the weeds has shown that the ears of the cereal were cut relatively high above the ground (fig. 14.5): no seeds of low species were encountered among the carbonised remains recovered from the settlements. The harvests may have been stored in attics in the southeast parts of the houses. In the last occupation phases in particular they were also stored in underground bottle-shaped, conical or cylindrical pits with volumes of about 2 m³. They must have been sealed with wooden covers, coated with daub to prevent the introduction of air from outside. Such silos could not be opened very often because otherwise the grain would start to decay.[7] It is therefore believed that these pits were used mainly for the storage of seed grain.[8] The grain intended for everyday consumption must have been obtained, in daily portions, from a different kind of storage area, for example an attic as mentioned above.

All this shows that the LBK farmers had an almost completely balanced mixed farming system that could be used at the same location for centuries. So why these farmers suddenly disappeared is not clear. One possibility is that they ultimately exhausted the soil around their traditional settlements, but there is no evidence to suggest that this was indeed the case.

THE EARLY NEOLITHIC B

The loess region

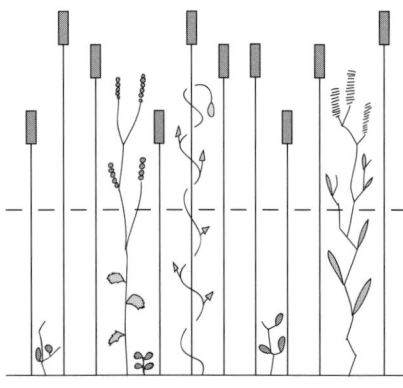

fig. 14.5

When cereals are cut halfway down the stems (dotted line) low-growing plants are left in the field. Seeds of climbing plants and plants of the same height as the cereal are harvested along with the cereal grain.

The LBK farmers were – after an interruption – succeeded by people of the Rössen culture. From an agricultural point of view the latter may indeed be regarded as the former's successors. Although they did not select the same locations as their predecessors – the only settlement known in the Netherlands, *i.e.* Maastricht-Randwijck, is not even situated in the loess region proper but on the Meuse lower

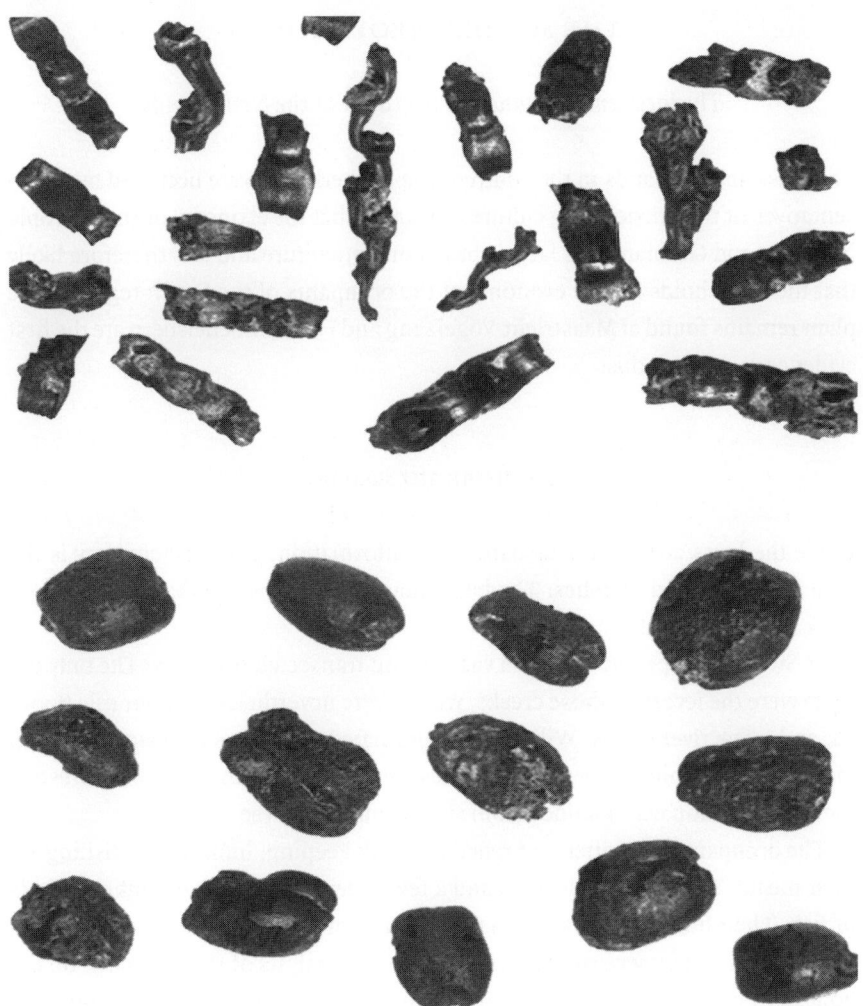

fig. 14.6
Bread wheat – grains and chaff – from the
Rössen settlement at Maastricht-Randwijck.
5 x actual size.

river terrace – all the evidence indicates that their economy was based on the same type of farming system. A difference between the two is that the range of crops of the Rössen culture included two new cereals, namely bread wheat and naked, six-rowed barley (fig. 14.6). These two species also originated in the Near East, but how they made their way into the fields of the farmers of the Rössen culture has not yet been adequately investigated.[9] A specific feature of these new species is that they are free-threshing wheats, which means that the grains can be detached from the glumes by beating the ears or walking over them. That does not hold true for emmer and einkorn, which are both glume wheat species; their glumes have to be removed by rubbing or pounding the spikelets, which implies extra work. That is the reason why these species are hardly cultivated anywhere nowadays. Nevertheless, after its introduction by the Rössen farmers, bread wheat, being a very demanding species, never caught on in the Netherlands in prehistoric times. Barley, on the contrary, did become popular and was to be cultivated on a large scale from then onwards.

Although the Rössen farmers lived essentially in the loess region, the wide distribution area of their characteristic perforated wedges (Breitkeile) indicates that their influence extended far beyond that area. We may therefore safely assume that crop cultivation and stock keeping were introduced in the rest of the Netherlands, too, in this period. This has, however, so far not been documented.

The loess and the sands in the south of the Netherlands

The loess and the sands in the south of the Netherlands were occupied by representatives of the Michelsberg culture. We know that the economy of these people in France and Germany was largely based on agriculture and it is therefore likely that the same holds for the economy of the occupants of the Dutch regions. The plant remains found at Maastricht-Vogelzang and Heerlen-Schelsberg are the first evidence to confirm this.

The freshwater swamps

While the loess zone offers us hardly any information, quite the contrary is the case in the lowland marshes. The best known sites are Swifterbant, Bergschen-hoek and Hazendonk.

In Swifterbant people lived in a vast swamp transected by creeks. The only dry parts were the levees of those creeks, which were nevertheless temporarily flooded, and a few river dunes. Willow carrs alternated with areas of open vegetation in the swamp, while the levees and dunes were covered with deciduous forests.[10] Most information was obtained from site S3, on a low levee.

The occupants of Swifterbant relied on stock keeping, hunting and fishing for their meat.[11] They kept cattle, pigs and a few sheep or goats and caught all kinds of fish. Their hunting efforts seem to have concentrated on wild boar and furred animals and to a lesser extent on waterfowl. The analysis of the cut marks on the bones of beavers and otters showed that those animals were not only caught for their furs but also for their meat (fig. 14.7). The large amounts of bones suggest that both species were very common in the environs of the settlement. Animals like red deer, aurochs, elk and horse, on the contrary, were rare, probably because the forests were so dense. The red deer remains consisted largely of fragments of

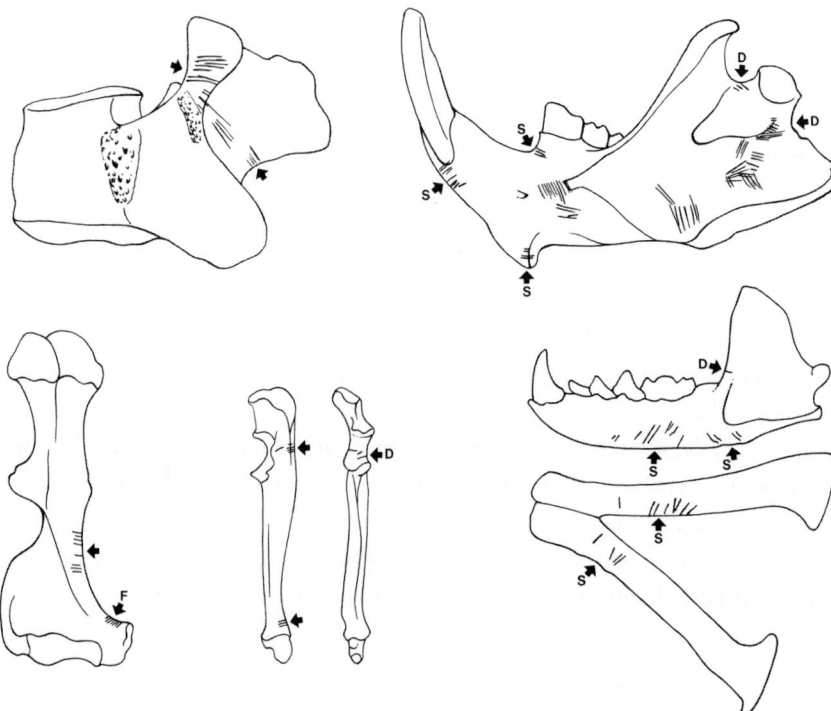

fig. 14.7
Cut marks on bones from settlement sites of the Swifterbant culture: lumbar vertebra of a brown bear (Hazendonk), lower jaw and *humerus* of beavers, *ulna* and lower jaw of otters (Swifterbant S3). Scale 1:2.

D = dismembering
F = filleting
S = skinning

antler, which were probably imported from elsewhere. Nevertheless, pig and cattle husbandry does not seem to have involved many problems in this area.

The presence of sheep/goat is a little surprising in view of the eggs of the liver fluke that were found in dog coprolites.[12] This parasite, which occurs in wet freshwater environments, is particularly lethal for sheep, so keeping sheep must have been quite risky. A comparison of the weights of bones, which provide a rough indication of the amount of meat yielded by a particular type of animal, showed that animal husbandry and hunting were about equally important as far as meat was concerned. Pig, wild boar and cattle were the main sources of meat. Little can be said about the importance of fishing as the total weight/skeletal weight ratio of fish is not dependent on the size of the fish, which means that we cannot use the weight of fish bones as an indication of the meat yield.[13] The large amounts of fish remains do indicate that we are not to underestimate the importance of fishing.

Besides meat and fish, the diet comprised plant food. The proportion of vegetables and fruit in the diet can no longer be ascertained as plant remains are even more difficult to interpret in terms of the amounts of food consumed than animal remains. What we do know is that the occupants of Swifterbant ate both gathered wild species (hazelnuts, wild apples, hawthorn berries, rose hips and blackberries, and cereals (emmer, barley). It is very unlikely that the cereals were grown at the site itself. Very little land suitable for the cultivation of cereal was available in this wet environment; the occupants would have to have cleared a large part of the dryer land to have been able to grow sufficient crops to support themselves. Such large-scale deforestation would have showed up in the pollen diagrams. And as this is not the case, the cereals must have been imported from elsewhere, unless they were consumed in only very small amounts. But where that 'elsewhere' was we do not know. Did the occupants of Swifterbant obtain their cereals from farmers elsewhere whose harvests were large enough to enable the exchange of surplus grain or did they live elsewhere themselves for part of the year?

The question whether the site was occupied on a seasonal, permanent or semi-permanent basis has been the topic of discussion for many years already. The environmental conditions would seem to argue against permanent occupation, but the archaeozoological data point to human activities in all seasons. There are two possibilities: either the site was continuously occupied, or it was occupied from the spring until the beginning of the autumn, after which the occupants returned to the settlement for short periods of time to perform specific activities during the winter. In the latter case we may assume that the occupants drove their cattle from their base camp to S3 in the spring, remained at S3 until the autumn and returned there for a short while during the winter to trap beavers and hunt waterfowl. The data relating to the ages at which the pigs and cattle were killed, however, seem to suggest that the animals were slaughtered mainly between the autumn and the spring. That brings us to a third possibility: when conditions on the levee remained favourable throughout the year the occupants did not leave the site, whereas they stayed there only from the spring until the autumn in years of less favourable conditions. This pattern of behaviour is in accordance with stratigraphic evidence, which indicated periods of frequent flooding alternating with periods of dryer conditions.

The second settlement, Bergschenhoek, was very small and was situated on a peaty shore in a freshwater to slightly brackish area dotted with lakes. The remains recovered in the excavation of the settlement included a few fish traps. The faunal spectrum is entirely different from that of Swifterbant. The only domesticated animal represented among the remains is dog; the great majority of the other remains

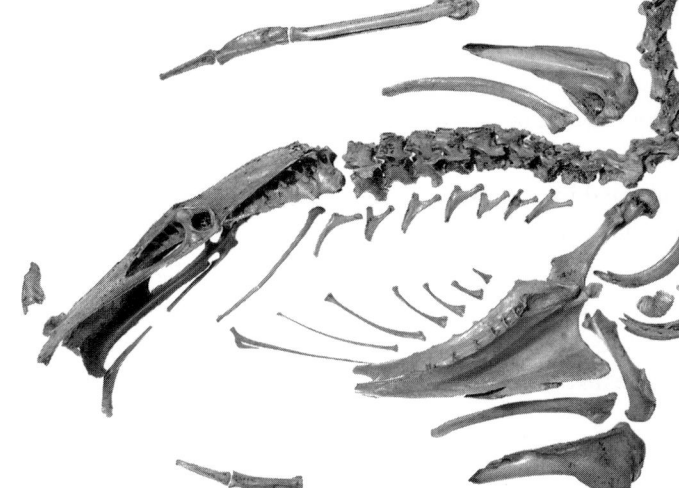

fig. 14.8
Remains of a Bewick's swan (*Cygnus bewickii*) found at the hunting camp of Bergschenhoek (fig. 12.12). Some of the bones are charred. The bird was apparently grilled, and its carcass subsequently buried. The head, legs and the majority of the wing bones are missing. They may have been used, possibly to make a decoy, together with skin and feathers.

belonged to birds and fish. There were also a few bones of wild cat, grey seal and otter.[14] The bird remains were of species that will have nested in that area and of species that overwintered there (fig. 14.8).[15] No remains of cultivated plants were found either. The identified food plants comprised only gathered fruits and nuts such as hazelnuts, wild apples and sloes.

The site was clearly a temporary camp that was used for fishing and hunting for several successive years. It is tempting to regard the remains of the wintering bird species as indications of the presence of human beings in the winter months. However, nowadays some of these species arrive in the Netherlands in September or October already and they sometimes remain in the country until the beginning of May. Moreover, it is not certain that the behaviour of migratory birds was the

fig. 14.9
Carred chaff (fragments of internodes) of barley found at the Hazendonk site, phase 1, c. 4000 BC (8 x actual size). Such remains are indisputable evidence of the consumption of cereals at a site, but not necessarily of crop cultivation: the grain may have been brought to the site in the ear. This grain assemblage is one of the earliest found to the north of the loess, but cereal cultivation may have been introduced a few centuries earlier.

landscape	culture	emmer wheat	einkorn wheat	bread and/or macaroni wheat	barley	pea	lentil	linseed	poppy
Early Neolithic A									
loess zone	Bandkeramik	•	•	-	-	•	•	•	•
Early Neolithic B									
loess zone	Rössen	•	•	•	•	-	-	-	-
Middle Neolithic A									
loess zone	Michelsberg	•	•	•	•	•	-	•	-
fresh water tidal marshes	Swifterbant, Haz. 3	•	-	(•)	•	-	-	-	•
coastal barriers and Older Dunes	Hazendonk 3	•	-	-	•	-	-	-	-
Middle Neolithic B									
Northern Netherlands upland	Funnel Beaker	•	-	-	•	-	-	•	-
fresh water tidal marshes	Vlaardingen	•	-	•	•	-	-	•	-
salt and brackish environment	Vlaardingen	•	-	-	•	-	-	-	-
Late Neolithic A									
Northern Netherlands upland	Single Grave	-	-	-	•	-	-	-	-
salt and brackish environment	Single Grave	•	(•)	•	•	-	-	•	-
Late Neolithic B									
fresh water tidal marshes	Bell Beaker	•	-	-	•	-	-	-	-

same in the Neolithic as it is today. The camp may in fact have been used mainly in the autumn, for hunting waterfowl, which were still meaty at that time of the year. The gathered fruits cannot throw any more light on this matter because, although they were picked in the autumn (and certainly not on the peat island itself), they could be kept for a very long time, either fresh or dried.

The third Middle Neolithic A site about whose subsistence economy we have some information is the Hazendonk, a site on top of a river dune in the area now known as the Alblasserwaard. This site was occupied in phases covering a total span of just under 2000 years. Phase Hazendonk 1 is more or less contemporary with the period of occupation of Swifterbant. Alder carrs alternated with lakes in the landscape surrounding the dune. The dune itself was covered with a deciduous forest. The area fit for occupation was only small: the dune itself measured no more than 1.2 ha. Other dunes were present in the immediate surroundings, but whether they were used at the same time is unknown.

The faunal spectrum resembles that of Swifterbant, with a predominance of cattle and beaver.[16] The range of gathered and cultivated plant species is also similar (table 14.1; fig. 14.9).[17] That means that we are faced with the same questions regarding the nature of the occupation. The site itself was far too small to have supported a farming community, even if it consisted of no more than one household. The total area of dry land is still quite small if we include the dry land available on nearby dunes, which would imply that the occupants would have to have paddled to and fro between their plots of arable and their pastures. Although the occupants may theoretically have used the dry land on the nearby dunes, it is more likely that the Hazendonk is an even better example than Swifterbant of a site oc-

table 14.1

Survey of crops grown in the Low Countries in the Neolithic. Crops indicated between brackets mean uncertain identifications. Since the writing of the text, remains of a range of crops dating from the Middle Neolithic A, and remains of emmer and barley dating from the Late Neolithic B, have been found. This new evidence has been included in the table.

cupied on a seasonal basis for specific activities focusing on hunting, fishing and pasturing small herds of cattle.

During the phases Hazendonk 2 and 3, the landscape became increasingly wet. Low swamp vegetations and open water expanded at the expense of the carrs and the dry areas decreased in size. In spite of these developments, the Hazendonk continued to be visited by human beings. Their presence in phase Hazendonk 3 is even visible in the pollen diagrams: they made the dry parts of land more open by felling trees.[18]

In Hazendonk 2 the subsistence activities were the same as in the preceding period. Hazendonk 3 is characterised by a decrease from 63% to 16% in the weight of cattle bones, which reflects a decrease in the importance of domestic animals in the economy. Hunting, which focused on red deer, beaver and wild boar, seems to have become far more important. This may be associable with the change towards wetter conditions and the resultant decrease in the grassland available for cattle. The faunal remains of Hazendonk 3 included bones of roe, an animal favouring a fairly open habitat, which is in accordance with the picture that emerges from the pollen diagrams. The plant foods were the same as those in the previous occupation phase.

Coastal barriers and Older Dunes

A former coastal barrier at Wateringen was occupied at the same time as Hazendonk 3. One had settled on the top of a low coastal dune, surrounded by fresh water marshes. Cattle dominates in the faunal remains, with pig and red deer second. The only crops established are emmer wheat and naked barley, that could very well have been cultivated locally.[19]

Survey

In the Middle Neolithic A, there were therefore both permanently settled farming communities (in the loess region and possibly on the southern sands as well) and societies whose subsistence base apparently comprised a broad spectrum of activities and was not yet dominated by the production of meat and plant food (in the swamps). The economy of the occupants of the swamps in the Middle Neolithic period A was based on a combination of foraging and farming focusing on a wide range of resources, like that of their predecessors. The differences between the phases Hazendonk 1 on the one hand and Hazendonk 2 and 3 on the other show that the emphasis could easily be shifted from foraging to farming or the other way round, in response to local conditions. We still do not know exactly what part agriculture, and in particular crop cultivation, played in the subsistence system of the marshland sites. If it was relatively important there must have been settlements in a complementary area where sufficient land was available for crop cultivation. The coastal dune landscape is perhaps a good candidate, but we should immediately add that we do not know anything in this respect from the other sandy uplands in the Netherlands.

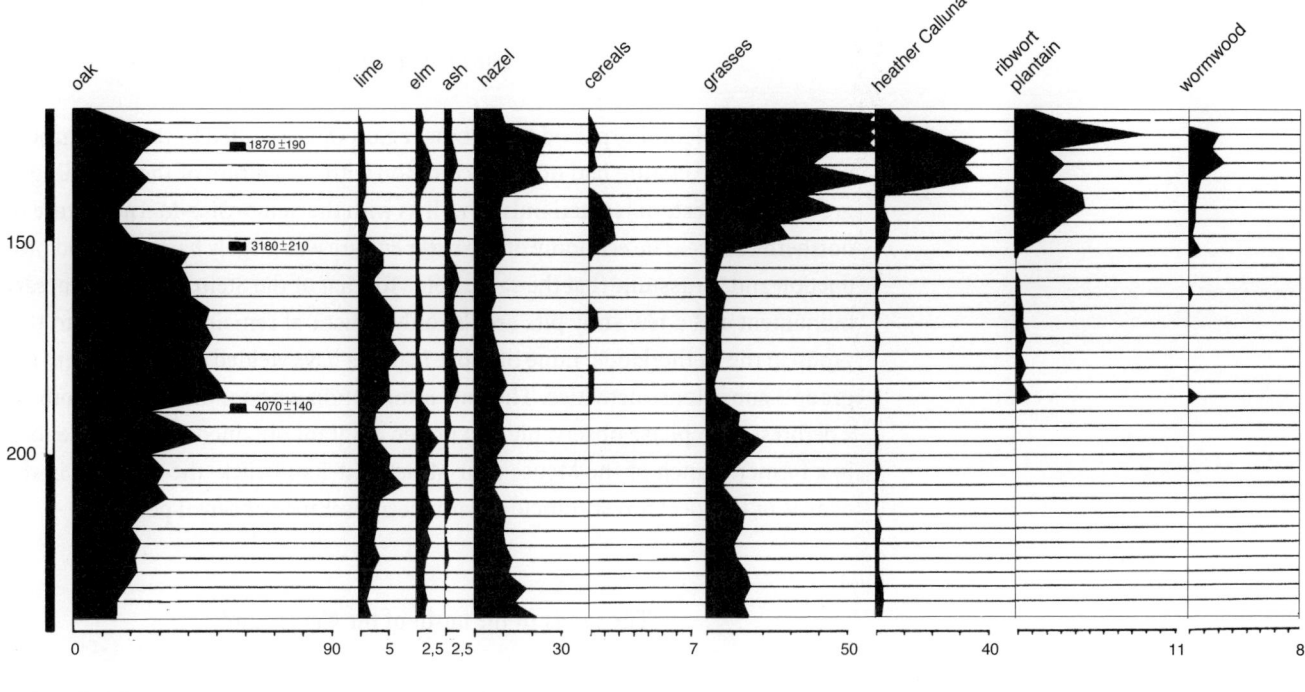

a

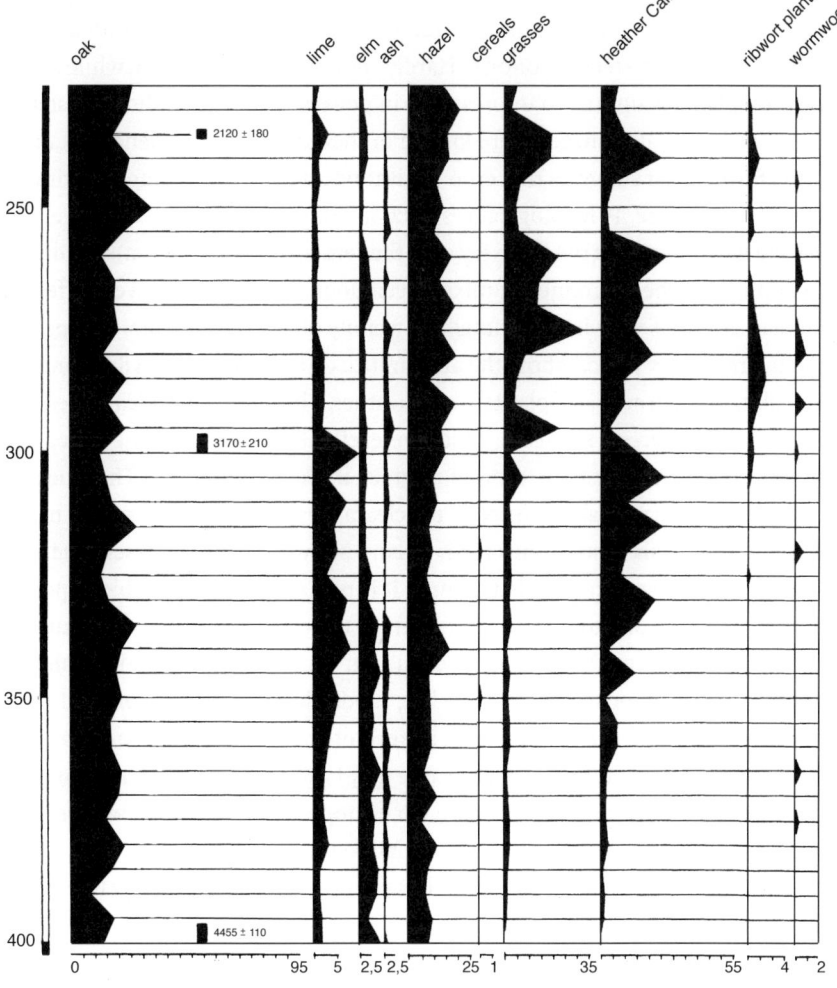

b

fig. 14.10

Two pollen diagrams, both from small peat bogs (so-called *Kesselmoore*) in the *Siedlungskammer* of Flögeln, northeast of Bremerhaven. The first diagram (a) relates to a bog that apparently lay close to a TRB settlement. The irregular oak curve is attributable to local disturbance of the forest. No such irregularities are observable in the oak curve in a second diagram (b) obtained for pollen from a similar contemporary peat bog lying a short distance from this settlement. Both diagrams however show a decline in lime in TRB times, around 3170-3180 cal BC, possibly attributable to cattle keeping. Cereal and wild herb pollen was found predominantly in the vicinity of the settlement (diagram a). All dates in cal BC.

The loess region

In the Middle Neolithic period B the loess region was occupied by the Stein group, a people whose culture had much in common with the culture of the Vlaardingen group of the western Netherlands as well as with the Seine-Oise-Marne culture of northern France. The economy of the latter culture was largely based on food production and we assume that the same holds for that of the Stein group. A funerary monument and a few stray pits are the only structural remains attributed to this group in the Netherlands; none of those features have yielded any insight into the group's subsistence activities. The only information we have on their economy is a deforestation phase observable in a pollen diagram obtained for a peat deposit in a former branch of the Meuse near Maastricht-Randwijck: the decrease in the density of the local forest coincides with the appearance of cereal pollen.[20]

The sands in the north of the Netherlands

We have no data on the sands in the south of the Netherlands. The sands in the north were occupied by the bearers of the TRB culture. Although these people left behind an abundance of remains, only few of those remains have provided information on their subsistence economy. Hardly any bones have survived, while information on plants is limited to impressions in pottery. The latter indicate that emmer, naked barley and linseed were known in these regions.[21] Evidence obtained in areas further east suggests that crop cultivation and stock breeding constituted the subsistence base. Palynological research in the settlement area of Flögeln in Germany has shown that the fields lay near the settlements (fig. 14.10a).[22] Oak and lime dominated the surrounding mixed deciduous forests, which were affected by human activities only in the immediate vicinity of the settlements. The pollen diagrams from this period show the appearance of cereals and of wild plants of open habitats, such as grass, plantain and heather. They imply that clearances had been made in the forests for fields, which were left fallow for some time after a few years of use. Cattle were then allowed to graze in the fallow fields. The wood of the felled trees was probably burned in the clearances, the ashes being used to enrich the soil. This slash-and-burn form of land use was termed 'Iversen *landnam*' after the Danish researcher of that name.[23] It is no longer demonstrable in pollen diagrams obtained one to two kilometres from the settlements, in which human impact is only apparent in the lime spectra (fig. 14.10b). That could indicate the use of lime leaves, or possibly even lime hay, as additional fodder. In forested areas with little grass cattle can be fed leaves instead of hay; cattle prefer lime leaves to oak leaves, which are more bitter. The cattle may have been fed lime leaves in periods in which ordinary fodder was scarce, for example at the end of the winter. This may have taken place in cattle pens of the kind found at Anloo.

Vague indications of the form of land use outlined above are observable in the pollen spectra obtained for the eastern part of the Drenthe Plateau (feature K). The soil of this region was a little poorer than that of Flögeln and more heather consequently grew in the clearances. That heather marked the small-scale beginning of the formation of the Dutch moors.

	culture	Swifterbant / Hazendonk 3			Vlaardingen							Single grave		Bell Beaker		
	site	Swifterbant S3 hand collected	Hazendonk phases Haz. 1-3	Wateringen 4	Leidschendam	Voorschoten-Boschgeest	Hekelingen 3	Vlaardingen	Hazendonk fase VL 1b	Hazendonk fase VL 2b	Ewijk	Kolhorn, noord en zuid	Aartswoud, trenches 1 en 2	Molenaarsgraaf	total	total / group
cattle	*Bos taurus*	321	46	284	200	254	162	334	6	24	197	200	313	218	2559	
pig	*Sus domesticus*	936	16	[77]	177	52	372	315	39	-	213	60	59	33	2349	
sheep/goat	*Ovis / Capra*	9	5		32	30	85	19	7	-	118	10	59	14	388	
	livestock															5296
dog	*Scanis familiaris*	49	10	40	-	8	8	12	8	49	6	116	15	+	321	
	dog															321
red deer	*Cervus elaphus*	39	78	155	28*	42*	274	700	154	8	13	-	-	4	1425	
wild boar	*Sus scrofa*	1205	63	[77]	-	5	38	558	39	82	1	-	-	1	2069	
roe	*Capreolus capreolus*	-	4	-	22	24	151	25	56	215	4	4	1	-	506	
elk	*Alces alces*	21	-	-	-	-	-	-	1	-	-	-	+	3	25	
aurochs	*Bos primigenius*	2	-	-	-	4	-	-	-	-	-	1	+	-	7	
horse	*Equus ferus caballus*	2	-	-	-	-	2	-	-	-	-	-	-	2	6	
	ungulates															4038
otter	*Lutra lutra*	511	94	7	-	-	21	26	57	57	-	3	-	-	776	
beaver	*Castor fiber*	491	319	10	1	-	93	218	110	227	2	3	2	8	1484	
	beaver and otter															2260
(pine) marten	*Martes martes*	-	-	-	1	-	10	21	4	-	-	-	-	-	36	
wild cat	*Felis silvestris*	1	-	3	-	-	4	20	1	4	-	1	-	-	34	
polecat	*Mustela putorius*	2	1	-	-	-	4	14	-	2	-	10	-	-	33	
brown bear	*Ursus arctos*	6	-	-	-	1	5	4	3	-	-	-	+	1	20	
fox	*Vulpes vulpes*	1	-	-	-	-	-	-	3	-	-	1	-	-	5	
badger	*Meles meles*	-	-	-	-	-	-	-	1	1	-	-	-	-	2	
wolf	*Canis lupus*	-	-	-	-	-	1	-	-	-	-	-	-	-	1	
	other fur animals															131
whale sp.	*Cetacea*	-	-		-	-	13	14	-	-	-	46	+	-	73	
bottle-nosed dolphin	*Tursiops truncatus*	-	-		-	-	19	1	-	-	-	-	-	-	20	
grey seal	*Halichoerus gryphus*	-	-	1	2	1	4	3	-	-	-	1	-	-	12	
common porpoise	*Phocoena phocoena*	-	-		-	-	-	-	-	-	-	9	-	-	9	
common seal	*Phoca vitulina*	1	-		-	-	-	-	-	-	-	-	-	-	1	
sperm whale	*Physeter macrocephalus*	-	-		-	1	-	-	-	-	-	-	-	-	1	
	sea mammals															116
	total	3597	636	654	435	380	1266	2284	489	669	554	465	449	284	12162	

table 14.2

Identifications of the bones of large mammals from a selection of relatively large assemblages from the period 4200-2000 BC. The Hazendonk 1, 2 and 3 assemblages were combined.

Pig bones were divided between wild and domestic swine on the basis of the ratios of the positive identifications. In the case of one assemblage (Wateringen 4) no distinction was made between wild and domestic swine and the identifications were divided on a 50/50 basis. It is incidentally not certain whether the different analysts based their identifications on uniform criteria.

The red deer scores are excluding antler, except where figures are marked with an asterisk (*).

The pronounced differences between domestic and wild animals in the case of the assemblages from the Swifterbant-Vlaardingen period are largely attributable to differences in the landscape of the sites' surroundings and differences in site functions.

After Clason 1967, 1990, Clason in Louwe Kooijmans 1974, Groenman-van Waateringe *et al.* 1968, Prummel 1987, Raemaekers *et al.* 1997, Van Wijngaarden-Bakker in Van Iterson Scholten/De Vries-Metz 1981, Zeiler 1997.

table 14.3 (next page)

Species identifications of bird bones from a selection of relatively large assemblages from the period 5500-2000 BC. Identifications according to genus or family (duck, *Anas*, *Aythya* and the like) are not included. Some figures include uncertain (probable) species identifications (*e.g.* white-tailed eagle, mute swan) or combined species (*e.g.* different plover species, red-throated/black-throated diver). The species and their frequencies present a highly distorted picture of the Mesolithic/Neolithic avifauna. The assemblages represent a hunting selection in the wet western part of the Netherlands and probably a small component of natural (background) fauna. Ducks account for almost 90% of the faunal remains whereas songbirds are almost completely absent! There are major differences between individual sites, in terms of both the represented species and their frequencies. Those differences reflect primarily the varying ecological zones in which the settlements were situated, but also a certain degree of specialisation or hunting preferences. Only a small number of species were represented at more than half of the sites; one of those species is the white-tailed eagle!

After Clason 1993, Clason/Brinkhuizen 1967, Gehasse 2001, Louwe Kooijmans 2001a and b, Prummel 1987, Raemaekers *et al.* 1997, Schnitger 1991, De Vries 2001, Zeiler 1997.

period / culture		Meso	Swifterbant / Hazendonk 3					Swift VL	Vlaardingen		Single Grave				total	total / group
site		Hardinxveld ph1	Bergschenhoek	Hardinxveld ph2	Hardinxveld ph3	Swifterbant S3	Wateringen 4	Hazendonk	Hekelingen III	Vlaardingen	Kolhorn	Aartswoud	Zeewijk	Mienakker		
teal	*Anas crecca*	4	2	1	1	.	.	.	.	1	.	.	36	1506	1551	
teal / garganey	*Anas crecca / querquedula*	.	.	.	.	.	.	.	.	.	566	.	.	.	566	
mallard	*Anas platyrhynchos*	169	8	153	39	102	240	15	2	62	32	44	36	.	902	
wigeon	*Mareca penelope*	4	1	11	4	.	38	.	1	.	1	21	15	.	96	
goosander	*Mergus merganser*	25	4	5	1	.	.	.	.	1	.	.	.	.	32	
goldeneye	*Bucephala clangula*	5	4	3	.	.	.	.	.	.	.	.	.	.	12	
eider	*Somateria mollissima*	.	4	.	.	.	6	.	.	.	.	1	.	.	11	
common scooter	*Melanitta (nigra)*	.	.	.	.	.	.	.	.	.	.	.	.	8	8	
garganey	*Anas querquedula*	.	1	.	.	.	.	.	.	.	6	.	.	.	7	
tufted duck	*Ayhtya fuligula*	1	1	.	.	1	.	.	.	.	.	1	2	.	6	
scaup	*Aythya marila*	3	1	.	.	.	.	.	.	.	.	.	1	.	5	
merganser	*Mergus serrator*	.	.	.	.	.	.	.	.	.	.	1	1	2	4	
pochard	*Aythya ferina*	.	.	1	.	1	.	.	.	.	.	.	1	.	3	
shel duck	*Tadorna tadorna*	.	.	.	.	1	.	.	.	1	.	1	.	.	3	
shoveler	*Anas clypeata*	.	.	.	.	.	.	.	.	.	3	.	.	.	3	
gadwall	*Anas strepera*	.	.	.	.	.	.	.	.	.	1	.	.	.	1	
red-crested pochard	*Netta rufina*	.	.	.	.	.	.	.	.	.	1	.	.	.	1	
	ducks															3211
mute swan	*Cygnus olor*	13	1	32	1	1	.	4	9	6	2	.	.	.	69	
whooper swan	*Cygnus cygnus*	10	.	2	.	.	.	1	5	.	.	.	.	.	18	
Bewick's swan	*Cygnus bewickii*	2	1	.	.	.	.	.	.	.	.	.	.	.	3	
	swans															90
(grey lag) goose	*Anser (anser)*	8	.	11	3	.	4	11	.	5	2	.	.	.	44	
brent goose	*Branta bernicla*	.	.	.	.	.	.	.	.	1	11	1	1	.	14	
bean goose	*Anser fabalis*	4	.	2	.	.	.	.	.	.	.	3	.	.	9	
barnacle goose	*Branta leucopsis*	.	.	.	.	.	.	.	.	2	.	.	.	.	2	
	geese															69
red- / black-throated diver	*Gavia stellata / arctica*	10	.	2	.	.	.	.	5	1	3	.	.	.	21	
coot	*Fulica atra*	10	.	1	.	.	1	.	.	5	.	.	.	.	17	
cormorant	*Phalacrocorax carbo*	10	1	.	.	2	.	.	.	.	.	.	.	.	13	
moorhen	*Gallinula chloropus*	7	.	3	1	.	.	.	.	.	.	.	.	.	11	
Dalmatian pelican	*Pelecanus crispus*	-	.	.	.	.	.	.	.	7	.	.	.	.	7	
water rail	*Rallus aquaticus*	1	.	5	.	.	.	.	.	.	.	.	.	.	6	
little grebe	*Tachybaptus ruficollis*	5	.	.	.	.	.	.	.	.	.	.	.	.	5	
little crake	*Porzana parva*	.	.	.	2	.	.	.	.	.	.	.	.	.	2	
great crested grebe	*Podiceps cristatus*	.	.	.	.	.	.	.	.	.	1	.	.	.	1	
	other water fowl															83
herring gull	*Larus argentatus*	.	.	.	.	1	.	.	.	.	3	.	.	.	4	
fulmar	*Fulmarus glacialis*	.	.	.	.	.	.	.	.	.	.	.	.	1	1	
gannet	*Sula bassana*	.	.	.	.	.	.	.	.	.	1	.	.	.	1	
guillemot	*Uria aalge*	.	.	.	.	.	.	.	.	.	.	.	1	.	1	
	sea birds															7
bittern	*Botaurus stellaris*	8	11	1	.	1	.	.	1	2	.	.	.	.	23	
grey heron	*Ardea cinerea*	.	.	6	.	.	+	.	.	1	.	.	.	.	7	
crane	*Grus grus*	1	.	.	.	.	.	.	1	4	.	.	1	.	7	
purple heron	*Ardea purpurea*	.	.	2	1	.	.	.	.	.	.	.	.	.	3	
greater flamingo	*Phoenicopterus ruber*	.	.	.	.	.	.	.	.	.	1	.	.	.	1	
	large waders															41
dunlin	*Calidris alpina*	.	.	.	.	.	.	.	.	.	32	.	.	.	32	
oystercatcher	*Haematopus ostralegus*	.	.	.	.	.	.	.	.	.	.	.	2	28	30	
plover	*Charadriidae*	7	.	.	.	.	1	.	.	.	3	.	2	2	15	
ruff	*Philomachus pugnax*	.	.	.	.	.	.	.	.	.	10	.	.	.	10	
knot	*Calidris kanutus*	.	.	.	.	.	.	.	.	.	8	.	.	.	8	
curlew	*Numenius arquata*	.	.	.	.	.	.	.	.	.	.	.	.	2	2	
godwit	*Limosa sp.*	.	.	.	.	.	.	.	.	.	.	.	.	1	1	
snipe	*Gallinago sp.*	.	.	.	.	.	.	.	.	.	.	.	.	1	1	
woodcock	*Scolopax rusticola*	1	.	.	.	.	.	.	.	.	.	.	.	.	1	
great snipe	*Gallinago media*	.	.	.	.	.	.	.	.	.	.	.	1	.	1	
	waders and meadow birds															101
(white-tailed) eagle	*Haliaeëtus (albicilla)/Aquila*	30	3	10	2	6	-	-	2	23	4	.	.	6	86	
eagle owl	*Bubo bubo*	1	-	5	3	-	-	2	-	-	.	.	.	.	11	
(marsh) harrier	*Circus (aeruginosus)*	.	.	.	.	.	.	.	.	.	2	.	.	5	7	
goshawk	*Accipiter gentilis*	.	.	1	.	.	.	.	4	.	.	.	.	.	5	
buzzard	*Buteo buteo*	3	.	.	.	.	.	.	.	.	.	.	.	.	3	
sparrow hawk	*Accipiter nisus*	3	.	.	.	.	.	.	.	.	1	.	.	.	4	
falcon	*Falco sp.*	.	.	.	.	.	.	.	.	.	.	.	1	.	1	
	birds of prey and owls															117
quail	*Coturnix coturnix*	.	.	.	.	.	.	.	.	.	2	.	.	.	2	
partridge	*Perdrix perdrix*	.	.	.	.	.	.	.	.	.	.	.	1	.	1	
	game birds															3
carrion crow / rook	*Corvus corone / frugilegus*	.	.	.	.	3	.	1	.	3	1	.	.	1	9	
great spotted woodpecker	*Dendrocopus major*	3	.	.	.	.	.	.	.	.	.	.	.	.	3	
reed bunting	*Emberizia schoeniclus*	2	.	.	.	.	.	.	.	.	.	.	.	.	2	
jay	*Garrulus glandarius*	.	.	.	.	1	.	.	.	.	.	.	.	.	1	
blue-headed wagtail	*Motacilla flava*	.	.	.	.	.	.	.	.	.	1	.	.	.	1	
	song birds															16
	total	350	39	257	58	120	290	34	29	125	698	73	102	1563	3738	

The freshwater swamps

The swamps, the dunes and the brackish regions were inhabited by the Vlaardingen group. We are very well informed about the subsistence economy of the occupants of the swamps thanks to the data that were obtained at four sites with the favourable preservation conditions characteristic of swamps: besides the aforementioned Hazendonk they are Hekelingen, Vlaardingen itself and Ewijk.

On a river dune

The excavations on the Hazendonk revealed three Vlaardingen occupation phases: Vlaardingen 1a, 1b and 2b. During Vlaardingen phase 1 the lakes became shallower, enabling the carrs to expand again in many areas. The landscape must have closely resembled that of the Hazendonk during phases 1 and 2. As the peat and the lacustrine deposits surrounding the river dunes had become thicker and hence also covered higher parts of the slopes of the dunes, the extent of dry land was smaller. The evidence for the felling of trees implies that both the deciduous forests in the dry areas and the carrs were more open. The lakes started to expand again in Vlaardingen phase 2 and that resulted in a landscape resembling that of Hazendonk 3, but with fewer and slightly smaller Pleistocene dunes. The only other relatively dry features were the levees of a few creeks that drained the swamps. They constituted a landscape that is difficult for us to imagine nowadays. The Hazendonk itself measured no more than 0.4 ha in this period.

Virtually all the recovered bones came from Vlaardingen layers 1b and 2b. The faunal spectrum shows a further decrease in the proportion of meat of domestic animals in Vlaardingen phase 1b, followed by a slight increase in Vlaardingen phase 2b. By far the greatest part of the meat, however, came from hunted animals: in Vlaardingen 1b mainly red deer, in Vlaardingen 2b beaver, roe deer and wild boar. Possible explanations for the conspicuous decrease in the proportion of red deer in Vlaardingen 2b are that the landscape had become too wet for this spe-

fig. 14.11
Half a carbonised apple found at the Hazendonk site, phase Hazendonk 3, c. 3600 BC., 2x actual size. Small wild apples can be stored relatively easily after being cut in half and dried. They are probably charred during the drying process.

fig. 14.12
Remains of a fish trap found in a gulley fill next to the eponymous Vlaardingen settlement site. The remains probably represent the trap's funnel-shaped entrance (cf. plate 19B).

cies, that red deer had been overhunted in Vlaardingen 1b or maybe a combination of the two.

The range of fur animals represented by the Vlaardingen bones is larger than that of the preceding periods. Cut marks on the bones show that the meat of virtually all the hunted animals was eaten, even that of wild cat, fox and badger. Fowling seems to have been of minor importance. The represented species will have nested in the vicinity of the sites. The abundance of remains of many different kinds of fish reflect the importance of fishing.[24]

The plant remains show that the subsistence pattern based on a combination of foraging and crop cultivation had not changed (fig. 14.11), only the relative importance of the different plant foods is not clear. Acorns, hazelnuts, sloes and hawthorn berries – examples of gathered fruit and nuts – may have been picked on the dune itself, but if they were staples in the diet the dune cannot have been the sole source. The same holds to an even greater extent for the crops, which comprised emmer and naked barley in Vlaardingen phase 1 and only barley in Vlaardingen phase 2. As in the case of the previous phases, we assume that the cereal was not grown at the site itself: an area of 0.4 ha (Vlaardingen 2b) that supported dwellings and working areas cannot possibly have yielded a cereal harvest too.

Along tidal creeks
The other sites in the swamps are all settlements on levees of creeks or rivers. These levees were covered with rich mixed deciduous forests and were surrounded by a landscape of carrs alternating with open areas and lakes.

The levees of Hekelingen and Vlaardingen were narrow. Hunting and fishing were the main subsistence activities. The picture that emerges for these two sites closely resembles that outlined for the swamp sites above. Between 50% and 60% of the weight of the identified faunal remains from Hekelingen III (Vlaardingen phases 1b and 2a) consisted of game, in particular red deer.[25] Remains of game amounted to two-thirds of the skeletal remains of Vlaardingen.[26] Cattle and pig seem to have been the principal domestic animals. Sheep or goats were kept in small numbers only, which is not surprising considering the wet environment.

Fowling seems to have played only a minor part. Fishing, on the contrary, was very important: all kinds of freshwater fish and migratory fish were caught (fig. 14.12).[27] A tributary creek at Hekelingen III was found to contain the remains of a wooden structure resembling a similar structure found at Vlaardingen, which has been interpreted as the remains of a fish weir which may have been used for catching sturgeon (fig. 14.13).[28] The Hekelingen structure may have served the same purpose, but the problem is that no pattern was recognisable in the configuration of posts.[29] Another possibility is that the posts supported hoop nets. With the exception of sturgeon, all the types of fish represented at Hekelingen could have been caught with the aid of hoop nets (fig. 14.14). Sturgeon can only be caught in wide-meshed nets or harpoons, whether or not in combination with a fish weir.

Besides gathered plant foods such as acorns, wild apples, hazelnuts, sloes, wa-

fig. 14.13
A series of posts found driven into the floor of a tidal gulley gave rise to this reconstruction of sturgeon fishing at Vlaardingen. The small side gulley has been blocked off and at the side of the main stream posts have been arranged in a funnel-shaped setting with a narrow entrance that can be closed off. The reconstruction is inspired by ethnographical examples.

ter chestnuts and tubers of lesser celandine, the plant remains comprised remains of the cultivated crops emmer, naked barley and linseed. The range encountered at Vlaardingen even included bread wheat.[30] It is however not very likely that crop cultivation played an important part on the narrow levees. In occupation phase 3 the Hekelingen levee for example was only 20 m wide. Any fields around the site would have been visible in the pollen diagrams obtained for deposits bordering the levee in the form of clearances, but that was not the case. It is not even certain whether all the wild plants were gathered in the immediate surroundings of the settlement: the levee was for example too low – and hence too wet – for oak to have grown there. That means that the acorns must have been gathered elsewhere too.[31]

The pollen diagram obtained for the creek at Vlaardingen, on the contrary, does indicate some degree of deforestation of the levee; it even includes cereal pollen.[32] However, this does not necessarily mean that cereal was actually cultivated at the site. The amount of pollen released in threshing by far exceeds that produced in the field. That is due to the fact that large quantities of pollen remain lodged between the glumes. Remains recovered in excavations show that in the Netherlands, at least in prehistoric times, grain was stored in semi-threshed condition, i.e. with the glumes still surrounding the grains. Grain is still stored that way today in areas where it rains fairly frequently and the same primitive wheat varieties are grown.[33] Pollen is then only released when the daily portion required for the meal is dehusked. Cereal pollen may therefore be encountered at any settlement, whether or not there were any fields nearby. Like that of Hekelingen, the levee that supported the Vlaardingen settlement was a little too small for crop cultivation of any significance. If cereal was a staple in the occupants' diet it must have been imported from elsewhere.

If we assume that the settlements of the Hazendonk, Hekelingen and Vlaardingen were all used as hunting and fishing stations for only part of the year and that some of the crops at least were not grown at the sites themselves, we may ask ourselves where those crops were then cultivated. The only possible answer is: there where crop cultivation was possible, i.e. at settlements in dry areas where there was sufficient room for fields. In the case of the Vlaardingen group we must look for such settlements on wide levees or in the coastal region.

On a river levee in the river clay district
One settlement on a really wide levee is that of Ewijk in the eastern peripheries of the river district. The faunal spectrum of this site differs markedly from that

fig. 14.14
Bone plate of a sturgeon as found in relatively large numbers at sites of the Vlaardingen group in the western Netherlands. These bone plates are reliable evidence of summer use of a site, because sturgeons are known to swim from the sea into the intracoastal delta area to spawn in early summer. The illustrated plate was found at the Vlaardingen settlement at Hekelingen III; scale 1:2. The rows of bone plates are clearly visible in the illustration.

of the sites discussed above. Fish remains were completely absent and only one (unidentifiable) fragment of a bird bone was found. The clay layers have, however, not been sieved. Moreover, no more than 7.4% of the total weight of the identified bones consisted of remains of game. Pig and cattle seem to have been the principal sources of meat, followed by sheep/goat.[34] Apparently the occupants of this site were already virtually entirely dependent on stock keeping for their meat. No botanical remains were collected at Ewijk.

The Older Dunes

The conditions of the coastal region were more favourable for stock keeping and crop cultivation than those of the swamps. The Vlaardingen settlements of Leidschendam and Voorschoten have yielded valuable information on the Older Dunes between the Rhine and the Meuse. These settlements lay on a former coastal barrier on which rows of low dunes had been formed. To the east, the coastal barrier was bordered by a vast swamp. To the west were series of parallel coastal barriers separated by brackish depressions. The occupation area itself was originally covered with dense deciduous forests.

More than 85% of the total number of identified skeletal remains were of domestic animals: at Voorschoten-Boschgeest mainly cattle, at Voorschoten-De Donk and Leidschendam cattle and pig. Sheep/goat were less well represented. Good pastures for the animals were to be found in the brackish areas and, to a lesser extent, in the dunes themselves. We have no direct evidence for the presence of fields, but peaks in the cereal curves in the pollen diagrams coincide with phases of occupation at the various sites and they therefore constitute proof of the frequent use of grain at least. Plant remains from the sites themselves have not been investigated.[35]

The saline and brackish environments

The Vlaardingen settlement Zandwerven lay on a dune in a saline/brackish environment. To the west of this dune were expansive mud flats and salt marshes,

fig. 14.15
Ard marks found in an excavation conducted at the Oostersingel site in Groningen. Two types of patterns, each comprising marks crossing one another at right angles, are clearly visible. They have been attributed to the TRB culture on the basis of the depth at which they were found (2 metres below present Mean Sea Level) and associated pottery sherds.

to the east was a vast brackish swamp. The landscape was traversed by creeks and was entirely or virtually devoid of trees. Some fifty bones of mammals were recovered during the excavation, the great majority of which were of cattle. The other identified animal species (pig, sheep/goat and porpoise) were represented by only one or two bones. A few bones of birds were found, but no fish remains, probably because wet sieving was not practised in those days.[36] We have no information on the weight distribution, but cattle seem to have been the main source of meat.

Two refuse pits yielded carbonised grains of emmer and naked barley, indicating that cereal at least was consumed. Gathered plant foods were poorly represented, the only finds consisting of a few fragments of hazelnut and a single dewberry seed.

Zandwerven, Leidschendam, Voorschoten and Ewijk are all good examples of the sites of the component of the Vlaardingen group that concentrated more on food production. At Zandwerven this was not only apparent from the faunal spectrum, but also from the ard marks which showed that crops had been grown at the site itself. Together with those observed at Groningen and Bornwird (see below), they are the oldest ard marks found in the Netherlands so far (fig. 14.15).[37] On the basis of observations in Britain and Denmark we must however assume that the ard was known in the Netherlands before then already.

Survey

The evidence discussed above leads to the conclusion that the people of the Vlaardingen group concentrated on food production in areas where sufficient dry land was available and on hunting, fishing and foraging in the swamps. At Hazendonk the importance of hunting and fishing apparently even increased or decreased as conditions became wetter or dryer, respectively.[38] What we still do not know for sure is whether the occupants of the swamps belonged to the same group of people as those who inhabited the dry areas; in other words: did some of the occupants of the dry areas move into the swamps for certain seasons or for certain activities, such as trapping or fishing for sturgeon? Another possibility is that the occupants of the swamps constituted a separate community with a slightly different way of life than the rest of the Vlaardingen group, with which it however did maintain contacts. The subsistence data do not yet allow us to choose between these options, but archaeological evidence seems to favour the first.

THE LATE NEOLITHIC A

The appearance of the Single Grave culture marks the beginning of the Late Neolithic A in the Netherlands. Elements of this culture have come to light in all of the natural landscapes distinguished above. However, settlement sites with refuse providing information on the subsistence economy have only been found in the sandy parts in the north of the Netherlands and in the saline/brackish regions.

The sands in the north of the Netherlands

No animal bones have survived at the sites in the sandy regions but plant remains are known from a pit at Eeserveld into which separate batches of emmer, naked barely and acorns had been dumped. Other finds were encountered among domestic refuse deposited on a plot of land that had been tilled with the aid of an ard at Bornwird: a few grains of naked barley and fragments of hazelnut shells. These finds could not be dated with certainty because the soil of the field was found to contain TRB remains besides sherds of the pottery of the Single Grave culture.[39] As carbonised cereal grains are not very resistant to mechanical influences we assume that they date from the last phase of the field's use. The field measured at least 50 x 50 m, but its exact limits were not determined. The furrows lay 30 cm apart and intersected one another perpendicularly, indicating that the field had first been ploughed in one direction and then again in the direction perpendicular to the first furrows. Ard marks are often seen to cross one another perpendicularly. As for the domestic refuse: there was nothing to suggest that the site of a former settlement had been ploughed over. The refuse must have been deposited there deliberately, possibly to enrich the soil. This means that the occupants must have had refuse heaps, but it does not necessarily imply that they also collected animal dung. Although they may well have done so, no features of structures in which manure may have been collected, such as stalls or cattle pens, have so far been found. As the wheel was known in this period it will have been possible to transport unwieldy loads such as manure without any difficulty.

The ard marks imply that the landscape was already substantially deforested and devoid of old tree-stumps when these areas were first brought into cultivation, because otherwise a hoe would have been a more efficient implement for tilling the soil. Pollen analyses have confirmed that the forest in the northern sandy regions had indeed degraded further since the arrival of the TRB settlers: the clearances were larger and grass and heather were expanding. The latter process took longer in areas with relatively rich soils with good hydrological conditions than in areas with poor soils: the forest of the Utrechtse Heuvelrug degraded at a much slower rate than that of the Drenthe Plateau.[40]

The saline and brackish regions

A few sites near the Vlaardingen/Single Grave settlement of Zandwerven have yielded exclusively finds of the Single Grave culture. They include Aartswoud, Kolhorn, Hoogwoud, Mienakker and Zeewijk. These settlements were all situated on levees bordering creeks in a treeless landscape of the same kind as that which surrounded Zandwerven.[41]

The faunal spectrum of Aartswoud is dominated by cattle, followed by sheep/goat and pig in equal proportions. The share of wild mammals is very small. The other remains are of birds (mainly waterfowl), fish (including sturgeon, salmon and pike) and large quantities of molluscs (oyster, mussel, cockle and whelk, plate 23A). The plant remains include emmer and naked barley, which are believed to have been the principal crops. Other plant remains are linseed and a few grains of bread wheat and hulled barley. Acorns, hazelnuts, apples and blackberries were gathered. The first three cannot have been gathered in the immediate vicinity of the site: the nearest areas where oak, hazel and apple were to be found in that period were Wieringen and Texel, both at least 15 km away. Although no remains of houses were found at Aartswoud, this site is believed to have been permanently occupied. It is assumed that cattle keeping on the brackish marshes and crop cultivation on the levees were the occupants' principal subsistence activities and that they augmented their diet with hunting. The menu was supplemented with molluscs.[42]

Cattle were also the principal source of meat at Kolhorn. Impressions of cattle hooves were observed in the bed of the creek that flowed next to what was described as the 'southern settlement' (plate 23B). Most of these tracks followed the same course, i.e. across the creek, from and to the settlement. Others were found to fan out from the centre of the settlement. This concentration of hoof impressions and their pattern can be explained by the presence of a fresh water well at the centre of the settlement.[43]

Sea mammals and fur animals were occasionally hunted too. The remains of a whale species probably belonged to a stranded animal. The only remains of red deer are antler fragments, which indicates that this species was not to be found in the immediate surroundings of the site. The most conspicuous aspect of the faunal spectrum of Kolhorn is the large proportion of bird bones: fowling was apparently far more important than hunting. Different duck species, in particular mallard, teal and garganey, were caught in large numbers. The most striking species is flamingo. If we compare these data with the remains of hunted animals from Early and Middle Neolithic sites in the freshwater swamps we note that the number of different species caught at Kolhorn is much larger, but so is the proportion of bird remains in the overall bone weight. In other words, fowling was more important at Kolhorn than at Swifterbant and the Hazendonk.[44]

The third source of meat at Kolhorn was fish. More than at Aartswoud, the emphasis was on saltwater fish and fish from brackish water. Flatfish (flounder, plaice) were about the only kinds of fish caught; other fish were caught only rarely. Finally, large concentrations of shells were found at Kolhorn, the great majority of mussels. Most of these shells were of adult mussels, which indicates that they were selectively harvested, most probably between the autumn and the early spring.[45]

The carbonised plant remains from the occupation layers included remains of emmer, naked barley and linseed and smaller amounts of hazelnut and apple remains. No house plans were found, in spite of the favourable preservation conditions. That suggests that Kolhorn was not permanently occupied.

The data from Hoogwoud closely resemble those of Kolhorn. Here too, the occupants caught large amounts of different duck species and fish, in particular cod and haddock. They had also consumed large quantities of molluscs. At this site, however, the remains of flimsy houses were found. Next to one of these houses was a pit that contained a batch of carbonised naked barley mixed with a few

fig. 14.16
Complete skeleton of an ox that was found at the Bell Beaker/Barbed Wire Beaker settlement of Molenaarsgraaf. The bones derive from a young animal. The hoof bones and some metapodals are missing, which could indicate that the animal was skinned. Such purposeful burials are seen as cult-related or ritual acts, reflecting the importance of cattle among the communities concerned.

grains of emmer. In spite of the house remains, it is assumed that Hoogwoud was
not occupied the whole year round either.

From what has been said above it can be inferred that the interpretations of the
nature of the occupation of the sites that have so far been published vary; some
are believed to have been permanently occupied, others semi-permanently or sea-
sonally. Their economic bases, however, do not vary very much. The ard marks
observed at Zandwerven indicate that crops were cultivated at the site itself; the
hoof impressions of Kolhorn are evidence of the presence of cattle inside the settlement. Food was definitely produced at these settlements. In addition, a wide
range of resources available in the surroundings was exploited. As far as subsistence is concerned, it would have been quite possible for the occupants to have
remained at the settlements all the year round. Those who chose not to must have
done so for reasons that were not related to their subsistence economy. The features of solidly built structures that have recently come to light in the excavation of
the settlement of Zeewijk did therefore not come as a surprise (feature J). Zeewijk
and Mienakker resemble Kolhorn closely in their animal and plant remains. The
people appeared, moreover, to have fished mainly flat fish in Zeewijk and Kolhorn,
as opposed to cod in Mienakker.[46]

THE LATE NEOLITHIC PERIOD B

The freshwater swamps

Good data on the Late Neolithic period B, the period of the Bell Beaker culture,
are only available for the swamps, in particular for Molenaarsgraaf.[46] This settlement was situated on a stream ridge which rose above the swamps surrounding
it. The ridge itself was densely forested originally. Pollen analysis has shown that
the forest had been cleared at the site of the settlement. Alder carrs alternated with
more open swamp vegetation in the wide surroundings. The majority of the bones
were of domestic animals, with a predominance of 81% cattle bones (fig. 14.16).
Pig and sheep/goat came second and third, respectively. It is uncertain whether
some horse remains relate to a wild or a domestic horse. The few remains of game
were of beaver, red deer, wild boar, brown bear and elk.[48] Fishing must have been
an important subsistence activity. This was not inferred from fish remains, which
were in fact absent at the site, presumably due to the non-optimum preservation
conditions. However, one of the three individuals whose graves were found at Molenaarsgraaf was accompanied by fish hooks (fig. 14.17), while another appeared
to have choked on a fish bone. Moreover, the remains of posts, which may have
held nets or hoop nets, were found in a creek near the site.

Plant remains were not collected, but a pollen diagram obtained for a sample from the creek includes cereal pollen. As already explained with reference to
Vlaardingen, this pollen only shows that grain was processed at Molenaarsgraaf.
The cereal may have been cultivated on the stream ridge itself, but that has not yet
been proven.

Molenaarsgraaf is believed to have been permanently occupied. There were
more sites from the Late Neolithic period B in this same swamp area, including
that of Hazendonk. It is not known whether the latter settlement was also permanently occupied in this period; so far, only acorns and hazelnuts datable to this
occupation phase have been found, *i.e.* evidence of foraging.

The only evidence of the farming activities of the Bell Beaker culture so far obtained in the rest of the Netherlands is that found in pollen spectra of surfaces

buried beneath Bell Beaker barrows on Pleistocene sands. These spectra closely resemble those of the Single Grave culture and indicate small clearances in a still densely forested landscape (feature J).[49]

FINAL CONCLUSIONS

The evidence discussed above clearly shows that the transition from the Mesolithic broad-spectrum hunter-gatherer economy to the production-based subsistence economy of the Neolithic proper did not take place at the same time in all parts of the Netherlands. There even appears to have been a kind of intermediate economy: every culture for which we have more than one well-investigated site proves to have comprised communities with a predominantly productive economy and communities that exploited mainly natural resources. The best example for which we also have the most evidence is the Vlaardingen group. However, even an essentially agricultural community like that of the LBK had settlements where game and fish were consumed on a greater scale than would be expected, for example Liège-Place St.-Lambert. Likewise, settlements of the agricultural TRB culture have been found, at least in northern Germany and southern Scandinavia, where hunting and gathering were still important. Examples of similar sites of the Single Grave and Bell Beaker cultures are mentioned elsewhere in this book.

Sites where hunting and fishing were practised on a large scale can be conceived as 'extraction camps', i.e. temporary bases for some members of a community whose economy was based on farming, who were sent out hunting or fishing. Bergschenhoek is a good example of such a site. According to another interpretation settlements yielding large amounts of remains of game and fish can also be regarded as seasonal bases, which were used for part of the year for pasturing the cattle and a little additional hunting. This one is proposed for some of the Single Grave settlements in the coastal region. A third possibility, however, is that the occupants of the wet parts of the Netherlands had a different way of life than those of the dry parts and consumed more game, fish or shellfish, depending on the availability of these resources in the vicinity of their sites. This interpretation implies a flexible approach to the ecological potential of the different environments. Long traditions, such as the Mesolithic roots of the prehistoric population of the western Netherlands, may have played a part in shaping the specific lifestyles of the occupants of the different environments, which were not necessarily conservative. Whatever the case, farming gradually became more important in the wet areas, too. By the end of the Neolithic all of the communities had switched to crop cultivation and stock keeping.

We are slowly obtaining more insight into the process of the transition to an economy based entirely on farming. An important question that still remains unanswered is, why did people actually start producing food? A functionalistic answer is that food production enabled more mouths to be fed per hectare of land. This could also answer the question as to why, in the Netherlands, this way of life was first adopted in one of the then most densely forested regions where relatively little game was to be found. The loess of southern Limburg constitutes an outcrop of the vast European loess which supported the LBK culture and that culture's farming system. The success of this culture, however, may very well be attributable to the poor opportunities that the dense deciduous forests offered hunter-gatherers. Why were the occupants of the Dutch swamps the last to adopt the Neolithic way of life? Possibly because they could manage very well in that environment without crop cultivation and stock keeping. The reasons why they, too, ultimately opted for a farming existence cannot have been purely economic.

Finally: the Neolithic farming economy proves to have been based on a combination of crop cultivation and stock keeping. The one was not practised without the other. The principal crops were emmer and naked barley; cattle were the most important animals in the stock system. The degree of integration of the two systems, *i.e.* the dependence of crop cultivation on stock keeping and vice versa, is not yet clear: too little is known about, for example, the use of straw as winter fodder and of the use of dung. In historical times, before the invention of artificial fertilisers, it was not possible to grow crops in poor soils without using manure. There was a relation between the amount of land under cultivation and the amount of land used for pasture. Finding archaeological evidence to demonstrate the use of such a ratio in prehistoric times is not easy. It is quite possible that a similar ratio, though probably less extreme than that of the Middle Ages, was used in prehistoric times too. But whether such a ratio was used in the Neolithic already – or whether there was indeed any need for one – is a different matter. In those early days the pressure on the soil and land was probably not yet very serious.

NOTES

1 Bakels 1978; Bakels/Rousselle 1985.

2 Bakels 1982a.

3 Bakels 1991.

4 Cordy/Stassart 1984.

5 Desse 1984.

6 Bakels 1982b.

7 Reynolds 1974.

8 Bakels 1990a.

9 Bakels 1990b.

10 Casparie *et al.* 1977; Van Zeist/Palfenier 1981.

11 Zeiler 1991, 1997.

12 De Roever-Bonnet *et al.* 1979.

13 Brinkhuizen 1989.

14 Clason/Brinkhuizen 1993.

15 Louwe Kooijmans 1985. The great majority of the current population of mute swans in Western Europe are descendants of birds that escaped or were released from captivity. Until some fifty years ago, mute swans brooded virtually exclusively in eastern and northern Europe and were observed in Western Europe in very severe winters only (Bekhuis *et al.* 1978).

16 Zeiler 1991, 1997.

17 Bakels 1981.

18 Bakels 1981; Van der Woude 1981.

19 Raemaekers *et al.* 1997.

20 Bakels *et al.* 1993.

21 Bakels 1991b.

22 Behre/Kucan 1986.

23 One speaks of *shifting cultivation* if people themselves move together with their shifting fields. Such a system may have been used on the Dutch upland sands.

24 Brinkhuizen 1979.

25 Prummel 1987. As the weights of the bones from Hekelingen I are not known it is not possible to estimate the importance of the different kinds of meat in the diet. Moreover, as the excavated soil was not sieved, most remains of fish and birds will have been overlooked. Nevertheless, the composition of the remains indicated that hunting must have been important, too, besides cattle keeping: 40% of the identified bones were of domesticated animals and 60% of wild animals (Clason 1967).

26 Clason 1967.

27 Prummel 1987.

28 Boddeke 1971.

29 Louwe Kooijmans 1987.

30 Van Zeist 1970.

31 Bakels 1988a.

32 Groenman-van Waateringe/Jansma 1969.

33 Hillman 1984.

34 Clason 1990.

35 Groenman-van Waateringe *et al.* 1968.

36 Clason 1967.

37 Fokkens 1982; Mook-Kamps/Van Zeist 1987.

38 It is hazardous to explain the activities of human beings primarily in the context of their natural environment. The authors are, however, of the opinion that the Hazendonk is an example of a site where environmental factors did indeed played a main role (see also Raemaekers 2001).

39 Fokkens 1982.

41 Van Heeringen/Theunissen 2001.

40 Casparie/Groenman-van Waateringe 1980.

42 Pals 1984.

43 Van der Waals 1988, 1989.

44 In the case of some species the season in which the birds must have been caught can be inferred. Garganey, quail and yellow wagtail are nowadays typical summer visitors that are to be found in the Netherlands from March/April until September/October. The brent goose arrives in October and remains until the end of April/beginning of May, although small groups regularly stay for the summer, too. The black-throated diver is observed in the Netherlands virtually exclusively between November and the end of March (Bekhuis *et al.* 1978), but, as in the case of Bergschenhoek, we must not jump to conclusions regarding the presence of human beings in a particular season.

45 Niclewicz-Hokse 1990.

46 Gerrets *et al.* 1988; see also De Vries 2001 and Gehasse 2001.

47 Louwe Kooijmans 1974.

48 Clason 1977. If wild, the horse remains would be very late; if domestic, very early.

49 Oostwoud: Van Giffen 1961; Groenman-van Waateringe/Casparie 1980.

pl. 17A Implements made of Rullen flint, identifiable by its orange colour caused by infiltration of iron, which were found in pits of the Rössen settlement of Maastricht-Randwijck in the valley plain of the Meuse.

pl. 17B Sherd from the Maastricht-Randwijck Rössen settlement showing remains of the white paste that was used to fill the grooves of the ornamentation. On the left is the imprint in the soil, on the right the sherd itself. Decorative patterns incised in pottery have been filled with white or red paste in other periods and cultures, too, but remains of the paste only rarely survive.

pl. 18A Swifterbant S2, burial of an adult man with a head ornament consisting of large rough pieces of amber and a pendant made from a flat pebble. Swifterbant culture, *c.* 4100 BC.

pl. 18B Section of the occupation level of the Swifterbant S3 settlement. The settlement was built on a natural levee of a freshwater tidal channel. The dark occupation level comprises layers of reed that was used to raise the surface of the land, domestic refuse and clay laid down during occasional floods. The grey and orange burned patches visible are the remains of the clay floors that the occupants created for their hearths.

pl. 19A Section of the Swifterbant culture camp at Bergschenhoek dating from around 4200 BC. Visible on a patch of peat (brown) is a hearth that was used in successive occupation phases. The yellow horizons are reed, the brown ones peat and the black ones charcoal. The sharp, frayed lower outline of the peat indicate that the peat did not grow here, but was torn loose elsewhere and embedded in clay. This took place after the site's formation.

pl. 19B Two more or less complete fish traps and parts of others were found close to the Bergschenhoek fishing and hunting camp. The traps were made from 1.5-m-long red dogwood branches. The technique of manufacturing such traps can be traced back to the Early Mesolithic; it continued to be used until recent times.

pl. 20A Jadeite axe found at Meerlo-Tienray (Limburg), length 11.7 cm. Green jadeite occurs in various varieties exclusively in the western Alps. Axes made of green jadeite have been found all over Western Europe, even at find spots far away in Scotland. Many of the axes have exceptional dimensions, implying that they were non-functional, symbolic objects. That does not hold for this axe, which is heavily worn from long use. Such axes are rare in the Netherlands.

pl. 20C Hoard consisting of seven axes and chisels of different types and a large scraper from the valley of the Reest near Pieperij in the southernmost part of Drenthe, a typical location for such a deposit. The objects date from the end of the TRB culture or the beginning of the subsequent Beaker period, roughly around 2900 BC.

pl. 20B A TRB axe blank made of the beautiful red flint of Helgoland (D). The axe comes from a hoard found at Een (cf. fig. G3). It is 20 cm long.

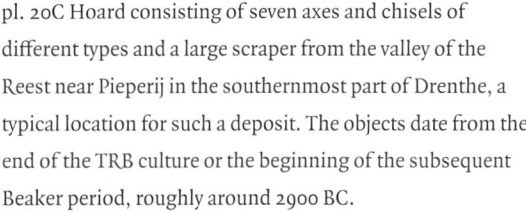

pl. 21A Two small, fairly crudely modelled axes from the Middle Neolithic that were found in the surroundings of Valkenburg (South Limburg), lengths 7.5 and 10.4 cm. The axes are made of a type of flint that is found only on the Lousberg near Aachen. The flint concerned is grey and occurs in the form of comparatively thin, irregular plates with a brown band on the outside caused by ferriferous groundwater. The left specimen is part of a broken-off cutting edge that was secondarily used for the production of flakes.

pl. 21C An almost completely natural deciduous forest in the Bialowieza nature resort in eastern Poland. Very little grows under the dense canopy of the sturdy lime trees. Rejuvenation occurs primarily in clearances created by fallen trees.

pl. 21B A blank and a finished axe of Valkenburg flint, found in the surroundings of Valkenburg (South Limburg), lengths 15.2 and 13.5 cm. Valkenburg flint is coarse-grained and light brown in its most characteristic form. It occurs in the southern slopes of the Geul valley and was exploited in the *Bandkeramk* period already. Radiocarbon dates demonstrated that it was mined in shafts in the Middle Neolithic period B. It is from that period that these axes are assumed to date. See also plate 16A.

pl. 22A The small *hunebed* of Loon, just north of Assen, has survived almost in its entirety. Clearly visible are the chamber, the short passageway and the stones marking the periphery of the mound that used to cover the stone structure.

pl. 22B The severely disturbed *hunebed* D49, known as Papeloze Kerk ('the Priestless Church'), between Noordsleen and Schoonoord has been restored to its original state, using erratic boulders from the surroundings.

pl. 23A Cross-section through the approximately 1-m-thick shell middens of a settlement of the Single-Grave culture at Aartswoud. The shells of consumed mussels and oysters are contained in a peaty clay matrix. Interspersed thin layers of clay show that the site was occasionally flooded.

pl. 23B Cattle hoof impressions associated with a settlement of the Single-Grave culture at Kolhorn. The impressions in the pale soft clay became filled with darker overlying soil. This evidence testifies to the importance of cattle in this period in this area.

pl. 24A Shortly after the excavation of the Vlaardingen settlement near Hekelingen in 1948 this artist's impression was published on the cover of the Dutch weekly magazine 'Panorama'. The setting is romanticised and the clothing inspired by that of classical antiquity rather than our knowledge of Neolithic technology. The artist clearly used his imagination to enhance the archaeological evidence (remains of pike, the pot).

pl. 24B Artist's impression from 1985 showing a Vlaardingen settlement on the Older Dunes. The drawing is based on the combined evidence obtained in the excavations of Haamstede-Brabers and Voorschoten-Bosgeest and is far more realistic than that from 1950.

pl. 25A The contents of a smith's burial found at Lunteren. The grave contained two bell beakers, one of which has since disappeared. They were accompanied by three cushion stones, which are assumed to be metal-working implements, a grindstone, a flint axe, part of a wristguard, a copper awl and six flint arrowheads.

pl. 25B Bell beaker of the Veluwe type from the environs of the Uddelermeer. Height 19.5 cm.

pl. 26 Beaker pot that was found in 1928 in the Stroesche Zand, municipality of Barneveld. Height 44 cm. These large pots with their plastic decoration belong to the settlement pottery of the Bell Beaker and Corded Ware culture. They were buried upside down, especially in the Veluwe area, presumably in order to protect votive gifts. The Stroe pot is assumed to date from the Barbed Wire beaker phase on the basis of its profile and perforated rim.

pl. 27A Hoard containing 18 bronze palstaves and one chisel that was found at Voorhout in 1907. The high lead content of the bronze and typological features of the axes indicate that the implements were made in Wales. This find shows that bronze was directly imported into the Netherlands from that area. In the past it was assumed that the bronze was traded by itinerant bronze smiths, but it is now believed that it was obtained in exchange and expeditions.

pl. 27B String of beads made of amber (orange), faience (blue) and tin (grey) with a bronze lock -a votive gift that was deposited in a bog in the Middle Bronze Age and recovered in 1881 during peat-cutting activities at Exloo. In former days this string of beads was taken to symbolise the wide-ranging Bronze Age trade networks. It is now, however, believed that the amber was not imported from Scandinavia, but picked up somewhere in the Netherlands. The segmented faience beads may also have been made in northwest Europe. The costly tin almost certainly came from Cornwall.

pl. 28 Imported bronze objects reflect the wide-ranging relations of the communities living in the Low Countries in the Bronze and Iron Ages.

No.	findspot	artefacts	date	origin
1	Nieuw-Weerdinge	neckring, two bracelets	Middle Iron Age	northern Germany
2	Uddelerveen	two neckrings	Early Iron Age	Germany
3	Nijenbeek	sword	Early Iron Age	England
4	Appelscha	'votive knife'	Late Bronze Age	manufactured locally
5	Bonnerveen	spectacle fibula	Late Bronze Age	Denmark
6	Heerde	*Bombenkopfnadel*	Late Bronze Age	western Alps
7	Exloërmond	basal-looped spearhead	Middle Bronze Age	England
8	Jutphaas	Plougrescant sword	Middle Bronze Age	Brittany
9	Steenwijk	flint dagger	Early Bronze Age	Denmark
10	Roermond	halberd blade	Early Bronze Age	Ireland
11	Haren	decorated flanged axe	Early Bronze Age	Ireland
12	Bargeroosterveld	dagger with horn strip	Early Bronze Age	central Europe

pl. 29 Three French flint daggers that were made around 2600 BC and found in the Veluwe district. The left dagger is made of the brown-white banded flint of Romigny-Léhry near Reims. This implement was most skilfully finished using parallel pressure flaking, but with unknown find context. The other two daggers are made of the honey-coloured flint of Le Grand-Pressigny at the Loire estuary. Both were part of a grave inventory with all-over ornamented beakers from Garderen and Emst (near Vaassen). The right tool was finished by grinding. The daggers are 19, 20 and 21 cm long.

pl. 30 The Nieuw Dordrecht bog trackway during its investigation in 1981. The trackway consists of transversely arranged tree stems resting on two stringers of longitudinally placed stems. With its date of around 2600-2500 BC, the period of the all-over ornamented beakers and the earliest bell beakers, this was for a long time the oldest trackway in Drenthe. However, new dates recently obtained for two similar bog trackways (Buinen and Smeulbranden) show that those trackways were built already in the days of the TRB culture.

pl. 31 The so-called southern bog footpath near Barger-Oosterveld during its excavation in 1961.
The trackway was built in the Middle Bronze Age, around 1350 BC, and leads to a part of the bog
that contained high-quality bog iron-ore. A 4-cm-long iron pin was found on one of the planks.
This confirms other evidence suggesting that iron was being processed on a small scale in the
Bronze Age already. The planks were floated apart shortly after the construction as a result of
continued peat growth, in spite of the long wooden pegs with which they where fixed into the
peat.

pl. 32A Artist's impression of a settlement at Molenaarsgraaf, dating from the transition from the Neolithic to the Bronze Age. Longhouses are set far apart on a 50-100 m wide strip of sand in the peat, on which the occupants also grow their crops. People can be seen fishing in the gulley. Horse bones were found at this site, but it is not certain whether these bones belonged to domestic horses, as implied in the drawing.

pl. 32B Artist's impression of the Middle Bronze Age settlement of Bovenkarspel in Westfrisia, which has been dated around 1200 BC. The settlement lies in an open landscape in which the longhouses have been arranged in a long row. On the left are fields on an old stream ridge, on the right are pastures in the backswamp. The cultivation plots are separated by ditches. Crops are temporarily stored in circular ditched enclosures near the yards. Here we see the main elements of what was over the centuries to evolve into the typical landscape of Holland.

15 The first farmers: synthesis

Annelou van Gijn and Leendert Louwe Kooijmans

The previous chapters covering the various periods of the Early and Middle Neolithic have focused on specific aspects of these periods, such as the settlement system, the burial rite and the material culture. Such a period-based approach however provides insufficient insight into the diachronic developments that took place in the Neolithic, for example the Neolithisation process. These developments will therefore be discussed separately in the present chapter.

ARCHAEOLOGICAL CULTURES AND ETHNICITY

The Neolithic is a period in which the archaeological concept of culture works remarkably well. In this period the Netherlands comprised clearly delimited areas, each with its own material culture. Most of these areas are style provinces, distinguished on the basis of differences between specific types of pottery and decorative motifs. There is for example a clear difference between the TRB pottery of the area to the north of the major rivers and the pottery of the Vlaardingen group to the south. There are no transitional types and very few problems arise in attributing pottery to these different cultures. These pottery provinces with their relatively sharp boundaries are much less easily recognisable in later periods. As for the meaning of these archaeological cultures, that is actually a difficult question. Archaeologists usually interpret differences in material culture in ethnic terms, basing themselves on anthropological evidence demonstrating strict links between the use of particular decorative patterns and specific ethnic groups.[1] Much of this anthropological evidence was however obtained in studies of ornaments, incised gourds and other perishable objects, whereas all that usually remains for prehistorians is flint and pottery. In recent years, the custom of equating archaeological cultures with social traditions and ethnic groups has excited much discussion, especially since anthropological studies have shown that the ways in which people express their identity in fact vary considerably, both in degree and in the materials employed for this purpose. The equation of material expression with a particular people has moreover acquired unpleasant connotations since certain pre-war German archaeologists, in particular Gustav Kossinna, misused archaeological evidence to corroborate the alleged superiority of the 'Aryan race'.[2]

Nevertheless, the concept of 'culture' still plays an important part in Neolithic research today. The existence of pottery provinces of course remains something which must be explained, only nowadays this is done on the basis of our more critical, modern understanding of the ways in which groups of people use their material culture to express group identity. An anthropological study among the peoples of the Baringo Basin in East Africa has shown that a greater diversity in decorative motifs observed in that area was in part related to food shortages.[3] It could well be that the deliberate group expression of some Neolithic 'cultures' is likewise attributable to extraordinary stress on the communities in question. Are we, in the absence of transitional types between different pottery assemblages, to conclude that there were no, or only few, contacts between the potters, or were such contacts perhaps expressed in different categories of materials, such as clothing, about which we are poorly informed? Could it be that there were contacts between TRB and Vlaardingen people which are not reflected in pottery styles?

A particularly intriguing problem is the meaning, in terms of social identity, of the differences between large, homogeneous pottery provinces with a clear style of their own, such as those of the *Bandkeramik*, Rössen, Michelsberg and TRB, and stylistically much less distinct groups such as the Swifterbant,[4] Hazendonk and Vlaardingen groups. Apparently pottery played a more prominent, more explicit, symbolic role among the communities with a way of life that was in effect based entirely on farming than among the more 'transitional' groups whose subsistence system was (still) largely characterised by mobility and the exploitation of natural resources.

SETTLEMENT SYSTEMS

The Neolithic saw the transition from mobile hunter-gatherers to sedentary farmers, from communities that exploited the natural resources of a large region to people who concentrated on a relatively small area around their settlements, into which they put a lot of energy, creating pockets of cultivated land in the wilderness. This led to a contrast between natural and cultivated landscape, between 'the domestic' and 'the wild'.[5] In an archaeological respect this is in principle observable in the changes that took place in the layouts of the settlements and the settlement system. Questions relating to permanent versus seasonal occupation, to base settlements versus special activity sites, to residential and logistic mobility[6] are particularly important with respect to the Neolithic, as is the issue of the representative of the often scarce evidence. In practice, these questions are not so easy to answer, because the visibility of the settlements varies considerably from one landscape to another and from one period to another.

In the loess zone the beginning of the Neolithic coincides with the appearance of the typical *Bandkeramik* settlements, settlements that were used on a continuous

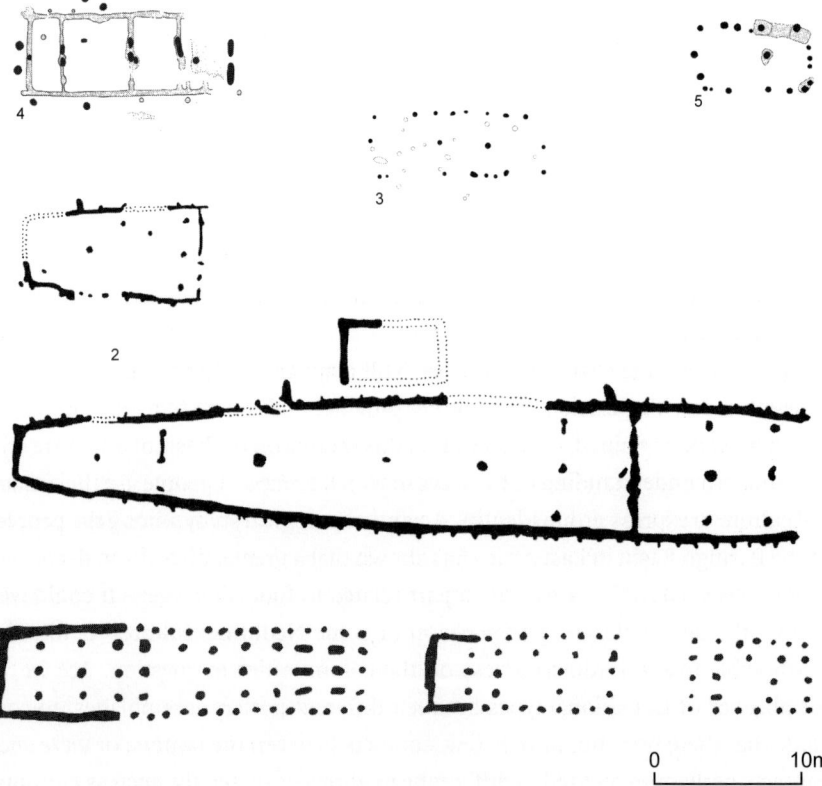

fig. 15.1
Development of houses during the Neolithic, from the large houses of the *Bandkeramik* and the Rössen culture to the small houses of Hazendonk 3, the TRB culture and the Vlaardingen group. All shown on the same scale (1:500).

5 Vlaardingen group Haamstede-
                             De Brabers

4 funnel beaker   Flögeln-Eekhöltjen

3 Hazendonk 3   Wateringen 4

2 Rössen culture   Inden

1 *Bandkeramik*

0   10m

basis, for long periods of time. Their layouts varied, depending on the local conditions, from relatively open, like the settlements in the Merzbach valley in Germany, to fairly compact, like those on the Graetheide plateau in the Netherlands. Although the custom of building new houses on virgin soil at the periphery of the occupied area caused these settlements to shift slightly, they were essentially immobile. Each settlement had its own, restricted, territory which contained arable land, a water supply and wood for construction and fuel. We are able to distinguish more or less unambiguous clusters of equivalent settlements whose occupants, we assume, herded their cattle and exploited raw materials like hard stone and flint in a large, communal home range.

Although the Rössen settlement system was in many respects different from that of the *Bandkeramik*, the two are actually not fundamentally different. The settlements of the Rössen culture were more compact and were shifted more often, but they nevertheless remained in use for a period spanning several house phases. It is not clear whether the clustering of settlements and the associated social context were the same as in the preceding period.[7] The smaller number of comparatively large houses points to larger basic social units, such as one or more extended families. We assume that the imposing *Bandkeramik* and Rössen dwellings were also material manifestations of the groups in the territories to which they laid claim (fig. 15.1). This assumption is based on the idea that in the vast wilderness a homestead will have symbolised the beginning of the 'domestication of the landscape'.

The 'ordinary' settlements of the Michelsberg culture are still largely unknown. We have no information on their size or layout, or on the length of time for which they were occupied. This could mean that the buildings were in use for shorter periods of time and were less solidly constructed, which would agree with the hypothesis that the Michelsberg groups manifested themselves in the landscape on a higher level of organisation. This hypothesis is based on the large, enclosed 'central sites', which are regarded as tribal centres rather than settlements.[8] The large-scale shaft-mining centres (feature E) that have been found at sites far removed from one another may likewise – on an even higher level – be regarded as locations to which communities in a large area attached great significance. The Belgian site of Spiennes in Hainault was such a location for the 'Chasséo-Michelsberg' of northern France and southern Belgium, while the Rijckholt mines served a similar function for the Rhineland and northwest groups of the Michelsberg culture. The changes in scale and mobility observable in the settlement system may be related to integration with late hunter-gatherer communities, for which we however still have only little concrete evidence.

We have virtually no information whatsoever on settlements after the Michelsberg culture. Some of the mining centres remained in use and a few new ones were created, but the enclosed 'tribal centres' were abandoned after this period.

Most of our information on the settlement systems of the communities in the northern plain comes from the wetlands. There, people lived on river dunes, the banks of rivers and creeks, salt marshes and coastal dunes. The earliest occupation phases are less well-known owing to erosion and sedimentation, but we seem to be obtaining more and more evidence suggesting that the settlement pattern in those phases was the same as that known from the later Vlaardingen period.[9] The crucial question is whether these areas were occupied by separate communities that specialised in the exploitation of the delta, or by groups who exploited both the sandy soils and the delta. In the wetlands proper, the locations and the small sizes of the sites and the nature of the finds give the sites a rather Mesolithic appearance. The same holds for sites where no features – or at most clusters of thin stakes – have been found: they are all sites where hunting and fishing dominated to varying extents and where no cereal will have been grown. They seem to have been non-permanent special activity sites in settlement systems based on the exploitation of different ecozones.[10] These sites show considerable logistic mobility, but, as in the case of the Swifterbant sites on the creek system in Flevoland, also the seasonal shifting of base camps. The main settlements of these communities lay elsewhere, but exactly where we do not yet know. It is likely that the 'dry' settlements were situated at the margins of the sandy areas and in stream valleys, where the old land surface now lies buried beneath thick layers of Holocene deposits,[11] but they may also have lain in the drier parts of the delta, for example on the coastal dunes and the levees in the river clay district. At such locations permanent occupation will have been possible. The distinctly agricultural nature of the evidence and the features of small, rectangular houses that have been found at some of the settlements at these locations indeed suggest that these settlements were permanently occupied.[12] The settlements in question were incidentally small, comprising not more than one or two houses, which were used for a relatively short time. In this respect they resemble the settlements that can be inferred from the scarce evidence available for the higher sandy soils. But alongside these settlements there were also special activity sites at many different locations, at which hunting and fishing continued to be practised throughout the entire Middle and Late Neolithic, until the end of the Beaker period.[13]

The many Michelsberg sites that have been discovered in the valley of the Meuse in Limburg have yielded extremely little information on settlement layout and the settlement system. At many of the sites that were found in surveys material from different periods had become mixed, and very few features were found at the small number of sites that have been excavated. By analogy with evidence obtained in Germany, it is thought that the TRB settlements of the central and northern parts of the Netherlands had a short life and were small, consisting of a single small house which was constantly rebuilt at a considerable distance from its predecessor. Such a high degree of residential mobility can be connected with a form of arable farming known as 'shifting cultivation', which is thought to have comprised ploughing, but no manuring, as a result of which people had to shift their settlement every time they had exhausted the surrounding land. Special sites, such as that of Anloo with its 'cattle pen', were more fixed elements in the settlement system. In the area around the Veluwe the internal arrangement of these first pockets of cultivated land in the relatively fertile, damp areas along the lower courses of the streams, and their later expansion in the Beaker period can be inferred from the distributions of TRB remains and the later Beaker barrows. In Drenthe we see how territories were claimed and marked as ancestral land by means of one or more *hunebedden*; in the Beaker period individual barrows were to take over this function from the *hunebedden*.

To summarise, the evidence available for the farmers in the loess zone seems to indicate increasing residential mobility and expansion of the social territories. Our understanding of the communities to the north of the loess and the low mountain ranges is still very poor. Sites in various parts of Europe have yielded evidence pointing to the emergence of more sedentary hunter-gatherer communities, such as cemeteries and settlements that were unmistakably used for long periods of time, but no such evidence has yet been found in the Netherlands. Another issue on which we have no information is the extent to which the slightly more visible territoriality and mobility of the small-scale settlements of the TRB culture differed from those of the preceding period. It could well be that the differences were actually fairly small. The fact that the wetlands of the delta continued to be exploited from seasonal camps throughout this entire period suggests that Mesolithic traditions persisted for a long time.

All over the Netherlands the clearances that had been created in the primeval forest for the first agricultural settlements were gradually expanded, in the loess region from the *Bandkeramik*, in the southern sandy zone from the Michelsberg culture and in the north from the TRB culture onwards, but the forests continued to dominate the landscape until the end of the Middle Neolithic.

WAY OF LIFE AND ECONOMY:
THE NEOLITHISATION PROCESS

The only way in which we can gain an understanding of the developments that took place in the Netherlands and surrounding areas in the Early and Middle Neolithic is by viewing them in the wider context of the course of events in northern Europe as a whole. Parallel developments took place in Great Britain and southern Scandinavia. Throughout the British Isles[14] the Mesolithic was around 4000 BC rather abruptly replaced by an Early Neolithic showing close affinities with contemporary cultures in the adjacent part of the continent. For a long time this transition was attributed to the immigration of farmers, but this interpretation model was ultimately rejected, primarily on the grounds of the complete 'disappearance' of the Mesolithic, the rapid diffusion of all the new phenomena to areas high up north and the impossibility of identifying a convincing area of origin of the alleged immigrants. It is now generally assumed that the native hunter-gatherer society underwent this drastic transformation within a short space of time.

In southern Scandinavia,[15] the Ertebølle culture, known from its *kjøkkenmøddinger*, or large shell middens, evolved around the same time as the Swifterbant group in the Netherlands. Besides two general similarities between the two – the technology and basic shape of the pottery and the use of the perforated Rössen axes – there are also fundamental differences: the flint industries are entirely different and Ertebølle sites have yielded no evidence whatsoever for animal husbandry

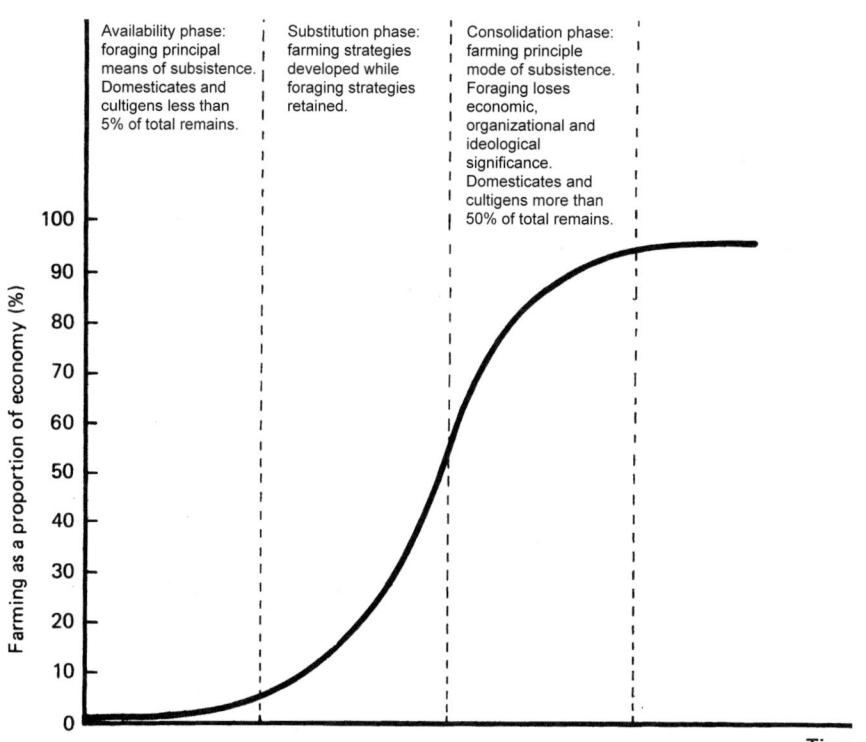

fig. 15.2

The 'availability model' developed by Zvelebil (1986) for the transition of the hunting-gathering way of life to agriculture. The S-shaped curve represents an ideal situation. The shape of the curve is under actual conditions determined by the length of the phases. The three phases were more or less arbitrarily defined on the basis of the ratios of bones of wild animals and domestic animals encountered at the settlements, with limits at 5% and 50%.

or the use of cereal. In Scandinavia, too, the years around 4000 BC saw a rapid transition to a farming culture, that of the TRB, which, even though it shows close stylistic links with areas further south, is nevertheless assumed to be essentially the outcome of a native development.

In both Great Britain and Denmark large, prestigious barrows were in this Early Neolithic erected for prominent members of society, and enclosed central sites resembling those of the Michelsberg culture described above were constructed for ritual purposes. We may speak of a convergence of the developments in the loess zone and those in northern Europe. Similar developments took place in the area of the northwest group of the Michelsberg culture in northern Belgium and the southern part of the Netherlands, except that no long barrows or enclosed sites were constructed there. The area of the Swifterbant culture, which seems to have extended to the Elbe, however shows different developments. Here the incorporation of animal husbandry and the cultivation of cereals in the broad-spectrum economy, around 4200 BC or possibly earlier, was not accompanied by drastic cultural changes. In this area the old cultural tradition was replaced by the TRB only around 3400 BC.

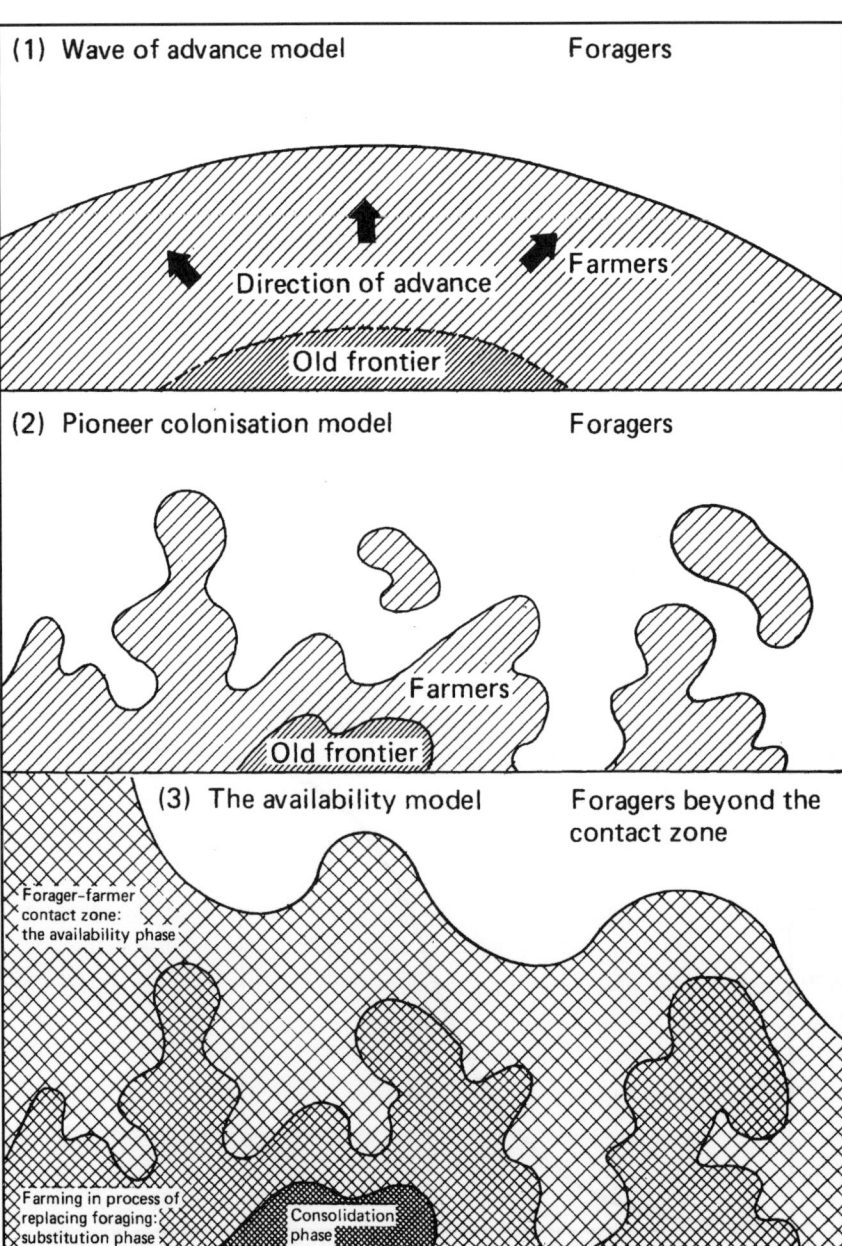

fig. 15.3

Three spatial models for agriculture frontiers, after Zvelebil 1986.

1 A frontier that is constantly advancing as a result of population growth and migration of the farming communities, the 'wave of advance' model developed by Ammermann and Scavalli-Sforza.

2 New settlements as centres of development beyond the front line of the farming community, the 'pioneer settlement' model proposed by Dennell.

3 Exchange of knowledge between hunter-gatherers and farmers on either side of a front line, the 'availability' model developed by Zvelebil.

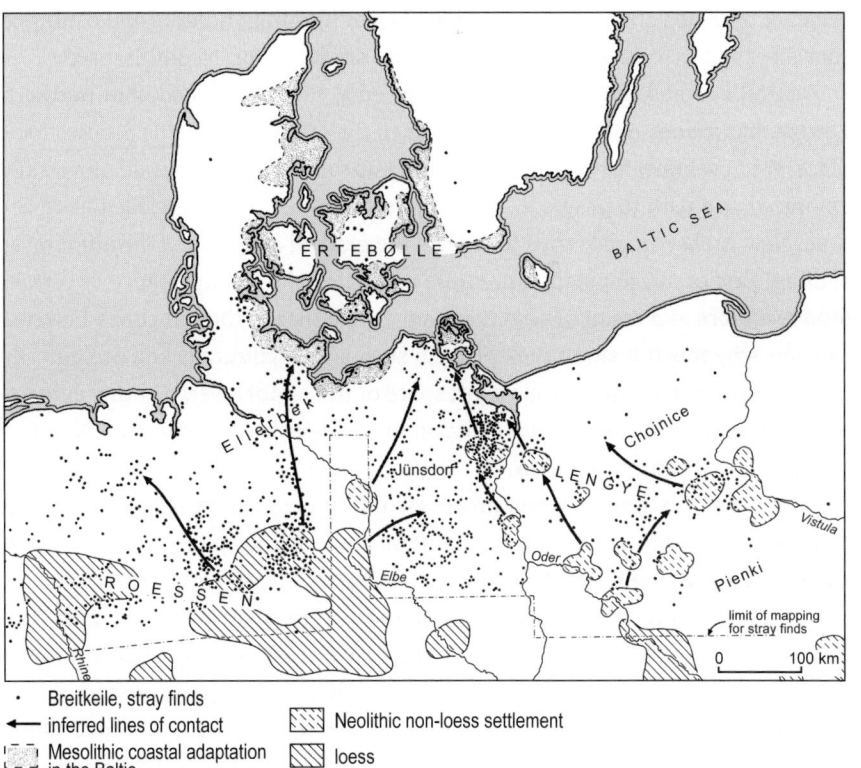

- · Breitkeile, stray finds
- ← inferred lines of contact
- Mesolithic coastal adaptation in the Baltic
- Neolithic non-loess settlement
- loess

fig. 15.4
Distribution of Rössen *Breitkeile* in northern Europe to the north of the loess zone, the result of exchange relations between the northern hunter-gatherers and the farmers further south.

All in all, this information constitutes a – still very incomplete but nevertheless sufficiently empirical – basis for a simple descriptive model for this period, which provides a geographical and chronological framework for the Neolithisation process. The period can well be described with the aid of a number of concepts introduced by Zvelebil, who distinguished three phases in the process of the introduction of farming (fig. 15.2):[16]

– an 'availability' phase, in which the new customs were known, but were not yet adopted;

– a 'substitution' phase, in which farming was adopted;

– a 'consolidation' phase, in which the communities derived their sustenance predominantly from farming.

Zvelebil fixed the boundaries between the three phases at 0% and 50% bones of domestic animals in the overall faunal spectrum, which are of course entirely arbitrary boundaries, but the same would hold for any other boundaries.

A similar distinction can be made in geographical terms within a single (short) period: we can distinguish availability, replacement and consolidation *zones* (fig. 15.3). The boundaries between these zones may be very sharp, they may remain stationary for long periods of time and they may be 'impermeable', in the sense that the communities on either side had very little (archaeologically traceable) contact. Or the boundaries may be 'permeable' and/or mobile, in the sense that there is evidence for contacts and/or the boundary shifted over time. In the Netherlands, this frontier was in essence stationary during the *Bandkeramik* and the Rössen cultures, but became increasingly 'permeable' (fig. 15.4). The Swifterbant culture represents a long replacement phase. This phase came to an end with the development of the northwest group of the Michelsberg culture in the southern part of the country and the appearance of the western group of the TRB culture in the north, but it seems to have continued until the end of the Vlaardingen culture in the wetlands. It is however difficult to apply the above concepts to communities with a complex settlement system. For example, in the case of the wetlands, the ample evidence obtained at the various settlements may highlight hunting and fishing to such an extent as to cause us to underestimate the degree of 'Neolithisation'.

Zvelebil's model can be aptly used to describe the Neolithisation of northern Europe, but it does not provide an answer to the question *why* this process took place. We now know for certain that farming was not immediately and universally embraced as a path to progress, as the old evolutionist outlook wished us to believe. New Archaeologists tried to explain the gradual adoption of farming by assuming, first of all, population pressure and, later, the disappearance of certain food resources as a result of climatic change.[17] Neither of these theories however explains why this transition took place in such a vast, culturally and ecologically highly diverse area within such a short space of time. Moreover, no other subsistence system will have been more resistant to small-scale environmental disasters than a broad-spectrum economy.

At present, the Neolithisation process is interpreted largely in terms of social acceptance: it is thought that crop cultivation and cattle keeping were first adopted by prominent members of society, such as lineage heads, after which the new practices were rapidly and widely imitated, in an atmosphere of social rivalry. The management of exotic animals and crops may have granted group leaders as much prestige as the possession of beautiful axes made of exotic types of stone.[18] The expansion of the range of food resources moreover implied less risk of food shortages, but that is a functionalistic argument. Something else we should consider is that intensive hunters and gatherers who were already practising systematic faunal management will have seen crop cultivation and cattle keeping not as exceptionally novel activities, but rather as more intensive versions of practices with which they were already familiar. By this time people had for example been keeping dogs as domestic animals for several millennia already.

The above arguments provisionally put an end to the debate concerning the interpretation of the transition to the farming way of life, but there is in fact another side to this problem and that is the question why some people did *not* (immediately) take this step and why – in the many centuries after 5300 BC – communities with different economies continued to live *side by side*.

FORAGERS AND FARMERS SIDE BY SIDE (fig. 15.5)

To obtain some understanding of such situations we can turn to recent hunter-gatherers or to descriptions of past communities of foragers and the reinterpretation of their status in the so-called revisionism debate in anthropology.[19] For many years such peoples, for example the pygmies, the African Bushmen and the North American Inuit, were portrayed as idealized hunting communities and it was incorrectly assumed that contacts with nearby farmers or 'more advanced' cultures further afield were a recent (acculturation) phenomenon that could be glossed over. Some foragers prove to have maintained close relations with nearby farmers for hundreds, possibly even thousands, of years. They exchanged ideas and goods with one another and from time to time the foragers even practised crop cultivation or animal husbandry themselves, too, or went to work for the nearby farmers. These additional activities formed an integral part of their traditional way of life and indeed seem to have contributed to their survival. Many hunter-gatherers prove to have voluntarily adhered to their traditional lifestyle instead of switching to a way of life that would have afforded them greater material property, among other advantages.

It would seem that we may apply such a view to the Neolithic frontline in north-

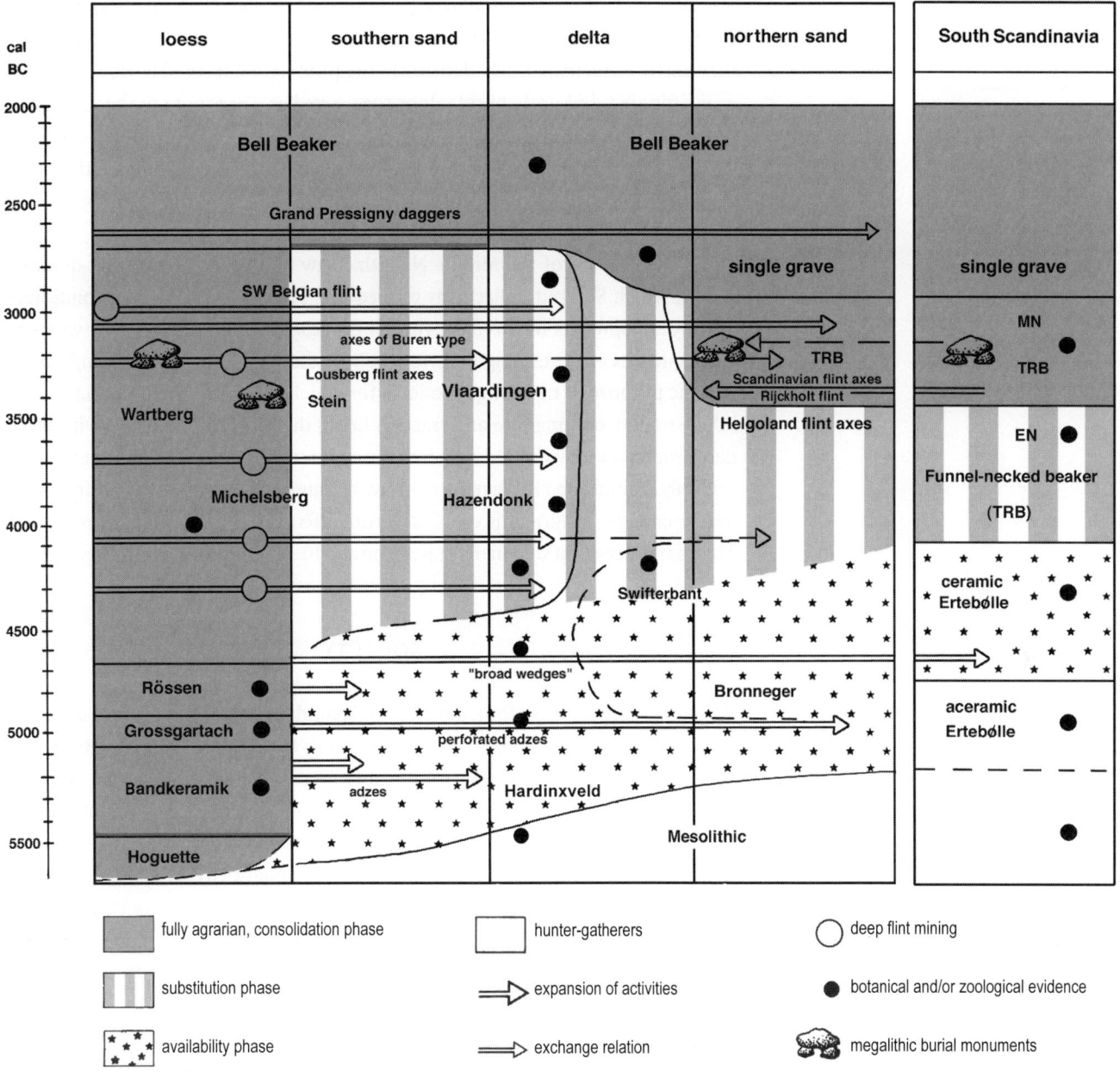

	loess	southern sand	delta	northern sand	South Scandinavia

cal BC

2000 —

Bell Beaker

Bell Beaker

2500 —

Grand Pressigny daggers

SW Belgian flint

single grave

single grave

3000 —

axes of Buren type

MN

Lousberg flint axes

TRB

Scandinavian flint axes

TRB

Stein   Vlaardingen

Rijckholt flint

3500 —

Wartberg

Helgoland flint axes

EN

Michelsberg

Funnel-necked beaker

Hazendonk

(TRB)

4000 —

Swifterbant

ceramic Ertebølle

4500 —

"broad wedges"

Rössen

Bronneger

aceramic Ertebølle

perforated adzes

5000 —

Grossgartach

adzes   Hardinxveld

Bandkeramik

5500 —

Mesolithic

Hoguette

Legend:

- fully agrarian, consolidation phase
- substitution phase
- availability phase
- hunter-gatherers
- expansion of activities
- exchange relation
- deep flint mining
- botanical and/or zoological evidence
- megalithic burial monuments

ern Europe, too. The principle of a symbiotic relationship chosen by the native population itself is an attractive explanation for the long 'availability phase' and the subsequent equally long 'replacement phase' in which certain – selected – Neolithic achievements were adopted. The great difference in the origins of the two communities and the associated differences in ideology and attitude towards the environment reflected by the archaeological evidence may have been important factors in this context.[20] On the other hand it is also known that considerable cultural differences, such as those between Papuans and Westerners, need not always prevent the rapid acceptance of cultural elements. But in these cases the nature of the contacts were different from those at issue here. The Late Mesolithic foragers descended from the Late Glacial *Federmesser* and tanged point groups. They had evolved a way of life based on the appreciation of a broad spectrum of food resources available in the rich, varied environment in which they lived. The *Bandkeramik* way of life, on the contrary, originated in the southeast and will have assimilated ideas and values from groups in southeast Europe, whose ideology was ultimately rooted in that of the earliest farming communities of the Near East. The two lifestyles first came into contact with one another around 5300 BC. The *Band-*

fig. 15.5

Schematic representation of the relations between the Neolithic communities in the loess zone (left) and those to the north of it (right) as reflected by imports of specific types of artefacts and stone. Also indicated are the periods and areas for which zoological and botanical evidence on subsistence is available.

keramik people selected very stereotype locations for their settlements and created their own cultivated micro-environments in the dense primeval forest, in which they practised their specialised form of food production. It could be that differences in attitude – and probably ideology too – acted as a barrier to the acculturation of the two communities and were partly responsible for their continued existence side by side. What is however difficult to explain is why the Late Mesolithic communities in Central Europe seem to have been far more receptive to innovations in an earlier stage of the Bandkeramik.

The final phase of the Middle Neolithic saw important agricultural developments, which Sherratt collectively termed the 'secondary products revolution'.[21] These developments involved the further domestication of nature. They were the consequences of the taming (domestication) of animals, namely breeding for the specific purpose of obtaining products for which the animals did not have to be killed: milk, wool, manure and traction being the most important. We have evidence for the use of wool and milk from an early stage of the Neolithic already, but it was only around 3000 BC that the ox-drawn plough and wagon were to bring about drastic changes in agriculture which were to affect the entire farming community. This marked the first step in the expansion and mechanisation of farming.

SOCIETY

It is not so easy for us to form a picture of Neolithic society. That is because there are no good reference points that we could use to compose such a picture. Our understanding of the Late Palaeolithic and Mesolithic is largely – and probably wrongly – based on evidence from groups like the Nunamiut and the Indians of the northwest coast of America, respectively, while our picture of Bronze and Iron Age societies is predominantly based on alleged similarities between their lifestyle and the historically known early twentieth century farming life. For the Neolithic there are however no attractive ethnographic analogies and we are hence primarily dependent on the archaeological evidence itself. There are arable farmers who still practise hoe agriculture today, for example in the Amazon and Orinoco Basins, New Guinea, Malaysia and other remote corners of southeast Asia, but their tropical contexts make them less suitable models for the Neolithic farmers of Northern Europe. The closest parallel is afforded by the original Indian farmers of northeast America, such as the Iroquois.[22] Most experts have for this reason avoided statements on Neolithic society. A few have ventured to propose imaginative reconstructions like that of the sturgeon fishers of the Vlaardingen group, dating from the 1950s (plate 24A). Our present understanding of Neolithic society is possibly somewhat romantic: the reconstruction of the farmstead on the edge of a dune in the coastal area is too idyllic (plate 24B). Like all archaeological interpretations, it is strongly influenced by the spirit of our times.

Because of this absence of a suitable analogy and the shortage of evidence shedding light on the social structure, we actually know very little about most of the Neolithic societies and the changes they underwent. An exception are the Bandkeramik communities, for which we have both a few cemeteries and a large amount of detailed settlement evidence. Modest differences in status and power have been expressed in the grave goods. The status was probably achieved, based on personal prestige or abilities achieved during one's lifetime. It is furthermore thought that the storage of the harvests was concentrated in a small number of households which consequently enjoyed a higher social position. The grave goods show no differences between men and women as far as the value of the goods is concerned, but they do differ in nature: men were accompanied by objects connected with strenuous woodworking and hunting, women by objects associated with crop cultivation and fertility. The communities were probably organised in kinship groups: families who traced their descent from a common ancestor and who lived close together on and around a communal yard. A number of such farmsteads together constituted a village. These villages were grouped in clusters, like that on the Graetheide in southern Limburg, and these clusters had contacts with one another. We can thus distinguish a spatial hierarchy, to which we would like to attribute a social meaning, which we are however unable to define or specify. We emphatically avoid using the term 'tribe'. One thing that is certain is that society was strictly ordered in the *Bandkeramik* period, unlike in the subsequent periods. This may have been a consequence of, first of all, the *Bandkeramik* people's colonist status and, later, their position relative to that of the Late Mesolithic hunter-gatherers living in their surroundings.

Even less can be said about social aspects of the later Neolithic communities, for which we have extremely little burial or settlement evidence. As far as the Michelsberg culture is concerned, the large central sites point to the existence of a level of organisation above that of the settlement. It is now furthermore believed that the large mining centres, such as those of Rijckholt and Spiennes, were not controlled by local groups, but were freely accessible to a very large community.[23]

The Swifterbant communities are thought to have been poorly stratified, like their Mesolithic predecessors. They were definitely characterised by less social ranking than the farming communities in the south. It is only with the TRB culture that we begin to regain some understanding of social organisation in this area. On the whole, the TRB communities seem to have been fairly egalitarian, too, although it was apparently possible for some individuals to distinguish themselves, for example in the construction of *hunebedden*. The evidence for long-distance exchange and the ritual deposition of axes of the northern rectangular type suggests that a few members of society indeed enjoyed a slightly higher status. But this status is not reflected in any recognisable form in the burial rite.

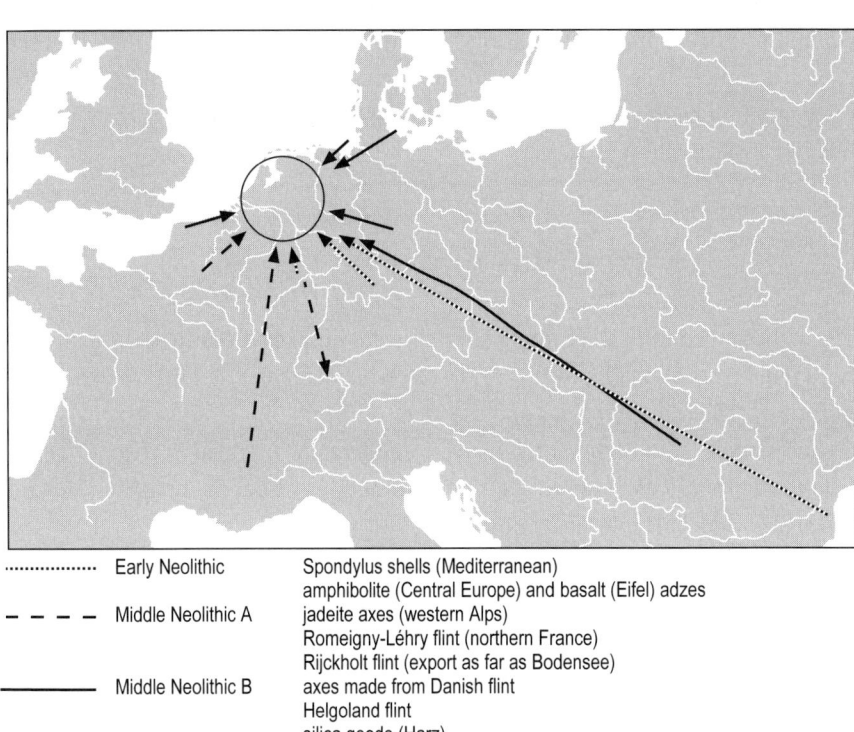

.... Early Neolithic   Spondylus shells (Mediterranean)
                                        amphibolite (Central Europe) and basalt (Eifel) adzes
– – – – Middle Neolithic A   jadeite axes (western Alps)
                                        Romeigny-Léhry flint (northern France)
                                        Rijckholt flint (export as far as Bodensee)
———— Middle Neolithic B   axes made from Danish flint
                                        Helgoland flint
                                        silica geode (Harz)
                                        Grand Pressigny flint (western France)
                                        copper spirals (southeast Europe)

fig. 15.6

The origins of artefacts made of exotic materials that were not regionally available in the Early and Middle Neolithic. See fig. 31.8 for the later periods.

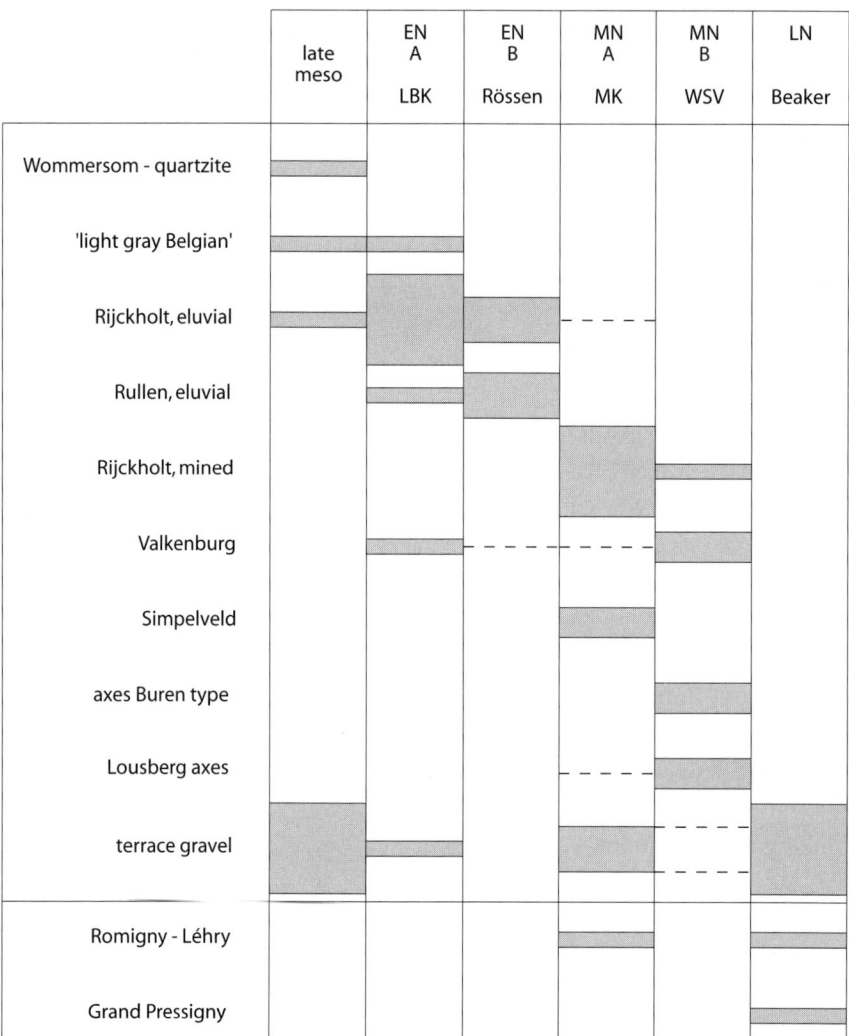

fig. 15.7

Survey of the types of flint and artefacts most frequently used in the Lower Rhine Basin in the successive phases of the Neolithic.

The Neolithic hence seems to be characterised by communities in which a few individuals possibly gained personal status through special achievements. The communities were probably organised in kinship groups who traced their descent from a common ancestor. Important social changes were not to take place until the beginning of the Beaker period. It is only then that we observe the signs of increased social differentiation.

EXCHANGE NETWORKS (fig. 15.6)

Throughout the entire Neolithic, materials were in many different ways exported from their areas of origin, over short to very long distances, in large to very small quantities. The transport lines and the areas of origin, but also the way in which artefacts made from these materials were deliberately intended for (ritual) deposition or for burial as grave goods, tell us something about the organisation and social networks of Neolithic communities.[24]

The chief aim of short-distance transport was to supply indispensable raw materials to regions where they did not occur naturally, such as flint and hard stone for the manufacture of querns and grindstones in the delta (fig. 15.7). This service was supported by the communities' own mobility in the context of, for example, seasonal migrations or special expeditions. The use, in the south of the Netherlands, of flint collected from the gravel deposits of the Meuse and the use of erratic flint in the north raises no questions. The occupants of Hekelingen, however, used fresh flint from a chalk region in such large quantities that we assume that they had direct access to the flint sources in question, which probably lay along the French Channel coast, some 150 km from their settlement.[25]

In addition to these fairly local raw material transport lines we can also distinguish patterns on a larger scale involving materials whose value was based largely on their distant provenance, such as axes of high quality, unusually coloured types of flint. They were distributed within traditional culture areas, but in some cases also far beyond their borders. The latter holds in particular for materials with an exclusively ascribed value, such as haematite, amber, jet and copper.

The contacts implied by these networks, or 'interaction spheres', may have been maintained by leading members of the communities, who are sometimes – somewhat exaggeratedly – referred to as an 'elite'. These leaders may have corroborated their position by exchanging exotic goods within their own circles and/or using such goods in (ritual) depositions on behalf of the group which they represented. Another possibility is that a much larger proportion of the community participated directly in the exchanges without there being any question of redistribution. It is generally assumed that the chief mechanism behind these exchange networks between the sedentary, territorially organised farming communities was a form of down-the-line exchange, via which objects were transported step by step, passing from hand to hand and becoming increasingly exotic and desirable as the distance from their sources increased. This form of exchange hence differed from the distribution of exotic materials by hunter-gatherers, in which group mobility played a dominant part. In the case of the farming communities, too little attention is still being paid to the possibility of different – possibly less organised – forms of mobility, for example of individuals or of groups of a certain age who, as part of their personal training, went out into 'the world' to return to their community after acquiring experience and material evidence of their journeys far afield.[26]

Our understanding of the larger-scale social networks is of course highly rudimentary. Only objects made of virtually imperishable materials can be recovered by archaeological means, and then chiefly those that were deliberately buried in the ground, as grave goods or in hoards. Highly valued materials will rarely have been lost or discarded.

There were very long lines of contact between *Bandkeramik* communities, through which ornaments made of *Spondylus* shells from the Adriatic or even the Black Sea made their way into Western Europe. In the lower Rhine region these ornaments have not survived owing to the decalcification of the loess. The stone adzes that have been found in the *Bandkeramik* area came from regions less far away: those of basalt and amphibolite possibly from the middle Rhine mountains and those of phtanite from central Belgium and the Ardennes. Rössen *Breitkeile* made their way to the northern communities, covering many hundreds of kilometres (fig. 15.4).[27] Jadeite axes have been distributed in the Middle Neolithic from a source in the western Alps all over Western Europe. From there these axes were distributed across the whole of Western Europe, even into Scotland. Rijckholt flint was transported from Limburg to Hessen in Germany and incidentally even deep into southern Germany. The occupants of Limburg in turn imported large flint blades from the surroundings of Reims, from the outcrops of Romigny-Léhry.[28]

As far as the Middle Neolithic is concerned, the copper spirals that were found in the *hunebed* of Buinen demonstrate contacts with Bohemia or possibly even the Balkans. Amber may have been picked up locally, along the coast or from ice-pushed Tertiary clay deposits in Overijssel, but that found in TRB contexts may well have come from Scandinavia and the same holds for large lumps of amber like that found in the cemetery of Swifterbant S2. The coast of northern France

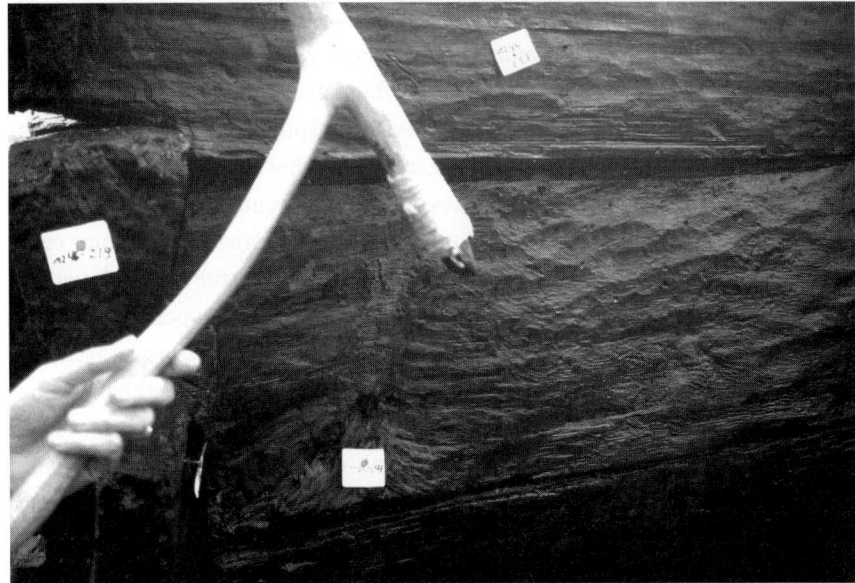

fig. 15.8
Reconstruction of a *Bandkeramik* adze with the lining of the Kückhoven well in the background (see plate 14A). The planks of the lining were made by cleaving the trunks of sturdy oaks and shaping them with the aid of adzes.

has been suggested as the source of the jet, the Rhineland and the Ardennes as that of the haematite or red ochre. The TRB people imported flint axes from southern Scandinavia and Helgoland in northwest Germany and axes made on quartz geodes from the German Harz mountains, but also axes of the Buren type from Belgium.

The continuous exchange of exotic materials that can be inferred from these materials' distribution patterns was – throughout the entire Neolithic – supported by networks of continuous social relationships which tell us that the communities were all in close contact with one another and that the horizons of the local communities were wider than is often assumed.

TECHNOLOGICAL DEVELOPMENTS

The Neolithic saw major technological innovations, which can be related to the changed, more sedentary, way of life and to the development of farming. Felling trees, woodworking and timber construction were important activities, as testified by the remains of houses, palisades, (bog) trackways, wagons with solid disk wheels, ploughs and, last but not least, the unique *Bandkeramik* well of Kückhoven (plate 14A, fig. 15.8).[29] The axe was the tool *par excellence* for both woodworking and felling trees. In the course of the Neolithic the axe was perfected through various

fig. 15.9
Haft and head of two different axe handles from the Vlaardingen 1b level at the Hazendonk, combined to reconstruct a Neolithic axe. Scale 1:4.

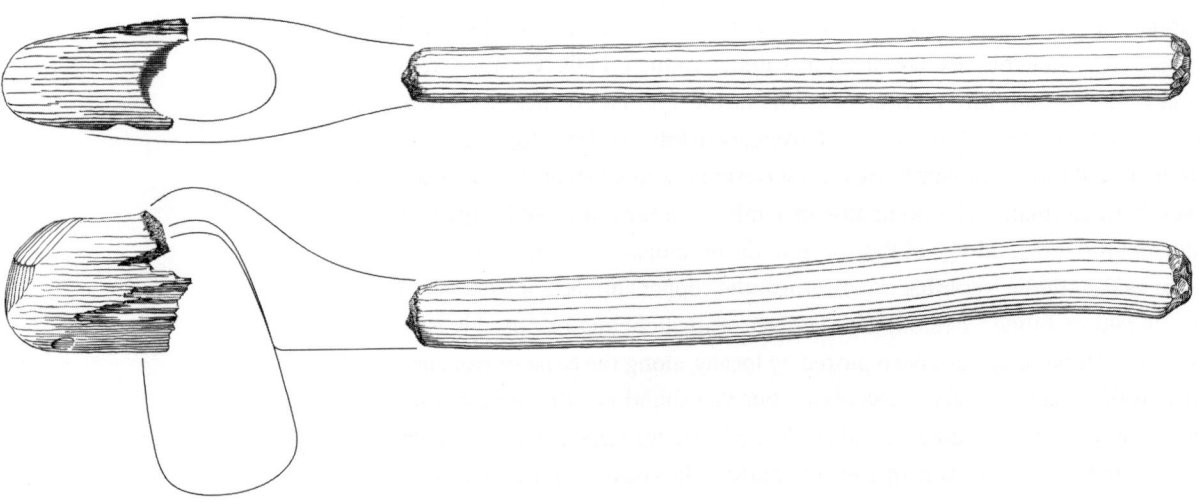

technical innovations affecting the blade, the haft and its attachment (fig. 15.9). Although the odd Mesolithic community (in Ireland and southern Scandinavia) had already produced simple polished axes, it was only in the Neolithic that man learned how to saw and drill hard stone and how to grind the even harder flint. Antler sleeves absorbed the heavy blows of the axes and prevented the risk of the ash hafts splitting.

Flint and stone remained of primary importance for the manufacture of all kinds of tools until in the Bronze Age, but the range of flint tools underwent fundamental changes reflecting a different attitude towards materials and tools, though it is difficult for us to determine whether the changes served a functional purpose or whether they had a symbolic value. The Early Neolithic range of flint tools is highly standardised, comprising clearly distinct types, the majority of which were intended for specific purposes. The tool kits of the early part of the Middle Neolithic, which were now made from mined flint, also included simple flakes made on local flint, which is regarded as a sign of continuity of Late Mesolithic traditions. Around the beginning of the Middle Neolithic B, c. 3400 BC, conspicuous changes took place in both the TRB culture and the Wartberg-Stein-Vlaardingen complex. Imported tools and blades disappeared entirely or almost entirely and both the size of the tools and the range of types decreased. The small disk scraper came to be the dominant tool type and in the flaking technology the emphasis increasingly shifted from the overall tool to the working edge.[30] Progressively less attention was hence paid to the procurement of high-quality raw materials and to the tools' design. But impressive examples of flint workmanship from the Beaker period, such as the Grand Pressigny daggers, the Early Bronze Age Scandinavian daggers and the carefully designed points, show that the technology was not lost and that exotic flint continued to be highly valued. In the Beaker period we discern a dichotomy between a 'casual' (ad hoc) technology for everyday tools and top-quality workmanship by specialist craftsmen for very special, prestigious artefacts.

Pottery was the first man-made material having different properties than the raw material from which it was made. Owing to its fragile nature, this novel material was however only suitable for use by more or less sedentary communities. Pottery will have replaced, or at least supplemented, all kinds of containers of perishable materials such as bags, baskets, hampers and wooden bowls. Illustrative in this respect is the fact that the earliest northern pottery was built from coils of clay, suggesting that its structure was copied from that of baskets and hampers made of wicker and coils of plant fibres.[31]

Throughout the entire Early and Middle Neolithic the pottery was shaped by hand and fired over open fires. The ceramic from the Bandkeramik period is already of good quality: its regular shapes, thin walls and fine, smooth finish show that it was made with great care. Particularly fine is the pottery of the Rössen and Michelsberg groups, the TRB and the later Beaker cultures. That of the northern 'transitional' communities, i.e. the Swifterbant, Hazendonk 3 and Vlaardingen groups and also the Stein people in the south, is however much poorer. The pottery of these groups is functional, but very simple in terms of technology, design and style.

WHAT NEXT?

The Neolithic has always held a special fascination, with its communities that are not as exotic and as far removed from us as the hunter-gatherers of the Ice Age, but that are neither as 'recognisable' as the mixed farming communities of the Bronze and Iron Ages. The Neolithic is also a period of major changes and important innovations (the invention of the wheel for example!), in which the first pockets of cultivated land were created in the otherwise virtually unspoilt nature. We now have a fairly good chronological and geographical view on this period of roughly three thousand years. Thanks to the expansion into the borders of the Netherlands of cultures that had been known for a long time (such as the Rössen and Michelsberg cultures), the discovery of entirely new units (such as La Hoguette and Limburg), which have made the Neolithic world more complex but also more interesting, and the definition of various phenomena specific to the Low Countries, such as Vlaardingen/Stein, Swifterbant and Hazendonk 3, the enormous hiatuses that formerly seemed to exist between the *Bandkeramik* and the TRB culture have largely been filled up, in a material respect at least. Although our understanding of the Neolithic is based on a very small number of sites and evidence from an even smaller number of excavated settlements, the gaps that still remain in the sequence for the Low Countries are actually quite small. A serious handicap and a major source of frustration in setting up a synthesis for the Neolithic are however the tremendous qualitative differences between the distinguished phases and regions, which are largely attributable to the frequent absence of burials and settlement features and, hence, of the information that can be derived from these sources, and the restriction of ecological and biological evidence to the delta and the odd site with favourable preservation conditions elsewhere. A great problem for archaeologists in the Low Countries is hence having to discount these huge differences in the – scarce – evidence in translating the *descriptive* model (what, where, when?) into a *dynamic* model. But at least we now have some idea of the developments, the transformation processes. There was clearly an area of tension between the south and the north, between the southern farmers and the northern foragers, both of whom were involved in a protracted process of interaction and drastic change which spanned the entire Neolithic. In spite of the tangibility and recognisability of the *hunebedden* and the flint mines and the 'historical experiences' evoked by some astonishing finds from the delta,[32] it is becoming more and more clear to us that these communities and their relationships with one another were in fact quite unique, with very few parallels in the ethnographic sources. And yet it is precisely anthropological considerations that help us understand *why* processes took place in the ways we believe we may infer from the evidence and *why* the 'Neolithisation' of Northwest Europe was seemingly such a protracted process.

There is little else for us to do but continue along the course we have taken and expediently take advantage of discoveries and process the information obtained at individual sites in thematic and regional studies.[33] Botanical and zoological research will remain of fundamental importance. It has moreover been found that much useful information can be obtained in microwear analyses of flint, both from the sites with poor archaeological records in the higher parts of the Netherlands and from the wetlands. Future regional research should focus on the former peripheries of the delta, which now lie buried beneath several metres of Holocene deposits. Thematic studies should be initiated in the fields of pottery technology, combined analysis of residues and use-wear traces, the location of flint sources and the further systematic analysis of the wide range of axes. Over the past few years, research into the Neolithic has benefited much from studies of material remains, but also from theoretical approaches which have shed a fresh light on the relations between farmers and foragers and the meaning of the archaeological remains of the material culture, and which have made us adopt a more critical attitude towards the relations between what we actually have, in archaeological terms, and what there once was.

1 Binford criticised the normative character of the archaeological concept of culture in 1965 already. Hodder (1977, 1982b) showed that ethnic groups express their social identity in different ways. Another problem that has led to discussions is the difficulty of defining the boundaries of cultures: the distributions of finds to a great extent dictate where boundaries are drawn, while the views of researchers determine where the boundaries are drawn in the case of transitional forms.

2 Van der Waals 1969.

3 Hodder 1985.

4 Raemaekers 1999.

5 Hodder 1990.

6 Binford 1982.

7 The only clearly distinguishable *Bandkeramik* settlement clusters are those which have been found on the Graetheide; most *Bandkeramik* settlement clusters are not or only very vaguely recognisable. The latter is always the case with settlement clusters of the Rössen culture. Apparently the available space was more equally used in the Rössen period and the 'empty' zones were filled in in a manner resembling that inferred by Kruk (1980) for the *Bandkeramik* and Lengyel periods in the Little Poland uplands.

8 The term 'tribal' is here used in the broadest sense, to refer to a regional group with a common identity and little social ranking.

9 This hypothesis, and also the impression that our picture of the early settlement patterns was highly distorted owing to factors of preservation and discovery, was confirmed by the discovery of the Hazendonk 3 farming settlements at Rijswijk and Wateringen (site 4) (Raemaekers 1999). The long, continuous use of the river dunes and of locations like P14 is also an argument for assuming that the settlement system did not change much.

10 The substantial differences in the sources of the various types of flint found at the Vlaardingen sites are a strong argument for assuming that there were closer contacts between these sites and their hinterlands than between the individual sites themselves (Van Gijn 1990; Louwe Kooijmans 1987, 1993).

11 Some examples are: Hoogevaart (southern Flevoland, Late Mesolithic/Swifterbant 1, Hogestijn *et al.* 1995); P14 (Noordoostpolder, Swifterbant 3 – Single Grave culture, Ten Anscher/Gehasse 1993, Gehasse 1995), Stenendam and Bornwird (Friesland, TRB/Single Grave culture, Fokkens 1982): Gassel and Kraaienberg (North Brabant, Hazendonk 3 and northwest Michelsberg, Verhart/Louwe Kooijmans 1989; Louwe Kooijmans/Verhart 1990).

12 Although Verhart (1992) prefers the alternative – seasonal occupation in a summer base camp – in the case of Haamstede.

13 Such as Bergschenhoek, Hazendonk, Hekelingen III phase 3 (Bell Beaker), Vlaardingen phase 2 (Bell Beaker), Oldeboorn (Louwe Kooijmans 1993b).

14 Thomas 1988, 1991.

15 Madsen 1986.

16 Zvelebil 1986a.

17 Ammerman/Scavalli-Sforza 1973; in particular in part of Denmark by Paludan-Müller 1978; Rowley-Conwy 1984.

18 Bender 1978; Thomas 1988.

19 See *e.g.* Lee 1992; Schrire 1984; Solway/Lee 1990; Stiles 1992.

20 Louwe Kooijmans 1998.

21 Sherratt 1981, 1983.

22 These 'Late Woodland' Indians and their historical successors, however, had no domesticated animals other than dogs. They lived in large communal houses. Their villages and fields, in which they grew maize, beans and squash, lay in clearances created in the woods and were surrounded by palisades (Ellis/Ferris 1990; Tuck 1971).

23 De Grooth 1991.

24 In Australia in particular, much ethnohistorical research has been carried out into the sociocultural meaning of exchange networks (*e.g.* McBryde/Harrison 1981). Bradley/Edmonds 1993 is an interesting case study on the mining centre of Great Langdale, northern England, and the social network behind it.

25 Van Gijn 1990: 97-132.

26 Works like Kelly 1992 and Shott 1986 discuss different forms of mobility from an archaeological viewpoint.

27 From the German Rhineland into the Netherlands and from Saxony into Denmark and southern Sweden (Van der Waals 1972; Brandt 1967).

28 Polman 1996.

29 Weiner 1992.

30 Van Gijn 1998.

31 Compare the plastic copies of traditional forms in our own century.

32 'Historical experience' is a concept from the philosophy of history (see Ankersmit 1993). Historical – and also archaeological – records may appear so recognisable that the difference in time between then and now seems to disappear. We then feel we can understand the past from our shared human background. This is for example the case at the camp of Bergschenhoek (Louwe Kooijmans 1987), although on further consideration important questions still remain unanswered at this site.

33 A number of regional projects are currently being carried out: the Meuse valley project (Wansleeben/Verhart 1990, 1992), the river dunes project (Verbruggen forthcoming) and the 'wet heart of Holland' project (Ten Anscher/Gehasse 1993).

Part III

Mixed farming societies

By the end of the Middle Neolithic crop cultivation and animal husbandry had become the mainstays of the subsistence system over almost the whole of the Netherlands, but it was only in the Late Neolithic that mixed farming proper, including cattle breeding and plough (ard) agriculture, started to be practised. The latter development went hand in hand with the introduction of innovations associated with this form of agriculture: the use of ox-drawn vehicles and the production of milk and wool. By the Middle Bronze Age the house-cum-byre had become the centre of the farmstead. The impact of man on the environment is clearly visible in the pollen diagrams in the form of indications of the development of heathlands and podzols due to the shorter fallow periods in the crop rotation cycles.

One of the many changes that took place in the Late Neolithic involved the replacement of collective funerary monuments such as hunebedden by barrows. It is for this reason that the first Late Neolithic culture is also referred to as the Single Grave culture; from this time onwards the standard burial rite comprised the inhumation of a single corpse.

As also in the areas surrounding the Netherlands, metal (copper and gold) started to be forged and used for the first time in the context of the Bell Beaker culture. That was followed shortly after by the introduction of bronze, the metal that gave the Bronze Age its name. The exchange networks that had to be established to obtain that bronze will certainly have played an important part in the social developments that took place in the Bronze Age communities. Competition for the leading positions within those communities was probably the impetus behind the emergence of more complex societies in later periods.

16 Late Neolithic, Early and Middle Bronze Age: introduction

Harry Fokkens

ENVIRONMENT AND SETTLEMENT

The Late Neolithic and the Early and Middle Bronze Age cover the part of the Holocene that is called the Sub-Boreal. In this period the climate was probably a little warmer than it is today. Although the difference in temperature will have been only small – a few degrees in terms of the annual average[1] – it may have had some influence on the vegetation and crop yields. What will have had a greater effect on the development of the landscape was the relative rise in sea level. Around 2000 BC the rate at which the sea level rose started to decrease, enabling the fen peat to expand further towards the sea. With time, a layer of infertile peat (raised bogs) developed on top of these fertile fen peat and gradually expanded inland. The resultant wide peat zone was not yet fit for occupation, but it was visited by the occupants of other areas. The many finds that have been recovered from this peat show that the raised bogs in particular occupied important places in what could be called the 'ritual landscape'.

From an economic viewpoint – and hence also from the viewpoint of settlement – the higher sandy soils and the clay regions will undoubtedly have appealed more to the Late Neolithic and Bronze Age farmers than the marshy parts of the Netherlands. Until the Late Bronze Age at least, mixed deciduous forests including oak and beech were dominant on the sandy soils. The vegetation of the transitional zones between the higher sands and the lowlands and stream valleys was more open, with lower trees like willows, alders and hazels. In the clearances that were created in the forests for crop cultivation on the marginal sandy soils heath began to grow, if still on a relatively small scale. The formation of these permanent clearances must be associated with changes in farming practices, in particular the introduction of the plough as a means for breaking up the ground and the intensive use of the clearances for pasturing.

Conditions in the coastal regions were also attractive for occupation when the sea permitted it. The higher parts were suitable for house construction and crop cultivation, while the low-lying parts constituted excellent pastures. That will have been a favourable combination of conditions for Bronze Age farmers in particular, in view of their heavy reliance on cattle breeding. The coastal deposits of Westfrisia, as these were silted up to a high level, were, for example, ideal settlement areas for cattle farmers. The dunes and the sandy deposits in the rivers area were also intensively used, as they had been in the previous period. The sediments of the tidal flats in the north of the Netherlands, however, were not yet sufficiently consolidated to allow occupation; they were not colonised until in the Iron Age.

In view of the great size of the coastal peatland, the expanding swamps in the area of the river Vecht in Overijssel and the poor accessibility of the rivers area, the occupants of the different parts of the Netherlands will not have maintained frequent contacts with one another (plate 4). It was probably still possible to travel from the northern Netherlands to the coastal area of Westfrisia across dry sand in the Late Neolithic, but by the Middle Bronze Age this route had been closed off as a consequence of the development of the raised bogs. The southern part of the plateau of Friesland and Drenthe was also increasingly enclosed by the peat expanding from the valley of the Vecht.

The rivers area constituted a distinct environmental unit whose specific settlement conditions led to unity in cultural terms, too. The same holds for the clay region of Westfrisia and the sandy soils of Brabant. The occupants of those different regions will undoubtedly have maintained contacts with one another, but it is likely that each region was occupied by different tribes, with their own regional traditions and their own cultural identity. As the economic basis of these regions was more or less the same, there were no great differences between the individual regions. Nevertheless, regional variations are observable in, for example, the motifs used to decorate the pottery, the plans of the houses, the burial rite, *etc.*

SOCIAL AND ECONOMIC CHANGES

The Late Neolithic: consequences of the 'secondary products revolution'

The early third millennium BC saw a number of – presumably closely related – developments. Around 3000 BC indications of the frequent use of *ards*, the introduction of the wheel, the development of wool production, *etc.* started to appear all over Europe.[2] Sherratt called this 'the secondary products revolution', by which he meant to indicate that although these innovations may have been introduced at an earlier date already, it was around this time that they found widespread acceptance.[3] The phase of experimentation was over: in the Late Neolithic the plough and wheeled vehicles – both drawn by a team of oxen – became integral parts of the agricultural system (fig 16.1). A little later, around 2300 BC, metal started to be used and forged in the Netherlands. The Late Neolithic is hence a period of major technological advance, too.

These innovations of course not only affected the food production, but also the social structure and the related framework of beliefs.[4] The changes observable in the material culture and burial rite are probably attributable to these same innovations. Some twenty years ago, however, it was still generally assumed that the sudden appearance of the Battle Axe or Corded Ware cultures over large parts of temperate Europe reflected the migration of tribes of warrior herdsmen, probably from the Pontic steppes bordering the lower reaches of the Volga; they were thought to have been the first speakers of an Indo-Germanic language to have arrived in this part

fig. 16.1

Two wooden one-piece disc wheels from the peat of the Smeulveen near Emmen (1) and Weerdinge (2). Scale 1:15. The earliest known wheels in Europe date from around 3000 BC. Fourteen of such wheels are known from the Netherlands. They were intentionally deposited in peat bogs, sometimes in pairs and in one case close to a trackway. All but one were found in the eastern part of the province of Drenthe, and all date from the same short period of around 2600-2500 cal BC.

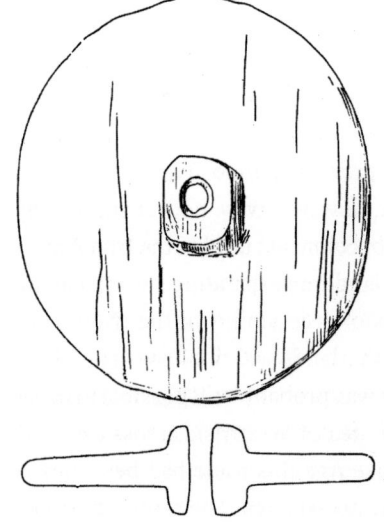
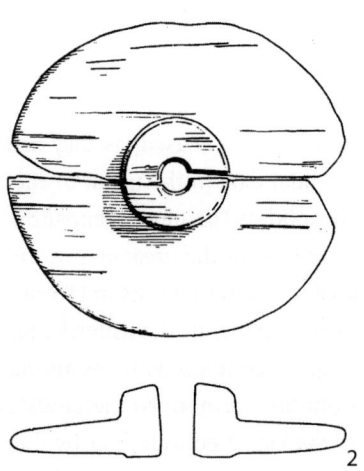

of Europe.[5] Likewise, the bell beakers were associated with people who had spread over Europe from the Iberian peninsula via the Atlantic coast, bringing along the knowledge of metal working together with their pottery. This picture has however recently been overthrown – in particular by evidence obtained in the Netherlands, discussed by Lanting and Van der Waals. The population movements which were in the past invariably invoked to explain all cultural changes are becoming increasingly less obvious explanations for such phenomena. That is not to say that population movements are always unacceptable as explanations for cultural changes, but in the cases discussed here a different explanation is now preferred. The model proposed by Lanting and Van der Waals assumes a continuous development from the Single Grave culture to the Bell Beaker culture.[6] Since its introduction, many archaeologists have adopted this 'Dutch Model', as Harrison called it.[7]

The Bronze Age: mixed farming

Within about a thousand years from the introduction of the innovations agriculture evolved into what may be called true integrated mixed farming. The sustainable balance of integrated crop cultivation and animal husbandry that was established in those early days was to remain the economic basis of many farms in the sandy part of the Netherlands until the 1960s. The changes that took place in the material culture and burial rite in the Late Bronze Age are hence more likely to have been the consequences of developments associated with the use of bronze than of economic instability.

The production and 'consumption' of bronze are indeed important aspects of the Bronze Age, if aspects about which we are still poorly informed. What is particularly difficult for us to understand is how the bronze objects found in the Netherlands were obtained and why they were 'discarded' in graves and deposits. This last problem has been the subject of extensive theoretical treatises on the functioning of the exchange networks: we prefer to use the word 'exchange' rather than 'trade' in this period. What does seem to be fairly certain is that the regional differentiation observable in the Late Neolithic persisted in the Bronze Age. Typological studies of the bronzes in particular have shown that the northern and eastern parts of the Netherlands formed part of the Scandinavian and northern German networks, whereas the southern part of the country belonged to the Belgian-French and, more generally speaking, the Central European exchange area. But how those networks functioned, who played the leading parts in them, what goods were circulated, these are still topics of discussion which will require further research.

CULTURAL UNITS: UNITY IN DIVERSITY

The Beaker cultures: uniformity in appearance only

Throughout long periods of prehistory, cultural differences were observable in the Netherlands, in particular between the two parts of the country separated by the major rivers. The differences in question were not all that great, though; in fact, they were rather comparable to the differences that are still observable between those parts today: the population of the area to the south of the rivers is largely Catholic and speaks a slightly different dialect from the people to the north, who are predominantly Protestant. Those differences cannot be traced back to a fundamental contrast between the two parts, but the division they imply is characteristic

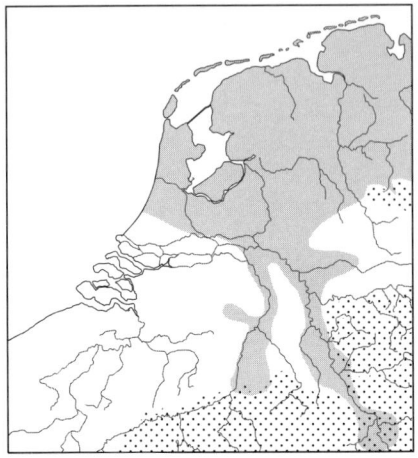

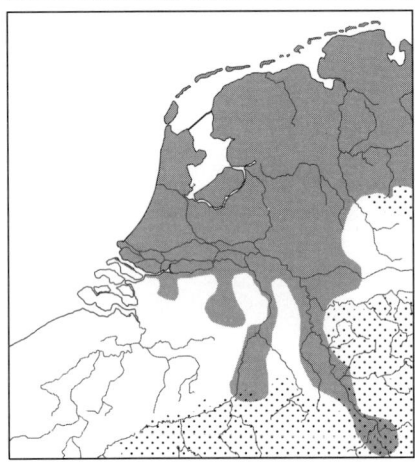

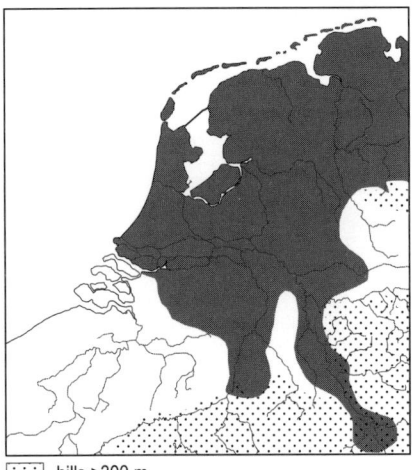

▦ hills >300 m

▪ Single Grave culture

▪ AOO phase and Bell Beaker culture

▪ Barbed Wire Beaker culture

fig. 16.2

Distribution of finds from three main phases of the Beaker cultures in the Netherlands and its environs.

of the Netherlands. We assume that the differences between the two parts of the country were of a similar nature in prehistoric times, only then natural and social barriers will have been less easily surmountable than they are today.

Hardly any signs of such differences are observable in the Late Neolithic; there are certainly no differences enabling us to distinguish different cultural groups within the Netherlands in this period. On the contrary, in fact: at first sight, there seems to be very little relation between the distribution areas of the Beaker cultures and the areas of the different cultures of the Middle Neolithic. Beaker pottery steadily spread across the whole of the Netherlands with the exception of the southernmost part. Finds of the Single Grave culture have been traced in the valley of the Meuse down to the central part of Limburg (fig 16.2), but none are known from the central part of Brabant; not many Bell Beaker sites have been found in that area, either. It is indeed not inconceivable that this area was only sparsely occupied in the Late Neolithic. That would agree with the evidence suggesting that the situation in the Middle Neolithic was very much the same, as that would imply that very little of the woodland had been cleared and made suitable for plough agriculture.

This picture of uniformity began to crumble in the late phase of the Bell Beaker period, when a distinct style of pottery decoration emerged in the Veluwe region and the hills of Utrecht. Beakers of this Veluwe type have also been found in northeast Brabant and the central part of Limburg, but only few findspots are known in the eastern and northern parts of the Netherlands and the adjacent part of Germany, where different types of bell beakers prevailed in this period.

The distribution pattern of the Corded Ware that is characteristic of the last phase of the Beaker cultures is largely the same as that of the Bell Beaker culture, but although Corded Ware has been found at many locations up to the Atlantic coast, its overall distribution area is much smaller than that of the bell beakers. The Netherlands occupies a special place within that area as the earthenware appears to have been distributed from here. As Corded Ware has been found both in barrows and in pits within settlements, archaeologists increasingly tend to speak of a Corded Ware culture, even though the number of finds so far recovered, especially the number of settlement finds, is actually quite small.

The Middle Bronze Age: regional differences

In the Middle Bronze Age, from c. 1800 BC onwards, regional differences became so pronounced as to enable us to distinguish different cultures, although it is not really possible to draw sharp lines between those cultures. The culture distinguished in the northern sandy region has been called the Elp culture, that observed in the central and southern parts of the country the Hilversum culture. The western Netherlands, where Middle Bronze Age settlements and barrows have been discovered at several sites in the dunes, is usually classed as part of the area of the Hilversum culture (fig. 16.3). In the last part of the Middle Bronze Age, however, a distinct regional group manifested itself in Westfrisia; that group's culture is referred to as the Hoogkarspel culture. Due to this area's isolated position, the colonists who settled here when the salt marshes had dried out sufficiently to allow occupation apparently rapidly evolved into a close community with a pottery tradition and burial rite of its own. Whereas the Middle Bronze Age burial rite of the rest of the Netherlands was characterised by burial in a central grave beneath a barrow which was often reused to accommodate secondary burials, no evidence of burials whatsoever has been found in Westfrisia, or at least no evidence from the mature phase of the Hoogkarspel culture.

The differences between the regions distinguished above concern the burial rite and the pottery and to a lesser extent the settlements. The settlements on the sandy soils probably consisted of no more than one or two contemporary houses of varying dimensions. The barrows were usually constructed in the vicinity of the settlements; it seems that new barrows were thrown up at new settlement sites every time the occupants moved on to a new location. In Westfrisia, and probably also in the rivers area, the environmental conditions led to a slightly different pattern. However, that does not mean that we are to assume an entirely different economic basis for those regions. The difference in settlement pattern was largely due to a lack of space on the higher parts of the elongated stream ridges and valley edges, which were the only areas where houses could be built in those regions. Consequently, the settlements in those regions were occupied for relatively long periods of time (several generations) and houses were often rebuilt at the same site rather than at a new location, as was the general custom elsewhere.

THE REPRESENTATIVITY OF THE EVIDENCE

The occupation remains from the Late Neolithic and the Early Bronze Age differ considerably from those from the Middle Bronze Age. This is not only due to post-depositional processes and research factors, but also to cultural formation processes, *i.e.* processes associated with prehistoric behaviour.

The graves

The hundreds of barrows known from the Late Neolithic and the Early and Middle Bronze Age represent only a small portion of the prehistoric population of those periods. On the one hand, many barrows will have been levelled or destroyed in ploughing over the ages. Such graves are discovered only very rarely; sometimes they come to light during settlement research, as at Angelslo, where sixteen destroyed barrows were excavated.[8]

On the other hand, it is believed that only a small portion of the population was buried beneath barrows in both the Late Neolithic and the Bronze Age. But what happened to the majority of the deceased who were not buried in barrows we don't really know. Although a number of flat graves have been found it isn't clear whether they are representative of the burial rite that was used for that part of the population. It is, for example, probable that children were buried in an archaeologically undetectable manner until the end of the Middle Bronze Age.[9]

Cultural formation processes are responsible for differences in the recognizability of the burials in a different manner, too. For example, there are marked contrasts between the Late Neolithic and the Bronze Age in the nature of the peripheral structures, the depth of the grave and the nature and number of grave goods. The graves from the Late Neolithic are on the whole fairly deep and contain well recognizable grave goods (a beaker, axes, flint knives, *etc.*), which makes them archaeologically fairly well detectable, even after ploughing or levelling. The deceased who were buried in the Bronze Age barrows, however, were placed in shallow pits or even in no pit whatsoever and were usually accompanied by only a few grave goods. The characteristic beakers of the previous period had moreover been replaced by much less durable forms of pottery, which were not or only rarely placed in central graves. The chance of graves from this period being discovered during levelling, land-reclamation, digging and other activities is hence far smaller.[10]

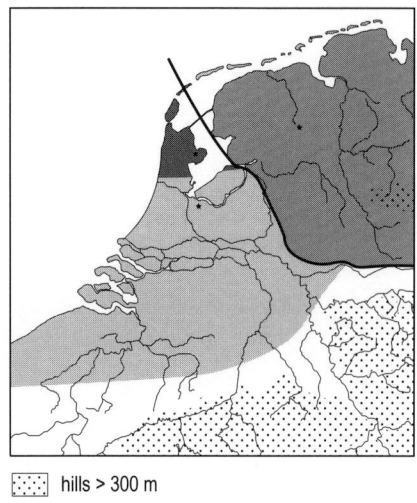

hills > 300 m

Hilversum culture

Elp culture

Hoogkarspel culture

fig. 16.3

Distribution of the culture groups (factually pottery traditions) in the Netherlands and its environs during the Middle Bronze Age. The solid line roughly indicates the boundary between the northern and the Atlantic exchange networks.

The recognizability of the settlements also varies: there are considerable differences in the recognizability of settlements from the Late Neolithic and the Early Bronze Age on the one hand and that of those from the Middle Bronze Age on the other. Those differences are due to cultural formation processes, but also to the nature of the subsoil. For example, virtually no Late Neolithic settlements are known in the sandy region, whereas quite a few have come to light in the clay regions. In the latter regions, the layers of domestic refuse characteristic of such sites have been preserved fairly well, whereas the majority of such layers in the sandy region have been destroyed in agricultural activities (fig 16.4). As excellent samples can be taken from the refuse layers preserved in the clayey subsoil, we have moreover been able to obtain a fairly good picture of the settlement pattern in regions like Westfrisia. Only a very small number of layers of settlement refuse have been found in the sandy region, at a few exceptional sites where those layers were covered with clay or peat deposits shortly after the site was abandoned.

Another reason why so few occupation remains from the Late Neolithic and the Early Bronze Age have been found is that the activities that were practised in those periods left behind little evidence in the form of postholes or pits. The absence of such features is particularly conspicuous at the Late Neolithic and Early Bronze Age settlements on the sandy soils. In those periods, people probably built fairly insubstantial houses and dug few pits. In the clay regions some configurations of postholes – that can be interpreted as house plans – have been found as well.

At Middle Bronze Age sites things are quite different. The farmyards from that period are easily recognisable because the occupants of the farms dug pits for different purposes, which they filled with soil mixed with refuse when they were no longer required. Apart from that, significant changes took place in a ritual context, too. Apparently, objects were more frequently than in the past deliberately buried in the ground. The pits in which they were buried may have been dug specifically for a ritual purpose. In that context it is conceivable that certain rules were employed for the deposition of waste, too.

Middle Bronze Age settlements are not only better recognisable on account of the presence of these pits, but also because the farmsteads were more soundly built than the structures of the preceding period. This was partly due to the fact that the occupants started to stall cattle inside the farm. Moreover, the farmyards were surrounded by fences, whose features often survive. Another important factor is that abandoned settlements probably remained visible in the landscape and

fig. 16.4
Shell midden with clay seams found at the sites of the Single Grave culture in the Westfrisia region. To the right is the Portelwoid site in 1989, to the left a narrow prospection trench dug at Aartswoud in 1972. *Cf.* plate 23A.

fig. 16.5
Ard marks dating from the Middle Bronze Age
B period (1400-1200 BC) in a stratification
of wind-blown sand and peat layers on the
landward side of the Older Dunes. Het Geest
site near Velserbroek.

sometimes were re-occupied in later times. That would explain why occupation remains from both the Bronze Age and the Iron Age have been found at so many settlement sites. A final explanation for the greater number of Bronze Age sites is that far more research into Bronze Age remains has been carried out over the past decades.

The subsistence data obtained in settlement research differ considerably from one environmental zone to another. We are for example far better informed about agricultural practices in the western Netherlands, especially in the clay regions of Westfrisia and the rivers area in the central part of the Netherlands, than about the practices of the sandy northern, eastern and southern parts of the country. This is largely due to the better preservation conditions of the clay regions.

Ard marks have been observed at various sites (fig 16.5). Many have been found buried beneath barrows, while others, for example in the dunes, have been preserved beneath layers of drift sand. These ard marks indicate areas of former fields, but tell us little about the shape or the size of those fields. We are relatively poorly informed about other aspects of farming methods, too, such as manuring, crop rotation cycles, the length of fallow periods and clearance methods.

Deposits

During dredging operations in rivers and lakes or during peat-cutting activities objects are frequently found which show that water and swamps played important parts in prehistoric rituals. These finds are referred to as 'deposits' to indicate that the objects in question were deliberately deposited in that particular environment. This custom had been practised in earlier times already; evidence attesting to this form of deposition in the Late Neolithic comprises, for example, wooden disc wheels, which were deposited in peat bogs. In the Bronze Age mainly bronze objects were consigned to the bogs and to water (chapter 29).

In comparison with for example Scandinavia, the Netherlands has yielded relatively few deposits. Although this difference in the number of deposits probably reflects an actual difference between the two regions, we may safely assume that many objects still remain buried in the Dutch peat while others will undoubtedly have been overlooked during peat-cutting activities in the past.

HISTORY OF THE RESEARCH

Until the end of the 1950s, Late Neolithic and Early Bronze Age research focused mainly on barrows. As a result, the definition of archaeological cultures and our image of the past were for a long time based largely on knowledge about the material culture, chronological sequences and the burial rite. It was only in 1954 that the first Middle Bronze Age settlement was discovered in the Netherlands (a settlement near Deventer). The excavation of the first Late Neolithic settlements, at Aartswoud and Bornwird, was to follow a few years later. Since then, our image of archaeological cultures has changed considerably and the emphasis has shifted from barrows to settlement research.

Barrows

The first barrows were excavated in the 18th and 19th centuries already, but it was only around the beginning of the 20th century that the first systematic research was carried out. The pioneers of that early research were J.H. Holwerda and later A.E van Giffen, in particular. Holwerda's excavation of two barrows near Hoog-Soeren is usually taken to mark the beginning of systematic barrow research in the Netherlands. In 1906 and the following years Holwerda excavated barrows in the Dutch crown estates at the request of Queen Wilhelmina, whose interest in archaeological research had been aroused by a visit to Pompeii and an article on Dutch archaeology written by Holwerda.[11]

The novelty of Holwerda's approach was that he investigated the barrows with the specific purpose of recording their structure and the context of the archaeological finds they contained. He also published his findings as soon has he had completed his research. Those findings almost immediately triggered a scientific debate, because Holwerda had interpreted the peripheral ditches and indications of burning that he had observed around the Bell Beaker burials as the remains of domed timber structures covered with sods (fig 16.6).[12] His interpretation agreed excellently with the diffusion model that Gordon Childe had advanced to explain

fig. 16.6
Model of a 'corbelled tomb' constructed from massive tree-trunks, as envisaged by Holwerda. The model was on show in the National Museum of Antiquities in Leiden until 1960.

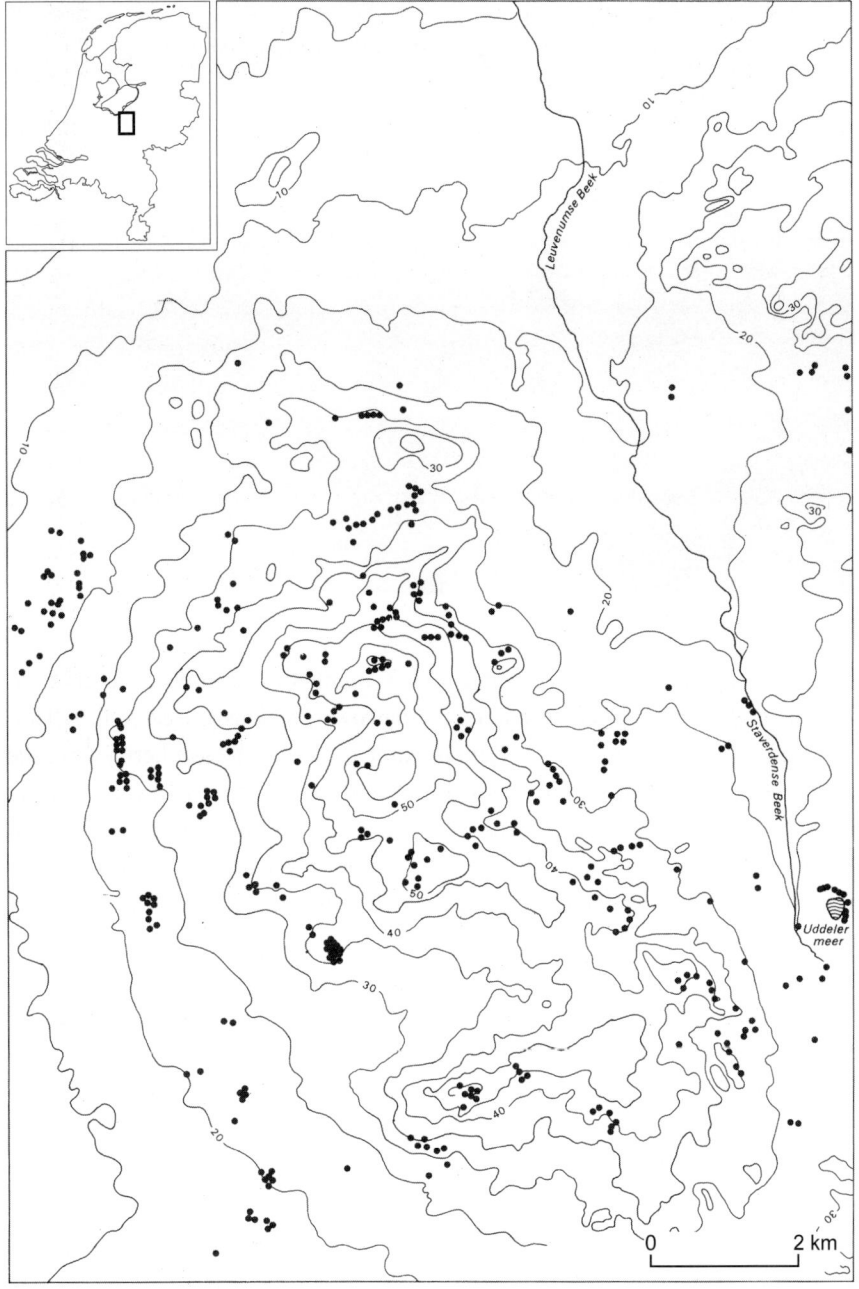

fig. 16.7

The barrow landscape of the northwestern part of the Veluwe region, between Putten and Lake Uddel. Scale 1:100,000.

cultural changes: Holwerda associated his 'corbelled tombs' with the Mycenaean tholos tombs with their corbelled roofs. However, apart from his successors, Remouchamps and Bursch, both from Leiden, only few archaeologists accepted Holwerda's reconstructions. Van Giffen in particular criticised Holwerda's methods for recording and interpreting features.

Van Giffen began investigating barrows at Harenermolen in 1916. From the very start he used the quadrant method, which he himself had developed to expose the barrow's structure in the clearest possible manner. One of the milestones of his work is *Die Bauart der Einzelgräber*, published in 1930, which presents a survey of all the observations made in Dutch barrows and the first relative chronological sequence for the burials.

In the 1930s and 40s, also during World War II, Van Giffen continued his barrow research in Drenthe, where he was later joined by his students Glasbergen, Van der Waals and Waterbolk. By this time, barrows had become the focus of scientific attention in other parts of the Netherlands, too. On the Veluwe, for example, members of the Dutch State Service for Archaeological Investigations (ROB),

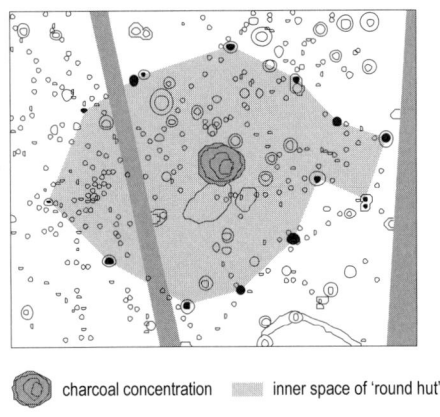

charcoal concentration inner space of 'round hut'

fig. 16.8
Two representations of the same 'round house plan' identified in the Middle Bronze Age settlement of Dodewaard, in a drawing (left) and a photo (right). It is now doubted whether the initial interpretation of the feature as the plan of a round house is correct. Drawing scale 1:200.

supervised by Modderman, excavated a large number of barrows from different periods and reinvestigated several of the barrows previously excavated by Holwerda (fig 16.7).[13] The most important research project in the southern part of the Netherlands is undoubtedly that which involved the excavation of the cemetery between Toterfout and Halve Mijl by Glasbergen.[14] In his dissertation, Glasbergen combined his observations with evidence obtained elsewhere in the Netherlands into a clear chronological framework. He also included palynological and physical-anthropological evidence in his research.

As the barrows of Toterfout-Halve Mijl all dated from the Bronze Age, Glasbergen had concentrated mainly on the monuments of that period. It was Lanting and Van der Waals who carried out the first systematic study of Late Neolithic barrows.[15] They gathered all the available data, excavated new barrows in salvage projects and also re-excavated barrows previously investigated by Bursch and Remouchamps. Their main aims were to demonstrate the cultural continuity of the Beaker cultures and to arrive at an accurate analysis of the burial rite. Their work still forms the basis for present-day Beaker research in the Netherlands and adjacent areas.

The excavation of barrows can be said to have come to an end in 1960, the year in which the Dutch Ancient Monuments Act became effective. Since then, only barrows threatened with destruction have been investigated. Nowadays, hardly any barrows at all are excavated, because almost all barrows are protected monuments. That does not mean that barrow research has come to a standstill. Fortunately, the evidence obtained in the excavations in the past proves to be suitable for modern forms of research such as that carried out by Lohof, who has re-examined Van Giffen's findings and interpreted them in terms of Middle Bronze Age social relationships.[16]

Settlements

In these early years settlements were usually excavated on a small scale only; very rarely were vast areas exposed, as at Elp. It is hence not surprising that the objectives of the earliest settlement research were very much the same as those of the barrow research of the preceding years, namely to obtain knowledge about material culture, chronological sequences, *etc*. The main aim of the first excavation of a settlement of the Single Grave culture was for example to establish a typological sequence for Beaker pottery. That is the reason why, in his research at Aartswoud, Glasbergen meticulously recorded the exact position of every diagnostic Beaker sherd he encountered in a number of 1-metre wide trenches, whereas he collected the undecorated pottery per square metre. Nowadays such research is seen to be almost tantamount to destruction. Nowadays, the main objective of settlement research is to study a settlement's structure and its economy. To that end, large areas are exposed, all the soil is screened and every posthole, pit and other feature is accurately recorded and excavated. The excavation at Kolhorn (North Holland)[17] can be said to mark the beginning of this new style of research, although – from a technical viewpoint – this excavation actually continued a tradition of research into older Neolithic sites such as the Swifterbant and Hazendonk sites (chapter 12).

Although larger areas are nowadays usually excavated at Neolithic settlement sites, too, the extent of the research bears no relation to that carried out at Bronze Age settlements. At the latter sites, the absence of refuse layers on the one hand and the larger area covered by the occupation remains on the other make it possible – but also necessary – to perform large-scale research. Excavating a total area of one hectare, as was done at Elp, is no longer considered a luxury, but rather an absolute minimum for arriving at sound conclusions regarding settlement forms and settlement systems. By 'settlement systems' we mean the relationships between different settlements and between settlements, arable land, cemeteries, ritual sites, etc. It is of course no coincidence that the amount of large-scale settlement research has increased tremendously since the first urban extension projects were launched. One of the first and finest examples of this large-scale research is that which was carried out at the sites near Emmen (Emmerhout, Angelslo) in the early 1960s.

Of great importance for our knowledge of Bronze Age settlements was the research that was carried out in Westfrisia. Thanks to this area's excellent preservation conditions, a wealth of botanical and zoological information could be obtained in this research. Although this agrarian evidence, which IJzereef discussed in his dissertation,[18] relates mainly to Late Bronze Age settlements, it can be used to model Bronze Age settlements in general. The results of the study of the features of these settlements still await publication in a definitive review.[19]

The same holds for the results of the excavations near Zijderveld and Dodewaard.[20] For many years the three-aisled house plans and the associated round features that were discovered in these relatively small-scale excavations served as the basis for reconstructions of the settlements of the Hilversum culture. Those round features were moreover regarded as important evidence supporting Glasbergen's migration theory, for round features were known from England, too! Only in the past ten years, in which more Middle Bronze Age settlements have been discovered in the southern part of the Netherlands, has it been found that the settlement form in this area is in fact comparable with that elsewhere in the Netherlands and that the existence of round structures is to be doubted at the least (fig 16.8).

Metal analysis

The study of metal objects, especially that aimed at establishing typological sequences of bronzes, is traditionally one of the most important branches of Late Neolithic and Bronze Age research. In the Netherlands, the study of metal objects has always been associated with J.J. Butler. Since the mid-1950s he has published a large number of articles on bronzes in the Netherlands, their typology and the sources of the raw materials. The sources of raw materials have been the focus of much research, especially in the years after Junghans, Sangmeister and Schröder carried out their impressive spectrographic analysis project.[21] Various archaeologists, among whom Butler and Waterbolk, criticised their approach and proposed a different quantification method instead.[22] In the meantime it has become clear that spectrographic analysis in fact yields little additional information on the sources of the metal, especially that of objects from the Late Bronze Age, when metal was reused to an increasing extent. Typological studies hence continue to play an important part in research into metal objects.

Current research topics

From what has been said above it will be clear that burial research determined the course of research projects for many years. Among the most important research objectives were the establishment of the relative chronology and regional distribution patterns of different types of burials and the grave goods they contained. In the 1950s and 1960s typological pottery sequences were published for the Late Neolithic and the Bronze Age which have remained of use to this day.[23] It has however been found that the detailed sequence set up for the protruding foot beakers (Single Grave culture) cannot be verified in settlement contexts. Neither is it possible to distinguish Drakenstein ware from Laren ware in settlement assemblages. The only types that can be recognised in settlement assemblages are the early Hilversum types; recently, a more detailed sequence has been set up for these early types.[24]

In the 1980s new developments in archaeological theory led to a new form of burial research. Nowadays, burials are considered potential sources of information on the social structure of prehistoric communities. They are studied for indications of differentiation in burial rites that could express differences in status.[25] A limiting factor is the representativity of the evidence, but as chapter 19 will show, certain conclusions can nevertheless be drawn from that evidence.

In settlement research the emphasis has shifted from typological sequences of house plans to settlement patterns and settlement locations. Recent studies focusing on the latter topics, especially those which were integrated with ecological studies, have yielded a wealth of new information. Good examples of studies of this kind are the Late Neolithic projects of the State Service for Archaeological Investigations (ROB) and the Groningen Institute of Archeology. Similar integrated research projects have been launched for the Bronze Age, too. In the western Netherlands, the Amsterdam Archaeological Centre of the University of Amsterdam did research in the surroundings of Velserbroek.[26] In the river district a vast Bronze Age occupation site near Wijk bij Duurstede has been investigated as part of the State Service for Archaeological Investigations' Eastern Rivers Project.[27] A number of Bronze Age sites have also been excavated in the trace of the Betuwe railroad.[28] Similar research is currently being carried out in North Brabant in the context of the Maaskant Project launched by the Prehistoric Department of Leiden University and the Southern Netherlands Project of the Free University of Amsterdam.[29]

One of the aspects that has been receiving more attention over the past few years is the problem of cultural changes. Whereas De Laet and Glasbergen[30] still ascribed almost all changes in material culture to migrations, most Dutch archaeologists nowadays tend to assume cultural continuity.[31] What has not yet been sufficiently investigated is the question why those changes took place. That is mainly due to the fact that the answers to that question lie in fields with which most Dutch archaeologists are fairly unfamiliar, namely anthropology and sociology. Nevertheless, theories from those fields will have to be studied in relation to archaeological considerations, because it is those theories that may be able to provide insight into social and economic processes on a larger scale, for example those involving exchange networks, which have so far received only little attention in the Netherlands.

NOTES

1 Zagwijn 1986, 8.
2 Sherratt 1980, Champion *et al.* 1984.
3 Sherratt 1981.
4 Gillman 1980, Fokkens 1986, 1998b.
5 Childe 1957, 146; 1959, 134.
6 Harrison 1980.
7 Lanting/Van der Waals 1976.
8 Butler/Van der Waals 1966.
9 Lohof 1991. Theunissen (1999) demonstrates that in the southern Netherlands in the Middle Bronze Age B, children were buried regularly, but not as a rule.
10 For a comprehensive analysis see Fokkens 1997.
11 Van der Waals 1973, 510.
12 Holwerda 1910.
13 Modderman 1954.
14 Glasbergen 1954.
15 Lanting/Van der Waals 1976.
16 Lohof 1991. Theunissen (1999) did the same for the barrows excavated by Glasbergen at Toterfout.

17 In 1979, under the supervision of J.N. Lanting and J.D. van der Waals.
18 IJzereef 1981.
19 See for example IJzereef/Van Regteren Altena 1991 for a preliminary report.
20 Theunissen 1999.
21 Junghans/Sangmeister/Schröder 1968. In 1974 the fourth and last part was published.
22 Waterbolk/Butler 1965.
23 Van der Waals/Glasbergen 1955, Lanting/Van der Waals 1976, A.E Lanting 1969, J.N. Lanting 1973.
24 Ten Anscher 1990; Fokkens 2001.
25 Lohof 1991; see also chapter 18.
26 Therkorn 1987.
27 Hessing 1991a.
28 Jongste/Van Wijngaarden 2002; Meijlink/Kranendonk 2002; Schoneveld/Kranendonk 2001; Schoneveld/Gehasse 2001.
29 Fokkens 1996; Roymans 1996.
30 De Laet/Glasbergen 1959; De Laet 1974.
31 Fokkens 1986; 1998b; Van der Waals 1984.

17 From stone to bronze
Technology and material culture

Jay Butler and Harry Fokkens

The period of the transition from the Late Neolithic to the Early Bronze Age saw a number of fundamental innovations in material culture and technologies. The extensive use of the plough and the wagon with solid wooden disc wheels marked revolutionary developments in agriculture and transport around 2900 BC. Of no less importance was the emergence of metal production a few centuries later. Numerous changes took place in pottery manufacture, too, both in style and in technology. Characteristic of the pottery of the Late Neolithic are the lavishly decorated, thin-walled 'beakers', which were produced alongside less sophisticated types, known as 'beaker pots' and 'pot beakers'. At the end of the Early Bronze Age an entirely different type of pottery started to be produced, consisting of virtually undecorated, thick-walled pots tempered with fine to extremely coarse grit. Another category of finds that underwent stylistic changes in the Late Neolithic is that of the stone artefacts, such as hammer axes and arrowheads. Several of these developments will be discussed below.

POTTERY

The earthenware of the northern and central parts of the Netherlands underwent great changes in the period coinciding with the emergence of the Single Grave culture, while that of the coastal plain remained unchanged for some time.

The pottery of the Single Grave culture can be divided into two categories: thin-walled (protruding-foot) beakers that were decorated with corded impressions or grooves and were often tempered with sand, and coarser beaker pots that were decorated with finger-tip impressions and raised cordons and were tempered with grit. In the past, the thin-walled beakers received the most attention as they were found predominantly in graves, which were for many years the main subjects of archaeological research. The first comprehensive typological sequence for this kind of pottery in the Low Countries was set up in 1964 by J.D. van der Waals and W. Glasbergen.[1] Twenty years later a few minor points of their sequence were adjusted, when Lanting and Van der Waals demonstrated that the pottery of the Single Grave and Bell Beaker cultures in fact represented a continuous development (fig. 17.1).[2] This entirely novel view caused much surprise in Europe, as most archaeologists had always assumed that the different kinds of pottery had been produced by different groups of immigrants: first the Single Grave people and later the Bell Beaker people. Since then, this 'Dutch model' has been generally adopted in other countries, too. Recently the occupation period of the Single Grave culture has been divided into four phases of about 100 years each[3] on the basis of typological characteristics of the hammer axes, which closely resemble Scandinavian examples for which sound dates have been obtained. This new chronological division indicates that the changes observable in the stylistic features of the decoration of the beakers are of only limited chronological value.

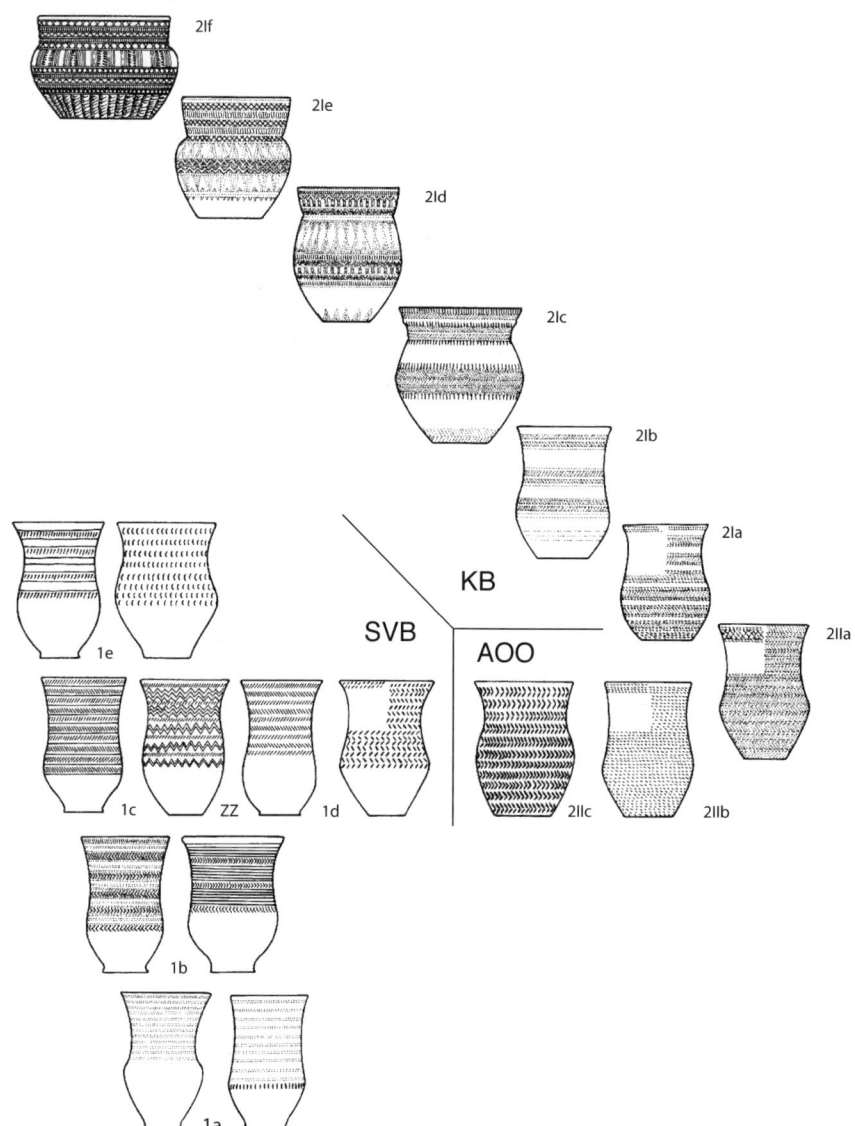

fig. 17.1
Beaker development, from the protruding
foot beakers and all-over ornamented beakers
of the Single Grave culture to the bell beakers
of the Bell Beaker culture, as presented by
Lanting and Van der Waals in 1976.

Thin-walled beaker pottery

Beakers started to be produced around 2900 BC. The first beakers were slender
vessels with S-shaped profiles whose decoration, consisting of twisted cord impressions, was limited to the zone above the belly. A little later, beakers adorned
with all kinds of grooved decorative motifs started to be produced alongside the
corded ware.[4] The decoration remained restricted to the zone above the belly until
2600 BC, when, for a short period of about 100 years, it expanded over the entire
surface of the pot, which retained its S-shaped profile. This is known as the 'all-
over ornamented' (AOO) phase of the Single Grave culture. Bell beakers, which
are characterised by bands of decoration alternating with undecorated bands over
the entire surface of the pot, started to be produced around 2500 BC. The decoration gradually became more exuberant, finally culminating in that of the Veluwe
bell beakers, which made their appearance around 2200 BC. The decorative motifs
consisting of lines and triangles with which the bell beakers were adorned were
executed with the aid of a fine-toothed spatula (fig. 17.2).

The lavish decoration disappeared in the Early Bronze Age, but, as Lanting has
demonstrated, this did not imply a break in the development of beaker pottery.[5]
The toothed spatula was replaced by an object around which a length of string

fig. 17.2

Detail of a bell beaker decorated with impressions made with a dentated spatula.

was wound, with which the distinctive impressions known as 'barbed wire impressions' or 'maggots' were produced (fig. 17.3).[6] This method of ornamentation remained popular from *c*. 2000 until 1800 BC. The barbed wire beakers mark the end of the beaker tradition in terms of pottery typology. After 1800 BC a different style of pottery started to be produced, whose squat shapes and crude workmanship suggest that they were not (drinking) beakers. These vessels have more in common with the coarse beakers encountered in settlement contexts from the beginning of the Late Neolithic onwards.

Coarse beakers and 'settlement pottery'

It is only in the past few decades that settlements of the beaker cultures have been discovered and excavated. Among the remains found at the first of those settlements were fragments of a different category of pottery, which had hitherto never or only rarely been encountered in graves and which was therefore termed 'settlement pottery' (fig. 17.4).

This category of pottery comprises pots that bear some resemblance to beakers as far as their shapes are concerned, but are generally much larger and more

fig. 17.3

Pottery with barbed wire decoration.

1 complete beaker that was found near the Renkumse Beek

2 detail of a sherd with a barbed wire stamp impression

373

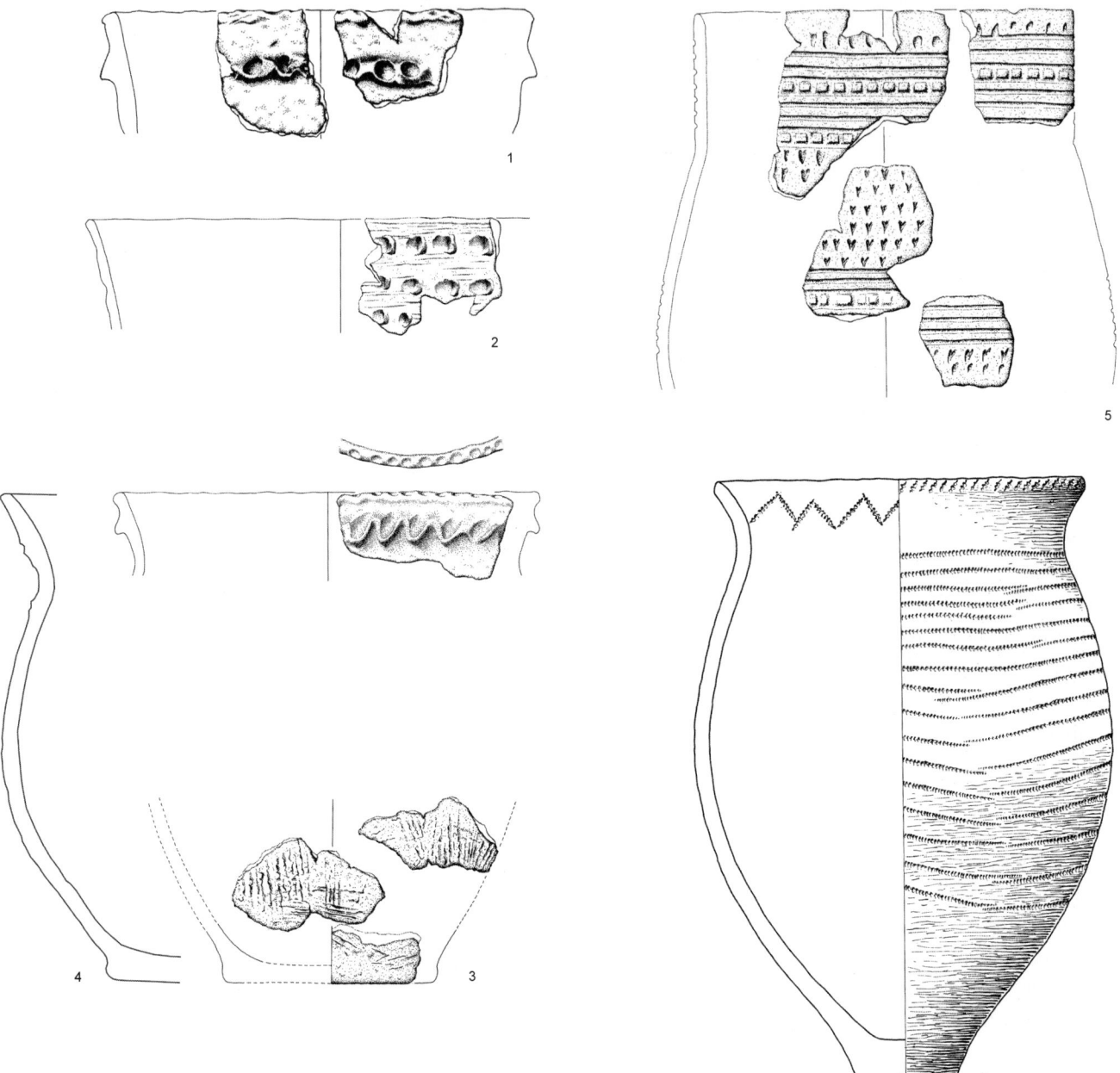

fig. 17.4
Settlement pottery of the Late Neolithic and
Early Bronze Age. Scale 1:4.

1-3   beaker with 'short wave moulding'
      (*Wellenbandbecher*) from the Single Grave
      culture settlement near Steenendam
4   complete profile of a *Wellenbandbecher*
      from a pit beneath a barrow near Putten
5   a 'pot beaker', Oldeboorn
6   a barbed wire beaker, Emmen

crudely decorated. Also these large types are widely distributed throughout Europe. The typical beaker pot of the Single Grave culture is referred to as a 'beaker with short wave moulding' as the rim and the zone bordering the rim are often adorned with a moulded decoration bearing finger-tip impressions. The bottom part of the pot is on the whole undecorated, like that of the thin-walled beakers, and often shows traces of scraping. Another characteristic that these pots share with the thin-walled beakers is the use of sand as temper. A type of vessels resembling the thin-walled pottery is encountered in bell beaker contexts. These vessels, which are known as 'pot beakers', are decorated with finger-tip and fingernail impressions, sometimes combined with grooves, arranged in zones over the entire surface of the pot (plate 26). A typological sequence has been set up for these pot beakers, too.[7] They were tempered with grit, like their Early Bronze Age successors, the barbed wire pots.[8] Only few of these are known, but then only one settlement has been investigated so far[9]; the lack of finds may therefore very well be due to insufficient research. The coarse beakers disappeared around the beginning of the Middle Bronze Age, but the production methods changed very little: the pot-

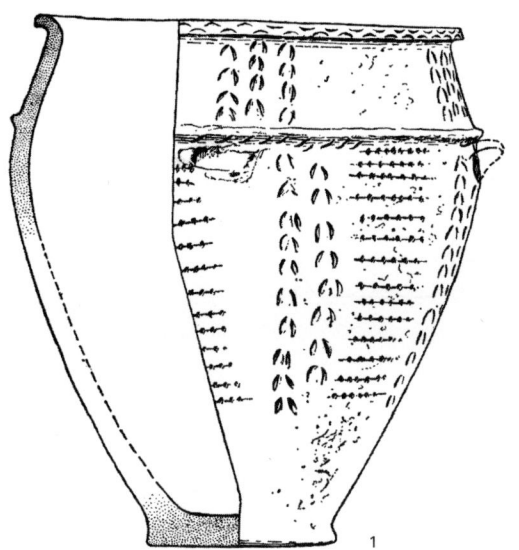

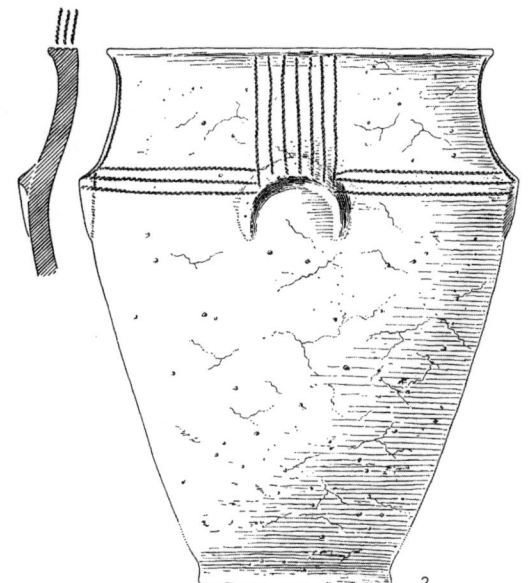

tery produced after that time was all crudely finished and tempered with grit or fine gravel.

Regional traditions in material culture become traceable again from about 1800 BC onwards, the beginning of the Middle Bronze Age. Characteristic of the northern and eastern parts of the Netherlands in this period is the Elp pottery,[10] the central and southern parts being characterized by the Hilversum-Drakenstein-Laren pottery. A different type of pottery was developed in Westfrisia: the Hoogkarspel pottery. The three traditions are closely related as far as manufacturing techniques are concerned: all three comprise barrel- or bucket-shaped pots with thick walls (sometimes up to 2 cm thick), tempered with grit and full of shrinkage cracks. In these respects the pottery of the Netherlands is no different from the bulk of the earthenware produced in Northern and Western Europe in this period.

However, the Dutch pottery does differ in terms of decoration, which is usually rare. Except for a few rare fingernail impressions, the Elp pottery shows no decoration whatsoever and for that reason no attempts have been made to set up

fig. 17.5

The urns from Vorstenbosch (1) and Budel (2). Scale 1:5.

The Vorstenbosch urn combines the shape and decorative motifs of early Hilversum pottery with impressions made with a cord stamp. Other aspects in which this vessel differs from early Hilversum pottery are the decoration of the surface of the pot below the shoulder and the absence of cord impressions as a decorative motif. The urn from Budel is decorated with cord impressions and has horseshoe-shaped handles. As far as the vessel's shape and the decorative motif are concerned, this urn is highly reminiscent of British examples, but comparable pots are also known from northwestern France .

fig. 17.6

Early Hilversum pottery from Empel (North Brabant) decorated with cord impressions arranged crosswise on the shoulder, fingernail impressions, reed impressions and raised cordons with nail impressions. Some of the vessels have small lugs. Scale 1:3.

fig. 17.7

Survey of the pottery from Hoogkarspel-Tolhek. Scale 1:10.

A (1-3) Hoogkarspel I (Middle Bronze Age B). Often fairly large, bucket-shaped vessels, tempered with grit and usually undecorated. A characteristic feature is a shallow groove beneath the rim.

B (4-31) Hoogkarspel II (Late Bronze Age). Considerable variation in types, including both fairly large biconical types and small bowls. The pottery is tempered with grit (thick-walled) or untempered (thin-walled). Decoration consists predominantly of fingernail impressions and grooves. A separate category of earthenware artefacts with an unknown function consists of discs with a central perforation (25-27) and perforated objects (24.)

a chronological sequence for it. Such a sequence has been established for the pottery of the Hilversum culture.[11] The earliest pottery of this sequence is decorated with a few rows of cord impressions beneath the rim and often has a cordon bearing finger-tip impressions on the shoulder. Another early feature of this pottery is the occurrence of horseshoe-shaped handles of the same kind as encountered on the Early Bronze Age pottery of northern France and Britain (fig. 17.5).[12] Other ornamental motifs besides cord impressions adorning the Hilversum pottery and also the Drakenstein pottery are fingernail and reed or bone impressions (fig. 17.6). The cord impressions below the rim disappeared around 1600 BC, when a barrel-shaped Drakenstein type decorated with a cordon bearing finger-tip impressions became the prevailing pottery type. Pots had been decorated in this fashion since c. 1800 BC already, but this form of decoration remained popular for far longer than the cord impressions, i.e. until in the Late Bronze Age.[13] There is also a category of vessels without any form of decoration, which, when encountered in graves, tend to be more bucket-shaped. Glasbergen was of the opinion that this type of pottery, which he called 'Laren ware', marked the end of the Middle Bronze Age sequence,[14] but evidence obtained in settlement research has proved this to be untrue. Laren ware, defined as undecorated Middle Bronze Age pottery, can consequently not be used as a basis for dating settlement remains.

After the colonisation phase, around the end of the Middle Bronze Age, a native style of pottery evolved in Westfrisia, which has been called 'Hoogkarspel ware' (fig. 17.7).[15] The manufacturing techniques of this pottery were much the same as those used elsewhere in the Netherlands, but the range of types is much wider and the decoration differs. Characteristic of the Hoogkarspel ware of the Late Bronze Age in particular are the finger-tip impressions covering the entire surface of the pot. The settlements of Westfrisia also yielded large numbers of spindle whorls, which are fairly rare at contemporary settlements outside this area, and conical objects whose function is still a mystery.

Funerary pottery and settlement pottery

Brief reference has already been made to the contexts in which the different categories of pottery have been found. Beakers with short wave moulding, pot beakers and barbed wire beakers are conspicuously absent in graves. On the other hand, the thin-walled beakers cannot be classified as typical funerary pottery as they have been encountered both in graves and in settlements. Indeed, they represent a large proportion of the pottery found in settlements.[16] The fact that thin-walled beakers are found in graves whereas beaker pots are not is in our opinion associated with a difference in function, the latter having been used mainly as kitchen ware and the former as tableware. If this interpretation is correct, the beakers that were placed in the graves may very well have contained foodstuffs or beverages, possibly intended to be consumed by the deceased on their journey to the other world. Indeed, some beakers found in graves still contained remains of food.[17] Pot beakers are sometimes found outside the actual grave, on the old surface beneath the mound or at the edge of the mound. Many pot beakers had been buried upside down, probably according to a burial practice that differed in some respects from the common practice known to us.

The pottery from the Middle Bronze Age shows no such difference between funerary and settlement ware. In the northern Netherlands the deceased were only rarely accompanied by pottery in that period and in the central and southern parts the same type of pottery as used in the settlements was also used for the burial of cremated remains. This shows that views on the burial of the deceased had changed in the course of the Early Bronze Age.

METAL PRODUCTION

Metalworking was certainly not invented in or even anywhere near the Low Countries.[18] The cradle of metalworking lies somewhere on the other side of Europe or in western Asia: in the ore-bearing Balkans and on the other side of the Bosporus in Anatolia. The oldest metal objects found in those areas – mainly beads and other ornaments – date from the 8th or 7th millennium BC. Metal tools and weapons made from hammered and cast copper were in common use in the Near East from the 4th millennium onwards. In the Low Countries, objects of metal (copper and gold) did not start to be produced until *c.* 2300 BC; they are associated with the

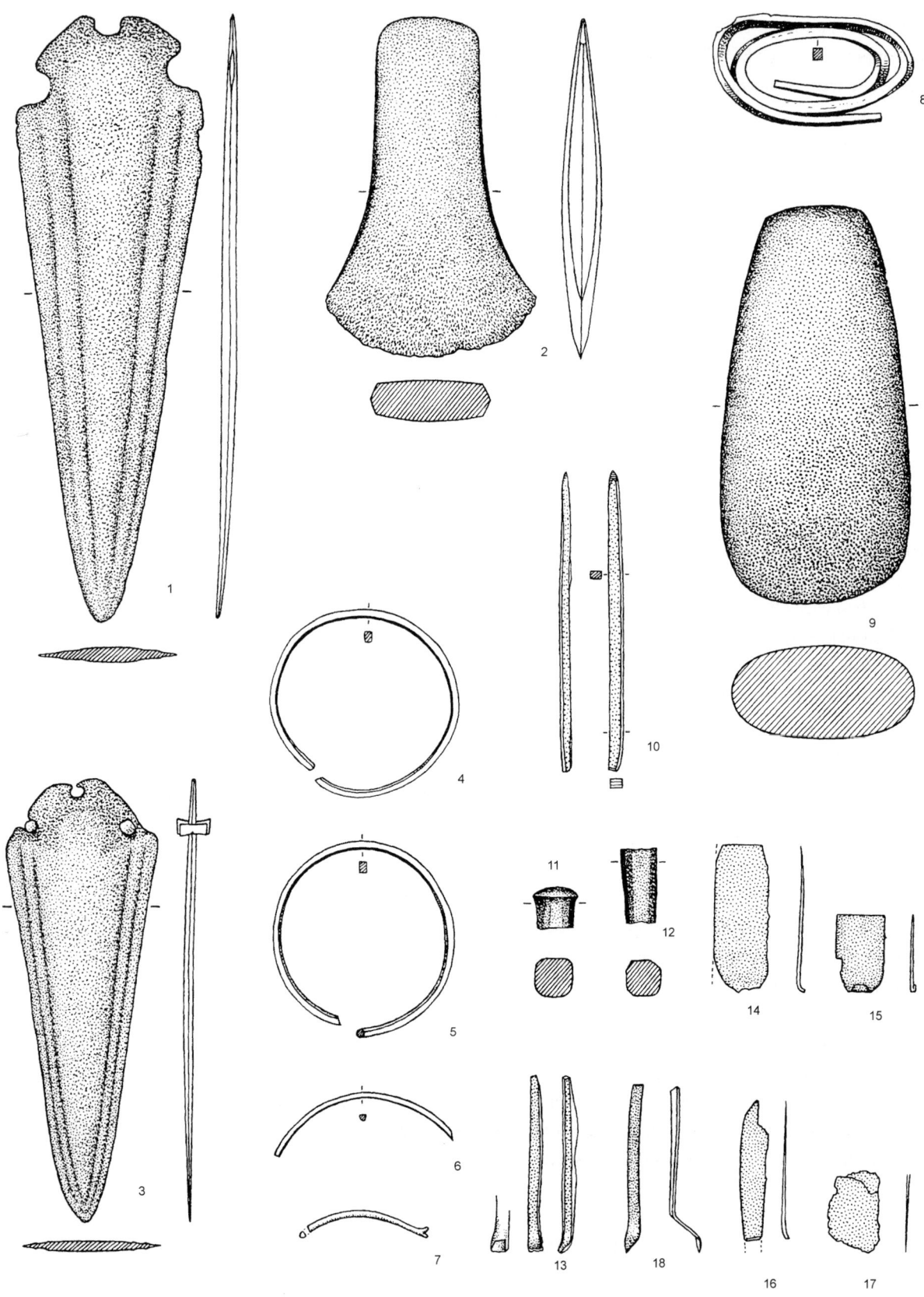

fig. 17.8

The Wageningen hoard, comprising objects made of copper and a stone axe, was deposited early in the Bronze Age in the Veluwe area, near the Rhine at Wageningen. The hoard was initially assumed to represent a travelling bronze smith's possessions. Although the concept of travelling smiths has meanwhile been largely abandoned, we do not have a good alternative explanation for this unique deposit. Scale 1:2.

1	halberd
2	flat axe
3	dagger
4-5	bracelets
6-8	copper waste fragments
9	stone axe
10	awl
11-12	unfinished halberd rivets
13-17	copper waste fragments

Bell Beaker culture.[19] The earliest metal hoard found in the Netherlands is that of Wageningen (c. 1900 BC). Besides unfinished rivets and bits of scrap, it contained various weapons and tools (flat axe, awl, dagger, halberd) and a few bracelets (fig. 17.8). They may have been produced locally from various types of copper imported from Central Europe.

Ore deposits and their exploitation

Copper

The earth's liquid core contains numerous metals. Via cracks in the earth's crust they flow to the surface, where they solidify, incorporated in for instance quartz and other igneous rocks. Prehistoric prospectors will probably have recognised outcrops of metallic veins by the white colour of the quartz and the bright colours of the oxidised metals. They indicated the places where the ore – the metal-bearing rock – could be exploited in open workings. When the parts of a vein close to the surface were exhausted, shafts had to be dug (shaft mining). At points where veins were intersected by running water the metals could be extracted by panning of gravels in the streambed. Sedimentary rocks, such as sandstone and limestone, sometimes also contain exploitable concentrations of copper ore, leached from the original veins. The first metal objects ever produced were manufactured from such readily accessible native (= pure) or oxidized ores obtained from outcrops.

Native copper ore and copper oxides found at the surface first had to be pounded with hammer stones to remove the adhering soil and rock. Then the metal-bearing components were ground with the aid of a grinding stone. The oxides were then mixed with charcoal and were reduced in a furnace by heating them to a temperature far above the melting point of copper (1083 °C). That necessitated the use of bellows, without which such a high temperature cannot be obtained.[20] Ores mined from deeper veins had to be subjected to additional processing because they usually contained sulphides. The sulphur had to be removed by roasting the ore in an open fire (artificial oxidation). Only after the release of this sulphur (in the form of volatile sulphur dioxide) could the ore be mixed with charcoal and reduced to pure or almost pure copper in a furnace.

A sulphide ore that was frequently used in the Bronze Age is the golden chalcopyrite. One of the main sources of this ore was the Mitterberg, to the south of Salzburg in Austria, where it was mined in deep shafts. So-called *Fahlerz* (brown or grey sulphuric copper ores) was also frequently used.

Other indications of prehistoric mining besides those in Austria (in particular on the Mitterberg) have been found in Spain (Rio Tinto), southern France, northern Italy, Ireland (in particular Mount Gabriel in County Cork), England, Scotland, Wales, Yugoslavia (Rudna Glava), Bulgaria (Aibunar), Anatolia, Cyprus and the Negev desert (Timna).[21] All these sites have been at least summarily investigated.

Tin, lead, silver and gold

Tin is much rarer than copper. Pure tin is usually reduced from tin ore (mainly cassiterite, SnO_2). Tin ore was won by panning the sand and gravel of stream beds, which had eroded from quartz and granite veins.[22] The tin that was – primarily or secondarily – used for the bronze objects that have come to light in the Low Countries is believed to have come from Cornwall and Devon. Objects of pure tin are rare. Well-known are the tin rivets that adorned the horn handle of an Early Bronze Age dagger found at Barger-Oosterveld (plate 28) and the tin beads which were found together with beads of faience and amber at Exloërmond (see below, plate

27B).[23] Both of these finds were recovered from the peat in Drenthe.

Lead and silver were used to manufacture objects in only a few areas in the Bronze Age (lead tableware is known to have been used in Anatolia, while silver objects have been found in Spain and other areas). No objects of these metals have so far been found in the Netherlands.

Gold does not oxidize and occurs exclusively in the native form. As it is also very easy to work, it was one of the first metals to be exploited by man. Being a very heavy metal, it could easily be separated from other types of stone in stream beds by panning. Gold does not become hard when hammered and does therefore not have to be annealed. It can be hammered endlessly and can easily be transformed into gold wire or gold sheet for the manufacture of ornaments, but it is far too soft for tools. The chief sources of gold in prehistoric times were in Transylvania and Ireland; gold was also found in some rivers, such as the Rhine.[24]

The composition of copper and bronze artifacts

Pure copper can be easily forged, but becomes hard and brittle when it is hammered. It can be made softer again by heating it (what is known as 'annealing'). By subjecting copper to alternating hammering and annealing one can shape it into ornaments, but also tools and weapons, providing they are relatively small and of simple design. Larger and more complex objects can be made by melting copper and then casting it into moulds. However, cast pure copper is soft and absorbs a good deal of oxygen, which makes it porous. It then has to be hammered for a long time. In spite of these disadvantages, large quantities of objects were made from pure or almost pure copper in the heydays of early metallurgy. They included both hammered objects and heavy, cast objects such as axes, hammer axes, chisels and battle axes.

By mixing copper with certain other minerals or metals, such as arsenic,[25] tin or lead – small amounts of which are sometimes already present in the ore – a so-called alloy is obtained, which is not only harder, but also less porous after casting. The mixture moreover has a lower melting temperature.

In the third millennium in particular much use was made of arsenical copper. Experimental research has shown that this type of copper can without any great difficulties be smelted directly from arsenical oxidized copper ore. Arsenical copper was used for manufacturing all kinds of objects, including tools such as flat axes, daggers and halberds and ornaments such as beads and pendants, in a very wide area, extending at least from Anatolia and the Caucasus to northern Germany, Poland and Denmark.

In what has been called the 'experimental period', c. 2500-1700 BC, more complex metal compositions started to be used all over Europe. It has been suggested that these new types of metal were a consequence of the development of shaft mining in zones of unoxidized, sulphuric primary ore. Besides copper, the ores from these zones contained other metals, too, such as arsenic, antimony, silver, nickel or combinations of those metals. Sometimes they were present in such concentrations as to give the copper the properties of bronze. A well-known example is the copper of the so-called 'Singen type', which was also used widely in the Netherlands in the Early Bronze Age.

Around 1700 BC tin-bronze – which is almost always an artificial alloy, because tin and copper rarely occur together in a natural form – became the standard alloy in the whole of Eurasia; it was to remain the most important metal for tools, weapons and ornaments until the emergence of iron technology heralded the end of the

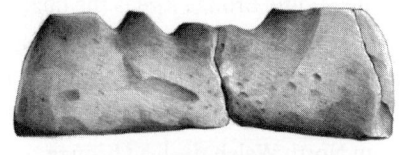

fig. 17.9

In 2001 part of a unique bipartite mould of a special fabric was found in a settlement pit near Oss (Horzak). One side contains the negative of a type of palstave with 'parallel sides', which Butler identified as native on typological grounds. That same side also contains the negatives of three tanged arrowheads which are sporadically found in rich graves. The other side contains the negative of a wheel-headed pin of a type of which two were found in a rich grave at Weerdinge and three more in the southern part of the Netherlands (see fig. 19.15). It was hitherto assumed that these objects were all imports. Scale 1:2.

Bronze Age, around 800 BC. The bulk of the tin that was used in prehistoric times is believed to have come from the southwest of Britain (Cornwall and Devon).[26] Between c. 1000 and 700 BC this tin was mixed with lead in some parts of Europe (e.g. southern Britain, Switzerland; in northern Wales from c. 1400 BC onwards). An alloy of bronze with tin and lead produces objects that are less hard than those of tin-bronze, but it flows better, which means that it fills the mould more easily.

It is interesting to observe the consequences of these developments in the Netherlands; as there are no natural ore deposits in the Netherlands, all the metal found here must have been imported.[27] The metal was probably imported in the form of finished objects or as scrap that could be melted down.

The early use of pure copper must have passed the Netherlands by completely; only one possible example of the use of pure copper has so far been attested. Arsenical copper has been found in the Netherlands mainly in the form of tanged daggers and other objects recovered from graves containing Late Neolithic bell beakers.

The Early Bronze Age hoard of Wageningen also included objects of arsenical copper (a dagger and a halberd) and of 'experimental' types of copper, but no tin-bronze. The earliest tin-bronze proper that has so far been found in the Netherlands is that of the low-flanged axes of British-Irish type and workmanship which came to light in the central part of the country. They were apparently imports. The native low-flanged axes of the Emmen type, which are encountered mainly in the northern parts of the country, consist largely of 'experimental' metal from Central Europe, in particular Singen metal.[28]

Around 1600-1500 BC tin-bronze became the standard alloy in the Netherlands too. An unusual find from the early part of the Middle Bronze Age is the hoard of palstaves that was found at Voorhout, in South Holland (plate 27A). Typological features suggest that almost all of the nineteen palstaves of this hoard – one of the largest ever found in the Netherlands – were imported from northern Wales; they were moreover found to have been made from North Welsh tin-lead bronze.

Casting methods

A great variety of different casting methods were developed in the course of the Bronze Age. The simplest method, which was used at a fairly early date already, entailed pouring metal into a cavity hollowed out in a stone. A major disadvantage of this method was that the cooling metal absorbed air and hence became porous. This could be prevented by covering the mould while the metal was poured into it. More complex objects could be cast in moulds consisting of two parts, in which shallow grooves were cut for the release of air and gases where necessary (fig. 17.9). Such moulds were made from heat-resistant types of stone, clay or even bronze. Any cavities required in the finished object, for example sockets, were created by placing moulded clay cores in the mould. Highly complex objects, finally, such as certain ornaments, figurines and ritual objects, were made by first modelling the desired object in wax. Wax can be easily modelled when warm and becomes hard when left to cool. The wax model was covered with clay and baked, during which process the wax melted and flowed from the mould. The cavity thus obtained was filled with molten metal, which was left to cool, after which the clay mould was broken away from the metal casting. This method, which is known as the lost wax, or *cire perdue*, technique, was being used for the manufacture of complex ritual and prestige objects in Israel around 3000 BC already.[29] The two small *cire perdue* bulls

fig. 17.10
Survey of various types of bronze axes that were common in the Netherlands in the Early and Middle Bronze Age. Scale 1:2.5.

Early Bronze Age 2000-1800 BC	flanged axe	1	low-flanged axe, Emmen type
Middle Bronze Age A 1800-1500 BC	flanged axes	2	*geknicktes Randbeil*, Sögel type
		3	high-flanged axe, Oldendorf type
		4	high-flanged axe, Oldendorf type Ekehaar variant
	stopridge axes	5	Plaisir type
		6	Vlagtwedde type
Middle Bronze Age B 1500-1100 BC	palstaves	7	wide blade, West European type
		8	regional type, with narrow midrib
		9	'plain' palstave
		10	arches on the side
Middle Bronze Age B (2nd half) 1300-1100 BC	winged axes	11	mid-winged axe (Grigny type)
Late Bronze Age 1100-800	winged axe	12	high-winged axe
	socketed axes	13	with imitation wings in relief
		14	Helmeroth type
		15	Plainseau type
		16	Wesseling type
Late Bronze Age (1st half) 1100-900 BC	socketed axes	17	with sawtooth decoration
		18	Nedermaas type
Late Bronze Age / Early Iron Age 900-600 BC	socketed axe	19	Geistingen type

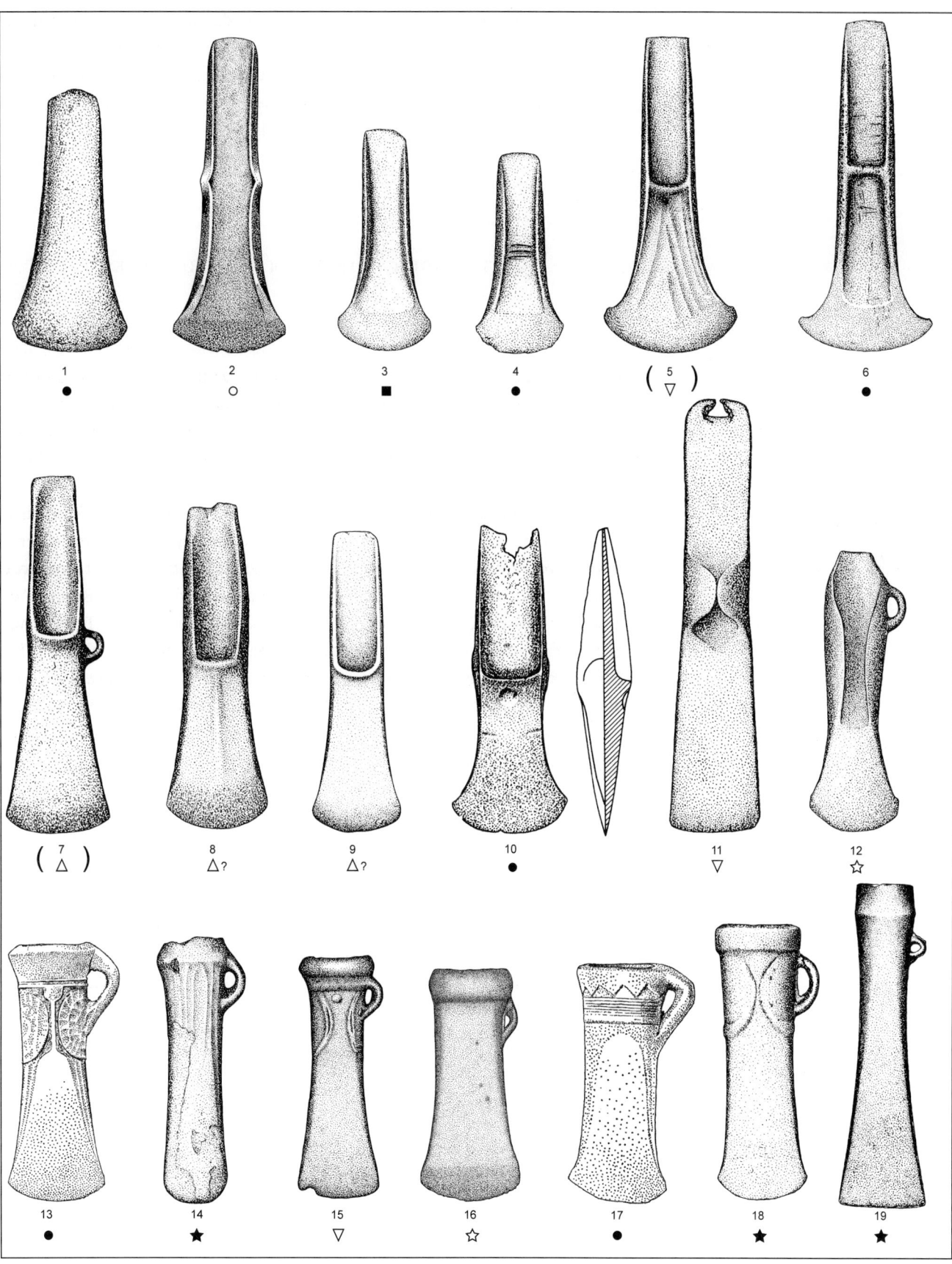

1 ●   2 ○   3 ■   4 ●   (5 ▽)   6 ●

(7 △)   8 △?   9 △?   10 ●   11 ▽   12 ☆

13 ●   14 ★   15 ▽   16 ☆   17 ●   18 ★   19 ★

■ common type

● local type of the northern Netherlands

○ import, predominantly in the northern Netherlands

★ local type of the southern Netherlands

☆ import, predominantly in the southern Netherlands, from western Germany

▽ import, predominantly in the southern Netherlands, from northern France

△ import, predominantly in the southern Netherlands, from western Europe

that were found together with a number of flat axes dating from the Copper Age in the hoard of Bytyń in Poland may have been produced around that same early date. In the Netherlands, however, the earliest indications of the use of this method date from the Late Bronze Age. A method that seems to have been used little in the Netherlands, but which was quite common elsewhere, involved manufacturing objects like bowls, copper cauldrons and buckets and weapons such as armour, shields and helmets from sheet metal.

METAL OBJECTS IN THE LOW COUNTRIES

Weapons, tools and ornaments of copper and bronze (plate 28)

The two copper coiled beads that were recovered from the hunebed of Buinen and a few stray finds of copper flat axes are believed to be the oldest metal objects so far found in the Netherlands. As the results of the analyses of the metal of these objects are rather ambiguous, it is however not clear whether they were produced in the TRB period or in the Early Bronze Age.

In total, about 2400 prehistoric copper and bronze artefacts have been found in the Netherlands. Only a relatively small number of these finds were recovered from graves. Rich graves are rare in the Low Countries; the few that have been found are moreover relatively poor when compared with the rich Bronze Age graves of Wessex (GB) and Brittany (Fr) or with the lavish Middle Bronze Age graves of Central and Northern Europe with their wealth of luxury objects. This difference may be due to a shortage of bronze in the Low Countries. However, the cause may also be of a more ideological nature: in some periods metal objects were not buried along with the deceased, but were removed from circulation in a different manner. The fact that a large proportion of the metal artefacts known in the Low Countries was recovered from rivers and swamps suggests that in these areas depositing objects in such watery contexts may have been considered more important than burying them in graves in the Bronze Age.[30] Bronze objects are only very rarely encountered in settlements in the Low Countries and no evidence whatsoever of bronze production (smiths' workshops) has been found, although a few Late Neolithic bell beaker graves have yielded hammers, anvils and other metalworking implements of stone (Lunteren, Soesterberg, Beers-Gassel, plate 25A). They show that copper and/or gold were already being worked in the Netherlands and that smiths were respected in those early days of metalworking. One of the few direct proofs that bronze was being worked in the Netherlands in the Middle Bronze Age is a single bronze mould; our assumption of a local bronze industry in that period is based entirely on typological evidence obtained in attempts to

fig. 17.11 (see page 385)
Bronze spearheads. Middle Bronze Age A
(No. 4) and B (others). Scale 1:2.

imports

1-2	socketed-looped and basal-looped spearheads from England	Veldhoven, Onstwedde
3	Tréboul type from Brittany	Witharen
4	Bagterp type from Denmark	Overloon
5	British socketed-looped, secondarily 'continentalized' by filing off the loops and drilling peg-holes	's-Hertogenbosch

regional types

6	flame-shaped spearhead	southern part of the Netherlands
7	'common' spearhead	all over the Netherlands

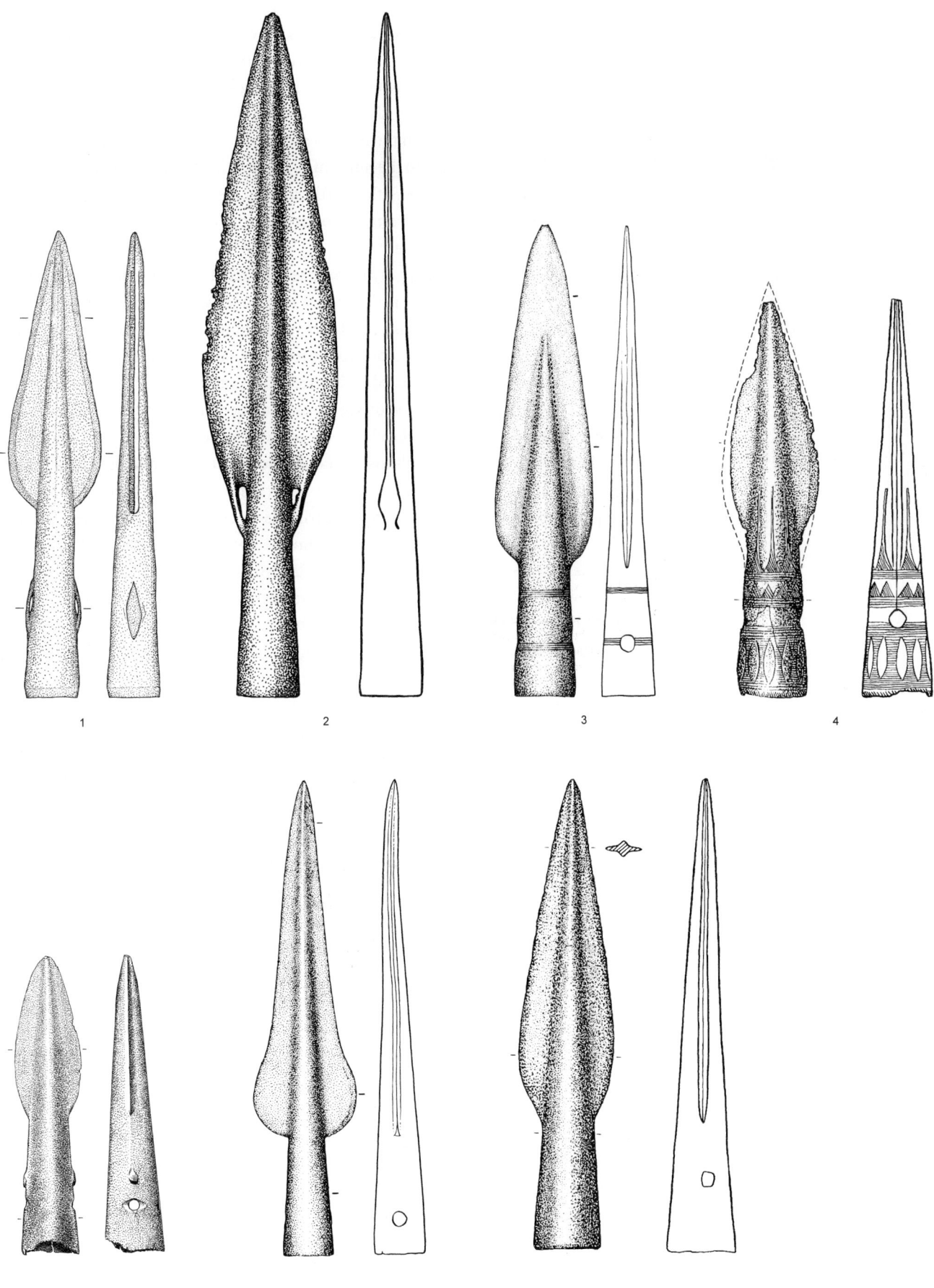

1   2   3   4

5   6   7

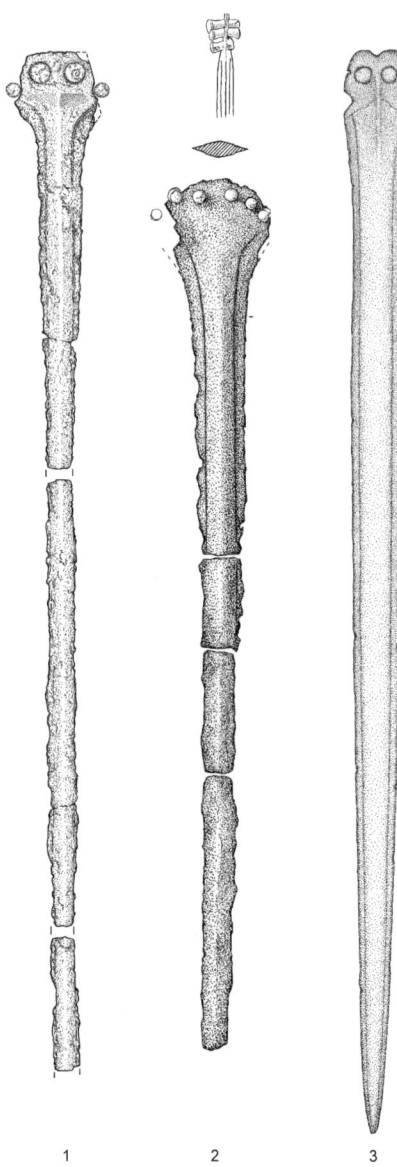

fig. 17.12

Middle Bronze Age rapiers from burials. The Meteren rapier was associated with at least two bronze arrowheads (fig. 17.16) and two bronze needles or awls. Scale 1:4.

1 Velserbroek (see fig. 19.6)

2 Zwaagdijk

3 Meteren

identify types that are absent or rare in other areas. In actual fact, the range of types that may have been produced in the Netherlands is only small. The majority of the approximately 900 axes that have so far been found here were produced locally (fig. 17.10). Regional differentiation is observable from the Early Bronze Age onwards. The British type of low-flanged axes are encountered mainly in the central part of the Netherlands, on both sides of the major rivers. The largest distribution area of the Emmen axes, which bear the closest resemblance to low-flanged axes from Westphalia, is in the northern part of the Netherlands. On the whole, there is a great difference between the flanged axes and palstaves of Middle Bronze Age date that have been found to the north of the major rivers and those that have been found further south: whereas the northern axes resemble types encountered in northwest Germany, those from the south are more like types found in England, Belgium and northern France.[31]

A second important category of bronze artefacts (7% of the total amount) is that of spearheads (fig. 17.11). They vary tremendously in size, from very small to extremely large specimens. The latter were almost certainly prestige objects. The spearheads found in the Low Countries are almost all socketed and have two holes through which pegs could be inserted to secure the spearhead to the shaft. The British basal-looped type of spearhead has been found only rarely. The 42-cm long basal-looped spearhead that was recovered from the peat at Exloërmond in Drenthe (plate 28) was almost certainly used for ceremonial purposes.[32] The socket loops of a smaller specimen from 's-Hertogenbosch had been removed and replaced by holes for pegs.[33] A few spearheads were imported from Scandinavia, for example the decorated spearhead from the hoard of Overloon.[34] Most spearheads are however so standardised that little can be said about their origins.

Few other types of bronze weapons have been found in the Netherlands. A few small copper daggers are known from the bell beaker period, but they are too small to be classed as weapons. An unusual find is the Early Bronze Age dagger with a horn handle decorated with copper and tin rivets that was found in the Barger-Oosterveld peat near Emmen.[35] Early Bronze Age daggers of flint (some of which were imported from Denmark or Schleswig-Holstein) are more common in the Netherlands than copper daggers (fig. 17.20).[36]

Rapiers were not to become popular until around the end of the Early Bronze Age (fig. 17.12). The earliest examples are associated with graves of the Sögel-Wohlde tradition, which are predominantly rich male graves. The richest grave of this tradition, which was centred around Lower Saxony and Schleswig-Holstein, is that which was found at Drouwen in Drenthe (fig. 19.11). In the course of the Middle Bronze Age the rapiers became longer, evolving into swords proper, and were produced in greater numbers. Most swords from this period were found in rivers or swamps; a few exceptional finds come from a hoard (Overloon) or from graves (fig. 17.13). Of special importance are two recent grave finds, brought to light in rescue excavations, containing long rapiers imported from southern Germany. One of these, from a plank-lined inhumation burial in a dune at Velserbroek, North Holland, had, in addition to the long rapier, a decorated palstave-axe of North German origin, probably a prestige axe rather than a chopping tool, and three gold wire earrings or hair-rings. These finds support the impression that in the Netherlands there were in the Middle Bronze Age warriors who were able to acquire scarce imported weapons and ornaments.[37] Some of the rapiers (those of the Rosnoën type) are believed to have been imported from western France (fig.17.14).

From a few exceptionally large examples we know that swords also served some ceremonial function; they were too large to have been used for the usual purposes. A noteworthy example is the excessively large sword that was deposited in a

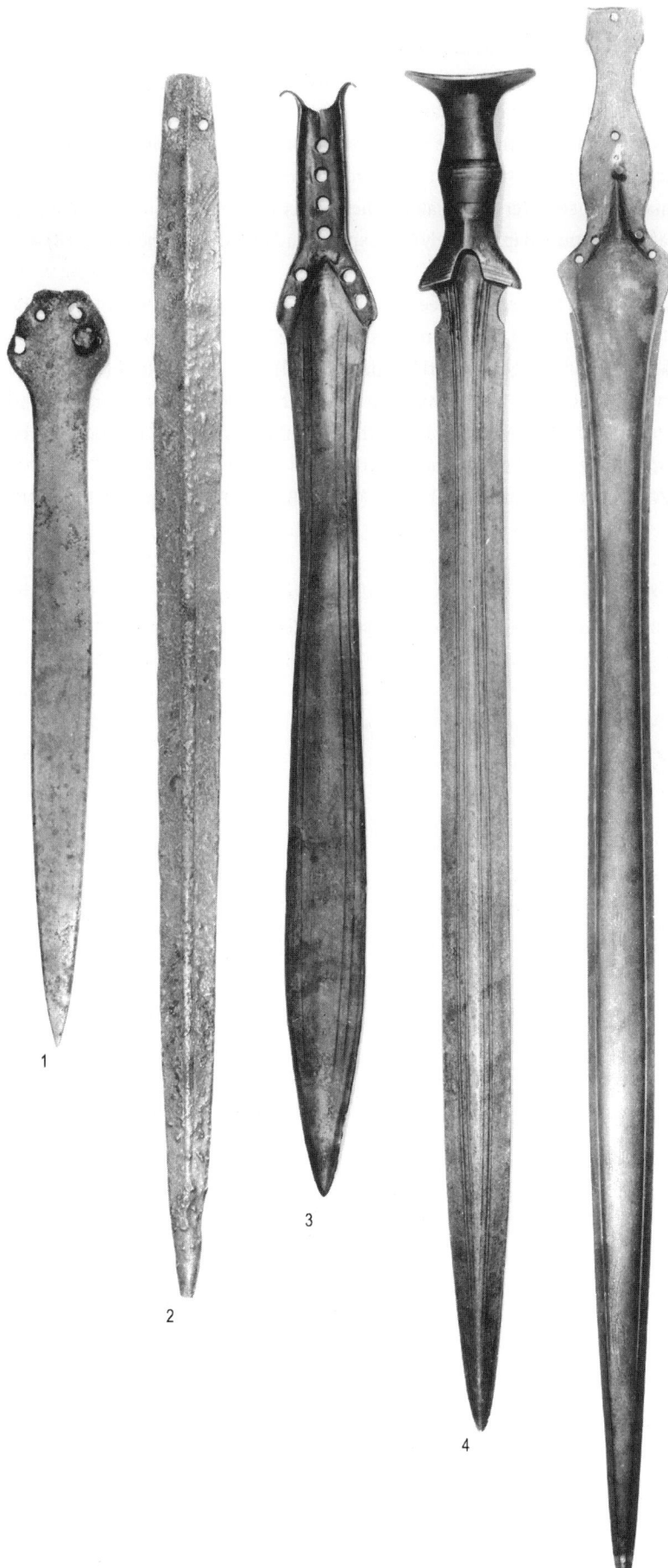

1

2

3

4

5

fig. 17.13
Rapiers and swords dating from the Middle
and Late Bronze Age from the (southern)
Netherlands, all dredged up from the river
Meuse. Scale 1:3.

Middle Bronze Age
  1 Wohlde rapier   Venlo
  2 Rixheim rapier   Stevensweert
Late Bronze Age
  3 *Griffzungen* sword   Venlo
  4 *Vollgriff* sword   Tegelen
Early Iron Age
  5 Gündlingen sword   Venlo

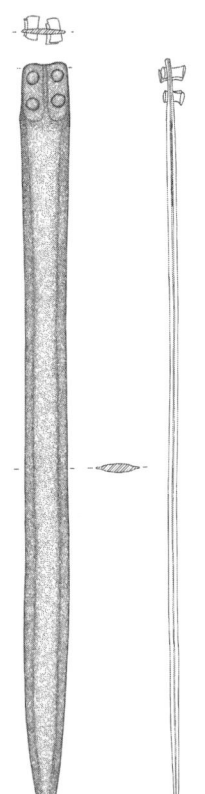

fig.17.14
Sword of the
Rosnoën type, found
in the valley of the
brook the Aa near
Den Dungen (N.Br.).
Scale 1:5.

swamp near Ommerschans along with other bronze objects, including a razor of Sicilian or Aegean origin.[38] An exact parallel of this sword is known from Plougrescant in Brittany; a smaller version was found near Jutphaas (plate 28).[39] A sword of very nearly identical form, decoration and size as those of Ommerschans and Plougrescant has recently been found in southeast England (fig. 17.15).[40] These objects were all produced in the same workshop (whether in Brittany or in southern England is unclear) and were all unfit for normal use. Apparently there was some exchange network via which such prestige objects, intended exclusively for ceremonial purposes, were circulated. The results of the metal analyses suggest that the aforementioned excessively large spearhead of Exloërmond (plate 28) was produced in the same workshop.

In several graves in Drenthe (Sleenerzand, Hijken-Hooghalen, Vries) and in the Betuwe (Meteren) as well as settlement sites in the Betuwe (Meteren, Eigenblok) bronze arrowheads (tanged or barbed-and-tanged) have been found (fig. 17.16). These finds show that for the Bronze Age society the bow and arrow continued to be an important weapon, whether for warfare or hunting, or both, throughout the Middle Bronze Age (see note 52 and feature L).

Bronze ornaments from the Early and Middle Bronze Age are rare in the Neth-

fig. 17.15
Ceremonial swords, apparently all by the same maker. Scale 1:4.

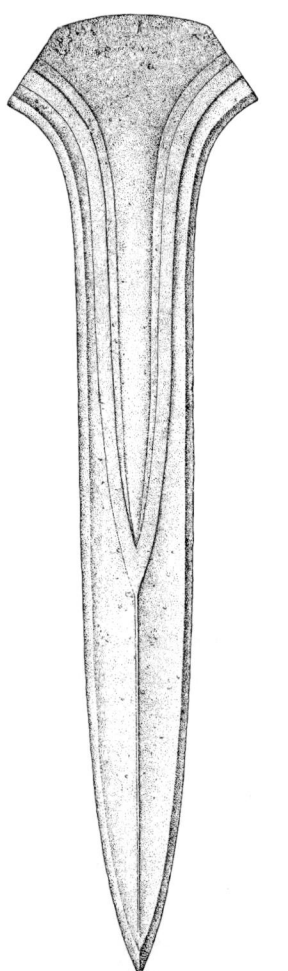

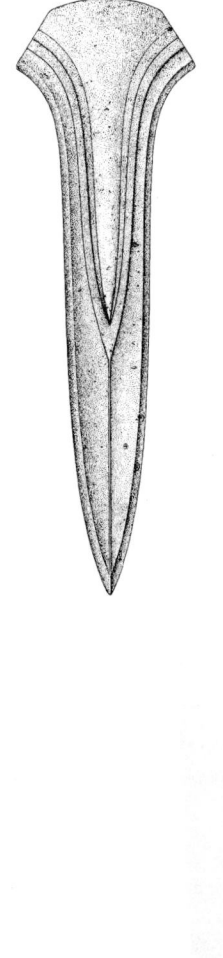

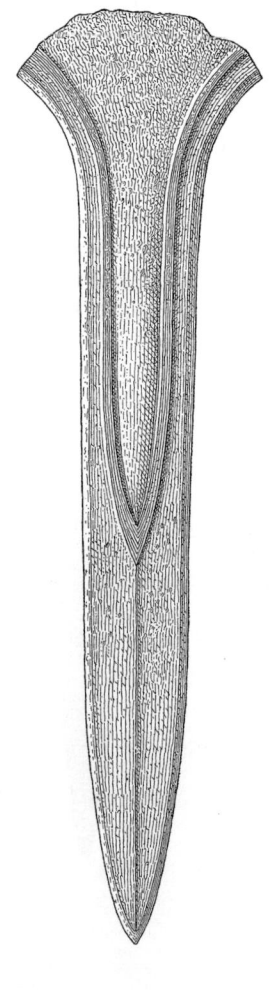

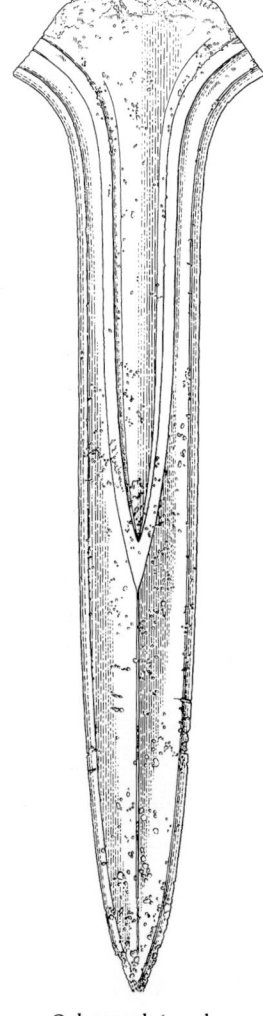

1 Ommerschans   2 Jutphaas   3 Plougrescant (France, Brittany)   4 Oxborough (southeast England, Norfolk)

fig. 17.16
Bronze arrowheads from Middle Bronze Age
burials. Scale 1:2.
1 Meteren-De Bogen
2 Geldermalsen-Eigenblok
3 Hijken

erlands. They are found mainly in graves, which are for that reason interpreted as female graves. One of the few examples of such rich female graves found in the Netherlands is that of the 'Weerdinge Lady', which yielded a string of amber beads, a bronze bracelet and four pins, including two with wheel-shaped heads. What makes this grave so unusual is that it contained a combination of objects that would cause no surprise in northern Hessen or Thüringen, but is in fact highly exceptional in the Netherlands. This led Butler to conclude that the 'Weerdinge Lady' was actually a 'Lady from Hessen', who had married a native chieftain.[41]

Gold ornaments

Among the bell beaker grave goods found in the central part of the Netherlands are a few ornaments made from lengths of gold wire whose ends had been flattened and then decorated with impressions. They include a pair of earrings (or lock rings?) from Beers-Gassel and a diadem from Bennekom. These ornaments may have been produced locally with the aid of stone tools of the kind known from Lunteren, Soesterberg and Beers-Gassel. Similar gold objects are also known from the British isles, Central Europe and Poland. A few Middle Bronze Age graves, for example at Drouwen and Hijken (Drenthe) and Velserbroek, yielded coils of single or double gold wire which were used as hair or ear ornaments. A necklace of four such double wire coils was found at Susteren. However, not one of the early gold finds recovered in the Netherlands is as rich as the exceptional treasure that was found in the peat near Lorup, in Emsland, just across the German border. Besides an amber bead, this deposit included no fewer than 34 gold coiled wire beads and pendants and two gold bracelets.[42]

All of the aforementioned gold objects that have been analysed were found to contain different amounts of silver, varying from 7% (Bennekom) to approx. 20-25% (Drouwen). This silver was probably not deliberately added to the gold, but accidentally mixed with it during the panning. In the Netherlands, the earliest objects of cast gold that also contain amounts of copper, deliberately added to obtain a harder metal, date from the Late Bronze Age.

WOODEN OBJECTS

Wood is only very rarely found in the sandy parts of the Netherlands. A few wooden objects have been recovered from deep wells or pits, but as only a small number of such wells and pits are known from the Neolithic or the Bronze Age, most of those objects are of later date.

Far more wooden objects have come to light in the peat regions, in particular in Drenthe. Although they were unfit for occupation, the raised bogs of these regions were regularly visited by human beings from the Neolithic onwards. This we know from such finds as the remains of bog trackways, a temple and the numerous objects that were deposited in the bogs, some of which were of wood.

Disc wheels

A remarkable category of bog finds is that of the solid wooden disc wheels, which date from a late phase of the Single Grave culture, c. 2500 BC. In total, fifteen specimens have been found in the peat of Drenthe (see fig. 16.1).[43] Almost all of these wheels had been made from a single piece of oak, which is why they are called 'disc wheels'. They were split vertically from the tree-trunk and were then shaped with the aid of adzes and hollowed out so as to create a raised hub at the centre.[44] At Midlaren an unfinished specimen was found, in which the hole for the axle had not yet been made.

Exactly how these wheels were used is not entirely clear. For example, we do not know whether they were mounted under two- or four-wheeled wagons, how the wagons were drawn or whether the wheels rotated with the axle or around it. The well-finished round hubs and the absence of a hole for a locking pin led Van der Waals to conclude that the wheels rotated around the axle.[45] Both two- and four-wheeled wagons were used in this period, so the wheels may have belonged to either.[46] It is generally assumed that the wagons were drawn by a pair of oxen, as illustrated by the copper statuette from Bytyń. Horses were not yet used as draught animals in those days.

Another interesting question is why the wheels were deposited in the bog within a relatively narrow time span. An obvious answer would be that they were dumped there, having become unfit for further use. However, only one of the wheels was found near a bog trackway (Nieuw-Dordrecht); several, including the unfinished specimen, had been deposited at quite a distance into the bog. That suggests that the wheels were votive deposits. Objects had been deposited in the bogs for many centuries already and this practice continued unchanged in the Bronze Age and Iron Age. Although only few votive deposits of the Single Grave culture are known, it is likely that the disc wheels recovered from the peat are to be classified in this category.

Bows, axe shafts and a 'hockey stick'

Various other wooden objects besides wheels have been recovered from the peat. Some of these are of help in completing the picture based on the stone objects recovered from other contexts: male graves of the Single Grave or Bell Beaker cultures sometimes yield stone shaft hole axes, arrowheads and hammer axes, but hardly ever the wooden shafts or bows with which they were buried. Those missing wooden parts have sometimes survived in peat. Two wooden bows are at present known, one from an unknown context near Noordwijk (De Zilk), the other from the peat near Onstwedde.[47] Only the latter bow is still intact; it is 1.70 m long and dates from c. 2500 BC. The bow from Noordwijkerhout, whose ends are missing, is believed to date from the Early Bronze Age.[48]

fig. 17.17
Stone hammer axe with a 70-cm-long handle of rowan wood that was found in a bog at Emmercompascuum. Scale 1:6.

Two other interesting wooden objects came to light during the excavation of the Late Neolithic bog trackway of Nieuw-Dordrecht: an adze shaft and a piece of wood that had been shaped into a kind of blade at one end, rather like a hockey stick.[49] It is difficult to determine the function of the latter artefact. Bottema, referring to ethnographic parallels, suggested that it may have been used to swat spawning fish, which often swim in shallow water.

Another rare find is the shafted hammer axe from Barger-Compascuum (fig. 17.17).[50] The 70-cm-long shaft was made of rowan wood. It projected through the perforated end of the hammer axe, which was not secured to the shaft. This find shows that hammer axes were used in very much the same way as stone axes, i.e. for slashing or cleaving. Whether they were indeed also used as weapons, as the frequently used term 'battle axe' suggests, is difficult to say. In view of their particular shapes and the fact that they were buried as grave goods, it is assumed that the hammer axes of the single-grave and Bell Beaker cultures were indeed also used as weapons.

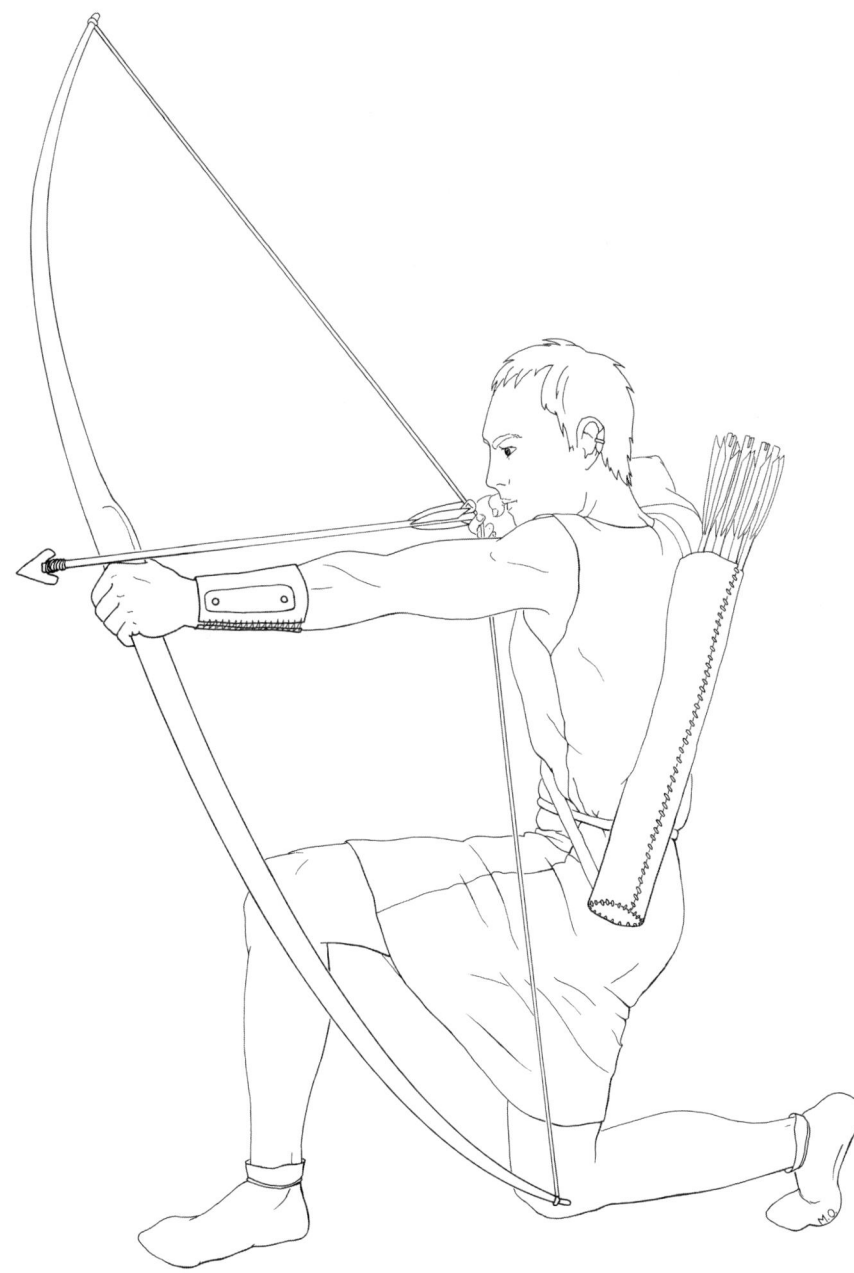

fig. 17.18
An archer of the Bell Beaker culture with a 'wristguard'. Contrary to the traditional interpretation, the stone 'guard' was probably a form of decoration worn on the outside of a leather wristband, which was the actual wrist guard. It was fastened to the leather guard with a thong or bronze rivets.

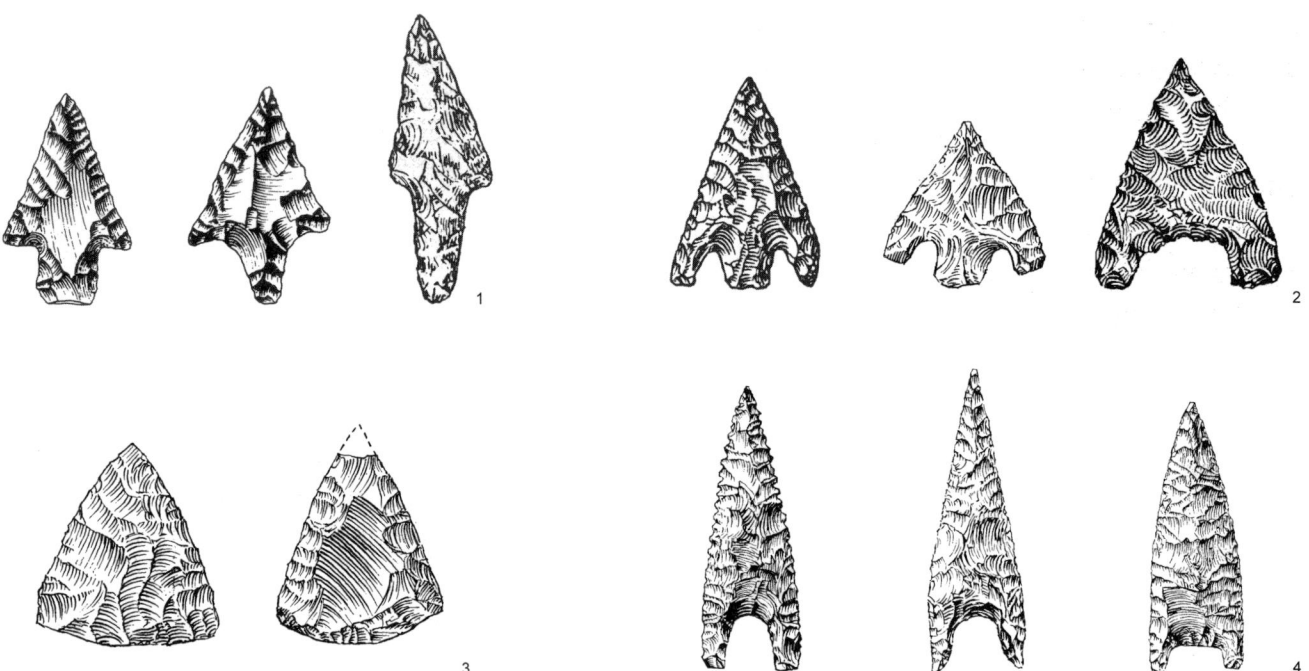

fig. 17.19

lint arrowheads from the Late Neolithic and
the Early and Middle Bronze Age. Actual size.

1	Vlaardingen group	Hekelingen III
1 right	Single Grave culture	Wijnjeterp
2, 3	Bell Beaker culture	Ede,
		Ginkelse Heide
4	Middle Bronze Age	Drouwen

WEAPONS, TOOLS AND ORNAMENTS OF STONE

Arrowheads and wristguards: the archer's equipment

The grave goods of the tribal communities of the Late Neolithic and the (Early) Bronze Age include a high proportion of objects of a distinctly warlike nature. Many of the deceased of the Bell Beaker culture in particular were accompanied by archer's equipment, comprising a bow and arrows, a wristguard and an implement for polishing arrow shafts (see fig. 19.10). Others were buried with 'battle axes', flint or copper daggers and, from the end of the Early Bronze Age onwards, swords, though all these weapons are found less frequently than archer's equipment.

One of the most curious objects associated with archery is the wristguard or bracer – a stone plate of a varying shape with two, three or four perforations. Most are of slate, which does not occur naturally in the Netherlands. It is usually assumed that these wristguards were tied to the inside of the wrist with the aid of leather thongs to protect the archer's wrist from injury due to the recoil of the bowstring when he shot an arrow. A trained archer would probably object that such a wristguard would in fact increase the risk of injury, due to the high probability of the string becoming caught behind the plate. It is indeed far more likely that the plate was worn on the outside of the wrist, as a kind of decorative clasp securing the actual (leather) wristguard (fig. 17.18).[51] That would also solve the problem of the wristguards with two or three perforations: it is difficult to imagine how they would have been attached to the wrist otherwise.

Another type of artefact associated with archery is the implement that is believed to have been used for smoothing arrow shafts and that is sometimes called an 'arrow straightener'. Occasionally a pair of such artefacts is found in a grave. In Late Neolithic contexts, these objects are found exclusively in bell beaker graves; the same holds for the wristguards.

And then there are the arrowheads themselves. These artefacts, which were made of flint, acquired a distinctive shape in the Late Neolithic. Those of the Single Grave culture are usually tanged, not barbed, whereas many of the Bell Beaker culture are barbed and tanged. The tanged type of arrowhead disappeared altogether in the Bronze Age (fig. 17.19). There was also a triangular type with a convex or concave base which started to be produced around 2200 BC. The characteristic type of the Middle Bronze Age is slender and barbed. This type is encountered in graves of the Sögel group, but has also been found in the southern part of the Netherlands.

The arrowheads of the Late Neolithic and the Bronze Age were carefully finished with pressure-flaked surface retouch. The greater attention that was apparently paid to the shape of the arrowheads in this period suggests that the weapons were not only used for hunting, but also – and above all – for tribal warfare.[52] Of interest in this context is the fact that they further support the impression that arrows were important weapons in Bronze Age society.[53]

Daggers and knives of flint

Some graves of the Single Grave culture were found to contain large flint blades that are interpreted as daggers or knives. The most remarkable are the daggers of (French) Grand Pressigny flint. Nine of these daggers have so far been found in the Netherlands (fig. 17.20, plate 29).[54] The blades of local flint are on the whole

fig. 17.20

Dolken uit het laat-neolithicum en de vroege bronstijd, grafgiften (1-3) en losse vondst (4).

Schaal 1:2.

1	blade knife	Single Grave culture	Sleen
2	Grand-Pressigny dagger	late Single Grave culture	Eext
3	copper tanged dagger	Bell Beaker culture	Ede
4	Scandinavian type	Early Bronze Age	Wollingboermarke

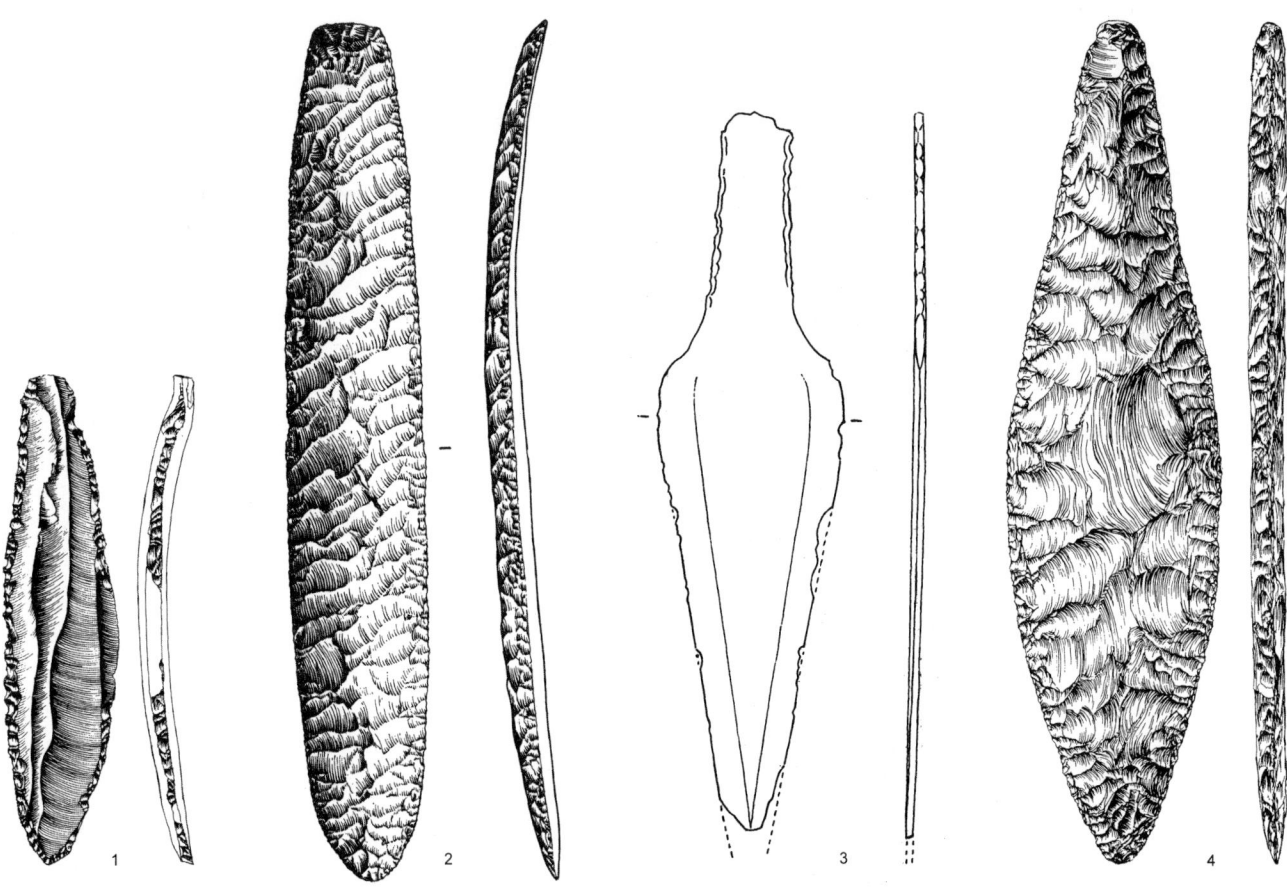

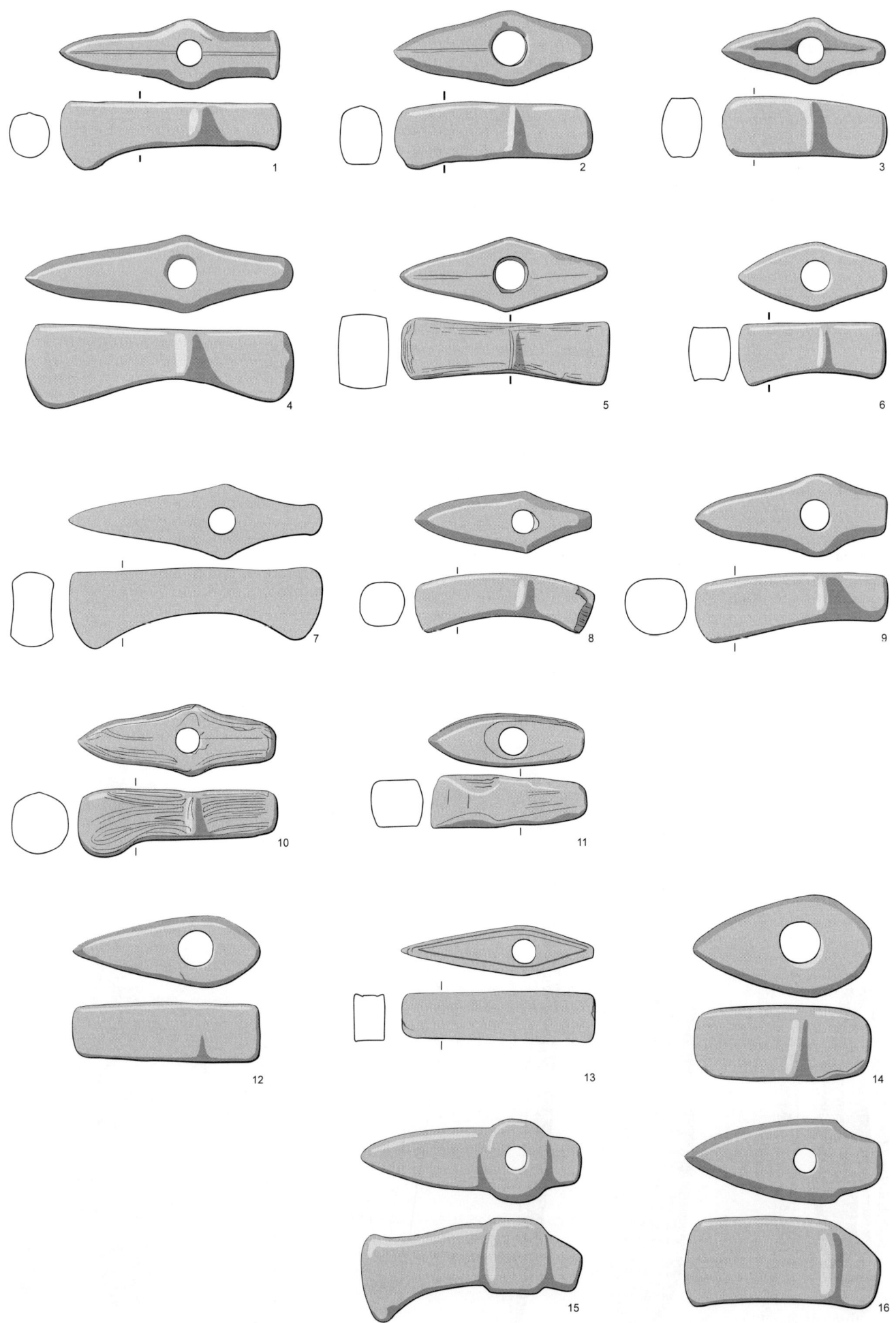

fig. 17.21 (page 394)
Survey of stone hammer axes from the Late
Neolithic, the Early and Middle Bronze Age
and the Early Iron Age. Scale approx. 1:4.

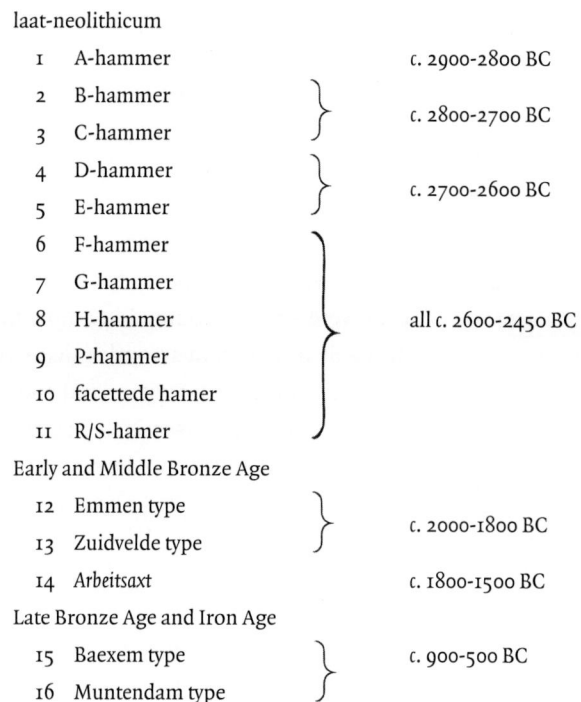

laat-neolithicum

1	A-hammer	c. 2900-2800 BC
2	B-hammer	c. 2800-2700 BC
3	C-hammer	
4	D-hammer	c. 2700-2600 BC
5	E-hammer	
6	F-hammer	
7	G-hammer	
8	H-hammer	all c. 2600-2450 BC
9	P-hammer	
10	facettede hamer	
11	R/S-hamer	

Early and Middle Bronze Age

12	Emmen type	c. 2000-1800 BC
13	Zuidvelde type	
14	Arbeitsaxt	c. 1800-1500 BC

Late Bronze Age and Iron Age

15	Baexem type	c. 900-500 BC
16	Muntendam type	

much smaller and less carefully finished; they are therefore sometimes referred to as 'pseudo-Grand Pressigny daggers'. This type is not encountered in the later bell beaker graves; it was replaced by small flint knives or copper tanged daggers.

In southern Sweden, Denmark and Schleswig-Holstein, where high-quality flint was mined on a large scale from the many flint veins that were to be found in the local chalk, large numbers of bifacial flint daggers were produced in the Late Neolithic and the Early Bronze Age. About fifty daggers of this southern Scandinavian flint – probably all imports – have been found in the northern and central parts of the Netherlands[55] – that is several times the number of early metal daggers found in the whole of the Netherlands.

Hammer axes or 'battle axes'

Although the Single Grave culture is in other countries also known as the 'battle axe culture', 'battle axes', or hammer axes, are in fact relatively rare; only about a quarter of the graves contained hammer axes and none whatsoever have been found in settlements. Perforated hammer axes have a long tradition which goes back to the Early Neolithic. However, that does not mean that they were always used for the same purpose or in the same context. During the period of the TRB culture hammer axes started to acquire a less practical shape. This development culminated in the frequently varying exotic shapes of the axes of the Single Grave culture (fig. 17.21). The latter artefacts can definitely no longer be regarded as tools; they were probably used as weapons in tribal warfare.

The practice of depositing hammer axes in graves came to an end in the course of the Early Bronze Age, around the same time that a comparable artefact made its appearance in settlement contexts. These tools, which were much coarser than the hammer axes and are assumed to have served a utilitarian function, are usually referred to by the German term *Arbeitsaxt*. By this time, bronze weapons had apparently replaced the former hammer axes in warfare. The *Arbeitsaxt* is believed to have remained in use until the Middle Bronze Age.[56]

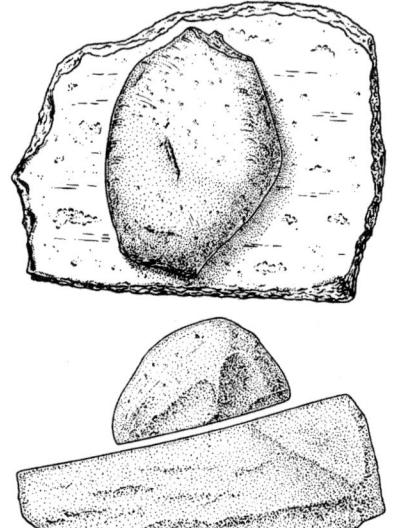

fig. 17.22

A granite quern from the Middle Bronze Age that was found at Hoogkarspel. Scale 1:8.

Stone axes

It is difficult to say what types of stone axes were still being used in the Late Neolithic. Flint and stone axes gradually decreased in size towards the end of the Neolithic. All of the axes from the bell beaker period that have so far been found in graves and settlements are relatively short (at most 14 cm long). This decrease in size may very well be associated with a change in the way in which the axes were shafted or in the purposes for which they were used. The large Middle Neolithic axes were simply mounted in a hole in the shaft, whereas the smaller ones were probably mounted in an antler sleeve of the kind found in large numbers in Late Neolithic contexts in Switzerland and northern France. These later axes have oval or rectangular cross-sections and are on the whole less carefully polished than their Middle Neolithic predecessors.

Metalworking implements

Four graves of the late Bell Beaker culture on the Veluwe and the hills of the Utrecht ridge yielded a small, but remarkable category of stone artefacts: small 'cushion-shaped' stones, which were used as anvils and hammers (plate 25A).[57] Only few parallels for these finds are known outside the Netherlands: a small number have been found in Germany (in rich graves), in Ireland[58] and in southern Russia. In the latter area such an object was found in a grave that also contained a few earthenware nozzles of bellows, which were probably used in a metalworkshop.[59]

The other objects found in the graves on the Veluwe clearly indicated that the implements had not belonged to full-time specialists or itinerant smiths: the deceased had been buried by their own relatives, according to local burial rites. The grave of Lunteren, for example, also contained a Veluwe bell beaker, a wristguard, arrowheads and a flint axe.

Querns and grinding stones

Querns and grinding stones constitute a poorly known find category. They are not often encountered in graves and are also quite rare in settlements of this period, of which only few have as yet been excavated.[60]

There are many different kinds of grinding stones, of many different sizes, varying from portable stones to large rocks in the ground. Most differ clearly from querns in that they are made of fine-grained sandstone, whereas querns are made of granite.[61] The portable grinding stones that were used for grinding or polishing stone axes are usually of a characteristic rectangular shape with rounded sides. Often, two of the sides were used for grinding or polishing the butt of an axe and the other two for polishing the cutting edge. It is assumed that these grinding or polishing stones were used until in the Late Neolithic, but none have been found in a datable context (fig. 13.8).

Smaller grinding stones have been found in Bell Beaker graves and in a few graves of the Early and Middle Bronze Age.[62] Among the objects in the aforementioned Ommerschans hoard were a few small stones which were probably used for polishing metal castings.[63]

Querns – or usually fragments of querns – are occasionally found in settlements. From intact specimens, some of which have been recovered from Vlaardingen contexts, we know that the querns that were used in the Late Neolithic and the

Bronze Age were hollow; the grain or other organic matter was ground in the cavity with the aid of a wide, flat stone (fig. 17.22).[64]

AMBER ORNAMENTS

From the Mesolithic onwards amber was in great demand for the manufacture of beads to be worn around the head or neck. One of the main sources of this fossil resin, which, on account of its static properties and its beautiful golden brown colour, was probably believed to possess magic powers, was the Baltic coast. From time to time, however, large lumps of amber are also washed up on the Dutch beaches.[65] The beads, conical buttons and crescent-shaped pendants of amber that have been found in a number of AOO and Bell Beaker graves may very well have been made from amber found in ice-pushed moraines or on the Dutch beaches (plate 25B). The beads from the Early and Middle Bronze Age, however, resemble types that have been found elsewhere, too, which suggests that they are imports. Objects of amber from the Baltic shores were also imported in other areas in Europe in the Middle Bronze Age. The fact that these objects were deposited in graves (or other contexts) indicates that amber was regarded as a prestigious material in that period.

Almost all the Early and Middle Bronze Age amber beads known in the Netherlands were found in the south of Drenthe, in particular in the surroundings of Emmen,[66] where they had been deposited in bogs or in women's graves. The best-known bog find is the Early Bronze Age necklace of Exloërmond (plate 27B). Besides beads and pendants of amber, this find also included beads of tin and faience, both of which are extremely rare in the Netherlands; they may have been imported via southern England. The beads of Roswinkelerveen and Emmer-Compascuum were also recovered from the peat. Amber beads have furthermore been found in relatively rich Middle Bronze Age graves such as that of Weerdinge (two separate interments), Emmerdennen and Hijken. Some were accompanied by bronze pins and bracelets or, in a few exceptional cases, a bead of glass or rock-crystal.

NOTES

1 Van der Waals/Glasbergen 1955.

2 Lanting/Van der Waals 1976a.

3 Drenth/Lanting 1991.

4 Drenth/Lanting 1991.

5 Lanting 1973.

6 Modderman 1955, Lanting 1969b.

7 Lehmann 1965; Lehmann inferred a development from necked pot beakers to pot beakers with an S-shaped profile. The beaker pot was probably a later development of the latter type (Lanting 1969b).

8 Lanting (1973, 252) uses the term 'beaker pot' for large to very large types from the Late Neolithic and Early Bronze Age. This term could also be used for the large beakers with short wave moulding.

9 Molenaarsgraaf (Louwe Kooijmans 1974).

10 This kind of earthenware was in the past described as Kümmerkeramik ('poor ware') because it appeared to have been poorly fired and was tempered with grit. In this book the less derogatory term 'Elp ware' will be used for this kind of pottery, which is associated with the Elp Culture, by analogy with the contemporary Hilversum ware, which is associated with the Hilversum Culture (Fokkens 1998a).

11 Glasbergen 1969, Ten Anscher 1990. Ten Anscher's classification into Hilversum 1, 2 and 3 ware is not used here because it essentially corresponds to Glasbergen's classification into Hilversum, Drakenstein and Laren ware. This is however not to say that we do not acknowledge the value of Ten Anscher's observations on the dating and typology of the Hilversum ware in particular, which are certainly relevant (see also Fokkens 2001).

12 This and several other similarities (see chapter 4) led Glasbergen to the hypothesis that the Hilversum Culture originated in Britain (De Laet/Glasbergen 1959, Glasbergen 1969). Nowadays the whipped cord ware and the pottery of the Hilversum and Elp Cultures are assumed to represent a continuous tradition.

13 Fokkens/Smits 1987.

14 Glasbergen 1969.

15 R.W. Brandt 1988a.

16 Kohlhorn (Van der Waals 1989), Oldeboorn (Fokkens 1998a).

17 Champion *et al.* 1984

18 For a general introduction (in Dutch) to the early use of metal, see Butler 1980 and the literature referred to in that work. The most important recent work (in English) on prehistoric metallurgy is that by Tylecote, 1992. Another interesting recent publication is the up-to-date, non-specialist, but scientifically sound German work by Steuer and Zimmermann (1993). See J.D. Clark (1991) for comparative ethnographic evidence. The Proceedings of the Freiburg Conference (Bartelheim *et al.* 2002) could not be taken into account here.

19 'Chalcolithic' literally means 'copper-stone age'. In the Low Countries this period is classed as part of the Late Neolithic, but in many other European countries a separate 'Copper Age' or 'Chalcolithic' is distinguished.

20 The copper is reduced (*i.e.* oxygen is extracted from it) because the oxygen in the copper reacts with the burning charcoal to form carbon dioxide ($CuO_2 + C = Cu + CO_2$).

21 For results of the recent explosive research into mining see *e.g.* Eibner 1982, Jovanovič 1982; Crew/Crew 1990, which contain many references.

22 Butler 1980, 113-130.

23 Butler 1990, 54-56, fig. 4.

24 See *e.g.* Hartmann 1970, 1979, 1982; Taylor 1980; Eluère 1982.

25 More recent works discussing the production and importance of arsenical copper are *e.g.* Bilgi 1990; Pollard, Thomas/Williams 1990; Frangipane 1985.

26 Whether any use was made of tin from Central Europe, Brittany or Ireland is still not clear. A Bronze Age tin mine has recently been discovered in Anatolia (Wilford 1994).

27 Butler/Van der Waals 1966, which contains illustrations and details of almost all the Neolithic and Early Bronze Age metal objects found in the Netherlands and provides the results of metal analyses and metallurgical data for some of those finds.

28 'Singen metal', or perhaps 'Singen-Nitra metal', which would be a more accurate term, is a type of copper that contains relatively large amounts of antimony and nickel and smaller amounts of arsenic and silver. It is believed to have come from the Alps and was frequently used in Central Europe in the Early Bronze Age, in particular by the representatives of the Singen, Nitra and Adlerberg 'Cultures'. It was also imported into the central and northern parts of Germany, southern Scandinavia and the Netherlands. For a detailed discussion see Krause 1988, 181 f.; and see Liversage/Liversage 1989, 1990; Liversage 2000. Some 40,000 spectral analyses have been published of metal objects of the European Copper Age and Early Bronze Age. Valuable detailed discussions, based on recent (and on-going) revaluations of this enormous material, can be approached with the help of (for example) the publications cited in Junk *et al.* 2001, 361-362, and Liversage 2001, 392-393.

29 Shalev/Northover 1993.

30 See chapter 20 for a further interpretation of hoards.

31 Butler 1963c. Butler 1995-'96 and Butler/Steegstra 1998-'99 provide complete catalogues of the Early and Middle Bronze Age axes found in the Netherlands. Comparision of the axe finds in the Netherlands with those of neighbouring areas has been made easier by publications such as Wegner 1996 and Laux 2000 for Niedersachsen, Kibbert 1980 for Middle West Germany, Vandkilde 1996 for Denmark.

32 Butler 1963a, 99 f., fig. 28.

33 Butler 1961a.

34 Butler 1990, 74-76, fig. 5.

35 Glasbergen 1956; 1960; Butler/Van der Waals 1966.

36 Bloemers 1978; it must however be borne in mind that objects of copper and bronze are less durable than objects of flint.

37 Butler 1969; 1986, 149-150, fig. 161-c; 1987b; 1990, 71-73 (Drouwen), 74-76 (Overloon), 94-95 (Velserbroek); Meijlink 2001, 2002 (Meteren, tumulus 'De Bogen').

38 Butler 1969; 1987b; 1990, 86-91, figs. 17 and 22; Butler/Bakker 1961.

39 Butler/Sarfatij 1970-'71.

40 Needham 1990; Briard 2001, 153-154; Fontijn 2001, 263-280.

41 Butler 1969, 114-116, fig. 51 (and photograph 12); 1979, 122-124, fig. 31 and 83; Butler 1990 (1992), 59-61, fig. 7. See Lohof 1991 for a more detailed version of this interpretation.

42 Tackenberg 1978; Wegner 1996, no. 203 (with colour photo).

43 Van der Waals 1964; Lanting/Mook 1978, 96. Six of the wheels were dated by means of ^{14}C analysis. It is difficult to calibrate the results because of their relatively large standard deviations; the average result yields a date of *c.* 2500 BC.

44 Van der Waals 1964a, 40.

45 Van der Waals 1964a, 45.

46 The fact that the wheels were found in pairs in three cases could imply that they belonged to two-wheeled wagons, but in one case (Gaselterboerveen) the wheels differed in size (Van der Waals 1964a, 48).

47 Clarke 1963; Brongers/Woltering 1978.

48 The narrowest range obtained after calibration of 3500 ± 100 BP is 2050-1610 BC (2 s). A probability of 68% (1 s) yields a range of 1960-1730 or 1720-1690 BC, *i.e.* in the Early Bronze Age.

49 Casparie 1984.

50 Glasbergen 1957.

51 This was suggested by J.N. Lanting, who was led to this hypothesis by the American Indian wristguards, which he saw while touring the US. They consisted of leather bands that were held in place on top of the wrist by a similar decorative (silver) plate.

52 Direct evidence for tribal warfare involving the use of arrows was found in the communal grave of Wassenaar (see feature L).

53 Butler 1990, 66, fig. 11a; 85, fig. 20; Meijling 2001, 407-409 with fig. 4, 424-425 (Meteren warrior grave); Hielkema 2001, 337-338, fig. 3 (Eigenblok).

54 Lanting/Van der Waals 1976a, Drenth 1991. Drenth is of the opinion that the true Grand-Pressigny daggers found in graves are insignia of the deceased's rank (see chapter 19).

55 Bloemers 1978, 47-110.

56 Lanting 1973.

57 Butler/Van der Waals 1966.

58 The Newgrange settlement from the Bell Beaker period: O'Kelly, M.J./C.A. Shell 1979, 127-144.

59 Butler/Van der Waals 1966, 74.

60 See *e.g.* Louwe Kooijmans 1974 (Molenaarsgraaf, Ottoland).

61 Fokkens/Schinkel 1990.

62 Butler 1990, 72, fig. 14:16 (Drouwen); 77, fig. 16:A3 (Monniken-braak).

63 Butler 1990, 86-91, numbers 17-18.

64 Harsema 1979a.

65 Waterbolk/Waterbolk 1991.

66 Butler 1990, 48-69.

I   Opening up the peat bogs
The timber trackways of Drenthe

Wil A. Casparie

Introduction

The expansion of raised bogs over large parts of Northwest Europe from *c.* 5000 BC onwards led to increasing compartmentalisation of the landscape. Vast environmental barriers were created as a result of the change towards wetter conditions. In the Neolithic the first timber trackways and footpaths were built to bridge the raised bogs or provide access to certain parts of them. These bog trackways are usually associated with the development of farming, from the Neolithic onwards. Many farming practices necessitated the trans-

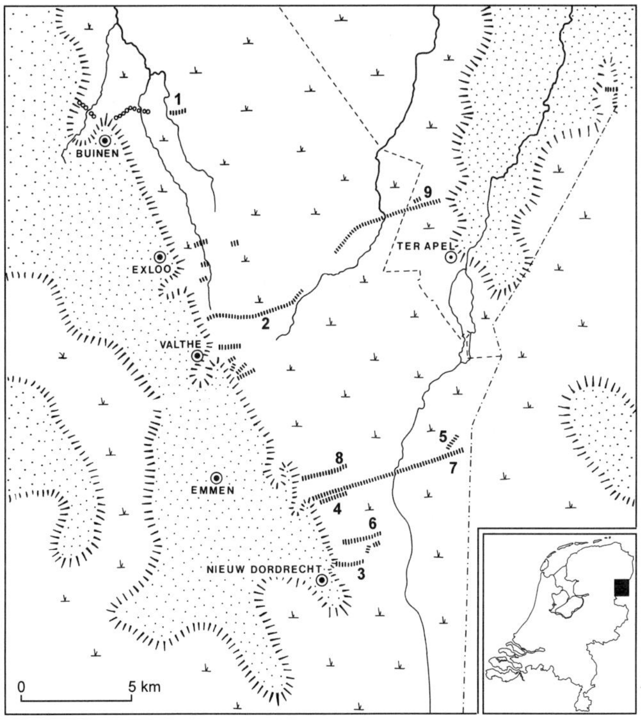

fig. I1

Wooden trackways and pathways in the part of the Bourtangerveen lying in the southeast of Drenthe and Groningen.

1 Buinen
2 Smeulbranden
3 Nieuw-Dordrecht
4 Southern footpath
5 Emmercompascuum
6 Klazienaveen-Noord
7 Northern footpath
8 Hurdle road
9 Valthe

portation of voluminous and sometimes also heavy loads between settlements, fields and pastures. That will have encouraged the construction of trackways and footpaths through poorly passable parts of the landscape, especially after the introduction of wheeled vehicles, around 3500 BC.[1]

The aim of the bog trackways was to enable people and animals to pass through the wet and poorly accessible bogs. This was done by creating a (large) supporting surface of timber which greatly reduced the pressure exerted by the person, cattle or vehicle moving across the soft marshy ground.

Timber trackways have been found in most peat bog regions in Northwest Europe. More than 2000 of such trackways are now known in Ireland.[2] A large number of trackways found in the wetlands of Somerset Levels in southwest England have been investigated.[3] Over 300 trackways and footpaths have been recorded in northwest Germany[4] and a small number have been excavated in Denmark.[5]

A modest total of slightly more than ten timber trackways (wider than 2.5 m) and footpaths (narrower than 1 m) have been well investigated in the area of the former raised bogs in the northeast of the Netherlands.[6] We have reports of a greater number of finds described as trackways, but in many cases it is doubtful whether the observed remains indeed represent a trackway or footpath. It is likely that not more than twenty trackways were constructed in the raised bogs in the northeastern part of the Netherlands in prehistoric times. Most of those trackways came to light in the part of the Bourtangerveen lying between southeast Drenthe and eastern Groningen (fig. I.1).

Renewed investigation of trackways, excavated long ago, indicates the onset of trackway construction in the Middle Neolithic B period. The trackways of Buinen and Smeulbranden (for a long time wrongly conceived as a 'northern branch' of the Valthe trackway) date from the period 3400-3100 BC. They can be attributed to the Funnel Beaker culture (fig. I.2).[7] In Ireland, England and northern Germany much older trackways are encountered, dating back to the beginning of the 4th millennium.[8]

Methods of construction (plates 30, 31)

Timber trackways mostly consist of a substructure or foundation and a surface layer. Sometimes the surface was covered

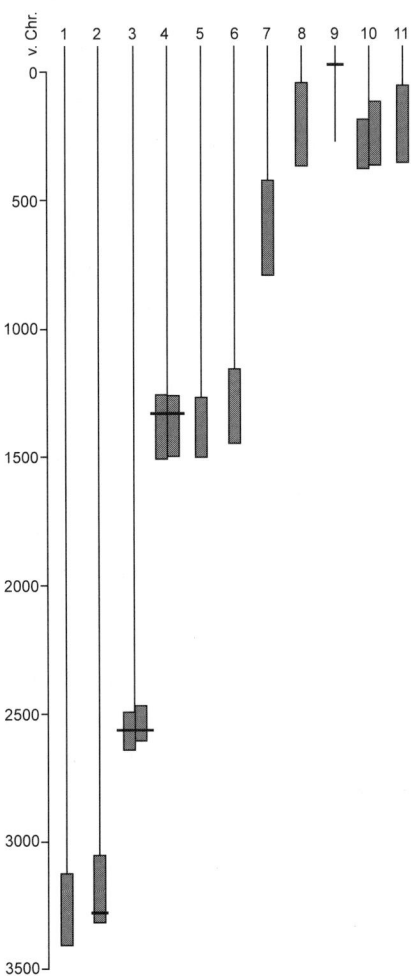

fig. 12

Dendrochronological and calibrated ¹⁴C dates obtained for the Dutch prehistoric wooden trackways. The dendrochronological dates are indicated by a line. The names commonly used for the trackways and their documentation codes are as follows:

1 Buinen   XII (Bou)
2 Smeulbranden   XXIX (Bou)
3 Nieuw-Dordrecht   XXI (Bou)
4 Southern footpath   XVII (Bou)
5 Emmercompascuum   XVI (Bou)
6 Klazienaveen-Noord XVIII (Bou)
7 Northern footpath   XV (Bou)
8 Hurdle road   XIV (Bou)
9 Valthe   I (Bou)
10 Smilde 1   I (Sm)
11 Hellendoorn   II (Eng)

with sods or small pieces of wood (fig. I.3). These structural elements were arranged horizontally. Pegs struck vertically into the peat prevented the risk of the structure sliding away or anchored the trackway to the surface of the bog; such pegs started to be used in the Bronze Age. The considerable differences in the methods of construction of the trackways and footpaths reflect the builders' great inventiveness in finding solutions to the problem of the impassability of the bogs (fig. I.4).

In most cases the substructure and the surface were built from planks or round timber, which was sometimes split. Woven mats (hurdles) were also used for the surface of the trackways (fig. I.6), while fascines sometimes served as the foundations. The elements of the surface layer were usually arranged close together, almost always in a direction perpendicular to that of the elements of the substructure, which were usually less carefully arranged. Some of the trackways have no substructure.

The larger the supporting surface, the greater the structure's stability. It was however not possible to achieve sufficient stability simply by using large amounts of timber, because then the structure would have become too heavy to have been supported by the marshy ground. No nailed joints have been found in the Netherlands. It may have been technically feasible to build rigid structures with large supporting capacity, but the bog's spongy structure (causing an effect known as *Mooratmung*) and the great variations in the bog surface's supporting capacity (due to the presence of hummocks and hollows) presented fundamental problems.

At Nieuw-Dordrecht small planks (slabs) had been used to smooth the Late Neolithic trackway surface. Whether this was also the case with the trackway known as the 'Buinerbrug' and the Smeulbranden track, we don't know. Even there where attempts were made to level the surface, riding across the trackway will have been most uncomfortable. The Bronze Age and Iron Age plank footpaths were good – if sometimes rather narrow (30 cm) – passageways, but as stretches of those footpaths often lay beneath the bog's water level the people who used them will have run the risk of getting their feet wet. The Bronze Age footpath of Klazienaveen-North (fig. I.5), with a negotiable width of over 50 cm, was very stable and lay above the bog's water level, but as it

fig. 13

The trackway Smilde 1 (Iron Age) after the removal of the overlying peat sods, 1983 excavation.

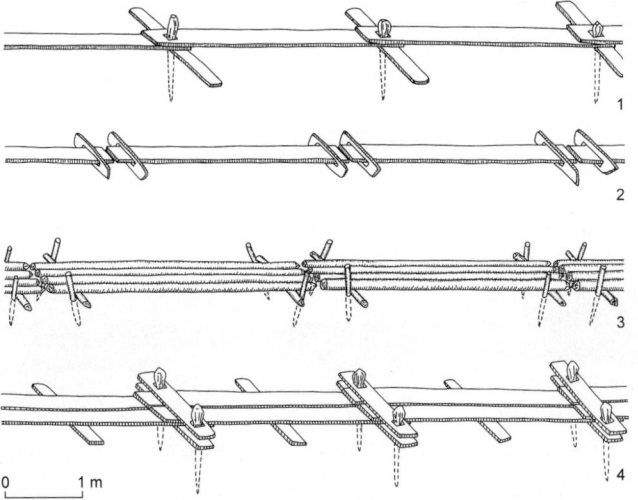

fig. l4

Structures of the four wooden foot paths in the southeastern part of
Drenthe, dating from the Middle Bronze Age (1-3) and the Early iron
Age (4).

1 Southern footpath
2 Emmercompascuum
3 Klazienaveen-Noord
4 Northern footpath

was made from longitudinally arranged round timber it will
have been difficult to negotiate.

The surface of the Buinen and Smeulbranden tracks consisted largely of thick round wood and a number of wide
planks.[7] These trackways can hardly have been fit for use
without a thick covering layer of for example sods. The surface of the 'Valthe bridge', excavated by J.W. Karsten in 1818
(the first excavation of a bog trackway in the Netherlands),
was made of carefully dressed planks.[8] This stretch must
have been suitable for vehicles having wheels with spokes.
The Emmerschans trackway, made from hurdles on a loose
frame of round timber, had a remarkably 'floating' surface,
which originally lay more than 15 cm above the surface of the
bog (fig. I.6). With its width of 2.8 m, the trackway was wide
enough for vehicles, but it is unlikely that any vehicles rode
over it because hurdles have little supporting capacity.

Prehistoric infrastructure?

An interesting question is whether the bog trackways formed
part of a road network. This seems to have been the case in
the northwest of Germany in 713 BC, at the beginning of the
Iron Age.[9] The regional road system in question may have
originated around the end of the Neolithic already. The landscape in that area was suitable for the development of such
a system, more so than in the northeast of the Netherlands.
A trackway, dated to 148 BC, crossing several bogs, has also

been found in the wetlands of central Ireland, but it is not yet
certain whether it formed part of an actual road system.[10]

Hardly any evidence for through trackways has been found
in the northeast of the Netherlands. Most of the trackways
in this region could have been used for only a short period
of time before they became overgrown. The small number
of finds that have been discovered along most of the trackways also indicates this. The majority, certainly the Neolithic
trackways of Smeulbranden, Buinen and Nieuw-Dordrecht
and the three Middle Bronze Age footpaths did not extend to
the other sides of the raised bogs. Nos. 4, 5, 6 and 8 probably
provided access to sources of bog iron ore.

The trackways that were built in the Iron Age suggest that
a (through?) road system did exist in this period. The northern plank footpath found in the Bourtangerveen may have
led to the eastern end of that bog, but the path was severely
damaged by erosion in the bog shortly after its construction,
after which large parts were made unfit for further use. At
first sight, the remains of the trackway called the 'Valtherbrug' seem to represent what must have been an imposing
connecting route. This trackway probably did not bridge the
entire about 12 km wide bog. It seems, moreover, likely it
concerns two different trackways, considering the two wig-
gle matching dates (c.16 BC and c.112 AD).

The two trackways found at Smilde measured 280 and 170
m. They formed part of an approximately 9-km-long traffic

fig. l5

Pathway, constructed from tree-trunks, positioned lengthwise and
fixed in the peat with wooden pegs, dating from the Middle Bronze
Age. Klazienaveen-Noord. 1930 excavation.

fig. 16
The Hurdle Road at Emmerschans, constructed from willow hurdles and dated to the Late Iron Age, 1962 excavation.

route that extended over sand ridges along the eastern edge of the Smilde bogs. They bridged two peat-filled depressions.

The use and production of timber, woodland management

Large quantities of timber were required to construct bog trackways: about 40 hectares of woodland were needed to build one kilometre of trackway.[11] With the exception of narrow zones of woods along their margins, the raised bogs were entirely devoid of trees. The timber that was used to build most of the bog trackways came from the higher sands.

It can be assumed for the two Middle Neolithic trackways of Buinen and Smeulbranden that the natural virgin forest was used for the wood supply. The felled areas can be estimated at 30 and 100 hectares, respectively. For the Late Neolithic Nieuw-Dordrecht trackway, initially forest stands separating (deserted) arable fields were felled, followed by secondary woodland on coversand and boulder clay, and at last bog margin forest, altogether over about 40 hectares.

There is an apparent shortage of timber wood, at least on the upland.

fig. 17
The 'Buinen trackway'. Its relatively high age was already assumed during the excavation in 1911, but this has been established only recently by means of a number of ^{14}C dates: between 3500 and 3200 cal BC, i.e. Funnel Beaker culture.

The plank footpaths from the Bronze Age and the Iron Age were made from oaks with diameters of 40-45 cm. The heartwood was used for the surface planks. The transversals and the pegs were made mostly from sapwood. According to Hayen's data on the amounts of timber required for trackway construction, about 21 hectares of woodland were needed to build footpath No. 4. An area of about 120 hectares may have been required for the construction of the more substantial and longer Iron Age footpath No. 7. In both cases no primeval wood was available in the vicinity, because by c. 1700 BC this whole area had been brought into cultivation. The fact that oak trees of a certain thickness had been selected for the planks points to woodland management or the import of timber from areas further away. There is no direct evidence for woodland management.

The Bronze Age footpath No. 6 was made from approximately 12-cm-thick bog pines – trees which grew extremely slowly. The pine forest, which may have measured 20 to 30 hectares, probably developed after the bog had dried out for a short while.

If the Valtherbrug was a single trackway with a length of at least 4 km, some 3000 trees will have gone into its construction, mainly oaks, alders and hazels. That corresponds to about 150 hectares of woodland. There can be no doubt that the construction of this type of trackways was based on a carefully planned supply of timber, which is a convincing indication of woodland management.

The surface and substructure of the short trackways of Smilde were made from alder wood which was covered with heather sods. The wood came from badly grown trees along the margins of the bogs. Osiers had been used specially for the construction of the hurdle trackway (fig. I.6). The osier thickets must have measured at least 18 hectares in the case of a four-year rotation cycle, which would imply a form of management which was in principle not different from present-day osier culture. We may assume that woodland was being managed in this manner in this area before 300 BC already.

Notes

1   Hayen 1987, 210-211.
2   Several dozens have been excavated by B. Raftery (e.g. 1990, 1996).
3   Coles et al. 1975-1989.
4   Hayen 1985, 1989.
5   Investigated by M. Schou Jorgensen (personal communication).
6   Casparie 1987. This publication presents a survey of the literature providing the most information on bog trackways, on which this feature is based. No reference will therefore be made to that literature here. See also Van der Sanden 2002d and Casparie et al. 2004.
7   Van der Sanden 2002d.
8   Raftery 1990, 1996; Coles et al. 1975-'89; Bauerochse/Metzler 2001.
9   Van Zeist 1958, fig. 16.
10 Van Zeist 1958, fig. 9-11.
11 Hayen 1985, 29.
12 Raftery 1990, 1996.
13 H. Hayen, personal communication.

18 Longhouses in unsettled settlements Settlements in Beaker period and Bronze Age

Harry Fokkens

As far as we know, the structure of settlements changed very little in the Late Neolithic. What did change was the subsistence system of the occupants of these settlements: innovations in farming practices that had been introduced in the Middle Neolithic, such as the use of *ards* and wagons, were commonly accepted in the Late Neolithic. From 3000 BC onwards the economy became increasingly dependent on cereal cultivation and stock keeping, although hunting and fishing remained important. In the course of the Bronze Age mixed farming became well-established all over the Netherlands. The appearance of farms with stall partitions in the Middle Bronze Age shows that cattle was the main stock. These farms formed parts of permanent settlements comprising one or more houses and outbuildings.

BEAKER SETTLEMENTS

The Single Grave culture

Our knowledge of the settlements of the Single Grave culture is still rather limited. A few settlements of this culture have been investigated in Westfrisia. They are all situated on clay deposited during the Calais IV transgression (Aartswoud, Hoogwoud, Kolhorn). In addition, the remains of a number of settlements have been found on the coastal barriers of the western Netherlands (Voorschoten, Zandwerven) and on the sandy soils of the northern Netherlands (Anloo, Bornwird, Steenendam). One group of barrows of the Single Grave culture has been identified to the south of the great rivers but no settlements associated with this culture have so far been discovered in this area.

The representatives of the Single Grave culture hence built their settlements in all types of landscape, with the exception of peat. This was a new development. In the Middle Neolithic there had been a clear distinction between the settlements of the Funnel Beaker culture, which were built exclusively on sandy soils, and those of the Vlaardingen group, which were concentrated in the coastal area and along the great rivers. In the past it was always assumed that the wide distribution area of the Single Grave culture was the result of migration. It may, however, be more correct to relate this change in distribution pattern to a change in farming practices, resulting from the large-scale use of ploughs. Plough agriculture, which could be practised in all types of landscape, marks the transition to integrated mixed farming. Beaker assemblages can be seen as symbols of these innovations in the economy and the related changes in social organisation.

Most of our knowledge of the settlements of the Single Grave culture is based on information obtained from the salt marshes in the western Netherlands. The reason for this is that the occupation remains of virtually all of the sites in this sedimentary environment are contained in archaeologically visible culture horizons. Culture horizons are layers of humic clays mixed with charcoal, remains of plants and seeds, bones and other settlement debris; they vary in thickness from a few to several dozen centimetres (fig. 16.4, plate 23A). The culture horizons of North Holland also contain large amounts of mussel and oyster shells. Culture horizons hence consist of layers of refuse formed during periods of occupation, which have been preserved by the clay that was deposited on top of them when the sea level rose and the peat that was later formed on top of this clay. The culture horizons contain large numbers of postholes but their diameters are usually too small to allow any reconstruction of house plans.[1] The general impression is that these settlements were occupied on a semi-permanent basis and that they comprised fairly insubstantial structures. However, as we know that houses were already being built in the Middle Neolithic it is not inconceivable that permanently occupied settlements comprising proper houses of the Single Grave culture will come to light in the future.

The settlement sites from this period, unlike those from later periods, contain few pits. At the settlement of Hoogwoud one pit was found, which contained a large amount of carbonised barley indicating that it may have been a storage pit. One of the most remarkable discoveries made at Kolhorn was a well that had been dug to 80 centimetres below the former water table. It is the oldest well that has so far been found in the Netherlands.[2]

The agrarian character of the settlements of this period is hence less apparent from the remains of dwellings than from the cereal remains and the bones of cattle, sheep, goats and pigs found in the occupation layers. At Kolhorn the clay subsoil moreover contained many impressions of hoofs of cattle (plate 23B). The layers of shells and bones of birds, fish and large game show that hunting and fishing were also important. The subsistence base of the occupants of these settlements hence comprised a wide range of activities. This kind of economy is also known as a broad-spectrum economy.[3]

As organic remains are not well preserved in sandy soils we know much less about the food economy of the settlements that were built on those soils. What we do have in these areas are plough marks. The best-known are the *ard* furrows found near Bornwird in Friesland.[4] Plough marks are also often found in the dunes of North Holland, but most of those are of a slightly later date (figs. 16.5, 22.5). The *ard* marks of Bornwird have been preserved so well because they were entirely covered by a layer of peat already around 2100 BC. Separate ploughing phases were distinguishable. The marks of most of these ploughing phases crossed one other perpendicularly, though in some cases all furrows were oriented in the same direction. The fact that separate ploughing phases were distinguishable probably indicates that the land was left fallow after periods of cultivation so as to allow it to regain fertility. These fallow periods were probably shorter than in the Middle Neolithic to avoid the risk of difficulties in ploughing caused by recovering roots and young trees growing on the untilled land; it is most likely that the land was left fallow for a few years only.[5]

The average distance between the furrows was 30 cm. Ards did not turn the turfs over and it is therefore assumed that they were used mainly to create furrows in which grain could be sowed in rows. The *ard* marks of Bornwird covered an area of at least 50 x 50 m; the limits of the field could not be determined.

Sherds of both funnel-beaker pottery (late Havelte phase) and protruding-foot-beaker pottery (Single Grave culture) were found in this field. They indicate continuity of use and this site hence plays an important part in the debate regarding the transition from the Funnel Beaker culture to the Single Grave culture.[6] The question is: how did these sherds end up in this field? There are no indications suggesting that the field was laid out on a former settlement site or that a settlement was later built on top of it. One of the hypotheses is that the sherds made their way onto the field mixed with manure: we know that household refuse was often dumped on manure heaps. However, we have no direct evidence that manure was indeed being collected in this period.

Another well-known settlement site was excavated at Anloo in 1958.[7] At first the palisade or fence of thick posts discovered at this site was interpreted as the remains of a cattle pen of the Single Grave culture, an interpretation that agreed extremely well with the then commonly accepted opinion that the representatives of this culture were groups of cattle herders without fixed settlements. However, it is now assumed that the fence was built by representatives of the Funnel Beaker culture, of which many finds were found at this site. The excavation brought to light no postholes or pits from the Late Neolithic but many stray finds and a few graves from the late phase of the Single Grave culture.

The Bell Beaker and Barbed Wire Beaker cultures

The amount of information available on the settlements of the Late Neolithic period B (c. 2500-2000 BC), the period of the Bell Beaker culture, is even smaller than that available for the Late Neolithic period A. In fact, virtually all of our information on the settlements of this period comes from one site: Molenaarsgraaf in the Alblasserwaard district (fig. 18.1, plate 32A).[8] Here, in a peat marsh, a silted up gully known as the Schoonrewoerd stream ridge was situated. On the highest parts of the ridge the remains of a number of occupation sites ranging in date from 2200 to 1800 BC were found. On either side of this ridge were clay deposits. The settlements were only small, measuring no more than 0.25 ha, and had been built at regular intervals across 6 km of the 30-km long and approximately 100-m wide ridge. Some of the settlements were probably occupied at the same time. At one of these settlements the plans of two two-aisled longhouses were found. The houses

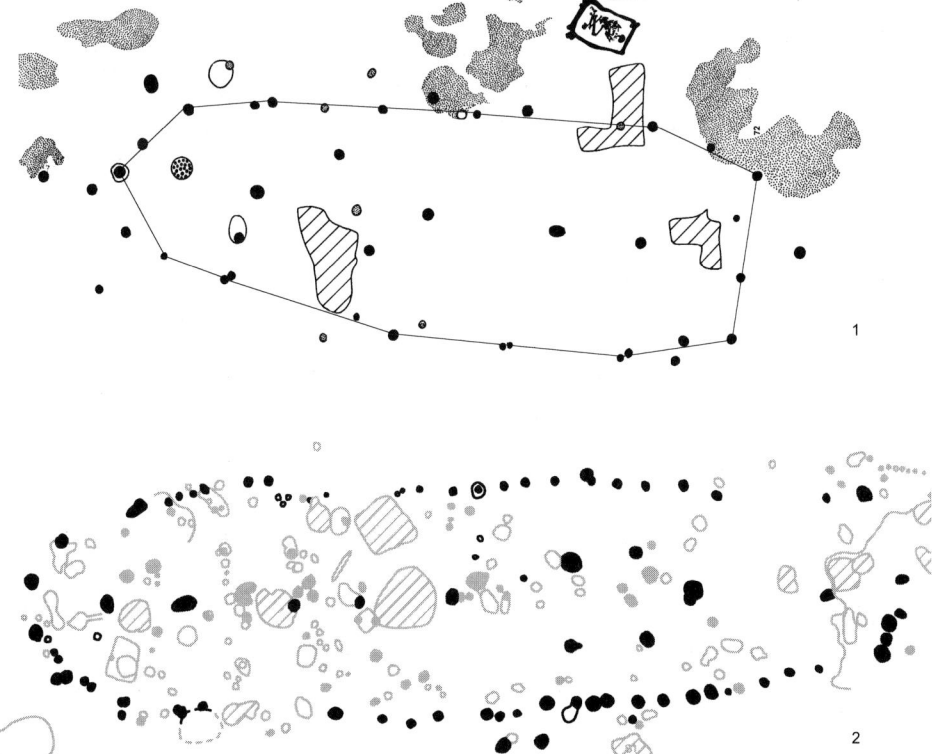

fig. 18.1
Two-aisled houses from the end of the Late Neolithic or the Early Bronze Age. The plan of Noordwijk has been published in several versions. The illustrated plan is the most recent version. Scale 1:200.
1 Molenaarsgraaf
2 Noordwijk

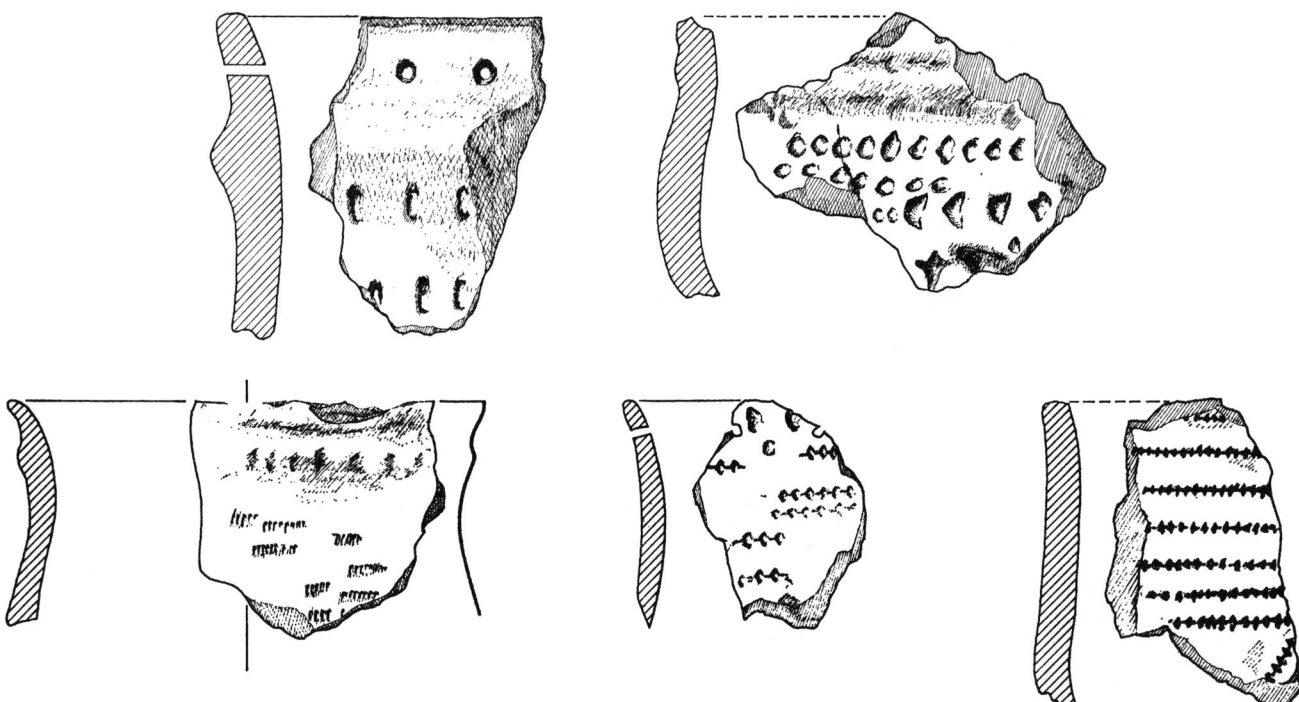

fig. 18.2
Settlement pottery from the Late Neolithic / Early Bronze Age transition from Molenaarsgraaf. Top row: rusticated Bell beakers, lower part: fragments of Barbed Wire Beaker pots. Scale 1:2.

had measured about 20 x 6 m.[9] It was not possible to identify separate residential and stalling areas. The excavator dated one of the plans to the Late Neolithic period B and the other to the Early Bronze Age, though it is more likely that both plans date from the Early Bronze Age.[10] Several postholes at this settlement were found to date from the Late Neolithic, but it was not possible to reconstruct any house plans from them. Besides these house plans a number of pits were found at this site. Four of these pits turned out to be graves; three contained human remains and one the remains of a young bovine.

The range of bones found at these settlements indicates that in addition to cattle, which was the main stock, the occupants kept pigs, sheep and goats and an occasional horse. Few remains of game were found. The specific location of the settlements, along the bank of a small gully, suggests that fishing was also important. Direct evidence for fishing was found in one of the graves, in which an adult male had been buried accompanied by three bone fish hooks, a pair of flint flakes and a large hook made of red deer antler, which was possibly used to lift nets (fig. 19.1). In another grave a 2-cm long piece of the bone of a pike was found near the larynx of the approximately fifteen-year-old boy who was buried there. It is possible that this fish bone was the cause of his death.[11] Research carried out at Oldeboorn in Friesland has shown that fishing and hunting were still important in the Middle Bronze Age in the sandy region, too.[12] Near the Boorne the remains of what was presumably a fishing camp were found on a river dune surrounded by peat. The culture horizon consisting of charcoal, pottery and fragments of bone dated from the Middle Bronze Age. But the site also yielded numerous sherds of Veluwe bell beakers and beaker pots, indicating that it had been used by representatives of the Bell Beaker culture as well (fig. 17.4). In view of the specific position of the site it is most likely that they also used it as a fishing and fowling camp. However, besides bones of the species that one would expect to encounter in this environment, the culture horizon contained bones of large mammals (cattle and pigs) as well. No postholes whatsoever were found here.

Apart from the aforementioned sites very few Late Neolithic and Early Bronze Age settlement sites are known. Now and then pits containing pottery dating from this period come to light but they are hardly ever accompanied by other features, such as postholes. The house plans of Molenaarsgraaf discussed above are the only evidence for dwellings from this period that has so far been found.[13]

The scarcity of house plans from the Late Neolithic and the Early Bronze Age is not a specifically Dutch problem: likewise, in the countries surrounding the Netherlands very few house plans from this period have been found. In England the remains of only a few round structures associated with the Bell Beaker culture have come to light. And in Denmark only recently house plans datable to before the Early Bronze Age have been found. The Danish Late Neolithic and Early Bronze Age house plans are in many respects comparable with the house plans of Molenaarsgraaf and Noordwijk.[14]

MIDDLE BRONZE AGE SETTLEMENTS

General characteristics

Our knowledge of the settlements of the Middle Bronze Age, from c. 1800 BC onwards, contrasts sharply with that of the settlements of the preceding periods. Large parts of settlement sites, some covering several hectares, including pits and the plans of houses and outbuildings, have been excavated in different parts of the Netherlands. One of the reasons why we are so well informed about this period is the large-scale research that is currently being done on Bronze Age settlements in the Netherlands. In this research much use is being made of digging machines, with which very large areas can be excavated. Such large-scale excavation methods cannot be used for the culture horizons of Late Neolithic settlements. The wealth of information that has thus been obtained in the Netherlands is unique in Northwest Europe. There are only very few examples of Bronze Age settlements that have been investigated in large-scale excavations in the countries surrounding the Netherlands. A number of house plans have been investigated in Denmark and Germany,[15] but the quantity and quality of the information obtained in the Netherlands is so far unequalled.

The typical Middle Bronze Age house plan encountered all over the Netherlands is three-aisled, comprising four rows of regularly spaced postholes, the holes of the outside rows (closest to the wall) often corresponding to those of the inside rows (fig. 18.3).[16] Sometimes the roof was supported by a few extra posts at the middle of the house; these posts give the plans of these houses a four-aisled appearance (fig. 18.3: 6, 7, 9). In the sandy areas traces of the walls are rarely preserved but in the clay areas the thin twigs of the wattlework are often still visible (fig 18.3: 6, 7). One of the short sides of the houses was often rounded; sometimes both were rounded. The short side contained an entrance to the byre. There were also entrances in the long sides. In North Holland in particular the outlines of stall partitions are sometimes found. They indicate that a maximum of 30-40 cattle could be stalled in the byre (fig. 18.3: 3, 6).

Out in the yards were four- or six-post structures, which are usually referred to as granaries, or *spiekers* in the Dutch literature. They are granaries with floors supported by posts above the ground (fig. 18.4). Sometimes there were also barns without internal divisions in the yard. Westfrisia is the only part of the Netherlands where no remains of the aforementioned type of granaries have been found. There is evidence that in that area unthreshed corn was stored inside circular ditches.[17] Corn may also have been stored in fairly deep, round storage pits of the kind encountered in a few houses in the north of the Netherlands and at the settlement near Nijnsel.[18]

Plough marks are often encountered in the dunes and in the salt marshes of

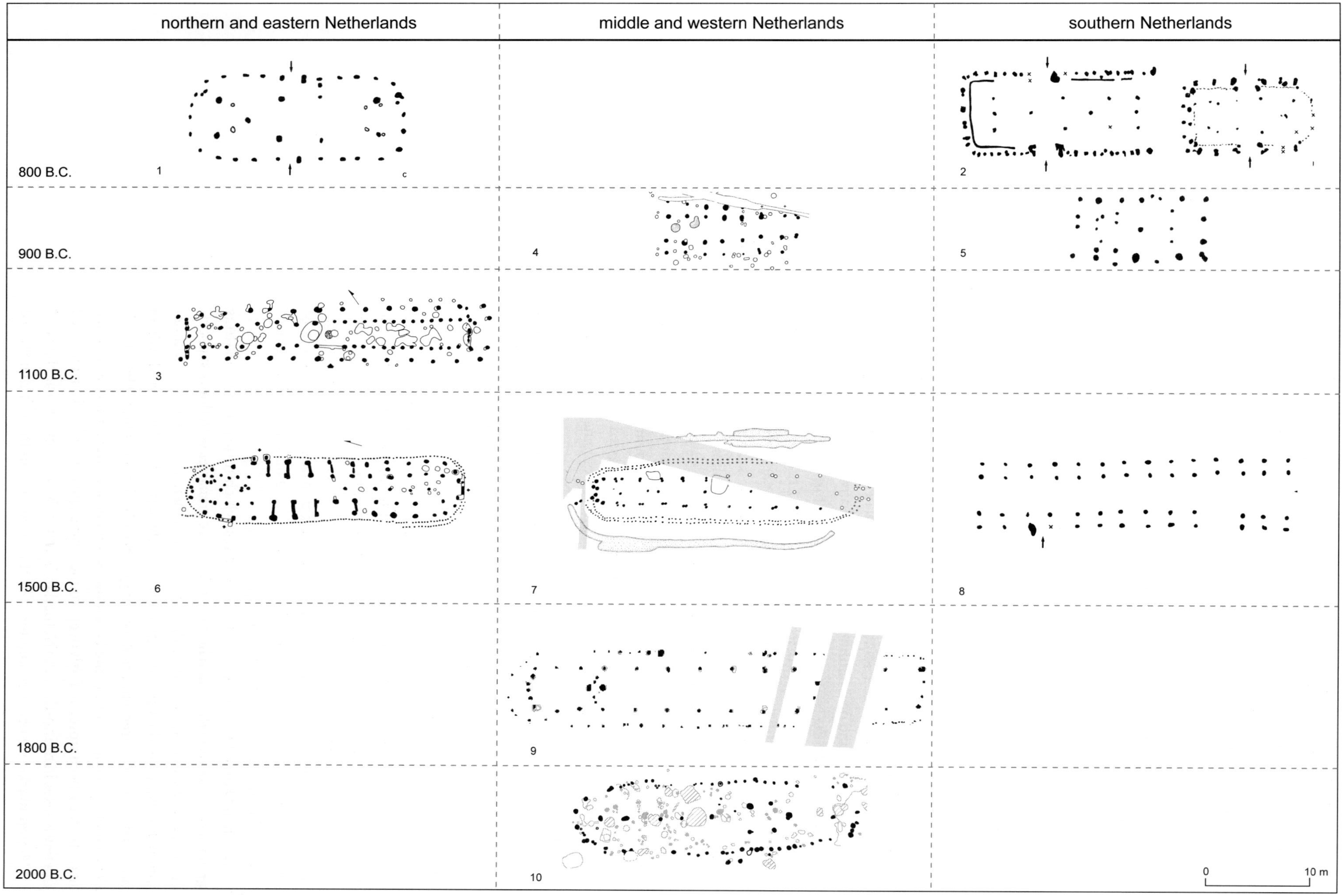

northern and eastern Netherlands

middle and western Netherlands

southern Netherlands

800 B.C.

900 B.C.

1100 B.C.

1500 B.C.

1800 B.C.

2000 B.C.

0   10 m

1

2

3

4

5

6

7

8

9

10

Westfrisia (fig. 16.5, 22.5). The range of bones found in these areas indicates that stock keeping concentrated on cattle. What we have here is the earliest evidence for what is known as integrated mixed farming. Cereal cultivation and stock keeping were integrated in one system: cattle were kept for their traction and for manure for the fields and this manure was mixed with cereal straw in the byres.

The layout of the houses and the settlement pattern were roughly the same all over the Netherlands and in the adjacent parts of neighbouring countries; slight regional differences appear to be essentially the results of adaptations to the local landscape. It is only the differences observable in pottery traditions and burial rites that distinguish the Elp culture in the northern and eastern parts of the Netherlands from the Hilversum culture in the central and southern parts.

The sandy soils of the northern and eastern parts of the Netherlands

The settlement of Elp, which was discovered in the northern part of the Netherlands during the excavation of a barrow in 1960, is still one of the finest examples of a settlement from the Middle and Late Bronze Age (fig. 18.4).[19] The settlement was located at the edge of a stream valley; over a period of about 700 years one or two farms and a number of outbuildings had stood at this site. The excavator is of the opinion that there was a period in which the settlement was temporarily not inhabited, during which a site some distance away was occupied. It was initially thought that the settlement had always comprised one large three-aisled building (25-40 m long and 5-6 m wide) and one smaller building (1-18 m long and 3.5-5 m wide) of the same layout. Now the excavator is of the opinion that there is a chronological difference between the two types of houses, the short houses being of Middle Bronze Age date and the larger ones of late Middle/early Late Bronze Age date.[20]

Fences of widely spaced posts enclosed some yards at Elp, measuring c. 500 m². In these oval yards the features of four-post granaries were visible; they may have been used for storing crops. In addition, some of the houses contained pits, which have been interpreted as storage pits. These pits and the ones that were found outside the houses yielded most of the finds. Like elsewhere in the Netherlands the postholes of the houses yielded virtually no finds. This – and the scarcity of pits – explains why it is so difficult to discover Bronze Age settlements in the sandy areas in field surveys.

The finest Middle Bronze Age house plans are probably those which were found at Angelslo-Emmerhout.[21] Unfortunately, only a brief preliminary report has so

fig. 18.3 (see p. 412)

Survey of the development of house plans in the Bronze Age and the Early Iron Age in the Netherlands.

1	Peelo	Hijken transitional type
2	Oss H112 and Oss H132	Oss types 2 (left) and 3 (right)
3	Angelslo	type Elp
4	Texel-Den Burg house J	
5	Boxmeer	
6	Angelso	type Emmerhout
7	Zijderveld	type Zijderveld
8	Oss	Oss 1 type
9	Voetakker house 28-1AH	
10	Noordwijk	

413

Elp

posscholes of houses and ancillary buildings
other postholes
stones
pits inside the house
other pits
grave
iron pan formation in and near houses

0   10 m

fig. 18.4 (see p. 414)
Plan of the barrow and settlement of Elp. An area of around 1 ha was excavated at this site. Scale 1:500

far been published on this site, which makes it impossible to discuss the structure of the settlement in any detail here. Figure 18.3: 6 shows the frequently published house plan, which is considered representative of the Emmerhout type. This is now assumed to be the oldest type of house plan in Drenthe, while the Elp type is dated to a later period, i.e. 1200-800 BC. The difference between the two types is that the postholes of the inside rows of the plan of Elp do not all correspond to those of the outside rows. Because of this the Elp type of plan looks less regular.[22] What is rather remarkable is that with the plans of the Emmerhout type encountered in Drenthe the byres are often positioned at the middle of the house, flanked by two parts without stall partitions. This tradition must have been restricted to the northern district, because plans of this type have rarely been found outside Drenthe.

The results of the excavation at Hijken are better known (fig. 18.5). At this site the plans of six Bronze Age longhouses were uncovered in an area of 2.5 ha.[23] The lengths of the houses varied from 14 to 27 m and their widths from 5 to 5.8 m; the

fig. 18.5
Late Neolithic flat graves (circular structures) and a Bronze Age settlement at Hijken; next to them is the plan of house 4, which has been dated to 3125 ± 65 BP (1520-1210 cal BC). Scales 1:1000 and 1:200.

The excavator interpreted the semicircular ditch feature with a palisade on its eastern side as part of a cattle enclosure that originally measured 40 x 90 m. The hatched plans represent houses that may have succeeded one another or – as the excavator assumes – may all have been in use at the same time as the cattle pen.

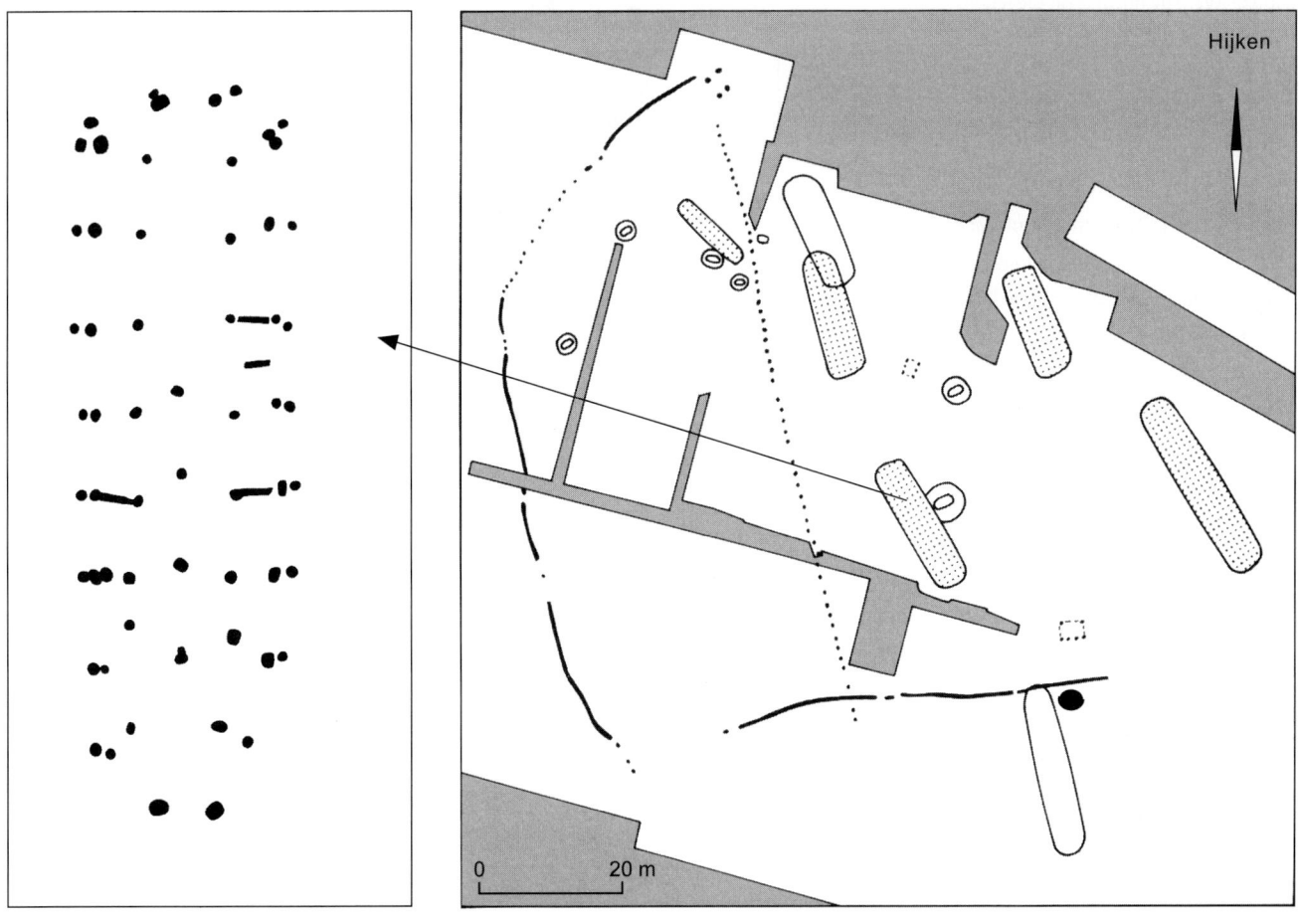

Hijken

0   20 m

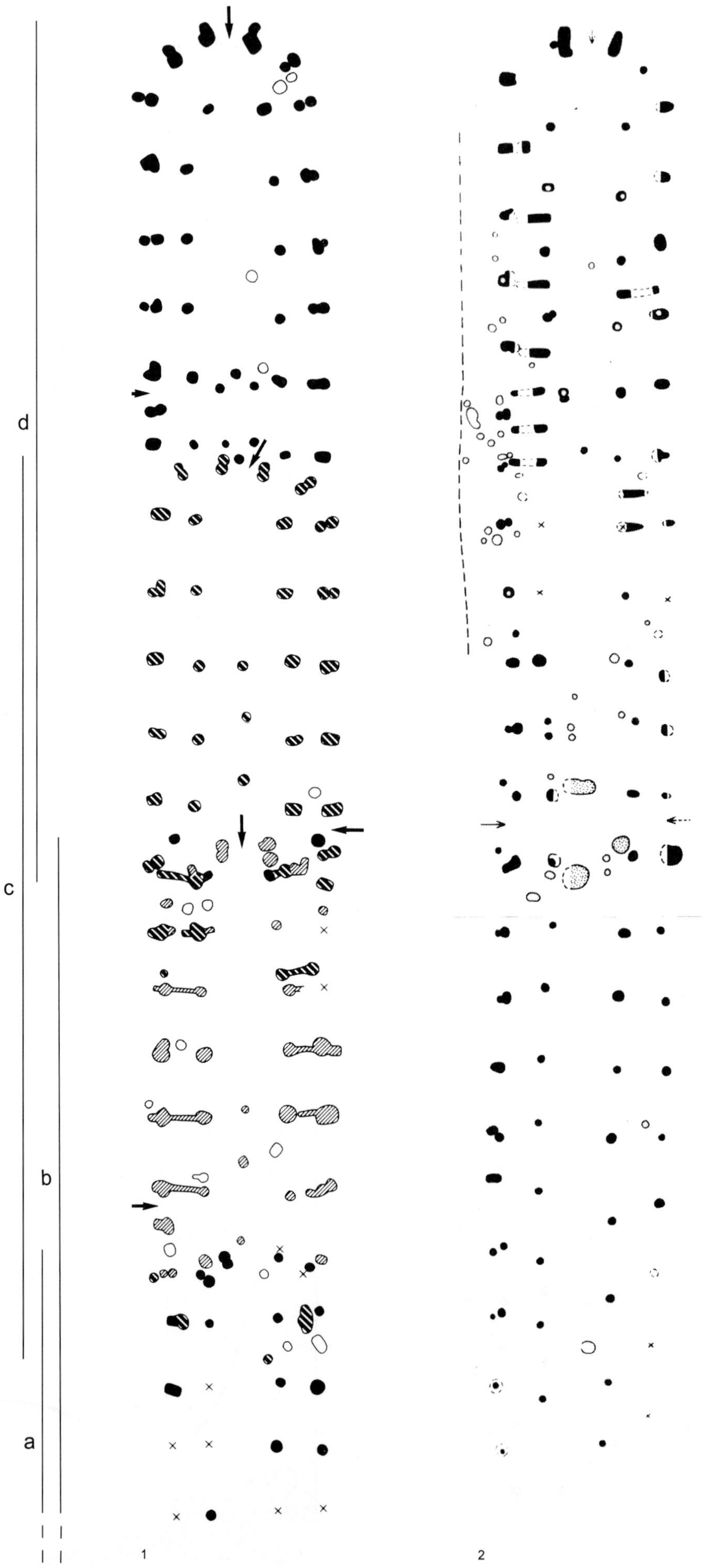

fig. 18.6
Two very long house plans from the Middle Bronze Age. The north is on the left; entrances are indicated by arrows. Scale 1:200.

1 Dalen IV, longer than 50 m
2 Rechteren, length 47 m

The excavator distinguished four occupation phases for the Dalen plan. The oldest house plan (a), which was only 10 m long, is partly disturbed. In phase b the original building was enlarged with a 13-m extension. Part of the resulting structure was evidently a byre, as indicated by the stall partitions. Phase c comprised another extension, on the eastern side. This new part was 12 m long, bringing the longhouse's total length to 29 m. By this time the greater part of the original western part had fallen into disrepair. Phase d, finally, comprised an extension on the eastern side and shortening of the western part, bringing the overall ultimate length to 27 m.

The excavator of the Rechteren plan described it as representing a single house, but the indentation in the central part suggests a phasing similar to that represented by the Dalen plan.

ends of the houses were rounded. A noteworthy element of the site at Hijken is the trapezoidal palisaded area, which the excavator interpreted as a cattle pen; it is probably of an earlier date than the house plans, though.[24]

Until fairly recently the presence of exceptionally long house plans was considered to be peculiar to the Middle Bronze Age settlements of the northern part of the Netherlands. Two such exceptionally long house plans were for example found on the Huidbergsveld near Dalen in 1990.[25] They were 51.5 and just over 50 m long (fig. 18.6: 1). The other two house plans found at this site had normal lengths of 20 and 25 m. Similar long house plans had previously been encountered at Elp and Emmerhout. Waterbolk is of the opinion that these long buildings had a special function. Harsema, however, has shown that the long plan found at Elp is probably the result of rebuilding.[26] Basing himself on the results of his research in Westfrisia, IJzereef had on an earlier occasion already argued that such long plans were the features of houses onto which extensions had been built.[27] At first this argument was met with scepticism. However, the evidence that has since then been obtained at Dalen leaves no room for doubt. Traces of the rounded original end of the house were still visible at the point where an extension had later been built onto the house. In the case of house plan III in particular it was quite clear that the house had been enlarged several times.

More and more settlements are coming to light in the eastern part of the Netherlands, where Middle Bronze Age settlement research started with the excavations at Deventer.[28] A very fine house plan has been unearthed at Rechteren (fig. 18.6: 2).[29] The length of about 46 m suggests that this plan is also the result of several building phases. There was clearly a byre at the eastern end of the house.

Between 1984 and 1986 the remains of four Middle Bronze Age longhouses were investigated on the Colmschater Es, near Deventer.[30] A noteworthy aspect of one of the house plans was the 2-m wide and 20-m long fenced cattle droveway leading up to the byre. Such droveways are often encountered in Westfrisia (e.g. at Bovenkarspel), only there they are flanked by ditches.

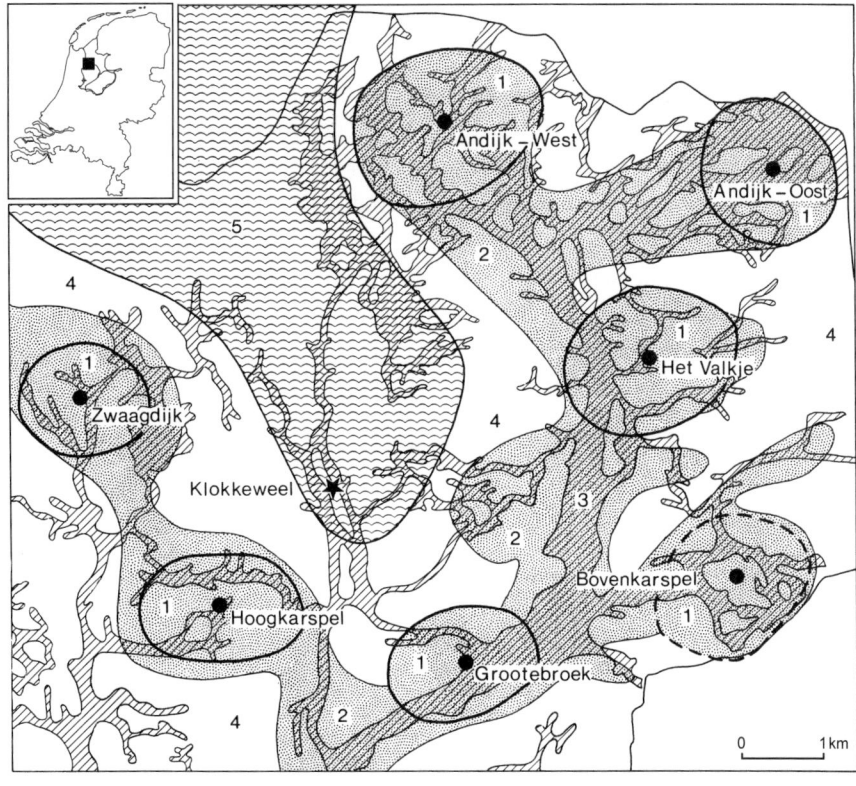

fig. 18.7

Schematic survey of the presumed settlement sites in the eastern part of Westfrisia. The first colonisation centres (1) are based on the distribution of barrows. The subsequent extension of the inhabited area is marked (2). The sites all lay on low ridges, representing sandy gulley fills (3), surrounded by low-lying backswamps (4) and adjacent to open water in the northwest (5).

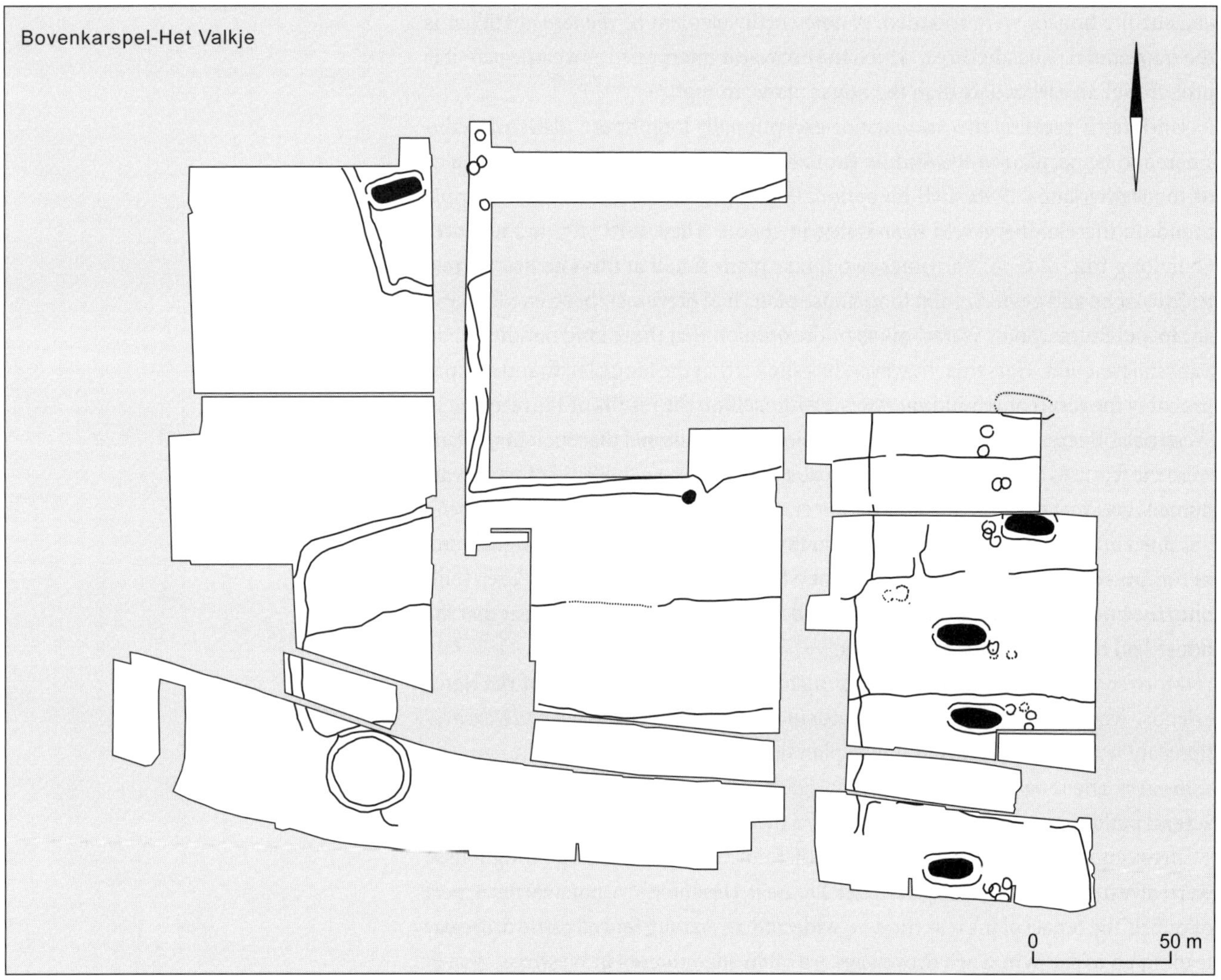

Bovenkarspel-Het Valkje

0   50 m

fig. 18.8

Part of the area excavated at Bovenkarspel-
Het Valkje. Visible in the eastern part of
this area are the plans of a number of
contemporary farmsteads whose yards
contain circular ditch enclosures and rings
of postholes which are thought to represent
granaries. To the west were the cultivation
plots, separated by ditches, and beyond them
lay a barrow from the settlement's earliest
occupation phase. Scale 1:2500.

The western Netherlands

The salt marshes of Westfrisia

For a long time Middle Bronze Age research in the western Netherlands focused
on the eastern part of Westfrisia because of the rather exceptional evidence that
came to light in that area. In the excavations that were carried out at Hoogkarspel
from 1955 to 1973 and the investigations at Andijk and Bovenkarspel a wealth of
information was obtained on the layouts of houses and their yards and on the
structure of the settlements.[31] After this eastern part of Westfrisia had fallen dry,
the salt marshes remained uninhabited for a long time. The first settlers, who arrived in this relatively wet area around 1500 BC, dug ditches around their houses

fig. 18.9

A house whose plan was found at Andijk-
Noord. The house was at some time rebuilt
and a small extension was added to it. Scale
1:200.

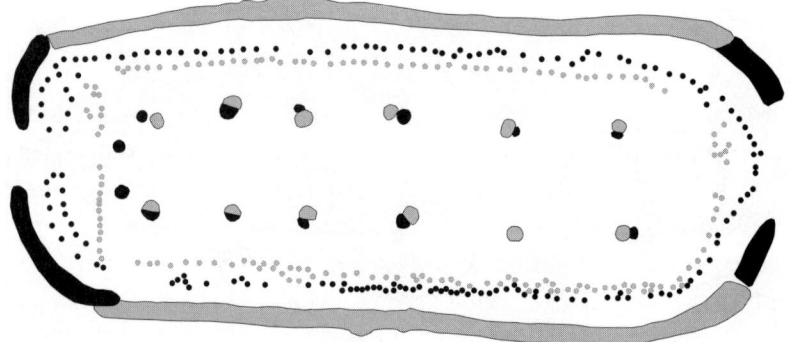

and their fields (fig. 18.7). These ditches now give us a very detailed picture of how the landscape was composed and how the land was used in the Bronze Age. They also show us how the yards, fields and pastureland were plotted out. At Hoogkarspel, for example, where a system of ditches covering a total area of some 20 ha was mapped, it was found that units of 4-6 ha had been split up into plots of usually 50 x 50 m, sometimes 80 x 80 m or 80 x 50 m.[32]

The information obtained at points at which the ditches intersected one another enabled more precise (relative) dating of the features. In this way a total of twenty-five occupation phases were distinguished for the earliest occupation period at Bovenkarspel (c. 1500-950 BC) and another six for the later period (c. 950-800 BC). This means that each phase, which comprised the period of occupation of a house and the time involved in rebuilding activities, lasted for about twenty-five years.

Instead of the remains of granaries, the yards contained circular ditches, which marked the outlines of corn- and haystacks, and circles of pits, which were in all probability dug around muck heaps (fig. 18.8, plate 32B).

At Andijk the parts of the Bronze Age features closest to the surface had been better preserved than at Bovenkarspel and the plans that were unearthed at this site hence yielded a good deal of information on the occupants' houses. For example, the plans clearly showed where the walls, which had consisted of fairly thin posts (7-10 cm thick), had been repaired and how the houses had been enlarged (fig. 18.9).

Close study of the features distinguishable at 78 house sites (constituting more than 200 individual plans) showed that at two-thirds of these sites more than one house had been built. No fewer than eleven different houses had been built at one of these sites. A remarkable aspect was that the size of the houses was found to decrease with time: the first plan had a length of more than 28 m whereas the last one, of a house that was built in the Late Bronze Age, probably more than 300 years after the first, had a length of only 12 m. The same trend has been observed at other house sites, where the overlapping ditches of successive house plans showed that the largest houses (with lengths of up to 32 m) dated back to the earliest period of occupation.[33]

Thanks to intensive field surveys and aerial photographs we are not only well informed about the structure of the settlements of the eastern part of Westfrisia, but also about the pattern of settlement of this area (fig. 18.7).[34] The first occupants built small settlements spaced some 3-4 km apart around an area with open water. These settlements are recognizable by the barrows in which, in the tradition of the sandy areas in this early period, the heads of the families or individuals with a comparable status were buried. The barrows were thrown up near the houses. Less important individuals were sometimes buried in flat graves. In later periods the dead were disposed of in a manner that is not archaeologically visible. Sometimes a human skeleton is found in a pit or a few stray human bones are encountered in ditches of house plans, but we do not really know exactly what burial rite was practised in Westfrisia after 1200 BC.

The Older Dunes
In the western Netherlands settlement sites have also been found in the Older Dunes. A small-scale excavation carried out at 'Het Geestje', near Monster, in the 1960s brought to light 5-6 horizons containing *ard* marks associated with pottery of the Hilversum culture.[35] At Vogelenzang a number of postholes and two pits yielded a large amount of pottery, bones and flint.[36] In the past few years large-scale research has been carried out at Velsen, in the Velserbroekpolder. A number of graves, overlapping house plans and fields have come to light. A particular ad-

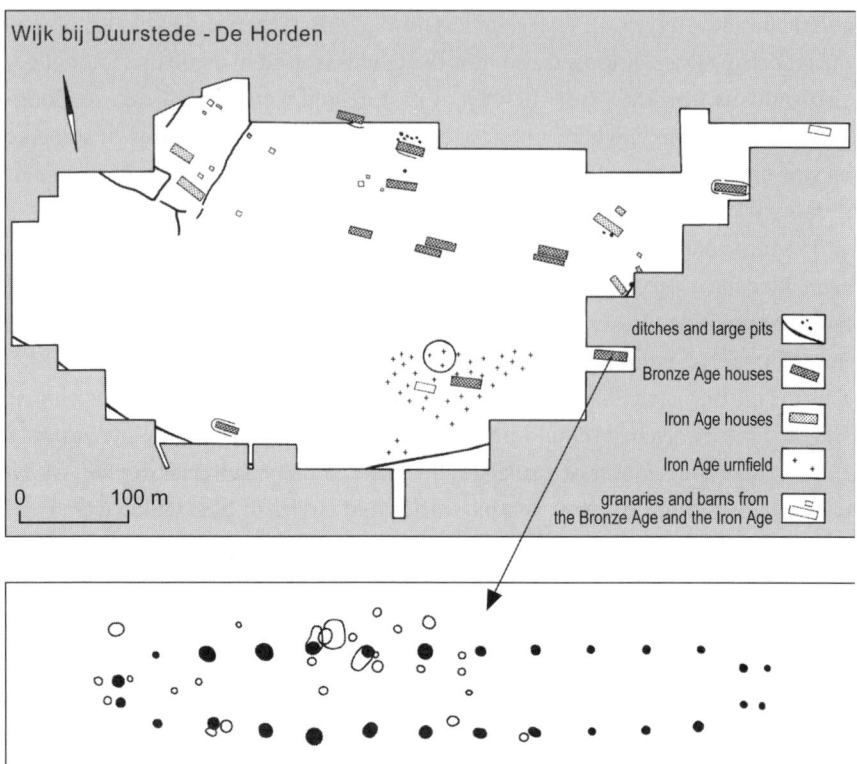

Wijk bij Duurstede - De Horden

ditches and large pits

Bronze Age houses

Iron Age houses

Iron Age urnfield

granaries and barns from
the Bronze Age and the Iron Age

0   100 m

fig. 18.10

Schematic survey of the excavation of De Horden near Wijk bij Duurstede. Beneath the survey is a detailed plan of house 10. The plan is of the Zijderveld type, with invisible walls (the walls were made of wattle or sods). Scale 1:200.

fig. 18.11

On the left are the features of a six-post granary dating from the Bronze Age at Oss-Mikkeldonk (approx. 1 x 1.5 m), on the right is a reconstructed granary (model).

vantage in this area is the good state of conservation of the bones that are unearthed. These bones enable excavators to determine the functions of the various pits that were dug on the settlement sites.[37] It has now become clear that a much larger number of pits than initially assumed served some ritual function.

The settlements in the Older Dunes were all positioned near the salt marshes, where the occupants could pasture their cattle. The same holds for the site near Den Burg on the island of Texel, where several overlapping Middle Bronze Age house plans have been investigated. These house plans bear a close resemblance to those of the farms of Westfrisia, but they are less detailed than the latter because of the poor conservation conditions of the sandy soils. Many pits were found at this site, some of which may have been wells, others probably storage pits. The yards contained the features of one or more four- or six-post granaries.[38]

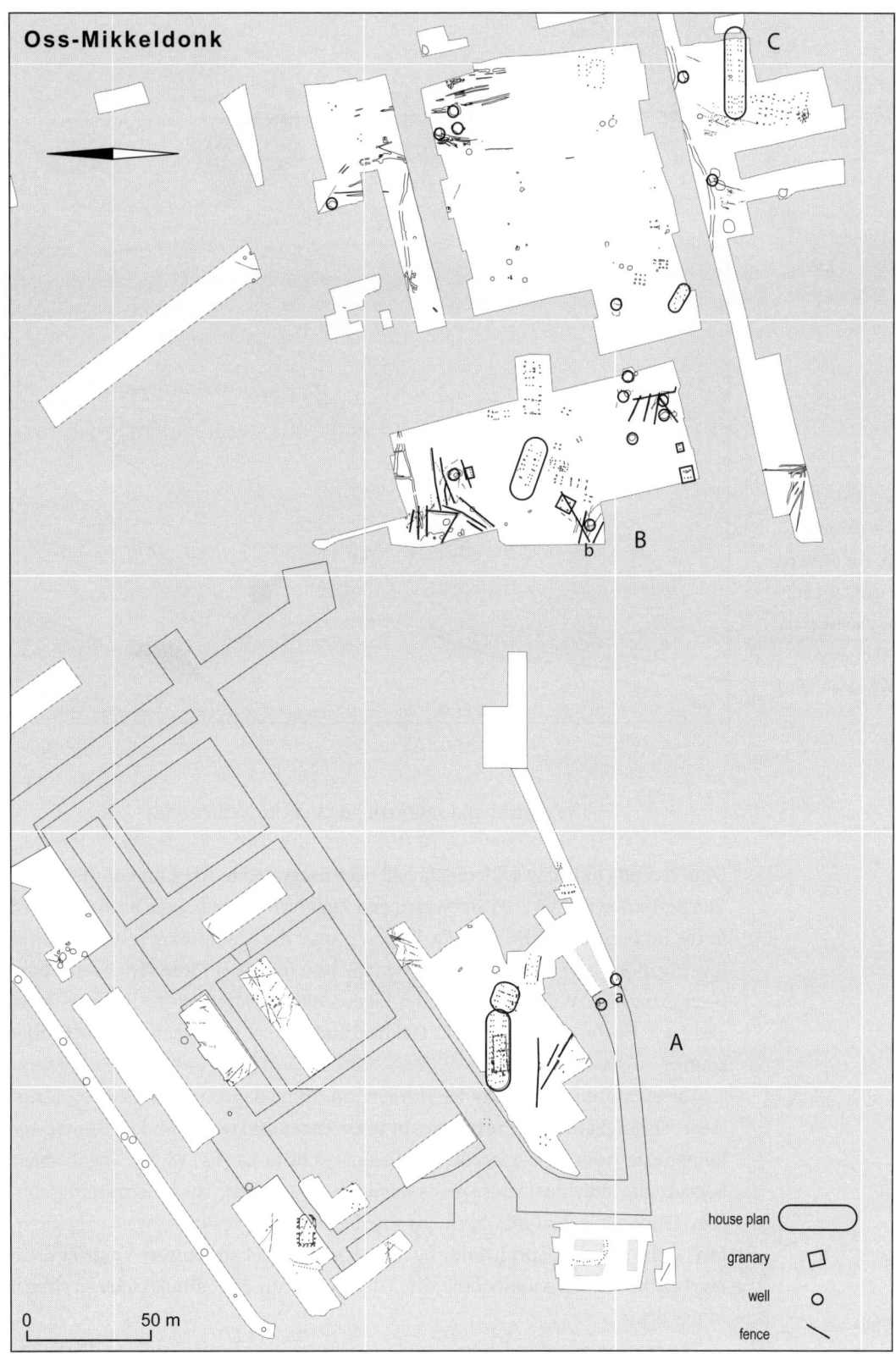

Oss-Mikkeldonk

C

B

b

A

a

house plan ⬭

granary ▢

well ○

fence ╱

0   50 m

fig. 18.12

Part of the Oss-Mikkeldonk site to the northeast of the town of Oss which was excavated in the
years 1986-1989. Clusters of features (including a house plan) that were discovered in this part,
which measures approx. 18 ha, are indicated by the letters A, B and C. The features date from the
Middle Bronze Age period B. A and B may have been contemporary, as the two wells lying in the
vicinity of these two houses were lined with hollowed-out parts of the trunk of the same tree (a
and b, see fig. 18.14). Cluster A is shown in greater detail in fig. 18.13. Scale 1:2500.

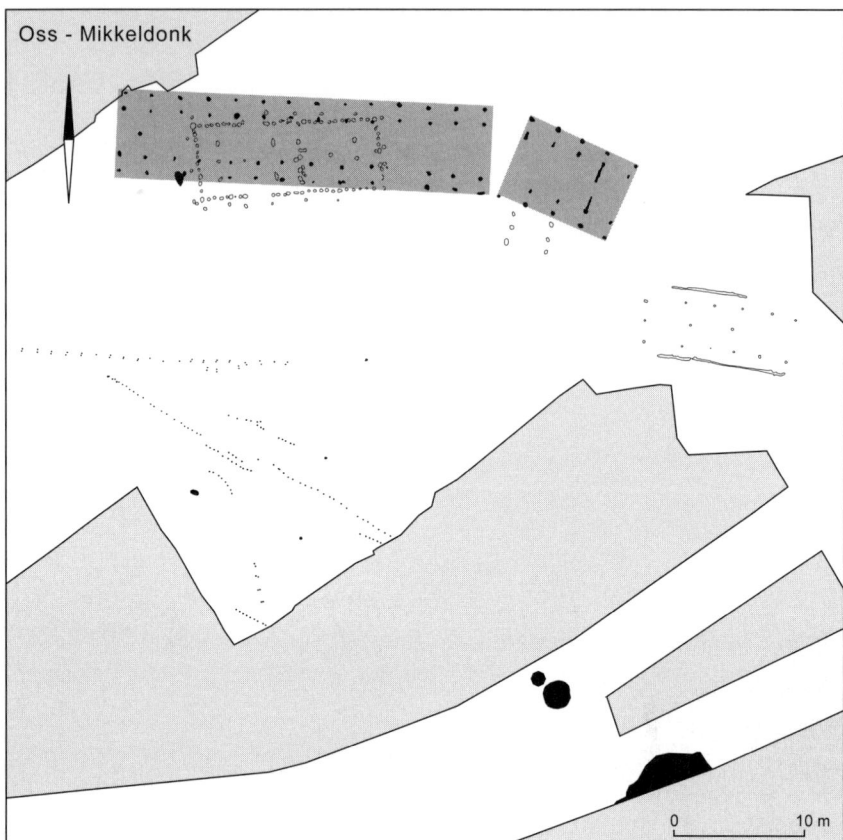

Oss - Mikkeldonk

0   10 m

fig. 18.13
A Bronze Age farm and yard at Oss-
Mikkeldonk that were reused in the Early
Iron Age (fig. 18.12, cluster A). The plans of
the Bronze Age house and an outhouse are
indicated in grey. The other two house plans
date from the Early Iron Age. Indicated in
black are two wells which may be associated
with this yard.

The central and southern parts of the Netherlands

Until recently only few settlements had been excavated to the south of the Rhine.
The best-known sites are Dodewaard and Zijderveld, which were both excavated
in the mid-sixties. Unfortunately, however, only the preliminary results of these
investigations have been published.[39] In the past few years more settlements have
been excavated: Wijk bij Duurstede, Eigenblok and Meteren in the rivers area,
and Loon op Zand, Oss, Blerick, Geldrop and Venray in the sandy areas further
south.[40]

The excavation of the site De Horden, on Rhine deposits near Wijk bij Duurstede,[41] brought to light the features of between ten and twelve Middle Bronze Age
longhouses from 1400-1200 BC within an area of 14 ha (fig. 18.10). The distance
between the individual house plans was at least 60 metres. The lack of stratigraphic evidence made it impossible to say whether any of these houses were contemporary; some were in all probability built to replace earlier structures. A narrow ditch
marked the southern limit of the site. There was a row of postholes along a stretch
of this ditch.

The houses varied in length from 20 to 26 m. It was impossible to determine
the width of any of the houses because no traces whatsoever had been preserved of
any of the walls or outer posts. All that had been preserved were the features of the
paired inside posts and, in some cases, a few ditches which probably contained
the posts that supported the edge of the roof. It is assumed that the houses were
of the usual three-aisled type. Near each of the houses was the feature of a four- or
six-post granary; a few of the yards contained patterns of postholes from which
in some cases the plans of barns could be made out (fig. 18.11). Only one house
plan was associated with pits; otherwise very few pits were found at this site. The
number of finds recovered was also small. There were no wells whatsoever. The

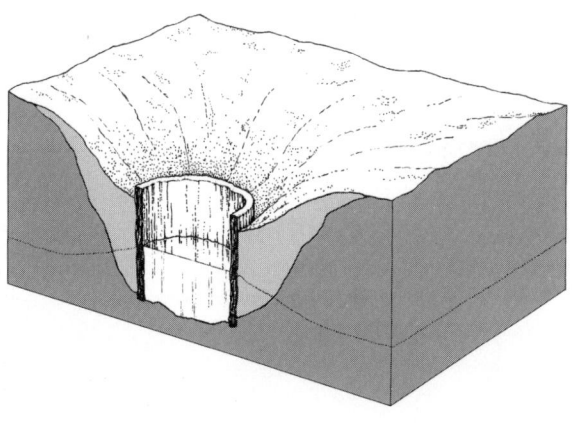

1

2

3

4

5

6

fig. 18.14

1 Block diagram of a wide well with a lining at the bottom of the pit. The lining prevented the risk of the walls of the well collapsing under the influence of the water flowing into it.

2 Section of the fill of a wide well with at the bottom a hollowed-out tree-trunk lining; the tree-trunk indicates the original depth of the well relative to ground level (approx. 1.50 m).

3 Tree-trunk well lining placed on its side after its excavation. Another part of the trunk of the same tree was used to make a second lining, which was found in a well 200 m away (figs. 18.12 a and b).

4 Tool marks made with a bronze axe visible on the tree-trunk lining shown in no. 3.

5 Wide well with a lining made of cleft wooden posts arranged in a ring.

6 The cleft posts after excavation.

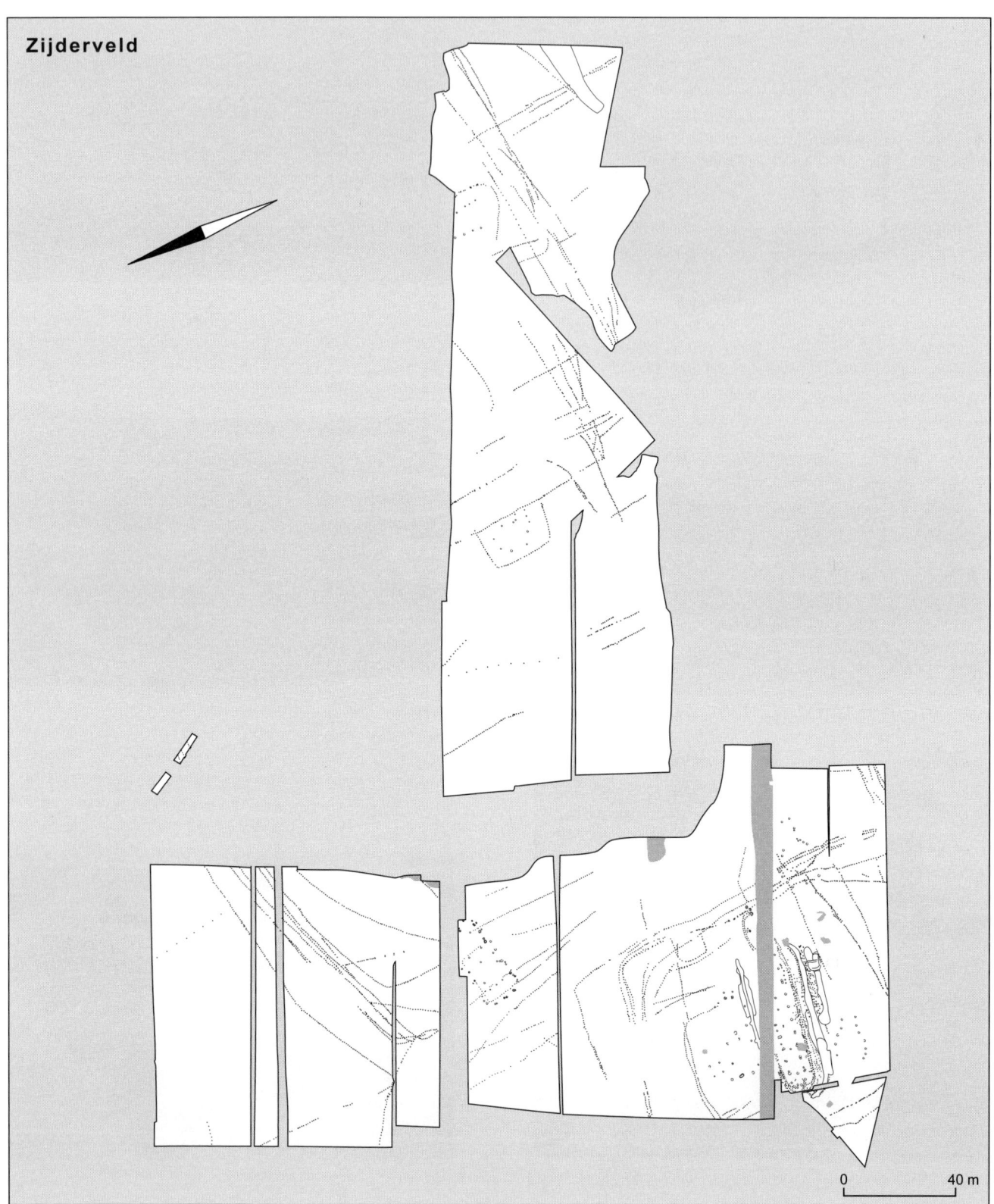

Zijderveld

fig. 18.15
Survey of the features of houses and yard and field boundaries at the Middle Bronze Age settlement at Zijderveld. At the bottom right is a yard with a house plan and the features of granaries dating from the Bronze Age. Scale 1:2000.

fact that hardly any Middle Bronze Age finds were found outside an area with a radius of about twenty metres around the houses suggests that the yards were not larger than 50 x 50 m. As already mentioned above, it is not really possible to say how many of these house plans are contemporary. The excavators are of the opinion that the settlement probably comprised at most two or three houses at a time and that these houses stood some distance apart and were later replaced by houses built in a different part of the site.

The information obtained at De Horden is comparable with that obtained at the site of Oss-Ussen (fig. 18.12).[42] The latter site yielded evidence for three different house sites spaced 100 to 150 m apart within an area of about 10 ha. The houses were over 30 m long (fig. 18.13). Traces of fences marking the limits of the yards were found here and there, but it was not possible to infer the size of the yards from them. The general impression is that the yards were not larger than 50 x 50 m.

Oss-Ussen is one of the very few sites at which the remains of a well have been found. Here the water table lay only about 1.5 m below ground level on the settlement site itself. Elsewhere in the Netherlands the wells were presumably sunk in depressions near the settlements but outside the excavated areas. At Oss it was found that an approximately 2-m deep pit had been dug to below the water table and that a hollowed tree-trunk or a ring of split thinner trunks or boards had then been placed at the centre of this pit (fig. 18.14). There were clear indications that the well had not been lined all the way up to ground level; the lining ended a few dozen centimetres above the floor of the well. The pit had not been backfilled with soil, but with sods. The well, which had a diameter of at most 40 cm, was hence lined with sods. Near several of the wells discovered so far were larger, unlined, pits, which may have served as watering places for the farm animals.

The finest example of a fenced yard surrounded by fields was found at Zijderveld (fig. 18.15).[43] Here a 28-m long three-aisled farmstead and a number of outbuildings were enclosed by a fence of closely set thin posts; the gaps between the posts had presumably been filled up with stacks of thin tree-trunks (fig. 18.16). Tracks, lined with fences, led to the fields, which were also enclosed by fences. The latter fences consisted of thin posts set about 50 cm apart, which were probably connected by wattlework.

The house plans that have been found in the central and southern parts of the Netherlands are all comparable, although they vary in length. The 20-m long plan that came to light at Loon op Zand is the shortest so far; the longest house plan, measuring 32 m, is that which was found at Oss-Ussen. Loon op Zand is the only site in this area where evidence for the stalling of cattle has been found (fig. 18.7).[44] A small part of the house plan found here contained the remains of stall partitions; this part of the house had been separated from the rest by a wall containing 'saloon doors'. Traces of such doorways have also been found at Oss-Ussen and Venray.

At some sites, for example Dodewaard, Wijk bij Duurstede and Zijderveld, extensions were found to have been built onto existing houses.

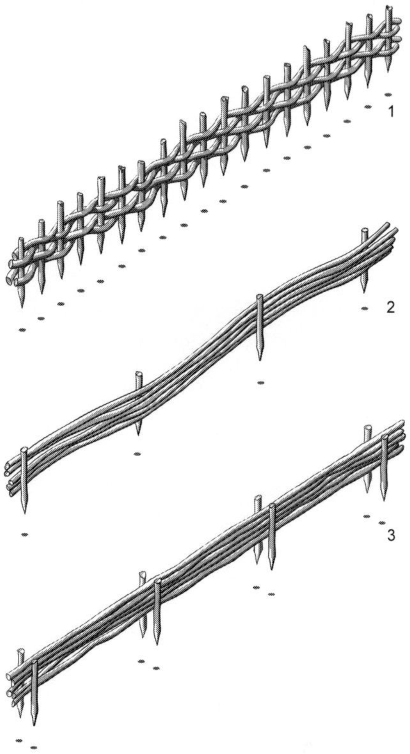

THE PROBLEM OF THE ROUND STRUCTURES

In excavations of Middle Bronze Age settlements carried out since the 1960s in the central and southern parts of the Netherlands, in particular the features of a

fig. 18.16
Features and reconstructions of three types of Bronze Age fences that have been encountered both in the rivers area and further south (at Oss).

a wattlework
b wattlework
c billet wood

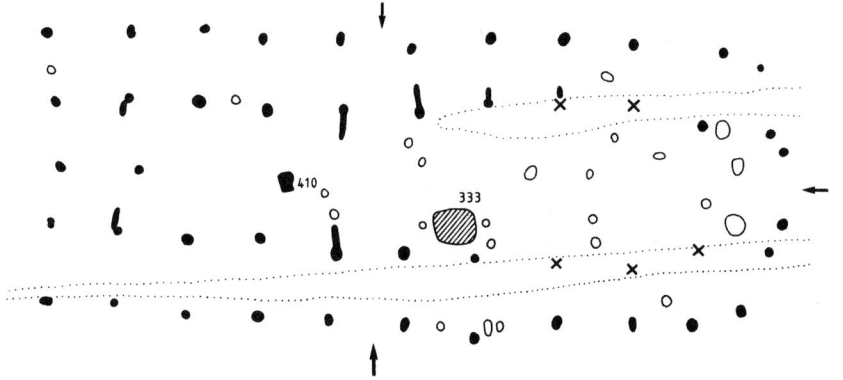

fig. 18.17
Middle Bronze Age house plan found at Loon-op-Zand. On the northern side of the right part are indications of cattle-stall partitions. The arrows indicate assumed entrances. Scale 1:200.

number of round structures have come to light (fig. 16.8). These round features have caused archaeologists many problems and they therefore deserve to be discussed in a separate section; that is also the reason why they have not yet been mentioned above. The first of these features were discovered at Nijnsel, Dodewaard and Zijderveld. Beex and Hulst interpreted them as the remains of round huts and as none of the settlements that had been discovered in the Low Countries until then had included such structures they took them to reflect influences from Britain, where round huts were common.[45] In the 1980s, however, this theory was abandoned and the original interpretation of the features started to be queried. The irregular outlines of the features and the fact that none of the published plans was complete increased the doubts.[46] In the 1990s more round features have been discovered, only now outside the distribution area of the Hilversum culture, the culture that was originally held responsible for the introduction of this foreign element. The most recent theory is that these features, which vary in date from the Middle Bronze Age to the Early Iron Age, are to be interpreted as the remains of cattle pens.[47] Many archaeologists reject this theory, too, because the newly discovered features show the same irregular outlines and are as incomplete as the first group. Moreover, the intervals between the postholes vary considerably. Phosphate analysis may be able to shed some light on the matter. The renewed analysis of the key sites Dodewaard and Zijderveld made clear that the interpretations of the 1960s no longer hold.[48]

SETTLEMENT PATTERN, ECONOMY AND SOCIAL ORGANISATION

It has already been pointed out above that the regional differences observable in settlement patterns are largely connected with differences in palaeogeographical conditions. These differences do not only concern soil conditions but also the surrounding landscape. The plateau of Friesland and Drenthe, for example, was split up into natural territories by the many streams that dissected it. In Westfrisia and the river area, on the other hand, the landscape features most suitable for habitation were the elongated stream ridges. In the case of some settlements, for example those of Elp and Bovenkarspel, overlapping features indicate that the sites in question remained occupied for a long time. This probably indicates that in that particular area only a relatively small amount of land was available or considered suitable for occupation. Elsewhere, for example at Oss and Angelslo, the centres of habitation were found to have moved laterally across fairly wide areas. In these cases the amount of land suitable for occupation was apparently less limited by environmental conditions. In view of these factors it would be unwise to make any general statements about what kind of sites were selected for occupation.

On the whole, the settlement pattern appears to have been more or less the same all over the Netherlands. Small settlements comprising two or three farmsteads probably exploited areas of 100 ha or more. The population density of these settlements was not very high. The farms were frequently rebuilt or replaced by new structures built nearby, as can be inferred from the complex patterns of dozens of house plans, many overlapping one another, which are observed at these sites. Bovenkarspel-Het Valkje is the only settlement that differed from those surrounding it in Westfrisia and in fact from all of the settlements investigated in the Netherlands. Owing to local geological conditions this settlement site was ribbon-shaped; the number of contemporary farms may have been twelve or more.[49]

The yards were probably quite small, at most 50 x 50 m. In the sandy areas the yards contained four- or six-post granaries and sometimes barns without internal divisions. The latter structures, which comprised between eight and ten posts, were used for the storage of crops, tools, wagons, *etc.* It is virtually impossible to say how long the farms were inhabited. The results of detailed research in Westfrisia suggest periods of approximately 25-40 years. Granaries were probably repaired or rebuilt more often than the farms.

The dead were usually buried in barrows which were thrown up probably not far from the yards. In Westfrisia and Drenthe (Elp, Angelslo) it was found that when the centre of occupation shifted, new barrows were built at the new settlement site. At other sites, for example Toterfout-Halve Mijl, clusters of barrows in what could already be termed cemeteries reflect long periods of use.[50]

The economic base was the same all over the Netherlands. The large house plans, some including stall partitions, indicate that cattle farming was of major importance, possibly also for the production of manure. The specific locations of the settlements also point to an integrated system of mixed farming: many of the settlements were positioned so that the occupants could cultivate crops on the higher grounds and graze their cattle in the salt marshes or stream valleys which were to be found all over the Netherlands with the exception of the forested parts of the sandy areas. In the faunal samples percentages for cattle are always highest, followed by those for sheep, goats and pigs. Horses were also kept, but presumably only for riding. Hunting and fishing were practised, but they were both clearly of lesser importance. Different models for the relative importance of cereal cultivation and stock breeding suggest ratios of 1:3 for a farm with 30 cattle, which would have required 2-5 ha of land for cultivation and a much larger area for pasture.[51]

Ard marks show that fields were often under cultivation for long periods, sometimes with interruptions caused by fallowing or a temporary shift of the centre of occupation. In the dune region layers of drift sand between field layers often indicate interruptions in use. The general impression, however, is that from the Middle Bronze Age onwards manuring formed an integral part of farming, enabling continuous use of a plot of land over a long period of time.[52] Owing to the scarcity of well-preserved seeds we are not very well informed about the crops that were cultivated. What we do know is that emmer wheat and barley were the main cereals and that linseed was also cultivated.[53]

The settlements tell us little about the social organisation of the their occupants. The largest farms may have been inhabited by extended families comprising parents, children and their spouses, and grandchildren to a total of ten to fifteen persons. Most will have been inhabited by smaller groups, though. There is no evidence for hierarchy or social differentiation within the settlements. The distribution pattern of the barrows largely confirms this picture: the fact that the barrows were constructed near the yards, as best exemplified by the earliest settlements of Westfrisia, suggests that they were intended for the most important members of a family rather than for an elite.

NOTES

1 At Kolhorn several attempts were made to recognize patterns in the postholes using statistical and other methods, but they were all unsuccessful (Kielman 1986). The two features at Hoogwoud-Mienakker that Hogestijn has identified as the plans of houses are very small (measuring approximately 20 and 35 m²) and irregularly shaped (Hogestijn/Van Haaff 1991). The interpretation as house plans can be disputed.

2 Hoogwoud: Hogestijn/Van Haaff 1991; Kolhorn: Van der Waals 1989.

3 Louwe Kooijmans 1993a.

4 Fokkens 1982.

5 Fokkens 1982, 1986.

6 For this debate see Fokkens 1982 and 1986; Van der Waals 1984.

7 Waterbolk 1960, 82.

8 Louwe Kooijmans 1974. A second site was recently excavated at Noordwijk, which yielded a good plan of a two-aisled house (Van Heeringen/Van de Velde/Van Amen 1999).

9 Louwe Kooijmans 1974.

10 Louwe Kooijmans 1993a.

11 Louwe Kooijmans 1974, 248.

12 Fokkens 1991a, 1998a.

13 Three plans found in Overijssel have been dated to the Late Neolithic or the Early Bronze Age but it is doubtful whether they have been correctly dated. Plan I at Vasse is comparable with the house plans of Molenaarsgraaf but no finds were recovered that could have yielded a date for the plan. Plan II is so irregularly shaped that it is very difficult to recognize a house plan in it. The feature of Zwolle-Ittersum, which has been described as a parallel of the house plans of Molenaarsgraaf, is too incomplete to be regarded as a house plan (Verlinde 1982, Clevis/Verlinde 1991). A well-documented settlement from the early Bronze Age is that at Noordwijk (Van Heeringen/Van der Velde/Van Amen 1998; Jongste/Meijlink/Van der Velde 2001). Jongste and Van der Velde also claim early houses at Rhenen-Remmerden and at Meteren-De Bogen. These are, however, less convincing (drawing board) reconstructions, than those of Noordwijk.

14 Jensen 1987a.

15 See Roymans/Fokkens 1991 for a survey.

16 Huijts 1992. This is Huijts' characterisation of the Emmerhout type of Drenthe, which resembles plans from the same period found in other parts of the Netherlands.

17 Buurman 1979, 1988.

18 Beex/Hulst 1968, fig. 6.

19 Waterbolk 1964, 1987.

20 Waterbolk 1987, 1989.

21 Van der Waals/Butler 1976, Harsema 1980.

22 Huijts 1992.

23 Harsema 1974, 1991.

24 Harsema 1991, 27. A sample from the bedding trench yielded a ^{14}C date of 3460 ± 55 BP (GrN-6642) but the excavator is nevertheless of the opinion that the palisade dates from the Middle Bronze Age. Also doubtful is his interpretation that five of the houses were contemporary.

25 Verlinde 1982, Kooi 1991.

26 Waterbolk 1985a; Harsema 1987, 109.

27 IJzereef/Van Regteren Altena 1991.

28 Modderman 1955.

29 Verlinde 1982.

30 Verlinde 1991.

31 Bakker et al. 1977; IJzereef 1981; IJzereef/Van Regteren Altena 1991. An import part of the data about Westfrisia was provided by G.F. IJzereef.

32 Bakker et al. 1977, 222.

33 IJzereef/Van Regteren Altena 1991.

34 IJzereef/Van Regteren Altena 1991.

35 Glasbergen/Addink-Samplonius 1965.

36 Groenman-van Waateringe 1966, Ten Anscher 1990.

37 Therkorn 1986, Therkorn/Van Londen 1990.

38 Woltering 1991.

39 Hulst 1973, 1991; Theunissen 1999.

40 Oss-Ussen: Fokkens 1986, 1991b. Wijk bij Duurstede: Hessing 1991. Loon op Zand: Roymans/Hiddink 1991. Nijnsel: Beex/Hulst 1968. See Theunissen 1999 for a survey of more recently excavated house plans (Venraij, Blerick, Geldrop).

41 Hessing 1991. The results of the excavation at Wijk bij Duurstede (De Horden) referred to in this chapter have not yet been published. They were kindly provided by W.A.M. Hessing and W.A. van Es (ROB).

42 Fokkens 1991b, Vasbinder/Fokkens 1987.

43 Hulst 1973, 1991; Theunissen 1999.

44 Roymans/Hiddink 1991.

45 Beex/Hulst 1968, Hulst 1973. The round feature of Nijnsel was not recognized in the field but on the drawing table (W. Beex, pers. com.). The features of Dodewaard and Zijderveld were 'recognized' in the field; their contours were indicated with markers which were then connected with string so as to make them stand out better. The postholes had not yet been sectioned at this stage. None of the Dutch archaeologists who visited the site saw the exposed features without these suggestive markings. See Theunissen 1999 for an extensive discussion.

46 It should be noted that in every publication these plans are shown out of context, i.e. without any indications of how they were reconstructed from concentrations of postholes and without illustrations showing the sections of the relevant postholes.

47 More round features have recently been recognized at Spoolde (Van Beek 1988), Zwolle (Clevis/Verlinde 1991), Dalen (Kooi 1991) and Elp (Van Beek 1991). Van Beek's publication, however, cannot be taken seriously because he reinterpreted the published, greatly reduced site plan (Waterbolk 1964) without consulting the drawings made in the field.

48 Theunissen 1999: Theunissen/Hulst forthcoming.

49 IJzereef 1981, IJzereef/Van Regteren Altena 1991.

50 Glasbergen 1954.

51 Fokkens 1991a, 1998a; IJzereef 1981.

52 Fokkens 1991a, 1998a; IJzereef 1981. Outside the Netherlands, on the island of Archsum in the Waddenzee, there was even evidence of sod manuring or Plaggen culture in the Middle Bronze Age (Kroll 1981). Of course we are here dealing with a rather exceptional situation.

53 See chapter 22 for more detailed information.

54 Fokkens 1999, 2002.

J   Shell fishers and cattle herders
Settlements of the Single Grave culture in Westfrisia

Willem Jan Hogestijn

The research into settlements of the Single Grave culture in Westfrisia has a long – but interrupted – history. The first settlement discovered, on a coastal barrier near Zandwerven, was investigated in 1929 by Van Giffen and in 1957 and 1958 by Van Regteren Altena.[1] Excavations have been carried out at Aartswoud[2] since 1972 and at two settlements near Kolhorn[3] since 1979, first by Lanting and later by Van der Waals. In 1986 Woltering excavated a small settlement near Keinsmerbrug. In an extensive survey in 1987 during the redivision of the region known as 'De Gouw' the RAAP Foundation discovered more than ten settlements of the Single Grave culture. As a result of this discovery the ROB launched a long-term protection and research project in 1989.[4] The area investigated lies to the north of the line that can be drawn from Hoorn to Bergen aan Zee.

Landscape and subsistence

With the exception of that at Zandwerven, all of the settlements discovered so far lie on Calais IVa2 levees (fig. J1). Pollen analysis shows that the landscape was fairly open at that time, *c.* 2600 BC. It consisted of extensive natural grassland, with an occasional willow and birch carr and some reed swamps. The use of heavy oak trunks for the construction of the big building at Zeewijk Oost, the many (charred) acorns at the Zeewijk site, and the charcoal analyses are, however, arguments in favour of occasional stands of trees on the slightly higher elevations, with oak, ash, alder and willow. Because of the decreasing influence of the sea and the gradually increasing influence of fresh water, from old courses of the IJssel and the Overijssel Vecht, among other sources, the landscape showed great ecological diversity. There were mud flats in varying degrees of desalination, numerous lakes and pools and above all endless reed marshes.

The pottery and a number of ^{14}C dates show that the aforementioned settlements, with the exception of that at Zandwerven, are datable to between *c.* 2600 and 2400 BC.[5]

The remains of all of the known settlements of the Single Grave culture were discovered close to the surface, above groundwater level; this means that the remains of this culture are being affected by oxidation and agrarian activities at a high rate. Sites of the Single Grave culture are hence usually recognised when the layer of organic remains that served as a platform for the raised settlements (the so-called culture horizon) happens to be partly exposed by ploughing.

Bones of domestic animals, especially cattle, ard marks, querns and seeds and pollen of naked barley and emmer indicate that the settlements were inhabited by an agrarian community. The large quantities of remains of game (especially of duck, but also wild boar, bear, red deer, roe deer, elk and aurochs), fish (for instance sturgeon, salmon, grey mullet, eel, cod, haddock and flatfish), shells (especially mussels, oysters and cockles) and nuts show that hunting, fishing and gathering were also very important in this economy.

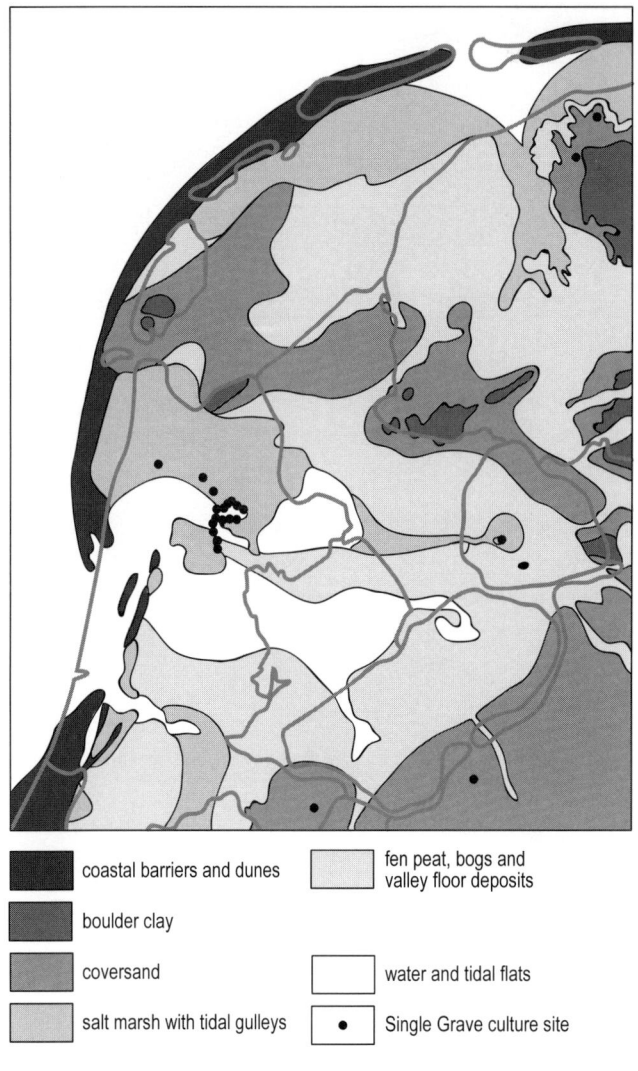

■ coastal barriers and dunes	▨ fen peat, bogs and valley floor deposits
▨ boulder clay	
▨ coversand	☐ water and tidal flats
▨ salt marsh with tidal gulleys	• Single Grave culture site

fig. J1

Palaeogeography of North Holland in the beginning of the third millennium B.C., with the location of Single Grave culture settlement sites.

Settlement form

The settlements can be divided into two groups on the basis of their size and former environment. The first group consists of sites larger than 3000 m², which were usually situated in the immediate vicinity of open water. The second group consists of much smaller sites (of approx. 300-400 m²) not situated in the immediate vicinity of open water (fig. J2-3). The difference in size could be interpreted as the result of a difference in the duration of occupation: the large sites may have been occupied for a longer period of time than the smaller ones. However, it seems not to be as simple as that. There are more differences between the large settlements and the small ones, for example:

– At large sites relatively larger amounts of butchering remains of domestic animals were found whereas at the smaller ones there were larger amounts of remains of game, especially of birds and fishes.

– Large sites are characterised by relatively larger amounts of bones of parts with relatively little meat, such as metapodials (metacarpals and metatarsals) and phalanges.

– the pottery of the large sites (fig. J4) shows great diversity: bowls, pots decorated with wavy bands, large beakers, baking trays or covers, for example, were found exclusively at the large sites. In addition, evidence for the secondary use of pottery has so far only been found at the large sites, for example: bases used as weights and wall sherds used as pottery burnishers;

– the diversity of stone and bone tools appears to be greater at the large sites;

– the average dimensions of postholes are larger at large sites;

– *ard* marks have so far only been found at or near large sites.

These differences seem to reflect differences in use and function between the two groups of sites. In the first place they may indicate differences in storage strategies: more storage evidence was found at the large sites, where storage was of greater importance.

Secondly, they may indicate differences in the size of the group of occupants, as appears from for example the fact that predominantly small cooking pots were found at the small sites whereas large ones were found at the large sites.

Thirdly, the differences may be attributable to differences in the nature and frequency of various subsistence activities. For example, hunting and fishing were of proportionately greater importance at the small sites, whereas agriculture was practiced near the large ones.

A fourth possibility is that differences in the period of use play a role: for example, smaller supplies may have been stored at the small sites. No large storage pots, which usually have longer lives, have been found up till now at the small sites.

The above considerations make it likely that the large sites are to be interpreted as base camps that were occupied for a long time, *i.e.* the actual settlements, and the small sites as logistic camps that were occupied for a short period of time; in other words, camps that were temporarily occupied in connection with specific, often seasonal, activities, such as hunting or fishing. Evidence supporting this interpretation is the fact that a large portion of the products of the small sites (hides, fish and perhaps even birds) was taken elsewhere, probably to the base camps.

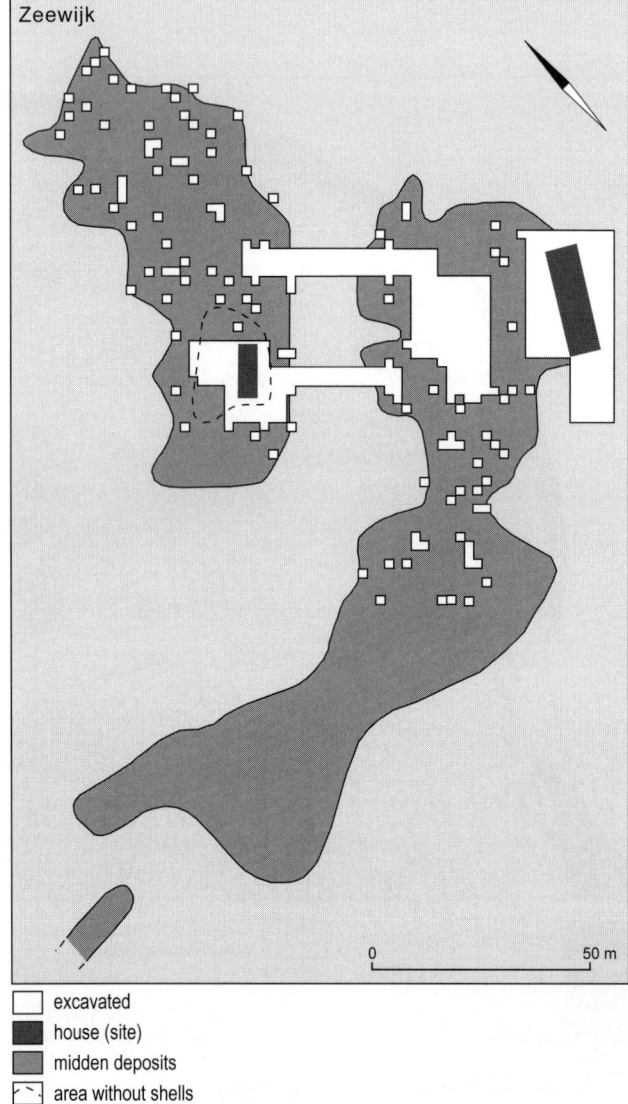

Zeewijk

☐ excavated
■ house (site)
▨ midden deposits
⌐⌐ area without shells

0   50 m

fig. J2
Plan of the Late Neolithic site of Zeewijk. The settlement was located on levee deposits at both sides of a former gulley, which had already been silted up completely.

Seasonal or permanent occupation?

One of the crucial questions is whether the area investigated was occupied throughout the year or for only part of it.

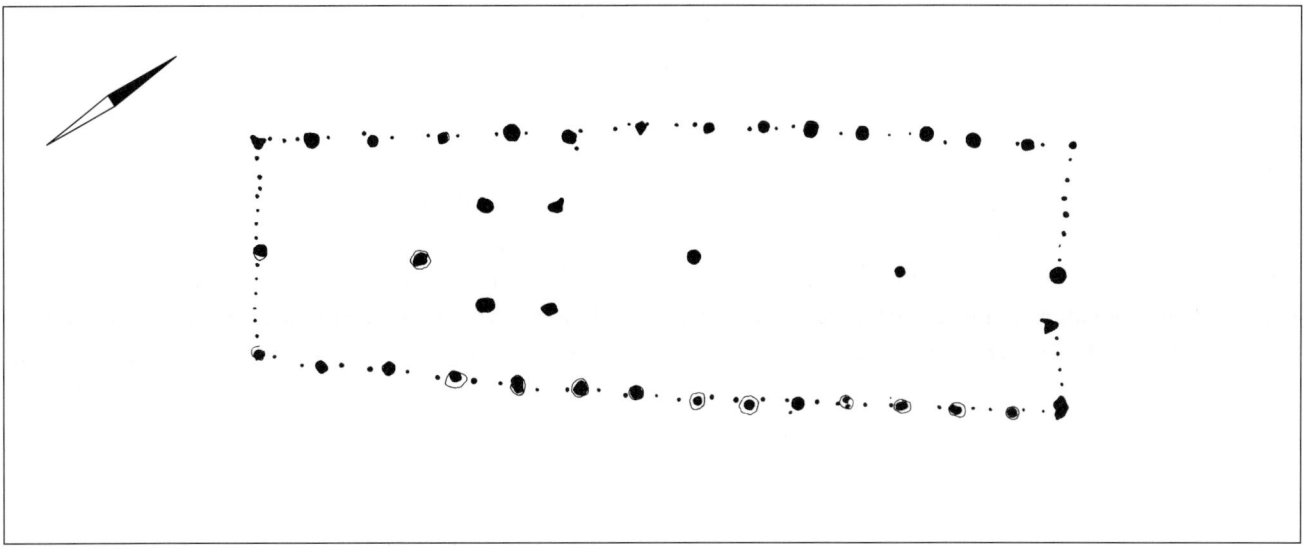

fig. J3
Zeewijk, plan of the 20 m long house, constructed from heavy posts, adjacent to the midden-deposits.
Scale 1:200.

Important information on this matter can be obtained from the analysis of the numerous remains of plants, seeds and bones that have been found at the base camps, but there are at least two general problems. The first problem is that the remains of plants or animals in principle provide an indication of the season in which they were harvested or killed, but can virtually never yield more precise information about the exact part of that season. For example, the bones of teal, a bird which is to be found in the Netherlands particularly in the winter half of the year, cannot tell us whether these birds were caught throughout the winter season or only for part of it. As teal bones are usually found in fairly large quantities, it seems less likely that they were caught during the summer half of the year.

The second problem is that the ecological remains can yield information about the time of harvesting or killing, but not necessarily about the time of consumption. It has been found that several sorts of food were stored for later consumption, for example cereal and nuts, but also cod and haddock and possibly meat, too. In the excavation of the small camp 'Mienakker' at Hoogwoud, for example, many remains of haddock, cod and whiting were found (3686 elements; 70% of the total number of fish bones). Analysis of these remains showed that of the large specimens especially the bones of the head and tail had remained. As there were no indications that the rest had decayed or had been eaten by for example dogs, we must assume that the fish were taken elsewhere after their heads and tails had been chopped off. They were probably dried or salted so that they could be consumed later.

Because of the aforementioned problems in the inter-

pretation of zoological and botanical remains, it is virtually impossible to prove whether Westfrisia was occupied in the winter months, when stored food was probably consumed. All that is certain is that this area was occupied from early spring until sometime in the autumn.

Besides ecological data, information obtained in research on pottery and other artefacts can also tell us something about the duration of occupation. For example, some settlements in Westfrisia have yielded axes of a type with an extended cutting edge, which is as yet unknown in the sandy regions. Elements characteristic of Westfrisia can be distinguished in the decoration of the pottery, too. Decorative patterns composed of vertical elements, for example, seem to

fig. J4
Beaker pottery from the settlement Zeewijk: represented are later
Single Grave culture types and all-over-ornamented beakers.

be more common in this area than in the rest of the Netherlands.

The regional differences may reflect a separate, regional, tradition and could be interpreted as an indication of the permanent occupation of the clay area of Westfrisia. It should however be borne in mind that the information obtained for the rest of the Netherlands comes largely from graves and not from settlements. Only when settlement research starts to yield more information for the rest of the Netherlands will it be possible to make sound comparisons.[6]

Notes

1   Van Regteren Altena/Bakker 1961.

2   Iterson Scholten/De Vries-Metz 1981; Pals 1984.

3   Van der Waals 1989a, 1989b; Zeiler 1989.

4   Hogestijn 1992; Pasveer/Uytterschaut 1992;

5   Lanting/Mook 1977.

6   Two publications appeared after this text was written: Van Ginkel/Hogestijn 1997 for a wider public, and Van Heeringen/Theunissen 2002 with a full documentation on behalf of archaeological heritage management.

19   Mounds for the dead
Funerary and burial ritual in Beaker period, Early and Middle Bronze Age

Erik Drenth and Eric Lohof

BARROWS AND FLAT GRAVES

Our knowledge of the Late Neolithic (Single Grave culture and Bell Beaker culture), the Early Bronze Age and the Middle Bronze Age is based largely on burial evidence, in particular on the information obtained in the excavation of barrows and flat graves.[1] A barrow or tumulus is a grave covered by a round or sometimes oval mound.[2] Being such conspicuous monuments, barrows have over the years attracted a good deal of interest from amateur and professional researchers. Flat graves, not being covered by mounds, are discovered only by chance, for example when grave goods are encountered during digging operations. Sometimes flat graves are found during large-scale excavations of, for example, settlements from an entirely different period. Because of this chance factor, flat graves are substantially underrepresented among the burials known from this period. Furthermore, we must allow for the possibility that the Late Neolithic and Early and Middle Bronze Age societies disposed of a certain percentage of their deceased, which is difficult for us to estimate, in a manner that left no archaeologically recoverable traces. However, with due cautiousness, this sample can nevertheless be used as a source of information on social relationships and the changes they underwent.

In the time span of almost two millennia discussed in this chapter (2900-1100 BC) the common burial practice comprised the inhumation of a single corpse in a flat grave or beneath a barrow, sometimes in a small necropolis. Within what was essentially a continuous tradition a number of more or less gradual changes took place, which resulted in a good deal of diversity in the burials over long periods of time. The distribution areas of both types of burials are largely limited to the Pleistocene sands, with major concentrations on the Drenthe plateau, on the Veluwe and in the Kempen region. To the south of the major rivers and in North Holland only burials from the late phase of the Single Grave culture onwards have been found, while no more than a few Bell Beaker burials and one or two Early Bronze Age flat graves have so far come to light in South Holland. No burials whatsoever have been discovered in Zeeland.[3]

Construction and situation

Several Late Neolithic flat graves have been found on settlement sites or in their immediate vicinity (fig. 19.1).[4] Sometimes they are grouped into small cemeteries; the largest concentration so far encountered consisted of eight flat graves.[5] Flat graves from the Early Bronze Age are virtually unknown in the Netherlands,[6] but Middle Bronze Age flat graves have been found, some in small groups in settlements or in the vicinity of or beneath barrows.[7]

Late Neolithic barrows are usually isolated monuments, but sometimes a group of (at most five) barrows of the same period is found.[8] By the Middle Bronze Age B some of these groups of barrows had expanded into *necropoles* of several dozens

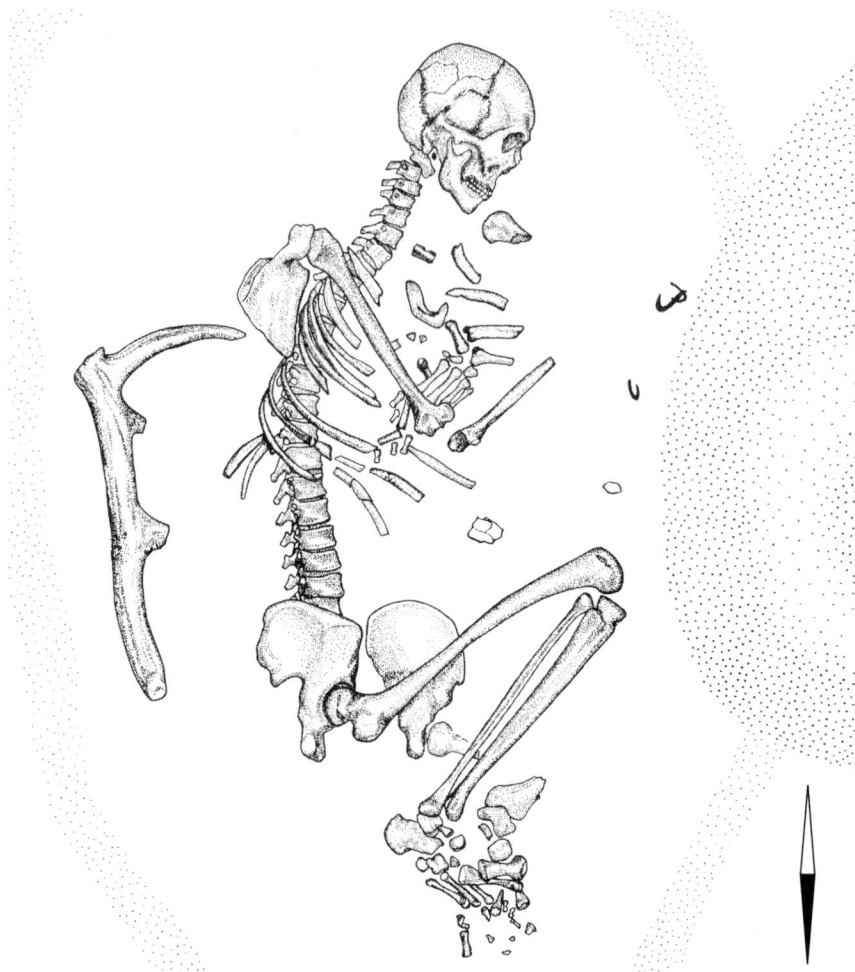

fig. 19.1

A flat grave from transition of Late Neolithic B to the Early Bronze Age at Molenaarsgraaf. The grave goods, in particular the bone fish hooks (fig. 14.17), suggest that the skeleton, of a man aged about 30, is that of a fisherman. The antler hook may have been used for lifting nets from the water and the flint artefacts for removing fish scales. Scale 1:10.

of mounds (plate 35A). In that period it also became customary to use existing barrows to accommodate new central burials (which resulted in what are known as 'multi-period barrows'). Sometimes barrows are found to lie in a row, suggesting that they had been sited along a road.[9] Many barrows were thrown up near the crests of natural elevations in the landscape.

Most of the barrows were constructed from sods, probably from the Late Neolithic onwards, but this is only apparent in the case of those from the Middle Bronze Age onwards: the sod structure of the earlier barrows is not clear because no well-developed podzols had yet been formed in the forests (plate 33A, 34A). Podzolisation did not take place until after a heather vegetation had developed in the permanent clearances that were created in the Late Neolithic.[10]

ASPECTS OF THE BURIAL RITE

The posture of the deceased

Direct evidence regarding the treatment of the deceased in the Late Neolithic and the Bronze Age is scarce because hardly any unburned skeletal remains have been preserved in the sandy region, the main distribution area of the barrows and flat graves. Silhouettes, sometimes still including the highly durable enamel teeth crowns, have survived as discolourations in the soil at only a small number of findspots with more favourable preservation conditions (fig. 19.2). Consequently, the sex and age of the deceased from this period can usually not be determined, at least not on the basis of skeletal evidence.

In most cases only one individual was buried in each grave. In the Late Neolithic and the Early Bronze Age the deceased were usually placed on their sides, in crouched position (plate 33B). The orientation of the body in the graves of the Single Grave culture was probably dependent on the sex of the deceased.[11] It is assumed that men were usually placed on their right sides, with their heads towards the west, and women on their left sides, with their heads towards the east; in both cases the face of the deceased was turned towards the south. As far as we know from graves outside the Netherlands, in the Bell Beaker period the usual position was the other way around: men were placed on the left side, women on the right. In the course of the Early Bronze Age the practice of extended inhumation was introduced (plate 34B).[12]

It is striking that in the case of almost all of the skeletons and silhouettes observed in the graves of the Bell Beaker culture the deceased had been placed in crouched position on their left sides.[13] This raises the question whether these graves all contained the remains of men, like those found abroad in which the deceased had been placed in the same position[14] or whether the former distinction between the sexes was no longer made in this period. Meanwhile it has become clear that both in flat graves and in barrows men were usually placed on their left sides, with their head towards the east, women on their right side with their head towards the west.[15]

fig. 19.2
The silhouette of a Late Neolithic body buried in a faintly crouched position beneath barrow II at Elp.

435

Different periods, but especially the Late Neolithic and the Early Bronze Age, are characterised by different grave orientations. The majority of the graves of the Single Grave culture were oriented E-W, with a maximum deviation of 45° towards the north or the south.[16] Graves containing so-called 'all-over ornamented' beakers from the last phase of this culture seem to have been oriented mainly NW-SE.

The majority of the Bell Beaker graves to the west of the IJssel were also oriented E-W, whereas some of those found to the north and east of that river were oriented N-S and some E-W. The differentiation in the latter area continued during the Early Bronze Age, while a few graves were also oriented NW-SE. In the Middle Bronze Age A the main orientation in that area became N-S, but some graves continued to be oriented E-W, especially those beneath mounds surrounded by a ring of stones, as was also the common tradition in northwest Germany and southern Scandinavia.[17] The Middle Bronze Age B saw another shift in orientation in Drenthe and on the Veluwe, this time to NW-SE, while the orientation in North Brabant shifted to NE-SW.

Inhumations and cremations

The aforementioned burials are all inhumation burials. Although being rare, cremation burials occurred during the Late Neolithic. No more than four cremation burials can be dated with any accuracy to the late phase of the Single Grave culture.[18] Twelve cremation burials have been dated to the Bell Beaker period, but only three from the Early Bronze Age. In the Middle Bronze Age A cremation was practised frequently all over the Netherlands. All of the Neolithic graves and most of those from the Bronze Age are of the type that is referred to as a *Brandskelettgrab* in Germany: a grave with the dimensions of an inhumation grave of an adult in which the cremated remains were spread out or deposited in a heap.

In the Middle Bronze Age A the number of barrows in the northern part of the Netherlands increased considerably. The increase concerns central cremation burials. This implies a marked change in the ratio of central inhumation and cremation burials beneath barrows: just over half of the barrows contain inhumation burials, the rest cremation burials. The same holds for the Veluwe, but in the southern part of the Netherlands the situation is different (fig. 19.3). There the great majority of the burials from the Middle Bronze Age onwards are cremation burials.[19] In the northern and central parts of the Netherlands the ratio changed again in the Middle Bronze Age B, when cremation was within a relatively short time almost completely replaced by inhumation.[20]

In the south of the Netherlands the cremated remains were often buried in urns of the Hilversum, Drakenstein or Laren types. However, contrary to what is generally assumed, these urns are only very rarely found in central burials.[21] They are more frequently encountered in secondary burials in barrows, especially the Drakenstein and Laren urns. To the north of the river IJssel the cremated remains were not placed in earthenware vessels in the Middle Bronze Age, but they were sometimes accompanied by small pots of the Elp type, though only in secondary burials.[22]

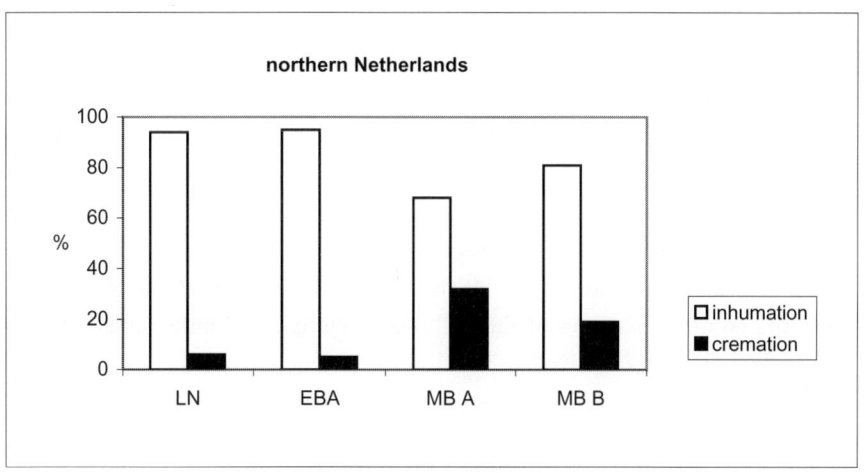

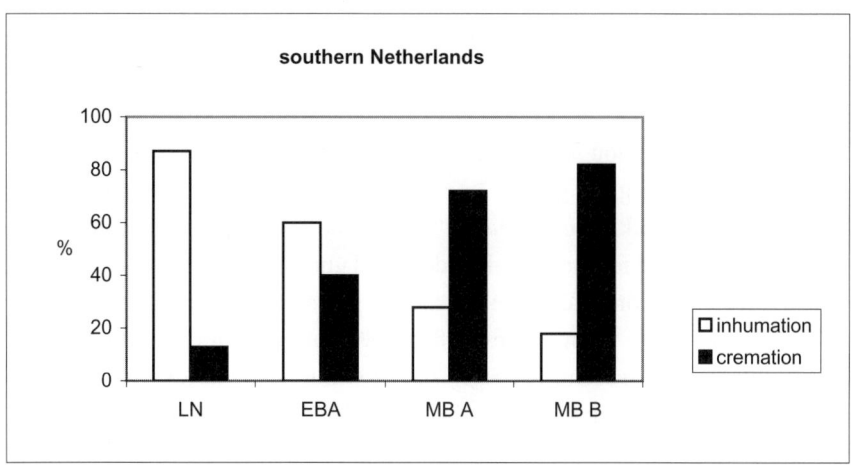

fig. 19.3
Developments in the treatment of the deceased in the northern and southern Netherlands during the Late Neolithic (LN), and the Early and Middle Bronze Age (MB A and B).

Collective burials and mortuary houses

On the whole, the burials from the Late Neolithic, the Early Bronze Age and the Middle Bronze Age are single burials, but some contain the remains of two or more deceased. A number of such collective burials are known from the Late Neolithic.[23] Collective inhumation burials of an adult and a child are known from the Middle Bronze Age.[24] Sometimes the cremated remains of one or more individuals were buried in an inhumation grave. A few *Brandskelettgräber* have also been found to contain the burned remains of several individuals.[25] An exceptional case is the Early Bronze Age collective burial of Wassenaar, in which the remains of twelve persons – men, women and children – who had met with violent deaths had been simultaneously buried (see feature L).[26]

Besides graves containing the remains of several deceased we also know of simultaneous burials in separate graves, from the Late Neolithic as well as from the Early and Middle Bronze Age. The best-known example in the Netherlands is that of the inhumation burials of three adults and two children that were found in the Middle Bronze Age barrow 75 in the Noordsche Veld near Zeijen (fig. 19.4).[27] Other simultaneous burials from this period comprise combinations of several compact cremation burials, *Brandskelettgräber* and cremation burials, inhumation and cremation burials or several *Brandskelettgräber*.

In the northern and central parts of the Netherlands 'mortuary houses' are frequently associated with two or more simultaneous Middle Bronze Age burials. So we may assume that there was a direct connection between the two. In those areas the mortuary houses had comprised four sturdy corner posts set around a central

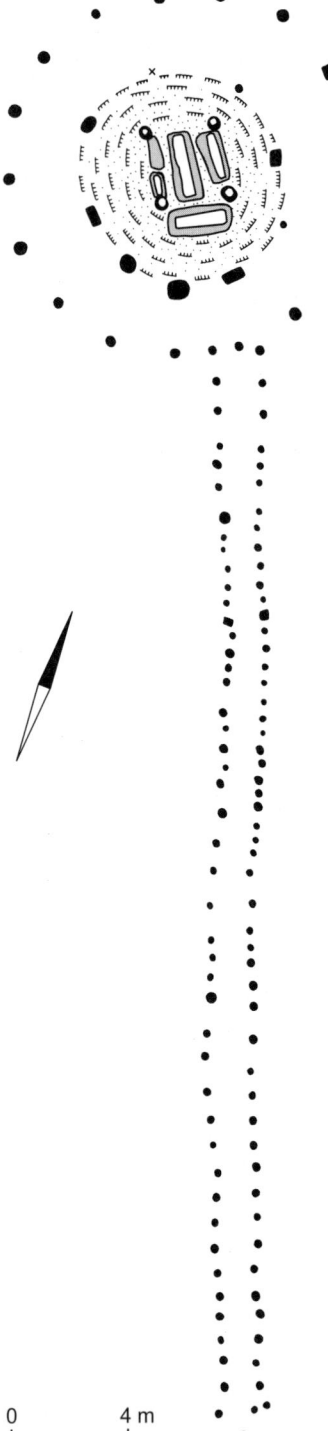

inhumation burial. In North Brabant some of the mortuary houses had comprised thin posts arranged around a central cremation burial underneath a barrow. Contrary to what is assumed to have been the case in the northern and central parts of the Netherlands, it would seem that these mortuary houses were removed before the cremated remains were deposited in the grave. Mortuary houses are also frequently associated with Middle Bronze Age flat graves, in which case they probably served to mark the graves aboveground. Only one mortuary house has been found in association with a grave of the Single Grave culture.[28] None has been encountered under barrows of the Bell Beaker culture and only one example is known from the Early Bronze Age.[29]

Other forms of burial

There are indications that deceased were also buried in different ways, besides in barrows or flat graves.

Several *hunebedden* have for example yielded artefacts of the Single Grave and Bell Beaker cultures;[30] although those artefacts were not associated with skeletal remains they could be grave goods. A small number of Early Bronze Age artefacts have also been found in hunebedden.[31] That could indicate that *hunebedden* were – sporadically – used for the 'burial' of deceased until in the Bronze Age.

If the aforementioned artefacts are indeed grave goods, they differ markedly from the grave goods recovered from flat graves and barrows. No or hardly any objects like (pseudo-)Grand-Pressigny daggers, flint arrowheads, (hammer) axes, wristguards and copper or bronze artefacts have come to light in *hunebedden*, whereas virtually none of the pottery types frequently found in *hunebedden*, such as amphorae, beakers with short wave moulding and beaker pots, has so far been encountered in single graves, although they are known from settlement contexts.[32]

The parts of skeletons that are sometimes found within settlements may indicate that some of the deceased were treated differently.[33] Those bones could be the remains of disturbed graves or they could have ended up in the settlement because they were treated as waste. Incomplete skeletons encountered in barrows are probably to be interpreted as remains that were reburied there some time after their original burial.[34]

THE STRUCTURE OF THE GRAVES

The shape and design of the grave pit

Most of the graves are rectangular to oval, their lengths varying from 1.5 to 2.5 m and their widths from 0.80 to 1.5 m. A small number of graves are smaller than 1.1 x 0.6 m; they are regarded as children's graves. The deepest graves have depths of over 2 m. In the northeast of the Netherlands the *Brandskelettgräber* are less deep

0   4 m

fig. 19.4

Barrow 75 on the Noordse Veld near Zeijen, scale 1:250. Two adults and two children were buried at the centre of the barrow, in a mortuary house covered with stones. A third adult was buried outside this mortuary structure. The capping stones were covered with sods. A double row of postholes marks a 34-m-long access route to the barrow. The outermost ring of postholes is thought to date from a following phase, in which the central cremation burial was created on the capping stones of the preceding period.

fig. 19.5
Plaster cast of the Late Neolithic grave 9 at Schokland (P14). A man aged 25-35 was buried without grave goods between two lengths of oak bark with his head in the west, facing the south.

than the inhumation graves, while secondary inhumation graves in barrows are generally slightly deeper than primary inhumation graves.[35]

A different form of graves are the graves known as ground graves, in which the deceased were not buried in pits, but were placed on the old land surface (which was sometimes levelled by removing sods) and were then covered with a mound. This form of burial was frequently practised from the late phase of the Single Grave culture onwards. It became particularly common in the northeastern part of the Netherlands in the Early Bronze Age. In that area many of the mounds erected over these burials contain rings of stones, usually halfway between the burial and the periphery of the mound. About 50% of the total number of Early Bronze Age central burials in the northeast of the Netherlands are ground graves,[36] but that decreased to just over one-third in the course of the Middle Bronze Age. In the adjacent part of northwest Germany, on the contrary, ground graves prevailed over other types of burials in the Middle Bronze Age.[37]

A special type of grave that is known from the Late Neolithic only is the so-called 'beehive grave', whose edges were deeper than the central part of the grave. Postholes and traces of wattle walls observed in these deeper parts indicate that they are in fact bedding trenches.[38] Beehive graves are known from the entire Single Grave period, both as flat graves and as central graves beneath barrows.[39] Beehive graves from the Bell Beaker period are rare and none whatsoever are known from the Bronze Age.[40]

Some graves showed discolourations suggesting that the grave was lined with timber. In the relatively well-preserved Late Neolithic flat grave cemetery that was found on plot P14 in the Noordoostpolder the deceased had been placed on pieces of wood, probably bark (fig. 19.5).[41] In one of the graves the deceased was found to have been covered with bark; this may have been the case in some of the other graves of this cemetery, too. The two long sides and the bottom end of a Middle Bronze Age A grave found at Velserbroek had been lined with planks, which still was covered with bark and then coated with a layer of clay. The deceased, an adult man, had been placed on a bed of sods (fig. 19.6), after which the grave had been covered with a bark lid.[42]

From the late phase of the Single Grave culture onwards (c. 2600-2500 BC) graves were occasionally lined with boulders. Several of such 'stone cists' are known from the Early Bronze Age, but only few from after that period. In the Middle Bronze Age it was more customary to cover graves with a cairn. The boulders (or sods) that are sometimes found inside graves probably served to prevent the

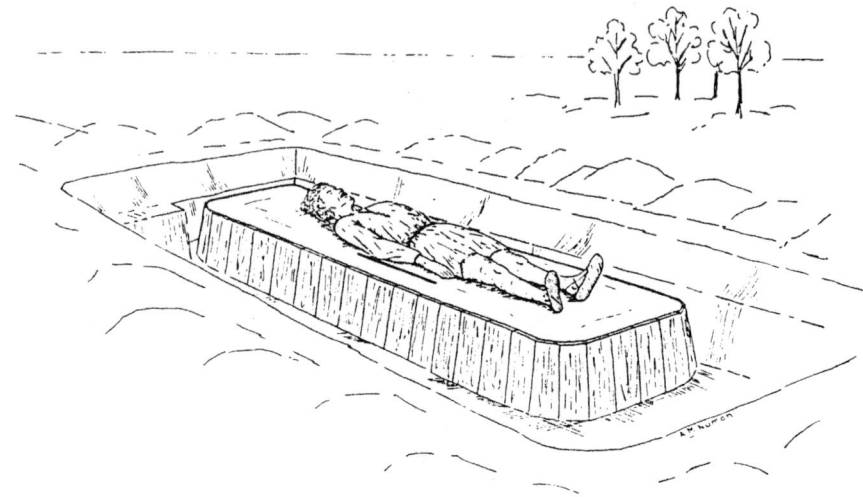

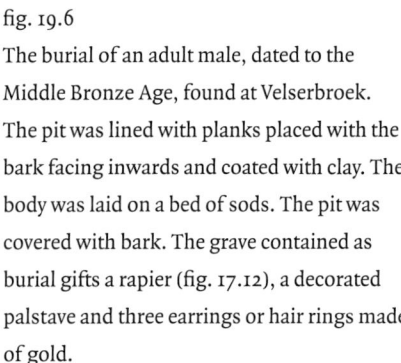

fig. 19.6
The burial of an adult male, dated to the Middle Bronze Age, found at Velserbroek. The pit was lined with planks placed with the bark facing inwards and coated with clay. The body was laid on a bed of sods. The pit was covered with bark. The grave contained as burial gifts a rapier (fig. 17.12), a decorated palstave and three earrings or hair rings made of gold.

semi-circular (tree-trunk) coffin from toppling over. Such forms of support are known from the early phase of the Single Grave culture onwards (from approx. 2800 BC); they were quite common in the Middle Bronze Age. The Middle Bronze Age custom of placing the deceased on hides or woollen blankets, surrounded by flowers and branches of hazel and other trees, attested in England and Denmark, may have been practised in the Low Countries, too, but no indications of this custom have survived in the sandy part of the Netherlands.[43]

Features surrounding the burials: rings of posts, circular ditched enclosures and other peripheral features

Many burials were surrounded by post circles or ditched enclosures. The shape of these features is usually characteristic of only one period and they are therefore of great help to archaeologists in the dating of the various funerary monuments (fig. 19.7).

Several Late Neolithic flat graves and burials beneath barrows were surrounded by more or less circular ditches. Some of those ditches were found to contain postholes. In the case of burials beneath barrows, the distance between these enclosures and the burial varied: a) some had been dug immediately around the central burial, b) some in an 'intermediate' position, about halfway between the burial and the periphery of the mound, and c) some beneath the periphery of the mound, but never outside the mound; the palisades that stood in the latter ditches may have served to temporarily screen off the area of the burial, before the mound was thrown up over it.[44] The intermediate enclosures containing postholes disappeared towards the end of the Bell Beaker period. Intermediate rings of stones, however, are known from the Early Bronze Age, especially from areas where ample stones were available.[45]

Characteristic of the Middle Bronze Age A are the mounds surrounded by circular ditches. They have been observed over a large area, from northern France to northwest Germany. Of relevance in this context is the discussion about a type of barrows with ditch and internal bank, which have been found in the southern part of the Netherlands.[46] In the 1930s, two different types of mounds surrounded by circular ditches were distinguished in the Netherlands: mounds with ditches that had been dug immediately around the periphery of the mound and mounds surrounded by ditches whose soil had been used to create a separate bank between the ditch and the mound. Glasbergen called the latter type a *ringwalheuvel* (literally: 'ringbank barrow'). In view of its resemblance to the English bell and disc bar-

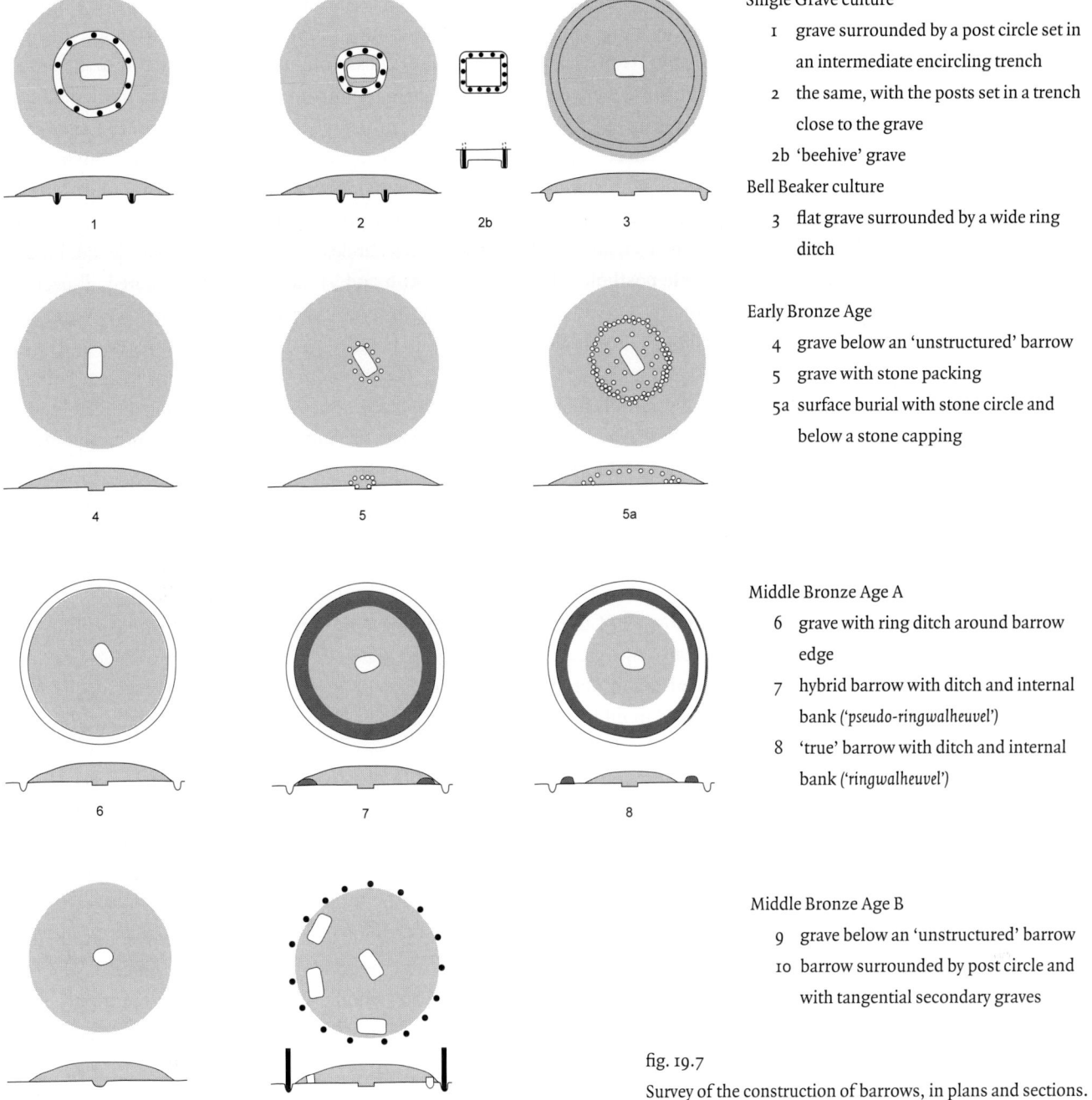

Single Grave culture
1 grave surrounded by a post circle set in an intermediate encircling trench
2 the same, with the posts set in a trench close to the grave
2b 'beehive' grave

Bell Beaker culture
3 flat grave surrounded by a wide ring ditch

Early Bronze Age
4 grave below an 'unstructured' barrow
5 grave with stone packing
5a surface burial with stone circle and below a stone capping

Middle Bronze Age A
6 grave with ring ditch around barrow edge
7 hybrid barrow with ditch and internal bank ('pseudo-ringwalheuvel')
8 'true' barrow with ditch and internal bank ('ringwalheuvel')

Middle Bronze Age B
9 grave below an 'unstructured' barrow
10 barrow surrounded by post circle and with tangential secondary graves

fig. 19.7
Survey of the construction of barrows, in plans and sections.

rows, he regarded this type as evidence indicating that the people of the Hilversum culture had crossed over to the Netherlands from England. It was subsequently discovered that in some cases barrow and bank were merged, which gave the barrow a similar appearance as the common barrow with circular ditch. This type was called a *pseudo-ringwalheuvel*.[47] The British relations were, however, disputed. In England the bank is usually outside the ditch and there is a berm between the mound and the ditch. Such barrows may be recognisable in Belgium, but not in the Netherlands.[48] But that doesn't alter the fact that bermed mounds with a bank inside the circular ditch occur in the southern part of the Netherlands. They were constructed in very much the same way as the mounds with circular ditches: the soil from the ditch was piled up on the inside of the ditch. The only difference is that the ditch of a 'true' *ringwalheuvel* had such a large diameter that a berm remained between the mound and the bank. This type of barrow may represent a regional development, specific to the Kempen region.[49]

In the Middle Bronze Age B the circular ditches were replaced by various types of circular settings of posts all over its Western European distribution area, except in Westfrisia, where circular ditches continued to be dug in this period, too.[50] The posts were erected around the burial before the mound was thrown up over it, during the burial rite associated with the central burial.[51] There are a number of pronounced geographical differences. In North Brabant, in particular in the Kempen region, circles of widely spaced paired postholes have been found, whereas rings of widely spaced single postholes prevail in the northern Netherlands (Glasbergen's types 4 and 3, respectively). Circles of closely spaced single, double and triple postholes (fig. 19.8, types 5, 6 and 7) have been encountered all over the country, but mostly in the south.[52] In some cases the mounds had been surrounded by a fence of closely spaced thin posts (type 9). In the northeastern part of the Netherlands such mounds have only been found in the Hijkerveld near Beilen.[53] A few burials in North Brabant had also been (temporarily?) surrounded by such fences.[54] The postholes of these fences lay halfway between the burial and the periphery of the mound.

GRAVE GIFTS

Almost all of the grave goods that have been recovered from Late Neolithic and Bronze Age graves are of inorganic material. The burned bone objects that have been found among cremated remains suggest that organic grave goods were placed in inhumation graves, but they have not survived in the sandy soils of the Netherlands.[55]

The majority of the Late Neolithic grave goods are earthenware vessels, mainly beakers, and flint or stone tools (fig. 19.9). Comparison with finds recovered from other contexts, especially from settlements, shows that these grave goods represent only a selection of the total range of artefacts used in this period. For example, beakers with short wave moulding, beaker pots and barbed wire pots, querns and flint scrapers are only very rarely found in barrows or flat graves. Usually, only one specimen of each category of grave goods is found in the graves of the Late Neolithic and those of the Early and Middle Bronze Age, with the exception of some categories, in particular pottery and flint arrowheads.

fig. 19.8
A barrow (tumulus 17) surrounded by a double ring of closely spaced postholes at Toterfout-Halve Mijl during its excavation by W. Glasbergen in 1948.

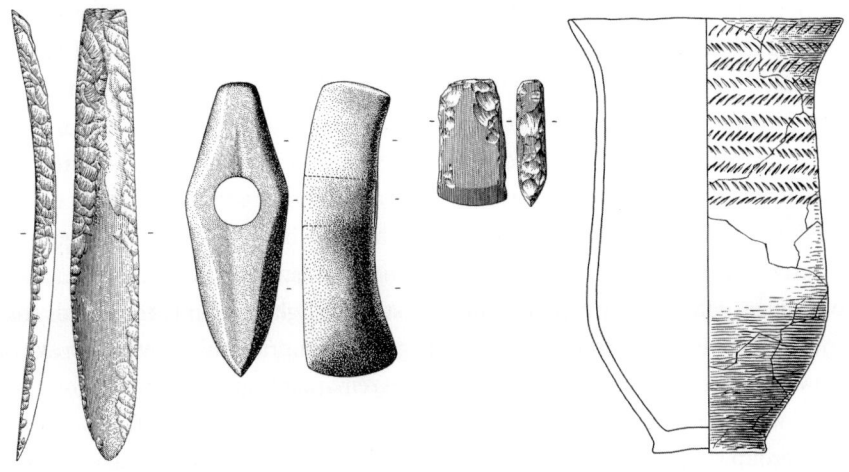

fig. 19.9

A burial of the Single Grave culture, tumulus II 'Galgenwandveen' near Eext, excavated in 1970. The grave contained a 1d beaker, a stone hammer axe, a Grand-Pressigny dagger and a flint axe. Scale 1:4.

By analogy with evidence obtained for Battle Axe and Bell Beaker cultures abroad it is assumed that the grave goods of the Single Grave culture were to some extent associated with the sex of the deceased. Stone hammer axes or battle axes, daggers of French flint (Grand-Pressigny daggers), flint arrowheads, grinding stones and flint chisels made on blades are believed to have been typical male attributes. Male grave goods of the Bell Beaker culture comprise stone hammer axes, flint daggers, flint axes and arrowheads, retouched flint knives, tanged copper daggers, gold ornaments, crescent-shaped amber pendants, stone wristguards and 'arrow straighteners', cushion stones and stone hammers (presumably used for metal working), strike-a-lights and wild boars' tusks (fig. 19.10, plate 25A and B). We may also assume that the majority of the axes known from burials from the Single Grave culture belonged to men.[56] Only very few typically female grave goods have been found in Late Neolithic graves. It is believed that dishes and bowls, and especially also the Dose of the Single Grave culture, were deposited mainly in female graves.[57]

Early Bronze Age grave goods are rare. Occasionally the deceased was accompanied by a Barbed Wire beaker or a retouched flint knife, which was probably worn strapped around the hip. In a few Late Neolithic and Early Bronze Age barrows sherds of vessels with short wave moulding, pot beakers and barbed wire pots have been found in an off-centre position. The vessels in question appear to have been deliberately broken during or shortly after the digging of the central grave.[58] Noteworthy is that these particular types of pottery are hardly encountered in the graves themselves.

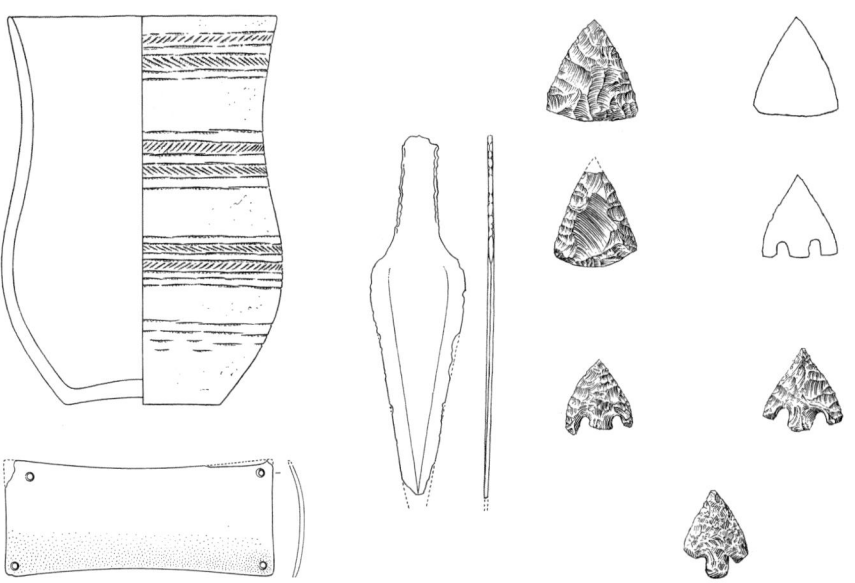

fig. 19.10

A burial of the Bell Beaker culture at Ede (Ginkelse Heide). The grave contained a maritime bell beaker (2Ib), a wristguard, a copper tanged dagger (all scale 1:4), seven arrowheads (scale 1:2) and a few strike-a-lights and flakes (not illustrated). The grave goods are associated with the cremated remains of two individuals: an adult (aged about 35) and an approximately 3-year-old infant.

In the northeastern Netherlands no more than about 10% of the graves from the end of the Early Bronze Age and the Middle Bronze Age A have yielded bronze artefacts, and in southern Netherlands even less. The number of finds that can be dated to the Early Bronze Age with any accuracy is particularly small. Most of these bronze artefacts are tools or weapons that may be regarded as parts of the deceased's personal equipment: swords, axes and arrowheads. Grave goods of this kind have only been found in central graves beneath barrows. The richest grave in this respect is a grave found at Drouwen, which yielded a sword, an axe and a razor of bronze, gold plait-rings, a whetstone, a strike-a-light and flint arrowheads (fig. 19.11).[59] Grave goods from contemporary graves comprise only a sword, an axe or a few arrowheads. These graves are akin to a remarkable group of graves found in northwest Germany: the Sögel graves, so called after a site near the Dutch border. This group is characterised by a range of grave goods consisting of a short bronze sword of the Sögel type, a curved type of bronze flanged axe and occasionally gold plait-rings and a strike-a-light. Comparable ranges of grave goods, but without the swords, are known from two other graves found in the northern part of the Netherlands.[60]

A grave has recently been discovered at Velserbroek which yielded a bronze axe imported from Scandinavia, a few composite gold rings and the corroded remains of a bronze rapier that has not yet been identified.[61] Two graves in North Brabant were found to contain a bronze axe, while two graves in Westfrisia contained a sword and graves on the Veluwe yielded a dagger, two axes and two swords.[62] These weapons are thought to have been typically male attributes. Female burials of this period are much harder to recognize.[63]

The central burials of the Middle Bronze Age B, on the contrary – and then only those found in the northern part of the country – have yielded only a few bronze chisels and axes but larger numbers of bronze pins. The greater number of secondary burials known from this period have yielded many grave goods: about 11% of the secondary inhumation burials discovered in the northern Netherlands were found to contain grave goods, notably strings of amber beads, bronze bracelets and finger rings. That is why the number of Middle Bronze Age B burials identified as female graves is far greater than the number of female burials known from the Middle Bronze Age A. The richest Bronze Age female grave known in the Netherlands is a secondary burial, which was found in a barrow at Weerdinge (fig. 19.15).[63]

In the south, where cremation was the most common form of burial, hardly any inorganic grave goods have been found.

REGIONAL DIFFERENTIATION

Regional differences are observable in the Late Neolithic and Bronze Age burials known in the Netherlands. These regional differences are essentially differences in emphasis; we cannot really draw any strict lines between the various regions. In the case of the graves of the Single Grave culture the distribution of the different types of hammer axes, the decorative motifs adorning the beakers and the burial customs all show regional differences. Beakers decorated with zoned corded impressions, for example, have been found predominantly in the central part of the Netherlands. In the early phase of the Single Grave culture hammer axes of type B appear to have been characteristic of the northern part of the Netherlands and facetted hammer axes of type 1 of the central part of the country.[65] Graves containing both AOO beakers and Grand-Pressigny daggers occur only in the central and southern part of the Netherlands.

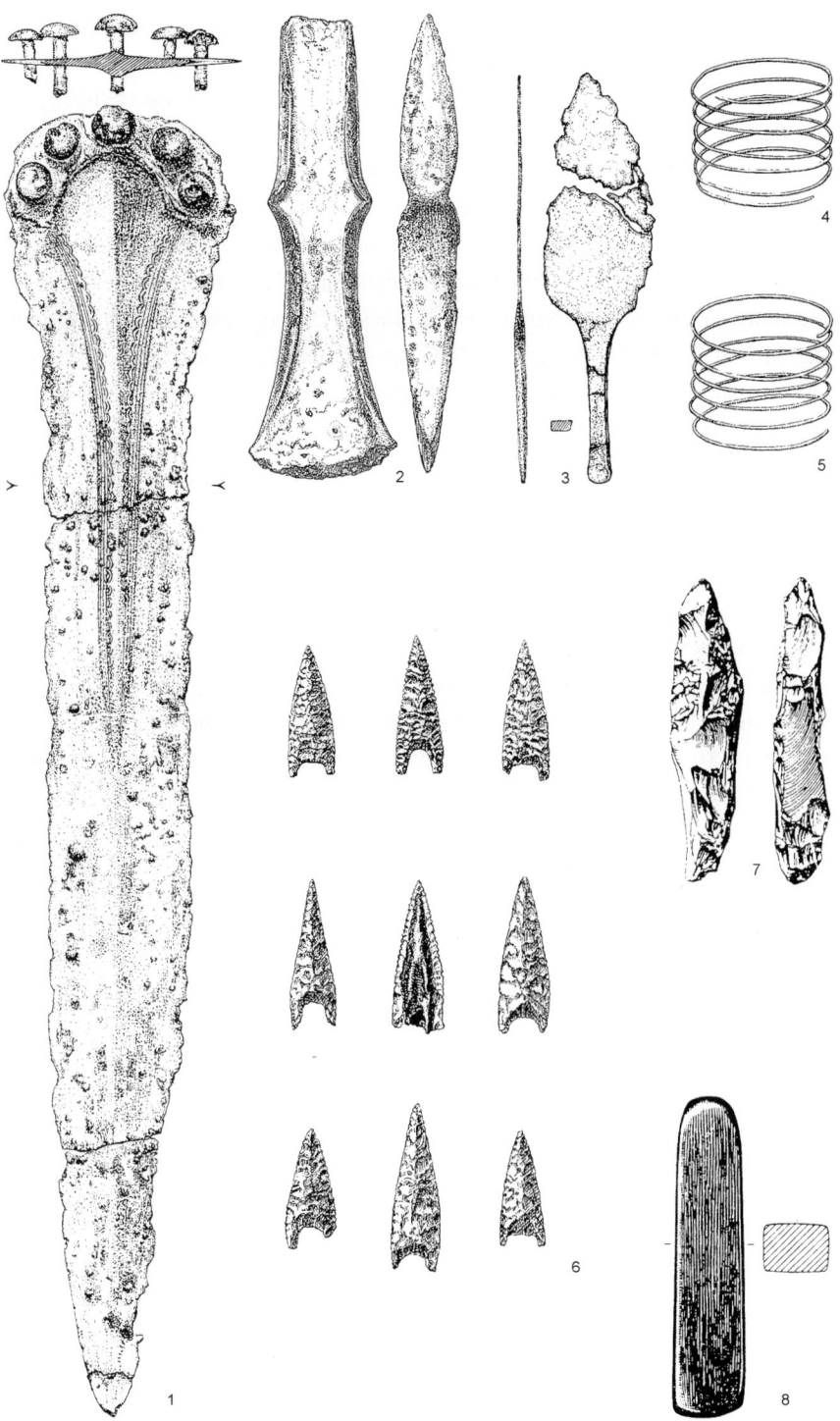

fig. 19.11

The inventory of the Sögel burial of Drouwen.

Scale 1:2.

1   sword, bronze

2   flanged axe with bent sides, bronze

3   bronze razor

4, 5 gold spirals, hair dress

6   flint arrowheads

7   a flint strike-a-light

8   a lydite whetstone

The difference in the orientation of the Bell Beaker graves between the northern and central parts of the Netherlands has already been mentioned above. Another difference concerns the earthenware: the Veluwe Bell Beaker is characteristic of the central part of the Netherlands, whereas the northern part had its own beaker earthenware.[66] In the north, the deceased were furthermore buried in stone cists. Regional differentiation is also observable in the distribution of the hammer axes: the Epe type has been found in the central part of the Netherlands, while the Zuid-velde and Emmen types are restricted to the northern part of the country.[67]

The regional differentiation is further emphasised by the fact that strike-a-lights, buttons with V-shaped perforations, crescent-shaped amber pendants and also copper and gold objects have been found predominantly in the central part of the Netherlands.[68] As also observed for the Single Grave culture, the burials of the

Bell Beaker culture in the southern part of the Netherlands are more akin to the burials in the central part of the Netherlands than to those further north.

More or less the same pattern of regional differentiation is observable in the Middle Bronze Age burial rite. The traditions of the area to the northeast of the IJssel closely resembled those in the west of Lower Saxony and Westphalia,[69] whereas those in the south of the Netherlands were more akin to rites in Belgium and northern France.[70] The main differences in the burial rite concern the aforementioned *ringwalheuvels* in the south of the Netherlands in the Middle Bronze Age A and the prevailing custom of urned cremation in the south as opposed to inhumation in the north in the Middle Bronze Age B. Other differences are observable in the design and use of mortuary houses, the orientation of the graves and preferences for different types post circles.

THE BURIAL RITE IN A SOCIAL PERSPECTIVE

In the preceding sections we have studied various aspects of the burial rite and have seen what changes they underwent in the period from the beginning of the Late Neolithic until the Late Bronze Age. Throughout this entire period, the burial rite remained based on the same principle, namely that of the inhumation of a single corpse. The existence of such a burial tradition and the changes it underwent were undoubtedly closely related to the society's ideology. For example, in the Late Neolithic as a rule only one individual was buried beneath each barrow, whereas the custom in the Middle Bronze Age was to bury a whole (kinship) group in each barrow; the latter barrows are sometimes even referred to as 'family barrows' (fig. 19.12). Such a shift in emphasis from the individual to the household can be seen as a consequence of a change in the community's social structure.[71]

We assume that the flat graves and barrows of this period were constructed according to a tradition associated with a clearly defined, structured set of standards and values. But this tradition was not static: it underwent changes because people 'manipulated' the burial rite. Changes observable in a particular tradition may reflect attempts to deny or on the contrary confirm certain aspects of that tradition (until fairly recently cremation was for example seen as a denial of the Christian belief in resurrection). The changes that took place in the burial rite in the Late Neolithic and the Early and Middle Bronze Age can hence tell us something about the relationships and dynamics of the societies of those periods. We will pay particular attention to these social aspects in the following sections.

The Beaker cultures

Differentiation on the basis of age and sex
From the relatively small number of burials known from the Late Neolithic and the small number of children's burials among those burials we may assume that in that period only a small percentage of the overall population was buried in flat graves or beneath barrows. The age of the deceased must have been one of the selection criteria for burial beneath a barrow, because no children were buried individually in central graves beneath barrows until in the Middle Bronze Age B. Moreover, the numbers and variety of grave goods found in children's graves are much smaller than those of the grave goods from graves of adults. Most of the few children's graves that have yielded grave goods contained only a beaker, which was smaller than beakers of adults. These differences show that children ranked

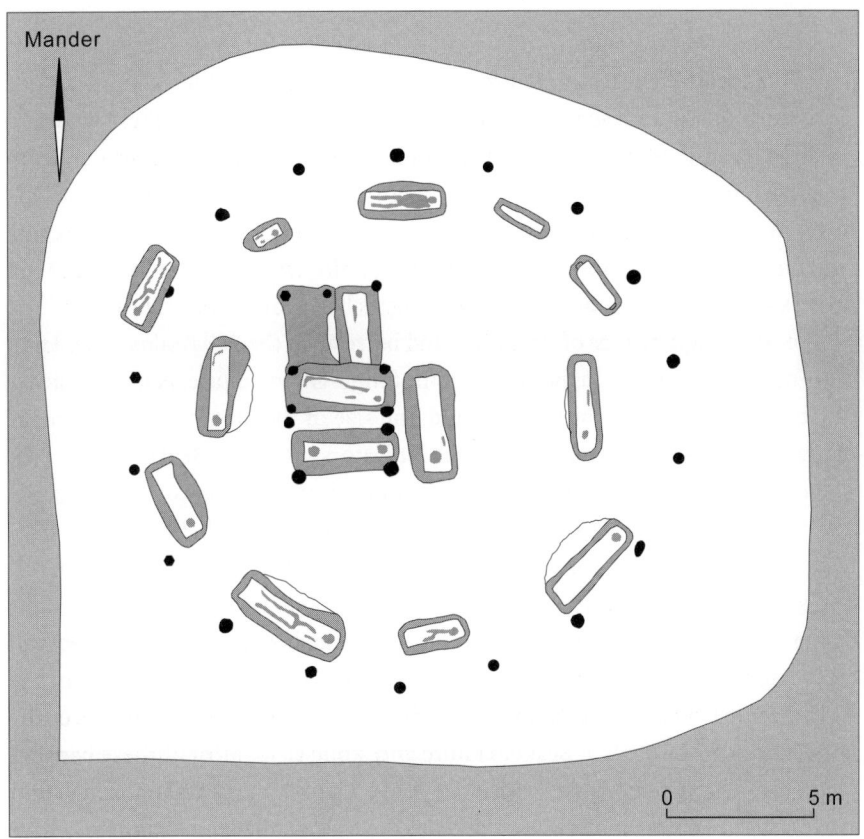

fig. 19.12
A so-called family barrow at Mander, dating from the Middle Bronze Age B. The four graves and the 'mortuary house' are thought to be older flat graves. The central burial is the approx. north-south oriented grave slightly to the east of the centre. The mound contained another 11 secondary burials. All the graves are inhumation burials. Scale 1:250.

lower in the social hierarchy than adults.[72] The sex of the deceased was probably also a criterion for differentiation in burial rite. It would seem that more men than women were buried in the barrows of the Single Grave culture and the same holds for the barrows of the Bell Beaker culture. Moreover, the richest burials of both the Single Grave culture and the Bell Beaker culture are almost all male burials.[73] This indicates that men generally enjoyed a higher status than women of the same age category and that they occupied what were formally the highest positions.

The relation between grave gifts and status
Late Neolithic flat graves and barrows have yielded various grave goods that were imported from distant regions, such as Grand-Pressigny daggers (fig. 19.9, plate 29), copper and gold artefacts, certain types of stone hammer axes, wristguards and relatively large flint axes and (retouched) flint blades. As most of these objects were found in male graves we may assume that the exchange networks were controlled by men.

All the available evidence suggests that in the late phase of the Single Grave culture the most important individuals, mainly adult men, were buried in ground graves.[74] These graves are all associated with relatively large barrows. Moreover, they have yielded the largest numbers of grave goods and also the richest grave goods. Those grave goods include Grand-Pressigny daggers and hammer axes and as Grand-Pressigny daggers have been encountered virtually exclusively in ground graves and hammer axes exclusively in relatively large barrows, most of which were thrown up over ground graves,[75] they will probably have symbolised a high male status. In the northern part of the Netherlands in particular a number of ground graves have been found in which men had been buried accompanied by both a hammer axe and a Grand-Pressigny dagger, but there is no reason to assume that their status differed fundamentally from that of the men who were buried in the central part of the Netherlands accompanied by only a Grand-Pressigny dagger. It is more likely that this difference represents a form of regional differentiation.[76]

An interesting question in this context is whether the large flint blades that are not made of French flint, but resemble French tools in shape and workmanship, show the same associations. This proves not to be the case: these so-called pseudo-Grand-Pressigny daggers have not been found in ground graves beneath large barrows, but only in flat graves and in graves beneath relatively small barrows. Moreover, the graves that yielded these pseudo-Grand-Pressigny daggers contained fewer and also less diverse grave goods. That makes it likely that the owners of the pseudo-Grand-Pressigny daggers had a lower social status.[77]

The social significance of flat graves and barrows in the Bell Beaker period was more or less the same as in the period of the Single Grave culture: generally speaking, the presence or absence of a mound, the size of the mound and the number of grave goods may be regarded as status indicators in the Bell Beaker period, too. The main grave goods associated with men in this period are stone wristguards and copper and gold objects. The latter objects, which are probably imports, have been found mainly in the central part of the Netherlands. They probably symbolised social positions comparable with those associated with the Grand-Pressigny daggers and hammer axes in the Single Grave period, because they were almost all recovered from large barrows.

In the north of the Netherlands there seems to be a close connection between the largest barrows of the Bell Beaker culture and stone cists. Most of these barrows contained no grave goods; those that did yielded hammer axes and retouched flint knives. In the central and southern parts of the Netherlands, cremation may have been a privilege reserved for important men: one of the richest Bell Beaker burials known in the Netherlands, that of Ede-Ginkelse Heide, is a cremation burial (fig. 19.10).[78] In Drenthe and Overijssel, however, cremation was a less exclusive form of burial: four of the five cremation burials known in those provinces were found in flat graves that contained only a few grave goods.[79]

To conclude, it appears that during the Single Grave culture social differences were increasingly emphasised by means of other variables besides grave goods. The size of the barrow in particular seems to have become more important. This development was undoubtedly associated with the observed increase in the number of burials in flat graves and barrows. The erection of a mound and its size were apparently regarded as means of distinction. The increase in the number of ground graves and the greater diversity observable in the grave goods can also be viewed

fig. 19.13
Excavation plan of the Galgenberg barrow at Sleen (scale 1:400) and the inventory of its primary burial (scale 1:2). The burial was surrounded by a ring of postholes (presumably the outermost) with a diameter of 19.6 m and was partly disturbed by a recently dug pit. The other burial structures date from two earlier barrow periods.

1 bronze axe
2 fragments of at least 11 bronze arrowheads
3 tweezers (fragment)
4 two gold rings
5 thin bracelet, bronze

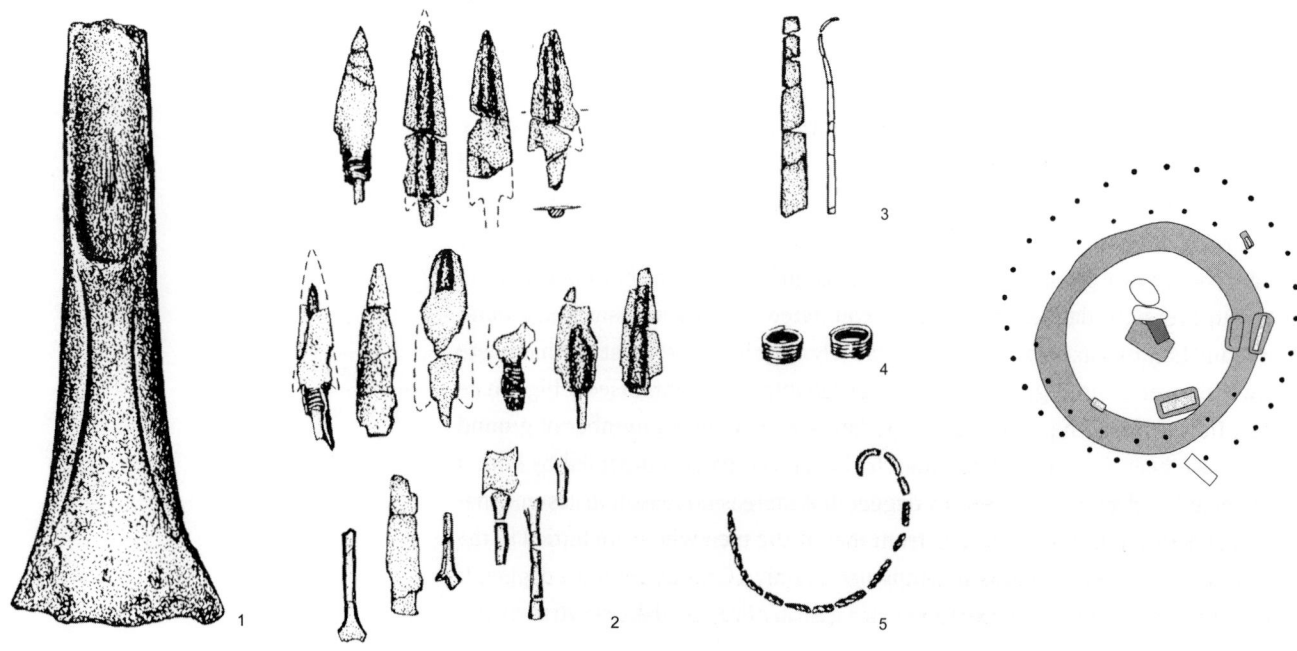

against this background. There are indications that the burial rite was in the Late Neolithic increasingly dominated by men. Whereas a certain – if small – number of the burials of the Single Grave culture can be identified as female burials on the basis of the grave goods associated with them, very few female burials are recognisable among the burials of the Bell Beaker culture. There are moreover indications that the range of typically male grave goods increased during the Late Neolithic.

The Early Bronze Age: towards new status positions

For a long time it has been suspected that only a select group of people was buried in barrows in the Late Neolithic and the Early Bronze Age. If we compare the number of burials from those periods with the number of burials known from the Middle Bronze Age B and if we then consider the lengths of those periods we must conclude that in the Early Bronze Age at most 15% of the population was buried in barrows. In Denmark this select group has moreover been found to have comprised twice as many men as women.[80] The absence of indisputably female graves of Early Bronze Age date suggests that the situation in the Netherlands may be quite similar.

The burial practice of the Early Bronze Age was a direct continuation of that of the Bell Beaker period, characterised by the inhumation of a single corpse beneath a barrow in which no or only very few secondary burials were accommodated and the virtual absence of flat graves. During the transition from the Early Bronze Age to the Middle Bronze Age A, however, a number of changes took place which indicate the emergence of new status positions, the most conspicuous of those changes being the appearance of a number of large barrows covering rich burials. Although the average mound diameters of the different periods do not differ all that much, the largest mounds – with diameters of 20 m or more – date from the transition from the Early Bronze Age to the Middle Bronze Age A. This group also includes the mound that was erected over the Sögel burial at Drouwen, with its diameter of (probably) 28 m.[81] As far as the number and diversity of grave goods are concerned, this is the richest of all known Sögel burials (fig. 19.11). That alone already indicates that the deceased must have enjoyed a high status. Similar gold plait-rings and strike-a-lights have been found elsewhere in Northwestern Europe in burials of men who are assumed to have had a high status.[82]

The more or less fixed range of grave goods of many Sögel burials and burials of a later date, such as those of Hijkerveld and Sleenerzand (fig. 19.13), seems to point to the existence of a social status position whose formal authority extended beyond a kinship group or a group of farmsteads. This position may have been held by only one individual per generation, possibly an individual with a status comparable with that of the persons who were buried in Schleswig-Holstein and Denmark accompanied by a folding chair and a sword that showed hardly any signs of wear.[83] But, as also observed for the Late Neolithic, there is no evidence to suggest that these status positions were hereditary.

The Middle Bronze Age A: the difference between cremation and inhumation

The Middle Bronze Age A saw a remarkable change in the burial rite: the number of cremations increased considerably and so did the number of burials per unit of time. The number of Middle Bronze Age A barrows known from the northern part of the Netherlands is about three times the number of Early Bronze Age barrows. The same trend has been observed in the central and southern parts of the Netherlands. Not only did the number of barrows increase, but also – within a relatively short period of time – existing barrows were enlarged with a second central grave in the top of the original mound, covered with a new raise of sods and surrounded by ditches or rows of posts. Multi-period construction seems to have become common practice, whereas in the Early Bronze Age barrows were only occasionally and with a much longer time interval erected over older (Neolithic) barrows or flat graves.

It was mostly the smaller barrows, covering *Brandskelettgräber* or cremation burials, that were selected to accommodate new burial 'periods', either out of preference or because people avoided the larger barrows covering central inhumation burials. A substantial increase in the number of cremation burials in *Brandskelettgräber* is observable in the northern part of the Netherlands in particular, where the transition from inhumation to cremation took place a little later than to the south of the major rivers (fig. 19.3). However, both in the south and in the north inhumation continued to be practised alongside cremation. This makes us wonder on what criteria this difference in the treatment of the dead may have been based. In our opinion, there are indications that in the north of the Netherlands inhumation was reserved for persons of a higher status or rank.[84] For instance, central inhumation burials are usually covered by larger mounds than central *Brandskelettgräber*. Where barrows contain both an inhumation burial and a cremation burial or a *Brandskelettgrab* it is found that the latter was added after the inhumation. This must hence be considered the most important, primary, burial. Thirdly, secondary inhumation burials have never been found in barrows containing central *Brandskelettgräber*, whereas both secondary inhumation burials and secondary cremation burials have been found in barrows containing central inhumation burials. This same phenomenon has also been observed in England.[85] And, finally, the majority of the bronze grave goods, which have been encountered in no more than 10% of the primary burials, come from inhumation burials. *Brandskelettgräber* have yielded few grave goods: some miniature Elp vessels or objects of flint.

The evidence currently available does not really allow us to answer the question whether this same distinction was also made in the south of the Netherlands. What does seem to suggest that the deceased who were cremated in the south likewise had a lower status than the individuals who were inhumed is the fact that the richest burial found in North Brabant, barrow IV on the Rechte Heide near Goirle, is probably an inhumation burial. Moreover, the majority of the bronze grave goods known from the south of the Netherlands came from inhumation burials,[86] although the total number of grave goods is small here too. Another possible argu-

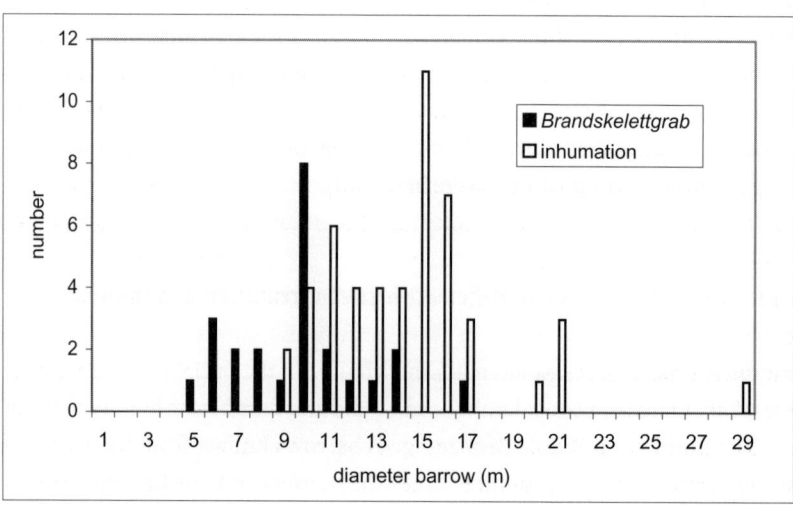

fig. 19.14
The difference in the diameters of barrows erected over a central cinerary burial (n=24) and a central inhumation burial (n=50).

ment for associating inhumation with a higher status is that *Brandskelettgräber* can be regarded as imitations of inhumation burials. The relatively fast rate at which the custom of inhumation was adopted in the north of the Netherlands and on the Veluwe in the Middle Bronze Age B furthermore suggests that the social group that initially had kept to the custom of cremation readily conformed to the practice of inhumation (fig. 19.14).

It is not possible to infer the sex of the deceased in Early and Middle Bronze Age burials from skeletal evidence. It is tempting to conclude from the grave goods that in the Middle Bronze Age A, men were more frequently buried in central graves beneath barrows than women. The general impression is that many of the central *Brandskelettgräber* from that period are female burials, but as the sex of only few cremated remains has been determined it is difficult to draw sound conclusions.[87] It would seem that when cremation started to be practised more commonly, burial in a central grave ceased to be the prerogative of a select group. The privilege of burial beneath a barrow was probably granted to a larger number of men, and later to women, too. It may well be that these groups or individuals had been buried in flat graves in the past, but as hardly any flat graves from the Early Bronze Age or Middle Bronze Age A are known, we have no evidence to confirm this.[88] Another possibility is that, in addition to the known forms of burial, there were also other forms of disposal of the dead which we are not (yet) able to detect archaeologically.

The Middle Bronze Age B

The barrow as 'family cemetery'

As already mentioned above, the number of barrows, and the number of secondary burials accommodated in them, increased considerably in the Middle Bronze Age B. The barrows, with their circular settings of posts, hence started to be used for a new purpose, namely for the burial of groups of individuals (fig. 19.12). On average, the Middle Bronze Age B barrows contain three secondary burials, whereas those of the preceding period contain only one. In the north of the Netherlands one or more secondary burials had been accommodated in 76% of the Middle Bronze Age B barrows, whereas only 34% of the Middle Bronze Age A barrows had been used for secondary burial. It is plausible that these secondary burials contain the remains of members of several, successive generations of one and the same household. Probably not more than one person per farmstead or household and per generation was buried in a central burial pit beneath a mound or a mound phase. The other members of that person's generation and his (or her) next of kin were then buried in that same mound in secondary pits. The barrows which had originally been intended for the burial of a single corpse hence evolved into 'family barrows' in the course of the Middle Bronze Age. As inhumation was the common form of burial in the north of the Netherlands in the Middle Bronze Age B, we have been able to infer from the lengths of the cists and the burial pits that a substantial portion of the secondary burials in that region are children's burials. They constitute 19% of the total number of known burials. It is assumed that babies and infants of under twelve months – the age group with the highest mortality rate in most comparable communities (20 to 30%) – were not buried in the barrows. That would mean that 19% of the children who survived the critical first twelve months did not live to become adults. Miniature pots of Elp ware are remarkably frequently found in children's graves and in a few graves which, on the basis of the other grave goods associated with them, can be interpreted as women's or girls' graves. The grave goods suggest that in this period, too, women

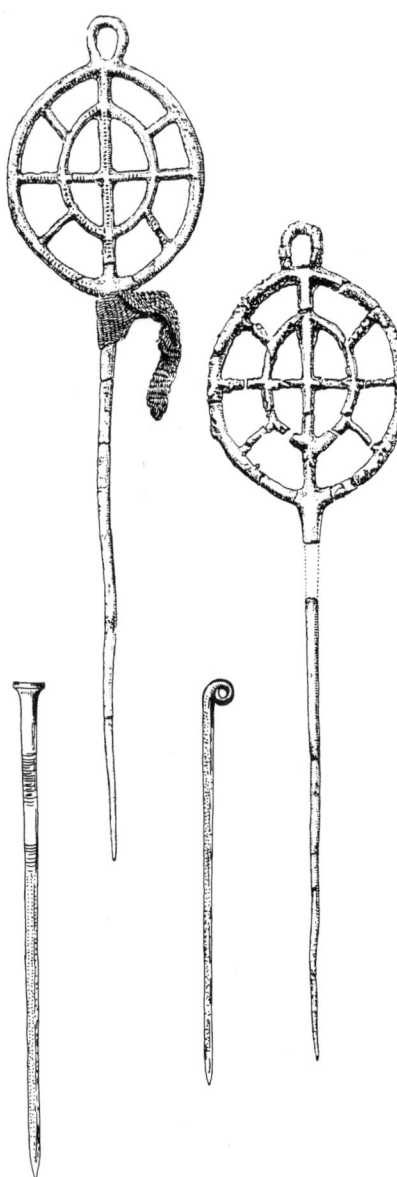

fig. 19.15
Two wheel-headed pins and two bronze
needles from the burial of 'the lady of
Weerdinge'. The pins probably came here
with a woman from the German Fulda/Main
region, where they formed part of the local
costume. Scale 1:2. See also fig. 17.9.

were more frequently buried in secondary graves than men. However, age and sex determinations of some cremated remains have shown that women and children were sometimes also buried in primary graves beneath small barrows.[89]

Grave gifts and status

In the period 1500-1100 BC (in the Netherlands this corresponds to the Middle Bronze Age B) the number of 'female' grave goods increased substantially over the whole of Northern and Northwestern Europe, to such an extent, in fact, that they came to dominate the archaeological record. Apparently the grave goods no longer solely expressed the position of a small group of adult men, but also reflected the importance of women and girls in the exchange systems, which were presumably still controlled by men. This development must imply a greatly improved political and social stability in a society in which men monopolised the formal positions and women – especially those of a reproductive age – played important parts as marriage partners in the establishment of alliances and new links in the exchange networks.

This starting point presents interesting possibilities for analysing such networks. For example, comparison of the bronze ornaments with which women were buried has shown that there were regional differences in female fashions, although no sharp lines can be drawn between the various regions; it is more a matter of a number of core areas separated by transitional areas.[90] At several findspots bracelets have been found which have such small diameters that it is assumed that they were forged around the wrists of the women, who then wore them for the rest of their lives.[91] When such a bracelet is found in association with ornaments of a fashion prevailing in a different region we may assume that the bracelet and the ornaments were not imported, but were brought along by a woman from a different region, who had most probably left her home region to marry. In Germany and Denmark several graves of women, in some cases quite young,[92] have been found to contain grave goods representing fashions that prevailed in different regions. These objects could be parts of dowries that the women's families had given them when they moved to their husbands' place of residence. A good example in the Netherlands is that of the grave goods including two wheel-headed pins that were found in the rich female burial of Weerdinge in the north of the country (fig. 19.15). The ornaments represent a fashion that is known only from the Fulda/Main region in Germany. It is likely that not only the pins, but also the woman herself, came from that region.

This assumed custom of giving brides-to-be a dowry and the mobility of marriageable women are compatible with a trend towards greater long-distance interaction and greater differentiation between (kinship) groups.[93] Such a trend presupposes greater political and social stability and the legitimation of the status of a social elite. A study into patterns of mobility, of both men and women, as reflected by the distribution patterns of grave goods of the kind discussed above may in the future yield valuable information on such social developments.

The socialisation of the burial rite, in the sense that the privilege of burial beneath or in a barrow started to be granted to (almost) everyone, marked the beginning of a development that was to culminate in the urnfields of the Late Bronze Age, in which social differences are less pronounced since everyone was apparently considered 'equal' after their death. The cause of this development was perhaps the breaking up of traditional lineages into smaller independent units whose members (almost) all qualified for burial beneath a barrow. This process possibly went hand in hand with the emergence of a more comprehensive form of organisation on a supra-regional level, which could explain the disappearance of the tradition of demonstrating high male status positions by means of bronze grave goods in the Middle Bronze Age A. It was probably this development, possibly in combination with economic changes such as the adoption of the 'Celtic' field system, that led to the fundamental and structural change that took place in the burial rite around the transition to the Late Bronze Age.[94]

NOTES

1 This chapter is based partly on information obtained from the unpublished catalogues of A.E. Lanting on burials of the Single Grave culture, and J.N. Lanting on AOO burials of the late Single Grave culture and the Bell Beaker culture. We are most grateful for having been granted access to these catalogues.

2 Not all barrows are round: some have shapes ranging from elongated oval to rectangular with rounded corners. Some fifteen Middle Bronze Age barrows of this kind are known in the northern and central parts of the Netherlands. Their deviating shape may be original, or it may be the consequence of the expansion of a round barrow. Surveys of investigated barrows of this type are to be found in Verlinde (1973) and Van der Veen/Lanting (1989, 195-196).

3 At present, at least 225 burials of the Single Grave culture (115 barrows, 75 flat graves, 35 indeterminate), c. 105 burials of the Bell Beaker culture (75 barrows, 20 flat graves, 10 indeterminate), just under 50 barrows from the Early Bronze Age, some 200 Middle Bronze Age A barrows and almost 300 Middle Bronze Age B barrows are known in the Netherlands. In addition, about 30 flat graves datable to this last period have been found.

4 For example at Sijbekarspel (Hogestijn/Woltering 1990) and Molenaarsgraaf (Louwe Kooijmans 1974).

5 Flat graves of the Single Grave culture near Sleen (Van Giffen 1937a).

6 One example is a burial found at Aalden (Modderman 1957).

7 Waterbolk 1962, 14-15 and fig. 4. Also at Anloo (Jager 1985, 245), Cuijk (Bogaers 1966, 123), Haps (Verwers 1972), and possibly Tilburg (Willems 1935, 140 and fig. 34:6) and Zwaagdijk (Modderman 1964a).

8 For example at Swalmen (Lanting/Van der Waals 1974). Barrows spaced at most 300 m apart were classed as belonging to one group.

9 Jager 1985.

10 Casparie/Groenman-van Waateringe 1980.

11 Single Grave culture: Lanting 1969; Lanting/Van der Waals 1976, 44.

12 Lohof (1991, 73-74) gives only one example of an extended inhumation burial from the Early Bronze Age in the northeast of the Netherlands, as opposed to five examples of silhouettes in crouched position. A crouched inhumation was also found beneath barrow I at St. Walrick (Groenman-Van Waateringe 1961, 73). Crouched inhumation silhouettes of Middle Bronze Age date are also known (Lanting 1973, note 3).

13 Only three examples of graves are known in which the deceased had been placed on his or her right side in crouched position, namely Burial III at Molenaarsgraaf (Louwe Kooijmans 1974, 260 ff), barrow II at Drijber (Lanting 1973, 273 ff) and a flat grave found beneath the 'Bergakkers' barrow III at Eext (Jager 1985, 237 ff and fig. 43). It is, however, doubtful whether the identification of the bones from Molenaarsgraaf as the remains of a female individual of 1.5 years old is correct, because human skeletons do not acquire sexual characteristics until puberty.

14 Harrison 1980, 40; Gebers 1984, 90 ff.

15 Beuker et al. 2001.

16 For a survey of the orientations of Late Neolithic graves, see Lanting 1973 and Lanting/Van der Waals 1976, 44 ff.

17 Ille 1991, 115.

18 For example Baarn (ROB 1988 Annual Report, 60) and Vaassen (ROB 1989 Annual Report, 82-83).

19 If the absence of a burial pit and charcoal or cremation remains is regarded as evidence of an unobserved inhumation ground grave, about one-third of the burials are inhumations.

20 Modderman 1954, 17-19.

21 The best-known examples are the Hilversum urns found in barrows 1b and 9 in the cemetery of Toterfout/Halve Mijl (Glasbergen 1954 I, 36 ff).

22 Lohof 1991, 244.

23 For example Niersen and Ottoland (Louwe Kooijmans 1974, 311 ff).

24 For example barrow I at Grootebroek (Van Giffen 1953, 36).

25 Examples are: Elp where several burial pits were found with each two inhumations (Waterbolk 1964); barrow III at Borger, which contained a Brandskelettgrab and a secondary cremation burial (Schoneveld 1988, 6-7); barrow III at Angelslo-Emmerhout, which contained an inhumation burial and a cremation burial (Van der Waals 1963, 252).

26 Louwe Kooijmans 1993.

27 Van Giffen 1949, 106.

28 Soesterberg, barrow 3 (Bursch 1934, 56 and fig. 32).

29 Aalden (Modderman 1957).

30 For example Bakker 1992, 58; Brindley 1983, 222 and fig. 7. Similar finds outside the Netherlands support such an interpretation (Körner/Laux 1981, 161-174; Gallay 1976).

31 Bakker 1992, 58; De Groot 1988, 93 and fig. 17: 132a-c, 133.

32 These finds may not be grave goods proper, but may have served some other purpose in the burial rite, possibly comparable with that of the pottery that has been found in barrows, but outside the burial pits themselves.

33 Disarticulated bones have been found for example in the settlements of the Single Grave culture at Aartswoud (F.R. van Iterson Scholten, personal communication) and Kolhorn (identified by T.S. Constandse-Westerman and H.T. Uytterschaut). They are also known from Middle Bronze Age settlements in Westfrisia (e.g. IJzereef 1981, 209 ff).

34 Niersen and Ottoland (Louwe Kooijmans 1974, 311-312). The burial of a child's skull in a Bell Beaker barrow at Velserbroek should also be mentioned here (Therkorn/Van Londen 1990, 304).

35 Lohof 1991, 145, 207.

36 Lohof 1991, 76.

37 Sudholz 1964, 9; Bergmann 1970, 16.

38 Two good examples of beehive graves whose bedding trenches contained wattle walls were found at Onnen (Van Giffen 1930, I, 124-128; II, Abb. 84-86a) and Putten (Van Giffen et al. 1971). Barrow 8 at Hooghalen is a good example of a beehive grave with postholes (Van der Veen/Lanting 1989, 213-214 and fig. 21).

39 Lanting/Van der Waals 1976, 43.

40 Lanting/Van der Waals (1976, 45) mention two graves in the Nutterveld cemetery.

41 Ten Anscher/Gehasse 1991, 123.

42 Therkorn/Van Londen 1990, 304.

43 Ashbee 1960, 89; Glob 1970, 93.

44 Modderman (1984) is, however, of the opinion that the ditched enclosures found in an intermediary position in Late Neolithic barrows are to be interpreted as the features of a structure that was erected around the periphery of the mound and collapsed over the ditch when the posts decayed.

45 They may be related to the aforementioned late Middle Bronze Age rings of stones found in the northern part of the Netherlands, which were however arranged around the foot of the mound.

46 See Lanting/Mook 1977, 100 for a discussion of this type of barrow.

47 Glasbergen 1954, but see also Van Giffen 1938a.

48 De Laet 1974, 311; Van Impe 1976.

49 Barrow 1 at Toterfout-Halve Mijl (Glasbergen 1954, 33); barrow 1 on 'de Rechte Heide' near Goirle (Van Giffen 1938a); a barrow near Kwaalburg (Beex 1964); barrow 'Zwartenberg' near Hoogeloon (Glasbergen 1954, I, 10-11; II, fig. 72).

50 Glasbergen distinguished nine types in the Netherlands; his classification is still used today (Glasbergen 1954 II, 77-79). See also Lanting/Mook 1977, 109, and Hermann/Jockenhövel 1975, 123.

51 Lohof 1991.

52 Glasbergen 1954 II, 74; Klok 1988.

53 Van Veen/Lanting 1989.

54 Glasbergen 1954 I, 53.

55 Fragments of bone objects, for example of awls, have been found for example in barrows near Oss (Bursch 1937, 3; Verwers 1966, 28 and fig. 5), in the Toterfout-Halve Mijl cemetery (Glasbergen 1954, II, 33, plate XII).

56 For instance Buchvaldek 1967, 74, Sangmeister/Gerhardt 1965.

57 Drenth (1992, 208).

58 Lanting 1973; Butler et al. 1972, 230 and fig. 6; Modderman/Montforts 1991, 145; Van Giffen et al. 1971, 119-120 and fig. 15.

59 Van Giffen 1930, 84-93; Butler 1969, 100-107; 1986, 149.

60 Barrow 9 in the Hijkerveld cemetery (Van Veen/Lanting 1989, 215-219, figs. 24-27, 39a), the 'Galgenberg' barrow in the Sleenerzand cemetery (Butler 1969, 110, fig. 27; Beuker 1991).

61 Bosman/Soonius 1990.

62 Klok 1988.

63 The reason why weapons are interpreted as male attributes and ornaments as female attributes is that weapons and ornaments, with the exception of pins, have never been found together in graves anywhere in northern or Central Europe (Laux 1971, 152; Primas 1977, 92; Willroth 1989; Wüstemann 1978, 198).

64 Van Giffen 1930, 76-80; Butler 1969, 114-116.

65 Drenth/Lanting 1991, note 3.

66 Lanting/Van der Waals 1976. Veluwe Bell Beakers have, however, been found in a few assemblages in the northern part of the Netherlands, too (Oldeboorn, Fokkens 1991, fig. 65).

67 Addink-Samplonius 1968; Lanting 1973; Lanting/Van der Waals 1976.

68 Butler/Van der Waals 1966, Lanting 1973.

69 Bérenger 1989.

70 Warmenbol 1989; Theunissen 1999.

71 Fokkens 1997; Lohof 1994.

72 Different researchers (including Pierpoint 1980, especially 224, 226; Shennan 1977; Siemen 1992) have arrived at the same conclusion for similar cultures.

73 Comparable results have been obtained for similar contemporary cultures (Case 1984, 44; Pierpoint 1980, 59 and 223; Shennan 1977, 54).

74 Drenth 1992.

75 Drenth 1990.

76 Drenth 1990, 109.

77 Drenth 1990. It is not certain to what extent pseudo-Grand-Pressigny daggers may be regarded as indications of the sex of the deceased. Associations with axes and in one case with a hammer axe suggest that some at least must have belonged to men. See also Drenth 1992, 211.

78 Butler/Van der Waals 1966.

79 E.g. Dalen (Lanting/Ufkes 1989) and Emmen (Beuker et al. 1991, 25 and fig. 21).

80 Randsborg 1974.

81 Butler 1986, 150.

82 Harrison 1980, 102; Sherratt 1986; 1987.

83 Kristiansen 1984; Willroth 1989, 94.

84 Lohof 1991, 113-120.

85 Bradley 1984, 84.

86 De Laet 1974, 309; Theunissen 1999; Fontijn 2003.

87 For a similar conclusion see Laux 1971, 130, 155. Examples of cremated males may be: the remains buried beneath barrow 3 at Bergsham on the Veluwe, which contained a sword of the Wohlde type (Van Giffen 1937b, 12); the remains buried beneath the 'Kwaalburg' barrow at Alphen, which contained a bronze axe (Beex 1964) and the remains buried in the Brandskelettgrab in barrow 3 at Annertol, which yielded a bronze dagger (Butler/Lanting/Van der Waals 1972).

88 The situation on the Danish islands is very much the same (Ille 1991, 112).

89 Barrows 5, 8 and 8a in the Toterfout-Halve Mijl cemetery (Glasbergen 1954, 141); barrow 37 at Gasteren (Van Giffen 1945, 73-78); barrow I at Grootebroek (Van Giffen 1953, 4 and 21).

90 Ille 1991, 103; Jockenhövel 1991; Lehmkühler 1991; Wels-Weyrauch 1989.

91 Laux 1989.

92 Lehmkühler 1991; Zich 1992.

93 Lohof 1991, 1994. But see Drenth 1994 for a critical view.

94 Fokkens 1997, Lohof 1994.

K   Barrow research and palynology
Methods and results

Willy Groenman-van Waateringe

The quadrant method

Until way into the twentieth century archaeological fieldwork in the Netherlands consisted mainly of the investigation of barrows, virtually the only prehistoric remains that were clearly recognizable as such in the Dutch landscape. The first scholar to have written about the *berghjes* ('little mounds') is Picardt.[1] He was followed by Van Lier, Van Cuyk, Westendorp, Reuvens, Janssen and Pleyte.[2] The last author brings us to the beginning of the twentieth century, in which barrow research has really boomed. With J.H. Holwerda and his pupils Remouchamps and Bursch, attention started to shift from the contents of the barrows, *i.e.* the finds, to their composition. The last of the pioneers is Van Giffen, who enhanced barrow research with a new, more systematic excavation method adopted from the study of wood anatomy. According to this method wood is examined in horizontal, vertical and radial planes. This is what is known as the quadrant method in barrow research (fig. K1). Van Giffen, however, was not the first to introduce scientific methods into barrow research. Earlier on, Professor Reuvens of Leiden University had had the different soil types of which barrows were composed chemically analysed. He had also instigated research on cremation remains. With his interdisciplinary approach he was far ahead of his time, at least in the Netherlands.

The quadrant method, though very useful in itself, presented a number of drawbacks when applied too mechanically. It sometimes proved difficult to stratigraphically and chronologically relate secondary burials that were not observed in the sections to the primary burial. Moreover, there was a risk of such secondary burials being missed altogether if they lacked clear finds or if their remains did not extend all the way to the old land surface. These drawbacks, however, did not discourage Van Giffen, who never tired of searching for new ways to improve barrow research, in particular through interdisciplinary cooperation. The possibilities of research on fossilized pollen (known as pollen analysis or palynology) were already appreciated before World War II and after the war radiocarbon analysis opened up new perspectives for obtaining information from charcoal samples collected from old land surfaces and from the various horizons distinguishable in barrows.

How can palynology be of use in barrow research?

The frequent lack of grave goods in Dutch barrows was one of the main reasons for the introduction, by Van Giffen, of palynological analysis into barrow research in the Netherlands. Systematic palynological research of old land surfaces beneath barrows, which in Denmark, where archaeologically oriented pollen analysis originated,[3] appears to be taking shape only now, was being carried out in the Netherlands already in the 1950s. The research method introduced

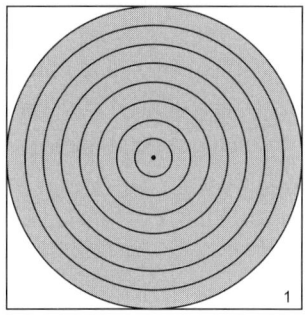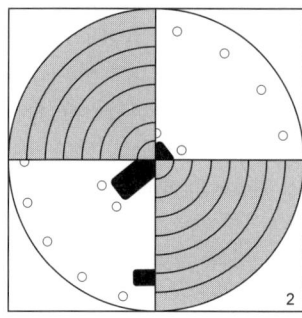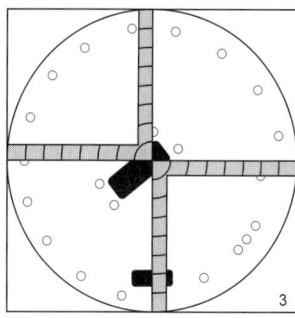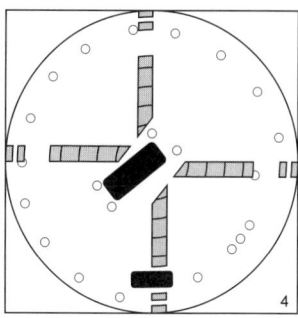

fig. K1

Schematic representation of the excavation of a barrow according to the quadrant method.

1 Schematic contour map of a barrow.

2 Excavation of the southwestern and northeastern quarters. Visible are post holes (white) and graves (black).

3 Excavation of both the other quarters. Profile banks are saved.

4 Full uncovering of the post circles and graves after the sections had been drawn.

fig. K2

The quadrant method in practice during the excavation of a multi-period barrow at Gasteren. In the first phase the barrow was a low mound without a clear sod structure surrounded by a shallow ring ditch. In the second phase the mound was raised with sods. Visible at the top is the present-day topsoil (turf).

by Van Giffen was further developed by Waterbolk and Van Zeist in particular.[4] Their work is now being continued by a younger generation of scientists.[5] In the past, archaeologists investigating barrows containing no grave goods often had nothing other than the structure of the mound to go by: Neolithic barrows tended to be fairly low mounds composed mainly of sand while Bronze Age and Iron Age barrows were more easily recognizable turf mounds (fig. K2, plates 33A, 34A). It was hoped that pollen analysis would constitute a more reliable means of dating such barrows. A few examples of the criteria used in palynological dating are: the total absence of pollen of beech in spectra obtained for Neolithic barrows and the gradual increase in beech pollen in Bronze Age spectra culminating in values of more than 5% at the beginning of the Iron Age. Furthermore, the pollen records show a decrease of lime with time and the spread of heather at the expense of forest. Besides dates, pollen analysis can yield information on the agricultural activities of the people who built the barrows. The importance of pollen analysis as a dating method has in fact decreased considerably since the introduction of radiocarbon dating. Nowadays, its main merit is as a source of information on the environment and the composition of the vegetation that surrounded prehistoric settlements. This of course implies the assumption that barrows were built in the immediate neighbourhood of settlements.

Method

Palynological barrow research is based on the fact that pollen grains survive in fairly acidic anaerobic conditions. The grains contained in samples collected in the field and prepared in the laboratory can be identified with the aid of a microscope (magnification at least 400 times; the grains measure approximately 20-100 μ) and the frequency of each individual pollen type can be determined. These data yield an impression of the composition of the vegetation that surrounded the barrow at the time of its construction, i.e. when the pollen was buried. A chronological sequence of samples, for example from successive horizons in a multi-period barrow, can provide information on the changes that took place in the vegetation during the period that the barrow was in use. The sods, of which the barrow was built, can be used for sampling as well.

In the past, samples were taken exclusively of the old land surface beneath the barrow, of the sods they built of and of the successive old surfaces in the case of multi-period barrows. Recent research, however, in particular by British archaeologists, has shown that much useful information can also be obtained from a series of samples collected from the old land surface downwards.[6] Such a series of samples can give us an impression of the development of the vegetation before the barrow was built. The same holds for a series of samples obtained from successive horizons in multi-period barrows (fig. K3).[7] The underlying principle is that different agents, in particular faunal, gradually transport pollen deeper down into the soil, which means that the age of pollen increases from the top of a section to the bottom.

Some results

When attention shifted from barrow to settlement research fairly little palynological barrow research was for some time carried out in the Netherlands. This changed drastically when, during their research on Beaker cultures, Lanting and Van der Waals started to re-excavate barrows with known find contents, or at least the remains that had survived from the earlier excavations, i.e. mostly baulks.[8] Their aim was to critically re-examine the phasing of the barrows and to collect samples for radiocarbon and pollen analysis.

The earliest palynological barrow research had concentrated on the barrows of Drenthe. It was mainly the results of this research that had led to the opinion that the main differences between the various Neolithic 'cultures' concerned the farming practices of their representatives. Besides small-scale crop cultivation, the Funnel Beaker and Bell Beaker peoples were thought to have practiced some kind of stock-breeding, in which the cattle were kept in byres all year round (the so-called Troels-Smith or small *landnam*). The people who built the Protruding-Foot-Beaker barrows, on the other hand, were thought to have deforested vast expanses of land for their cattle (Iversen or *Plantago landnam*). Now that more information has been obtained from other parts of the Netherlands, we know that pollen records and the impact of man on the surrounding vegetation vary from one region to another, dependent on, in particular, hydrological conditions and local soil types. The agricultural activities of the prehistoric occupants of Drenthe, for example, led to deforestation and the spread of heather at a much earlier stage than elsewhere in the country. In that area human activities had a great effect on the composition of the forest in particular: research on the old land surfaces buried beneath *hunebedden*[9] has shown that the rich types of vegetation, characterized by the presence of elm and lime, were the

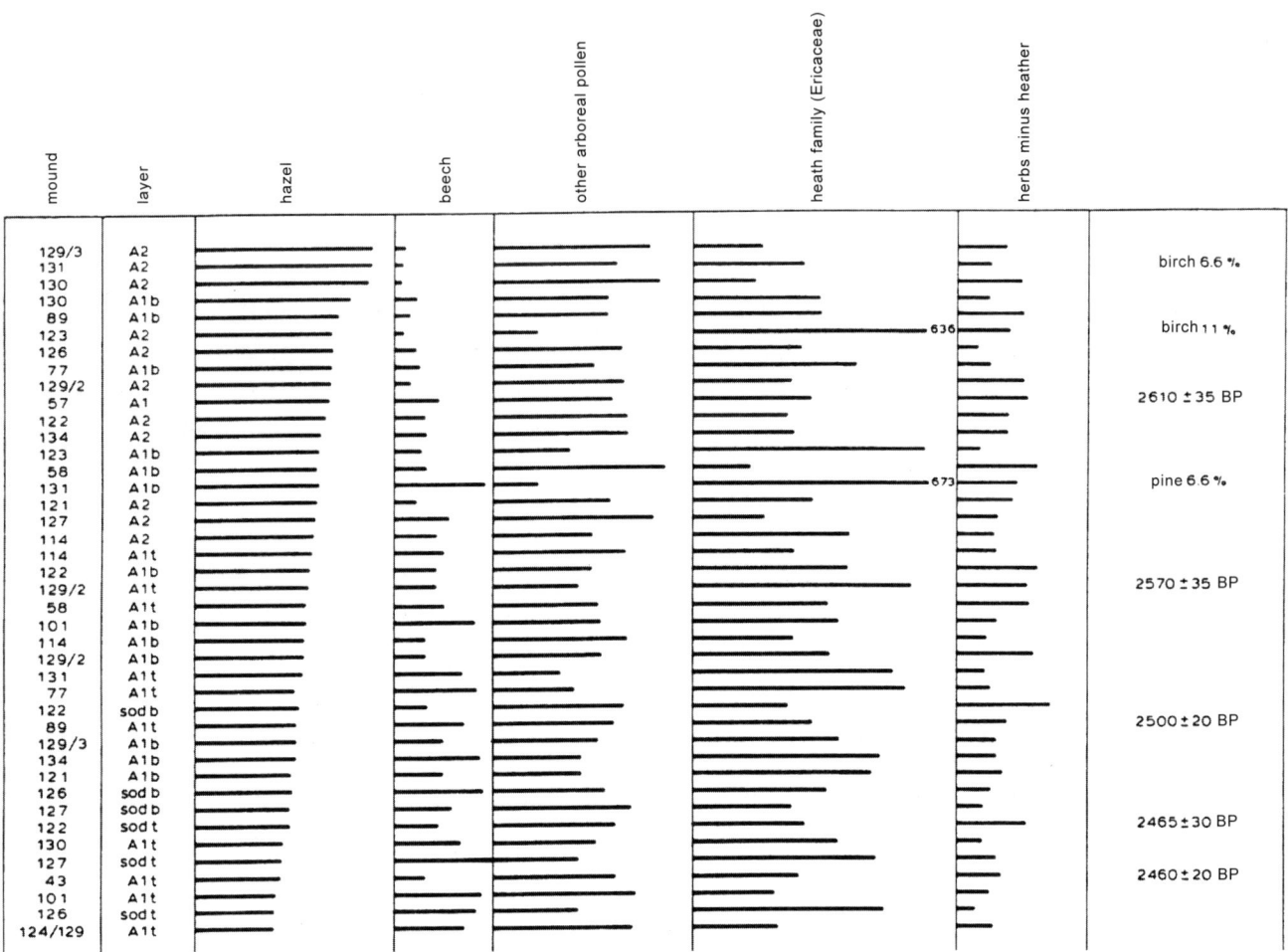

fig. K3
Pollen spectra of samples of A2 and A1 soil horizons from the Boshoverheide urnfield near Weert, arranged according to the decreasing hazel values.

457

first to suffer. If any regeneration ever took place, it was with poorer variants of the original forests, composed largely of oak and birch. In some cases barrows appear to have been constructed at the site of an abandoned settlement or in a former field; they were rarely thrown up in fields still under cultivation or in their immediate surroundings. Pollen records obtained for one and the same culture appear to vary considerably, indicating environments ranging from vast expanses of open land with much evidence for stock-breeding to closed forests with only very small clearings for crop cultivation and forest grazing.

It is not possible to determine the extent or the relative importance of crop cultivation and stock-breeding via pollen analysis, but pollen spectra can give us an impression of any shifts that may have taken place. They are expressed in increases and decreases in certain indicators in a chronological sequence of samples obtained from, for example, multi-period barrows.

For considerable time the Dutch State Service for Archaeological Investigations (ROB) has been paying much attention to the restoration of surviving excavated and unexcavated barrows. In many cases only a small part of a section is exposed to determine the original slope and size of the mound and to take samples. Sometimes the results obtained in such investigations lead to large-scale excavations, such as in the case of the restoration of the Boshoverheide urnfield near Weert (fig. 21.5).[10]

Systematic pollen research of old land surfaces and of turf in barrows has shown that the earliest barrows were constructed on open patches of heather in forests. The decrease in the amount of hazel pollen in the examined samples shows that the heather spread to form a heath as the urnfield expanded. Very little evidence for crop cultivation or stock-breeding has been found in samples collected from such urnfields, even in those obtained from beneath a long barrow. This confirms Professor Bakels' opinion that urnfields containing long barrows are not to be interpreted as ritual fields.[11]

Notes

1   Picardt 1660.
2   Brunsting 1947.
3   Iversen 1941.
4   Waterbolk 1954; Van Zeist 1955.
5   Casparie/Groenman-van Waateringe 1980.
6   Dimbleby 1985.
7   Groenman-van Waateringe 1986, 1988.
8   Lanting/Van der Waals 1976.
9   Bakker/Groenman-van Waateringe 1988.
10 Bloemers 1990; Groenman-van Waateringe 1988.
11 Bakels 1975.

L   Bronze Age war
A collective burial at Wassenaar

Leendert Louwe Kooijmans

The grave

In 1987 a discovery was made at Wassenaar that has shed a somewhat different light on the Bronze Age.[1] It all started

with some flint and a few bell beaker sherds found during construction work for the new district Weteringpark. It was a great surprise when the small-scale salvage excavation that was then carried out brought to light a large burial pit

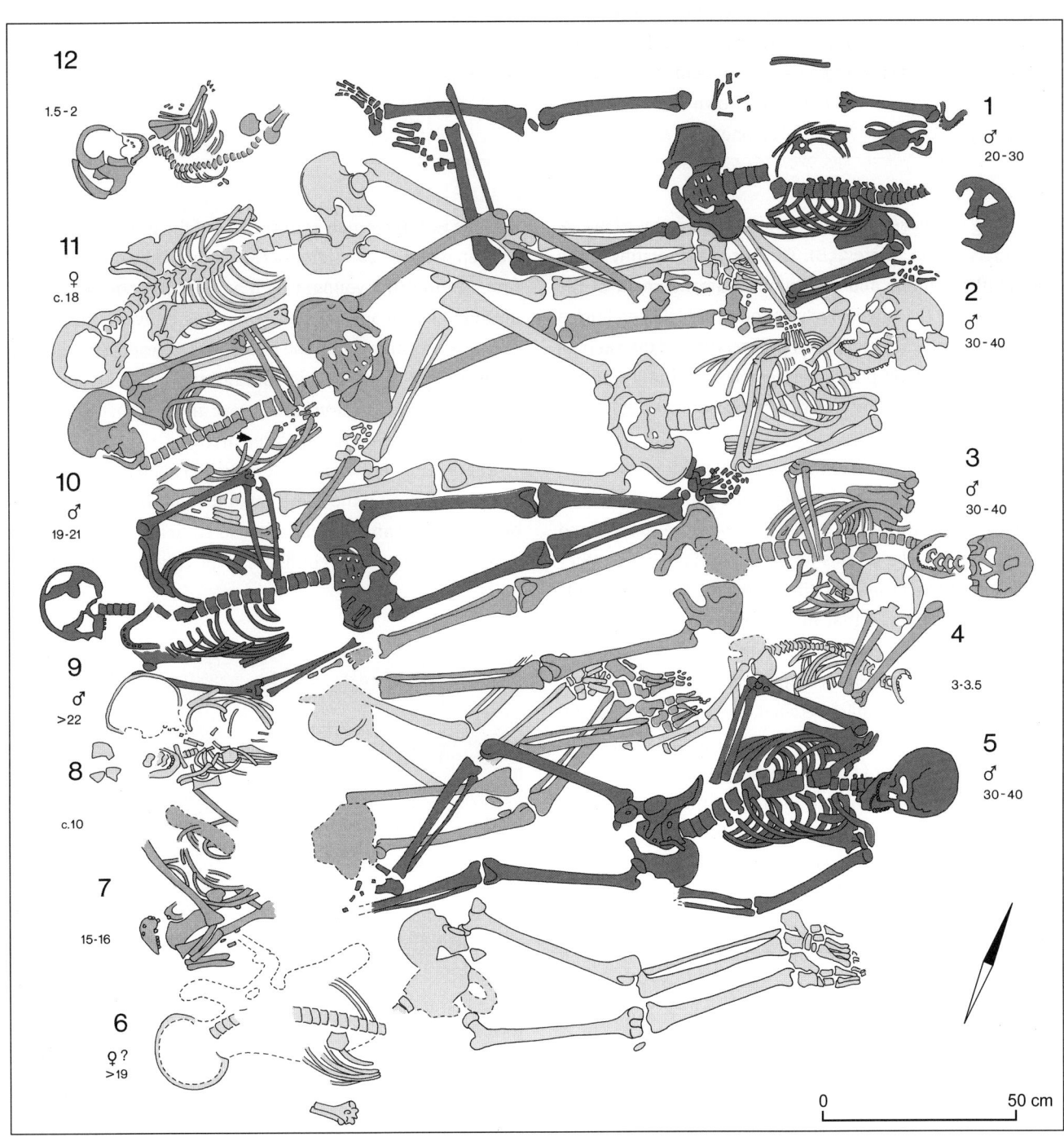

fig. L1

Excavation plan of the Wassenaar burial, with skeleton numbers, sex and age determinations. The position of the arrowhead is indicated in skeleton 10.

ind.	age (years)	sex	stat. (cms)	burial posture	traumatology
1	20-30	♂	167	one leg bent	–
2	30-40	♂	182	one leg bent	blow, lower jaw
3	30-40	♂	176	streched on back	blow, right humerus
4	3-3,5	–	–	on one side	skull separate
5	30-40	♂	169	one leg bent	blow, frontal bone
6	>19	♀?	170	face down	–
7	15-16	–	ca. 170	?	–
8	ca. 10	–	–	on one side	–
9	>22	♂	176	streched on back	–
10	19-21	♂	177	one leg bent	shot-in arrow
11	ca. 18	♀	182	face down	–
12	1,5-2	–	–	on one side	–

Wassenaar, composition of the burial group

fig. L2

Wassenaar. Group composition.

containing the more or less orderly buried remains of twelve individuals (fig. L1, plate 35B). The microstratigraphy of the superimposed limbs and the compact arrangement of the bodies showed that these twelve people had all been buried at the same time. The degree of preservation of the skeletal remains ranged from poor to extremely poor but it was still sufficient to allow some basic anthropological data to be drawn from them.[2]

The pit contained the remains of two children, two adolescents and eight adults: five men, one young woman and two individuals whose sex could no longer be determined (fig. L2). At first, the bodies appeared to have been rather hastily and haphazardly deposited in the pit, but closer study of the remains showed that they had on the contrary been buried according to careful rules. In the first place, all of the men had been deposited face upwards; the oldest (No. 3), whose legs were both fully stretched, had been placed at the centre of the grave and the four younger men had been arranged on either side of him in a rather remarkable posture: one of their legs was bent and the foot of that leg had been placed against the shin of the other leg. The children and adolescents had all been deposited on their sides, with slightly bent knees. The posture of the woman (No. 11) who was accompanied by the remains of a very young infant at one end of the row of skeletons was rather exceptional: she had been deposited face downwards. The posture and position of the second skeleton with stretched legs at the centre of the grave (No. 9) suggested that that too represented the remains of an adult male of over thirty, while the second individual who had been buried face downwards at the other end of the row (No. 6) was probably a woman, just like No. 11. The fact that limbs of the deceased had apparently been rearranged during the burial procedure made it impossible to determine the order in which the bodies had been interred. It is most likely

that the two older men at the centre of the grave and the two women with the two infants (Nos. 4 and 12) were deposited first and that the younger men and adolescents were then arranged in the open spaces remaining between them. This arrangement shows that the bodies were buried according to some precise ritual, in which the age and sex of the deceased determined the position in the grave and the posture and order in which they were deposited in it.

There is no doubt about the facts that all of the individuals were killed during the same calamity and that they were all buried shortly after. There are also sufficient arguments to assume that an armed conflict was the cause of their deaths.

fig. L3

Arrowhead, as shot in between the ribs of individual 10.

First of all, a flint arrowhead was found in the chest of individual No. 10 (fig. L3-4). Other indications are the gashes in the lower jaw of No. 2, in the right upper arm of No. 3 and in the skull of No. 5. We must bear in mind that a violent death need not necessarily leave any visible marks on skeletal remains, that any evidence of violence may have vanished in the case of poorly preserved bones and that skeletal remains are often shifted from their original positions by burrowing animals, uprooting or rooting. None of these, however, can explain the position of the skull of the body of the young child (No. 4): the skull was separated from the body spatially, but also by the left arm of the older man beside it (No. 3) and, as gruesome as it may seem, it must have been buried like that too. Finally, the composition of the group, in which able-bodied men predominate, brings to mind an armed conflict between neighbouring communities in which 'innocent civilians' fell victim, too. The careful burial rite suggests that the deceased were buried by surviving relatives rather than by their opponents.

The conflict took place around the transition from the Early to the Middle Bronze Age. Samples of charcoal from the burial pit yielded two ^{14}C dates of 3420 ± 80 BP (GrN 14949) and 3380 ± 80 BP (GrN 14950). The date of about 1700 BC obtained after calibration agrees well with the typological resemblance of the arrowhead to arrowheads in an assemblage from Vogelenzang that also included some sherds with 'barbed wire' impressions.[3]

The Bronze Age context

The Wassenaar grave is unique in the archaeology of the Netherlands, but that is no reason to regard it as evidence for a highly exceptional event, such as a once-only conflict in an otherwise peaceful Bronze Age. Graves of this kind are archaeologically invisible because they are not marked by funeral monuments and contain no grave goods. Moreover, skeletal remains buried under such conditions are not usually preserved. There is very little we can say about the frequency of the conflicts that led to such massacres. Neither

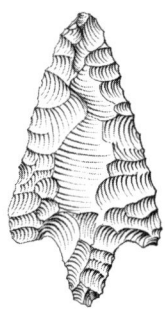

fig. L4
Arrowhead from the rib cage of individual 10. Natural size.

the settlements nor the graves of the Bronze Age conjure up images of warlike or aggressive communities. As far as we know, no fortifications were built in the Netherlands in the Bronze Age and, unlike in many other areas in Europe, the deceased were only rarely accompanied by weapons. Nevertheless, we should seriously consider the possibility that armed conflicts which left very few traces in the archaeological record formed a structural part of Bronze Age life in the Netherlands.

Ethnographic frame of reference

Ethnography provides us with a clarifying frame of reference for the issue of warfare in prehistoric societies, in particular tribal communities, although only little systematic research has been carried out so far.[4] A carefully conducted world survey of fifty primitive communities ranging from band societies to chiefdoms and from hunter-gatherers to plough agriculturists led the American Keith Otterbein to the conclusion that practically all communities wage aggressive and/or defensive wars at varying frequencies.[5] The more complex the society, the more complex the weapons and the higher the degree of organisation of the wars. Tribal societies have few defences, they cause relatively little havoc, they do not include special groups of warriors and their weapons are not very specialised. In other words, an armed conflict between groups of this type would leave little trace in the archaeological record.

There are two contrasting forms of tribal warfare: duelling warfare and raids. Duelling warfare is best known from Papuan groups such as the Tsembaga and the Dani. Their duels have been described as a rather rough kind of sport. The place, time and form of the duel are all regulated by rules and mutual agreements. Groups, usually neighbouring tribes, take up a position opposite one another and then shoot arrows or throw spears at one another until someone is injured or the two parties have had enough. Sometimes things get out of hand and the duel degenerates into a massacre in which women and children are occasionally killed, too. This duelling warfare is a fine example of a (be it imperfect) form of conflict control in which 'accidents' occur from time to time.

Raids are in our eyes less sporting activities. They are conducted furtively, preferably before daybreak and often at a long distance – several days' marching – from home. The aim is to steal horses or cattle or to abduct women. Raids are usually violent affairs which often involve casualties and in which old people and children are rarely spared. Well-known examples are the raids of Amazon Indians (for example the Yanomamö) and of several North American plains Indians and east African cattle breeders such as the Nuer.

Both kinds of warfare are endemic, which means that there is often no real reason for them and that there is no end to them either. They are a structural part of life. Any trifling matter, such as the theft of a pig, may be the cause of a duel or a raid or they may form part of an endless sequence of revenge and retaliation.

Tribal warfare in European prehistory

There are now three very different arguments for extrapolating the ethnographic picture of endemic warfare amongst tribal communities to a prehistoric context.

The first argument is of a functionalistic nature. Endemic tribal warfare, it is argued, is good for the team spirit, it gives men the opportunity to show their courage and strength, it provides some distraction in an otherwise uneventful and monotonous existence and aspiring leaders can prove what they are worth. It must have meant very much the same to prehistoric tribal societies as it does to the communities mentioned above.

Secondly, elsewhere in Europe, if not in the Netherlands, there is plenty of evidence for warfare in the Late Bronze Age and Iron Age. Fortifications, specialised offensive and defensive weapons, warrior graves and hoards of weapons are all directly associated with warfare. Besides fairly complex, centrally organized societies, these finds imply a relatively sophisticated level of warfare, which must have evolved from earlier, simpler, forms of armed conflict that are less clearly visible in the archaeological record.

Thirdly, all kinds of collective burials with varying evidence of violence have been found all over Western Europe, if sporadically. Their dates vary from the *Bandkeramik* via the Michelsberg, Funnel-Beaker and SOM periods to the Beaker period. In many cases the deceased were simply dumped in a pit or in a cave, sometimes accompanied by hundreds of arrowheads. In this respect the Wassenaar grave is far from unique, although the grave's relatively late date and the evidence for the careful burial rite do set it apart from the others.

We would like to conclude with an answer to the question, 'raids or duels?', but that does not appear to be possible. On the one hand the possibility of conflicts between civilian communities seems quite feasible in the presumably densely occupied dune area, but on the other hand the specialised cattle breeding of Bronze Age farmers may have been a good context for cattle raids. Whatever the answer to this question may be, the discovery of this grave has lifted the idyllic haze from the Bronze Age and forces us to take another look at the periods that preceded and followed it.

Notes

1 This is an abbreviated and slightly altered version of Louwe Kooijmans 1990 and 1993c. Preliminary discussion in Jungerius/Smits 1988.
2 In view of the poor condition of the remains, this was done in the field by the anthropologist Mrs E. Smits.
3 Groenman-van Waateringe 1966, fig. 46; Ten Anscher 1990.
4 References in Louwe Kooijmans 1993c.
5 Otterbein 1969.

20 Mixed farming societies: synthesis

Harry Fokkens

Chapters 17-19 discussed various aspects of archaeological cultures from the Late Neolithic and the Bronze Age. In those discussions developments in material culture, settlements and burial practices were covered in separate chapters, as though they were more or less unrelated features of culture. But this was done for practical purposes only; in actual fact, these elements are of course all closely linked. In this chapter the emphasis will therefore be on the connection between issues like settlement, subsistence, dwellings, religion and social structure. An attempt will be made to relate the changes observable in the various aspects of the archaeological record to one another and to explain them.

CHANGES AT THE BEGINNING OF THE THIRD MILLENNIUM BC

The early third millennium BC saw the rise of the Beaker cultures over a large part of Northwest Europe. In the Low Countries they succeeded megalithic cultures in the sandy areas, like the TRB culture and the Seine-Oise-Marne culture, and the Vlaardingen group in the western coastal and rivers area. The most conspicuous change in the sandy areas is the replacement of collective burial in a stone tomb by individual burial beneath a barrow. Another noteworthy development is the transition from a diversity of cultural groups to a single, ubiquitous archaeological culture – first the Single Grave culture, then the Bell Beaker culture.

How we are to interpret the emergence of the Single Grave culture has already been briefly discussed in chapter 16. It was argued that this was the consequence of social and economic changes. This is an entirely different view than the traditional immigration theory proposed by Gordon Childe, who was of the opinion that this culture was introduced by cattle-herding invaders from the Pontic steppes. That these people must have been cattle herders he inferred from the absence of remains of houses, and his interpretation of them as belligerent invaders was based on the 'battle axes' found in their graves. For a long time pollen analysis seemed to confirm this view.

The migration model still exists today, but a lot has changed since Childe advanced his hypothesis. Over the years, many settlements of the Single Grave culture have come to light, especially in the Netherlands, and they have not yielded any evidence for cultural discontinuity. Now that the theory of itinerant cattle herders is no longer supported by palynological evidence either,[1] archaeologists are searching for alternative explanations for the strikingly rapid transformation in material culture that took place in many parts of Central and Northwest Europe around 2900 BC.[2] One of the alternative explanations that has been proposed for the rapid emergence and diffusion of the Beaker cultures revolves around a combination of ideological and social changes and agricultural and technological innovations.

Innovations associated with the Single Grave culture are the use of the ard and cart and of oxen as a source of traction.[3] This is not to say that the ard and the wheel had not been used previously (outside the Netherlands), for we have unmistakable evidence that this was indeed the case. The early evidence of their use however fits well into geographical models describing the introduction of innovations. These models show that innovations are adopted on a large scale within a fairly short time only after a long period of hesitant and experimental use. This period could be correlated with the emergence of the Single Grave culture.

The question is: why did the ard imply such a major improvement that people started using it everywhere? The answer probably lies in the development of the landscape under the influence of man. In areas with a forest vegetation an ard is impractical because the trees' root systems are too dense and too thick. But in a more open landscape the ard is an ideal means for breaking up the ground and drawing furrows. The fact that the ard was usually used for cross-ploughing is not surprising: in countries like Turkey, where ards are still being used today, this form of ploughing and sowing is used because it reduces the risk of weeds emerging. It is thought that the use of the ard also implied a change from broadcast sowing to sowing in furrows,[4] which will – probably unintentionally – have led to higher yields.

The use of the ard also had consequences for the composition of the livestock, for it implied a demand for draught animals in addition to manpower. It is likely that oxen were used as a source of traction from the outset. From for example the great care with which pairs of oxen were buried by Late Neolithic groups in eastern Europe we know that oxen had a special meaning in these early times. Besides for pulling ards, oxen could also be used for drawing carts. It hence comes as no surprise that the wheel and the ard were introduced more or less simultaneously. That the wheel was in these early days also regarded as something special is apparent from, for example, the Late Neolithic wheel deposits that have been found in the peat bogs in Drenthe.

The beginnings of mixed farming

In chapters 16 and 18 it was argued that mixed farming originated in the Bronze Age. In the Late Neolithic, mixed farming, i.e. an agricultural system in which stock keeping and crop cultivation are combined in a mutually beneficiary manner, seems to have still been in a formative phase. No longhouses incorporating cattle stalls – the type of farm typically associated with mixed farming in the lowlands[5] – are for example known from this period. From the Middle Bronze Age onwards this type of building was however to be found all over the Low Countries and their wide surroundings, from northern France to southern Scandinavia, where it has in fact remained in use until the present. The origins of this type of dwelling are difficult to explain. In our temperate region the need to stall cattle in the winter owing to cold weather is hardly a convincing argument. One reason for combining living areas and a byre beneath a single roof may have been that cattle yielded warmth from which human beings could also benefit, but that cannot have been the chief reason for stalling the cattle. Cattle can easily be driven together for milking outside, and giving the animals supplementary food outdoors is no problem either. What is however more difficult when cattle roam around outdoors is collecting manure. One of the explanations for the appearance of stalls is hence that stalling cattle presented the possibility of collecting manure in sods or litter.[6] That does however not explain why cattle was stalled under the same roof with the people. That has to have also a social meaning: the byre house symbolizes a strong bond between men and cattle. Cattle guaranteed fertile soil and provided traction, food, clothing. But apart from that – through its role in exchange networks – it probably enabled people to enter into social relations like alliances and marriage bonds.

THE SETTLEMENT FORM: SCATTERED FARMSTEADS

The term 'settlement' usually conjures up an image of a group of (relatively) close-ly arranged houses which constitute a unity on account of their spatial clustering, but which are also linked in a social sense – whose occupants, in other words, constitute a village community. In the Low Countries there were, however, hardly any such spatial clusters of houses until in the Late Iron Age. The farmsteads lay scattered across the landscape, rather like the farmsteads that are still to be found here and there in the Dutch Achterhoek region today. So whereas it will have been possible to make out groups from a great height, this was virtually impossible at ground level.

The almost complete absence of spatial clustering does however not imply the absence of feelings of solidarity or group cohesion, or a lack of social control. It could well be that the farms scattered across a particular area were linked by kin-ship ties, which bound them into a social unit even though that unit was not spa-tially recognisable in the form of a village. That spatial unity was probably more evident from the long-term use of a particular settlement territory within which the farms were regularly shifted from one location to another.

The size of the farms suggests that married children continued to live with their parents until well into the Middle Bronze Age. The occurrence of annexes may well be associated with this form of cohabitation in so-called extended families. Such cohabitation secured the continuity of the farm in its territory. It may more-over be regarded as a form of safety: a larger unit is better capable of distributing its manpower and is also more resistant to influences from outside. The head of the family will often have been the most powerful individual, but the oldest son also held an important position. Age and sex are in such a simply structured or-ganisation important factors for determining social rank. This picture seems to be confirmed by the information on social organisation that can be inferred from burials. It could be argued that the right of being buried in a primary grave be-neath a barrow pertained to the heads kin groups that consisted of a few of such extended families (fig. 20.1).

A LINK BETWEEN BARROWS AND PLOUGH AGRICULTURE?

Chapter 19 gave a detailed account of the meaning of the contents and the shapes of barrows, but it did not explain the transition to the individual barrow as a uni-versal form of burial. This development, which is associated with the Single Grave culture, took place at the beginning of the Late Neolithic. Instead of depositing their dead in a megalithic tomb that was used for collective burial for a relatively long period of time by a large group of individuals, people started to bury them separately, beneath individual barrows or in individual flat graves.[7] This does not mean that everybody was given an archaeologically visible grave. As in the Middle Neolithic, this privilege was reserved for only part of the population. That may

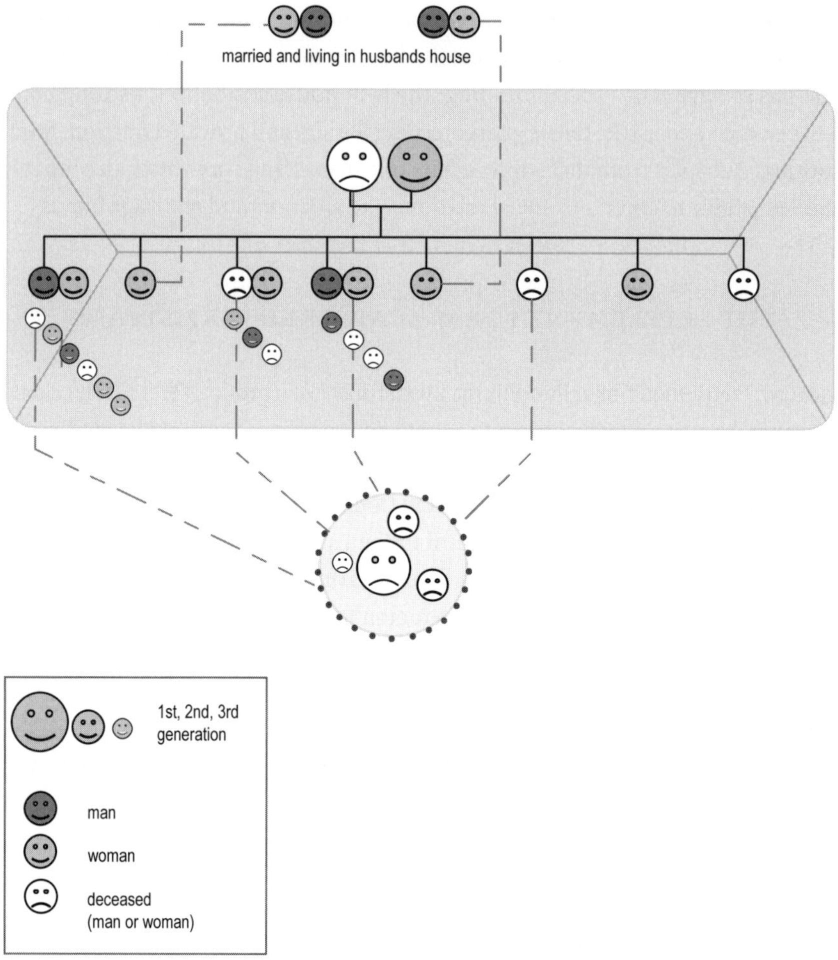

married and living in husbands house

1st, 2nd, 3rd generation

man

woman

deceased
(man or woman)

fig. 20.1

Model showing the relation between
household and cemetery. According to this
model Middle Bronze Age local communities
consisted of a group of 10-25 persons, an
extended family comprising parents with
their married sons and grandchildren, living
together in one long house. Adult deceased
were interred as a secondary burial in the
barrow of a (direct) ancestor. Infants and
grandchildren were not buried in the barrow,
with the exception of – in this example – the
oldest grandson. Only heads of families were
entitled to a burial covered with a mound or
with a new mound period.

incidentally quite possibly have been the same part of the population that was previously buried in the megalithic tombs.[8]

For a long time this change was related to an immigration of Beaker peoples who brought the custom of burial beneath barrows along with them. As already mentioned above, there is however no concrete evidence to support this. And since the archaeological remains on the contrary seem to suggest cultural continuity, it is better to search for a different explanation. Something that should be pointed out in this context is that such drastic changes in cultural patterns cannot be explained with the concept of 'fashion'. They were without doubt associated with changes in ideology, which is understood to include issues like religion, views on 'proper' behaviour, taboos and also the burial rite.

The ideological development reflected by the changing burial rite at the beginning of the Late Neolithic could be characterised as a shift in emphasis from the collective to smaller units forming part of it, such as kinship groups and families.[9] This shift can possibly be understood by relating it to the changes in the economy outlined above and assuming that the stone tombs belonged to 'corporations', groups of people who had the customary right of using the land in a particular area.[10] The collective tomb was the symbol of such a group and probably served as a ceremonial centre for all kinds of rituals. It is believed that the system of shifting cultivation assumed for these groups involved very little awareness of personal 'possession' of fields or other plots of land, because only little time and material were invested in preparing the land for use, and it is moreover assumed that sufficient land was available for small-scale crop cultivation.

All this probably changed with the introduction of the plough: farmers then had to invest more time, energy and 'capital' in tilling the soil. They had to remove stumps and plough the soil, they needed a team of oxen, the soil had to be manured after some time, *etc.*[11] It is quite conceivable that these increased investments in the soil led to an increasingly tighter bond with the tilled land, which ultimately resulted in the farmer who tilled the soil with the help of his relatives claiming exclusive rights of use.

The 'corporations' consequently disintegrated into smaller units like kinship groups. This also implied the end of the use of the collective tombs, the *hunebedden*. They came to be seen as symbols of the old system, and were probably also respected as such, but they were no longer used as burial monuments. Instead, people buried their dead beneath barrows. The location of those barrows was probably very important to the deceased's relatives. Thrown up in abandoned fields[12] in the territory over which the relatives claimed the right of use, the barrows symbolised the relatives' ties with the land (fig. 20.2).[13]

The barrows were hence boundary markers, as it were, in a 'land of the ancestors' which at first probably bore a fairly close resemblance to the actual territorial division. After some time people presumably forgot to what person, group or territory a particular barrow belonged, but it is also possible that the memory was kept alive for a fairly long time by passing the information on from generation to generation. This was almost certainly the case with the family barrows of the Middle Bronze Age (see chapter 19), which probably represented more than ties with the tilled land alone. The positions of the secondary burials seem to reflect the contemporary hierarchical relations within the kinship groups: the primary graves contain predominantly the remains of older men, the secondary burials those of women and also children. All this changed in the Late Bronze Age, when this hierarchy seems to have been deliberately negated in the urnfields, as suggested by the many separate burials. This again indicates an important change in ideology. The emphasis seems to have reverted to the individual again, to an even greater extent than in the past. But the great variation in the shapes and dimensions of the burial monuments shows that the degree of equality had by no means increased.[14]

The question as to how we are to interpret this trend towards even further fragmentation of the social units, and apparently also towards greater differences between the individual units, brings us to an aspect of culture that has received virtually no attention so far: the economic and social use of metal.

THE BRONZE TRADE: ITINERANT SMITHS OR EXCHANGE NETWORKS?

One of the most influential – technical and social – developments in later prehistory was without doubt the discovery of metals like copper, gold and iron. In the Low Countries, the use of copper and bronze was introduced during the Bell Beaker period, by which time these metals had already been in use for a long time elsewhere. As already discussed in chapter 17, copper and bronze started to be used on a relatively large scale in the Early Bronze Age, when the development of alloys and casting techniques widened the range of products and applications for which these metals could be used.

Until fairly recently, great emphasis was placed on the technologically innovative aspect of the use of copper and bronze. Even today, a distinction is in many countries still made between a Copper and a Bronze Age, as though they were clearly distinct periods.[15] Research, especially settlement research, has however

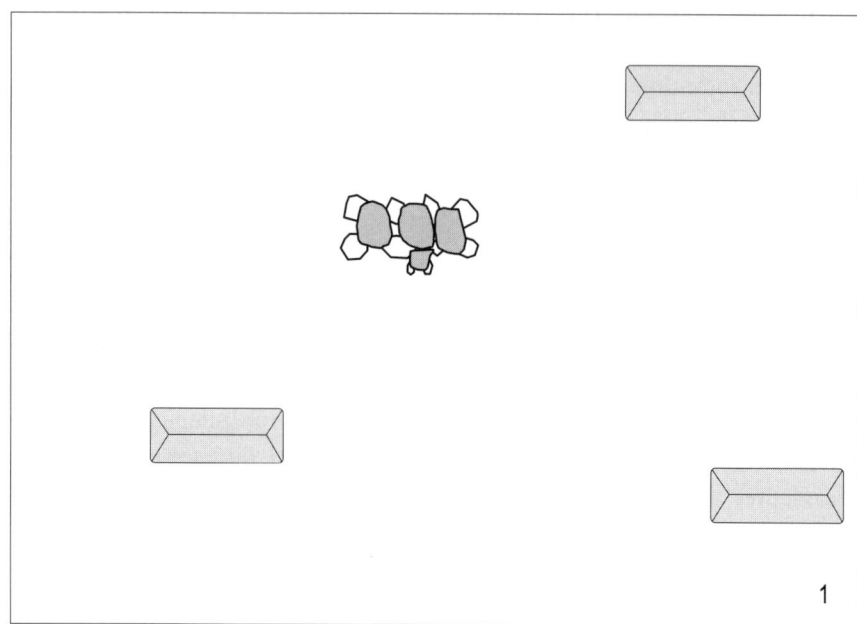

fig. 20.2
Schematic models showing changes in social organisation and the associated settlement structure in the Middle Neolithic B, the Late Neolithic and the Bronze Age.

1 The focus of the *hunebed* corporations of the Middle Neolithic was a single *hunebed* or a different type of megalith. It is assumed that extended families lived together in single houses.

2 In the Late Neolithic the corporations fell apart into kinship groups, which buried their deceased beneath a barrow in the area they regarded as their ancestors' traditional territory. Such groups are defined as 'local communities'. The dotted lines mark very vague limits, which will in the past probably have been primarily natural boundaries (streams, valleys, low-lying areas, *etc.*).

3 From around 1000-900 BC onwards people no longer lived in longhouses in an extended-family context, but as separate households in different parts of the territory. The urnfields symbolized the unity of the local community and were usually laid out in relation to older burial monuments. All three models represent a hypothetical area measuring at least 20 km² and comprising at least 60 occupants.

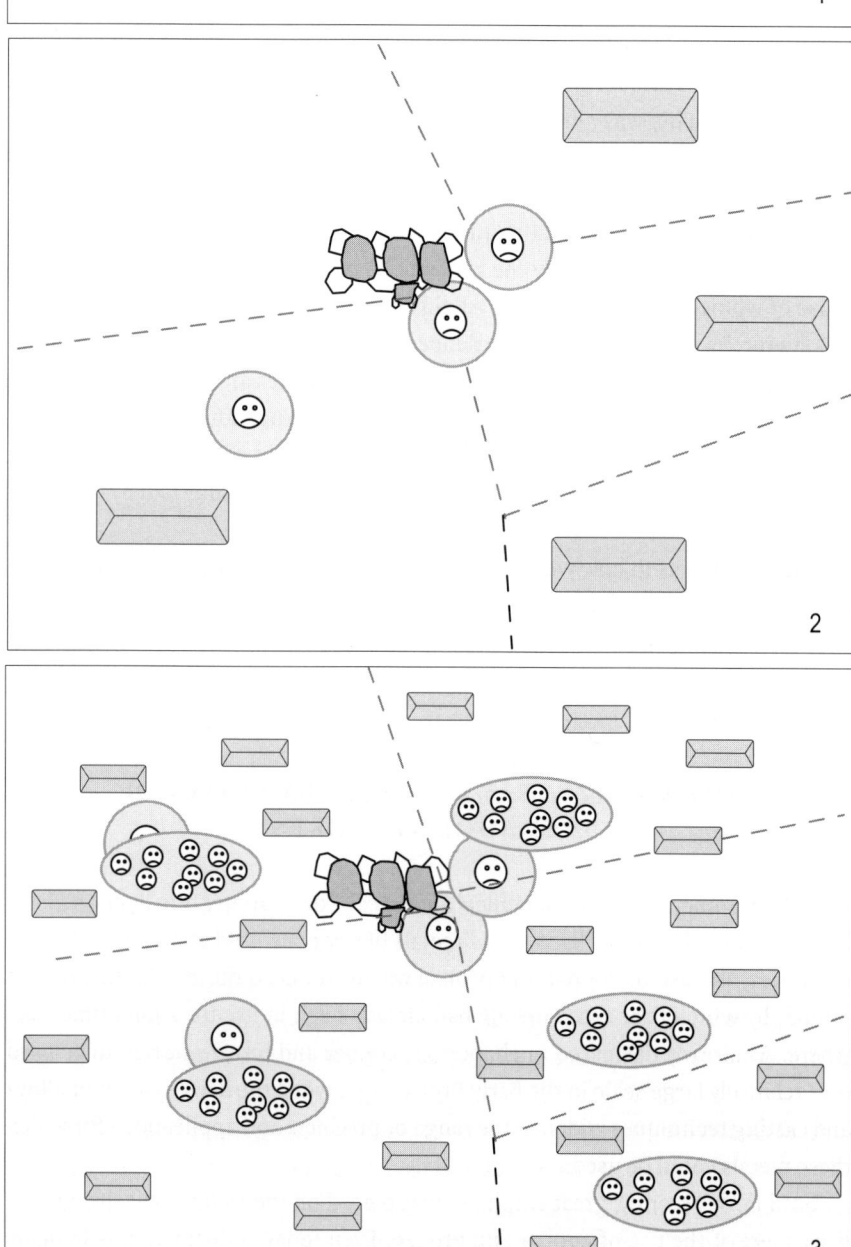

shown that neither settlements nor cemeteries show any signs of the divisions suggested by the technological model.[16] The earliest occurrence of copper and bronze can be dated via grave goods and hoards, but that is not the time when these materials came into common use. As already mentioned above, most prehistoric innovations were universally accepted only after a relatively long period of tentative use, which is in the archaeological record often associated with special persons or locations, after which the novelties started to be used by all the members of the community within a relatively short time. This probably also holds for copper and bronze. This model for the introduction of novelties may also explain the rapid diffusion of the so-called Bell Beaker assemblage, a term often used to indicate the fairly uniform association of grave goods in Bell Beaker graves. The range of metal objects was limited at first, comprising small daggers, axes and a few ornaments. However, the discovery of the techniques of alloying and casting copper greatly widened the field of application and all kinds of weapons, implements and ever more ornaments started to be made of bronze.

Objects of bronze were undoubtedly highly coveted, especially in view of the metal's scarcity. As almost everywhere else in Europe, all the copper and bronze had to be imported, and this is one of the reasons why we assume that these metals came to play important parts in a social context. Under the influence of Gordon Childe it was assumed until the 1970s that bronze objects were distributed by itinerant traders who were also smiths[17] and who were given food and drink in exchange for their services. Some objects were thought to have been distributed by means of barter: a bronze axe was bartered for, say, a cow's skin or a sheep. But anthropological research has shown that this is a typically Western interpretation.[18] In societies without a market economy people are mainly dependent on good contacts with other groups for obtaining goods from outside the community; barter not involving relations is extremely rare in moneyless economies. In such economies barter is almost always based on a complex network of relations, with each community having its own agreements as to who can and may exchange goods with one another, what may be bartered for what and what (social) obligations the transactions involve.

We assume that similar exchange networks existed in prehistory, too. Much research is currently being devoted to this issue, but it is of course a topic that excites many discussions because it is difficult to infer such networks from the available evidence. In the Netherlands, few articles have yet been published on this topic, because our research tradition has offered little scope for such studies. But research into exchange networks could throw an interesting light on social aspects of prehistoric communities and this question therefore deserves attention.

Exchange networks in the Low Countries: the differences between the north and the south

Although there is little evidence to prove it, we may assume that the nature and composition of the existing networks changed at the beginning of the Bronze Age, for the exchange of flint, hitherto one of the most important raw materials for tools and weapons, did not necessarily take place in the same network as that of bronze. New contacts were required and different principles came to govern the exchanges. This is not to say that flint disappeared from daily life at the beginning of the Bronze Age; on the contrary, flint was for a long time to remain an important raw material for certain tools, such as sickles, and weapons, such as arrowheads. So it is unlikely that the existing networks suddenly collapsed; instead, they probably changed in character and content over the years, with new networks emerging alongside them.

The research into burials in particular has shown that the diffuse boundary between the northern and southern parts of the Netherlands observable in the Late Neolithic persisted until in the Middle Bronze Age: the northeastern part of the country formed part of the networks oriented towards Scandinavia, while the southern and central parts focused on Belgium, France and Britain.[19] The ranges of products that circulated in the two networks were almost the same, but there were clear regional differences in types.

Gift exchange: a brief theoretical introduction

The bronze 'trade' will certainly have been an important aspect of exchange networks, but the networks will have had a much wider function. Anthropological research among present-day communities suggests that their most important function may have been as a means for establishing and maintaining contacts with other groups.[20] Contacts can be important in times of need, for example during a famine or war, but they can of course also be used as a source of prestige.

We assume that the exchange of gifts was one of the most important mechanisms for creating and maintaining networks;[21] the presentation of a gift creates a bond between the donor and the recipient. What this bond exactly implies, and what form the gifts should take, will vary from one community to another. In theory the 'debt' can be redeemed by returning the gesture with a gift of a similarly standardised form. Such behaviour is known to us from the Kula exchange system among the people of the Trobriand Islands.[22] In some communities the debt is

fig. 20.3

Model representing two 'dimensions' of a local Bronze Age community. A represents the environmental situation of two Bronze Age households which together constituted a local community. B represents the ideal dimensions of the same situation along with possible meanings of certain elements of the environment: bogs, areas where streams merged and forests are in this model associated with deities and barrows with ancestors. The exchange relations with various elements are indicated in italics.

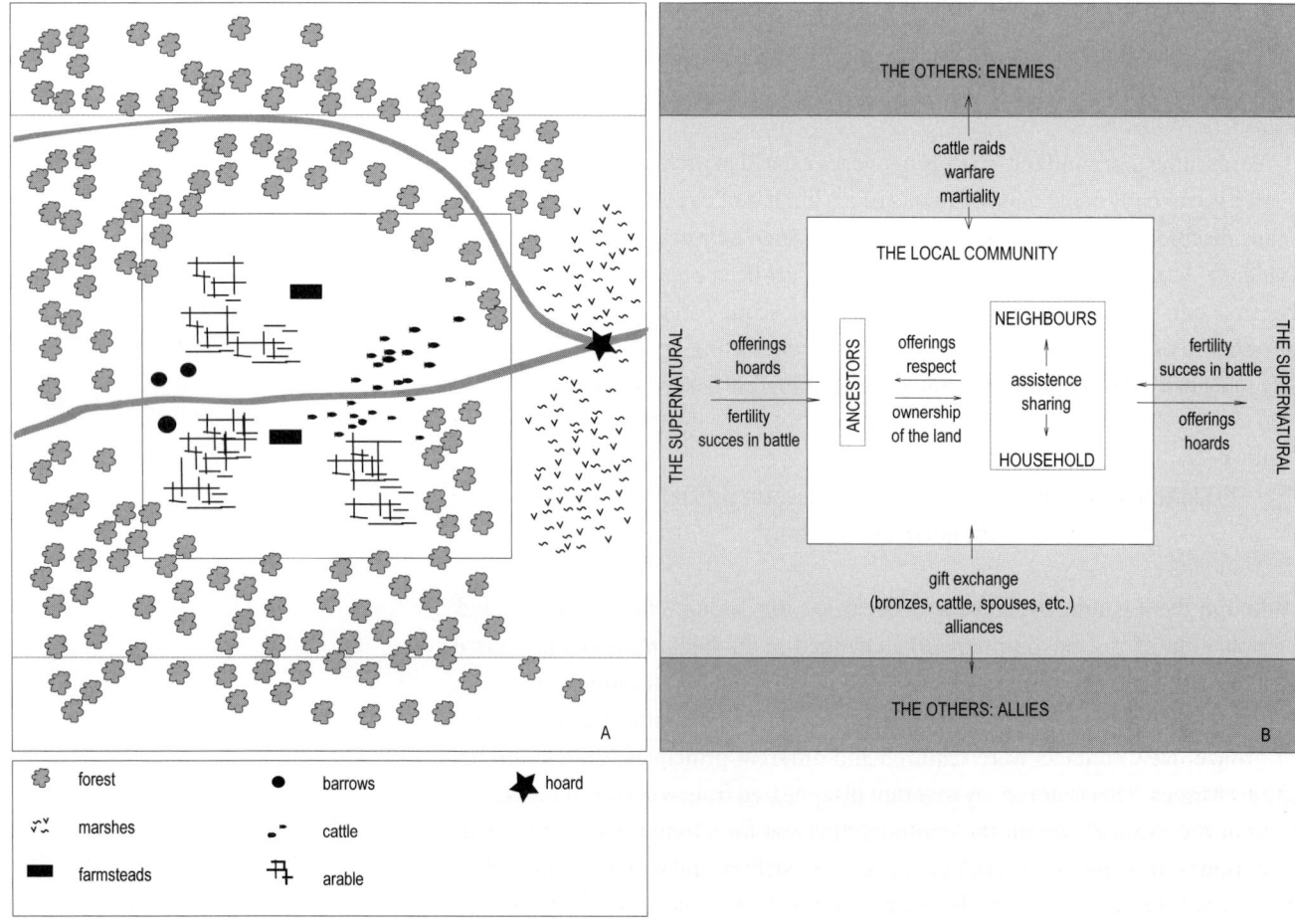

forest   barrows   hoard

marshes   cattle

farmsteads   arable

however never redeemed, but is constantly reversed by returning the gesture with a gift of a greater value. This is known as 'competitive gift exchange'.

As exchange based on such mechanisms involves more than economic transactions alone, the exchange acts themselves are often accompanied by ceremonies. Those ceremonies may involve only a small number of individuals, but sometimes they may extend to entire families, kinship groups, villages or even tribes. The protagonists are often the dominant male members of those groups: village chiefs or tribal or lineage heads, who gain prestige from their prominent roles.

Besides the presentation of gifts, their destruction may also be a source of prestige. The recipient may accept the offered gifts to then, for example, break or burn them. Such an act symbolises his great disdain of property and the strength of his spirit (as in the case of the 'potlatch' discussed in chapter 29). At the same time, it grants him prestige. The effect of this ceremonial destruction may be to put an end to an escalated cycle of competitive gift exchange. After the destruction ritual a new cycle starts, but with gifts of a much lesser value than those with which the previous cycle ended.[23]

So besides the giving of gifts, their exchange – often referred to as consumption – may also have an important social function. A special form of destruction is to irrevocably part with valuable goods by depositing or discarding them in inaccessible places like peat bogs, springs or rivers, as offerings to deities or ancestors. In the archaeological record we find only the traces of gifts thus 'consumed'. Some of the bronzes that have come to light may of course represent tools or ornaments that were lost or that were deposited in a pit as waste after they had fragmented, but the cases in which such a form of deposition can be demonstrated are rare. Bronze objects are for example only very rarely found in settlement contexts, in the Low Countries at least, while most fragmented bronzes are recovered from contexts that show that they were deliberately buried there. That fragmented bronze was not readily discarded is no cause for surprise: the material was scarce and could be easily melted down for reuse. The study of bronze hoards has therefore become an important means for investigating exchange networks and the ideological aspects of the custom of depositing bronzes.[24]

SOCIAL ASPECTS OF THE USE AND DISCARDING OF COPPER AND BRONZE

In what ways were copper and bronze used and discarded in the Low Countries? We must ask ourselves this question in order to find out something about the social aspects of the use of metal. The trends reflected by the grave goods have already been discussed with reference to the burial rite in chapter 19. It seems that from the Late Neolithic onwards the deceased were accompanied by predominantly items of personal gear: copper daggers, a few bronze axes or swords, sometimes a bracelet or a neck ring (pottery is here left out of consideration). Judging from the grave goods, the personal gear was fairly sober, but this impression is of course greatly influenced by traditions and taboos associated with the burial rite. Apparently bronzes were virtually not removed from circulation in the form of grave goods.

An entirely different picture emerges from the finds that have been recovered from swamps, rivers and river valleys (chapter 29). The practice of depositing objects at watery locations seems to have existed since the Neolithic. From the distribution of the finds we may infer that swamps, springs and other places where water seeps to the surface, the sources of rivers and points where rivers flow together were particularly popular locations for 'offering' objects. The offerings even included objects that were made specifically for the deposition ritual, such as the swords from Jutphaas and Ommerschans (chapter 17). Especially from the Late Bronze Age onwards, such categories of objects were not deposited in graves. We know nothing about the size of the groups who witnessed such depositions, but from the many rock engravings showing processions that have been found in Scandinavia we may infer that fairly large gatherings attended these events.

We get the impression that bronze thus came to play an increasingly important part in manipulating social relations. But if the social structure described above is correct, only a select group of individuals will have been 'entitled' to participate in the transactions in the exchange networks. The challenging of these individuals' monopoly positions may ultimately have led to the disintegration of the existing social structure of autonomous kinship groups led by a lineage head. The evidence obtained in excavations of settlements and cemeteries suggests that from the Late Bronze Age onward, the family came to play a more important part as the smallest social unit. From this perspective it is easy to understand why the number of primary burials beneath a barrow increased in the course of the Middle Bronze Age, and why, in the Late Bronze Age, this form of burial subsequently gave way to burial in an urnfield, in which (almost?) everybody was entitled to a 'primary' grave.

WHAT NEXT?

On the preceding pages an attempt has been made to present a coherent picture of the social and economic developments that took place in the Late Neolithic and the Middle Bronze Age. In some cases it has been briefly mentioned along what lines these developments continued in the subsequent Late Bronze Age and Early Iron Age. Although the appearance of the urnfields is often regarded as a major turning point, marking the end of the Middle Bronze Age, it is very likely that this change can also be traced back to developments that started in the Middle Bronze Age already. What we do know for certain is that it, too, represents an important ideological transformation and not a new fashion or the immigration of a foreign people.

Many aspects of the picture presented in the previous sections require further research. Although we are reasonably well-informed about house construction and settlement layout in the Middle Bronze Age, our knowledge of these issues in the Early Bronze Age and the Late Neolithic is still poor. A few chance discoveries have given us some idea of the settlements, but the evidence is too scanty to enable us to construct a sound model. It is hoped that the research in West-Friesland will alter this situation (feature J).

Although the Dutch model of shifting farmsteads for Bronze Age settlement is well founded, much research still remains to be done in the field of settlement archaeology. For example, no attention – other than in a technological sense – has yet been paid to the dynamics of the movements of the farmsteads.[25]

Another topic requiring further study is the ways in which settlements, cemeteries and ritual sites were viewed in relation to the surrounding landscape and the ways in which they acquired new meanings over the years.[26] This question could be approached by studying for example how settlements and cemeteries were treated after they had been abandoned: were they respected or did groups who later arrived at the site take them into use again or erect new buildings over their remains and, if so, in what period? There where it is found that the site of a former settlement was reused for occupation shortly after it had been abandoned, as took place at, for example, Elp and, on several occasions, Oss, we may assume that the farmsteads had remained recognisable as such.[27] Research into this topic is currently being carried out on a settlement level and a (micro)regional level.[28] The realization that landscape has cultural as well as physical aspects seems to be an important discovery that will certainly lead to new ideas on people's attitudes towards the organisation of their surroundings and the meanings they attached to their surroundings. Research into large adjoining areas within a restricted region is important for gaining a better understanding of this issue.

An important source of information which has by no means been exhausted yet is metal. While most research so far has focused on the provenance of the various materials, future studies will have to concentrate on the context of deposition. Only such research may provide information on the social and ideological aspects of the ways in which metal was used and discarded. An interesting area of research in this context is that of the dynamics of the exchange networks, in which due attention should be paid to the fact that the Netherlands occupied a special position at the border of two spheres of exchange, the Atlantic and the Scandinavian.

Another field, finally, in which much still remains to be done is palaeoecology. Although we are now reasonably well-informed about the range of foodstuffs consumed by the Late Neolithic and Bronze Age occupants of the Netherlands, we still have much to learn about farming practices. Too little attention is still being paid to issues like forms of manuring, the cultivation methods employed, the situation and size of the fields, the relation between crop cultivation and cattle keeping, the origins and nature of the Celtic field system (chapter 22), *etc*. Such research is especially important if we wish to make well-founded statements on the meaning of the landscape and man's conscious shaping of his surroundings. These issues in fact present a new communal area of research for palaeoecologists and archaeologists.

NOTES

1   Casparie/Groenman-van Waateringe 1980.

2   The curious thing, incidentally, is that a migration model has recently been advanced in Scandinavia (Kristiansen 1990), where a model based on continuous developments has hitherto always been used. It has however not yet gathered a following.

3   See *e.g.* Champion *et al.* 1986 for a survey.

4   Slicher van Bath (1978, 37) writes that in the Middle Ages sowing in furrows led to higher yields than broadcasting.

5   Roymans/Fokkens 1991.

6   Fokkens 1991a, 128-129; 1998a.

7   Which is not to say that no flat graves are known from the period before the Single Grave culture.

8   Fokkens 1991, 1997.

9   Fokkens 1986, 1998b.

10 See Bloch 1971.

11 Gilman 1981.

12 Casparie/Groenman-van Waateringe 1980.

13 Some archaeologists assume that the *hunebedden* were also territorial markers. It is however difficult to assume a one-to-one relation between a *hunebed* and the surrounding territory for the developed phase of the TRB culture, because the distribution area of the settlements is then much larger than that of the *hunebedden* (Fokkens 1986; 1991a, 102; 1998).

14 Fokkens 1997, 2002; Roymans 1991; Roymans/Kortlang 1999.

15 In 1978 Brongers and Woltering, for example, wrote (p. 86): 'There is only little piece of evidence for continuity from Late Neolithic Bell Beaker metallurgy to the Early Bronze Age'.

16 Roymans/Fokkens 1991; Lanting 1973.

17 Brongers/Woltering 1978, 86; Bloemers *et al.* 1981, 54.

18 Rowlands 1971.

19 Butler 1973; Brun 1991.

20 See for example Mauss 1950; Gregory 1982; Weiner 1992.

21 Mauss 1950.

22 Gregory 1982, 60. Gregory is here quoting Boas, the ethnographer who first described the Kwakiutl potlatch.

23 Malinowski 1922; Weiner, 1988. Malinowski (1922, 83) puts this as follows: 'The ceremonial exchange of the two articles is the main, fundamental aspect of the Kula. But associated with it, and done under its cover, we find a great number of secondary activities and features. There, side by side with the ritual exchange of arm-shells

and necklaces, the natives carry on ordinary trade, bartering from one island to another a great number of utilities, often inprocurable in the district to which they are imported and indispensable'.

24 Fontijn 2003.

25 For a social explanation see Gerritsen 2001.

26 Fokkens 1996; Fontijn 2003; Gerritsen 2001.

27 Fokkens 1993, 42.

28 See for example Roymans 1995.